THE DICTIONARY OF

Physiological and Clinical Psychology

THE DICTIONARY OF

Physiological and Clinical Psychology

EDITED BY

Rom Harré and Roger Lamb

ADVISORY EDITORS

Dennis Gath
Linda Patia Spear
Norman E. Spear

The MIT Press
Cambridge, Massachusetts

First MIT Press edition, 1986

LIBRARY OF CONGRESS CATALOGING-IN-PUBLICATION DATA

The Dictionary of physiological and clinical psychology.

Revised portions from: The Encyclopedic dictionary of psychology, 1983.
Includes index.
1. Clinical psychology — Dictionaries. 2. Psychology, Physiological — Dictionaries. I. Harré, Rom.
II. Lamb, Roger. III. Encyclopedic dictionary of psychology.
RC467.D48   1986   150'.3'21   86-14379
ISBN 0-262-58075-6 (pbk.)

This book was set in 9 on 10pt Linotron Ehrhardt
and printed and bound in Great Britain.

CONTENTS

PREFACE

The highly successful and comprehensive *Encyclopedic dictionary of psychology* included a dozen psychological specialities. The editors have selected, updated and supplemented material from the original dictionary to provide in this and similar volumes a compact but compendious coverage of the most widely studied of these specialities. In preparing the independent dictionaries we have had in mind the needs of both students and practitioners in many branches of psychology and allied fields. In addition to this volume which concentrates on physiological and clinical psychology, three further volumes cover personality and social psychology, developmental and educational psychology, and ethology and animal learning.

The selected articles have been brought up to date, and the bibliographies have been revised to include the most recent publications. Many new entries have been added to fill the inevitable gaps of the first edition. The number of biographies of great psychologists has been increased to help to bring the research process and its scientific findings to life.

Psychology has developed within several different conceptual frameworks, often treating the same subject matter with very different assumptions and methods. We have tried, we hope without being uncritically eclectic, to reflect a wide range of approaches to human thought and behavior, including those popular in academic, applied and clinical branches of psychology.

Rom Harré and Roger Lamb

ACKNOWLEDGMENTS

The Editors and Publisher are grateful to Bridget Cook who compiled the index. They are also pleased to acknowledge permission from the publishers to reproduce the following illustrations:

brain and central nervous system

1 W. H. Freeman and Company. (Redrawn from R. W. Sperry, "The great cerebral commissure", *Scientific American* (January 1964).)

2 Blackwell Scientific Publications. (Redrawn from J. G. Beaumont, *Introduction to neuropsychology* (1983), p. 37.)

3 Blackwell Scientific Publications. (Redrawn from J. G. Beaumont, *Introduction to neuropsychology* (1983), p. 37.)

4 Macmillan Inc. (After Penfield and Rasmussen, *The cerebral cortex of man* (1950).)

5 Blackwell Scientific Publications. (Redrawn from J. G. Beaumont, *Introduction to neuropsychology* (1983), p. 28.)

6 Blackwell Scientific Publications. (Redrawn from J. G. Beaumont, *Introduction to neuropsychology* (1983), p. 37.)

7 Blackwell Scientific Publications. (Redrawn from R. Passmore and J. S. Robson, eds., *Anatomy, biochemistry, physiology and related subjects*, vol. 1, 2nd. edn. (1976), p. 25.23.)

8 Blackwell Scientific Publications. (Redrawn from J. F. Stein, *Introduction to neurophysiology* (1982), p. 253.)

9 W. H. Freeman and Company. (Redrawn from J. D. French, "The reticular formation", *Scientific American* (May 1957).)

10 Hodder & Stoughton Educational. (Redrawn from David Le Vay, *Teach yourself anatomy*, p. 425.)

11 Blackwell Scientific Publications. (Redrawn from J. F. Stein, *Introduction to neurophysiology* (1982), p. 316.)

12 W. H. Freeman and Company. (Redrawn from T. H. Bullock, *Introduction to nervous systems*, p. 87.) Also Blackwell Scientific Publications. (Redrawn from J. F. Stein, *Introduction to neurophysiology* (1982), p. 215.)

13 Holt, Rinehart & Winston, CBS College Publishing. (Redrawn from Peter Milner, *Physiological psychology* (1971), p. 84.)

14 Holt, Rinehart & Winston, CBS College Publishing. (Redrawn from Peter Milner, *Physiological psychology* (1971), p. 89.)

15 Harper & Row Inc. (Redrawn from R. F. Thompson, *Foundations of physiological psychology*, p. 96.)

16 Rockefeller University Press. (After D. M. McLean, "The triune brain, emotion and scientific bias". In *The neurosciences: second study program* (1970).)

17 John Wiley. (After J. de Groot, in *Sex and behavior*, ed. F. A. Beach (1965).)

18 Blackwell Scientific Publications. (Redrawn from J. F. Stein, *Introduction to neurophysiology* (1983), p. 189.)

19 Williams & Wilkins Co. (After R. C. Truex and M. B. Carpenter, *Strong and Elwyn's human neuroanatomy*. 5th edn. (1964).)

20 McGraw-Hill. (After E. L. House and B. Pansky, *Neuroanatomy* (1960).)

21 McGraw-Hill. (After E. L. House and B. Pansky, *Neuroanatomy* (1960).)

22 Academic Press. (Redrawn from *Hormones and behavior*, ed. Seymour Levine (1972), p. 4.)

23 Blackwell Scientific Publications. (Redrawn from J. F. Stein, *Introduction to neurophysiology* (1982), p. 95.) Also Academic Press. (Redrawn from P. H. Lindsay and D. A. Norman, *Human information processing* (1977), p. 73.)

24 Blackwell Scientific Publications. (Redrawn from J. F. Stein, *Introduction to neurophysiology* (1983), p. 124.)

25 Hafner (Macmillan Inc.). (After G. L. Walls, *The vertebrate eye and its adaptive radiation* (1942).)

26 Murray Hill. (After H. Davis, *Hearing and deafness: a guide for laymen* (1947).)

27 Henry Kimpton. (Redrawn from N. B. Everett, *Functional neuroanatomy*. 5th edn. (1965), p. 101.)

28 McGraw-Hill. (After E. L. House and B. Pansky, *Neuroanatomy* (1960).)

29 McGraw-Hill. (After E. L. House and B. Pansky, *Neuroanatomy* (1960).)

31 Liverpool University Press. (After A. L. Hodgkin, *The conduction of the nervous impulse*. 4th impression (1971), p. 17.)

32 Blackwell Scientific Publications. (Redrawn from R. Passmore and J. S. Robson, eds. *Anatomy, biochemistry, physiology and related subjects*, vol. 1, 2nd. edn. (1976), p. 25.15.)

33 McGraw-Hill. (After E. T. Morgan and C. Stellar, *Physiological psychology* (1950).)

34 Blackwell Scientific Publications. (Redrawn from J. F. Stein, *Introduction to neurophysiology* (1982), p. 124.)

RNA, DNA

Churchill Livingstone. (After G. H. Haggis et al., *Introduction to molecular biology* (1964), p. 217.)

CONTRIBUTORS

Jeffrey R. Alberts — JRAl
Indiana University

Irving E. Alexander — IEA
Duke University

John Archer — JA
Preston Polytechnic

Charles W. Baatz — CWB
State University of New York, Binghamton

Paul Bebbington — PBe
Medical Research Council Social Psychiatry Unit, London

Sidney Bloch — SB
Warneford Hospital, Oxford

David E. Bond — DEB
Royal School for the Deaf, Margate

James N. Butcher — JNB
University of Minnesota

Gillian Butler — GB
Warneford Hospital, Oxford

George E. Butterworth — GEB
University of Southampton

J. Catalan — JC
Warneford Hospital, Oxford

Stephen C. Chamberlain — SCC
Syracuse University

Neil M. Cheshire — NMC
University College of N. Wales, Bangor

Rebecca M. Chesire — RMC
University of Hawaii at Manoa

David D. Clarke — DDC
University of Oxford

Cary L. Cooper — CLC
University of Manchester

Thomas R. Cox — TRC
University of Nottingham

John H. Crook — JHC
University of Bristol

Christopher Dare — CD
University of London

Nancy Datan — ND
West Virginia University

Richard J. Davidson — RJD
State University of New York, Purchase

D. W. Dickins — DWD
University of Liverpool

Rene Drucker-Colin — RD-C
Universidad Nacional Autonoma de Mexico

Adrian J. Dunn — AJD
University of Florida

J. A. Edmondson — JAE
University of Texas, Arlington

Roger P. Elbourne — RPE
Brunel University

Christopher G. Fairburn — CGF
University of Oxford and Wellcome Trust

Gillian C. Forrest — GCF
Park Hospital for Children, Oxford

K. W. M. Fulford — KWMF
University of Oxford

Adrian Furnham — AF
University of London

David M. Galloway — DMG
University of Wellington

Dennis Gath — DG
Warneford Hospital, Oxford

Kenneth J. Gergen — KJG
Swarthmore College, Pennsylvania

Richard L. Gregory — RLG
University of Bristol

Rom Harré — RHa
University of Oxford

Keith E. Hawton — KEH
Warneford Hospital, Oxford

Paul Heelas — PLFH
University of Lancaster

Ray J. Hodgson — RJH
University of Wales and South Glamorgan Health Authority

Robert Hogan — RHo
Johns Hopkins University

Gary P. Horowitz — GPH
State University of New York, Binghamton

Sonja M. Hunt — SMH
University of Edinburgh

Robert A. Jensen — RAJ
Southern Illinois University of Carbondale

E. Roy John — ERJ
New York University Medical Center

Derek Johnston — DWJ
University of Oxford

David L. Julier — DLJ
University of Oxford

David Kennard — DK
Leicester University

Raymond P. Kesner — RPK
University of Utah

Jennifer King — JK
Wallingford, Oxford

Marcel Kinsbourne — MK
Eunice Kennedy Shriver Center for Mental Retardation

Ron Kurtz — RK
Hakomi Institute, Boulder

Roger Lamb — RL
University of Oxford

Howard Leventhal — HL
University of Wisconsin, Madison

Barbara B. Lloyd — BBL
University of Sussex

J. W. Lloyd — JWL
Abingdon Hospital, Oxford

Donna A. Lupardo — DAL
State University of New York, Binghamton

D. J. McFarland — DJM
University of Oxford

N. J. Mackintosh — NJM
University of Cambridge

Salvatore R. Maddi — SRM
University of Chicago

Aubrey W. G. Manning — AWGM
University of Edinburgh

W. A. Marshall — WAM
University of Technology, Loughborough

Maryanne Martin — MM
University of Oxford

Richard A. Mayou — RAM
University of Oxford

J. H. Mellanby — JHM
University of Oxford

Alexandre Métraux — AM
University of Heidelberg

Martin C. Mitcheson — MCM
University College Hospital, London

J. D. Mollon — JDM
University of Cambridge

Neville Moray	NM	Larry R. Squire	LRS
University of Toronto		*University of California, San Diego*	
Peter Mühlhäusler	PM	Diana Staples	DS
University of Oxford		*Nuffield Orthopaedic Centre, Oxford*	
Michael W. Orr	MWO	Charles T. Tart	CTT
Horton General Hospital, Oxford		*University of California, Davis*	
W. Ll. Parry-Jones	WLlP-J	Colin Tatton	CT
University of Oxford		*International Transactional Analysis*	
Addie L. Perkins	ALP	*Association, Birmingham*	
University of Michigan		David C. Taylor	DCT
Terry L. Powley	TLP	*University of Manchester*	
Purdue University		Insup Taylor	IT
G. P. Pullen	GPP	*University of Toronto*	
Littlemore Hospital, Oxford		Talbot J. Taylor	TJT
Benjamin E. Reese	BER	*College of William and Mary, Virginia*	
University of Oxford		Noel M. Tichy	NMT
V. Reynolds	VR	*University of Michigan*	
University of Oxford		Michael J. Tobin	MJT
Trevor W. Robbins	TWR	*University of Birmingham*	
University of Cambridge		Peter Trower	PET
Daniel N. Robinson	DNR	*University of Leicester*	
Georgetown University		J. O. Urmson	JOU
R. Rodnight	RR	*Stanford University (Emeritus Professor)*	
University of London		Carol Van Hartesveldt	CVanH
John C. Rowan	JCR	*University of Florida*	
London		Boris M. Veličkovkij	BMV
Richard C. Saunders	RCS	*Moscow*	
University of Oxford		Dirk H. G. Versteeg	DHGV
Lindsay T. Sharpe	LTS	*State University of Utrecht*	
University of Freiburg		Nigel Walker	NDW
John J. Sidtis	JJS	*University of Cambridge*	
Cornell University		Patrick D. Wall	PDW
W. T. Singleton	WTS	*University of London*	
University of Aston		Nancy C. Waugh	NCW
Ben R. Slugoski	BRS	*University of Oxford*	
University of Oxford		Kevin Wheldall	KW
Peter D. Spear	PDS	*University of Birmingham*	
University of Wisconsin			

Andrew Whiten — AW
University of St Andrews

Diana Whitmore — DW
Psychosynthesis and Education Trust, London

Glayde Whitney — GW
Florida State University

K. V. Wilkes — KVW
University of Oxford

Glenn D. Wilson — GDW
University of London

Gordon Winocur — GWi
Trent University, Ontario

Linda A. Wood — LAW
University of Guelph, Ontario

Clifford Yorke — CY
The Anna Freud Centre, London

EDITORIAL NOTE

Asterisks against titles in the bibliographies indicate items suitable for further reading. The convention 1920 (1986) indicates a work first published in 1920 but widely accessible only in an edition of 1986, to which the publication details given refer.

Cross references to other entries are printed in small capitals in the text. Leads to further additional information can be found from the index.

A

acetylcholine A neurotransmitter in both the peripheral and central nervous system. Acetylcholine is synthesized from choline. Once released at the SYNAPSE it interacts with postsynaptic receptors, and is then degraded enzymatically by acetylcholinesterase. There are two types of acetylcholine (cholinergic) receptors. Nicotinic receptors are mimicked by nicotine and blocked by α-bungarotoxin. Synapses involving nicotinic receptors are excitatory and have been postulated by McGeer, Eccles and McGeer (1978) to be ionotropic: that is, the interaction of acetylcholine and nicotinic receptors causes a direct change in the ion permeability of the postsynaptic membrane. Muscarinic receptors are mimicked by muscarine and blocked by atropine. These synapses can be excitatory or inhibitory and are thought to be metabotropic, using cyclic AMP as a second messenger (see ADENYL CYCLASE). Peripheral actions of acetylcholine include parasympathetic (muscarinic) innervation of smooth muscles and glands and nicotinic innervation of skeletal muscle (see NEURONS, ALPHA AND GAMMA MOTOR). Centrally, acetylcholine is found predominantly in LOCAL CIRCUIT NEURONS, primarily in the EXTRAPYRAMIDAL MOTOR SYSTEM, THALAMUS and CEREBRAL CORTEX. In addition, there are cholinergic projections from portions of the LIMBIC SYSTEM to HIPPOCAMPUS. Central cholinergic synapses are predominantly muscarinic. Cholinergic systems are involved with movement and behavioral inhibition. (See also NEUROTRANSMITTER SYSTEM.)   GPH

Bibliography

Gundersen, C.B. 1980: The effect of botulinum toxin on the synthesis storage and release of acetylcholine. *Progress in neurobiology* 14, 99–119.

Kruk, J.L. and Pycock, C.J. 1983: *Neurotransmitter drugs*. 2nd edn. Beckenham, Kent: Croom Helm. pp. 22–41.

Kuffler, S.W. Nicholls, J.G. and Martin, A.N. 1984: *From neuron to brain*. 2nd edn. Sunderland, MA: Sinauer Associates Inc. pp. 207–40.

McGeer, Patrick L., Eccles, John C. and McGeer, Edith G. 1978: *Molecular neurobiology of the mammalian brain*. New York and London: Plenum.

ACTH Adrenocorticotropic hormone, a 39 amino acid peptide found in the anterior lobe of the PITUITARY. Its secretion from the pituitary is promoted by a chemical factor (CRF) released from the HYPOTHALAMUS (see BRAIN AND CENTRAL NERVOUS SYSTEM: ILLUSTRATIONS, fig. 22). On release from the pituitary into the blood stream, e.g. in response to stressful stimulation, ACTH reaches the adrenal gland where it stimulates the growth of the adrenal glands and the synthesis and release of steroid adrenal hormones. ACTH is also found in the brain, even following removal of the pituitary in laboratory animals. There is increasing evidence that, like the ENDORPHINS, ACTH may function as a neuromodulator in the central nervous system (CNS) (see NEUROMODULATORS). First, ACTH and the endorphins appear to be derived from the same macromolecular precursor and can be found in the same overlapping neural pathways. Second, ACTH can interact with opiate receptors and many of its effects are reversible by opiate antagonists. Finally, administration of ACTH (or its fragments) directly into the CNS have been shown to have dramatic effects on such diverse behavior as grooming and retention of avoidance learning in experimental animals.   GPH

action potential The pattern of electrochemical changes that are propagated

1

along the length of the axon of a neuron. It is the basic mechanism by which information is transmitted from one place to another in the nervous system. The basis of the action potential is the difference in electrical potential that exists across the cell membrane of each neuron; the inside is negatively charged relative to the surrounding by approximately 70 mV. This resting potential results from the movement of positively charged potassium ions moving from the inside of the cell, where they are found in fairly high concentrations, across the cell membrane, to the outside where there is a higher concentration of positively charged sodium ions which do not freely penetrate the cell membrane (see BRAIN AND CENTRAL NERVOUS SYSTEM: ILLUSTRATIONS, figs. 30 and 31).

When a cell is stimulated by the release of neurotransmitters from other neurons it may become depolarized to a critical value called threshold. When threshold is exceeded, the membrane's resistance to the entry of sodium ions collapses resulting in a rapid influx of sodium ions and within 1 msec there is a transient reversal of polarity of the membrane potential at the junction of the cell body and the axon, a region known as the axon hillock. The resting potential at the axon hillock is then restored by an outward flow of potassium ions. Sodium influx at the axon hillock causes the adjacent region of the axon membrane to be depolarized to threshold too and in this way the action potential proceeds down the length of the axon toward the synaptic terminals of the cell. The amplitude of the action potential is unaffected by the intensity of the depolarizing stimulus and proceeds without diminution the entire length of the axon. The rate of generation of action potentials is an important way that the nervous system uses to code information such as stimulus intensity. In myelinated axons, action potentials occur only at breaks in the myelin sheath, called nodes of Ranvier, resulting in much more rapid conduction of information. RAJ

Bibliography

Ardley, J.D. 1975: *The physiology of excitable cells*, 2nd edn. Cambridge: Cambridge University Press.

Kuffler, S.W. and Nicholls, J.G. 1984: *From neuron to brain*, 2nd edn. Sunderland, MA: Sinauer Associates Inc. pp. 111–32.

Wright, Samson. 1982: *Applied physiology*. 13th edn. eds. C.A. Keele, E. Neil and N. Joels. Oxford: Oxford University Press. pp. 267–77.

adaptation in infants Those characteristics and processes which, in the course of development, fit the infant to the environment. Some characteristics of the newborn are preadapted to the evolutionarily predictable structures of the physical and social milieu. Behaviors essential for survival, such as sucking, are well organized and may even have been "practiced" in utero. Other behavior such as neonatal imitation, reaching for objects or looking in the direction of sound may also be preadapted, although they undoubtedly undergo further development. The process of adaptation may depend upon a considerable degree of PLASTICITY in the nervous system. There is evidence that the nervous system adapts to repeatedly encountered characteristics of the environment during the early months of life. For example, cells in the visual cortex responsible for coding spatial orientation are subject to considerable modification in the first few weeks of life depending on the particular characteristics of the visual environment. GEB

Bibliography

Walk, Richard and Pick, Herbert L. Jr. 1978: *Perception and experience*. New York and London: Plenum.

adenyl cyclase cAMP and second messenger systems One of the ways in which the signal from a NEUROTRANSMITTER, NEUROMODULATOR or HORMONE is translated into physiological changes in the target neuron or organ. In the case of synaptic transmission, neurotransmitters, e.g. NOREPINEPHRINE (NORADRENALINE), are released into the synaptic cleft by the presynaptic neuron (see SYNAPSE AND SYNAPTIC TRANSMISSIONS). The neurotransmitter interacts with its receptor on the membrane of the postsynaptic neuron (see BRAIN AND CENTRAL NERVOUS SYSTEM: ILLUST-

RATIONS, fig. 32). In certain types of synapses, termed metabotropic synapses, this interaction effects a series of metabolic changes in the postsynaptic neuron. It has been postulated that the neurotransmitter-receptor interaction activates an enzyme, adenyl cyclase. When activated, adenyl cyclase causes the conversion of adenosine triphosphate to cyclic adenosine mono-phosphate (cAMP). Cyclic AMP acts as a second messenger by catalyzing the phosphorylation of membrane proteins by another enzyme, protein kinase. By some mechanism which is yet to be elucidated, these phosphorylated proteins alter the permeability of the postsynaptic membrane to certain ions which are important in synaptic transmission. The series of events is terminated by two other enzymatic reactions by which both phosphorylated proteins and cAMP are inactivated. Other possible second messenger systems have been reviewed by Greengard (1976).   GPH

Bibliography

Aurbach, G.D. 1982: Polypeptide and amine regulation of adenylate cyclase. *Annual review of physiology*, 653–66.

Bowman, W.C. and Rand, M.J. 1980: *Textbook of pharmacology*, 2nd edn. Oxford: Blackwell Scientific Publications. Sections 2, 20–24.

Greengard, P. 1976: Possible role for cyclic nucleotides and phosphorylated membrane proteins in postsynaptic actions of neorotransmitters. *Nature* 260, 101–8.

adrenal glands (See BRAIN AND CENTRAL NERVOUS SYSTEM: ILLUSTRATIONS, fig. 22). Small, triangular organs located at the upper pole of either kidney. They consist of two distinct parts: an outer part, the adrenal cortex and a center part, the adrenal medulla which is homologous to a sympathetic ganglion. Interest in the adrenal glands was sparked by Addison's description in 1849 of patients with what we now know was an insufficiency of the adrenal cortex (Addison's disease). The adrenal cortex synthesizes and secretes a number of steroid hormones (see STEROIDS) which are essential for HOMEOSTASIS. These steroids can be divided into three groups: glucocorticoids, mineralocorticoids and

sex steroids. The latter are normally secreted at a low rate. The synthesis and release of glucocorticoids is under the control of the pituitary hormone ACTH (see PITUITARY; ACTH); that of the principal mineralocorticoid aldosterone is regulated by the renin-angiotensin system. Other examples of diseases of the adrenal cortex, in addition to Addison's disease, are Cushing's syndrome due to a sustained overproduction of the principal glucocorticoid hydrocortisone, and Conn's syndrome due to primary aldosteronism. The adrenal medulla is the site of synthesis and release of EPINEPHRINE (ADRENALINE).   DHGV

Bibliography

O'Riordan, J.L.H., Malan, P.G. and Gould, R.P. 1982: *Essentials of endocrinology*. Oxford: Blackwell Scientific Publications. pp. 58–91.

affective disorders States in which mood is abnormally depressed or elated, often with associated behavioral and cognitive changes. They comprise manic-depressive psychosis, a wide variety of other less specific depressions – sometimes referred to as neurotic or reactive – and some illnesses occurring in particular settings such as puerperal psychosis and abnormal grief reactions. Although the term "affect" has strictly a wider connotation, tradition dictates that affective disorders encompass only those disturbances where depression and elation are the moods principally involved. Mood disturbances secondary to other illnesses, for example lability accompanying an organic brain disease or the blunted emotional responsiveness sometimes seen in chronic schizophrenia, would usually not be included.

Variations of mood are of course a common and natural phenomenon, indeed an essential ingredient of our emotional lives. It is not always easy to know when such variations should be regarded as abnormal; consideration may be given to several factors: duration of the mood swing, its intensity, apparent disproportion between the circumstances and the mood, or the specific nature of the change, which in florid cases leaves the observer in no doubt about the abnormality. In practice affective disorders are seen to include brief depressive or manic reactions, more sustained states which are exaggerations of the individual's natural pattern, and distortions of emotional and cognitive functioning of all degrees of severity. Mood swings may be classed as reactive or endogenous (the latter meaning arising from within); alternatively as neurotic (understandably related to the individual's constitution) or psychotic (with depressive delusions, loss of insight and of contact with reality).

The question whether neurotic and psychotic depressions are two distinct disorders has aroused much controversy. Kendell (1968) concluded that they should be viewed as forming a single continuum; the symptoms of an individual case could be scored in such a way as to assign him or her a position on this continuum and to indicate the likely response to treatment. BIPOLAR DEPRESSION – where a manic swing has also occurred – tends to be associated with a psychotic symptom pattern. Many other types of classification have been proposed and are reviewed by Paykel and Rowan (1979). Paykel's cluster analysis subdivided depressed patients into four groups: psychotic, anxious, hostile, and younger depressives with personality disorders. Earlier writers had emphasized the separate status of involutional melancholia as a form of depression affecting those aged over forty-five years and characterized by agitation and hypochondriacal preoccupations. However recent studies have failed to confirm this. The place of anxiety states remains controversial; by convention pure states without significant mood change are usually classified with the neuroses.

Depression is in its many forms a common disorder. In western society prevalence rates of 3–4 per cent have been quoted, but the figures vary greatly with the criteria for defining cases. Women seem to be affected about twice as commonly as men, this difference being only partially attributable to puerperal depressions. The peak age of onset is around sixty for psychotic depression and thirty for neurotic depression.

Research into the etiology of depression has identified a large number of predisposing and precipitant causes of which several may be operative in any one individual. Certain genetic, developmental, cognitive, psychodynamic, social and biochemical factors can be considered here. Genetic studies have shown a higher risk of manic-depressive psychosis (12 per cent) among the relatives of affected individuals; this is probably due to the inherited predisposition, since monozygotic twins have a higher concordance rate (68 per cent) than dizygotic twins (23 per cent). Unipolar and bipolar disorders may be genetically distinct. In the course of a child's development the prolonged absence of a parent seems to predispose to a later tendency to depression, either by undermining the individual's sense of security or by coloring his or her interpretation of experiences of separation and loss. Such experiences are the focus of various psychoanalytic views of depression; in particular it is suggested that the deprived individual blames himself for such losses and turns his anger inwards upon himself. Repeated experiences of being powerless to avoid emotional or physical trauma can lead to a state described by Seligman as LEARNED HELPLESSNESS. Another cognitive theory of depression was put forward by Beck (1967) who suggested that negative evaluations of the self, the environment and the future, acquired by past experience and activated by stresses, generate a corresponding mood of despondency. Many social factors lead understandably to depressed mood; Brown and Harris (1978) identified several conditions which render women vulnerable to depression: preschool children at home, absence of a job or of a supportive marital relationship. Depression is a familiar accompaniment to many physical, hormonal and biochemical abnormalities, such as electrolyte imbalance and thyroid deficiency. In addition certain drugs such as anti-hypertensives often provoke depression. In primary depression complex patterns of imbalance have been found in

NEUROTRANSMITTERS (chemicals which enable the nerve impulse to pass from one brain cell to another), particularly NORADRE-NALINE, SEROTONIN and DOPAMINE. Anti-depressant drugs have important effects on these neurotransmitters.

The diagnosis of depression is based on the symptoms and signs. These include sustained lowering of mood, sometimes with diurnal variation (usually lifting in the evening): diminished interest, energy, concentration and capacity for enjoyment; headaches, heaviness in the limbs; insomnia; dry mouth, gastrointestinal discomfort, constipation, poor appetite and weight loss. Psychotic depression may show additional features: retardation or agitation, delusions of guilt, of worthlessness, of poverty and bodily disintegration (nihilistic delusions), persecutory ideas, hallucinations of a depressive nature, pessimism and suicidal impulses. In masked depression the normal diagnostic features are unclear and other problems present: hypochondriacal preoccupations, facial pain, obsessional activity or uncharacteristic delinquent behavior (such as shop-lifting); in the elderly disturbance of intellectual function gives rise to PSEUDO DEMENTIA. There are no confirmatory tests for depression, but the severity can be rated on a number of scales, for example the Beck (subjective) and the Hamilton (objective).

The choice of treatment depends on the pattern and severity of the symptoms; the more severe and the more clearly psychotic the depression the greater the likelihood of response to physical treatments. These are principally ELECTROCONVULSIVE THERAPY (ECT; see Kendell 1981), and anti-depressants of the tricyclic (imipramine, amitriptyline), quaternary (mianserin), or more rarely monoamine oxidase inhibitor (MAO: tranylcypromine, phenelzine) groups. Medication continued for several months after recovery tends to prevent relapse. Lithium is a dramatically effective prophylactic in many cases of recurrent depressive or manic-depressive illness. Psychotherapy, cognitive therapy and social intervention grow in importance as the symptom pattern approaches the neurotic end of the continuum.

Mania (the term hypomania is often used for minor degrees of the condition) is a less common disorder, occurring in perhaps ten per cent of those subject to severe depressive illness, and rarely seen in the absence of depressive swings. Women predominate, but less so than with unipolar depression. According to some studies the incidence increases steadily with age. Stressful life events play a less important role in precipitating episodes of mania than of depression, and interact with effects of predisposition (largely genetic) and vulnerability.

Central symptoms of mania include: elated, disinhibited, impulsive and irritable mood; increased energy, activity, speech, social contact and enterprise; teeming thoughts and grandiose delusions. There is often an admixture of depressive mood, and where this is marked, the diagnosis of mixed affective state may be made. Hospitalization may be required to secure rest and sleep, nutrition and hydration, and to limit the consequences of the individual's distorted judgment and extravagance.

Specific treatment relies heavily on major tranquilizers (neuroleptics such as chlorpromazine and haloperidol): the manic patient may need surprisingly high doses to achieve sedation. Lithium has an important part to play, both in the acute phase and more especially in long-term prophylaxis. The course of severe unipolar and bipolar disorders tends to be one of erratic or sometimes cyclical relapses; up to 15 per cent of sufferers die by suicide, but lithium can vastly improve the prognosis.

Puerperal psychosis, occurring after about 1 in 200 births usually takes the form of a psychotic depression, the symptoms tending to be florid and varied, but the prognosis is good. The term maternity blues refers to a transient despondency often experienced soon after childbirth. The menstrual cycle is commonly associated with mood changes, often with despondency and irritability in the pre-menstrual phase; hormone adjustment and, in severe cases, lithium may be tried. Bereavement is accompanied by lowered mood lasting perhaps several months; in abnormal grief reactions the normal response may be inhibited, exaggerated or prolonged (Parkes 1972).

Future researchers will undoubtedly discover more about the biochemical mechanisms of affective disorders, leading to more effective GENETIC COUNSELING, prevention and treatment. At some distant point we may have to decide whether man should have total control over his mood.

DLJ

Bibliography

Beck, A.T. 1967: *Depression: clinical, experimental and theoretical aspects*. New York: Harper and Row.

———, Rush, A.J., Shaw, B.F. and Emery, G. 1983: *Cognitive theory of depression*. New York: Guildford Press.

Brown, G.W. and Harris, T. 1978: *Social origins of depression; a study of psychiatric disorder in women*. London: Tavistock; New York: Free Press.

Kendell, R.E. 1968: *The classification of depressive illnesses*. London: Oxford University Press.

——— 1981: The present status of electroconvulsive therapy, *British journal of psychiatry* 139, 265–83.

Parkes, C.M. 1972: *Bereavement: studies of grief in adult life*. London: Tavistock; New York: International Universities Press.

Paykel, E.S. ed. 1982: *Handbook of affective disorders*. London and New York: Churchill Livingstone.

Paykel, E.S. and Rowan P.R. 1979: Affective disorders. In *Recent advances in clinical psychiatry*, K. Granville Grossman. 3rd edn. London and New York: Churchill Livingstone.

alcoholism Most psychologists prefer the terms "alcohol dependence" or "problem drinking" to refer to the excessive and compulsive use of alcohol, since the label "alcoholism" is too closely associated with a simple disease model. A distinction is made between *dependence* upon alcohol and the harm caused by excessive consumption. Alcohol dependence refers to the strength of the habit, the subjective experience of compulsion and the difficulty in resisting alcohol across a wide variety of situations.

There is a physiological component in dependence. It is usually called neurologi-cal adaptation, the state in which the brain adapts to the presence of alcohol. This state results in tolerance of alcohol and also withdrawal symptoms when blood alcohol levels decline. It is important to emphasize that neurological adaptation does not always lead to psychological dependence. For this reason the term neuroadaptation is preferable to the term physical dependence. The distinction between neurological adaptation and psychological dependence also applies to the effects of other drugs. A surgical patient, given morphine to reduce pain, for example, might experience withdrawal symptoms, but not a desire to continue using the drug. Neurological adaptation can be conditioned so that it is aroused by signals or conditional stimuli in the absence of alcohol. This leads to behavioral tolerance and conditioned withdrawal.

Psychological models of alcohol dependence can be understood by considering the three stages of relapse. After a period of abstinence, a severely dependent problem drinker will usually start to drink again as a response to psychological and social events. Social anxieties, social pressures to drink, depression, frustration, boredom and loneliness have all been implicated in this first stage of relapse. The second stage involves the cognitive and psychophysiological effects of a few drinks. It is the processes involved in this stage which provoke the most debate. The simple disease model espoused by Alcoholics Anonymous includes the notion that "one drink leads to one drunk". Experimental work has shown that, for the severely dependent drinker, a desire to drink can be primed by a few drinks, but "loss of control" is not the inevitable result. Other processes are also involved at this stage, especially the "abstinence violation effect", a cognitive process which occurs when a resolution is broken and a feeling of helplessness sets in. In the final stage of relapse, after several days of heavy drinking, withdrawal symptoms are clearly expected when drinking stops. At this stage, one reason for continuing is to escape these unpleasant experiences.

The drinker learns to expect a variety of

short-term and long-term consequences if he drinks or resists at each stage. Every antecedent event or signal is therefore linked to a pay-off matrix of expected consequences. A functional analysis is an attempt to identify important antecedent events, along with the associated pay-off matrix. Most psychologists base their treatment upon such a detailed functional analysis. Psychological treatments usually involve three related approaches. In the first, an attempt is made to *enhance sobriety* so that there is a good reason to resist drinking. For example, job-finding clubs have been used to deal with unemployment that may be consequent on heavy drinking. The second approach involves facing up to temptation as a way of reality testing and altering the pay-off matrix. Deliberately accepting all invitations to events involving drink would be an example of this approach, which is sometimes called *cue exposure*. Finally, there is a great deal of emphasis upon the development of self-control or *coping strategies* to counteract craving.

As a working hypothesis, many psychologists believe that severe dependence is the result of learning and conditioning. Psychological treatments might therefore be developed which reverse this process. The simple disease model espouses the view that alcoholism is an irreversible disease and total abstinence is, therefore, the only route to recovery. Psychologists have been closely involved in the debate about whether some alcoholics can return to controlled drinking as an alternative to total abstinence for life. The research evidence indicates that severely dependent alcoholics do have great difficulty in achieving controlled drinking. On the other hand, for the early problem drinker who is less severely dependent, a goal of total abstinence is much more difficult to achieve than one of controlled drinking.

The development of dependence is not simply the result of an aberrant gene or an addictive personality. There are many routes to dependence. Research has identified links with cultural norms, as well as price and availability. In wine-producing countries, for example, continuous drinking is easy, cheap and socially acceptable. Consequently these countries have to cope with severe alcohol-related problems. Type of occupation is another associated factor: company directors, bartenders, theater managers, actors, entertainers, musicians, cooks and seamen tend to have a high death rate as a result of excessive consumption. Other influences are parental modeling and peer group pressures, as well as personality.

Psychological models of the development, nature and treatment of alcohol dependence are not very different from psychological models of any other area of human behavior and experience. This may appear to be a trite and commonsense observation, but in the last twenty years such an approach has been closely associated with a paradigm shift in the area of alcohol consumption. The simple disease model has now been replaced by a more complicated set of working hypotheses based, not upon irreversible physiological processes, but upon learning and conditioning, motivation and self-regulation, expectations and attributions. (See also DRUG DEPENDENCE; KORSAKOV'S PSYCHOSIS; WERNICKE'S SYNDROME.)   RJH

Bibliography
Marlatt, G.A. 1983: *Relapse prevention.* New York: Guildford Press.
Orford, J. and Keddie, A. 1985: Gender differences in the functions and effects of moderate and excessive drinking. *British journal of clinical psychology* 24, 265–79.

amnesia: retrograde, anterograde
The partial or total loss of memory for events that occurred shortly before brain trauma or physiological treatment that affects brain processes is called retrograde amnesia. For mild trauma, the amnesic period may encompass only a few seconds of time before the injury, but for more serious brain trauma it may be much longer. Retrograde amnesia is evidence that a serious injury to the central nervous system has occurred and it is usually thought to arise from the interruption of consolidation of memory.

The loss of memory for events that happen after injury to the central nervous system, disease, or administration of certain drugs is called anterograde amnesia. Anterograde amnesia can also result from psychosis, delirium, or the effects of drug-induced alterations in consciousness which cause inattention to stimuli and events.

Psychological factors such as anxiety, conversion and dissociative reactions, phobias, and obsessive-compulsive conditions can also induce amnesia. These types of amnesia do not involve any damage to the nervous system and the recovery of memory is sometimes spontaneous or can be achieved through professional psychological help.

(See also MEMORY AND LEARNING DISORDERS.)   RAJ

Bibliography

Diamond, R. and Rozin, P. 1984: Activation of existing memories in anterograde amnesia. *Journal of abnormal psychology* 93, 98–106.

Stern, L.D. 1981: A review of the theories of human amnesia. *Memory and cognition* 9, 247–62.

Weingartner, H., Grafman, J., Boutelle, W.C., Kaye, W. and Martin, P.R. 1983: Forms of memory failure. *Science* 221, 380–2.

amygdala (Greek, almond) A LIMBIC SYSTEM structure located medial to the temporal lobe near the ventral surface of the brain (see BRAIN AND CENTRAL NERVOUS SYSTEM: ILLUSTRATIONS, figs. 15, 17 and 21). The amygdala is divided into corticomedial and basolateral regions which in turn subdivide into smaller nuclear groups. Both areas project directly to the HYPOTHALAMUS but corticomedial nuclei send fibers, via the stria terminalis, primarily to diencephalic and forebrain areas while basolateral nuclei project more ventrally to midbrain and BRAIN STEM (figs. 5 and 6). Historically associated with a wide range of functions (e.g. olfaction, sexuality, information-processing), the amygdala is most consistently linked to emotional reactivity. The basolateral region appears to mediate an excitatory function in emotion since electrical stimulation of this area produces aggressive and other emotional responses while lesions have a general dampening effect. The opposite pattern is observed with respect to the corticomedial region, indicating an inhibitory function. Recent evidence suggests that the amygdala, in conjunction with the HIPPOCAMPUS, may contribute to basic learning and memory processes.   GWI

Bibliography

Rolls, E.T. 1984: Connections, functions and dysfunctions of limbic structures, the prefrontal cortex and hypothalamus. In *The scientific basis of clinical neurology*, eds. M. Swask and C. Kennard. London; Churchill.

anorexia nervosa A psychiatric disorder in which there is self-induced weight loss with severe inanition; persistent amenorrhoea (or an equivalent endocrine disturbance in the male); and extreme concerns about shape and weight. An intense desire to be thin leads to food avoidance and in some cases self-induced vomiting, excessive exercising and purgative abuse. Most of the physical features of the condition are the result of starvation. The disorder is largely confined to developed countries in which slimness is considered attractive. Onset is usually during adolescence. The majority of cases are female and the prevalence is thought to be increasing. Most treatment approaches are helpful in the short-term, at least as regards weight gain, but initial response to treatment does not predict enduring improvement. The long-term outcome is highly variable.

See also NEUROSIS.   CGF

Bibliography

Darby, P.L., Garfinkel, P.E. Garner, D.M. and Coscina, D.V. 1984: *Anorexia nervosa — recent developments*. New York: A.R. Liss.

Garfinkel, P.E. and Garner, D.M. 1982: *Anorexia nervosa: a multidimensional perspective*. New York: Brunner/Mazel.

McLeod, S. 1981: *Art of starvation*. London: Virago.

anxiety A crucial concept, especially in psychoanalytic theories, where it is seen to be of primary importance in the dynamics of behavior. It is often said that the state or feeling of anxiety is more closely associated with uncertainty than is the feeling of fear. The agitation produced in animals which cannot distinguish signals for shock from signals for food may be regarded as an analogue of human anxiety. The feeling is accompanied by fairly well-defined bodily changes which are manifested in raised heart-rate and GALVANIC SKIN RESPONSE (GSR). The primacy of uncertainty in the causes of anxiety was shown by Epstein (1972), who found that people who were told that they had a 5% chance of receiving an electric shock had higher heart-rate and GSR than people who were told they had a 95% chance.

In FREUD's earlier writings (1917), anxiety is said to result from the undischarged energy of the id, which expresses itself in this form when there is a lack of libidinal gratification. In his later theory (1926) the ego 'inoculates' itself with anxiety when the gratification of a desire will cause more pain than pleasure. To avoid this experience of anxiety the ego makes use of DEFENSE MECHANISMS, both to prevent the unacceptable gratification and to resolve the conflict by allowing the urge to be expressed in a socially acceptable form. Both these explanations can be seen to involve the elements of uncertainty or inability to act effectively to fulfill a desire.

In the writings of the neo-Freudians Horney and Sullivan anxiety is said to result from feelings of insecurity, which begin in infancy and may be due to actual helplessness or to the experience of parental disapproval. Both Horney and Sullivan stress the importance of relationships in causing and reducing insecurity.

Anxiety includes PHOBIAS, panic, obsessive-compulsive states and generalized anxiety. BEHAVIOR THERAPY (in vivo exposure) has proved quite effective with simple phobias, and COGNITIVE THERAPY is also used. Obsessive compulsions have been treated with exposure and response prevention (see Parloff et al. 1986). Drugs (benzodiazepines such as valium) reduce anxiety, but may have sedative effects, and lead to dependence and withdrawal symp-

toms. Physical signs of anxiety such as raised heart rate, nausea, sweating and palpitations may be treated with β-adrenoceptor blockers. These however have cardiovascular effects and may be inappropriate in many cases.

Spielberger (1971) distinguished the transitory emotion or mood of anxiety from the characteristic of being an anxious person. This distinction between state and trait anxiety has informed a good deal of recent research. Individuals who have more than usual trait anxiety also have unusually intense state anxiety in response to stressors, particularly to psychological rather than physical threat (Lamb 1978). In Cattell's work trait anxiety is one of the two best replicated second-order factors produced by factor analyzing the intercorrelations among his 16 'source traits'. As such it is probably to be identified with Eysenck's dimension of neuroticism. (See also NEUROSIS.)   RL

Bibliography
Epstein, S. 1972: In Spielberger 1972. op. cit.

Freud, S. (1917) 1963: *Introductory lectures on psychoanalysis*. Trans. J. Strachey. London: Hogarth.

—— (1926) 1963: *Inhibitions, symptoms and anxiety*. Trans. J. Strachey. London: Hogarth.

Lamb, D. 1978: Anxiety. In *Dimensions of personality*, eds. H. London and J.E. Exner. New York: Wiley.

Parloff, M.B., London, P. and Wolfe, B. 1986: Individual psychotherapy and behavior change. *Annual review of psychology* 37, 321–49.

Spielberger, C.D. ed. 1971, 1972: *Anxiety: current trends in theory and research*. 2 vols. New York: Academic Press.

aphasia Any disorder of speech resulting from brain damage. *See* speech disorders.

arousal A psychophysiological concept that is used in all branches of psychology, particularly personality theory. The idea of arousal can be traced back to Pavlovian ideas of the excitatory strength of the nervous system, but is perhaps more widely known in the work of Eysenck (1967) and Gray (1971). Both see arousal level as an inherited biological phenomenon on which individuals may differ along a dimension. Furthermore both have the notion of an optimal level of arousal.

Russian and Polish researchers have looked at arousal in terms of the concept of reactivity of the nervous system — that is the relationship between the intensity of the stimulus and the amplitude of response. Stimuli of equal physical activity are demonstrated to evoke a lower level of arousal in low-reactive than in high-reactive subjects. The low-reactive individual augments stimulation, and the high-reactive individual reduces stimulation, both aiming at maintaining or restoring a genetically fixed optimal level of activation.

Eysenck (1967) has argued that extraversion and introversion are closely related with habitual levels of arousal in the cortex (particularly the reticular activating system). Introverts have a higher level of arousal and hence are more inhibited, seek less stimulation and are better at learning and remembering are easily conditioned. Extraverts have a lower level of arousal and hence are more excitable, seek more stimulation and are not so good at learning or remembering or so easily conditioned.

Numerous studies have looked at the relationship between various self-report and physiological measures of arousal (see Paisey and Mangan 1980). Much work in human experimental psychology has also concerned the effects of induced rather than inherited levels of arousal on performance. An inverted U curve has been found for the relationship between arousal level and performance at a wide variety of different tasks. At very low levels of arousal the nervous system may not function properly, whereas at very high levels it may lead to intense emotions that disrupt performance. A moderate optimal level of arousal tends to produce alertness and interest in the task at hand.

(See also SLEEP AND AROUSAL: PHYSIOLOGICAL BASES). AF

Bibliography

Andrew, R.J. 1974: Arousal and the causation of behaviour. *Behaviour* 51, 135–65.

Eysenck, H.J. 1967: *The biological basis of personality*. Springfield, Ill.: Thomas.

Gray, J.A. 1971: *The psychology of fear and stress*. London: Weidenfeld and Nicolson; New York: McGraw-Hill.

Paisey, T. and Mangan, G. 1980: The relationship of extroversion, neuroticism, and sensation-seeking to questionnaire derived measures of the nervous system. *Pavlovian journal of biological science* 15, 123–30.

auditory nervous system The neural structures which participate in the conversion of physical sound waves into the sensations and perceptions of hearing. Sound waves interact with the external ear, ear canal, eardrum and three ossicles (malleus, incus and stapes) to produce a traveling wave along the basilar membrane in the cochlea (BRAIN AND CENTRAL NERVOUS SYSTEM: ILLUSTRATIONS, figs 26 and 27). Movement of the auditory receptors (hair cells) which rest on the basilar membrane causes sensory transduction initiating the chain of neural events that results in hearing. The auditory perception of pitch largely results from the frequency of the sound stimulus. Different frequencies in the sound stimulus cause different portions of the basilar membrane to move maximally: high frequencies stimulate the basilar membrane in the base of the cochlea; low frequencies, the basilar membrane in the apex of the cochlea. The orderly representation of stimulus frequencies as response maxima along the basilar membrane is a spatial mapping or tonotopic organization that is maintained in central auditory pathways.

The hair cells of the cochlea are innervated by NEURONS that form the spiral ganglion and give rise to the auditory branch of the eighth nerve. Fibers from the spiral ganglion terminate in the cochlear nucleus on the lateral surface of the BRAIN STEM. The interconnections of higher auditory centers are exceedingly complex. Auditory structures in the medulla include the nuclei of the superior olivary complex. At the level of the pons, ascending auditory fibers form a fiber tract (lateral lemniscus) to the nuclei of the lateral lemniscus and the inferior colliculus. The medial geniculate body is the auditory center in the THALAMUS. The primary auditory cortex lies in the superior temporal gyrus (Heschle's gyrus) (see BRAIN AND CENTRAL NERVOUS SYSTEM: ILLUSTRATIONS, fig. 3). Other cortices involved in hearing and speech include Wernicke's area which is important for speech comprehension, the angular gyrus which receives both auditory and visual inputs, and Broca's area which controls the motor speech centers. Although there is bilateral representation of the cochlear map in primary auditory cortex, secondary auditory cortex (Wernicke's area) is often enlarged on the left side of the human brain, suggesting lateralization of language function to the left hemisphere of the CEREBRAL CORTEX.

Many parts of the auditory system are innervated by descending fibers from higher centers, including fibers from the auditory cortex to the medial geniculate, fibers from the inferior colliculus to the cochlear nucleus, and fibers in the olivo-cochlear bundle from the superior olivary complex to the cochlear hair cells and the afferent neurons of the spiral ganglion that innervate them. The function of these feedback connections is not well understood. Possible functions include the selective direction of attention to a particular sound.   SCC

Bibliography

Brugge, J.F. and Geisler, C.D. 1978: Auditory mechanisms of the lower brainstem. *Annual review of neuroscience* 1, 363–94.

Dallos, P. 1973: *The auditory periphery, biophysics and physiology*. New York and London: Academic Press.

Evans, E.F. 1974: Neural processes for detection of acoustic patterns and for sound localization. In *The neurosciences, third study program*, eds. F.O. Schmitt and F.G. Worden. Cambridge, Mass. and London: MIT Press.

Geschwind, N. and Levitsky, W. 1968: Human brain: left-right asymmetries in temporal speech region. *Science* 161, 186–87.

Keidel, W.D. and Neff, W.D. eds. 1974: *Handbook of sensory physiology* vol. V/1. *Auditory system; anatomy, physiology (Ear)*. Berlin and New York: Springer-Verlag.

——— eds. 1975: *Handbook of sensory physiology*, Vol V/2. *Auditory system; physiology (CNS), behavioral studies. Psychoacoustics*. Berlin and New York: Springer-Verlag.

von Békésy, G. 1960: *Experiments in hearing*. London and New York: McGraw-Hill.

autism Infantile autism is a rare condition, affecting about two children per 10,000, and was first described by Kanner in 1943. The main features are: a failure to develop social relationships; specific abnormalities of language; an insistence on "sameness"; and onset before thirty months of age. Three quarters of autistic children also have mental retardation. Stereotyped repetitive movements (e.g. finger flicking), overactivity and epilepsy are common. Although it is classified with the childhood psychoses, it bears little resemblance to adult psychoses such as schizophrenia. Autistic children come from predominantly middle-class families, and this observation was thought at one time to have causal significance. However, the true nature of the condition remains obscure, and the current view is that autism is a non-specific syndrome of biological impairment. Treatment is aimed at helping social and linguistic development, often using BEHAVIOR THERAPY. Involvement of the family in treatment is important and special schooling is usually necessary. Prognosis is closely linked to the degree of mental retardation present, and the severity of language impairment.   GCF

Bibliography

Rimland, B. 1978: Savant capabilities of autistic children and their cognitive implications. In *Cognitive deficits in the development of mental illness*, ed. G. Serbon. New York: Brunner/Mazel.

Rutter, M. and Schopler, E. 1978: *Autism – a reappraisal of concepts and treatment*. New York: Plenum.

autogenic training A therapeutic system developed from the original work of Oskar Vogt by Johannes Schultz. It is similar to self-hypnosis, but is taught in graded steps: subsequent steps are not practiced until earlier steps are mastered. In a comfortable posture, in graded steps, patients learn to feel heaviness and warmth in their arms and legs, to experience the autonomy of their breathing process ("it breathes me") and feelings of peacefulness, to calm and regularize their heart beat, and to experience warmth in their solar plexus area along with coolness of their forehead. The process produces a highly relaxed state which is useful as an adjunct to many other kinds of therapy, as well as combating stress *per se*. More advanced forms of autogenic training involve specific therapeutic suggestions. The standard reference book is by Schultz and Luthe (1959).   CTT

Bibliography

Schultz, J. and Luthe, W. 1959: *Autogenic training: a psychophysiological approach in psychotherapy*. New York: Grune and Stratton.

autonomic nervous system The portion of the peripheral nervous system that innervates visceral organs, glands, and blood vessels in the control of basic vegetative functions (BRAIN AND CENTRAL NERVOUS SYSTEM: ILLUSTRATIONS, fig. 11). The autonomic nervous system, whose cell bodies are arranged in ganglia outside the SPINAL CORD, consist of sympathetic and parasympathetic divisions. The sympathetic division receives preganglionic fibers from motor cells in the thoracic and lumbar sections of the spinal cord, while the parasympathetic division originates in the cranial and sacral sections. The sympathetic division is responsible for mobilizing bodily resources and organizing physical activity appropriate to exciting or emergency conditions. Thus, sympathetic activation leads, for example, to increases in cardiac activity, blood flow to skeletal muscles, respiration rate, oxygen intake, and sweat gland activity to cool the body during exertion. On the other hand, digestive processes and activities associated with a relaxed state are inhibited. In contrast, the parasympathetic division acts to conserve bodily resources and maintain a state of relative quiescence. Thus the effects of parasympathetic activation are opposite to those of sympathetic activation. In general, the two systems may be regarded as working in a correlated but antagonistic fashion to maintain an internal equilibrium.

Autonomic activity is controlled by a part of the brain called the HYPOTHALAMUS. It is closely associated with the action of various hormones, particularly the EPINEPHRINES (ADRENALINES). Autonomic activity is important in situations involving aggression and fear and is involved in all aspects of emotion. (See also EMOTION AND THE AUTONOMIC SYSTEM.)   DJM/GWi

aversion therapy A procedure based on classical conditioning (see PAVLOV) that attempts to reduce the attractiveness of a particular stimulus by pairing it with an unpleasant event, for example, an alcoholic patient may receive a severe electric shock as soon as alcohol touches his lips. Aversion therapy found its main use in the treatment of alcoholism and various sexual "perversions", including homosexuality. Changed social attitudes toward homosexuality and the rise in the use of self-control procedures (see BEHAVIOR THERAPY) have made most uses of aversion therapy obsolete and it is now regarded primarily as of historical significance as an early and systematic attempt to apply a paradigm from experimental psychology to the treatment of maladaptive behavior.   DWJ

B

basal ganglia A group of forebrain subcortical nuclei located deep within the cerebral hemispheres (BRAIN ILLUSTRATIONS, fig. 15). The major structures include the caudate nucleus and putamen (collectively called striatum), globus pallidus, and claustrum. The amygdala, subthalamic nucleus, and substantia nigra are also sometimes included. The basal ganglia maintain vast connections with structures throughout the brain and particularly with the cortex and THALAMUS. It is a major integrative center for the EXTRAPYRAMIDAL MOTOR SYSTEM and as such plays an important role in the regulation of voluntary motor activity. Striatal influence in this regard appears to be primarily inhibitory since restrictive damage to this region induces, in animals, persistent circling movements and a hyperactive condition known as obstinate progression. In humans, a variety of motor disorders follow basal ganglia damage. Degenerative changes in the globus pallidus and substantia nigra are associated with Parkinson's Disease, a condition characterized by rigidity, tremor, and difficulty in initiating voluntary movements. Damage to the putamen results in athetosis in which the patient assumes abnormal postures, displaying slow and repetitive movements. Huntington's chorea, a hereditary disease characterized by jerky involuntary movements as well as by speech problems and progressive dementia, involves extensive damage to the striatum.   GWi

Bibliography

McKenzie, J. and Wilcox, L. 1984: *The basal ganglia: structure and functions*. New York: Plenum.

behavior genetics Is concerned with the effects of genes on the expression of behavior. Any form of genetic analysis requires the identification of differences. This may take the form of a clear distinction between the behavior of two individuals, or there may be continuous variation in the expression of some type of behavior within a population. Breeding tests or examination of relatives can then be made to establish how far such differences are genetic. Behavior genetics is not a unified field of investigation and within this broad outline are to be found a diverse set of aims and approaches which may have little contact with each other. Fuller and Thompson (1978) provide much the best survey of the whole field.

On the one hand, much research is directed toward the nature of gene action upon behavior. Single gene mutations are studied in convenient organisms such as *Drosophila* or mice, and attempts are made to relate behavioral differences between mutant and normal individuals to gene action on physiology, neural structure or neurochemistry. At the other end of the range the techniques of quantitative genetics are used to analyze the variation within a population for a complex trait like learning ability. This will certainly involve many genes and there is no possibility of identifying the action of any one, the aim may be to use genetic analysis to help partition the trait and distinguish between variation of genetic and environmental origin.

There is an inevitable diversity imposed on the field by the nature of the character being studied. Some branches of genetics are concerned with systems whose control is quite well known and where it is possible to relate the known action of genes (i.e. controlling the synthesis of proteins) to the end product. It is no coincidence that the most spectacular recent advances in genetics have come at its interface with molecular biology. Behavior presents many more problems for genetic analysis. Firstly, the phenotype itself is extremely diverse and indeed demands many completely different levels of analysis. We may be interested in the phototactic behavior of fruit flies, the control of balance and locomotion in mice, the maze-learning of rats, levels of aggression in different breeds of dog, courtship displays in chickens or spatial components of intelligence tests in human beings (all of which have been the subject of behavior-genetic analysis). Secondly, for many such phenomena the gap between gene action at the cellular level and the end-product we are studying is maximal. Nor can we expect to be able to generalize about the pathways along which genes operate to exercise their effects on such diverse behavioral phenotypes. Not all the pathways are of much interest in any case – a mutant mouse may show inferior avoidance learning, but turn out to have an elevated pain threshold to the electric shock which serves as reinforcer in the learning situation. It will always be necessary to screen out trivial effects of this type.

It has been argued that since behavior is usually manifested only intermittently as a sequence of events through time, its genetic basis exists only in so far as we can identify some underlying structure upon which it is based. Certainly some people feel that only by working with identified single genes of known effect can we hope to make any progress (see Quinn and Gould 1979 for an extreme statement of this reductionist position). However this type of approach is scarcely possible, except in one or two favored invertebrates whose genetics are well known, and much more that is of interest to psychologists has been achieved by behavior genetic analysis at other levels. We can consider some examples of each type.

Single-gene studies

There has been extensive work on *Drosophila melanogaster* where hundreds of mutant stocks are easily available, but these may have diverged genetically in other ways over generations of culturing, so it is often more useful to treat normal flies with a mutagen and screen the progeny for behavioral changes. Using this technique mutants have been isolated which affect a wide variety of behavioral phenotypes: phototaxis, locomotor activity, circadian rhythms, courtship behavior and learning ability (see Benzer 1983). Screening for behavior mutants requires some ingenuity and many trivial effects will have to be discarded along the way, e.g. flies which fail to respond because they cannot walk properly. The mutants affecting learning were mostly derived from a screening test in which flies learnt to avoid an odor which had been associated with electric shock. As their names, *dunce*, *amnesiac* and *turnip*, suggest their effect is to reduce learning and retention. It is obviously important to discover whether such mutants affect only olfactory conditioning, or whether they act more generally. It is not easy to get a range of learning situations for *Drosophila* but some visual, and simple operant conditioning has proved possible; *dunce* and *amnesiac* flies show some learning ability in these situations but certainly reduced from normal, (see Folkers 1982). The genes appear to have both general and specific effects and attempts are being made to link them with changes to brain biochemistry. Using special stocks of *Drosophila* it is possible to generate flies some of whose cells express the effects of a mutant gene while others are normal. Study of such mosaic individuals helps to reveal in which parts of the body the gene acts to produce its effect – its "primary focus"; (see Hotta and Benzer 1972).

Behavioral analysis involving many genes

The great majority of behavioral characteristics will be affected by many genes and we may not be able to identify the effects of any particular locus. Nevertheless the study of different strains of breeds or inbred lines of animals has often yielded interesting results. Nearly always they show differences on a wide variety of behavioral measures which can be shown to be of genetic origin, but the scale and sometimes direction of such genetic effects can be markedly affected by the environment. For example Henderson (1970) compared mouse strains reared in complex or standard cage environments in a feeding situation which involved exploratory behavior and agility. The genetic contribution to variance between the strains was four times greater in mice from complex cages, indicating extreme gene/ environment interaction. We must expect such interactions to be the rule in behavioral development.

Artificial selection for behavioral characteristics has often been successful and reveals that natural populations are variable for genes affecting behavioral traits. Aggression in mice, mating speed in *Drosophila*, maze learning in rats – all have responded strongly to selection. Tryon's experiment with maze learning was one of the first of its type. He produced "maze-dull" and "maze-bright" rats with virtually no overlap in performance. However, when tested in other types of learning situation the brights performed no better or even less well than the dulls. Analysis showed that Tryon's selection had isolated factors relating to the main cues the rats responded to when learning the maze. The brights were genetically predisposed to concentrate on kinesthetic cues in which Tryon's original maze was rich; the dulls' behavior was more visually controlled. Such a result contributed to our understanding of learning and illustrates the use of genetics as a tool for the study of behavior itself over and above its intrinsic genetic interest (see Manning 1976). By separating and exaggerating the effects of components which are normally associated with each other behavioral analysis is facilitated.

Human behavior genetics

Human behavior genetics mainly operates in two highly contrasted areas. First there is the study of gross genetic abnormalities, both those associated with single genes such as phenylketonuria or microcephaly, and also the chromosome abnormalities responsible for Down's syndrome, Turner's syndrome and others. With the single genes the nature of the primary action is often a clear enzyme deficiency which can be related to the effects on the

functioning of the nervous system and it can sometimes be counteracted using a controlled diet. Study of the genetics of brain metabolites backed up with experimental animal studies may help us to understand certain types of mental illness where neurochemistry is implicated (see Petersen, Collins and Miles 1982; Kety 1982).

The other type of human behavior genetics uses quantitative genetic approaches to study continuously varying traits such as intellectual ability and personality. The genetic analyses can be of impressive sophistication with data from extended families, mono-and dizygotic twins reared together and apart etc. The unresolved problem concerns the realistic separation of genetic and environmental influences upon such complex and controversial traits.

(See also GENETICS, EVOLUTION AND BEHAVIOR). AWGM

Bibliography

Benzer, S. 1983: The Croonian Lecture. Genes, neurons and behavior in *Drosophila*. *Proceedings of the Royal Society B*.

Folkers, E. 1982: Visual learning and memory of *Drosophila melanogaster* wild type C-S and the mutants *dunce, amnesiac, turnip* and *rutabaga*. *Journal of insect physiology* 28, 535–39.

Fuller, John L. and Thompson, William R. 1978: *Foundations of behavior genetics*. C.V. Mosby, St Louis: No UK edn. *but* distributed in UK by: London: Y.B. Medical Publishers.

Henderson, N.D. 1970: Genetic influences on the behavior of mice can be obscured by laboratory rearing. *Journal of comparative physiological psychology* 72, 505–11.

Hotta, Y. and Benzer, S. 1972: The mapping of behavior in *Drosophila* mosaics. *Nature* 240, 527–35.

Kety, S. 1982: Neurochemical and genetic bases of psychopathology: current status. *Behavior genetics* 12, 93–100.

Manning, A. 1976: The place of genetics in the study of behavior. pp. 327–43. In *Growing points in ethology*, eds. Paul P.G. Bateson and Robert A. Hinde. Cambridge and New York: Cambridge University Press.

Petersen, D.R., Collins, A.C. and Miles, R.G. 1982: An overview of the genetics of psychopathology. *Behavior genetics* 12, 3–10.

Quinn, W.G. and Gould, J.L. 1979: Nerves and genes. *Nature* 278, 19–23.

behavior modification A generic term referring to the applied use of behavioral psychology to bring about changes in human behavior by workers in the helping professions (clinical and educational psychologists, social workers, teachers, etc). Based on Skinner's operant conditioning paradigm, its central tenet is that all behavior is primarily learned and maintained as a result of an individual's interaction with his environment, which includes other individuals, and is hence susceptible to change by control over features of that environment. The three-term analysis of behavior (or ABC model) indicates that behavior change may be achieved by manipulating either the antecedent conditions for behavior, or the consequences following behavior, in line with the law of effect. Simply stated, this means that rewarded behavior will tend to increase in frequency, while behavior followed by punishing consequences will tend to decline.

(See also BEHAVIOR THERAPY.)   KW

behavior therapy Also called behavior modification, is the application of the methods and findings of experimental psychology to the alteration of maladaptive behavior. Rimm and Masters (1979) suggest that behavior therapy has eight main features. (1) Relative to PSYCHOTHERAPY behavior therapy tends to concentrate on behavior itself rather than some presumed underlying cause. (2) It is assumed that maladaptive behavior is to a considerable degree acquired through learning. (3) It is assumed that psychological principles, especially learning principles, can be effective in modifying maladaptive behaviors. (4) It involves setting specific clearly defined treatment goals. (5) It rejects classical trait theory. (6) The therapist adapts his or her methods of treatment to the client's problem. (7) The therapy concentrates on the here and now. (8) Therapists place great value on obtaining empirical support for their techniques.

Behavior therapy has its roots in two seminal publications in the 1950s. Wolpe (1958) described his work on experimental neurosis in cats and the clinical techniques he had developed from that work, the most important and enduring of which has been systematic desensitization. Skinner's book *Science and human behavior* (1953) was equally influential in suggesting how the principles derived from the study of operant conditioning and in particular the effects on learning of the consequences of behavior, could be applied therapeutically. The 1960s and '70s saw a rapid increase in the use of behavior therapy and it is now the major form of therapy practiced by clinical psychologists in much of the English speaking world. Scientific publications on behavior therapy have increased explosively and there are now numerous journals in this field in general and on specific aspects of it; the three best known are *Behaviour research and therapy*, *Journal of applied behavior analysis* and *Behaviour therapy*. The main changes in the theoretical and empirical background to behavior therapy since the 1950s have been the increasing influence of other aspects of experimental psychology as well as learning theory and in particular the role of social and cognitive factors which have been incorporated in social learning theory (Bandura 1977) which now provides the main theoretical basis for behavior therapy.

Five stages in behavioral treatment can be recognized. (1) Behavioral analysis – a detailed analysis of a client's problems and factors related to them. This is done on the basis of data gathered in various ways, including interviewing the client, direct observation of his or her behavior and self-monitoring of this behavior. There is considerable emphasis on the collection of objective numerical data, i.e. the number of journeys from home if the patient is agoraphobic, the frequency of incontinence in an encopretic child. (2) The determination of specific goals for treatment. (3) The development of a treatment plan involving the use of those techniques of behavior therapy which are applicable to the particular problem. (4) Implementation of the treatment plan.

(5) Objective evaluation of the results of treatment with modification and extension of the treatment plan based on the feedback provided by such evaluation.

Applications of behavior therapy

Behavior therapy has now been applied with considerable success to a wide variety of the problem behavior traditionally seen as falling within the province of psychiatry, including phobias, obsessions, generalized anxiety, depression, enuresis and encopresis, drug and alcohol abuse, the effects of longterm institutionalization in psychotic patients and the mentally handicapped, marital discord, sexual inadequacy and, decreasingly, sexual deviation, aggression, delinquency and eating disorders. In addition to the application of behavioral techniques in the traditional areas of psychiatry, treatment has now been extended to deal with the problems of physical illness in a sub-specialization of behavior therapy called behavioral medicine. Among the problems treated in this area are smoking, obesity, compliance with medical regimes, rehabilitation from physical illness, the direct treatment of psychophysiological disturbances such as high blood pressure, asthma and headache, and the alteration of self-damaging patterns of behavior such as the coronary-prone TYPE A behavior pattern.

Techniques of behavior therapy

Since behavior therapy is essentially applied experimental psychology, the specific techniques are numerous and in some respects less important than a general attitude toward therapy and the collection of objective data. Five categories of therapeutic technique, not necessarily mutually exclusive, can be discerned: (1) exposure based methods; (2) contingency management procedures; (3) cognitive behavior therapy; (4) assertive and social skills training; (5) self-control procedures.

Exposure methods

Much anxiety and anxiety-related behavior, such as phobic avoidance or obsessional compulsions, arises in response to particular events. Behavior therapy tries to extinguish the anxiety and associated behavior by systematic exposure of the patient to the feared situation. The actual form of exposure varies and can be very gradual with minimal anxiety as in SYSTEMATIC DESENSITIZATION or rapid and fear-inducing as in FLOODING (IMPLOSION) and can be to the real situation or to imaginal representations of it. Modeling procedures are also used, in which the patient observes the desired behavior being carried out by someone else before attempting it. There is now a consensus that exposure to the real situation (in vivo exposure) is most effective. In the treatment of obsessional behavior, such exposure is often used in conjunction with response prevention to stop the patient carrying out rituals associated with exposure to the feared or contaminating object.

Contingency management

The central tenet that behavior is maintained by its consequences forms the basis of contingency management, an all-pervasive component of behavioral practice. Behavior therapists try to determine the consequences of disturbed behavior and to ensure that such behavior is not followed by positive consequences and that desired behavior does receive positive reinforcement. Such contingency management is usually applied as part of an overall behavioral approach which uses some of the other techniques described. For example, a therapist treating an agoraphobic woman would try to ensure that her family did not attend to her solely when she was panicking and housebound and that they did positively reinforce her efforts to go out. With the very young or with institutionalized individuals with very limited behavioral repertoires contingency management may constitute the main form of behavior therapy as in a token economy in which practically all forms of the patient's behavior earn tokens which can later be cashed in for material rewards or privileges. Using such methods the more damaging effects of chronic institutionalization can be averted or reversed and patients can be taught to attend to their own physical well-being, their ward tasks and increased social interaction with other patients.

Cognitive behavior therapy

Possibly because of its roots in behaviorism and in the rejection of psychoanalytic theory, behavior therapy has until recently fought shy of dealing with non-observable private cognitive events. However, practically all therapists working with non-institutionalized adults now concern themselves to some extent with the thoughts and beliefs of their clients. Most cognitive therapies have arisen outside the field of behavior therapy but they are increasingly being incorporated into that therapy and have more affinities with it than with the more traditional psychotherapies. The three main variants of cognitive behavior therapy are Ellis's rational emotive therapy (RET) Meichenbaum's self instructional training (SET) and Beck's cognitive therapy. All these therapies are broadly similar and all attempt to enable cognitive change, now frequently called cognitive restructuring. Ellis claims that most disturbed behavior is based on irrational beliefs which he tries to change, primarily by logical argument. He claims that there are many irrational beliefs common to mankind, including for example, the belief that one must have the love and approval of all significant people in one's environment at all times. RET attempts to modify such irrational core beliefs. SET is more concerned with specific idiosyncratic irrational beliefs and attempts to modify them by making the patient first of all aware of them, and then instructing the patient in countering them by making appropriate statements while performing the desired behavior. Beck has concentrated primarily on the role of cognitions, and cognitive therapy in depression. He regards depression as having a central cognitive element and claims that the depressed display various cognitive distortions. For example, the tendency to refer all external events to oneself or to apply absolute standards in one's thinking so that everything is either all good or all bad. While Beck uses many of the behavioral techniques, particularly early in therapy with the most depressed

patients, the core of his therapy is a cognitive therapy that attempts to alter distorted thinking by, for example, helping the patients to consider their problems in alternative, solvable terms, or actually to assess the extent to which their problems can be attributed to their own actions.

(See also AFFECTIVE DISORDERS for different approaches to depression.)

Assertive and social skills training

Many interpersonal difficulties and resultant maladaptive behavior arise because of patients' inabilities to assert themselves, i.e. express positive or negative emotions clearly. Assertive and SOCIAL SKILLS training have been used with a wide variety of patients in an attempt to overcome these difficulties. The most widely used techniques in this area are behavioral rehearsal, modeling and information feedback in which the patient and therapist act out troublesome situations. The therapist first of all models the correct response, then the patient produces that response while the therapist provides feedback on the patient's behavior. If the patient is markedly socially unskilled a detailed analysis of his social deficits may be followed by extensive training on specific aspects of social interaction.

Self-control

It is a common misbelief that behavior therapy is applied by potent, or even omnipotent, therapists to passive clients. Some of the early theoretical writings on behavior therapy encourage this misconception but in reality most therapy involves the active participation of the client and increasingly therapy aims to teach the client methods of self control that will enable him or her to cope with problem situations. Practically all the techniques described above can be used by the patient as a self-control aid, and patients can therefore learn that they must, for example, expose themselves to the fearful situation if the phobia returns, that they should rehearse difficult social situations before entering them, and that they should arrange reinforcement for their positive actions and ensure that the actions they wish to discontinue are not being reinforced. In addition to the use of these standard techniques as self-control techniques, a number of procedures uniquely related to self-control have been developed, the most prominent of which is BIOFEEDBACK, a technique in which the subject learns to control his own physiological responses by receiving augmented feedback, usually through some electronic device, on the activity of the physiological system in question. Such techniques have been applied to a multitude of psychophysiological disturbances, most successfully in the treatment of headache, using muscle and skin temperature feedback, and in the treatment of encopresis using feedback from the anal sphincters.

Behavior therapy offers a complex and comprehensive treatment approach to almost the complete range of maladaptive behavior. The influential review of the effects of psychological treatment by Rachman and Wilson (1980) makes it clear that behavior therapy is effective and offers an enduring solution to many patients' problems, a solution that is often more effective than that offered by the traditional psychotherapist. Behavior therapy is also largely free of negative side effects and in particular the prediction on the basis of psychoanalytic theory that maladaptive behavior successfully treated by behavioral methods would reappear in some other form ("symptom substitution") has not been confirmed. When behavior therapy has effects beyond the particular maladaptive behavior targeted these effects are likely to represent further gains for the patient. DWJ

Bibliography

Bandura, A. 1969: *Principles of behavior modification*. New York: Holt.

—— 1977: *Social learning*. Englewood Cliffs, N.J.: Prentice-Hall.

Eysenck, H.J. 1979: The conditioning model of neurosis. *Behavioural and brain sciences* 2, 155–99.

Kovel, J. 1981: *A complete guide to therapy*. London: Penguin.

Rachman, S.J. and Wilson, G.T. 1980: *The effects of psychological therapy*. Oxford and New York: Pergamon.

Rimm, D.C. and Masters, J.C. 1979: *Behaviour therapy. Techniques and empirical findings*. London and New York: Academic Press.

Skinner, B.F. 1953: *Science and human behavior*. New York: Macmillan.

Wolpe, J. 1958: *Psychotherapy by reciprocal inhibitions*. Stanford, Calif.: Stanford University Press.

biofeedback A technique which can enable individuals to learn to control such internal bodily processes as heart rate, blood pressure, skin temperature, or degree of muscle relaxation by obtaining immediate information (feedback) about the state of the internal conditions through the use of monitoring equipment. Information about internal states is usually not available to the conscious experience except through the sensors of the biofeedback instrumentation. By providing feedback about the consequences of certain actions, many internal processes can be brought under some degree of conscious control.

Currently, the best explanations of biofeedback appear to be operant conditioning and servosystem models. Biofeedback is a relatively new therapeutic technique and consequently there are unanswered questions about its theoretical basis and continued utility once use of the monitoring equipment is discontinued.

(See BEHAVIOR THERAPY; MEDITATION.) RAJ

Bleuler, Eugen (1857–1959). A Swiss psychiatrist who was for many years director of the Burghölzli Clinic, near Zurich. Bleuler's major works on SCHIZOPHRENIA, PARANOID STATES and ORGANIC MENTAL STATES were based on close and detailed clinical observations. In 1911 he extended Kraepelin's clinical description of dementia praecox, introducing the term schizophrenia to emphasize the splitting (or fragmentation) of the personality and to avoid the implication that deterioration is inevitable. He acknowledged the help of C.G. JUNG in his main aim of applying FREUD's theories of psychological processes. Bleuler distinguished "fundamental symptoms": AUTISM, loosening of associations, THOUGHT DISORDER and changes in emotional reactions. He had a more optimistic view of social outcome than KRAEPELIN but believed that subtle signs of an illness process could usually be detected in the premorbid personality and invariably after clinical recovery. These ideas have had very considerable influence on many later definitions of schizophrenia (especially in the United States) and on psychological theories of etiology.   RAM

Bibliography

Bleuler, E. 1950: *Dementia praecox: the group of schizophrenias.* New York: International Universities Press.

blind, the: psychology and education

There is still no internationally-agreed definition of blindness, and in most countries the term is not restricted only to those who are totally lacking in sight. No reliable statistics are available, therefore, about global incidence, and even within any given nation the medico-legal criteria used for classification or registration purposes will encompass a very heterogeneous population. In some countries, for example the UK and the USA, the statutory regulations specify upper limits of acuity for distant vision and lower limits for width of visual field, and result in the majority of the "legally blind" having some potentially useful residual sight. A group that is so heterogeneous in visual functioning will vary also in its educational and psychological needs, as is seen by the emergence of a term such as "educationally blind" which is used for those who have to use braille for reading and writing. The age of onset of the visual impairment and the presence of additional handicaps add to the heterogeneity of those labeled as blind.

Nevertheless, some order can be obtained by partitioning along the two independent dimensions of degree of residual vision and age of onset. The growing interest in the needs of the majority of the registered blind, those at the upper end of the blindness continuum, has its origins (1) in the confirmation of

ophthalmologists that most ocular disabilities cannot be made worse by normal use of sight; (2) in the findings of experimental psychologists that various aspects of perception can be improved by training; and (3) in improvements in the quality and variety of magnifiers and low vision aids. Educators (e.g. Barraga 1964) seized upon the implications of these developments and proceeded to devise assessment and teaching procedures aimed at encouraging greater reliance on and interpretation of quite meagre visual information for orientation, mobility, object perception and even the reading of print (the latter now being facilitated by the use of closed circuit television magnifiers). The classification of a child or adult as blind is no longer regarded by teachers and rehabilitation staff as sufficient reason for assuming vision to be unusable, and when there are no contra-indications from the ophthalmologist, the common practice is for them to assess whether and how the learner uses, or could use, any remaining sight in recreation, classroom, and work and to devise training programs with that information in mind.

When the cut is made along the other axis – age of onset – a new set of problems arises. For those who become blind after extensive experience of operating visually, the concepts "readjustment" and "rehabilitation" are used but they seem less useful when applied to those who are born blind. This does not imply that congenital blindness has no impact on cognitive, perceptual and social development but rather that the growth of the total personality has its own unique shape and integrity. The handicapping consequences of blindness will be understood later, and then initially through the mediation of other people. There will be no sense of loss of body parts or functioning, nor the expectation by parents, family and advisers of overt or disguised feelings of hostility, depression and demoralization. These, however, are major problems for the newly-blinded, and are bound up with archetypal anxieties and attitudes about blindness that are themselves not just to do with the loss or absence of one of the major sensory modalities. Blindness has a symbolic content related to light and darkness, and to loss of power and control (see, for example, Monbeck 1973). It is perhaps for this reason that rehabilitation programs for the blind are a compound of skills training (to replace the lost power and control) and counseling, with the counseling sometimes extending to the members of the immediate family to enable them to accept the blindness and understand the feelings it evokes both in them and in the blind relative. Great though the difficulties of the later-blinded may be in acquiring braille, independent mobility, and daily-living skills, there is ample objective and anecdotal evidence testifying to the value for the individual of having had the power of sight, even if only for a few years. In relation to learning, this provides a framework against which new experiences can be set and evaluated.

Extensive evidence from behavioral scales and checklists has shown that, as a group, congenitally blind infants and young children reach certain developmental milestones later than the normally sighted. Many of the items where delays are observed involve locomotor and self-care skills. In later childhood, there is evidence too of the slower growth of various perceptual and cognitive competencies, for which the expression "developmental lag" is often used. It has, however, little explanatory value. More recent research is attempting to move on from merely recording these differences to an examination of the conditions that can mitigate the deleterious effects of visual loss. The wide variations among totally, congenitally blind children are being seen as informative about the constellation of necessary conditions for activating what Russian psychologists describe as the "safe analysers" (the remaining sensory channels). Western researchers may cast the procedure in terms of selecting alternative coding strategies, and then point to the role of the parents whose own feelings about the child's lack of sight may affect the initiation and development of their own parenting skills. As an example we may cite the importance for later language development

of the ability of mother and baby to monitor one another's line of gaze and so share a frame of reference and know what the other is "thinking" about, before any mutual verbal communication is possible. In the absence of this visually-based component of pre-speech communication, the mother may herself be deprived of some important stimulus and feedback, and need to be taught how vocalization and then speech may have unusual functions for the blind child – for sensing objects, for maintaining contact, for obtaining attention, and for spatially locating himself in relation to others. The fact that language seems eventually to develop normally, that object permanence and constancy are achieved, that walking may be accomplished without a preceding crawling stage, and that some blind children achieve these and other attainments at ages not very different from those of their sighted peers, may be interpreted as proof that blindness is not inevitably a brake on development. This does not deny that it can very easily restrict opportunities for learning and interfere with the emergence of facilitative behavior on the part of the care-givers.

As with sighted children, reading occupies a central place in the educational curriculum of the blind. Although modern technology is making access to information easier through cassette-recorders and devices that can convert print into a tactile format and into spelled out or synthetic speech, braille remains the dominant system. This is because it is a reading-and-writing medium, and one that preserves the information-rich characteristics of whole-page lay-out (the ability to emphasize by indenting, paragraphing, italicizing, etc.) and the facility for rapid backward and forward checking and scanning. However, print can be read two to three times more quickly than braille, and makes smaller demands on storage capacity (short-term memory). The various explanations for the relative slowness of tactual reading can be seen to have physiological and psychological bases. The width of the finger-pad, the "tactual window", is smaller than the eye's visual field, thus reducing the amount of information that can be picked up in one fixation. The speed of movement and powers of acuity of the eye are inherently superior; the sensations in the finger leave fast-decaying traces, easily obliterated by succeeding stimuli and thus not accurately identified and transferred to longer-term storage centers. Recognition of shapes by touch is akin to recognition through blurred vision. Textural (dot density) features of braille are coded as well as the global and spatially-related characteristics, and especially in the early phases of learning, this can result in the adoption of inefficient strategies of coding. Also, the low levels of redundancy characteristic of the structure of the braille cell (as compared with printed letter shapes), combined with multiple meanings for the symbols and complex rules about the use of contracted forms, impose perceptual and cognitive loads of a higher order than those encountered in print reading. Some of these hypotheses are now being adequately operationalized (e.g. Millar 1981) and there is reason to expect significant advances in our understanding of the factors that influence braille letter and word recognition. Among the already well-attested findings are those of Nolan and Kederis (1969) to the effect that (i) growth of some of the factors basic to reading readiness occurs very slowly in blind children, (ii) the correlation between intelligence quotient and reading is significantly higher for braille than for print reading, and (iii) the recognition times for braille words are longer than the sum of the recognition times of the individual symbols in the words, a position which is the reverse of that found for print. Whatever the causation of the slower processing of tactually-presented information, the blind are at a disadvantage vis-à-vis their sighted peers, requiring considerably more time to cover the same curriculum content and finding graphical illustration in mathematics, geography, and other science subjects difficult to interpret.   MJT

Bibliography

Barraga, N. 1964: *Increased visual behavior in low vision children*. New York: American Foundation for the Blind.

Millar, S. 1981: Tactual shapes. In Portwood and Williams, op. cit.

*Monbeck, M.E. 1973: *The meaning of blindness: attitudes toward blindness and blind people*. Bloomington and London: Indiana University Press.

Nolan, C.Y. and Kederis, C.J. 1969: *Perceptual factors in braille word recognition*. New York: American Foundation for the Blind.

*Portwood, P.F. and Williams, R.S., eds. 1981: *The visually handicapped child*. Division of Educational and Child Psychology, Occasional Papers, vol 5, no. 1. Leicester: The British Psychological Society.

*Warren, D.H. 1977: *Blindness and early childhood development*. New York: American Foundation for the Blind.

blood-brain barrier A mechanism which interferes with or selectively prevents certain types of chemicals borne in the general circulatory system from entering the brain (Kalat 1981). The barrier is actually an interface of the capillaries supplying blood to the brain with certain types of glial cells, namely astrocytes (see GLIA). The foot-like projections of the astrocytes tightly pack the capillary membranes, resulting in an insulating glial sheath around the capillaries. In order to enter the brain chemicals leaving the blood stream must pass through not only the capillary membranes, but also the glial sheath. In general, lipid soluble chemicals cross the blood-brain barrier more readily than do water soluble substances. For example the increased potency of heroin, relative to morphine, is due to its greater permeability through the blood-brain barrier, rather than any differential affinity for opiate receptors. The lack of passive diffusion across the barrier for certain compounds can be overcome by active transport mechanisms, such as for certain amino acids. The barrier presumably functions to preserve and protect the chemical environment of the brain, and is not fully developed at birth in humans.   GPH

Bibliography

Kalat, James W. 1981: *Biological psychology*. Belmont, Calif.: Wadsworth.

Wright, Samson 1982: *Applied physiology* 13th edn., eds. C.S. Keele, E. Neil and N. Joels. Oxford: Oxford University Press. p. 368.

body centered therapy A relatively new term referring to a host of therapies whose common goal is the altering of self-image or personality through work with the physical body, either exclusively or as a major component of the therapy. Among the more influential and widely practiced therapies of this type four stand out as very distinct in their methods, while still sharing this common goal. These four are: bioenergetics, Rolfing (also called structural integration), Feldenkrais method (also called functional integration) and body centered psychotherapy (a major form of which is called Hakomi method). Other body centered therapies include: psychomotor therapy, developed by Albert Pesso, Lomi work developed by Robert Hall, Ellisa Hall, Catherine Flaxman and Richard Heckler and the Alexander technique, developed by F. Mathius Alexander. Also related, peripherally, are dance and movement therapies and the traditional approaches like Hatha Yoga and such oriental martial arts as Tai Chi, Aikido and Tai Kwan Do. Though these do not by any means exhaust the body centered therapies, they provide a wide and representative sample.

The various body centered therapies work with the body in very different ways. Primarily these are work with: (1) slow, precise movements, as in Feldenkrais Method, Tai Chi and Alexander Technique (all three entail a careful sensing of body position and experience); (2) expressive movements and stressful postures, used to access emotionally charged material, as in bioenergetics and dance therapy; (3) the manipulation of body tissue, especially the fascial sheaths to restructure the organization of the muscles of the body and the relation of the whole body to gravity, as in Rolfing and its many offshoots; (4) the body as an expression of character and the use of touch, movement and physical interactions with the therapists in an attempt to understand and

process emotionally charged issues (as in bioenergetics, body centered psychotherapy and psychomotor therapy); (5) general conditioning and toning of the body to enhance health, feelings of well-being, and the development of the skills of self defense and personal control, as in Yoga and oriental martial arts. The common element among these different approaches is their use of some aspect of work with the body to influence mental health and well being.

Bioenergetics is an offshoot of Reichian therapy developed by Alexander Lowen and John Pierrakos, both of whom worked and studied with Wilhelm Reich. It is strongly influenced by PSYCHOANALYSIS and uses an elaborate theory of character which is seen as being intimately related to such aspects of the body as posture, structure, "energy flow" and tensions. The therapy combines a minimum of discussion with strong expressive movements and stress postures to promote the release of "blocked" or repressed emotions. The stress postures, combined with breath work, are used to exhaust those muscles which inhibit expression, breath and the full, free experience of feelings. The therapist will use his or her fingers and fists to open blocked areas by exerting pressure or by palpating or massaging. The therapist will often encourage the client to deepen the expression of his or her feelings by pounding, kicking, sobbing or screaming till these begin to happen in a spontaneous and natural way. It is postulated that through this contact with and expression of strong emotions, especially those that have been repressed, such as hate, anger, pain, sadness and sexual feelings, an understanding and a working through of significant emotional issues can and often is accomplished. In addition, the tensions that segment the client's body can be released and a new integration formed.

In Rolfing, the practitioner, for the most part abstains from any psychotherapeutic intervention. In theory at least, Rolfing is done on the body. The intention, however, is to create changes in the client's self image and feelings about him or herself, through integration of the myofascial system (the system which binds and gives shape to the muscles of the body) and integration of the whole body in the field of gravity. Since a lot of feeling comes up and is released during the treatment, some interchange along these lines does occur. But, generally, Rolfing is totally body-orientated, a systematic attempt to realign the structure of the body. The Rolfing practitioner uses his or her fingers, knuckles and elbows to stretch muscles that need length, to separate muscle bundles that have become stuck together through improper use and to stretch and move the fascial tissue that surrounds all muscle. The Rolfer works with the fascial tissue to restore proper balance, coordination and freedom of movement. A minimum of ten one-hour sessions is given, with more if needed. These ten hours follow a set routine during which layer after layer of fascial muscle is stretched and realigned until the entire body has been covered. In the process breathing and energy level improve significantly and the emotional effects are often as dramatic as the changes in body structure. A very important adjunct to Rolfing is Rolf Movement Work which, by its use of movement and awareness, has a great deal in common with Feldenkrais floor work, though most Rolf Movement Work is done standing and sitting.

Feldenkrais Method combines two ways of working with the body. One consists of a one-to-one manipulation of the body, the second is a method of movement work done with a leader directing any number of people through a series of gentle movements, done mostly on the floor. What is common to both forms is the use of heightened attention to the fine details of slow, gentle movement, whether the practitioner manipulates the client's limbs, etc., or the client makes the movements, guided by a leader. This process, which Moshe Feldenkrais developed is also called Functional Integration. The general idea is to impress upon the nervous system a detailed image of the body. Feldenkrais's second book on his method is entitled, *Awareness through movement*. By moving small segments at first and then combining these into larger and more complicated patterns, always with patient, careful attention and many repetitions, the client's body image (literally the image the client's nervous system has of his or her body) is enhanced and the possibilities of movement and the movement functions, given this new body image, are much improved. Since the method is directed at creating changes in the nervous system, it is not surprising that it has found application and notable success in diseases such as cerebral palsy, polio and meningitis. Its effects on self-image are seen as directly parallel to its effects on body image and it is through these that psychological changes are made.

Body centered psychotherapy, of all of these, is the most directly psychological method. Its connections with the body therapies are: (1) its extensive use of the body to evaluate the client psychologically, as in reading the body for character, and (2) the use of physical interventions such as touch, expressive movements, etc., as a vehicle for understanding mental life, and (3) its view of the mind/body split as the central issue in therapy of the character processes. In both the Hakomi Method, developed by Ron Kurtz, and the Psychomotor Therapy of Pesso, the therapist combines discussion, action and awareness to access and process important emotional material. The therapist may use fantasy, psychodrama, movement, touch and, in groups, the assistance of one or more people, to create the safety and structure necessary for powerful, emotional changes. The body centered psychotherapies have borrowed widely from the fields of movement, dance, drama and all manner of psychotherapy, from analysis to Gestalt. Their unique flavor and effectiveness is in the subtle and powerful use they make of the bodily manifestations of the client's psychological makeup.   RK

Bibliography

Alexander, F.M. 1974: *Resurrection of the body*. New York: Delta (Dell Publishing Company).

Feldenkrais, M. 1972: *Awareness through movement*. New York: Harper and Row.

Kurtz, R. and Prestera, H. 1976: *The body reveals*. New York: Harper and Row.

Lowen, A. 1971: *The language of the body*. New York: Macmillan.

Rolf, I. 1975: *Structural integration*. New York: Viking/Esalen.

body image The perceptions, conscious or unconscious, of one's own body. It may be distorted in personality and neurotic disorders. Examples are ANOREXIA NERVOSA and overpreoccupation with the appearance of particular body parts. Organic lesions of the parietal lobe may cause partial or complete unawareness and neglect of parts of the body. Body image concepts have been used to explain the occurrence and nature of somatic symptoms in neurotic and psychiatric disorder.
RAM

Bibliography

Schilder, P. 1950: *The image and appearance of the human body*. New York: International University Press.

borderline states The category borderline state (or syndrome) has been used in the United States to cover psychiatric conditions believed to be intermediate between SCHIZOPHRENIA and NEUROSIS, and PERSONALITY DISORDER. There is no generally accepted definition and the term is not widely used outside the United States. There are three main usages: (1) an independent entity quite separate from all other diagnostic categories; (2) a mild expression of schizophrenia, called schizotypal personality in the current American classification, DSM III (American Psychiatric Association 1980); (3) a form of personality disorder with features of impulsiveness, unstable relationship, identity disturbance, unstable mood and boredom (borderline personality in DSM III).
RAM

Bibliography

American Psychiatric Association 1980: *Diagnostic and statistical manual* III.

Claridge, G. 1985: *Origins of mental illness*. Oxford: Basil Blackwell.

Liebowitz, M.R. 1979: Is borderline a distinct entity? *Schizophrenia bulletin* 5, 23–28.

brain and central nervous system: illustrations *See* pp. 26–37; figs. 1–34.

brain and nervous system: chemistry of A major biochemical discipline, generally known as NEUROCHEMISTRY, concerned with the chemical composition of neural tissues and the functioning of the nervous system at the molecular level. Neurochemistry originated with the nineteenth-century pioneers of organic chemistry, neurophysiology and neuroanatomy, but its undoubted founder was J.L.W. Thudicum, a mid-Victorian expatriate German physician. While practicing medicine in London, Thudicum, supported by grants from government sources, conducted extensive research into brain chemistry culminating in the publication in 1884 of the classic treatise *The chemical constitution of the brain* (see Drabkin 1958). Slow but steady progress over the next sixty years was followed in the post war era by an explosive growth in neurochemical knowledge. Modern neurochemistry is represented by the International Society for Neurochemistry which publishes a major journal (*Journal of neurochemistry*) and several substantial textbooks (see below). It should also be emphasized that modern neurochemistry is increasingly becoming interwoven with other major disciplines in the neurosciences (e.g. neuroanatomy, neuropathology, neurophysiology, neuroendocrinology and neuro- and psychopharmacology).

Gross chemical composition. This reflects the exceptionally high ratio of surface membrane area to cell volume in the nervous system. Lipids, prominent constituents of membranes, are remarkably enriched in the brain and contribute about 50 per cent of its dry weight. Examples of lipids found only in neural tissues include galacto cerebroside (the characteristic lipid of myelin) and components of the complex class known as the gangliosides. Similarly neural tissues are greatly enriched in proteins with properties characteristic of membranes. Among the many brain-specific proteins already identified are neurafilament protein, the S-100 protein

25

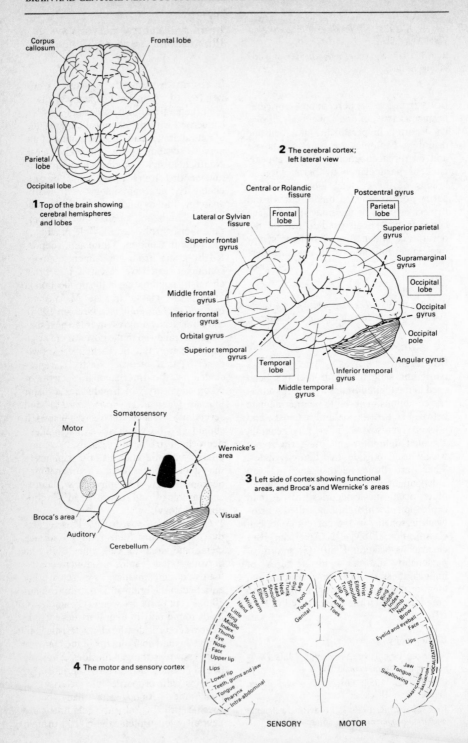

1 Top of the brain showing cerebral hemispheres and lobes

2 The cerebral cortex; left lateral view

3 Left side of cortex showing functional areas, and Broca's and Wernicke's areas

4 The motor and sensory cortex

SENSORY   MOTOR

5 The regions of the brain

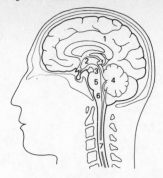

6 Principal structures of the brain stem and cerebellum

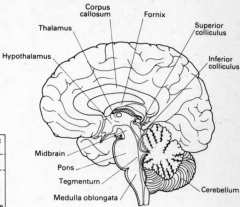

BRAIN				
	FOREBRAIN (prosencephalon)	TELENCEPHALON (end brain) (1)	cerebral cortex	
		RHINENCEPHALON	limbic system	
		DIENCEPHALON (interbrain) (2)	thalamus hypothalamus basal ganglia internal capsule	
BRAIN STEM — reticular formation	MIDBRAIN	MESENCEPHALON (midbrain) (3)	midbrain	
			cerebellum (4)	
		METENCEPHALON (afterbrain)	pons (5)	
		MYELENCEPHALON (narrow brain) (6)	medulla oblongata	
SPINAL CORD (7)				

7 Dorsal view of the brain stem. The right half of the cerebellum has been removed. The left half has been drawn over to the left to expose the floor of the IVth ventricle

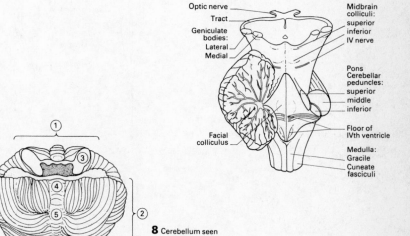

8 Cerebellum seen from below

1. Anterior lobe 2. Posterior lobe 3. Cerebellar peduncles
4. Flocculus nodule 5. Uvula

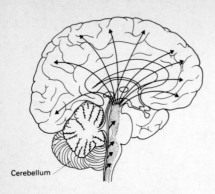

Cerebellum

9 The reticular formation is the shaded area. A bodily sense organ is connected to sensory areas in the brain by a pathway extending up the spinal cord. This pathway branches into the reticular formation. When a stimulus travels along the pathway, the reticular formation may "awaken" the entire brain (arrows)

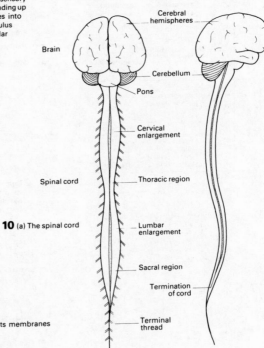

Brain

Cerebral hemispheres

Cerebellum

Pons

Cervical enlargement

Spinal cord

Thoracic region

10 (a) The spinal cord

Lumbar enlargement

Sacral region

Termination of cord

Terminal thread

10 (b) Cross-section of the spinal cord and its membranes

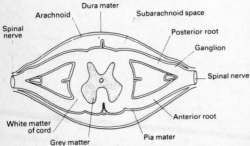

Dura mater

Arachnoid

Subarachnoid space

Spinal nerve

Posterior root

Ganglion

Spinal nerve

White matter of cord

Anterior root

Grey matter

Pia mater

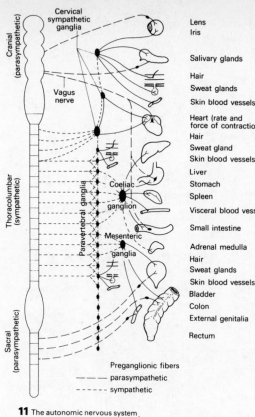

Cranial (parasympathetic)

Cervical sympathetic ganglia

Vagus nerve

Thoracolumbar (sympathetic)

Paravertebral ganglia

Coeliac ganglion

Mesenteric ganglia

Sacral (parasympathetic)

Lens
Iris

Salivary glands

Hair
Sweat glands
Skin blood vessels

Heart (rate and force of contraction)

Hair
Sweat gland
Skin blood vessels

Liver
Stomach
Spleen
Visceral blood vessels

Small intestine

Adrenal medulla
Hair
Sweat glands
Skin blood vessels
Bladder
Colon
External genitalia

Rectum

Preganglionic fibers
——— parasympathetic
- - - - sympathetic

11 The autonomic nervous system

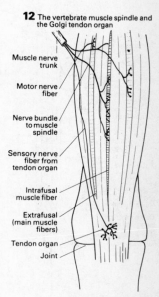

12 The vertebrate muscle spindle and the Golgi tendon organ

Muscle nerve trunk

Motor nerve fiber

Nerve bundle to muscle spindle

Sensory nerve fiber from tendon organ

Intrafusal muscle fiber

Extrafusal (main muscle fibers)

Tendon organ

Joint

A whole muscle and its tendon

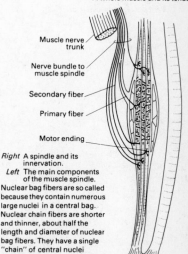

Muscle nerve trunk

Nerve bundle to muscle spindle

Secondary fiber

Primary fiber

Motor ending

Primary ending annulospiral

Plate ending

Nuclear bag fiber

Nuclear chain fiber

Trail endings

Secondary ending flower spray

Right A spindle and its innervation.
Left The main components of the muscle spindle.
Nuclear bag fibers are so called because they contain numerous large nuclei in a central bag. Nuclear chain fibers are shorter and thinner, about half the length and diameter of nuclear bag fibers. They have a single "chain" of central nuclei

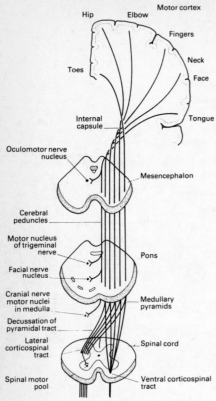

13 Pathway of the pyramidal tract

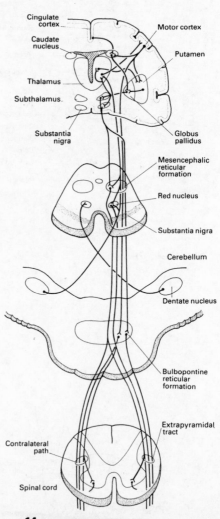

14 The extrapyramidal system.
The sections are not all to the same scale

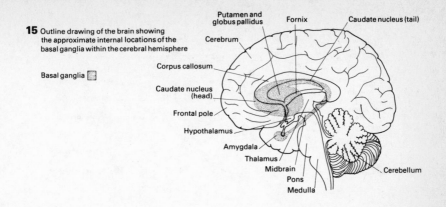

15 Outline drawing of the brain showing the approximate internal locations of the basal ganglia within the cerebral hemisphere

Basal ganglia

Putamen and globus pallidus
Fornix
Caudate nucleus (tail)
Cerebrum
Corpus callosum
Caudate nucleus (head)
Frontal pole
Hypothalamus
Amygdala
Thalamus
Midbrain
Pons
Medulla
Cerebellum

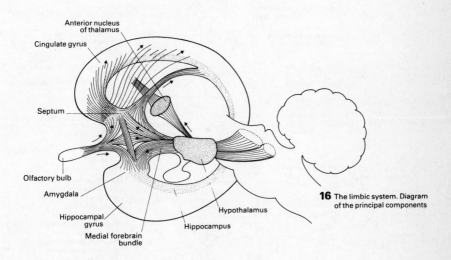

Anterior nucleus of thalamus
Cingulate gyrus
Septum
Olfactory bulb
Amygdala
Hippocampal gyrus
Medial forebrain bundle
Hypothalamus
Hippocampus

16 The limbic system. Diagram of the principal components

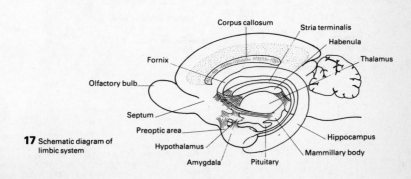

Corpus callosum
Stria terminalis
Habenula
Thalamus
Fornix
Olfactory bulb
Septum
Preoptic area
Hypothalamus
Amygdala
Pituitary
Hippocampus
Mammillary body

17 Schematic diagram of limbic system

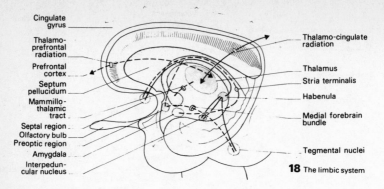

Cingulate gyrus

Thalamo-prefrontal radiation

Prefrontal cortex

Septum pellucidum

Mammillo-thalamic tract

Septal region

Olfactory bulb

Preoptic region

Amygdala

Interpeduncular nucleus

Thalamo-cingulate radiation

Thalamus

Stria terminalis

Habenula

Medial forebrain bundle

Tegmental nuclei

18 The limbic system

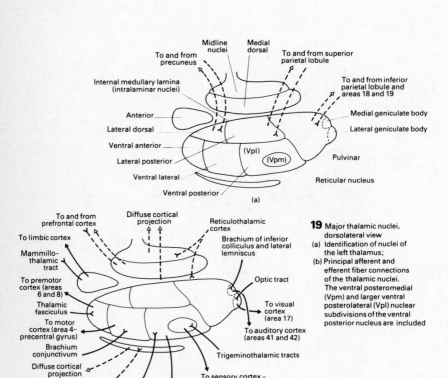

Midline nuclei

Medial dorsal

To and from precuneus

To and from superior parietal lobule

Internal medullary lamina (intralaminar nuclei)

To and from inferior parietal lobule and areas 18 and 19

Anterior

Medial geniculate body

Lateral dorsal

Lateral geniculate body

Ventral anterior

Lateral posterior

(Vpl)

(Vpm)

Pulvinar

Ventral lateral

Reticular nucleus

Ventral posterior

(a)

To and from prefrontal cortex

Diffuse cortical projection

Reticulothalamic cortex

To limbic cortex

Brachium of inferior colliculus and lateral lemniscus

Mammillo-thalamic tract

To premotor cortex (areas 6 and 8)

Optic tract

Thalamic fasciculus

To motor cortex (area 4– precentral gyrus)

To visual cortex (area 17)

Brachium conjunctivum

To auditory cortex (areas 41 and 42)

Diffuse cortical projection

Trigeminothalamic tracts

Reticulothalamic fibers

Medial lemniscus, spinothalamic tracts

To sensory cortex – face area

To sensory cortex – neck, trunk and extremities area

(b)

19 Major thalamic nuclei, dorsolateral view
(a) Identification of nuclei of the left thalamus;
(b) Principal afferent and efferent fiber connections of the thalamic nuclei. The ventral posteromedial (Vpm) and larger ventral posterolateral (Vpl) nuclear subdivisions of the ventral posterior nucleus are included

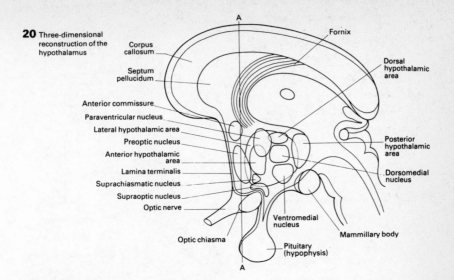

20 Three-dimensional reconstruction of the hypothalamus

Corpus callosum
Septum pellucidum
Anterior commissure
Paraventricular nucleus
Lateral hypothalamic area
Preoptic nucleus
Anterior hypothalamic area
Lamina terminalis
Suprachiasmatic nucleus
Supraoptic nucleus
Optic nerve
Optic chiasma
Ventromedial nucleus
Pituitary (hypophysis)
Mammillary body
Fornix
Dorsal hypothalamic area
Posterior hypothalamic area
Dorsomedial nucleus

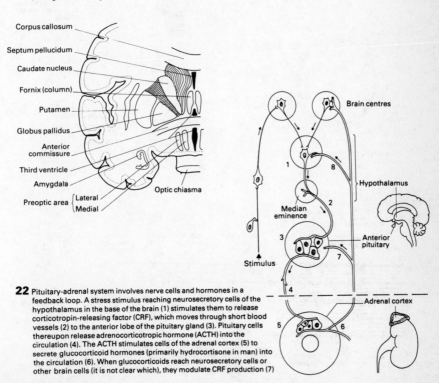

21 Cross-section of the hypothalamus (through line A on Fig. 20)

Corpus callosum
Septum pellucidum
Caudate nucleus
Fornix (column)
Putamen
Globus pallidus
Anterior commissure
Third ventricle
Amygdala
Preoptic area { Lateral / Medial
Optic chiasma

Brain centres
Hypothalamus
Median eminence
Anterior pituitary
Stimulus
Adrenal cortex

22 Pituitary-adrenal system involves nerve cells and hormones in a feedback loop. A stress stimulus reaching neurosecretory cells of the hypothalamus in the base of the brain (1) stimulates them to release corticotropin-releasing factor (CRF), which moves through short blood vessels (2) to the anterior lobe of the pituitary gland (3). Pituitary cells thereupon release adrenocorticotropic hormone (ACTH) into the circulation (4). The ACTH stimulates cells of the adrenal cortex (5) to secrete glucocorticoid hormones (primarily hydrocortisone in man) into the circulation (6). When glucocorticoids reach neurosecretory cells or other brain cells (it is not clear which), they modulate CRF production (7)

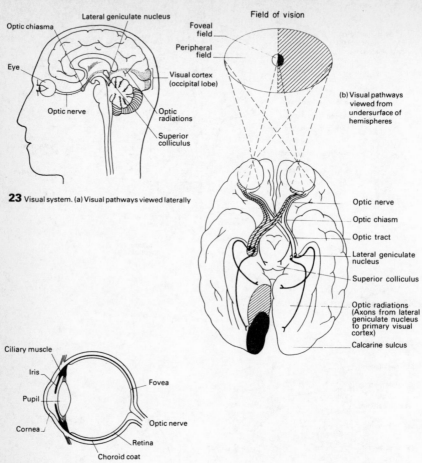

23 Visual system. (a) Visual pathways viewed laterally

(b) Visual pathways viewed from undersurface of hemispheres

24 Cross-section of the eye

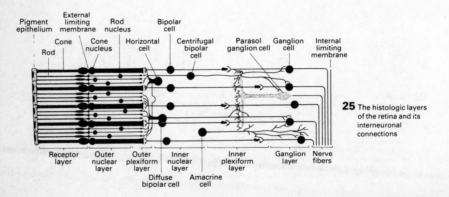

25 The histologic layers of the retina and its interneuronal connections

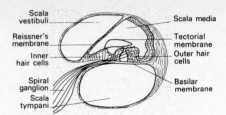

26 (a) Cross-section through cochlea

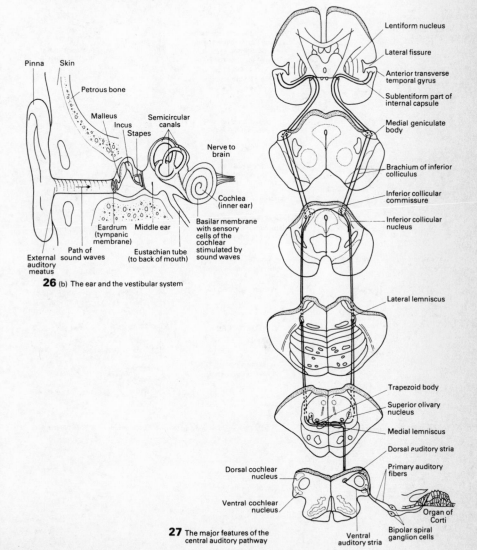

26 (b) The ear and the vestibular system

27 The major features of the central auditory pathway

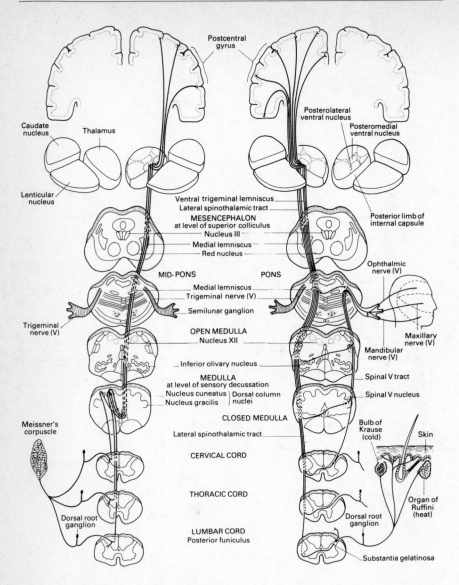

Postcentral gyrus

Caudate nucleus

Thalamus

Posterolateral ventral nucleus

Posteromedial ventral nucleus

Lenticular nucleus

Ventral trigeminal lemniscus
Lateral spinothalamic tract
MESENCEPHALON
at level of superior colliculus
Nucleus III
Medial lemniscus
Red nucleus

Posterior limb of internal capsule

MID-PONS   PONS

Medial lemniscus
Trigeminal nerve (V)
Semilunar ganglion

Ophthalmic nerve (V)

Trigeminal nerve (V)

OPEN MEDULLA
Nucleus XII

Maxillary nerve (V)

Mandibular nerve (V)

Inferior olivary nucleus

Spinal V tract

MEDULLA
at level of sensory decussation
Nucleus cuneatus
Nucleus gracilis } Dorsal column nuclei

Spinal V nucleus

CLOSED MEDULLA

Bulb of Krause (cold)   Skin

Meissner's corpuscle

Lateral spinothalamic tract

CERVICAL CORD

THORACIC CORD

Organ of Ruffini (heat)

Dorsal root ganglion

Dorsal root ganglion

LUMBAR CORD
Posterior funiculus

Substantia gelatinosa

28 Pathway for tactile discrimination

29 Pathway for pain and temperature, including the types of receptors

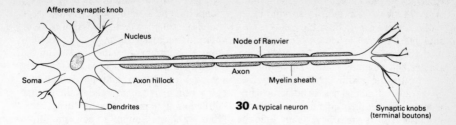

Afferent synaptic knob
Nucleus
Node of Ranvier
Soma
Axon hillock
Axon
Myelin sheath
Dendrites
Synaptic knobs
(terminal boutons)

30 A typical neuron

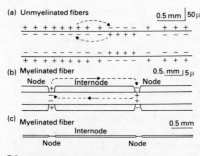

(a) Unmyelinated fibers 0.5 mm $|50\mu$

(b) Myelinated fiber 0.5 mm $|5\mu$
Node Internode Node

(c) Myelinated fiber 0.5 mm
Internode
Node Node

31 Propagation of impulse along a nerve fiber. In (a) there is only one line of current flow drawn in. In (b) the propagation is in a myelinated fiber, with the current flow restricted to the nodes. The dimensions in (b) are transversely exaggerated as shown by the scale, but are correctly shown in (c)

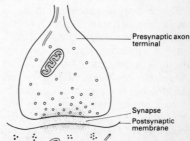

Presynaptic axon terminal

Synapse
Postsynaptic membrane

32 Diagram of a synapse. The presynaptic fiber swells to form a terminal bouton. This contains the chemical transmitter. The bouton membrane is polarized. The action potential depolarizes the membrane and the transmitter is released

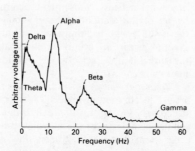

Delta
Alpha
Theta
Beta
Gamma
Arbitrary voltage units
Frequency (Hz)
0 10 20 30 40 50 60

33 The frequency spectrum of brain waves. Alpha waves, 10 Hz; beta waves, 20 to 25 Hz; gamma waves, 40 to 60 Hz; and delta waves, 1 to 2 Hz. Waves of 4 to 7 Hz, between the delta and alpha waves, are called theta waves

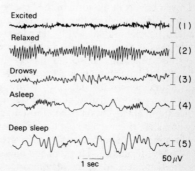

Excited (1)
Relaxed (2)
Drowsy (3)
Asleep (4)
Deep sleep (5)
1 sec
$50\,\mu V$

34 EEG waves: (1) β(desynchronized) wave when alert and excited; (2) α(synchronized) wave when eyes are closed and subject relaxed; (3), (4), (5) successive stages of sleep. The EEG becomes more synchronized, slower and greater in amplitude (specific to glial cells) and numerous enzymes involved in neuron-specific biosynthetic processes. Other important constituents of neural tissues are nucleic acids, nucleotides, carbohydrates, amino acids, amines and vitamins. The compounds in these categories, with certain exceptions, are found in all animal tissues but it must be emphasized that their quantitative patterns in the nervous system have many unique features.

General metabolism. The average adult human brain consumes about 49 ml of oxygen per minute or 20 per cent of the resting total body oxygen consumption. In infants this value rises to 50 per cent of the total. Under normal conditions glucose is the only substrate oxidized. Moreover the brain, unlike other organs, has only limited carbohydrate reserves and is therefore highly dependent on glucose supplied by the blood stream and exceptionally vulnerable to hypoglycaemia. In chronic starvation, however, the situation changes and the brain begins to oxidize other substrates, notably the ketone β-hydroxy-butyrate, a substance β-derived from the catabolism of fat. This explains the remarkable ability of the brain to function during prolonged starvation. The exceptionally fast rate of oxygen consumption of the brain reflects its high requirement for metabolically-derived energy in the form of the "energy-rich" compounds creatine phosphate and adenosinetriphosphate (ATP). The former functions as an energy store and the latter as the immediate source of energy for function. Both compounds are synthesized in neural tissue by enzymic pathways (glycolysis and oxidative phosphorylation) that are qualitatively similar to those in all mammalian tissues. The pattern of energy utilization in the nervous system, however, is highly distinctive. Here, major energy sources are needed for the maintenance of the ionic gradients across the nerve cell membrane that determine the membrane potential and form the basis for the conduction of the nerve impulse. (See BRAIN AND CENTRAL NERVOUS SYSTEM: ILLUSTRATIONS, figs. 30 and 31.) During conduction sodium ions enter and potassium ions leave the nerve cells through permeability

changes that are independent of energy supplies. The resulting shift in membrane potential causes a relative loss in excitability and eventually the cessation of conduction. Restoration of excitability is achieved by the active transport (a process requiring energy) of sodium and potassium ions across the nerve membrane in the reverse direction. The machinery for this process (the "sodium pump") consists of a membrane-bound enzyme (known as the sodium ion-dependent adenosinetriphosphate (ATP)). The energy released through this hydrolysis is coupled to ion transport by mechanisms poorly understood. In this way the incessant electrical activity of the living brain is highly dependent on a constant supply of energy, thus explaining why the brain fails so rapidly when deprived of oxygen. Other neuron-specific, though quantitively less impressive, reactions utilizing the energy of ATP include the synthesis of acetylcholine, axoplasmic transport and many signal transducing processes in the sense organs.

The *in vivo* coupling of energy utilization to function in discrete areas of animal brain has been greatly advanced by the introduction by Sokoloff of the deoxyglucose technique. Carbon-labeled deoxyglucose is used as a tracer. When injected into animals the brain cells accumulate this substance at a rate proportional to their functional activity. Subsequent determination of the amount of radiocarbon in the tissue by the technique of radioautography gives an accurate quantitative measure of the activity of individual neuronal systems.

Chemical anatomy. This term covers the precise localization of molecules in tissue structures. Owing to the extraordinary cellular complexity of the nervous system progress in this area has been slow: yet such knowledge is clearly essential for the formation of hypotheses regarding the functional significance of the chemical constituents of nervous tissue. Traditional methods of regional and micro dissection, cell fractionation and the preparation of subcellular structures (nuclei, mitochondria etc.) have provided limited information, but the striking advances have come from new approaches to the problem. First, extensive information on neuronal pathways has been gained by lesioning techniques in which degeneration of specific neuronal tracts is induced, either by surgical intervention or by the injection into the brain of specific cytotoxins. Subsequent analysis of the lesioned tissue alongside normal tissue from the same area provides information on the original composition of the degenerated neurons. For example the cytotoxin 6-hydroxydopamine, which causes a specific degeneration of neurons utilizing catecholamines, has been extensively used to map the projections of the DOPAMINE and noradrenaline (see NOREPINEPHRINE) neurotransmitter systems. Secondly new developments in histochemistry have made equally major contributions. Fluorescent microscopy, a technique due to Falck and Hillarp from Sweden, has permitted the detailed mapping in the brain of neuronal systems utilizing SEROTONIN and catecholamines as neurotransmitters. More recently immunocytochemical methods have proved invaluable, particularly since they permit the localization of antigenic molecules (e.g. enzymes and neuropeptides) to be studied at the very high magnifications available in the electron microscope. Two striking examples of the application of immunocytochemistry to the chemical anatomy of the nervous system are: the specific localization of the enzyme glutamic acid decarboxylase (responsible for the synthesis of the inhibitory neurotransmitter γ-aminobutyric acid) in the nerve terminals of the Purkinje cells in the deep cerebellar nuclei; and the demonstration of the coexistence of several neuropeptides with monoamine neurotransmitters in NEURONS.

Chemistry of synaptic transmission (see BRAIN AND CENTRAL NERVOUS SYSTEM: ILLUSTRATIONS, figs. 30, 32). Communication between neurons in the mammalian nervous system occurs almost exclusively by chemical transmission. Neurotransmitters (see NEUROTRANSMITTER SYSTEMS) are chemical messengers synthesized by enzymes present exclusively in the nerve axon terminals (or pre-synaptic "boutons") and stored in structures known as synaptic vesicles (see SYNAPSE). In general each nerve cell synthesizes and stores only one neurotransmitter, which is released into the synaptic cleft by nerve impulses traveling down the axon. After diffusing across the gap the neurotransmitter is bound to specific proteins located on the surface membrane of the postsynaptic neuron, known as receptors. The binding of neurotransmitter to its receptor initiates changes in the permeability of the postsynaptic cell membrane that either increase (excitatory neurotransmitters) or decrease (inhibitory neurotransmitters) its level of excitability, and therefore its tendency to transmit by conduction the message to further nerve cells.

The molecular events that underlie the several stages of chemical neurotransmission are only partly understood. The most complete evidence concerns the enzymic reactions involved in neurotransmitter synthesis, which are known in detail in the case of ACETYLCHOLINE, γ-aminobutyric acids, dopamine, noradrenaline and serotonin. Much evidence is also available for mechanisms responsible for the inactivation of these neurotransmitters, the process that terminates transmission. Acetylcholine is hydrolyzed by the enzyme acetylcholinesterase; histochemical studies have shown this enzyme to be highly localized in the region of the synaptic cleft. The choline liberated by acetylcholinesterase action is transported back into the presynaptic terminal and utilized for further synthesis of acetylcholine. For the other neurotransmitters mentioned above inactivation occurs either through reuptake of the unchanged molecule or enzymic degradation; for example the enzyme monoamine oxidase serves to inactivate the neurotransmitters serotonin, dopamine and noradrenaline. The molecular events involved in the process of neurotransmitter release and in neurotransmitter-receptor interaction are being intensively studied, but the current picture is far from complete. However, extensive knowledge is now available on the molecular structure of the acetylcholine receptor and work on the γ-aminobutyric acid receptor is well advanced.

Chemistry of the nervous system in man. By far the greater part of contemporary knowledge of the chemistry of the nervous system has come from studies in animals. The development of human neurochemistry has inevitably been slow because of the inaccessibility of the brain in the living subject and the unavailability of fresh human neural tissue for analysis. However, recent work has shown that for many purposes it is possible to obtain useful data by analyzing tissue from cadavers taken at autopsy many hours after death. At present analysis of such material indicates that the chemistry of the human nervous system closely resembles that of other mammalian species, although it is possible that more extensive studies will reveal significant differences.

In the medical field important advances in our understanding of the pathogenesis of certain diseases of the nervous system have accrued from chemical analysis of brain tissue taken from patients after death. In Parkinson's disease (the "shaking palsy") the work of Hornykiewicz and others demonstrated a dramatic decrease in the concentration of the neurotransmitter dopamine in the BASAL GANGLIA (a brain region concerned with the control of voluntary movement – see BRAIN MECHANISMS OF MOVEMENT) of patients dying with the disease. This discovery led to the introduction of treatment of Parkinson's disease with levodopa, a drug that increases dopamine concentrations in the basal ganglia and ameliorates many of the symptoms of the disease. In another disorder of movement, Huntington's chorea, analysis of autopsy tissue has demonstrated a significant loss of the neurotransmitter system utilizing γ-aminobutyric acid, and to a lesser extent of the acetylcholine system. In dementia a more specific loss of the acetylcholine neurotransmitter system has been demonstrated.   RR

Bibliography

Drabkin, D.L. 1958: *Thudicum: chemist of the brain*. Philadelphia: Saunders.

McIlwain, H. and Bachelard, H.S. 1985: *Biochemistry and the central nervous system*. 5th edn. Edinburgh: Churchill Livingstone.

Siegel, George J. et al. eds. 1981: *Basic neurochemistry*. 3rd edn. Boston: Little Brown.

Siesjo, B.K. 1978: *Brain energy metabolism*. Chichester and New York: John Wiley.

brain damage: recovery of function

See recovery of function after brain damage.

brain mechanisms of movement

Studied most often in psychology using animal models of the symptoms of movement disorders. This approach provides an understanding of the neural bases of normal movement, and leads to discoveries of the brain areas and neurotransmitter systems responsible for abnormal movement.

Laboratory studies of brain mechanisms of movement usually take two general forms: (1) the use of experimentally-induced brain damage and/or (2) the administration of centrally acting drugs. Techniques used to produce experimental brain damage include procedures such as electrolytic or radio frequency lesions (which destroy tissue), direct infusion of neurotoxic substances into the brain (such chemicals destroy particular neuronal systems relatively selectively), aspiration of tissue and tissue transection (cutting). Centrally acting drugs are administered systemically (orally or through the muscles, skin, abdominal cavity or veins), or directly into the brain and, in general, such drugs either elicit disturbances in movement or restore more normal movement to damaged subjects. Any of these techniques may be combined in a single experiment.

The areas of greatest interest to psychologists who study movement are the motor areas of the cerebral cortex (BRAIN AND CENTRAL NERVOUS SYSTEM: ILLUSTRATIONS, figs. 3 and 4), the so-called EXTRAPYRAMIDAL MOTOR SYSTEM which includes a number of structures collectively referred to as the BASAL GANGLIA, the BRAIN STEM (a lower area), and the CEREBELLUM (a lower motor integration area). Areas often of special interest also include the median raphé nucleus and the lateral hypothalamic area (figs. 5–8, 15 and 20). Damage or chemical manipulation of these areas can produce a variety of symptoms (varying by area) that mimic those observed in certain neurological disorders such as Parkinson's disease, EPILEPSY and Huntington's chorea. Some commonly studied symptoms are: Akinesia or bradykinesia (a loss or slowing of locomotion and movement), hyperkinesia (an abnormal quickening of locomotion and movement), seizure, catalepsy (the maintenance of awkward postures for long periods of time), drug-induced dyskinesias (involuntary movements of several types), tremor, muscular rigidity (which prevents normal movement), abnormalities in postural support, and impairment of righting reflexes (for detailed definitions, see Klawans 1973). Several forms of repetitive, stereotyped movements (such as those produced by amphetamines) are also studied.

A number of substances normally produced by the brain ("endogenous" substances) are known to regulate or affect movement. A few of these (putative neurotransmitters) are DOPAMINE, ACETYLCHOLINE, NOREPINEPHRINE, SEROTONIN, and γ-aminobutyric acid (Klawans 1973). Certain endogenous opiates, such as β-endorphin (Tseng et al. 1980) are also believed to affect movement. Selected symptoms, and their possible neurochemical and anatomical bases will be discussed.

Akinesia/bradykinesia often appears when dopamine systems are disrupted. In particular, manipulations that disturb the nigrostriatal dopamine system (a system that begins in the substantia nigra (fig. 14) and projects to the neostriatum) result in akinesia/bradykinesia (Hornykiewicz 1975). Thus, normal locomotion and movement depend, in part, upon intact dopamine systems. Techniques used to disrupt brain dopamine systems include focal (on a particular place in the brain) or intraventricular (through the brain's ventricles) infusion of the neurotoxin 6-hydroxydopamine (Ungerstedt 1971), a chemical that selectively destroys dopamine and norepinephrine neurons; systemic administration of drugs such as haloperidol (Hornykiewicz 1975) which block brain dopamine receptors; and electrolytic

lesions of the lateral HYPOTHALAMUS (Levitt and Teitelbaum 1975), through which the nigrostriatal dopamine system courses (Ungerstedt 1971). Akinesia can also be produced by systemic injection of sufficient amounts of drugs such as reserpine (Hornykiewicz 1972), which depletes levels of dopamine, serotonin and norepinephrine; morphine and other opiatelike substances (DeRyck, Schallert and Teitelbaum 1980; Tseng et al., 1980); and general anesthetics. In Parkinson's disease (a disease in which akinesia is a prominent symptom), there is a loss of nigrostriatal dopamine neurons that can be compensated for, in part, by administration of drugs such as Levodopa which increase brain dopamine function (Barbeau 1962). However, the loss of excitatory dopamine systems is probably not the only mechanism that interferes with kinesia. Recent research has shown that methysergide (a serotonin receptor blocker) can reverse the profound akinesia produced by lesions of the lateral hypothalamus (Chesire and Teitelbaum 1982), and that atropine (a drug that antagonizes acetylcholine) can reverse the akinesia produced by 6-hydroxydopamine. Thus, the loss of excitatory dopamine systems in conjunction with active inhibition by intact systems may combine to produce certain forms of akinesia. *Hyperkinesia* is also a feature of certain neurological disorders, including some forms of Parkinsonism (Parkinson 1817). Hyperkinetic disorders take several forms, and vary in expression from choreatic (jerking) movements (a symptom of Huntington's chorea) to rapidly accelerating forward locomotion (seen in some forms of Parkinsonism). Lesions of the caudate nucleus (part of the neostriatum) are often used as an animal model of Huntington's chorea (figs. 14 and 15). Caudate lesions elicit a form of "cursive" hyperkinesia or "running headlong forward" during which the animal runs straight forward and is not inhibited by obstacles (Mettler 1942). In Huntington's chorea, jerky movements have been attributed, in part, to excessive effects of dopamine on neurons that have been damaged or changed by the disease process

(Klawans et al., 1981). Another area that appears to be involved in hyperkinesia is the median raphé nucleus, a serotonin-rich area that is part of a system involved in sleep and waking (Jouvet 1968). Although the experimental results are controversial, lesions of this nucleus can produce excessive activity and locomotion (Jacobs, Wise and Taylor 1974). Serotonin may inhibit locomotion via other areas of the brain as well. Lesions of the nucleus reticularis tegmenti pontis in the brainstem of rats produce rapidly accelerating forward locomotion that (similar to some Parkinson's patients) can coexist in the presence of severe dopamine deficiency (Cheng 1981).

When such animals recover, so that their locomotion is no longer so rapid, the serotonin receptor blockers methysergide and metergoline can fully reinstate the previous level of rapid locomotion (Chesire, Cheng and Teitelbaum 1982). Furthermore, the administration of L-5-hydroxytryptophan (which increases levels of brain serotonin) can inhibit these animals (1982). Interestingly, animals with damage in this nucleus are not inhibited by doses of morphine that render normal rats completely akinetic (1983). Thus, the nucleus reticularis tegmenti pontis may be part of a final common system that inhibits locomotion (see 1982, 1983, 1984).

Among the drugs that can produce experimental *catalepsy* are haloperidol, morphine and reserpine. Reserpine is widely used in the treatment of Huntington's chorea, which has sometimes been described as the reverse of Parkinsonism (Klawans et al., 1981). Haloperidol and morphine appear to produce two very different forms of catalepsy that may reflect different adaptive states (De Ryck, Schallert and Teitelbaum 1980). Although sufficient amounts of either drug result in complete akinesia for several hours, the morphine-treated rat lacks postural support and righting reflexes (two abilities that are retained by haloperidol-treated rats). The morphine-treated rat, although rigid, lies in a posture resembling that of forward locomotion, while the haloperidol-treated rat sits crouched with a hunched spine. Thus, De Ryck, Schallert and Teitelbaum have proposed that morphine catalepsy may be organized to permit readiness for forward locomotion, while haloperidol catalepsy seems organized to permit the maintenance of stable equilibrium.

Seizure can originate at virtually any location in the brain, and may remain local or spread and become generalized (Klawans et al., 1981). There are many possible causes of seizure, including tumors, epilepsy, and brain diseases. Drugs that interfere with normal inhibitory substances in the brain can also induce seizure. These include drugs that antagonize γ-aminobutyric acid (such as picrotoxin and bicuculline), and other convulsants (such as strychnine). Many drugs show anticonvulsant activity, including some barbiturates such as phenobarbital.

Two forms of *tremor* are frequently distinguished:
(1) intention tremor (a symptom of Wilson's and other diseases) which occurs during voluntary movement and
(2) resting tremor (a feature of Parkinsonism) which usually occurs when the involved area is not engaged in voluntary movement, but may continue when such movement is initiated (Klawans 1973). Tremor may be partly dependent on serotonin systems, for it is one symptom of Parkinsonism that does not always respond as well as others to Levodopa (Klawans 1973). In monkeys, resting tremor can be produced by lesions of the ventromedial tegmental area, and such tremor has been alleviated by administering serotonin or dopamine agonists (drugs that facilitate these systems) (Goldstein et al. 1969). However, the role of serotonin agonists in Parkinson's and other disease states has not been completely investigated, and controversy still exists (Birkmayer and Riederer 1978).

Drug-induced dyskinesias are frequently choreatic in appearance, and can occur after prolonged treatment with Levodopa or neuroleptic drugs ("Tardive" dyskinesia) that are used to treat mental disorders (Klawans 1981). Amphetamine abuse may also produce dyskinesias (Klawans 1981). In Parkinson's disease, dyskinetic movements are frequently associated with the use of Levodopa in high doses, or at lesser doses but in patients with a long duration of the disease (Klawans et al. 1981). In all three cases (Parkinsonism, Tardive, and Amphetamine abuse), the appearance of dyskinesia is believed to be partly a function of excessive sensitivity of dopamine receptors to the drugs (Klawans et al. 1981).   RMC

Bibliography

Barbeau, A. 1962: The pathogenesis of Parkinson's disease. A new hypothesis. *Canadian medical association journal* 87, 802–7.

Birkmayer, W. and Riederer, P. 1978: Serotonin and extrapyramidal disorders. In *Serotonin in mental abnormalities*, ed. D.J. Boullin, New York: John Wiley.

Cheng, J.T. et al. 1981: Galloping induced by pontine tegmentum damage in rats: A form of "Parkinsonian festination" not blocked by haloperidol. *Proceedings of the National Academy of Sciences USA* 78, 3279–83.

Chesire, R.M. and Teitelbaum, P. 1982: Methysergide releases locomotion without support in lateral hypothalamic akinesia. *Physiology and behavior* 28, 335–47.

Chesire, R.M., Cheng, J.T. and Teitelbaum, P. 1982: Reinstatement of festinating forward locomotion by antiserotonergic drugs in rats partially recovered from damage in the region of the nucleus reticularis tegmenti pontis. *Experimental neurology* 77, 286–94.

—— 1983: The inhibition of movement by morphine or haloperidol depends on an intact nucleus reticularis tegmenti pontis. *Physiology and behavior* 30, 808–19.

—— 1984: Reversal of akinesia and release of festination by morphine or GABA applied focally to the nucleus reticularis tegmenti pontis. *Behavioural neuroscience* 98, 739–42.

De Ryck, M., Schallert, T. and Teitelbaum, P. 1980: Morphine versus haloperidol catalepsy in the rat: A behavioral analysis of postural support mechanisms. *Brain research* 201, 143–72.

Goldstein, M. et al. 1969: Drug-induced relief of the tremor in monkeys with mesencephalic lesions. *Nature* 224, 382–84.

Hornykiewicz, O. 1972: Biochemical and pharmacological aspects of akinesia. In *Parkinson's disease*, ed. J. Siegfried, Bern, Stuttgart, Vienna: Hans Huber.

—— 1975: Parkinsonism induced by dopaminergic antagonists. In *Advances in neurology*, eds. D.B. Calne, T.N. Chase and A. Barbeau. New York: Raven Press.

Jacobs, B.L., Wise, W.D. and Taylor, K.M. 1974: Differential behavioral and neurochemical effects following lesions of the dorsal or medium raphé nuclei in rats. *Brain research* 79, 353–61.

Jouvet, M. 1968: Insomnia and decrease of cerebral 5-hydroxytryptamine after destruction of the raphé system in the cat. *Advances in pharmacology.* 6B, 265–79.

Klawans, H.L. 1973: *The pharmacology of extrapyramidal movement disorders*. Basle: S. Karger.

—— et al. 1981: *Textbook of clinical neuropharmacology*. New York: Raven Press.

Levitt, D.R. and Teitelbaum, P. 1975: Sòmnolence, akinesia and sensory activation of motivated behavior in the lateral hypothalamic syndrome. *Proceedings of the National Academy of Sciences USA* 72, 2819–23.

Mettler, F.A. 1942: The relation between pyramidal and extrapyramidal function. *Research Publications of the Association of Nervous and Mental Diseases* 21, 150–227.

Parkinson, J. 1817 (*1955*): An essay on the shaking palsy. Reprinted in *James Parkinson*, ed. M. Critchley. London: Macmillan (1955).

Tseng, L.F. et al. 1980: β-Endorphin: Central sites of analgesia, catalepsy and body temperature changes in rats. *Journal of pharmacology and experimental therapeutics* 214, 328–32.

Ungerstedt, U. 1971: Adipsia and aphagia after 6-hydroxydopamine-induced degeneration of the nigrostriatal system. *Acta physiologica Scandinavica* Suppl. 367, 95–122.

brain stem The hind-and mid-brain area of the brain, located between the spinal cord and diencephalon (BRAIN AND CENTRAL NERVOUS SYSTEM: ILLUSTRATIONS figs. 5–7). The principal structures of the hind-brain are the medulla, pons, and cerebellum. The medulla is the most caudal structure in the brain stem. Several ascending and descending pathways as well as cranial nerves pass through this region which also contains nuclei concerned with basic life systems (e.g., heart action, respiration). The pons, located just anterior to the medulla, contains cell bodies for cranial nerves serving the head and face regions as well as a number of nuclei which interconnect separate brain structures. In particular there are major connections with the CEREBELLUM, located dorsal to the medulla and pons, and primarily involved in motor coordination. Anterior to the hind-brain is the mid-brain which consists of the tectum and tegmentum. The tectum contains two prominences – the superior colliculus, involved in processing visual information and the inferior colliculus, which serves a similar function in audition. The tegmentum is an extension of the brain stem reticular formation which forms a central core of nuclei and pathways transmitting impulses dorsally to specific processing points at higher brain levels as well as motor impulses ventrally to the spinal cord. A separate reticular system (fig. 9) projects diffusely to cortical regions, mediating an activating function that is important for sleep, arousal, and attentional processes.   GWi

Bibliography

Wright, Samson 1982: *Applied physiology*. 13th edn. eds. C.A. Keele, E. Neil and N. Joels. Oxford: Oxford University Press. pp. 293–7.

brain stimulation and memory (For

sites see BRAIN AND CENTRAL NERVOUS SYSTEM: ILLUSTRATIONS, figs. 2, 17, 19 and 21.) Brain stimulation via electrodes has been used as a tool for analyzing the neurology of memory. PENFIELD and his colleagues provided some of the first reports of subjective effects of intracranial stimulation in conscious human patients during the course of surgery on the temporal lobe, as an aid to locating epileptic foci (see Penfield 1958). In roughly one third of the patients, the stimulation mimicked their characteristic epileptic auras, including not only bodily sensations, but also apparently memorial effects. For example stimulation of the medial temporal lobe induced feelings of strangeness in the present surroundings and déjà vu, whereas similar stimulation of lateral aspects of the temporal lobe repeatedly resulted in banal and stereotyped recollections, often related to emotionally significant events. Although both auditory and visual experiences

occurred, together with the appropriate emotional tone, the minute detail and sense of immediacy experienced was different from that of normal recollection and resembled hallucinations. For a small number of patients the subjective sensations were not directly related to the experiential content of their spontaneous seizures.

Many aspects of Penfield's findings have been replicated. For example Bickford et al. (1958) found similar results with implanted electrodes and repeated testing involving interviews. Elicitation of that same memory could be achieved providing that stimulation parameters and neuroanatomical placement were held constant, although other studies have emphasized the variability of the responses (Stevens et al. 1969).

Although Penfield's results have been widely used in the context of the neurology of memory and in support of psychoanalytic concepts such as REPRESSION (see Kubie 1953), they can now be seen to be of more limited value. This is because the apparently memorial effects could not often be related to actual events in the subject's previous experience. The hallucinatory quality of the lateral temporal lobe effects, in particular, make it likely that many of the responses were confabulated. Mahl et al. (1964) found that momentary predispositions and thoughts at the time of stimulation were important determinants of the response. Furthermore, although the quality of the subjective phenomena has a degree of neuroanatomical specificity, similar results have been reported not only following stimulation of the HIPPOCAMPUS and AMYGDALA which are closely related to the temporal lobe, but also in medial thalamic regions (Flanigin et al. 1976). These results therefore limit the neurological significance of the effects.

Penfield also found some amnesic effects following temporal lobe stimulation, particularly in the recall of words or names. Similar effects have been found by Ojeman (1982), but also at frontal and parietal cortical sites. Ojeman has also characterized deficits in short term verbal memory resulting from stimulation to discrete frontal, parietal and occasionally temporal sites which are dissociable from sites producing naming or motor deficits in speech. Effects more similar to the amnesic syndrome have been reported in *two* patients following deep temporal lobe stimulation, including a retrograde AMNESIA for events up to a few days before the stimulation and a permanent anterograde amnesia for a short time afterwards (Bickford et al. 1958).

These results have encouraged the use of post-trial brain stimulation following training in animals to identify precise neural sites for memory processes. At currents below the threshold for seizures, motor or rewarding effects, intracranial stimulation can produce amnesia which depends on the site of stimulation and the nature of the memory task (see Kesner and Wilburn 1974).   TWR

Bibliography

Bickford, R.G. et al. 1958: Changes in memory function produced by electrical stimulation of the temporal lobe in man. In *The brain and human behavior*, eds. H.C. Soloman, S. Cobb and W.E. Penfield. Baltimore: Williams and Wilkins.

Flanigin, H.F. et al. 1976: Stimulation of the temporal lobe and thalamus in man and its relation to memory and behavior. In *Brain stimulation reward*, eds. A. Wauquier and E.T. Rolls. Amsterdam: North-Holland/Elsevier.

Kesner, R.P. and Wilburn, M.W. 1974: A review of electrical stimulation of the brain in the context of learning and retention. *Behavioral biology* 10, 259–93.

Kubie, L.S. 1953: Some implications for psychoanalysis of modern concepts of the organization of the brain. *Psychoanalytical quarterly* 22, 21–52.

Mahl, G.F. et al. 1964: Psychophysical responses in the human to intracerebral electric stimulation. *Psychosomatic medicine* 26, 337–68.

Ojeman, G.A. 1982: Interrelationships in the localization of language, memory and motor mechanisms in human cortex and thalamus. In *New perspectives in cerebral localization*, eds. R.A. Thompson and J.R. Green. New York: Raven Press.

Penfield, W. 1958: Functional localization in temporal and deep Sylvian areas. *Association for research into nervous and mental disorders* 36, 210–26.

——— and Perot, P. 1963: The brain's record of auditory and visual experience: a final summary and discussion. *Brain* 86, 595–696.

Squire, L.R., Slater, P.C. and Chance, P.M. 1975: Retrograde amnesia: temporal gradient in the very long-term memory following electroconvulsive treatment. *Science* 187, 77–9.

Stevens, J.R. et al. 1969: Deep temporal stimulation in man. Long latency, long lasting psychological changes. *Archives of neurology* (Chicago) 21, 157–69.

Thompson, L.I. and Grossman, L.B. 1972: Loss and recovery of long-term memories after ECS in rats. *Journal of comparative physiological psychology* 18, 248–54.

Whitty, C.W.M. and Zangwill, O.L. 1977: *Amnesia*. 2nd edn. London: Butterworth.

bulimia nervosa In the United States the term bulimia refers both to a pattern of behavior ("binge-eating") and to a specific psychiatric syndrome in which binge-eating is the principal feature; in Britain the equivalent syndrome is named bulimia nervosa. Binge-eating may be defined as a an episode of eating which is experienced as excessive and beyond voluntary control. In bulimia nervosa, binge-eating is accompanied by compensatory behavior such as extreme dieting, self-induced vomiting and the taking of purgatives and, in addition, there are extreme concerns about shape and weight similar to those found in anorexia nervosa. Although almost 50 per cent of patients with bulimia nervosa have had ANOREXIA NERVOSA in the past, their body weight at presentation is usually within the normal range. Like anorexia nervosa this disorder is confined to countries in which slimness is considered attractive. Most cases are female. The prevalence of the condition is not known. Vulnerability to OBESITY and to DEPRESSION appear to be predisposing factors. Treatment is difficult and the long-term outcome is not known.

See also NEUROSIS.   CGF

Bibliography

Fairburn, C.G. 1984: Bulimia: its epidemiology and management. In *Eating and its disorders*, eds. A.J. Stunkard and E. Stellar. New York: Raven Press.

Schlexer-Stropp, B. 1984: Bulimia: a review of the literature. *Psychological bulletin* 95, 247–57.

C

cardiac control *See* emotion and cardiac control.

catatonia *See* schizophrenia.

catharsis (Also known as abreaction.) The release of anxiety and tension by reliving and expressing an intense emotional experience. In Aristotle's *Poetics* catharsis is said to come about by watching grand tragedy on the stage. FREUD incorporated the concept into psychoanalytic therapy by emphasizing the release of repressed emotions as the first step in understanding and eliminating an underlying psychic conflict.   RHo

cerebellum A large, convoluted structure in the hind-brain situated behind the medulla and pons (BRAIN AND CENTRAL NERVOUS SYSTEM: ILLUSTRATIONS figs 5–8). The cerebellum consists of two hemispheres, each covered by a cortex of gray matter which surrounds a core of white matter. A cortex contains three distinct layers in which are embedded various cerebeliar nuclei. The cerebellum is attached to the BRAIN STEM by means of three pairs of peduncles containing afferent and efferent tracts which also link the structure to other parts of the central nervous system, most notably the CEREBRAL CORTEX, BASAL GANGLIA, and SPINAL CORD. A central component of the EXTRAPYRAMIDAL MOTOR SYSTEM, the cerebellum functions as part of an interconnecting system of pathways with the responsibility of coordinating motor activity in a timed and integrated fashion. The cerebellum is organized according to three functionally differentiated lobes – the flocculonodular lobe concerned with orientation and postural adjustments, the posterior lobe which exerts inhibitory control over voluntary movements, and the anterior lobe which regulates muscle tonus. A variety of motor defects follows cerebellar damage with tremor, ataxia and hypotonia among the most common symptoms.   GWi

Bibliography
Eccles, J.C., Ito, M. and Szenthagothai, J. 1967: *The cerebellum as a neuronal machine*. Berlin: Springer-Verlag.
Wright, Samson 1982: *Applied physiology*. 13th edn. eds. C.A. Keele, E. Neil and N. Joels. Oxford: Oxford University Press. pp. 303–13.

cerebral blood flow The normal brain, whether the body is sleeping or awake, requires an enormous amount of energy relative to the rest of the body. Since the metabolism of the brain is almost exclusively aerobic (i.e. oxygen requiring) and since the source of brain energy metabolism is almost exclusively glucose, under normal conditions cerebral blood flow, glucose uptake and oxygen consumption are highly correlated. This correlation can be disturbed in various pathological states, such as coma (Sokoloff 1976). The energy and oxygen requirements of the brain are reflected in the fact that, while the brain accounts for only about 2 per cent of an adult's body weight, it receives 15–20 per cent of the body's total cardiac output and accounts for about 20 per cent of the body's oxygen consumption. Recent technological advances have allowed a finer examination of blood flow to specific brain regions during various forms of mental and physical activity. One interesting suggestion from such research is that blood flow increases in the left, relative to the right, side of the brain during verbal activity.

(See LATERALIZATION.)   GPH

Bibliography

Meyer, J.S. and Schade, J.P. eds. 1972: *Cerebral blood flow. Progress in brain research*, vol. 35. Amsterdam: Elsevier.

Rasmusen, K. and Lassen, N.A. 1974: *Brainwork and the coupling of function, metabolism and blood flow through the brain*. New York: Academic Press.

Sokoloff, L. 1976: Circulation and energy metabolism of the brain. In *Basic neurochemistry*, eds. G.J. Siegel et al. 2nd edn. Boston: Little Brown and Co.

cerebral cortex The mantle of gray matter that surrounds the cerebral hemispheres (BRAIN AND CENTRAL NERVOUS SYSTEM: ILLUSTRATIONS, figs 1, 2, 5). Ninety per cent of cerebral cortex is classified as phylogenetically recent neocortex which is composed of six structurally defined layers. The convoluted surface provides numerous elevations (gyri) and depressions (sulci or fissures) which serve as useful landmarks for dividing the cortex into four principal regions: frontal, parietal, temporal and occipital lobes. The most developed part of the brain, the cortex as a whole has long been regarded as the seat of higher cognitive and intellectual function. There is also considerable localization of function, particularly involving sensory and motor processes (figs. 3 and 4). Visual information is processed in an area of the occipital lobe, audition within the temporal lobe, and somatosensory input projects to the parietal lobe. A motor area in the frontal lobe is responsible for initiating movement. The capacity for speech is localized unilaterally in frontal and parietal/temporal lobe areas. Adjacent to the primary sensory and motor areas are secondary or association areas. The motor association areas are concerned with complex motor skills, while the sensory association areas integrate, store, and correlate information that is necessary for thought and perception. Damage to association areas can produce various deficits affecting the execution of skilled movements (apraxia), the ability to recognize or be aware of objects (agnosia) and the comprehension or expression of language (APHASIA).   GWi

Charcot, Jean Martin (1825–1893). A most distinguished neurologist and director of the Salpêtrière Hospital in Paris, provided first descriptions of many neurological syndromes. He used the same methods of precise clinical examination and description to study HYSTERIA. Charcot believed this to be an inherited brain disease in which "stigmata" and seizures are triggered off by "hysterogenous" zones. He suggested that hysteria could be cured by hypnosis, a process which he classified into an elaborate series of stages and phenomena. Charcot's enduring importance for psychology and psychiatry results not from his beliefs, which were soon disproved, but from the interest he aroused in the study of neuroses and their treatment. He was a prominent public figure with many literary and medical friends and his regular clinical demonstrations attracted large audiences. FREUD and JANET were among his pupils.   RAM

chemotherapy *See* psychopharmacology.

child and adolescent psychiatry Is concerned with persistent disturbance of emotions or behavior which affects the child's social relationships or development, and is out of keeping with the child's sociocultural background and developmental level. Psychiatric disorder may be caused by factors within the child himself, his family, or his environment. In assessing disturbed children therefore, it is necessary to examine not only the child but also the family and school and social circumstances. A multidisciplinary team approach is widely used to achieve this, with medically qualified child psychiatrists working closely with psychologists and social workers. This model forms the basis of Child Guidance Clinics.

The incidence of psychiatric disorder in school children has been estimated at between five and fifteen per cent; and ten to twenty per cent in adolescents (Rutter, Tizard and Whitmore 1981). These figures, however, do not reflect the number of children presenting for treatment, and factors such as parental anxiety may be as important as the severity of a child's disturbance when treatment is sought. Boys are twice as commonly affected as girls. Although the rate of disorder is highest in inner city areas there is no clear association with social class alone: other associated factors are parental mental illness and criminality, family discord and disruption, early separation experiences and social disadvantage. Children with central nervous system abnormalities, mental handicap, or EPILEPSY, and children who have been abused, form a high risk group. There has recently been considerable interest in "protective factors" (Rutter 1981), which enable some children to survive gross deprivation and psychosocial stress. Examples are: an adaptable temperament; isolated rather than all-pervasive stress; a good relationship with one parent.

The two main groups of child psychiatric disorders, which together cover more than 90 per cent of psychiatric disorder seen in children are disorders of conduct, where the child behaves in socially disapproved-of ways, e.g. lying, stealing, disobedience (see CONDUCT DISORDER) and emotional disorders, characterized mainly by anxiety symptoms, which may be accompanied by tearfulness, sadness, social withdrawal or relationship problems. They occur equally commonly in girls and boys, and are relatively short-lived compared with adult neuroses. They usually develop in response to stress in the child's environment, e.g. parental disharmony, illness in a family member. Certain children, those with especially anxious temperaments, are vulnerable to minor stresses, and it is thought that there are also critical periods in a child's life when specific stresses have a major impact, e.g. bereavement in the third or fourth years of life. Treatment usually consists of understanding the stress, and either modifying it or helping the child develop better resources to cope. The prognosis for recovery and adjustment in later life is very good.

Children diagnosed as "psychotic" are generally withdrawn and unable to form emotional relationships with adults or other children. They frequently have mannerisms such as finger flicking, twirling or spinning objects. PSYCHOSIS in childhood is very rare and is a confused area. This is partly owing to the difficulties inherent in applying adult diagnostic criteria to children who are usually unable to verbalize their inner feelings and experiences; partly also because any process which affects relationship formation in infancy interferes with normal development. It may thus be difficult to distinguish psychosis in young children from mental retardation. Three subgroups are recognized:

(a) late-onset psychosis: these are adult-like psychoses (e.g. SCHIZOPHRENIA or BIPOLAR DEPRESSION) occurring in late childhood and adolescence. The treatment and prognosis is the same as for the adult condition.

(b) disintegrative psychoses: these present around the age of four with social withdrawal and loss of skills, including speech. They are due to an underlying degenerative disorder of the central nervous system, and treatment is mainly palliative and symptomatic.

(c) infantile AUTISM.

The outlook for recovery from psychotic conditions in childhood is not good.

In ORGANIC MENTAL STATES there is impairment of brain-functioning with "delirium" — confusion and hallucinations, which are usually visual in children. The commonest causes in childhood are high fevers accompanying infections such as measles, meningitis or pneumonia. They may also be caused by accidental self-poisoning, by overdoses of drugs such as sedatives or anticonvulsants; and by drug abuse (e.g. glue sniffing, LSD or amphetamine intoxication). Treatment is directed at the underlying cause, and the episode of delirium is usually short lived.

A number of conditions which occur on their own, not as part of a more widespread emotional or behavioral disturbance can be grouped under the heading *monosymptomatic disorders*. They include tics, enuresis (bedwetting), encopresis (soiling), night terrors, head banging, thumb sucking. Many of these can be regarded as developmental, i.e. they arise as part of a developmental stage, and resolve spontaneously with increasing age and maturity. However, treatment may be sought because of parental anxiety, or because of the child's distress if symptoms are interfering with his or her functioning or relationships.

Educational problems form another group of conditions. There are many reasons for a child failing to learn.

(a) General intellectual impairment, which will affect all areas of learning.

(b) A specific learning disability, affecting only one area, such as reading or arithmetic. (See DYSLEXIC CHILDREN.)

(c) Temperamental factors: restless, fidgety children with poor concentration and high distractibility often fail to learn in ordinary classroom settings.

(d) *Conduct disordered children* have a high incidence of reading retardation. The nature of this association is not well understood. Background family factors (e.g. dismissive attitudes to learning or authority) may be relevant; or the child's failure in the classroom may lead him to act out as an alternative strategy to impress his peer group and boost his own self esteem.

(e) *Stress* – such as divorce, bereavement, illness of a family member – may lead to loss of concentration and a temporary interruption of the child's progress.

(f) *Mental illness* – depressive disorder or schizophrenia arising in adolescence interferes with learning. The teacher may be the first to notice signs of the illness as school performance declines.

Wherever a child is failing educationally, there are likely to be secondary emotional problems – poor self esteem and loss of self confidence – which may need attention in their own right.

Treatment of disturbed children, like assessment, requires a multidisciplinary approach, and inpatient, day patient or outpatient care may be necessary. The focus of treatment may be on the individual child, e.g. through individual PSYCHO-THERAPY, play therapy, BEHAVIOR THERAPY, remedial tuition, or placement in a special school. On the other hand, the focus may be on helping the family to change, and for this family therapy, or parental counseling,

may be required. Liaison with schools, nurseries, and play groups may be necessary, and close working relationships with social services departments are vital for children in care, or those who are suspected of emotional or physical neglect and abuse. The combined efforts of the child psychiatric team with pediatricians, physiotherapists, speech therapists, or teachers may be needed to help children who are physically or mentally handicapped in addition to any psychiatric disturbance. Drugs are little used in child psychiatry apart from the treatment of the hyperkinetic syndrome and the adult-like psychoses.

Child abuse; non accidental injury Each year about six children per 1,000 are abused physically, emotionally or sexually. Such children may grow up to be permanently affected by their early experiences, with impairment of their capacity to form loving relationships. Abused children may present at accident departments with multiple fractures, burns and bruising; or with failure to thrive and developmental delay. They commonly show "frozen watchfulness" in the presence of adults. Research suggests that the failure of parent-child attachment often predates the abuse, and a number of high risk factors have been identified which provide clues for possible early intervention (Lynch and Roberts 1982). These include young maternal age, a history of parental psychiatric illness; the parents themselves being abused as children; separation of mother and baby in the neonatal period, and multiple social problems. The management of child abuse may involve permanently removing the child from its parents; helping develop parenting skills in a mother and baby unit or special day center; or setting up early intervention programs for high risk mothers and their new born babies to try and promote attachment.   GCF

Bibliography

*Barker, P. 1979: *Basic child psychiatry*. London: Granada.

Lynch, Margaret A. and Roberts, Jacqueline 1982: *Consequences of child abuse*. London: Academic Press.

*Rutter, M. 1975: *Helping troubled children*. Harmondsworth: Penguin; New York: Plenum.

—— 1981: Stress, coping and development: some issues and some questions. *Journal of child psychology and psychiatry* 22 (4), 323–56.

——, Tizard, J. and Whitmore, K. eds. 1981: The Isle of Wight and its services for children. In *Education, health and behavior*. New York: Robert E. Krieber.

chromosome abnormalities Chromosomes are those parts of the body cells which carry the genetic code. In humans, the normal cell contains 46 chromosomes, 44 of which are common to both sexes (autosomal chromosomes) and 2 which differ between the sexes (sex chromosomes). In males these consist of one X and one Y (XY); in females, two matching X chromosomes (XX). A variety of abnormalities of both autosomal and sex chromosomes have now been identified, the commonest being too many or too few chromosomes. Autosomal chromosome abnormalities are generally associated with marked physical malformation and mental retardation (e.g. DOWN'S SYNDROME). Sex chromosome abnormalities are less closely associated with mental retardation; malformation of the sex organs is the most common physical abnormality and psychiatric disorder may occur. Prenatal diagnosis of chromosome abnormalities is possible by sampling the amniotic fluid surrounding the fetus (amniocentesis). Subsequent termination can thus prevent the birth of an abnormal child. GENETIC COUNSELING for parents and relatives of affected children can help them decide about future pregnancies.   GCF

Bibliography
Therman, E. 1980: *Human chromosomes*. Heidelberg and New York: Springer-Verlag.
DeGrouchy, J. and Thurleau, C. 1978: *Atlas of chromosome abnormalities*. New York: John Wiley.

circadian rhythm A cycle of internal bodily activity level with a period of about twenty-four hours. Such rhythms can be detected by measurements of body temperature, heart rate, urine secretion, plasma content or indeed any measure which indicates metabolic rate. Measurements reveal a cycle which is roughly sinusoidal with a peak at about 4.00 p.m. and a trough at about 4.00 a.m. The cycle is disturbed if there is a change in the pattern of daily activity owing for example to starting night work or to flying across the world to a different time-zone. The rate of adjustment to a new cycle varies extensively. In some individuals the phase change occurs almost at once; in others it takes weeks. On average it takes about three days for a twelve hour shift to occur.

Although these rhythms are reflected subjectively in different feelings of arousal and lassitude it is difficult to obtain a direct correlation with changes in measures of performance either in the laboratory or in the field. Such changes do occur, but they are not large and there are extensive individual differences.

Thus, although circadian rhythms are clearly relevant to policies concerning shift work or working hours of intercontinental aircrews, recommendations cannot be definitive and must also take account of psychological, social and even cultural variables.   WTS

Bibliography
Wilkinson, R. 1978: Hours of work and the 24 hour cycle of rest and activity. In *Psychology at work*, ed. P.B. Warr. Harmondsworth: Penguin.

clinical psychology A branch of psychology concerned with the practical application of research findings and research methodology in the fields of mental and physical health. Clinical psychologists, whatever their theoretical backgrounds, share a strong belief in the understandability of human behavior. They are specifically skilled in the application of objective methods of observation, normative data and theories of change to human thought, feeling and action. When faced with dysfunctional behavior they will attempt to explain it in terms of normal processes, and to modify it by applying principles acquired from the study of normal learning adaptation and social interaction.

The term was first used by Witmer in 1896 to refer to assessment procedures carried out with retarded and physically handicapped children. The development of assessment procedures was further stimulated in the United States by the first world war and in the United Kingdom by the work of the War Office Selection Board during the second world war. Since then increasing numbers of nations have incorporated psychologists into their health services (Trethowan 1977), and have drawn up codes of professional practice (the American Psychological Association 1963). During the 1960s and 1970s the emphasis on assessment declined after the expansion of behavioral and many other eclectic therapies, and clinical psychologists started to draw on sources other than traditional experimental psychology, e.g. social, occupational and environmental psychology and ethology. Clinical psychology is now therefore enormously variable, as a description of the training and functions of those who make up the profession will illustrate.

Training includes the university level study of general psychology as well as specialist clinical experience, taking overall five to six years. (In some countries subsequent additional clinical experience is required before professional certification or licensing.) The graduate clinical psychologist will know something about most or all of the following:
(1) how individual experience of the world is modified by the processes involved in perception, thinking and the use of language and imagery
(2) the processes involved in learning, memory and adaptation
(3) what motivates human behavior, recognizing that unconscious as well as conscious motivation is possible
(4) the course of human psychological development
(5) norms and scales of measurement and their application to individual differences
(6) interpersonal interaction, the formation of groups and emergence of leaders
(7) the principles of individual and mass communication, and of the formation of attitudes, opinion and prejudice.

According to Hetherington (1964) the clinical psychologist will, above all, have had a training in the careful observation, assessment and recording of the way people behave, and of the experiences they say they have, whether or not this behavior and experience is considered normal. This background knowledge, together with a special interest in the field of abnormal psychology (Eysenck 1973) and a variety of clinical experience, qualifies the clinical psychologist both to act as a consultant and to perform the functions outlined below.

Assessment: The purpose of assessment may be either descriptive or functional, and will vary according to which aspect of behavior, physiological, psychological (covert), or behavioral (overt) is being assessed. Descriptive assessment was primarily used (a) to compare an individual with others in a valid and reliable way, using standardized norms, e.g. an IQ test or (b) to describe characteristics associated with disorder as an aid to diagnosis (e.g. the MMPI). Diagnostic assessment is no longer so predominant, and newer descriptive techniques are more clearly related to the problems and progress of particular individuals. For example recent developments in behavioral assessment (Hersen and Bellack 1976) make more use of direct observation and of rating methods and take account of situational and environmental as well as individual variation. Descriptive assessment still plays an important role, e.g. in work with children with learning difficulties, with the mentally or physically handicapped and in neuropsychology. Functional assessment has increased in importance as it is a necessary first step in constructing psychological treatment programs. Its functions may be to determine the type of intervention likely to be of most value, to measure the effects of intervention or of change during therapy, or to identify factors responsible for change (Mittler 1973).

Treatment: An individual may be referred to a clinical psychologist if some aspect of the way in which he or she thinks, feels or acts is itself a problem, is causing a problem or if changing it may ameliorate a problem. The range of referrals is growing and now includes medical, developmental and rehabilitative problems as well as psychiatric ones. The precise function of clinical psychologists in treatment (rehabilitation, behavior modification, therapy, counseling, crisis intervention etc.) varies therefore according to the setting in which they work, and their theoretical orientation. Particular psychologists may specialize in BEHAVIOR THERAPY, GROUP THERAPY, FAMILY THERAPY, PSYCHOANALYSIS, or other PSYCHOTHERAPY and in applications to physical medicine or in rehabilitation, but they should be sufficiently well acquainted with the principles and methods of other approaches to make appropriate referrals if they do not themselves have the necessary skills. They may intervene directly with an individual or indirectly through contact with family members or direct care staff.

Because of the emphasis placed on the scientific nature of their profession, clinical psychologists have played a major part in the development of those therapies theoretically founded in academic psychology – the behavior therapies. The value of some of these procedures is now well recognized, for instance in the treatment of phobias, learning difficulties and sexual dysfunctions, and in the use of operant methods. Other areas, COGNITIVE THERAPY in particular, are not yet so well recognized, but are fast developing.

Research: Clinical psychologists have a particularly important contribution to make in the field of research since they have been trained in the use of experimental design and statistical procedures. They should for example be able to make proper use of control groups, or randomization procedures, and also remain sufficiently objective in the interpretation of observations to be willing to abandon cherished theories in the face of disconfirming evidence. They are well placed to carry out research projects as individuals or as part of multidisciplinary teams, and to advise others on appropriate use of research methodology and statistics. In performing this function the clinical psychologist is aiming to evaluate critically his own work and that of other professionals so as to contribute as an applied scientist to the advancement of the health services. Examples include investigations into the value and cost effectiveness of health care interventions, into the design of health centers, or into doctor–patient communication, controlled treatment trials, testing hypotheses about the precise nature or course of dysfunctions, and detailed studies of single subjects.

Teaching: Because of their training as scientists, and their background knowledge of normal psychological development and processes, clinical psychologists are expected to contribute to the training of other health care professionals. The latter will need information about fundamental psychological principles as well as particular skills and knowledge relevant to their own specialization and interests, for instance in the cognitive changes expected with age, in the acquisition of basic skills by the mentally handicapped, in interviewing and communication skills, or in preparation for surgery. Psychologists will also be required to contribute to training for their own profession and to train others in the use of therapeutic techniques.

Administration: The deployment and organization of psychologists is of enormous importance in a small but fast growing profession. Clinical psychologists contribute to the planning and administration of health services in general, and are represented on international bodies such as the World Health Organisation (WHO 1973).

The five functions outlined above are performed in a wide variety of contexts: in psychiatric or general hospitals, in community based health centers or social work departments, in centers for the mentally or physically handicapped or for other disadvantaged groups such as geriatrics, drug addicts or epileptics, in counseling centers of all kinds and also in research establishments and government departments. The distribution of energy between functions will be determined partly by individual preferences and job demands and partly by the degree to which each country has been able to develop its psychological services within a health service or in private practice. The profession is constantly developing, as can be seen from a glance at some of the issues still under discussion. These include questions about the source of referrals to psychologists, about clinical responsibility, about the division of labor over function, and how to make best use of therapists as a scarce resource. The way in which these and other issues are resolved will determine some of the future characteristics of clinical psychology together with its national variations. GB

Bibliography

American Psychological Association 1963: Ethical standards of psychologists. *American psychologist* 18, 56–60.

Bellack, A.S. and Hersen, M. 1980. *Introduction to clinical psychology*. Oxford and New York: Oxford University Press.

Eysenck, H.J. 1973. *Handbook of abnormal psychology*. London and New York: Pitman.

Hersen, M. and Bellack, Alan, S. 1976: *Behavioral assessment*. Oxford and New York: Pergamon.

Hetherington, Ralph, R. 1964: The psychologist's role in society. *Bulletin of the British Psychological Society* 17, 9–12.

Korchin, Sheldon, J. 1976. *Modern clinical psychology*. New York: Basic Books.

Mackay, D. 1975. *Clinical psychology: theory and therapy*. London and New York: Methuen.

Mittler, P. 1973: *The psychological assessment of mental and physical handicaps*. London: Methuen.

Shapiro, M.B. 1985: Reassessment of clinical psychology as an applied science. *British journal of clinical psychology* 24, 1–13.

Trethowan, W.H. 1977: *The role of psychologists in the health services*. London: HMSO.

World Health Organisation 1973. *The role of the psychologist in mental health services*. World Health Organisation, Copenhagen.

cognitive therapy A form of psychotherapy developed by Aaron Beck in the United States in the 1960s. Beck postulates that a person's thoughts (cognitions is the favored term here) primarily determine his or her behavior. In neurosis, and particularly in depression, where poor self-regard is a common feature, the patient's thoughts about himself are said to be incorrect because of faulty learning: erroneous premises and misconceptions

are the source of such thoughts as for example, that he has achieved nothing, deserves criticism or has little to offer. Misinterpretations of reality become automatic and entrenched. In cognitive therapy the chief priority is to correct faulty conceptions and thereby eradicate negative automatic thoughts and promote realistic thinking. The therapist adopts an active role in making the patient aware of his automatic thoughts and helps him to realize that they are not true.

(See also BEHAVIOR THERAPY; CLINICAL PSYCHOLOGY.) SB

Bibliography

Beck, A.T. 1976: *Cognitive therapy and the emotional disorders*. New York: International Universities Press.

——, Rush, A.J., Shaw, B.F. and Emery, G. 1983: *Cognitive therapy of depression*. New York: Guildford.

Teasdale, J.D. 1985: Psychological treatments for depression: how do they work? *Behavior research and therapy* 23, 157–67.

color blindness In Caucasian populations about 8% of men exhibit an hereditary deficiency or anomaly of color vision. Some are *dichromats*, that is to say, they need only two variables in a color-matching experiment rather than the three required by the normal trichromat (see COLOR VISION). The most plausible explanation of dichromacy (first advanced in 1781 by von Gentilly) is that one of the three classes of cone photopigment is missing. A milder type of color deficiency is exhibited by *anomalous trichromats*, who require three variables in color-matching experiments, but make matches different from those of normal observers; it is thought that one of their three types of photopigment has been replaced by a pigment with a shifted peak sensitivity. In the hereditary forms of color blindness it is almost always either the long-wavelength pigment or the middle-wavelength pigment that has been affected; defects attributed to loss or alteration of the long-wave pigment are called *protan* and defects attributed to loss or alteration of the middle-wave pigment are called *deutan*. *Tritan* defects – disorders of the short-wave receptors – are only rarely inherited.

Overt, hereditary, color blindness is much rarer in women than in men (the incidence in women is less than 0.5%). The long- and middle-wave pigments appear to be specified by genetic loci on the X chromosome and thus a woman, having two X chromosomes, must inherit abnormal alleles (variant forms of a gene) from both her parents if she is to be overtly color deficient, whereas a man, having only one X chromosome, will necessarily be color blind if he inherits the abnormal allele from his mother. However, the 16% of women who are carriers of color deficiency do exhibit subtle abnormalities of color perception; for example, carriers of protan alleles reliably reveal themselves by being less sensitive to red light than are other women.

The color sense is a very delicate one and *acquired* deficiencies of color discrimination arise in a number of diseases. Interestingly it is the short-wavelength receptors that are most frequently disturbed in diseases (such as diabetes mellitus) that affect the retina. These tritan disorders are characterized by a confusion of yellow and white. Diseases that affect the optic nerve (such as multiple sclerosis) may lead to a generalized deterioration in hue discrimination, although the patient may pass tests designed to detect the genetically color blind. Very rarely, a central lesion may produce a total loss of color discrimination, while leaving unimpaired the patient's ability to read small print. Cases of the latter kind hint at some independence in the central analysis of color and form.

JDM

Bibliography

Cruz-Coke, R. 1970: *Color blindness.* Springfield, Illinois: Charles Thomas.

Pokorny, J., Smith, V.C., Verriest, G. and Pinckers, A.J.L.G. 1979: *Congenital and acquired colour vision defects.* New York: Grune and Stratton.

color vision The ability to distinguish different wavelengths of light (or different mixtures of wavelengths) independently of their luminance. Our color discrimination is strictly limited: mixtures of light that are physically very different may look identical to us. This limitation derives from the most fundamental property of human color vision, that of trichromacy. Consider a circular matching field subtending two degrees of visual angle and divided into two halves (see figs. (a) and (b)). Suppose that we can illuminate the field with three fixed wavelengths, λ_1, λ_2 and λ_3, and that we also have a variable light λ_4, which may be any wavelength or mixture of wavelengths. By arranging the lights in one of the two ways shown in the figure, it will be possible, by adjusting the intensities of λ_1, λ_2 and λ_3, to cause the two sides of the field to match. The choice of the fixed wavelengths is arbitrary (provided only that no one of them can be matched by a mixture of the other two) and they may themselves be replaced by mixtures.

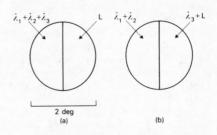

Color vision

In primitive form the fact of trichromacy was expressed by J.C. Le Blon in his *Coloritto* (c.1725), but he, and most eighteenth-century authors, took it to be a property of the world rather than of man. Thomas Young in 1802 made clear that trichromacy was a physiological limitation and we now know that it arises because there are just three types of cone receptor in the retina, each containing a different photo-sensitive pigment (see VISUAL PERCEPTION). When measured by microspectrophotometry the peak sensitivities of the three classes are found to lie at 420, 530 and 560 nm, but each type responds over most of the visible spectrum and there is no wavelength that stimulates only one class.

Cones are thought to obey the *Principle of univariance*: although the input to a cone can vary in intensity and wavelength, the cone's output signal can vary in only one dimension. This means that any individual cone is color blind; and thus, if the visual system is to extract information about wavelength, it must compare the rates of absorption of photons in different types of cone. This comparison is carried out by types of post-receptoral neuron that receive excitatory signals from one or two classes of cone and inhibitory signals from other cones; these *color-opponent* neurons are excited by some visible wavelengths and inhibited by others and thus they exhibit a color specificity not exhibited by the cones themselves. The most common type of color-opponent cell draws inputs of opposite sign from the long-wave and middle-wave receptors (i.e. the cones maximally sensitive at 560 and 530 nm). Since the excitatory and inhibitory inputs derive from different concentric retina areas, this type of cell also carries spatial information and, for stimuli of high spatial frequencies (see VISUAL PERCEPTION), ceases to be color-opponent. Thus information about color and form is not separated at the early stages of visual analysis. However, recent electrophysiological studies of monkeys suggest that there are discrete patches of striate cortex devoted to the analysis of color; and one whole region of pre-striate cortex seems specialized for color.

The short-wave cones of the retina (i.e. those with peak sensitivity near 420 nm) are sparse, constituting less then 5% of all cones in the retina. Consequently our spatial resolution is very poor when it depends on the short-wave cones alone; and when a stimulus becomes small or brief our color discrimination collapses to the "tritan" form characteristic of the rare dichromats who lack the short-wave cones (see COLOR BLINDNESS). No spatial opponency is exhibited by the relatively rare type of post-receptoral cell that receives opponent inputs from the short-wave receptors on the one hand, and from some combination of the long- and middle-

wave receptors on the other; that is to say, the excitatory and inhibitory inputs to these cells are drawn from congruent retinal areas.

The color-opponency seen in physiological recordings from the visual system is reflected in the psychophysical phenomenon of *combinative euchromatopsia*. Suppose that the threshold for a violet (420 nm) target is first measured on a blue (473 nm) "adapting field". If now we add increasing quantities of yellow (570 nm) light to the blue adapting field, the threshold for the violet target will fall, even though the composite adapting field is now much brighter. And the threshold is minimal when the ratio of the blue and yellow components is such that the composite field looks whitish. Analogous results are found if the target and the initial adapting field are red, and if green light is then added to the field. Combinative euchromatopsia is a striking failure of WEBER'S LAW and it suggests that the color-opponent channels of our visual system are most sensitive when they are in the middle of their operating range when, say, we are detecting slight departures from white.

Many have hastened to identify the color opponency revealed by physiology and by combinative euchromatopsia with the *opponent processes* that were classically postulated by Ewald Hering (1834–1918). Hering was concerned to explain some phenomenological aspects of our color sensations. He noted we never experience reddish greens or yellowish blues; and there are some hues (a red, a green, a blue, and a yellow) that look to us "unmixed", whereas in the case of other hues, such as orange or purple or cyan, most observers say they see more than one component. Hering was led to postulate "red-green" and "yellow-blue" processes in the visual system; each process was opponent so that say, redness and greenness could not be concurrently signaled. Unhappily, the opponent channels of the peripheral visual system (see above) do not map comfortably on to Hering's opponent processes. Thus the channel that draws opposing inputs from the long- and middle-wave cones (a channel misleadingly called the "red-green" channel in some textbooks) is strongly polarized by blue light, whereas Hering's red-green process would be left in equilibrium by a blue that is neither reddish nor greenish.

One of the most important phenomena of color vision is that of *color constancy*. Our perception of the color of a given object is remarkably stable, despite large changes in the wavelength composition of the ambient illumination, and thus in the wavelength composition of the light reflected to us by the object. For example, a piece of white paper continues to look white whether we examine it in the yellowish light of a domestic tungsten bulb or in the bluish light of the northern sky. To achieve this constancy the visual system must be taking into account the spectral balance of stimulation across a more than local region of the retina. Some colors, such as brown and olive green, are seen *only* in complex scenes and there is no mixture of wavelengths that will generate them when a spatially homogeneous patch of light is viewed in isolation. The mechanism of color constancy is the subject of current research.   JDM

Bibliography

Boynton, R.M. 1979: *Human color vision*. New York: Holt, Rinehart and Winston.

Gouras, P. 1984: Color vision. *Progress in retinal research* 3, 227.

Mollon, J.D. 1985: Studies in scarlet. *The Listener* 10 January, 6–7.

conditioning A form of associative learning which results in changes in an organism's behavior as a consequence of exposure to certain temporal relations between events. It is customary to distinguish two forms of conditioning, classical or Pavlovian conditioning on the one hand, and instrumental or operant conditioning on the other. In experimental studies of both varieties, the experimenter presents an event of biological or motivational significance usually termed a reinforcer; it may be food, water, or access to a sexual partner; or it may be a painful or distressing event such as a brief electric shock or the administration of a drug which causes nausea. Classical and instrumental conditioning differ in the other event with which this reinforcer is associated.

In classical conditioning the occurrence of a reinforcer is signaled by the presentation of a particular stimulus. In Pavlov's original experiments (1927) the reinforcer was either the delivery of food or an injection of a weak solution of acid into the dog's mouth, both of which caused the dog to salivate. Because they unconditionally elicited this response, they were called unconditional stimuli (abbreviated to US), and the salivation they elicited was an unconditional response (UR). The delivery of the reinforcer or US was preceded by the presentation of a neutral stimulus, a flashing light, a tone or buzzer or the ticking of a metronome. After a number of joint presentations of, say, the light and food, the dog would start salivating as soon as the light was turned on, before the food arrived. The light was referred to as a conditional stimulus (CS) and the response of salivating to the CS was called a conditional response (CR); the term refers to the fact that the CR is conditional upon the joint presentation of CS and US: if the light were now presented alone for a number of trials, it would lose its ability to elicit salivation. A mistranslation of "conditional" as "conditioned" meant that in English the CS and CR were referred to as a conditioned stimulus and conditioned response, and the verb "to condition" was derived to refer to the process responsible for the establishment of the new CR.

Classical conditioning experiments have employed a variety of events as CS and US, and have recorded CRs ranging from discrete, reflexive responses such as salivation to food or acid as the US, blinking to a puff of air directed at the eye or flexion of the leg to a shock to the foot, to more general changes in behavior such as approaching and contacting an object associated with the delivery of food, withdrawal from an object associated with danger, or rejection of a normally palatable food of which ingestion has been artificially associated with illness and nausea. The defining criterion for saying that these are all experiments on classical conditioning is that the experimenter's rules for delivering the reinforcer or US make no reference to the behavior of his subjects. In Pavlov's experiments the dog receives food on every conditioning trial regardless of its behavior when the CS is turned on; the puff of air is directed at the eye, the shock applied to the animal's foot, or the emetic drug injected after the animal has consumed some food, and there is nothing the animal can do to prevent these things happening.

This marks the distinction between classical and instrumental conditioning. In an instrumental experiment the delivery of the reinforcer depends on the experimental subject's performance of a designated, instrumental response. The first systematic study of instrumental conditioning was by Thorndike (1911), who trained a variety of animals to escape from a puzzle box and thus gain access to food by pressing on a catch, pulling a loop of string or undoing a latch. The most commonly used procedure for studying instrumental conditioning is that developed by Skinner (1938): a rat is placed in a small chamber and presses a bar or lever protruding from one wall in order to obtain a pellet of food delivered automatically into a recess in the wall. As in Pavlov's original experiments, the reinforcer is food, but here the delivery of the reinforcer is not dependent on the occurrence of a CS, but rather on the rat's performance of a particular response, that of pressing the lever. The experimenter may be said to be rewarding this response, or if the reinforcer is an aversive or painful event, punishing it, and instrumental conditioning has occurred if the subject's behavior changes as a consequence of these "contingencies of reinforcement" (in Skinner's phrase), that is to say if the subject comes to perform the rewarded response or refrains from performing the punished response.

The difference between classical and instrumental conditioning is thus defined in terms of the experimenter's rules for delivering a reinforcer. But this is hardly sufficient to prove that there is any fundamental distinction between the two. The fact that the experimenter can describe his experimental manipulations or

operations in different ways does not imply that the subject's description matches the experimenter's or that fundamentally different processes are responsible for the changes in behavior observed in the two cases. But many psychologists have followed Skinner's lead in believing that the operational distinction may have some further significance. In the end the question is a theoretical one: whether a single theory of conditioning can encompass all the phenomena of both types of experiment.

An adequate theory of conditioning must explain why Pavlov's dog starts salivating to the CS. Pavlov's own explanation, expressed rather more clearly by his Polish successor Konorski (1948), was rather simple. Salivation is part of the set of responses unconditionally elicited by food; as a consequence of the experimenter's pairing a CS with the delivery of food the two events are associated by the subject; an association of the two events ensures that the presentation of one will activate a representation of the other; the presentation of the CS will activate a representation of food and this activation will elicit salivation just as it would have if generated by the presentation of the food itself. Classical conditioning thus depends upon the establishment of an association between CS and US, and the CS thereby acquiring the ability to elicit responses normally elicited by the US alone.

It does not seem easy to apply this explanation to a case of instrumental conditioning: when a rat is rewarded with food for pressing a lever, this new response, not previously elicited by food, increases in probability. It is true that the last thing that will normally happen before a pellet of food is obtained is that the rat will have been in contact with the lever, sniffing it or touching it with its paw, but it remains to show how any association between these stimuli and the delivery of food could generate, via the Pavlovian mechanisms outlined above, the efficient instrumental response that rapidly emerges from the rat's initially accidental or exploratory contacts. In at least some cases, however, it turns out to be possible to apply a Pavlovian analysis. Another common instrumental procedure is to train pigeons to peck a small illuminated plastic disk on the wall of a Skinner box, rewarding them with food whenever they perform the required response. But pecking is, in fact, the pigeon's natural consummatory (or unconditional) response to food, and it turns out that the pigeon will peck the disk just as rapidly if the experimenter simply arranges to illuminate it for a few seconds before he delivers food regardless of the pigeon's behavior. The association between illumination of the disk (CS) and the delivery of food (US) is sufficient to ensure that the former comes to elicit the pecking response normally elicited by the latter alone. Here then is a purely Pavlovian explanation of what had always been regarded as a case of instrumental conditioning (Brown and Jenkins 1968).

But the fact remains that this analysis will not easily work for many cases of instrumental conditioning. It cannot easily explain why rats learn to press levers for food, still less why they can be trained to press the lever with a particular force (Notterman and Mintz 1965) or to hold it down for a particular length of time (Platt, Kuch and Bitgood 1973). It is equally unsuccessful at explaining why a dog should learn to flex a leg either to obtain food (Miller and Konorski 1928), or to avoid a puff of air directed at its ear (Fonberg 1958). Here and elsewhere instrumental conditioning occurs in accordance with Thorndike's law of effect which stated that responses are modified by the consequences, increasing in probability if followed by a satisfying consequence, decreasing if followed by an aversive consequence. Whether the law of effect is a theory or a circular description of observed data has from time to time been disputed, but it certainly captures what we intuitively see as the essential feature of voluntary actions – that they are performed because of their consequences.

If we cannot explain or describe instrumental conditioning without recourse to the law of effect, then the distinction between classical and instrumental conditioning can only be denied by dismissing Pavlov's account of classical conditioning and applying the law of effect here also. Several psychologists, notably Hull (1943), have attempted to do just this, but their attempts do not seem entirely successful. A pigeon conditioned to peck a disk whose illumination has served as a CS signalling food, will continue to do so even if the delivery of food is canceled on those trials when the pigeon pecks at the disk. The only way for the pigeon to earn food now is to refrain from pecking when the disk is illuminated, but it is unable to do so. The association between light and food remains strong, so the pigeon cannot help approaching and pecking the light in spite of the adverse consequences of its actions (Williams and Williams 1969). There are many other examples of involuntary responses being conditioned by Pavlovian procedures in spite of their having adverse consequences. It is difficult to see how such conditioning could be analyzed in terms of the law of effect.

Unless a new, all-embracing theory is proposed, therefore, there is reason to believe that the distinction between classical and instrumental conditioning is real and important. This is not entirely surprising, for it corresponds roughly to the distinction we intuitively draw between involuntary and voluntary responses. Involuntary responses are evoked or elicited by stimuli which have been associated with, and thus make us think of, certain consequences: we cannot help salivating if we imagine someone squeezing a lemon into our mouth, or help blushing or sweating if we recall an embarrassing or frightening incident. Voluntary actions are those which we perform or refrain from carrying out because we have learned what their consequences are and because of the value we put on those consequences. We may often be mistaken in our belief that a particular response is voluntary or involuntary: the pigeon's pecking response seemed a voluntary act until experimental analysis suggested otherwise; and there is good evidence that responses we should normally regard as involuntary can sometimes be brought under voluntary control (this is the basis of BIOFEEDBACK). It is possible that the difference is one of degree rather than of kind. But that does not diminish its importance, and this suggests that we should acknowledge the reality of the two types of conditioning.   NJM

Bibliography

Brown, P.L. and Jenkins, H.M. 1968: Auto-shaping of the pigeon's key peck. *Journal of the experimental analysis of behavior* 11, 1–8.

Fonberg, E. 1958: Transfer of instrumental avoidance reactions in dogs. *Bulletin de l'Academie Polonaise des sciences* 6, 353–56.

Hull, Clark L. 1943: *Principles of behavior.* New York and London: Appleton-Century-Crofts.

Konorski, Jerzy 1948: *Conditioned reflexes and neuron organization.* Cambridge: Cambridge University Press. Reprinted 1968. New York: Hafner.

*Mackintosh, N.J. 1983: *Conditioning and associative learning.* Oxford and New York: Oxford University Press.

Miller, S. and Konorski, J. 1928: Sur une forme particulière des reflexes conditionnels. *Comptes rendus des séances de la Société de Biologie* 99, 1155–57.

Notterman, Joseph M. and Mintz, Donald E. 1965: *Dynamics of response.* New York and London: Wiley.

Pavlov, Ivan P. 1927: *Conditioned reflexes.* London: Oxford University Press. Reprinted 1960. New York and London: Dover.

Platt, J.R., Kuch, D.O. and Bitgood, S.C. 1973: Rats' lever-press durations as psychophysical judgments of time. *Journal of the experimental analysis of behavior* 19, 239–50.

*Schwartz, B. 1978: *Psychology of learning and behavior.* New York: Norton.

Skinner, Burrhus F. 1938: *The behavior of organisms.* New York and London: Appleton-Century-Crofts.

Thorndike, Edward L. 1911: *Animal intelligence.* New York: Macmillan. Reprinted 1965. New York and London: Hafner.

Williams, D.R. and Williams, H. 1969: Auto-maintenance in the pigeon: sustained pecking despite contingent non-reinforcement, *Journal of the experimental analysis of behavior* 12, 511–20.

conduct disorder The commonest type of child psychiatric disorder, characterized by behavior which is antisocial, e.g. lying, stealing, aggression, firesetting, truancy. Conduct disorder occurs more commonly in boys than girls, and children from large or disrupted families living in poor social conditions are especially at risk. There is a marked association with reading retardation, and there may be associated emotional symptoms such as anxiety and low self esteem. In up to 50 per cent of children, the disorder persists into adolescence and may develop into delinquency. Psychiatric treatment may take a variety of forms. Behavioral treatments consist of setting clear limits of acceptable behavior for the child, and encouraging parents and teachers to work together in a consistent approach. Individual therapy aims at developing the child's skills and self esteem and exploring any areas of conflict; family therapy may be aimed at trying to change rejecting family attitudes. If these approaches fail it may be necessary to remove the child from the home environment, by placing him or her in a residential school, children's home, or foster family.

(See also CHILD AND ADOLESCENT PSYCHIATRY; DELINQUENCY.)   GCF

Bibliography

Robins, L. 1966: *Deviant children grown up.* Baltimore: Williams and Williams.

consciousness disorders Disorders of the awareness of the self and the external environment. The main abnormalities include lowering of consciousness, dream-like disorders, and narrowing of consciousness.

(1) lowering of consciousness: *clouding of consciousness* is a reduced state of awareness, ranging from slight lowering of consciousness to stupor and coma. It is accompanied by impairment of attention, memory and perception in varying degrees. Clouding of consciousness is characteristic of organic states (see ORGANIC MENTAL STATES).

(2) dream-like disorders: *delirium* includes severe impairment of consciousness, with disorientation in time and place, perceptual abnormalities such as illusions and hallucinations, and motor abnormalities, such as restlessness and agitation. Delirium is also a typical picture in organic states (see ORGANIC MENTAL STATES).

(3) narrowing of consciousness: twilight states where the individual remains aware of only part of the environment, as in hypnotic states, or where marked and sudden changes in consciousness are accompanied by dramatic expression of emotion such as anger or fear, and sometimes by hallucinatory experiences. Psychogenic twilight states can occur in hysteria. Organic twilight states are more often seen in epilepsy.

Psychomotor seizures are epileptic manifestations characterized by disorders of consciousness and behavior, and include epileptic automatisms, petit mal states, fugues and post-ictal disorders (see EPILEPSY). Disorders of consciousness and behavior can also occur in relation to sleep, as in the narcoleptic syndrome, somnambulism and night terrors (Fenton 1975). JC

Bibliography

Fenton, G.W. 1975: Clinical disorders of sleep. *British journal of hospital medicine* 14, 120–45.

Lishman, W.A. 1978: *Organic psychiatry: the psychological consequences of cerebral disorder.* Oxford: Blackwell Scientific: St Louis, Missouri: C.V. Mosby.

contingent visual after-effects A class of after-affects in which an illusory perception on one visual dimension (e.g. color, movement, tilt) is contingent on the value of a second dimension. The most celebrated, and the most robust, of this class of phenomena is the McCollough effect. To secure this effect one adapts to, say, a vertical grating of red and black bars and a horizontal grating of green and black bars. The adapting stimuli should be alternated every few seconds for several minutes. If then one examines a black and white grating, it will look pale green when its orientation is vertical and will look pink when its orientation is horizontal. The after-effect is called *contingent* because the illusory hue depends on the orientation of the grating. The most curious aspect of the McCollough effect is its long persistence: after an adaptation period of several minutes, the after-effect may last for hours or days (even for months), although it is seen only when an appropriate grating is present.

A widely favored explanation of such effects attributes them to the presence in our visual system of neurons specific to color and to some other attribute of the retinal image. We are to suppose that our perception of the color of a black and white grating depends on the relative activity in a population of neurons all specific to the same orientation but differing in the color to which they most strongly respond. If we selectively adapt the neurons specific to red and to vertical edges, these neurons will not make their normal contribution when a black and white grating is observed and so the grating will appear pale green.

An alternative theory likens the McCollough effect to Pavlovian conditioning. Not only is the effect peculiarly persistent, it also exhibits spontaneous recovery; and its decay is said to depend on the frequency of extinction trials (i.e. on exposure to the black and white test grating). To explain why the after-effect is negative – the after-effect of adapting to a red grating is greenish – we must suppose that the unconditioned response of the visual system to an excess of redness in the world is to turn down the gain of the red-sensitive channels; a correlated visual attribute, such as orientation, then becomes the conditioned stimulus for this response and is analogous to the bell in Pavlov's paradigm. Notice that this theory is different from the first in its level of explanation; and the two theories are not entirely exclusive. JDM

Bibliography

Stromeyer, C.S. 1978: In *Handbook of sensory physiology*, vol. 8, eds. R. Held and H. Leibowitz. Berlin: Springer-Verlag.

Siegel, S. and Allan, L.G. 1985: Overshadowing and blocking of the orientation-contingent color aftereffect: evidence for a conditioning mechanism. *Learning and motivation* 16, 125–38.

coronary-prone behavior Usually refers to the Type A coronary-prone personality pattern described by Friedman and Rosenman (see TYPE-A PERSONALITY). Other psychometric work has been done, however, linking personality factors to coronary heart disease (CHD).

The conclusion from six studies using the Minnesota Multiphasic Personality Inventory (MMPI) seems to be that before their illness, patients with coronary disease differ from persons who remain healthy on several scales of the inventory, particularly those in the "neurotic" triad of hypochondriasis (Hs), depression (D), and hysteria (Hy). The occurrence of manifest coronary heart disease increases the deviation of patients' MMPI scores further and, in addition, there is ego defense breakdown. As Jenkins (1971) summarizes: "patients with fatal disease tend to show greater neuroticism (particularly depression) in prospective MMPIs than those who incur and survive coronary disease".

Three major studies have utilized the sixteen Personality Factor inventory. All three investigations portray patients with CHD or related illness as emotionally unstable and introverted, which is consistent with the six MMPI studies. The limitation of these investigations is that they are, on balance, retrospective. That is, anxiety and neuroticism may well be reactions with CHD and other stress-related illnesses rather than precursors of it. Paffenberger, Wolf and Notkin (1966) report an interesting prospective study in which they linked university psychometric data on students with death certificates filed years later. They found a number of significant precursors to fatal CHD, one of which was a high anxiety or neuroticism score for the fatal cases.   CLC

Bibliography

Jenkins, C.D. 1971: Psychological and social precursors of coronary disease. *New England journal of medicine* 283, 244–55.

Paffenberger, R.S., Wolf, P.A. and Notkin, J. 1966: Chronic disease in former college students. *American journal of epidemiology* 83, 314–28.

criminal psychology The study of offenders' motives, personalities and decisions. The motives for most offenses – whether acquisitive, violent, sexual or connected with traffic – are normal in the sense that they are of kinds experienced by ordinary adults from time to time: greed, rage, lust, impatience, the desire for excitement. What has interested clinical psychologists, psychiatrists and psychoanalysts is the motive which is abnormal either in its strength, so that the offender finds it difficult to resist even when it is clearly dangerous to yield to it, or in its nature, sadism or pedophilia being examples.

Explanations of such motives belong to abnormal psychology. A few forms of mental disorder seem to be associated with certain kinds of objectionable behavior, although there is no good evidence that mental disorder in general increases the likelihood of being in trouble with the law. People who have committed serious personal violence are not infrequently found to be depressed, schizophrenic or "aggressive psychopaths". Some chronic confidence tricksters are said to have hysterical personalities. Some sexual offenders, especially against children, are found to be mentally handicapped. Arson, when committed for excitement rather than for gain or revenge, often seems to be compulsive.

The extent to which a predisposition to anti-social forms of behavior can be congenital has long been the subject of research and controversy. What cannot be disputed is the genetic transmission of a few diagnosable disorders (such as Huntington's Chorea) which sometimes involve sufferers in social trouble. There are also indisputable chromosomal abnormalities (not necessarily inherited) such as the XYY condition, which is associated with above average height, below average intelligence and a slightly increased likelihood of being involved in violence, including sexual violence.

The overwhelming majority of offenders are not suffering from such abnormalities. Their offences are often simply the result of circumstances: a speeding driver may have been late for an appointment; an assaulter may have been provoked by taunts; a sexual offender's self-control may have been reduced by alcohol or the behavior of his companion. (Indeed it is sometimes the victim's conduct that calls for explanation.) When the offence is premeditated or repeated, however, we feel the need for a fuller explanation. This may be the offender's imprudence or deliberate risk-taking; it may be lack of conscience or shame; or it may be a preference for the criminal's way of life.

In other contexts what seems to call for explanation is not the frequency with which an individual offends but the frequency of offences of certain kinds among certain groups, such as vandalism among schoolboys. Current explanations may emphasize child-training methods, the values of a culture or subculture, low intelligence or impaired capacity for social learning. *Child-training methods* are important because they may fail to result in the child internalizing the rules of conduct of the culture or sub-culture to which he belongs. In this case he will be readier to breach them when it seems in his interest to do so. Internalization seems most likely to take place when parents explain the reasons for a rule and withdraw affection when the child breaks it. Physical punishment, especially if harsh or erratic, seems less effective (and may teach the child violent behavior). The effect is also weaker if parents' reactions are inconsistent, or if the child's dependence on their affection is weakened (e.g. by frequent absences). There are also types of anti-social conduct which become likely only in the teens or later, when children are less influenced by their parents and more by their peers (e.g. the abuse of drugs). It may be significant that the rate of DELINQUENCY rises with every year of compulsory schooling, and begins to decline at about the age when most young people leave school and mix with older people.

In any case, the child, the teenager or the adult may belong to a *subculture* whose values do not condemn everything that the law forbids. It may for example view dishonest acquisition no more seriously than many motorists regard speeding. It may respect rather than censure a man who uses violence to settle a quarrel. In some white-collared subcultures tax evasion and the acceptance of corrupt favors are "smart". Again, an individual may belong to, or join, a subculture which condones what he or she likes doing. Even in societies which condemn pedophilia (as not all do) pedophiles can sometimes join or form like-minded groups. Such groups often adopt "neutralizing" arguments to counterbalance the condemnation of others (or in some cases their own consciences). Pedophilia is said to benefit children by introducing them to a more mature kind of affection than they get from their contemporaries. Burglars assure themselves that householders' insurance policies indemnify them. Football fans excuse their violence to rivals by claiming that the latter "began it", or "asked for it" by entering their territory. Like other groups, such as street gangs or terrorists, they may invoke loyalty to a group or a cause, which can be used to justify revenge for an injury to a group member, or an unprovoked assassination. Another technique is the denial of legitimacy: "Property is theft". The concept of "neutralization" is more often used by sociologists than psychologists, perhaps because of the latter's preoccupation with measurable characteristics.

A controversial figure is "the psychopath" (see PSYCHOPATHIC PERSONALITY). Many psychologists and psychiatrists believe that even when allowances are made for the influence of subcultures which are tolerant of dishonesty, violence, sexual promiscuity, drug abuse and other hedonistic conduct, there are some men and women whose proneness to one or more of these kinds of behavior is so impulsive or unheeding of other people's disapproval that it is in some way pathological: attributable, that is, to some sort of defect. Descriptions and explanations of the defect vary, from congenital abnormalities or perinatal brain damage to grossly affectionless upbringing. Some investigators find that samples of "psychopaths" contain individuals who do not show the normal responses to stimuli which should arouse anxiety, although the samples also seem to include others whose responses are more or less normal. Psychiatrists have succeeded in having the concept of psychopathic disorder written into legislation. For example, Section 1 of the Mental Health Act 1983 defines it as "a persistent disorder or disability of mind... which results in abnormally aggressive or seriously irresponsible conduct..." In the USA statutory definitions (e.g. of "sexual psychopaths") vary from state to state. The more precise term now approved by the American Psychiatric Association (in its *Diagnostic and Statistical Manual*) is "anti-social personality disorder" in which there is "a history of continuous and chronic anti-social behavior in which the rights of others are violated, persistence into adult life of a pattern... that begins before the age of fifteen not due to... severe mental retardation, schizophrenia or manic episodes". These definitions, however, are descriptive and generic, leaving room for a variety of more specific diagnoses, such as those of the International Classification of Disorders (published by the World Health Organization). It is possible that this generic group will eventually prove divisible into sub groups with more or less specific etiology; but this is unlikely to happen until research workers develop more exact diagnostic criteria and explanatory hypotheses.

An aspect of law-breaking which is only beginning to receive attention is what can be loosely called the decision-making stage, although many offenses are the result of processes which can hardly be called "decisions", being impulsive, compulsive, negligent or habitual. These apart, however, even very strong motivation does not mean that every opportunity for the offense will be taken. The situation may be perceived as too risky, the penalty as too great, accomplishment as too difficult (as when a car thief is attracted by a car but desists because he would be too conspicuous, because he knows that his next prison sentence would be a long one, or because he knows that its lock is hard to force). NDW

Bibliography

Feldman, M.P. 1977: *Criminal behaviour: a psychological analysis*. New York and London: John Wiley.

Walker, N. 1977: *Behaviour and misbehaviour: explanations and non-explanations*. Oxford: Basil Blackwell: New York: Basic Books.

West, D.J. 1982: *Delinquency: its roots, careers and prospects*. London: Heinemann; Cambridge, Mass.: Harvard University Press.

crisis intervention A brief form of psychological treatment used in the case of a person whose usual methods of coping have become ineffective in the face of some personal crisis. The result is acute distress and the associated failure to function adequately in customary social roles. Crises are conveniently classified as developmental, such as adolescence and retirement, and accidental, such as a major disappointment or a breakdown in an important relationship.

The aim of therapy is relief from the effects of the crisis and possibly the development of new effective methods of coping and solving problems. The therapist provides a supportive framework within which the transiently disabled patient can have a breathing space, feel hopeful about obtaining help and receive reassurance and guidance. The patient temporarily forgoes some measure of independence, but resumes former responsibility for himself as he comes to feel and function better. SB

Bibliography

Ewing, C.P. 1978: *Crisis intervention as psychotherapy*. New York: Oxford University Press.

critical periods and the nervous system Periods during ontogeny when specific conditions are necessary for the normal development of the nervous system. If the nervous system has been exposed to abnormal conditions its ability to recover from this exposure decreases quickly after the critical, or sensitive, period. Different critical periods may exist for different aspects of neural development, and although they may overlap in time, they exert their effects by different mechanisms. Nutritional deficiencies may markedly influence the overall growth and synaptogenesis of the nervous system, depending upon the time of the exposure, whereas sensory deprivation or restriction may produce selective effects upon the physiological properties of cells within sensory systems (see SENSORY DEPRIVATION AND ENRICHMENT). The nervous system's response to brain damage may also vary according to the time of occurrence of the injury, yielding different prospects for functional recovery depending upon the system involved (see RECOVERY OF FUNCTION AFTER BRAIN DAMAGE). For example, humans will show linguistic competence following damage to the language-dominant cerebral hemisphere if the injury occurs within the first decade of life. (See also PLASTICITY: PHYSIOLOGICAL CONCEPT.)   BER/RCS

Bibliography

Lund, R.D. 1978: *Development and plasticity of the brain: an introduction.* Oxford: Oxford University Press.

D

defense mechanism: in psychoanalytic theory One of a number of techniques used by the ego to defend itself from ANXIETY, which may arise from three sources: when an instinctual impulse in the Id is pressing for gratification; when the Superego exerts moral pressure against a wish, intention or idea; or when there is a realistic danger of pain or injury (ego-anxiety). The aim of defense mechanisms is to divert anxiety away from the ego's consciousness. This can be done in about a dozen different ways, according to psychoanalytic literature, which vary in the extent to which they are consistent with reason and perceived reality; one that is consistent is "ego-syntonic", and one that is not is "ego-dystonic". The severity of a psychological disturbance is often assessed by the quality (in terms of ego-syntonicity) of the prevailing defenses, which PROJECTIVE TESTS especially are designed to elicit. The ego-defenses have been extensively discussed by Anna Freud (1937) and by Laughlin (1970).

The principal defense is REPRESSION, which covers both preventing a mental element (idea, wish, anxiety, impulse, image) from becoming conscious, and rejecting from consciousness to the unconscious mind an element which had been conscious. The commonest of the others are: "projection", by which one attributes to others a property of oneself and can therefore blame them instead of feeling guilt (a form of anxiety) oneself; "reaction-formation", by which one's anxiety about (say) aggressive feelings towards someone is kept at bay by overtly adopting the opposite attitude of solicitude and compliance; "identification", by which either depressive anxiety over "object-loss" is mitigated by perpetuating in one's own behavior some psychological property of (say) a parent or spouse who has been emotionally lost (cf. Freud on depression: 1917a, p. 239), or the threat of an aggressor is annulled by one's adopting his/her characteristics; "denial", a relatively ego-dystonic defense because if some unpleasant feature of the perceptual world is simply denied, then this defies the "reality principle" and may lead to delusion or hallucination, whereas, if one denies some painful aspect of one's emotional make-up (say depression), one is tending towards mania; "sublimation" and "rationalization", both much more ego-syntonic, and the latter meaning to give an intellectual rationale for what was in fact an emotionally-determined action or response; "isolation" by which the mental image of a disturbing experience or action is disconnected in one's thinking from its temporal and associative context, drained of its feeling-tone, and left cognitively and emotionally isolated; "splitting", by which a single "object" is treated as two separate ones so that a separate set of feelings can be directed to either part-object, and the anxious dissonance between (say) wanting and rejecting the same thing be consequently resolved; "regression", by which one reverts to the gratification techniques of an earlier psychosexual stage to compensate for a current anxiety.

The theoretical relation between repression and the other defenses is problematic, with the exception of REGRESSION. For the latter is the only one which depends upon the chronology of personality development (Freud 1917b, ch. 22). FREUD recognized (1926, ch. 11A) that he had been using the word repression to cover different forms of defense against anxiety (on the assumption that all defenses except regression would involve repression). He proposed to revert to the concept of a class of defense-mechanisms of which repression would be a particular case. Madison (1961) has argued that Freud does not maintain this program in subsequent writings. Freud also considers (1926) the possibility that the neuroses should be understood in terms of which defense mechanisms dominate their respective psychopathologies, and Fairbairn (1941) proposed a realization of this idea in the context of "object-relations theory".

Kline has reviewed a great many ingenious empirical investigations into defense-mechanisms (1981, ch. 8), and concludes that, although a number of them are poorly designed or irrelevant, there is undoubted support for repression, and a certain amount for isolation, projection, reaction-formation and denial. NMC

Bibliography

Eichenbaum, L. and Orbach, S. 1983: *Understanding woman*. London: Pelican.

Fairbairn, W.R.D. 1941 (1952): A revised psychopathology. Reprinted in *Psychoanalytic studies of the personality*. London: Tavistock.

Freud, Anna 1937: *The ego and the mechanisms of defence*. London: Hogarth; New York: International Universities Press (1946).

Freud, Sigmund 1917a: 1917b: 1926: Mourning and melancholia (vol. 14); Introductory lectures (vol. 16); Inhibitions, symptoms and anxiety (vol. 20). In *Standard edition of the complete psychological works of Sigmund Freud*, vols. as indicated. London: Hogarth Press; New York: Norton.

Kline, Paul 1981: *Fact and fantasy in Freudian theory*. London and New York: Methuen.

Laughlin, Henry P. 1970: *The ego and its defenses*. New York: Appleton-Century-Crofts.

Madison, Paul 1961: *Freud's concept of repression and defense*. Minneapolis: Minnesota University Press.

delinquency Conduct disorder in young persons involving offenses against the law. In Britain, juvenile delinquents could be considered legally as persons under the age of seventeen with criminal convictions. However, no widely accepted definition exists, the term often including any antisocial, deviant or immoral behavior whether or not it forms part of a criminal offense. Delinquency is a serious cause for concern worldwide, but rates are difficult to estimate reliably. West and Farrington (1973) showed that 30.8 percent of working-class boys in London had at least one conviction at twenty-one years. Boys have outnumbered girls in a ratio of up to ten to one. The most common offenses involve theft. A popular distinction is drawn between socialized and unsocialized delinquents (Hewitt and Jenkins 1946).

Causation is multifactorial, including genetic, psychological, social and cultural factors. Over-simplified causal explanations are misleading. Prevalence is high in depressed urban environments and one view relates delinquency particularly to disadvantaged subcultures. There is a well established connection between delinquency and disturbed home background and family conflict. Schools may have differing rates of delinquency and may play a part in fostering delinquent behavior (Reynolds 1976). Longitudinal studies suggest that future delinquents may be differentiated from others during late childhood on the basis of their attitudes and behavior (West and Farrington 1973). The "labeling" of children as failures and troublemakers, especially by teachers, contributes to the acquisition of deviant status (Hargreaves 1975). WLIP-J

Bibliography

Hargreaves, David H., Hester. F. and Mellor, S. 1975: *Deviance in classrooms*. London and Boston: Routledge and Kegan Paul.

Hewitt, Lester E. and Jenkins, Richard L. 1946: *Fundamental patterns of maladjustment: the dynamics of their origin*. Springfield, Ill.: State of Illinois.

Reynolds, D. 1976: The delinquent school. In *The process of schooling*, eds. Martyn Hammersley and Peter Woods. London and Boston: Routledge and Kegan Paul.

Rutter, M. and Giler, H. 1983: *Juvenile delinquency: trends and perspectives*. Harmondsworth, Middx: Penguin.

West, Donald J. and Farrington, D.P. 1973: *Who becomes delinquent?* London: Heinemann Educational.

*——— 1977: *The delinquent way of life*. London: Heinemann Educational.

delusion A delusion is a false belief, held despite evidence to the contrary, and one which is not explicable in terms of the patient's educational and cultural background. It is held with complete conviction and cannot be shaken by argument. Delusions must be distinguished from culturally acceptable beliefs and from more idiosyncratic convictions that are understandable in terms of the patient's background. The latter are called overvalued ideas. Primary delusions are those that appear to have arisen suddenly and fully formed while secondary delusions can be seen as derived from hallucinations or other psychotic beliefs. Delusions are seen most often in SCHIZOPHRENIA, severe AFFECTIVE DISORDER and ORGANIC MENTAL STATES. The content of the delusion may have diagnostic significance, for instance delusions of guilt are associated with depression.　　　　RAM

Bibliography

Jaspers, K. 1959: *General psychopathology*. Trans. J. Hoenig and M.W. Hamilton. Manchester: Manchester University Press.

dendrites and dendritic spines (See BRAIN AND CENTRAL NERVOUS SYSTEM: ILLUSTRATIONS, fig. 30). Processes of a NEURON characterized by cytoplasm like that of the cell body and often bearing numerous lateral spines. The definition is cytological. Dendritic cytoplasm is an extension of the cell body cytoplasm (perikaryon) and possesses in particular rough endoplasmic reticulum (Nissl substance) which distinguishes it from axoplasm. Dendrites are usually rapidly tapering extensions from the cell body which repeatedly branch at acute angles. They are typically packed in satellite glial cells without an individual sheath (see GLIA). Dendrites are generally the principal receptive and integrative regions of a neuron and usually do not conduct ACTION POTENTIALS. The geometry of the "dendritic tree" determines how much various inputs will change the membrane potential at the axon hillock where nerve impulses are triggered.

Although the dendritic tree is generally regarded as the input stage of a neuron (the axon is the output stage), outputs from dendrites to other dendrites are actually quite common. Such dendro-dendritic connections would appear to represent an economical way to minimize the space required for synaptic interactions. Reciprocal synapses between dendrites have been termed microcircuits and represent the most compact synaptic circuit known. Sites of reciprocal dendro-dendritic circuits include the retina, olfactory bulb, CEREBRAL CORTEX, BASAL GANGLIA, and THALAMUS.

Dendritic spines are a common feature of neural dendrites and are well displayed by the Golgi method of neuron staining. They vary from long and thin to short and fat, but a common form consists of a ball on a short thin stalk. Spines appear to be specializations for receiving synaptic inputs, although many fibers SYNAPSE onto the dendrite shaft, not onto spines. The increase in area represented by dendritic spines may be accessory to some other function since on most dendrites much of the membrane area is covered by glial processes rather than synaptic inputs. The structure of dendritic spines suggests that they help electrically to isolate groups of inputs from the electrical environment of the dendrite proper.

The above definition of dendrite is a simplification, however, and many cases arise where the term "process" may be preferable to either dendrite or axon (see Shepard 1979, for a discussion of this issue).　　　　SCC

Bibliography

Peters, A., Palay, S.F., and Webster, H. de F. 1970: *The fine structure of the nervous system: the cells and their processes*. New York and London: Hoeber Medical Division, Harper and Row.

Shepard, Gordon M. 1979: *The synaptic organization of the brain*. 2nd edn. New York and Oxford: Oxford University Press.

depression *See* depression, bipolar; affective disorders.

depression, bipolar Where an individual has suffered abnormal swings of mood in both directions, that is both depressive and manic illnesses, his disorder may be termed bipolar. Recurrent illnesses which are all depressive or all manic (the latter being rather rare) may be called unipolar. Perris (1976) provides evidence that unipolar and bipolar disorders are genetically distinct, but in practice it is often difficult to say with confidence that an individual belongs to the unipolar depressive category, since manic spells may go unrecognized and their emergence may be long delayed (see AFFECTIVE DISORDERS). Frank illnesses may be preceded by a tendency to the minor mood swings which characterize the cyclothymic personality.   DLJ

Bibliography
*Paykel, E.S., ed. 1982: *Handbook of affective disorders*. London and New York: Churchill Livingstone.
Perris, C. 1976: Frequency and hereditary aspects of depression. In *Depression: behavioral, biochemical, diagnostic and treatment concepts*, eds. D.M. Gallant and G.M. Simpson. New York: Spectrum.

deprivation: human parental This term covers the many ways, emotional and physical in which parental care may be inadequate, and which may have immediate and long term consequences for the child. Bowlby (1951) suggested that separation of a young child from its mother not only causes immediate distress (protest followed by despair and detachment) but also predisposes to later PSYCHOPATHIC PERSONALITY disorder and vulnerability to AFFECTIVE DISORDER. Since then it has become apparent that the effect of separation depends on many factors including the age of the child, its previous relationship with its mother and father, and the nature of the separation. It is also apparent that the various types of parental deprivation have quite different longterm consequences. For example, lack of environmental stimulation and encouragement to learn in infancy is associated with educational under-achievement, whereas poor early emotional attachments may result in difficulties in adult social relationships.

Awareness of the consequences of maternal separation and other forms of parental deprivation has been a major influence in the development of ideas of child care whether it is undertaken by the parents, by substitute parents or by any form of educational or residential institution.   RAM

Bibliography
Bowlby, J. 1951: *Maternal care and mental health*. Geneva: WHO.
Rutter, M. 1981: *Maternal deprivation reassessed*. 2nd edn. Harmondsworth and New York: Penguin.

desensitization, systematic A highly influential form of BEHAVIOR THERAPY primarily used in the treatment of phobic behavior in which fear is reduced by exposing the patient to the feared object in the presence of a stimulus that inhibits such fear. It was developed by Wolpe (1958) on the basis of his work on the experimental neurosis in cats. In therapy the client imagines a series of phobic situations of ever increasing fearfulness while anxiety is inhibited by muscular relaxation. Systematic desensitization was the first behavioral technique to receive extensive experimental investigation, and numerous studies on volunteers with fears of small animals such as spiders or rats and in clinical populations with major disabling fears have shown that desensitization is an effective treatment for such behavioral disorders. In clinical practice it has now largely been superseded by exposure to the situation in reality without relaxation training.   DWJ

Bibliography
Wolpe, J. 1958. *Psychotherapy by reciprocal inhibitions*. Stanford, Calif: Stanford University Press.

development of the nervous system The growing ability of the nervous system to coordinate the organism's responses to simple and complex stimuli, together with the structural and physiological changes on which this ability depends. Development is most dramatic during intra-uterine and early postnatal life. This discussion will be confined to the central nervous system and excludes physiological topics which are too complex for the space available (see also BRAIN AND CENTRAL NERVOUS SYSTEM: ILLUSTRATIONS, figs. 5 and 6).

Gross structure

Two and a half weeks after conception the disk-shaped human embryo is less than 1 mm in diameter. Some cells on the dorsal surface fold to form a gutter-like "neural groove". Adjacent cells multiply and form raised walls whose top edges bend toward each other and fuse to form the neural tube, the front end of which dilates to form the brain while the remainder gives rise to the spinal cord.

Six weeks after conception five separate regions can be identified in the enlarged front end of the neural tube (Patten 1968). The hindmost will become the medulla oblongata, the next will become the pons and in front of this lies the mesencephalon or mid-brain (fig. 5).

In front of the mid-brain lies the forebrain which is itself divided into the diencephalon, in which the THALAMUS and HYPOTHALAMUS will eventually develop, and two enlargements which will become the cerebral hemispheres.

During infancy the brain grows rapidly but at a steadily decreasing rate. The BRAIN STEM, i.e. the mid-brain, pons and medulla oblongata, which contain centers essential for the maintenance of life, are quite well advanced in growth by the time of birth and show very little increase in size after the end of the first year. Nearly half the postnatal growth of the cerebral hemispheres has usually been completed by the end of the first year and they are close to their adult size by the tenth year. This growth is largely due to increase in volume of the white matter.

Cellular structure

Multiplication of "neuroblast" cells which will develop into NEURONS is most prominent from the tenth to eighteenth weeks

after gestation (Dobbing 1981). The neurons grow rapidly through the remainder of pregnancy while cell multiplication declines. In late intra-uterine life, and during the first four years or so after birth, elaboration of dendritic processes (see DENDRITES) is associated with development of increasing neuronal function. Simultaneously, proliferation of the glial cells (see GLIA) continuing to the second postnatal year (Dobbing and Sands 1973), provides the main connective and supporting structure of the brain.

Myelinization begins at about the fourth fetal month, in the dorsal and ventral roots of the SPINAL CORD. The fibers connecting higher centers in the cerebral hemispheres are generally later and some tracts are not completely myelinated for several years. After a fiber has become myelinated the thickness of the myelin sheath may continue to increase for a number of years.

The CEREBRAL CORTEX develops rather slowly and it is not until the seventh fetal month that the six cell layers characteristic of the adult are apparent.

While the brain is developing its biochemical and electrical characteristics are also changing. These changes continue beyond childhood.

The development of function

Evidence of the degree of functional development in the central nervous system of the early embryo is provided by its movements in response to stimuli. For example, closing of the hand when the palm is touched has been demonstrated during the third fetal month. At about nine weeks, touching the mouth with a fine hair leads to bending of the whole body whereas by twelve and a half weeks, the mouth closes when it is touched and, if the touch is repeated several times, the fetus will exhibit swallowing movements. Thus a general response is replaced by a localized one appropriate to the stimulus and requiring a more highly developed nervous system.

Infants born prematurely have been studied at the gestational age of twenty-eight weeks (Saint-Anne Dargassies 1966). They close their eyes if a light is shone on them. Nerve pathways in the midbrain and pons, which would be essential for this response, must therefore be functioning. A loud noise will awaken the infant and cause generalized movement. There is evidence of a sense of smell at this stage and there may be some taste sensation. The rooting reflex, i.e. opening the mouth and turning the head towards a part of the face which is touched, and the walking reflex are also present. The latter is demonstrated by holding the baby upright with the feet on a flat surface and moving it forward. It will walk with high stepping movements. Thus the basic functional connections in the nervous system required for the movements of walking are well developed.

By thirty weeks the neuronal connections which allow the pupil to contract when a light is shone into the eye are established. The movements of sucking and swallowing are well coordinated in relation to breathing so that the infant can suck without choking. Also, the legs stiffen when the infant is held upright, an indication that the steady output of impulses from the lower end of the spinal cord, which will later be responsible for the maintenance of muscle tone, has begun.

Premature babies of thirty-two to thirty-five weeks' gestation usually appear much more alert than younger infants. This suggests that the "arousal" mechanism within the brain may be beginning to function. Improved coordination of movement shows further development within the nervous system.

When the prematurely born infant reaches a gestational age of forty-one weeks, it will follow a light with its eyes. This implies some form of vision but does not necessarily indicate that what the infant sees has great significance for it. It does suggest that further functional links have been established between the visual input to the brain and the outflow to the eye muscles. The infant tends to respond selectively to sounds such as that of the human voice. The differences in behavior between a child born at forty-one weeks and a premature infant who has reached this age are usually slight. Whether the infant has remained in utero or has been exposed to the external environment for the preceding month or two seems to have little effect on the development of the central nervous system. The movements of the newborn full term infant are largely reflexes but they become more controlled after about five or six months, as higher centers begin to process information and relate it to movement. Responses may be observed to many different stimuli, e.g. pain, touch or pressure, changes in temperature, taste, and certain odors.

By two months of age the visual system is sufficiently well developed to allow size and shape discrimination (Fantz and Miranda 1975). The vestibular apparatus, which provides the brain with information about the position and movement of the head in space, is functioning to some extent at birth but the child is usually ten or twelve weeks old before sensory input from the eyes, the vestibular apparatus and the receptor organs in the muscles and joints become fully integrated within the central nervous system. This integration is an essential basis for well controlled voluntary movement.

Infants over the age of twelve weeks show considerable variation in the rates at which their central nervous systems develop. Ages at which developmental "landmarks" are said to be reached are generalizations and many entirely normal children will reach them either earlier or later than the norm.

After the first three months the cerebral cortex begins to influence the postural reflexes which have recently become integrated. The action of the cortex is usually to inhibit these reflexes so that the child has more voluntary control of its posture.

Effective activity in the motor areas of the cerebral cortex is shown at about the fourth or fifth month by voluntary goal-directed movements, such as grasping at an object in the field of vision. These movements become increasingly skillful as the corpus striatum, motor cortex and pyramidal tracts develop further but even after two or three years the movements may still be clumsy.

The walking reflex, which is coordinated

in the spinal cord, disappears completely some months before the infant begins to crawl or walk alone because it is inhibited by higher centers of the brain as these develop. The development of independent locomotion follows a sequence which reflects the order of maturation in the regions of the motor area of the cerebral cortex in which different parts of the body are represented. The infant can creep with the help of its arms before it can use its legs to crawl, stand or walk.

(See also BRAIN MECHANISMS OF MOVEMENT.)   WAM

Bibliography

*Dobbing, J. 1981: The later development of the brain and its vulnerability. In *Scientific foundations of paediatrics*, eds. J. Dobbing and J.A. Davis. London: Heinemann.

Dobbing, J. and Sands, J. 1973: The quantitative growth and development of the human brain. *Archives of disease in childhood* 46, 757–67.

Fantz, R.L. and Miranda, S.B. 1975: Newborn infant attention to form and contour. *Child development* 46, 224.

Patten, Bradley M. 1968: *Human embryology*. 3rd edn. New York and Maidenhead: McGraw-Hill.

*Saint-Anne Dargassies, S. 1966: Neurological maturation of the premature infant of 28 to 41 weeks' gestational age. In *Human development*, ed. F. Faulkner. Philadelphia and London: Saunders.

developmental psychobiology

Sometimes referred to as developmental biopsychology (e.g. Tobach et al. 1977) this is the study of biological processes that determine and constitute the development of behavior and its psychological components. As its name suggests, developmental psychobiology represents an amalgamation of *developmental psychology* and *psychobiology*. Developmental psychobiology encompasses all stages of life during which the foundations for behavior are established.

The roots of developmental psychobiology can be traced to the turn of the century when many ontogenetic issues were in the limelight of scientific debate. Experimental embryology had emerged as a discipline and from within it arose some model approaches to developmental studies that were to have broad and long-lasting influences. W. Preyer (1841–1897), in particular, attempted to unify developmental studies in physiology, neuroanatomy and behavior. Preyer's celebrated works included comparative studies of behavioral embryology and developmental studies of the maturation of children.

Charles Darwin (1809–1882) can also be seen as an early advocate and practitioner of developmental psychobiology. In particular, his *The expression of emotion in man and animals* (1872) reflects some of his views of developmental study as a tool to an understanding of comparative-evolutionary aspects of behavior, as well as the nature of brain-behavior relations. Claparède (1911) was perhaps the first developmentalist to use the term "psychobiological" in his treatment of human attention, and asked "is that which really interests us, which holds us enthralled, always that which *ought* to interest us from the point of view of our preservation, from the biological point of view?" Thereafter, as Konner (1977) points out, most of the major advances in twentieth century developmental psychology, notably those associated with Freud, Piaget, Hall, Baldwin, Gesell, Carmichael, Bower, Bowlby and Brown have been based on biological constructs.

Links with evolutionary theory and genetics

The Darwinian framework was incorporated into the thinking of many developmental psychologists (e.g. Baldwin 1895) during the later nineteenth century. Their acceptance of evolutionary views was influenced by those of contemporary embryologists who suggested that individual development (ontogeny) appears to replay (or recapitulate) the evolutionary development of the species (its phylogeny). To apply to mental development the doctrine that "ontogeny *recapitulates* phylogeny", it was assumed by many early developmental psychologists that studying the psychological development of children would provide an account of the otherwise inaccessible phylogenetic evolution of the human mind. Today, most developmentalists do not accept such views. Instead of asking what modern children can tell us about human evolution, contemporary interest tends to focus on how the nature of childhood and the developmental rules which guide it have themselves evolved (Bruner 1972; Konner 1977).

Some psychobiologically-oriented researchers conduct developmental studies because they are interested in problems derived from ethology, comparative psychology, or animal behavior. Indeed, ethological and comparative traditions, as articulated by Konrad Lorenz, Niko Tinbergen, T.C. Schneirla and Daniel Lehrman, placed great value on ontogenetic analyses. In particular, one goal of such behavioral approaches is to clarify *adaptive or functional* aspects of behavior, that is, to understand the means by which behavioral traits enable organisms to meet various environmental challenges and in the face of such forces of natural selection be maintained or reinforced in the species' repertoire. From this tradition comes interest in the behavior and behavioral development of young in relation to their social and physical environments. Parent-offspring relationships, affiliative behavior, the organization of motor patterns, play, imitation, recognition of parents, kin, food, prey, and basic vegetative activities have, for example, been involved in studies of the adaptive aspects of behavioral development.

The function of developmental processes is in general the achievement of adult competence. The adaptive significance of some aspects of the behavior of young, then, may lie in converting neonatal competence to adult competence: it is thought to be the case for infantile play, for example, that adaptive benefits are realized *in later life*.

By contrast, some of the behaviors of young may not perform this function at all, but instead have survival value *at that point* in development. Bowlby has proposed that one such function of the human infant's attachment to its parents has been protection from predators and other threats of the environmental "niche" experienced by the

infant at this vulnerable stage in its life.

The development of species-typical behavior and its evolutionary implications brings with it an appreciation of and interest in *heritable* factors that are expressed in behavior. Thus, the field of BEHAVIOR GENETICS has a relevant alignment with developmental psychobiology. Heritability, however, is a parameter of populations, not individuals, so the role of some aspects of behavior genetics exists most precisely on the level of population characteristics.

The historical persistence of the so-called "nature–nurture" controversy in developmental psychobiology can be understood, in part, as a problem that has been difficult to resolve because the adversaries in the controversy are often confronting one another with analyses that are appropriate either to individuals or to populations. Behavior genetics is, however, increasingly influenced by revelations of modern molecular biology and genetics.

The complexity of modern psychobiology: parent-offspring relations

Although developmental psychobiology has a tradition of comparative study that ranges across many species, mammalian development is emphasized. This can be understood in terms of its relevance to humans, and because mammalian offspring tend to present interesting ontogenetic pictures for study – their life histories usually include dramatic transformations from infancy to adulthood. It is possible to make such a generalization because mammals are defined, as a group, on the basis of common reproductive–developmental features: live birth and the provision of milk via specialized glands on the female's body. Mammary glands are an anatomical signpost for maternal behavior. The developmental psychobiology of mammals, therefore, necessarily includes the analysis of maternal behavior or, more accurately, *parental* behavior since in many species, including man, nurture is provided by adults other than, and in addition to, the mother. Parental behavior is, in fact, a prominent feature of the reproductive efforts of many non-mammalian animals, such as some species of fish and many species of birds.

The inclusion of parental behavior in the mandate of developmental psychobiology brings with it special conceptual and methodological demands. Parental behavior is not a static or fixed form of input. The quantity and quality of parental attention tends to change over time, usually in a manner suited to the developmental status of the offspring. It is important to recognize the *developmental* nature of parental care.

The concept of developmental synchrony is very important because it stimulates awareness of the existence of the different means by which such interindividual synchrony is achieved. The effect of a parent (caregiver) on the offspring and the effect of the offspring on the parent often must be analyzed separately in order to understand the nature of their *reciprocal* controls. Developmental studies have been enhanced considerably by ability to understand the mechanisms of interactions within dyads, such as parent-offspring units.

Links with neuroscience

The problems and methods of contemporary psychobiology, physiological psychology, and the neurosciences in general, contribute to the scope and conduct of developmental psychobiology. Developmental analyses continue to be applied as *tools* to study other processes. Thus, many topics of psychobiological interest, such as learning and memory, feeding and drinking behavior, sensory processes, sleep, reproductive behavior and communication, are studied developmentally, with the aim of learning more about each problem as a result of better understanding the factors that contribute to its development.

In addition, the *methods* of contemporary neuroscience have influenced the conduct of the developmental work. In some instances a new technology has been applied to a developmental problem. This would include, for instance, basic studies of the development of neurochemical systems of the brain, behavioral pharmaco-logy in immature animals, and neuroanatomical studies of the developing nervous system. Some of these efforts resemble or are identical to research in developmental neurobiology, a closely-aligned discipline which is best discriminated from developmental psychobiology by greater emphasis on intrinsic properties of neural tissue and systems, rather than in their relations to behavior.

The application of modern anatomical and physiological techniques of neurobiology to behavioraly-oriented investigations is usually done through "descriptive–correlative" studies, which are typical of preliminary analyses. In developmental psychobiology there are several significant examples of this approach. Neural changes during development have been described with the aid of numerous neurobiological measures, ranging from molar levels of analysis such as brain size, cortical depth and myelination patterns, to more molecular analyses such as neuronal counts, cell size and shape, or arrangement of dendritic spines. Such morphological measures are then correlated with onset of function or level of performance. Alternatively, the same kinds of neural measures can be used correlatively to assess the consequences of different early environmental conditions for rate or level of neural development.

Relevance of early experience

Ontogenetic stages during which behavior and/or morphology undergo rapid or dramatic changes are, generally speaking, especially attractive to developmental psychobiologists. It is generally believed that periods of rapid changes are more susceptible to extrinsic influences than are ontogenetic stages of stability. The assumption is that living systems in the process of reorganization or change are more easily affected by environmental events, natural or artificial, than are systems that are operating in a relatively steady state. It is for this reason, at least in part, that developmental psychobiologists are attracted to analyses of "early experience", because the "early" period is usually part of the postnatal phase when development is rapid and dramatic.

The same assumptions that highlight early life as an important period during which development is shaped, also apply to the study of the early influence of toxins or teratogens (substances that can have detrimental effects on the organism). Hence, the methods and data of developmental psychobiology are often relevant to toxicologists and teratologists interested in some organismic effects of a toxin. Toxicologists who study, for instance, potentially harmful effects of drugs on developing animals are particularly aware of the special interpretive problems, particularly in organisms that engage in extensive parent-offspring interactions. The problem is that a drug can directly affect the young organism in at least two different ways. First, the drug can act directly on the organ systems of the young animal, and perhaps have more dramatic effects than on an adult, whose tissue is less susceptible to perturbation. The second potential source of effect is less direct but can be as significant. Alterations in physical or behavioral characteristics of offspring can produce changes in the quantity or quality of parental care. Moreover, many aspects of parental care are determined, in part, by responses to proximate cues from the offspring. Drug effects, even transient ones, can affect the parent's response which, in turn, can alter the condition of the young. These effects can produce chains of interaction that can extend beyond the immediate drug effect, in time and in kind of action.   JRAI/AW

Bibliography

Baldwin, J.M. 1895: *Mental development in the child and in the race*. London: Macmillan.

Bateson, P.P.G. 1981: Ontogeny. In The *Oxford companion to animal behavior*, ed. D.J. MacFarland. Oxford and New York: Oxford University Press.

Bruner, J. 1972: The nature and uses of immaturity. *American psychologist* 27, 687–708.

Claparède, E. 1910 (1911): *Experimental pedagogy and the psychology of the child*. London.

Darwin, C. 1877: A biographical sketch of an infant. *Mind* 2, 285–94.

Gould, S.J. 1977: *Ontogeny and phylogeny*. London: Belknap.

Hofer, M.A. 1981: *The roots of human behavior*. London: Freeman.

Konner, M. 1977: Evolution of human behavior development. In *Culture and infancy*, eds. P.H. Leiderman, S.R. Tulkin and A. Rosenfeld. London and New York: Academic Press.

Piaget, J. 1967 (1971): *Biology and knowledge*. Edinburgh: Edinburgh University Press; Chicago: University of Chicago Press.

Tobach, E., Aronson. L.R. and Shaw, E. 1971: *The biopsychology of development*. London and New York: Academic Press.

Trevarthen, C. 1980: Neurological development and the growth of psychological functions. In *Developmental psychology and society*, ed. J. Sarts. London and New York: Macmillan.

dissociation An unconscious DEFENSE MECHANISM in which a group of mental processes are separated (or split) from the remainder of the person's activity. This may result in dissociative disorder (see HYSTERIA) in which there is a narrowing of consciousness; typical symptoms are fugues (wandering states) and multiple personality. Dissociation may also lead to conversion symptoms.   RAM

dopamine One of the catecholamine neurotransmitters (see NEUROTRANSMITTER SYSTEMS). Dopamine is synthesized indirectly from the amino acid tyrosine. Although dopamine has been found in certain ganglia of the peripheral nervous system, most work has concentrated on its role in synaptic transmission in the central nervous system (CNS). There are two major dopaminergic pathways in the CNS. The cell bodies of the nigrostriatal pathway are located in the substantia nigra, and the neurons project to the BASAL GANGLIA (see EXTRAPYRAMIDAL MOTOR SYSTEM; BRAIN AND CENTRAL NERVOUS SYSTEM: ILLUSTRATIONS, figs. 5, 6 and 14–16). The cell bodies of mesolimbic dopaminergic neurons originate from the ventral tegmental region and project to various structures in the LIMBIC SYSTEM. Dopaminergic neurons from both sites of origin may project to certain cortical areas as well. The majority of dopaminergic synapses are suggested to be metabotropic (see ADENYL CYCLASE) and inhibitory, although excitatory dopaminergic synapses have recently been reported in the caudate nucleus. Central dopaminergic pathways are involved in the mediation of movement and emotional states, and in certain pathological states, including Parkinsonism and, perhaps, SCHIZOPHRENIA. GPH

Bibliography

Rolls, E.T. 1984: Activity of neurons in different regions of the striatum of the monkey. In *The basal ganglia: structure and function*, eds. J. McKenzie and L. Wilcox. New York: Plenum.

Down's syndrome This condition, known as mongolism until the early 1960s, accounts for 25 per cent of the severely mentally retarded and is caused by a CHROMOSOME ABNORMALITY. The main clinical features are a small round head, eyes which slant upwards and outwards (giving the "mongoloid" appearance); minor abnormalities of hands and feet, and moderate to severe mental retardation. There may also be abnormalities of the heart and digestive tract. It occurs in approximately 1 in 600 live births, and the incidence increases with maternal age. The chromosome abnormality consists in over 90 per cent of cases of an extra autosomal chromosome (Trisomy 21) with a recurrence rate of 1 in 100. More rarely, there is a translocation defect of chromosomes D/G, with a high risk of recurrence; or a mixture of some cells in the body with normal chromosomes and some with abnormal chromosomes (mosaicism). The diagnosis can be made in early pregnancy by examining the amniotic fluid surrounding the fetus (amniocentesis), and it is now common practice to offer this to all older women and those who already have an affected child. GENETIC COUNSELING is important. GCF

Bibliography

Smith, G.F. and Berg, J.M. 1976: *Down's anomaly*. Edinburgh: Churchill Livingstone.

dreaming Hallucinatory experience during SLEEP, often bizarre in the telling, but usually convincing at the time. There is no clear understanding of its function. A distinction may be made between dream interpretation, based on psychoanalytic theories of personality and dream investigation, a branch of cognitive psychology.

Since dreams are not accessible to direct observation, for most of the history of dream exploration there was no other source of information about them than the subjective memory of the dreamer. The discovery in the early 1950s of a relationship between rapid eye movement (REM) sleep and the reporting of dreams in the sleep laboratory seemed to provide an objective measure of the frequency and duration of dreams. However, it is now generally accepted that there is no straightforward relationship between a particular brain state and type of mental activity, since dreamlike mentation occurs intermittently throughout sleep. RPE

Bibliography

Cartwright, Rosalind 1978: *A primer on sleep and dreaming*. Reading, Mass. and London: Addison-Wesley.

Crik, F. and Mitchenson, G. 1983: The function of dream sleep. *Nature* 304, 111–14.

drug dependence Drug dependence has been defined by the World Health Organisation as: "A state psychic and sometimes physical, resulting from the interaction between a living organism and a drug, characterized by behavioral and other responses that always include a compulsion to take the drug on a continuous or therapeutic basis in order to experience its psychic effects, and sometimes to avoid the discomfort of its absence. Tolerance may or may not be present. A person may be dependent on more than one drug."

This replaces former definitions which attempted to sustain a distinction between drug addiction and drug habituation. The WHO Committee emphasized that the general definition should be applied separately in connection with specific drugs since the nature of the dependence varies to some extent with the type of drug (WHO 1964). This definition of dependence would exclude much consumption of psychoactive drugs. Taking drugs for medical or quasi-medical purposes to relieve specific symptoms does not constitute dependence, provided that it is for a limited period of time and that the patient experiences neither withdrawal symptoms nor a desire to continue consumption of drugs when the medication is stopped. Social consumption of drugs for hedonistic purposes, when the substance is taken on an occasional basis and where the consumer is able on each occasion to make a choice to take the drug without experiencing pressure or compulsion, may be harmful but is not drug dependence. In various societies alcohol, cannabis (both the resin and the vegetation usually referred to as marijuana) and the psychedelic drugs are usually consumed in this non-dependent fashion. Amphetamines and cocaine are also primarily taken on an intermittent basis but here the tendency to progress to a more compulsive pattern of use is greater. Sedatives such as the barbiturates and the benzodiazepine tranquilizers, and the opioid group of drugs are more likely to be consumed compulsively and continuously.

Within this range of drugs the first and most commonly consumed are likely to be those most readily available and socially accepted – in western society nicotine and alcohol. A substantial group of consumers may proceed to those drugs which are moderately disapproved of – cannabis, tranquilizers and sedatives taken for nonmedical purposes, and psychedelics and amphetamines taken orally. Only a minority progress to the injection of the most disapproved drugs – cocaine and opioids including heroin (Kandel 1975).

Attempts to understand drug dependence solely on the basis of the pharmacological properties of the drug, or of a simple interaction between a drug and an animal are insufficient. Dependence is a complex interaction to which the pharmacology of the drug, the personality and situation of the subject, and the culture of the society contribute in variable degrees in varying circumstances. Social factors are inevitably involved in the interaction and include, in addition to physical access to drugs, a milieu in which drugs are socially acceptable and even, at times, within specific subcultures, encouraged. Economic and political factors are also of relevance. In particular, drug-taking may provide an alternative activity where groups or individuals are deprived of the potential to gain success and status by legitimate means.

Dependence must be understood as a continuing process. Becoming dependent may involve important factors other than those which determine the process of progression to further drug use, and again differing from the predominant factors which maintain a state of dependence once drug-taking has become a regular and established part of the individual's life.

Social factors predominate in determining the initial consumption of drugs: availability and acceptability of certain drugs; access through subcultures to the illegal drug market; the support of drug users by peers and/or a disregard of, or rebellion against the social mores of non-drug-users. Among individual factors it has been suggested that an underlying personality inclined to immediate satisfaction in disregard of possible long-term adverse consequences may pre-dispose to drug experimentation.

Continuing drug consumption will be influenced by the same factors and will be facilitated by pleasurable experiences derived from drug-taking and by an increasing identity with other drug users.

Progression to a drug-centered lifestyle or state of "addiction" will be most likely to occur when in addition there is: social support for drug-taking behavior; a lack of gratifying alternatives, such as employment or training, and, in many individual cases, a relief from psychic or physical discomfort and pain.

The relative importance of these inter-related factors will vary between cultures and individuals and over time. Where an individual lacks personal resources and confidence to change, and where there is an obvious disparity between a society's wider expectation and the individual's capacity to achieve what are effectively unobtainable goals, the risk of progression to heavy drug use is high.

Coincidentally various factors resulting from drug-taking may amplify or reinforce this process. Developing the skills to obtain illegal drugs can earn approval within a deviant subculture and disapproval by wider society, and can modify an individual's self-image. Investment of time and energy in such activities reduces the probability of learning the skills valued in conventional society. The development of tolerance to the actions of drugs requires larger doses to maintain drug effect and hence more work is invested in obtaining supplies. The occurrence of unpleasant withdrawal symptoms which can be immediately avoided by drug administration increases the conditioned aspect of drug-taking. These factors have been elaborated in sociological and psychological theory in terms of deviancy amplification, social learning theory, and classical and operant conditioning. (See Becker 1973; Wickler 1973; Lindsmith 1968; and Young 1971.)

Conflicts between differing theories of addiction can only be reconciled by appreciating the very different circumstances pertaining in laboratory experiments with animals, pharmacological studies on human volunteers in hospital or penal settings, social studies of non-dependent cannabis consumption, and observations of the heavily dependent both on the street and in treatment.

Measures to reduce the harm of drug-taking are correspondingly complex. There is qualified support for the view that the number of individuals harmed by drug-taking will vary simply as a factor of the number of individuals who consume drugs within a society, e.g. the numbers dependent upon or suffering complications from alcohol consumption will vary according to the frequency and amount of alcohol consumption by the wider population. Hence primary prevention measures are aimed at reducing overall consumption. Most societies attempt to restrict access to drugs by increasing the cost both by taxation and by making the possession of some drugs illegal. This in turn increases the cost to the consumer both financially and in terms of time spent to acquire the

drugs. Educational programs aim at persuading people to avoid or reduce their consumption of drugs. In this context simply providing information or propaganda is insufficient and increasing emphasis is being placed on helping people to improve their ability to take decisions based on such knowledge in anticipation of events (Dorn 1981). Prevention is also aimed in a general manner at providing adequate experience and skills to enable young people to cope both with intrapsychic stresses and with societal demands as adolescence and adult life are reached. However, these measures can themselves have adverse consequences. Educational programs can have the unwanted effect of stimulating interest in drugs in many young people, which may make them more likely to experiment. Increasing the price of drugs will add to the burden upon the dependent user thereby reinforcing any tendency to finance drug-taking by crime. Outlawing a drug has the inevitable consequence of ensuring that only persons prepared to break the law by supplying drugs will profit from effective monopoly of supply. Decisions regarding education and social policy must therefore be based on information about the availability and demand for drugs within any particular culture.

Management of the individual's dependence upon drugs also varies. In the UK between 1920 and 1960 a few hundred opiate-dependent patients introduced to drugs in the course of medical treatment were satisfactorily managed, at least from society's point of view, by continued medical maintenance of their addiction. The same policy applied to younger gregarious drug-users in the 1960s was associated with a rapid escalation of heroin use. New users initiated with heroin from diverted medical maintenance prescriptions in North America over the past fifty years, and in Europe during the 1970s, have developed the extensive use of illegal drugs. This has been mainly in youth cultures and has been sustained primarily by illegally imported drugs. The medical management of individual users ranges from indefinite continued maintenance to immediate in-patient withdrawal. Generally it is agreed that it must include extensive social and psychological measures to enable the patient to resume a role acceptable to the wider society. The simple provision of maintenance supplies generally maintains the user within the drug subculture and on its own will rarely prevent the additional consumption of other illegal drugs. In the USA the substitution of long-term supervised maintenance with oral methadone appears to have enabled many former heroin addicts to alter their lifestyle and attain or resume conventional lives. It would be a mistake, however, to see the role of methadone in this context as purely a pharmaceutical replacement of heroin. It represents a change of status for the participant, who is no longer a person obtaining and injecting illegal drugs but one who accepts certain restraints and consumes a regular dose of medicine. That is not to dispute that even when persons have been stably maintained on methadone for a number of years they experience physical and psychological instabilities when the dose is reduced and terminated. However, provided the period of maintenance has been utilized to reverse many of the social consequences of addiction and the learned patterns of behavior required to maintain an illegal drug habit, the individual is better placed to persevere through the period of discomfort and drug craving which generally follows withdrawal from opiate drugs.

A contrasting approach is practiced in drug-free therapeutic communities where the initial drug withdrawal is accompanied by considerable support from the community, and then followed by intensive use of the therapeutic community to enable the individual to learn first how to handle the difficulties without having recourse to drugs, and subsequently to generalize the skills through a progressive re-entry into society.

Morbidity and mortality rates among drug users are many times higher than among others of the same age group. The proportion of drug users able to make use of a treatment program at any one time is limited; but despite this lack of immediate cures it seems probable that in the longer term a reasonable proportion of individuals are able to avail themselves of one or another form of assistance.   MCM

Bibliography

Becker, Howard S. 1973: *The outsiders; studies in the sociology of deviance.* 2nd edn. New York: Free Press.

Dorn, N. 1981: Social analysis of drugs in health education and the media. In *Drug problems in Britain, a review of ten years*, eds. G. Edwards and C. Busch. London: Academic Press.

Jaffe, J.H. 1980: Drug addiction and drug abuse. In *The pharmacological basis of therapeutics.* 6th edn., eds. Alfred G. Gilman, Louis S. Goodman, and Alfred Gilman. New York: Macmillan.

Kandel, Denise 1975: Stages in adolescent involvement in drug use. *Science* 190, 912–14.

Lindsmith, Alfred R. 1968: *Addiction and opiates.* Chicago: Aldine.

Wickler, A. 1973: Dynamics of drug dependence, implications of a conditioning theory for research and treatment. *Archives of general psychology* 28, 611–16.

World Health Organisation 1964: *13th Report of WHO Expert Committee on Addiction Producing Drugs.* Technical Report Series no. 273.

Young, Jock 1971: *The drugtakers: the social meaning of drug use.* London: MacGibbon and Kee.

drugs, depressant A classification of psychoactive agents, the administration of which produces a general inhibition of central nervous system functions and behavior. The majority of depressant drugs are termed sedative-hypnotics, which include the barbiturates (e.g. phenobarbital), minor tranquilizers (e.g. the benzodiazepines), nonbarbituric sedatives (e.g. chloral hydrate) and alcohol (Julien 1978). In increasing doses all sedative-hypnotics can produce anxiolytic effects, excitement and euphoria (due to the inhibition of inhibitory centers in the brain), sedation, sleep and general anesthesia (the loss of consciousness, sensation and reflexes). In lethal doses these agents can result in death due to respiratory paralysis. In appropriate doses chronic administration of all sedative-hypnotics can lead to tolerance and physical dependence. In addition two or more sedative-hypnotics administered simultaneously have at least additive effects with each other. Finally, virtually all sedative-hypnotics show cross tolerance and cross physical dependence with each other.

(See also DRUGS, TOLERANCE AND PHYSICAL DEPENDENCE.) GPH

Bibliography

Julien, R.M. 1978: *A primer of drug action.* 2nd edn. San Francisco: Freeman.

drugs, stimulant A group of psychoactive agents which increase activity and mental alertness. Most drugs in this class have both central and peripheral nervous system effects. Stimulant drugs differ markedly in both chemical structure and mechanism of action. Amphetamines, cocaine and methylated xanthines such as caffeine all cause peripheral sympathetic nervous system activation. The central effects of amphetamines are caused primarily by their ability both to stimulate release and block re-uptake of norepinephrine and dopamine, while cocaine primarily blocks the re-uptake of norepinephrine and, to a lesser extent, dopamine. Caffeine and other methylated xanthines increase the basal metabolic rate of all cells, including neurons. While the central alerting effects of amphetamines and cocaine may be mediated primarily via stimulation of the reticular activating system, areas of the cerebral cortex may be more sensitive to caffeine than are centers in the brain stem. Nicotine is clearly a stimulant drug, as evidenced by its effects on the electroencephalogram, but both its peripheral and central mechanisms of action are complicated and dependent on time since administration. Both catecholamine and acetylcholine neurotransmitter systems appear to be involved.

(See also DRUGS, TOLERANCE AND PHYSICAL DEPENDENCE.) GPH

drugs, tolerance and physical dependence Two phenomena associated with continued use of certain drugs.

Tolerance refers to a waning responsiveness following repeated administration of a given dose of a drug, or put the other way round, with repeated exposure, greater doses are needed to maintain some desired effect of the drug. Tolerance can be either dispositional (i.e. metabolic), behavioral (e.g. learning to compensate for the behavioral effects of the drug) or pharmacodynamic (i.e. decreases in the efficacy of the drug once it reaches its site of action, which may reflect compensatory alterations at the synapse). Physical dependence is a state in which the drug is needed for the body to maintain normal functioning. It is usually inferred from the consequences of terminating drug administration (i.e. withdrawal or abstinence syndrome). Interestingly, withdrawal responses are often opposite in direction from responses to initial administrations of the drug. Cross tolerance results when chronic use of one drug lessens an initial response to a different drug. Cross dependence is inferred when one drug can block the abstinence syndrome following withdrawal from chronic use of a different drug (Julien 1978). GPH

Bibliography

Julien, R.M. 1978: *A primer of drug action.* 2nd edn. San Francisco: Freeman.

dyslexic children Controversies surrounding the concept of dyslexia have given rise to much heated argument, and there is no universally accepted definition for the group of children suffering from this handicap.

The term "dyslexia" generally refers to a developmental abnormality in which there exists a difficulty in reading which is out of all proportion to the individual's intellectual competence. The definition proposed in 1968 by the World Federation of Neurology's research group on the subject, chaired by Macdonald Critchley, implies a constitutionally based reading disability free from correlates of reading failure like low intelligence, socio-cultural deprivation and gross neurological deficits. While an exclusionary definition of this type is justifiable for practical reasons, it is unsatisfactory because of its failure to aid conceptual clarity and its limitations for diagnosis. An amended definition by Critchley includes erratic spelling and lack of facility in handling written language as identifiable symptoms and suggests that the defect is capable of improvement. Nonetheless, the negative correlates continue to be central to the definition. Although Critchley insists that the diagnosis is a medical responsibility, dyslexia is not viewed basically as a medical problem by the British Medical Association (1980), which states that most doctors are not competent or willing to diagnose dyslexia without the assessment of an educational psychologist.

The first reference to such a disorder was made in a report in the British Medical Journal in 1896 describing "the paradoxical case of an intelligent boy of 14 who was incapable of learning to read". The validity of supposing that dyslexia in children is a specific inherent disorder is based on the analogy of its symptoms to the acquired loss or impairment of the ability to read, caused by cerebral damage. In order to distinguish the two conditions, it is common practice to reserve the term "alexia" for all acquired forms of reading impairment and the term "dyslexia" for the inability to learn to read. In the vast majority of cases of dyslexia, there is hardly any evidence for anatomical or physiological brain deficits. The remarkable preponderence of boys who are dyslexic makes it more difficult to explain the condition on the basis of brain damage.

The primary basis for the sustained interest in dyslexia in children is the promise that they hold as a distinct sub-group of reading disabled pupils. Although symptoms vary from child to child, case studies of dyslexic children refer to persistence in letter and word reversals, (e.g. confusions between b-d; was-saw); difficulty in repeating polysyllabic words; poor recall of sequences of letters or digits; bizarre spelling; disordered writing; frequently a history of clumsiness and late speech development. The presence of similar characteristics in many children who experience difficulty in learning to read has caused skepticism about the existence of dyslexia in children as an identifiable sub-type of reading disability. Most psychologists and educators would agree that a small proportion of problem readers may in fact have a specific learning defect which is inherent and independent of intellectual shortcomings. The symptoms of the sub-type in its current use do not help to differentiate dyslexic from non-dyslexic failing readers.

Increasing recognition that reading disability is not homogeneous has sustained the search for homogeneous sub-groups of reading-retarded children. Eleanor Boden's (1973) attempt to divide these children into those with psychological and those with visual problems is an example. Theoretical notions about neuropsychological processes concerned with reading have been the basis for several studies using a variety of classification approaches (Vellutino 1979). No doubt these attempts provide insights on different sub-types. However, despite their appeal for clinical and educational practice, they require evidence to show that they really are distinctive sub-types. The more recent diversity models proposed for dyslexia, as part of a continuum of language learning difficulty, hold more promise because of the shift in emphasis from treating these children as victims of pathology to providing opportunities for optimal development.

SDS

Bibliography

Applebee, A.N. 1971: Research in reading retardation: two critical problems. *Journal of child psychology and psychiatry*.

Benton, A.L. and Pearl. D. eds. 1979: *Dyslexia: an appraisal of current knowledge*. Oxford and New York: Oxford University Press.

Boden, E. 1973: Developmental dyslexia: a diagnostic approach. *Developmental medicine and child neurology* 15, 663–87.

Mathis, S. 1981: Dyslexia syndromes in children: towards the development of syndrome-specific treatment programs. In *Neuropsychological and cognitive processes in reading*, eds. E.J. Pirozzolo and M.C. Mittrock. New York and London: Academic Press.

Pavlidis, G.T. and Miles, T.R. eds. 1981: *Dyslexia research and its applications to education.* London: John Wiley and Sons Ltd.

Tansley, P. and Panckhurst, J. 1981: *Children* *with specific learning difficulties: a critical review of research*. London: Nelson.

Vellutino, F. 1979: *Dyslexia: theory and research.* Cambridge, Mass.: MIT Press.

E

electroconvulsive therapy (ECT) A form of therapy for the psychoses initially used to treat schizophrenics, but currently used primarily in the treatment of severe endogenous depression in individuals for whom drug therapy is either ineffective or contraindicated. With current methods patients are pretreated with a muscle relaxant to avoid undue stress on muscles and bones. An electrical current (110–170v, low fixed amperage) is applied briefly to the head, resulting in electrical seizures. Treatment is usually given no more than three times per week, for up to three to four weeks. In many individuals the treatment is remarkably effective in reducing severe depression. Side effects include temporary changes in the ELECTROENCEPHALOGRAM and transient RETROGRADE and ANTEROGRADE AMNESIA. This latter effect can be minimized by unilateral current administration. (See PSYCHIATRY: PHYSICAL TREATMENTS) GPH

electroencephalogram (EEG) A graphic representation of the electrical activity of the brain over time (BRAIN AND CENTRAL NERVOUS SYSTEM: ILLUSTRATIONS, figs 33 and 34). EEG records are typically recorded from the surface of the scalp with an array of six or more electrodes placed at different locations on the head. The electrical potentials of the EEG are very small, ranging from around 5 to 150 microvolts, and therefore they require substantial amplification. EEG activity ranges in frequency from 0.5 to 50 Hz.

Several characteristic EEG rhythms are seen in normal individuals.

Alpha rhythms have a frequency of 8 to 13 Hz and are usually observed when the subject is calm and relaxed with eyes closed. Beta rhythm is low-voltage fast activity above 13 Hz and is often seen when a subject is alert or aroused. Delta rhythms are large amplitude slow waves with frequencies of 0.5 to 4 Hz. Delta activity is seen during deep (stage 3 and 4) sleep. Theta rhythms have a frequency of 4 to 7 Hz and have been associated with memory storage processes in some studies. (See also MEDITATION) RAJ

emotion: neurobiological approach to Since the brain was first recognized as the organ of behavior scientists have been searching for the underlying brain systems which regulate and control emotional behavior. This investigative effort has primarily involved studying the effects of experimentally produced localized brain lesions on the behavior of various animal species as well as examining the emotional consequences of brain damage and the neural dysfunctions associated with psychiatric illnesses in humans.

The LIMBIC SYSTEM refers to a set of related neural structures and pathways in the brain which are importantly involved in emotion. The term is derived from *le grand lobe limbic* which was introduced by the French neurologist Paul Broca in 1878. Although Broca is best known for his discovery of the cerebral localization of certain language problems his neuroanatomical observations led him to describe the limbic lobe, which consisted of the HIPPO-CAMPUS and parahippocampal gyrus, structures which formed the underlying limbus or border of the cerebral cortical hemispheres (See BRAIN AND CENTRAL NERVOUS SYSTEM: ILLUSTRATIONS, figs. 15–17). Anatomists working at the turn of the century conducted the first comparative anatomical studies and described a group of cerebral structures which appeared to be closely linked to the olfactory system, such as hippocampus, olfactory lobe, septal region and thus these structures were collectively named the "rhinencephalon" or olfactory brain. The AMYGDALA was also viewed as having olfactory functions since its location deep within the temporal lobe was in close proximity to the nucleus of the olfactory tract. The rhinencephalic structures identified by these anatomists were recognized to be phylogenetically older than other prominent cortical formations such as the neocortex.

A number of studies in the late 1920s linked various brain lesions to disturbances in emotional behavior (e.g. Bard 1928). However, it was not until 1937 that the rhinencephalic region came to be associated with any function other than olfaction. In that year Papez proposed that a set of anatomically related structures, which included the hypothalamus, anterior thalamic nuclei, cingulate gyrus and hippocampus, mediated emotional expression and viscero-endocrine responses. Papez's suggestion was controversial at the time since it challenged existing notions of the olfactory brain. However, it was becoming more apparent that the term rhinencephalic was something of a misnomer. A clear example of this was the observation that certain limbic structures are highly developed in animals which are anosmatic (e.g. the dolphin).

Papez's proposed mechanisms of emotion were elaborated upon further by MacLean (1949) who introduced the concept of the *limbic system*. MacLean noted that various rhinencephalic, thalamic and cortical structures had close anatomical connections with the HYPOTHALAMUS and argued that these circuits modulated the affective response to stimuli and were responsible for autonomic effector mechanisms. He suggested that the structures of the rhinecephalon were strategically situated so as to be able to associate internal events with external stimuli. In this way, MacLean believed that the limbic system provided the emotional coloring to perceptual and cognitive processes.

The idea of an "emotional brain" was received favorably because of the popularity of Freudian thinking at the time. The concept of an ancient, deep part of the

central nervous system which controls emotions and instincts unconsciously was naturally appealing to a Freudian-based psychology which ascribed great importance to the unconscious.

Around the time of Papez, Kluver and Bucy (1939) rediscovered a behavioral syndrome first observed by Brown and Schaefer (1888). Kluver and Bucy's experiments have had a major impact on understanding the neurobiological substrates of emotion. They found that bilateral removal of the temporal lobe in monkeys resulted in profound changes in affective and social behavior. The lobectomized animals, formerly quite wild, became docile and tame and showed no fear reactions toward normally frightening stimuli. They displayed indiscriminate dietary behavior expressed in eating many types of previously rejected foods and attempting to eat inedible objects. Their sexual behavior changed dramatically with an increased incidence of autoerotic, homosexual and heterosexual activity. They showed a tendency to attend and react to every visual stimulus, termed "hypermetamorphosis" by Kluver and Bucy. They also showed a tendency to examine all objects by mouth, along with displaying signs of visual agnosia.

The Kluver–Bucy syndrome is not a phenomenon restricted to experimentally-lesioned animals. Many of the symptoms associated with this syndrome have also been observed in humans with a variety of neurological disorders (see e.g. Marlowe, Mancall and Thomas 1975). Additional research has indicated that the appearance of this syndrome requires both the amygdala and inferior temporal cortex to be removed bilaterally.

The functions subserved by the amygdala and hypothalamus are probably better studied than those for any of the other structures which comprise the limbic system. The amygdala receives input from all cortical sensory regions as well as from the internal visceral sensoria. It projects to hypothalamic, mesencephalic and lower brainstem structures. Electrical stimulation of the amygdala induces a wide variety of autonomic changes, including effects on heart rate, respiration and blood pressure. The most commonly reported behavioral change following amygdalectomy is the loss or dimunition of the normal reaction to fear-provoking stimuli and the inability to produce appropriate defensive behavior. These findings have led investigators to associate the amygdala with species-typical defensive behavior.

It is not possible to specify a single or even major function of the hypothalamus given the complexity and anatomical diversity of this structure. It is intimately concerned with the regulation of fundamental drives and bodily needs such as feeding, drinking, sexual behavior and avoidance of injury. There appear to be both facilitory and inhibitory systems within the hypothalamus for at least some of these functions. For example lesions in the ventromedial hypothalamus induce excessive eating and eventual obesity in animals while lateral hypothalamic damage abolishes the feeding or drinking response to internal events such as changes in glucose concentration, cellular dehydration or hypervolemia.

In addition to the various subcortical structures within the limbic system, certain regions of the cerebral cortex are known to be importantly involved in emotional behavior. Jacobson (1935) was the first to report that frontal lobe removals produced dramatic affective changes. In the course of studying the behavior of chimpanzees on a variety of learning tasks following frontal lobotomy, he noticed that some of the animals became more placid after the surgery.

Jacobson's observations on chimpanzees led Egas Moniz, a leading Portuguese neurologist, to propose that similar lesions in humans might relieve certain behavioral problems. In addition to establishing the questionable practice of PSYCHOSURGERY, these findings highlighted the important contributions of certain cortical regions to emotional behavior. A growing body of research indicates that the frontal and temporal regions play significant roles in affective behavior in humans. For example, frontal lesions have been found to reduce the production of spontaneous facial expressions (e.g. Kolb and Milner 1981).

Recent findings on both normal and clinical populations suggest that the frontal lobes are lateralized for different affective processes (Davidson 1983). Specifically, activation of the right frontal region appears to be associated with certain negative affects while activation of the left frontal region is associated with certain positive affects. This asymmetry may represent a fundamental lateralization for approach and avoidance behavior. A number of experiments have shown that when normal individuals are exposed to negative emotional stimuli and report negative affect, EEG recorded from the left and right frontal regions shows increased right-sided activation. In response to positive affective stimuli, the EEG shows increased left-sided activation. This basic pattern has recently been observed in subjects as young as 10 months of age (Davidson and Fox 1982). Similar findings have been reported for patients with unilateral anterior cortical lesions. When the lesion is on the left side, patients are reported to display more negative emotion compared with comparable sized right-sided lesions.

The study of neurobiological substrates of emotion may provide important insights for understanding the disorders of brain function associated with various psychiatric illnesses. Already, significant advances have occurred in the treatment of schizophrenia and depression. In many important respects, these developments emerged from basic research on the neurobiology of emotion.   RJD

Bibliography

Bard, P.A. 1928: A diencephalic mechanism for the expression of rage with special reference to the sympathetic nervous system. *American journal of physiology* 84, 490–513.

Brown, S. and Schaefer. E.A. 1888: An investigation into the functions of the occipital and temporal lobe of the monkey's brain. *Philosophical transactions of the Royal Society* 179B, 303–27.

*Davidson, R.J. 1983: Affect, cognition and hemispheric specialization. In *Emotion, cognition and behavior*, eds. C.E. Izard. J. Kagan and R.

Zajonc. New York and Cambridge: Cambridge University Press.

Davidson, R.J. and Fox, N.A. 1982: Asymmetrical brain activity discriminates between positive and negative affective stimuli in human infants. *Science* 218, 1235.

Isaacson, R.L. 1974: *The limbic system*. New York: Plenum Press.

Jacobson, C.F. 1935: Functions of the frontal association areas in primates. *Archives of neurology and psychiatry* 33, 558–69.

Kluver, H. and Bucy, P.C. 1939: Preliminary analysis of function of the temporal lobe in monkeys. *Archives of neurology and psychiatry* 42, 979–1000.

Kolb, B. and Milner, B. 1981: Observations on spontaneous facial expression after focal cerebral excisions and after intracarotid injection of sodium amytal. *Neuropsychologia* 19, 505–14.

MacLean, P.D. 1949: Psychosomatic disease and the "visceral brain." *Psychosomatic medicine* 11, 338–53.

Marlowe, W.B., Mancall, E.L. and Thomas, J.J. 1975: Complete Kluver-Bucy syndrome in man. *Cortex* 11, 53–9.

Papez, J.W. 1937: A proposed mechanism of emotion. *Archives of neurology and psychiatry* 38, 725–43.

Rolls, E.T. 1985: A theory of emotion and its application to understanding the neural basis of emotion. In *Neuronal and endogenous chemical control mechanisms in emotional behavior*, ed. Y. Oomura. New York: Japanese Scientific Societies Press and Springer-Verlag.

emotion and cardiac control Voluntary control of cardiac rate with BIOFEEDBACK and other procedures has been found to produce changes in emotion. It is known that heart rate changes during various emotions and recent evidence suggests that controlling heart rate through either biofeedback or verbal instructions changes emotional behavior. For example, when people are trained to lower their heart rates with biofeedback, they become more pain tolerant in response to noxious stimulation. When heart rate and blood pressures are lowered simultaneously, individuals report feeling particularly relaxed. Recent evidence suggests that anger, fear and sadness are associated with greater heart rate elevations compared with happiness, surprise and disgust. Therefore a lower heart rate would be expected to have a greater effect on decreasing the intensities of the first three emotions while increasing heart rate would be expected to have the greatest effect on intensifying the latter three emotions. RJD

emotion and cardiovascular disease At least two lines of investigation have linked cardiovascular disease to emotion. One is based on the hypothesis that stress causes premature illness and was advanced in 1897 by Sir William Osler, who suggested that "working the machine to its maximum capacity" may be the cause of coronary artery disease. Studies of the Type-A behavior pattern, i.e. the time urgent, competitive, hard driving individual who is over-involved in tasks, rapid and emphatic in speech, and appears to ignore his internal states of emotional stress, shows these behaviors statistically associated with high rates of morbidity and mortality that may be mediated by stress (emotion) induced activation of the autonomic and neuroendocrine systems. The second psychosomatic approach links cardiovascular disease or high blood pressure to specific emotions, i.e. anger that is suppressed because of fear of retaliation. Evidence is accumulating implicating suppressed anger or hostility in cancer as well as cardiovascular disease. The two lines of study should converge during the coming years. HL

Bibliography

Friedman, M. and Rosenman, R.H. 1974: *Type A behavior and your heart*. New York: Knopf.

Glass, D. 1977: *Behavior patterns, stress, and coronary disease*. Hillsdale, N.J.: Erlbaum.

Graham, D.T. 1972: Psychosomatic medicine. In *Handbook of psychophysiology*, eds. N.S. Greenfield and R.A. Sternbach. New York: Holt, Rinehart and Winston.

Krantz, D.G. and Marwick, S.B. 1984: Acute psychophysiological reactivity and risk of cardiovascular disease: a review and methodological critique. *Psychological bulletin* 96, 435–65.

Matthews, K.A. 1982: Psychological perspectives on the Type A behavior pattern. *Psychological bulletin* 91, 293–323.

emotion and neurological damage

Neurological damage produces changes in emotional behavior. Experiments in animals have demonstrated that damage to the frontal and temporal lobes, as well as to certain subcortical structures which comprise the LIMBIC SYSTEM, produces dramatic changes in emotional responsiveness. Removal of the frontal lobes has been found to produce behavioral placidity while removal of the temporal lobes along with the AMYGDALA diminishes fear normally elicited by threatening stimuli. This latter effect is part of a syndrome produced by bilateral temporal lobectomy known as the Kluver-Bucy syndrome (see EMOTION: NEUROBIOLOGICAL APPROACH). In humans and certain other species damage to the left versus right side of the brain produces different emotional effects. In general anterior damage to the left side results in a more negative emotional response compared with damage to homologous right hemisphere regions. Posterior right-sided damage often results in deficits in the perception of emotional stimuli such as facial expressions.   RJD

emotion and physical illness

Over the centuries, moralists have attributed illness to lack of balance, and overstimulation. The idea that any adaptive demand, positive or negative, evoked a common stress response, e.g. alarm, defense and exhaustion of a pituitary-adreno-cortical response pattern, was developed by Hans Selye. The hypothesis led to the studies of retrospective and prospective relationships between scores on life event scales and various illness measures. Recent studies suggest negative rather than positive life events, and the individual's perception of the event and coping skills determine the degree to which it is stressful and disease inducing. The approach of psychosomatic psychiatry is more similar to that of differential emotion theory in that particular attitudes, i.e. interpretations and modes of coping with situations, give rise to specific emotions and particular diseases, e.g. feeling deprived and wanting to get even leading to duodenal ulcer or feeling out in the cold and wanting to shut out the situation leading to asthma. Two key issues await resolution: one is the way in which short term emotional states lead to clinical disease; and the other is why stressed individuals develop different diseases.   HL

Bibliography

Graham, D. 1972: Psychosomatic medicine. In *Handbook of psychophysiology*, eds. N.S. Greenfield and R..A. Sternback. New York: Holt, Rinehart and Winston.

Dohrenwend, B.S. and Dohrenwend, B.P. eds. 1974: *Stressful life events: their nature and effects*. New York: Wiley.

Levi, L. ed. 1971: *Society, stress and disease*, vol. 1. *The psychosocial environment and psychosomatic diseases*. London: Oxford University Press.

Grosserth-Maticek, R., Bastiaans, J. and Kanazir, D.T. 1985: Psychosocial factors as strong predictors of mortality from cancer, ischaematic heart disease and stroke: the Yugoslav prospective study. *Journal of psychosomatic research* 29, 167–76.

emotion and the autonomic system

Emotional behavior has historically been thought to involve arousal in the autonomic nervous system (ANS). Changes in ANS activity are believed to be a necessary, but not sufficient condition for the elicitation of emotion. A relatively large proportion of the research in autonomic psychophysiology has involved the study of emotion (e.g. Grings and Dawson 1978).

Many common-language phrases which refer to emotion include descriptions of autonomic changes. For example, "white with fear" and "red with anger" presumably refer to blood flow changes in the face while "butterflies in the stomach" refers to alterations in gastric motility. While these descriptions imply that different emotions are associated with different patterns of ANS activity this is a matter which is surrounded by considerable controversy. William James (1890) was one of the first psychologists to suggest that different emotions involve different patterns of ANS changes. James, and independently the Danish physiologist, C.G. Lange, theorized that the perception of these autonomic changes was critical for the subjective experiences of emotion. This position became known as the James-Lange theory of emotion. The theory specifically states that certain stimulus situations produce particular bodily reactions (e.g., pounding of the heart and other visceral responses) and the perception of these reactions *is* the emotion. James (1890) explains the theory in the following way:

> Common sense says, we lose our fortune, are sorry and weep; we meet a bear, are frightened and run; we are insulted by a rival, are angry and strike. The hypothesis here to be defended says that this order of sequence is incorrect . . . that the more rational statement is that we feel sorry because we cry, angry because we strike, afraid because we tremble. (pp. 449–450)

The James-Lange theory was seriously challenged by Walter Cannon in the early 1900s (see Cannon 1927). Cannon presented a number of criticisms of this theory, the most significant of which include: (1) similar bodily reactions occur in widely varying emotional states, hence such changes cannot be responsible for the qualitative differences across emotion; (2) the viscera are relatively deficient in sensory nerves, and therefore we are not likely to be aware of changes occurring in these structures; and (3) autonomic reactions often have relatively long latency periods, whereas the time between the occurrence of a critical stimulus and a change in the subjective experience of emotion is often considerably shorter.

The Cannon critique of the James-Lange position was and still is very influential in psychology. The claim that patterns of autonomic arousal are similar across emotions has led to the search for the factors that are responsible for the qualitative differences in subjective feeling among emotions. The most influential theory of emotion predicated on the assumption that emotions do not differ in patterns of autonomic arousal is that proposed by Schachter and Singer (1962), who argued that emotion consists of (a) the activation of autonomic activity; and (b) the interpretation of this arousal as a

function of environmental events. Schachter and Singer performed a series of studies designed to illustrate this theory. For example in one experiment they manipulated autonomic arousal by giving injections of EPINEPHRINE (ADRENALINE) to one group of subjects and placebo injections to another. Cognitive factors were varied by providing accurate information about the drug's effect to some subjects, and misinforming and not informing other subjects. All the subjects were then left in a waiting room with an experimental accomplice who acted in either a euphoric or angry fashion. The emotional reactions of the subjects in this situation were then evaluated to determine how the combination of drug or placebo and information about the drug's effect would influence reactions to the accomplice. Schachter and Singer predicted that when subjects were not provided with accurate information about the drug's effects they would be more likely to evaluate their environment and find cues to explain their arousal. Therefore, they expected that the misinformed and uninformed groups would report themselves to experience more happiness and anger (depending upon the conditions) compared with the correctly informed group. The results from this experiment were interpreted as providing general support for the Schachter-Singer theory, although the study has been criticized on methodological and conceptual grounds (Plutchik and Ax 1967). One major problem with their conclusion about similar autonomic arousal accompanying different emotions was that no comprehensive assessment of physiological state was performed. Therefore, subjects might indeed have displayed different patterns of autonomic arousal following exposure to the happy versus angry stooge.

Although the Schachter and Singer view has been persuasive in psychology, a number of older studies have uncovered fairly convincing evidence of physiological differentiation among at least certain emotions. Both Ax (1953) and Funkenstein (1955) found that fear and anger could be distinguished on the basis of certain physiological measures. For example, Ax

(1953) found that anger was associated with larger increases in diastolic blood pressure compared with fear.

Research on psychosomatic disease also supports the hypothesis of physiological differentiation among emotions. One influential theory of the etiology of psychosomatic disorders is known as the specific attitude hypothesis which asserts that (a) each psychosomatic disease is associated with its own specific attitude, and (b) each attitude has its own specific physiological characteristic (Graham 1972). Graham has found that individuals with different PSYCHOSOMATIC DISORDERS report consistently different emotional attitudes. For example patients with ulcerative colitis feel that they are injured and degraded and want to get rid of the responsible agent; those with essential hypertension feel threatened with harm and have to be alert.

One of the most striking ways in which this theory has been tested was to take healthy subjects and hypnotically induce certain emotional attitudes which had previously been found to be associated with particular psychosomatic disorders. Changes in the relevant physiological measure could then be examined to determine whether the attitudinal induction produced specific physiological patterns. In one study (Graham, Stern and Winokur 1960) subjects were hypnotized and then given instructions for the attitude associated with hives or Raynaud's disease. Hives is accompanied by increases in skin temperature while Raynaud's disease is associated with decreases in this measure. The differential effects on skin temperature of the hives versus the Raynaud's attitude could then be assessed. The predominant attitude reported by patients with hives is that they feel as though they are taking a beating and are helpless to do anything about it. The attitude associated with Raynaud's disease is that they want to take hostile gross motor action. Graham et al. (1960) found that after the attitude induction, a small but reliable difference in hand temperature developed between conditions with the induction of the hives-relevant attitude producing increases in temperature while the Raynaud's-relevant

attitude produced temperature decreases. These findings support the suggestion that emotions are indeed associated with different patterns of autonomic activity and challenge the Schachter and Singer view which asserted that the same pattern of autonomic arousal occurs across emotions.

The inability of some investigators to find different patterns of ANS activity in different emotions may in part have been a function of the imprecision with which they classified emotional states. In some experiments, it was assumed that individuals would experience a particular emotional state if they were exposed to a stimulus which was selected to elicit that emotion. However, affective reactions are quite variable across people and rarely are instances of "pure" emotion elicited. In the Schachter and Singer experiment referred to above, the stooge who behaved in an angry versus joyful fashion might not have invariably elicited anger or happiness. The emotional responses of the subjects may have been a complex blend of many basic emotions. It may have been for this reason that robust ANS discrimination was not observed.

New and sophisticated methods have recently been used to measure the facial expression of emotion to select epochs of relatively "pure" emotion based upon the presence of the unique relevant facial expression. A battery of autonomic measures were recorded while subjects' self-generated emotion and the ANS measures were compared for those epochs during which pure facial expressions were present. The data from this study revealed the most robust ANS discrimination among emotions which has been found to date.   RJD

Bibliography

Ax, A.F. 1953: The physiological differentiation between fear and anger in humans. *Psychosomatic medicine* 15, 433–42.

Cannon, W.B. 1927: The James-Lange theory of emotions: A critical examination and an alternative theory. *American journal of psychology* 39, 106–24.

Funkenstein, D.H. 1955: The physiology of fear and anger. *Scientific American* 192, 74–80.

Graham, D.T. 1972: Psychosomatic medicine.

In *Handbook of psychophysiology*, eds. N.S. Greenfield and R.S. Sternbach. New York: Holt.

Graham, D.T., Stern, J.A. and Winokur, G. 1960: The concept of a different specific set of physiological changes in each emotion. *Psychiatric research reports* 12, 8–15.

*Grings, W.W. and Dawson, M.E. 1978: *Emotions and bodily responses*. New York: Academic Press.

James, W. 1890: *The principles of psychology*. New York: Holt.

Plutchik, R. and Ax, A.F. 1967: A critique of determinants of emotional state by Schachter and Singer (1962). *Psychophysiology* 4, 79–82.

Rolls, E.T. 1985: A theory of emotion and its application to understanding the neural basis of emotion. In *Neuronal and endogenous chemical control mechanisms in emotional behavior*, ed. Y. Oomura. New York: Japan Scientific Societies' Press and Springer-Verlag.

Schachter, S. and Singer, J.E. 1962: Cognitive, social and physiological determinants of emotional state. *Psychological review* 69, 379–99.

encephalins/endorphins Two types
of endogenous opioid peptides. After the discovery by several investigators of specific opiate binding sites in both central and peripheral mammalian systems, it was thought that these systems might also contain endogenous opioid substances which would interact with these receptors. Subsequent research has revealed two major families of endogenous opioids, both of which can interact with opiate receptors. Encephalins are pentapeptides, with two natural forms (met and leu) differing from each other only in the terminal amino acid. Endorphins are components of β-lipotropin, a pituitary factor. The primary endorphin, β-endorphin, is a 30 amino acid peptide and is found both in the PITUITARY and in the brain. Other endorphins have also been reported, including both α-and γ-endorphin. Although the amino acid sequence for met-encephalin is contained within the β-endorphin molecule, it is now apparent that encephalins are not formed as degradation products from β-endorphin. Finally, although the distributions of both encephalin-containing and endorphin-containing neurons overlap to

some extent, these distributions appear to be distinct neuronal systems. Although both encephalins and endorphins may modulate the perception of pain, endorphins may also be important in modulating mood and responses to stressful stimuli.

GPH

Bibliography
Beaumont, A. and Hughes, J. 1979: Biology of opioid peptides. *Annual review of pharmacology* 19, 245–67.

Bennett, G.W. and Whitehead, S.A. 1983: *Mammalian neuroendocrinology*. London: Croom Helm/Oxford University Press. ch. 10.

Rossier, J. 1982: Opioid peptides have found their roots. *Nature* 298, 221–2.

encephalization The extraordinary
development of the CEREBRAL CORTEX in humans has distinguished the human brain as being more than just a larger version of the brains in lower animals. Greater development of the neocortex was accompanied by innovations of brain function, but for the most part the changes can be described as a migration of functions from lower brain centers (brain stem, midbrain, diencephalon) to higher levels (neocortex) (see BRAIN AND CENTRAL NERVOUS SYSTEM: ILLUSTRATIONS, fig. 5). Within the cerebral cortex greatest development has occurred in the "association" and "motor" areas. This has allowed for the greater learning and memory capacities and for the fine motor control man possesses. Transfer of functions from lower brain centres to higher centres is readily seen by the expansion in scope of the sensory cortices. For example, in the frog all visual processing is controlled by the tectum, a midbrain structure. The equivalent in man, the superior colliculus (fig. 6), retains some visual functions, but it is the visual cortex (fig. 3) that has become most important and allows for the greater range of vision possessed by humans. The linguistic ability of humans is an example of functional innovation. In the frontal and temporal "association" cortex specialized areas have evolved for the production and comprehension of language. RCS/BER

encephalopathy *See* Wernicke's syndrome.

endocrine disorders Conditions due to abnormal functioning of the endocrine glands which result in pathologically high or low levels of circulating HORMONES in the blood stream. In addition to their effect on bodily functions endocrine disorders have prominent effects on mental functions and behavior, and commonly the psychological manifestations are a characteristic feature of the clinical picture. The disorder may be due to dysfunction of the peripheral gland (e.g. thyroid, testicle), or it may be the result of abnormalities at the level of the hypophysis or the diencephalon. Endocrine disorders are caused by a variety of agents, among them: tumors, infections, trauma, immunological factors and external administration of hormonal preparations, while in a proportion of cases the cause remains unknown.

The following are examples of endocrine disorders with significant psychological and behavioral manifestations:

(1) thyroid disorders: hyperthyroidism (Graves' disease) and hypothyroidism (myxoedema).
(2) adrenal gland disorders: adrenal insufficiency (Addison's disease), endogenous overproduction of cortisol (Cushing's syndrome), phaeochromocytoma.
(3) parathyroid gland disorders: hyperparathyroidism and hypoparathyroidism.
(4) pituitary gland disorders: hypopituitarism and acromegaly.
(5) gonads: hypogonadism in man, and disorders of menstrual cycle in women.
(6) pineal gland disorders: pinealomas.
(7) pancreatic disorders: diabetes mellitus and insulinomas.   JC

Bibliography

Hall, R., Anderson, J., Smart, G.A. and Besser, M. 1974: *Fundamentals of clinical endocrinology*. 2nd. edn. London: Pitman.
Lishman, W.A. 1978: *Organic psychiatry: the psychological consequences of cerebral disorders*. Oxford: Blackwell Scientific; St Louis, Missouri: C.V. Mosby.

enuresis A medical term applied to the involuntary passage of urine by persons more than three years old. Distinctions are made between enuresis which occurs only during the night, nocturnal, and that which happens during the day, diurnal. Two thirds of the reported cases among children involve nocturnal enuresis. The reported frequency of enuresis in childhood is a function of the social characteristics of the sample studied. Rates vary for normals, children with behavior problems, institutionalized and retarded children. Rates also vary with cultural background and training. Among children whose parents have sought psychiatric advice enuresis is almost twice as common in boys as in girls and peaks between the ages of eight and eleven years. In adulthood and old age a lack of voluntary control over the discharge of urine and feces is labeled incontinence.   BBL

epidemiology *see* life events; social psychiatry.

epilepsy Acute and transitory brain dysfunction which may take the form of motor disturbances, such as convulsions, or of psychological and behavioral abnormalities. It develops suddenly, ceases spontaneously, and has a tendency to recur. It is usually accompanied by disturbances of consciousness.

Epilepsy can be classified by reference to the characteristics of the seizure, or by the nature of the cause or the underlying pathology. The study of the electrical activity of the brain by means of electro-encephalography (EEG) has advanced considerably our understanding of this condition, helping to clarify its mechanisms and contributing to the process of making the diagnosis.

There are two main types of epilepsy: generalized epilepsy and focal epilepsy. *Generalized epilepsy* results from abnormalities below the cerebral cortex, and tends to spread to all parts of the cortex simultaneously, impairing consciousness from the beginning of the seizure. The attacks can take the form of "petit mal" or brief attacks usually involving disturbance of consciousness without convulsions, or "grand mal" seizures, characterized by severe and generalized convulsions with loss of consciousness. *Focal epilepsy* is due to abnormalities of specific areas of the cerebral cortex, although the electrical discharge can spread to other cortical or sub-cortical areas. The attack is usually preceded by characteristic subjective experience (aura) which can suggest the part of the brain where the discharge has its origin. For example, a discharge starting on the visual cortex tends to have an aura characterized by visual abnormalities.

The cause of epilepsy is often unknown in the case of the generalized type, although hereditary factors appear to play some part. Focal epilepsy is usually due to lesions of the particular area of the cortex involved. A variety of factors may cause such damage, among them: birth injury, congenital abnormalities, head injury, infections and tumors. Persistent febrile convulsions in childhood appear to be important in the development of temporal lobe epilepsy.

The treatment of epilepsy is mainly by means of medication, but it is important to investigate the patient carefully to rule out the presence of other conditions, such as a tumor or infection, which would require a different approach.

(See also EPILEPSY, CHILDHOOD.)   JC

Bibliography

Lishman, W.A. 1978: *Organic psychiatry: the psychological consequences of cerebral disorder.* Oxford: Blackwell Scientific; St Louis, Missouri: C.V. Mosby.

epilepsy, childhood Recurrent, transient brain dysfunction with altered consciousness, associated with paroxysmal electrical discharges in the brain, which may be detectable by an electroencephalograph, and diverse objective and subjective phenomena depending upon developmental age and the location of the discharge within the brain. It is best understood as one form of brain dysfunction which may betoken the existence of other forms of dysfunction (see GABA) or damage especially where the epilepsy starts early in life (particularly in the first year where there is a mortality of about ten per cent) and is persistent. Most children survive and recover. Those who do not are more likely to show evidence of other cerebral impairments in cognition and in behavior. Otherwise behavior disorder and psychiatric disorder are increased as a function of: the socially aversive nature of seizures leading to dread and to prejudice; the general problems of living with a chronic illness; impaired parenting of a vulnerable child; the unwanted effects of drug treatment and restrictive regimes; and poorly managed treatment programs.

Such factors in combination readily account for the 60 per cent rate of psychiatric abnormality found in children with epilepsy and brain lesions. The child's development may be biased by the brain abnormality before the onset of seizures or as a function of the disturbances in parenting engendered by the seizures. These will vary with the child's developmental age at their onset. Increased irritability and dependency, reduced learning capacity and some increased tendency towards psychosis are noted. The abnormality of parenting includes extreme over-solicitude or severe rejection, or, what is worse, intense ambivalent wavering between these two responses to the remembered, imagined, or ever present threat of death which seizures inspire and which their mortality intermittently re-enforces.   DCT

Bibliography

Meldrum, B.S. 1978: GABA and the search for new anticonvulsant drugs. *Lancet* 11, 304–6.

Reynolds, E.M. 1978: Drug treatment of epilepsy. *Lancet* 11, 721–5.

Sloper, J.J., Johnson, P. and Powell, T.P.S. 1980: Selective degeneration of interneurones in the motor cortex of infant monkeys following controlled hypoxia: a possible cause of epilepsy. *Brain research* 198, 204–9.

epinephrine (adrenaline) The principal compound synthesized and secreted by the adrenal medulla (see ADRENAL

adrenaline HO—⟨benzene ring⟩—CH—CH$_2$—NH—CH$_3$
HO—   OH

GLANDS; BRAIN AND CENTRAL NERVOUS SYSTEM: ILLUSTRATIONS, fig. 22). The chemical structure of epinephrine was elucidated in 1901 by Takamine (see fig. above). Epinephrine was the first hormone to be synthesized (by Stolz in 1904). The N-methylated derivative of NOREPINEPHRINE (NORADRENALINE) is the transmitter of the post ganglionic sympathetic nerves. The adrenal glands release substantial amounts of epinephrine into the circulation in response to stressful situations. Epinephrine has profound autonomic (sympathicomimetic) and metabolic effects which together prepare the organism for the fight, flight and fright reactions. Though the presence of epinephrine in the brain was first reported in the early 1950s, it was not until 1974 that it was found in distinct neuronal systems with cell-bodies in the medulla oblongata. As central transmitter, epinephrine is thought to be involved in the regulation of neuroendocrine and autonomic processes (see TRANSMITTER SUBSTANCES). There is particularly convincing evidence for its role in the central control of cardiovascular functions.   DHGV

Bibliography

Bowman, W.C. and Rand, M.J. 1980: *Textbook of pharmacology*. 2nd edn. Oxford: Blackwell Scientific Publications.
Kruk, Z.L. and Pycock, C.J. 1983: *Neurotransmitters and drugs*. 2nd edn. Beckenham, Kent: Croom Helm.

est An acronym for Erhard Seminar Training and Latin for "it is". *Est* is a corporation which provides "a sixty-hour educational experience which creates an opportunity for people to realize their potential to transform the quality of their lives" (*est* 1980). Attempts by outsiders to characterize more exactly this optimistic organization – as, for instance, a form of PSYCHOTHERAPY or as a mass-psychological religious movement – are not well received by insiders, although there is probably consensus that *est* belongs to the human potential movement.

One reason why *est* is not easy to characterize is that Werner Erhard, who founded the organization in 1971, drew upon a range of traditions: some religious (zen, yoga, taoism, Subud, the protestant ethic and positive thinking), some psychological (GESTALT, encounter, Mind Dynamics, PSYCHODRAMA), not to speak of scientology, and what he had learnt from his work in commerce and from his reading in philosophy.

While the education received by trainees has diverse roots it is highly structured. There are two consecutive weekend sessions, 250 typically middle-class trainees spending sixty hours with a trainer. Having paid in the order of $250 each ($200 if booked in advance), and having agreed to abide by a number of ground rules (for example, to forgo intoxicants, and to stay seated and silent unless called upon by the trainer), participants experience the results of the standardized techniques employed by the trainer.

The goal is "IT" and associated "recontextualization". His own "catalytic" experience of "IT" prompted Erhard to recognize that, "you can't put it together. It's already together and what you have to do is experience it being together" (see Rosen 1978, p.56). In other words, to use an *est* distinction, one cannot do much to change the "content" of life (e.g. a pressing debt), but one can change the "context" in which the content is "held" (one's experience of the debt is "transformed" if the correct context is applied) (see *est* 1980).

But what exactly is the "IT" which provides the correct context? Writes Erhard, "IT is you experiencing yourself without any symbology or any concept. Normally, I experience myself through my thoughts; I think who I am ... Well, IT is you experiencing you directly without any intervening system" (see Rosen 1978, p.63). Since this "real" self is "actually satisfied" and "perfect" (p.61), it provides the context, "power" or "source ('it cause')" to "transform your ability to experience living so that the situations you have been trying to change or have been putting up with clear up just in the process of life itself" (*est* 1980).

The strategies used by trainers are designed to "realize" the self and its powers. Two main components are "processes" (e.g. the "Danger Process" in which twenty-five trainees stand facing the audience and are reprimanded if they are not themselves) and lectures (e.g. the six-hour "Anatomy of the Mind" discourse explaining, among other things, the nature of suffering) (see Finkelstein et al. 1982). "Tapes", or patterns of thought and feeling that prevent one from experiencing one's perfection (or "completing" experiences) are destroyed; energy and satisfaction, what you create or decide, the freedom of immediate experience, take over.

Whether the strategies are best understood in terms of Erhard's rather metaphysical formulations (real and perfect self, the primacy of self/experience/ consciousness/choice over the public self/ objective world/belief/intellect/ necessity, or whether they are best understood in terms of the more scientific language of psychotherapy raises difficult issues. (Finkelstein et al., 1982, treat *est* in terms of behavior and cathartic therapies, for example.) What is clear, however, is that the great majority of the 250,000 + *est* graduates are satisfied customers (1982).

The challenge for psychologists is both to devise more fideistic measures of the results of est (how does one quantify "wholeness"?) and somehow to accommodate the possibility that "recontextualization", for example, is just as efficacious (if not more so) as more scientifically reputable processes such as flooding and social reinforcement. But perhaps *est* cannot be captured in terms of quantification and experimentally derived theorizing: perhaps Rosen is justified in claiming that Erhard "is, truly, providing a third dimension, opening up a 'space' for people to glimpse that cosmic perspective on their problems which is so hard to achieve in a cluttered life" (1978, p.60).   PLFH

Bibliography

*Bartley, W.W. 1978: *Werner Erhard.* New York: Clarkson N. Potter.

*Est 1980: *Questions people ask about the est training.*

*Finkelstein, P., Wenegrat, B. and Yalom, I. 1982: Large group awareness training. *Annual review of psychology* 5, 15–39.

*Rhinehart, L. 1976: *The book of est.* New York: Holt, Rinehart and Winston.

Rosen, R.D. 1978: *Psychobabble.* London: Wildwood House.

evoked potential A transient change in electrical activity that can be recorded from the brain in response to sensory stimulation. When recorded from the scalp, evoked potentials are comparable in amplitude to ELECTROENCEPHALOGRAM (EEG) waves which are occurring at the same time. Studies of evoked potentials have made important contributions to our understanding of neural systems that respond selectively to different types of sensory stimulation and to the mapping of the projections to cortical and subcortical regions of the brain. Evoked potentials reflect the presence of synaptic activity but not ACTION POTENTIALS. Computer-based averaging techniques are used to separate evoked potentials from a background of random brain activity.   RAJ

existential analysis A form of psychotherapy concerned with reestablishing meaning in the lives of persons who have lost it. This psychotherapy is practiced by existential psychologists who have been influenced by philosophers such as Kierkegaard, Heidegger and Sartre. In synthesizing the work of existential psychologists and philosophers Kobasa and Maddi (1977) delineate the major assumptions about personality as follows:
(1) persons create meaning through the decision-making process;
(2) decisions invariably take the form of choosing the future (the unknown) or the past (the already familiar status quo);
(3) although choosing the future brings anxiety (fear of the unknown), choosing the

past brings guilt (a sense of missed opportunity);

(4) choosing the future is desirable because it is the way of continued growth through creating meaning, whereas choosing the past leads to stagnation and eventual meaninglessness;

(5) in order to tolerate the anxiety associated with choosing the future, persons need to have developed hardiness (defined as attitudes of commitment rather than alienation, control rather than powerlessness, and challenge rather than threat) in early life;

(6) persons who tend to choose the future become individualistic, continue to grow, and feel vitality based in an expanding and deepening sense of life's meaningfulness;

(7) in contrast, persons who tend to choose the past become conformists, who change little, and increasingly experience boredom, stagnation, meaninglessness and despair about life. In addition they are vulnerable to stress-related disorders, because they experience changes as stressful, and are relatively unable to cope with them.

Although existential analysis can be and is used on the entire range of psychopathological symptoms, it is especially relevant to states of meaninglessness and stress-related disorders. In providing an illustration of this approach, Maddi has synthesized the techniques employed by several existential psychotherapists, such as Binswanger, Boss, Frankl, Gendlin, Kobasa, May and himself. Existential analysis emerges as a confrontational approach, in which the therapist is active in asking difficult questions, indicating that he is not convinced, and requiring that the client accept responsibility for both actions and passivity. Needless to say, the confrontations are done in an overall context in which the client knows that he or she is cared for and supported in his or her efforts to construct a meaningful life. Therapy sessions emphasize the present and the future, dwelling less on events of the remote past. Further, the waking state is regarded as the most relevant datum, existential analysis not concerning itself with supposedly unconscious mental

states. As such, there is little discussion of dreams, and when they are discussed it is in the same terms as waking experiences.

Existential analysis contrasts sharply with such humanistically-oriented therapies as ROGERS' person-centered counseling in being more confrontational, and such dynamic approaches as PSYCHOANALYSIS in putting more emphasis on conscious experience. Typical techniques of existential analysis which underline its differences from other approaches are discussed by Maddi as follows:

(1) *Paradoxical intention*, a technique of value when clients have symptoms which frighten them because they do not seem to be able to exercise any control over them. For example, a business executive may worry because he blushes whenever any pressure is put on him. He may feel that his whole career is jeopardized by this tell-tale sign of weakness. In employing paradoxical intention, the therapist encourages the client to exaggerate the symptom and try to blush even more under even more circumstances, so that everyone will know how threatened he feels. Clients usually resist intending paradoxically at first, then see the humor of the situation, and, once they actually adopt the suggestion, find that the symptom diminishes. From an existential viewpoint, the client has gained control over the uncontrollable symptom by attempting to increase it and thereby facing up to his or her worst fears.

(2) *Focusing*, a technique whereby clients can identify their real feelings about a problem and then transform those feelings into something less debilitating. When the client comes up with a problem, he is asked to concentrate on the feeling it provokes. He then lets an aspect of the feeling dominate his attention. Then he is asked to find some new words or pictures to capture the feeling. The new words or pictures become the felt meaning derived from focusing. In focusing on the problem of not being able to study, clients can transcend the conventional conclusions that they are merely "lazy" or "full of self-pity", understanding instead that they are too frightened of failure to perform.

(3) *Situational reconstruction*, a technique

whereby clients can construct a sense of options and of immutable givens in problematic circumstances. When a stressful event has occurred (e.g. a manager has been unfavorably evaluated by his superior, and failed to get promotion), he is encouraged to imagine three ways in which the situation could have been worse, and three ways in which it could have been better. Clients typically resist this instruction when they are obsessively preoccupied with the troublesome event as they remember it. But once they have succeeded in the imaginative task, they can better see the lines along which the event can be transformed mentally. Furthermore, they will have provided themselves with ideas about how to change the circumstance itself. These ideas about change in one's person and in one's circumstances form a basis for dealing with the current problem, but also for anticipating future events beneficially. (4) *Compensatory self-improvement*, a technique whereby clients confronted with a debilitating problem with which they appear incapable of coping can increase their sense of worth and control by improving their capabilities in some other area of life. If no amount of situational reconstruction produces a sense that stressful events can be transformed, the meaning of those events is temporarily or permanently a given. In such instances attention is profitably shifted to some important deficiency that seems more changeable. By improving themselves in this fashion, clients remind themselves that they can still exercise control in other areas of life. Sometimes, they can even return to the original recalcitrant problem with greater conviction that they can cope with it.

The four techniques mentioned are useful in building hardiness. The commitment aspect of hardiness increases as the client is able to deal with problematic events of everyday life in the supportive, caring setting of psychotherapy. The control aspect of hardiness increases as the client is better able to identify feelings, discern possibilities, improve deficiencies and transform unpleasant circumstances by thought and action. The challenge aspect is increased as discussions between client and therapist clarify how the presenting problems came about because of adherence to convention and a tendency to choose the past, and how the future must be approached in a different way. This process of learning hardiness takes place simultaneously with actual attempts to choose the future in everyday life. The therapist provides understanding support in the early stages of this effort. When future-oriented decisions are reasonably common, the time to terminate therapy is near.

The techniques of existential psychotherapy are specific to it, but in the overall aim of increasing hardiness and encouraging future-oriented choices they resemble other humanistic approaches to some degree. Gestalt psychotherapy and rational-emotive therapy are fairly close in spirit to existential analysis.   SRM

Bibliography

Kobasa, Suzanne C. and Maddi, Salvatore R. 1977: Existential personality theory. In *Current personality theory*, ed. R. Corsini, Itasca. Ill.: Peacock.

expressed emotion It was noted twenty-five years ago that schizophrenic patients discharged to family homes did less well than expected. The concept of Expressed Emotion (EE) has been developed to measure aspects of familial interaction which can be used to predict relapse in schizophrenics. The behavior of the key relative is assessed in an interview during the patient's admission, relying particularly on critical attitudes or over-involvement, and appears to be independent of the clinical state of the patient at discharge. EE's measurement and value are now well established. Patients who return to high EE relatives with whom they are in close contact have a greater than even chance of relapse in the following nine months, even if they are on phenothiazine medication. In contrast, the relapse rate in patients returning to low EE homes is only 10 per cent. Recently Leff and his colleagues have reduced relapse rates in patients in close contact with high EE relatives to 10 per cent by reducing EE or the degree of contact with relatives. They used a composite package of education of relatives, relatives' groups and a form of FAMILY THERAPY. The clinical implications of this work are likely to be very important.   PBe

Bibliography

Bebbington, P.E. and Kuipers, L. 1982: The social management of schizophrenia. *British journal of hospital medicine* 28, 396–403.

Brown, G.W. Birley, J.L.T. and Wing, J.K. 1972: Influence of family life on the course of schizophrenic disorders: a replication. *British journal of psychiatry* 121, 241–58.

Leff, J.P. et al. 1982: A controlled trial of social intervention in schizophrenic families. *British journal of psychiatry* 141, 121–34.

Leff, J.P. and Vaughn, C. 1985: Expressed emotion in families: its significance for mental illness. London: Guildford Press.

extrapyramidal motor system (See BRAIN AND CENTRAL NERVOUS SYSTEM: ILLUST-RATIONS, fig. 14). Includes the BASAL GANGLIA (fig. 15) and their associated subthalamic and BRAIN STEM nuclei and connections (figs. 6 and 7). Classically the three subdivisions of the motor system are the pyramidal system (fig. 13) which connects directly from the motor cortex to the SPINAL CORD and was thought to be involved with skilled voluntary movements; the extrapyramidal system, concerned with postural adjustments; and the cerebellar system (fig. 6), involved with coordinating movement. Actually these three parts are complexly interconnected and function as a single system. The pyramidal system is phylogenetically the newest portion of the system, and its development permitted higher animals to exert separate control over individual muscles. As the pyramidal system developed, the spinal connections of the extrapyramidal system appear to have become relatively less important. In higher mammals the major action of the extrapyramidal system seems to be through the pyramidal system.

Kornhuber (1974) has suggested that both the basal ganglia and the CEREBELLUM are movement pattern generators, and that

sophisticated somatosensory regulation of generated movements is accomplished by the motor cortex. In his view, the cerebellum generates patterns for fast movements and the basal ganglia patterns for slow movements (see DeLong 1974). As the somatosensory and motor portions of CEREBRAL CORTEX (fig. 3) evolved, control of those movements requiring or benefiting from elaborate analysis of tactile inputs during movement moved to the motor cortex and utilized the pyramidal system. Those movements not requiring such analysis remained in the centers of the extrapyramidal system and may still use the descending pathways of that system.

The main structures of the extrapyramidal system are the basal ganglia (caudate nucleus, putamen, and globus pallidus), the subthalamic nucleus, the substantia nigra and the red nucleus. The major inputs to the extrapyramidal system are from the cerebral cortex (including, but not solely, the motor cortex), and the thalamus (figs. 18–19). The major output is to the THALAMUS with other connections to the spinal cord via the brain stem.

Motor disorders, such as Parkinson's disease and Huntington's chorea, involve lesions of the basal ganglia. Parkinson's disease has been an important model system for the study of neural pathology resulting from a defect in neurotransmitter metabolism.   SCC

Bibliography

*Côté, L. 1981: Basal ganglia, the extrapyramidal motor system, and diseases of transmitter metabolism. In *Principles of neural science*, eds. E.R. Kandel and J.H. Schwartz. New York and Oxford: Elsevier/North-Holland.

DeLong, M.R. 1974: Motor functions of the basal ganglia: single-unit activity during movement. In *The neurosciences*, Third Study Program, eds. F.O. Schmitt and F.G. Worden. Cambridge, Mass. and London: MIT Press.

Kornhuber, H.H. 1974: Cerebral cortex, cerebellum, and basal ganglia: an introduction to their motor function. In *The neurosciences*, Third Study Program, eds. F.O. Schmitt and F.G. Worden, Cambridge, Mass. and London: MIT Press.

McKenzie, J. and Wilcox, L. 1984: *The basal ganglia.* New York: Plenum.

F

family therapy The treatment of the family group as a unit rather than of its individual members. This form of therapy developed in the USA during the late 1940s and 1950s at a time of growing recognition of the connection between disturbance in the child and parental problems. During the last decade the family approach has become increasingly popular in the mental health field. Early family therapists worked with families containing severely disturbed individuals, but they were later joined by those who were moving away from traditional psychoanalytic approaches to treatment of individuals. A major impetus was given by studies of communication in the families of patients suffering from schizophrenia by G. Bateson and others, which generated new concepts about family interaction, including the double-bind hypothesis, pseudo-mutuality, schism and skew in family relationships. Ackerman (1958) was one of the early pioneers.

Ideas from general systems theory, cybernetics, BEHAVIOR THERAPY (Patterson 1971), group analysis and communication theory (Watzlawick et al. 1967) have been incorporated. General systems theory has provided the most comprehensive and widely used framework, providing a model for various approaches to therapy involving intervention in the family system to change it, such as "structural family therapy" (Minuchin 1974) and "strategic therapy" (e.g. Palazzoli 1978). The theoretical base, however, remains incomplete, with no uniform agreement about the most effective use of diverse strategies. An eclectic approach in the formulation of the family's problems and treatment plan is the most appropriate. Marital or couples therapy has developed alongside family therapy. In 1967 Dicks pioneered conjoint treatment and important contributions have been made by behavioral (Jacobson and Margolin 1979) and group analytic methods. Techniques such as family sculpting, role-playing and play-back of video recordings are often employed.

A wide range of methods of family assessment are in use (e.g. Minuchin 1974) reflecting the numerous conceptual models of how families function. Data employed range from current interactional phenomena in the family to information about the family's developmental history, the families of origin and transgenerational influences, such as family myths. The McMaster Model of Family Functioning has been influential. It is concerned with information about problem solving, communication, roles, affective responsiveness, affective involvement and behavior control. There are widely differing opinions about the precise indications and contraindications for family therapy. In general, its consideration is appropriate in disorganized, dysfunctional families, when problems are presented in relationship terms, e.g. marital problems or parent-child separation difficulties, or when an individual's symptoms appear to be the outcome of emotional conflict in the family. Outcome studies tend to have methodological weaknesses including a lack of consistency in techniques employed, poor outcome measures, and the absence of control groups. As a result, despite much partisan enthusiasm, evaluation of the efficacy of family therapy and its place in psychiatric treatments is rudimentary.   WLIP-J

Bibliography

Ackerman, N.W. 1958: *The psychodynamics of family life*. New York: Norton.

*Barker, P. 1981: *Basic family therapy*. London: Granada: Baltimore: University Park Press.

Dicks, H. 1967: *Marital tensions*. London:

Routledge and Kegan Paul: New York: Basic Books.

Jacobson, N.S. and Margolin. G. 1979: *Marital therapy: strategies based on social learning and behavior exchange principles.* New York: Brunner/Mazel.

Minuchin, S. 1974: *Families and family therapy.* Cambridge. Mass. Harvard University Press.

Palazzoli, M.S. et al. 1978: *Paradox and counterparadox.* New York: Jason Aronson.

Patterson, G.R. 1971. *Families: application of social learning to family life.* Champaign, Ill.: Research Press.

*Skynner, A.C.R. 1976: *Our flesh: separate persons.* London: Constable.

Watzlawick, P., Beavin, J.H. and Jackson, D.D. 1967: *Pragmatics of human communication.* New York: Norton.

feedback The effect of the consequences of behavior on future behavior. Negative feedback occurs when the consequences diminish the level of performance of, or probability of, future behavior. The consequences of feeding (i.e. intake of food) have a diminishing effect upon hunger, and the animal is less likely to eat in the near future. Positive feedback occurs when the consequences increase the level of future behavior. In some cases, for instance, it is possible for feeding to have a temporary incremental effect upon appetite and so increase the apparent level of hunger. Positive feedback tends to be unstable, leading to escalation of the behavior, and in nature it is usually kept in check by simultaneous negative feedback (as in the case of feeding) or by environmental constraints.

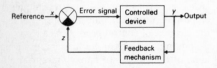

Negative feedback processes tend to have a stabilizing influence and they are particularly important for the maintenance of equilibrium in, e.g., homeostasis and orientation. The essential elements of a negative feedback process are illustrated in the figure. The reference x represents the required level of output, and is usually supplied from some other part of the system. The error signal is the difference between the reference x and the feedback signal z. The error signal actuates the controlled device which produces an output y. In animal behavior studies y is usually some aspect of the behavior of the animal. The feedback mechanism monitors some aspect of the output and translates this into a signal z, which is subtracted from the reference x to give the error signal $(x-z)$. For example, the body temperature $x = 39°C$ may be compared with a feedback signal (actual body temperature) of 38°C, giving an error signal of 1°C. This actuates the warning mechanisms of the body (controlled device) to increase heat output y. The consequent rise in body temperature is sensed by the feedback mechanism, and z consequently becomes larger. The feedback mechanisms that operate in real physiological and behavioral control systems are considerably more complex than that illustrated here, but the principle remains the same (see HOMEOSTASIS; HORMONES). DJM

flooding (implosion) Techniques designed to elimate fear and avoidance by extinction. As originally described by Stampfl, the techniques require the patient to imagine the feared or avoided object in as vivid and fear-inducing form as possible while the therapist applies an additional fear-inducing commentary. Imaginal exposure to the fear object continues for some time until fear can no longer be elicited. As originally described by Stampfl, imaginal exposure to the supposed psychodynamic origins of the fear or feared situation was also attempted but his practice did not find general acceptance. While controlled trials suggested that flooding was effective in reducing phobic and obsessional behavior, it did not prove to be more powerful than other less unpleasant behavioral techniques and has now largely been superseded by real life exposure to the feared object without other fear-inducing procedures. (See also BEHAVIOR THERAPY; DESENSITIZATION, SYSTEMATIC). RAM

Bibliography

Stampfl, T.G. and Levis, D.J. 1967: Essentials of implosion therapy: a learning theory-based psychodynamic behavioural therapy. *Journal of abnormal psychology* 72, 496–503.

forensic psychiatry The branch of psychiatry concerned with mentally disordered offenders. It embraces assessment, expert testimony, and treatment in various settings: ordinary psychiatric facilities, secure units, special hospitals and prisons. Many offenders show sociopathic traits, and for these the appropriateness of psychological treatment is debatable. However, one-third to one half of prison inmates suffer from other and more specific psychiatric conditions, including MENTAL HANDICAP, SCHIZOPHRENIA, EPILEPSY, ALCOHOLISM and DRUG DEPENDENCY, while profound personality disorders are common among, for example, arsonists and sexual offenders. The challenge for psychiatric workers is to select those who may be helped by treatment.   DLJ

Bibliography

Gunn, J. 1977. Criminal behaviour and mental disorders. *British journal of psychiatry* 130, 317–29.

Freud, Anna The youngest of Sigmund and Martha Freud's six children, Anna was born in Vienna on 3 December 1985. Although best known as a pioneer of child psychoanalysis, she is highly regarded for her contributions to developmental psychology, to work with adults, and to applied PSYCHOANALYSIS in a number of different, if related, disciplines.

She was educated at the Cottage Lyceum in Vienna, and returned there to begin her professional life as a teacher. Her interest in understanding the psychological as well as the educational needs of children deepened during the five years she worked there, and led ultimately to her wish to work as a psychoanalyst. In May 1922 she wrote her first published paper on fantasy life in children (*The relation of beating phantasies to a daydream* 1923.) This resul-

ted in her election to membership of the Vienna Psychoanalytic Society.

During the early years of her career as a psychoanalyst she attended the Psychiatric Clinic in Vienna, headed by Wagner-Jauregg, and was taught there by Paul Schilder and Heinz Hartmann. She regarded a knowledge of psychiatry as a necessary requirement for the practice of clinical psychoanalysis. Her early publications in the field of child analysis include *Introduction to psychoanalysis: Lectures for child analysts and teachers* (1922–35), and *Introduction to the technique of child psychoanalysis* (1927). Her best known work, written before exile and published in 1936, was *The ego and the mechanisms of defence*. This influential book has continued to be read widely in its many translations.

Following the Anschluss in 1938 she left Vienna with her father and other members of the family and settled in England. Together with Dorothy Burlingham, a friend of many years' standing, she opened the Hampstead War Nurseries in London. These residential nurseries provided care for some 80 children whose family life had been disrupted by war-time conditions. Two important works, written in collaboration with Mrs Burlingham, emerged from these experiences: *Young children in wartime* (1942), and *Infants without families* (1943). The nurseries closed in 1945 but many of her students and gifted collaborators urged her to initiate a comprehensive training in child psychotherapy. Together with a number of senior psychoanalysts she set up a formal course which led, in 1952, to the foundation of The Hampstead Child-Therapy Course and Clinic. Now, following her death, this has been renamed The Anna Freud Centre for the Psychoanalytic Study and Treatment of Children. The Centre continues to provide a comprehensive child psychoanalytic training and services.

During these years her writings were extensive and reflect her interest in the relationship between so-called normality and pathology, and her belief that the study of the one contributes to the knowledge of the other. The integral development of her ideas can best be understood from her book *Normality and pathology in childhood* (1965). This is a distillation of her work on children and her thinking about child development up to this time.

This work initiated a new phase of activity in which the ideas expanded in the book were extensively elaborated and augmented. From the time of its publication until her death she studied and wrote extensively on the assessment and diagnosis of childhood disturbances, developmental psychopathology, mental health and illness in terms of internal harmony and disharmony, and the distinctions between pathology based on such disharmonies and those leading to neurotic symptom formation. She elaborated her views on aggression (1972), discussed critically changes in psychoanalytic practice and experience (1976a), developed and discussed her views on psychoanalytic training (1976b) and contributed to many clinical topics, including fears, anxieties and phobic phenomena (1977) and the role of insight in psychoanalysis and psychotherapy (1979).

During these same years, she made a number of contributions to applied psychoanalysis. Two influential books addressed to problems of divorce, adoption, fostering and related matters were written in association with Albert J. Solnit and Joseph Goldstein and entitled *Beyond the best interests of the child* (1974) and *Before the best interests of the child* (1979). Her active work with pediatricians led to a paper on the interaction of pediatrics and child psychology (1975), and further contributions to education are to be found in such papers as *Dynamic psychology in education* (1976c) and *The nursery school from the psychoanalytic point of view* (1976d). Her early interest in psychiatry was reflected in studies with psychiatric colleagues over many years, and influenced the publication of works on psychoanalytic psychiatry by these colleagues. An account of this work can be found in the Bulletin of the Hampstead Clinic (*Psychoanalytic psychiatry: some past and present studies at the Hampstead Clinic* (1984).

Her interest in all these activities was maintained during intermittent, but disabling, illness in the last year of her life, and continued almost to the time of her death on 9 October 1982.   CY

Bibliography

Freud, A. 1922–1935: *Introduction to psychoanalysis: lectures for child analysts and teachers.* New York: International Universities Press.

—— 1923: The relation of beating phantasies to a daydream. (1928) *International journal of psychiatry* 4.

—— 1927: *Introduction to the technique of child psychoanalysis.* New York: Nervous and Mental Disorders Monograph Series 48; London: Imago (1948).

—— 1936: *The ego and the mechanisms of defence.* London: Hogarth Press.

—— 1943 (1973): Infants without families. In *The writings of Anna Freud*, vol. 3. New York: International Universities Press.

—— 1965 (1973): *Normality and pathology in childhood.* London: Hogarth Press.

—— 1972: Comments on aggression; 1975: Interaction of paediatrics and child psychology; 1976a: Changes in psychoanalytic practice and experience; 1976b: Remarks on the problems of psychoanalytic training; 1976c: Dynamic psychology in education; 1976d: The nursery school from the psychoanalytic point of view; 1977: Clinical topics including fears, anxieties and phobic phenomena; 1979: The role of insight in psychoanalysis and psychotherapy. In *The writings of Anna Freud*, vol. 8. 1981: New York: International Universities Press.

—— and Burlingham, D. 1942: *Young children in war-time.* London: Allen and Unwin.

—— , Goldstein, J. and Solnit, A.J. 1974: *Beyond the best interests of the child.* New York: Macmillan Publishing Co. Inc.; London: Collier Macmillan.

—— et al. 1979: *Before the best interests of the child.* New York: Macmillan Publishing Co. Inc.; London: Collier Macmillan.

Freeman, T., Wiseberg, S. and Yorke, C. 1984: Psychoanalytic psychiatry: Some past and present studies at the Hampstead Clinic. *Bulletin.* Hampstead Clinic 7.

Freud, Sigmund (1856–1939) Founder of the branch of psychological theory and psychotherapeutic practice known as psychoanalysis. Born on 6 May 1856 in Freiberg, Moravia, which was then within the Austro-Hungarian Empire (now Pribor in Czechoslovakia), Sigmund was the first child of the second marriage of a Jewish wool-merchant Jakob Freud, whose two sons by a previous marriage were already grown up; one of them was married and the father of a small boy, so that Freud was an uncle at birth. He had seven brothers and sisters.

The family moved to Vienna when Sigmund was only three, and the half-brothers emigrated to England (Manchester) at this time. Thereafter Freud lived in Vienna for the rest of his life, except for the last fifteen months when he too settled in England (London) after being forced to flee from Nazi persecution at home. Although family finances were very limited, the eldest son's education was fostered, and his intelligence and academic industry won him a place at the local *gymnasium*. Here, in addition to German literature and some English, he studied mainly the language and literature of the Greek and Latin classics. In his latter years at school he was consistently top of his class, putting to good use an exceptionally retentive visual and auditory memory, and his flair for writing was singled out as unusual by one of his teachers. Formal recognition of his literary achievement as an adult came with the award of the Goethe Prize at Frankfurt in 1930, three years before Hitler ordered his books to be burned in Berlin.

By the time he left school, his career plans had changed from becoming a lawyer to "desire to eavesdrop on the eternal processes" of nature, as he wrote to his boyhood friend Emil Fluss (Schrier 1969, p. 424). In practice this meant registering in the medical faculty of Vienna University to study biology, physiology and anatomy. But Freud did not abandon his earlier interest in cultural and philosophical matters, for during his first few years he also sat at the feet of Franz Brentano whose theories about the object-orientation of mental processes may have influenced his own later psychological formulations. As a third-year student he did laborious work on the reproductive system of the eel, but was later able to concentrate under Ernst Brucke upon neuroanatomy, the field in

which he published his first scientific observations (1877). It was Brucke who eventually had to persuade Freud that he could not make a living as a research-worker and had therefore better take his medical degree. This he did in 1881.

The need for a financially gainful career became more urgent the following year when he became engaged to Martha Bernays of Hamburg. The next four years, which took him to establish such a career as a basis for marriage, produced an assiduous two-way correspondence which is a rich source for biography as well as for glimpses of Freud's view of women. The couple were married in 1886 and eventually had six children; the marriage lasted until Freud's death.

During his engagement he was working in the Vienna General Hospital, mainly on neurological problems, and trying to make a mark in the medical world. He did so in 1884 with his pioneering paper on the medical and psychotropic properties of cocaine, and he consolidated this success by acquiring in the following year a teaching post at the university (*Privat-dozent*) and a traveling scholarship to visit the eminent psychiatrist Jean-Martin CHARCOT in Paris. Charcot was well known for his particular interest in the pseudo-neurological symptoms (such as anesthesia, amnesia, paralysis, dysphasia) produced by some patients suffering from HYSTERIA, and in using hypnosis for their treatment. He also intuited the sexual component in many of these disturbances. It may almost be said that Freud went to Paris as a neurologist and came away as a psychotherapist. For although, when back in Vienna, he worked for another two years or so in brain-pathology (especially with children) and gathered material for an important later monograph (1891) on speech disorders arising from brain-damage (APHASIA), he soon began to collaborate with Joseph Breuer in the psychological treatment of a number of hysterics. From these case-studies, published in 1895, emerged several hypotheses which have remained central in psychoanalytic theory. The question of the relation between Freud's early neurological preoccupations and his later psychological theories also remains, but at the outset he was certainly concerned to sketch an elaborate and detailed neurological model for his psychological postulates. This seminal *Project for a scientific psychology*, as it is now known in English, was written only four years after the study of aphasia, but this was not published until 1950 (*Standard edition*, vol. 1).

Crucial ideas to emerge from these first psychotherapeutic researches were:
(1) that the neurotic symptom, and the pattern of such psychological disturbance as a whole, are a symbolic reaction to an emotional shock;
(2) that the memory of this shock, and its associated feelings, are so distressing that they have been banished from conscious recall by the mind's processes of defending itself against anxiety (see REPRESSION);
(3) that these repressed elements, now located in "the unconscious", are not dormant but are part of a system of non-rational associations and transformations (the "primary process") which can indirectly influence and disrupt conscious feelings, trains of thought, recollections and perceptions, and which are most clearly evident in dreams;
(4) that the business of therapy is to identify the repressed material and the reasons for its repression, and to enable the patient to accept them consciously and rationally;
(5) that, in order to gain access to the unconscious, the therapist must bypass the limitations and obstructions of conscious mentation, either by hypnosis (Breuer's method, leading to the purging or "catharsis" of the repressed anxieties) or by the interpretation of free-associations, dream-material and incidental but symptomatic lapses of psychological function (Freud's substitute method based on the pervasive assumption that all such phenomena are systematically "determined");
(6) that in the course of treatment a patient forms a dependent, child-like and sometimes sexualized relationship to the therapist, in which he or she transfers to the therapist feelings, dispositions and assumptions which are derived from other relationships, especially (but not exclusively) from the childhood relationship with parents;
(7) that this "transference-relationship" is a principal context for discovering and unlearning neurotic responses to anxiety and for learning healthy ones in their place (see PSYCHOANALYSIS).

The greater part of Freud's subsequent work consisted of the investigation, modification and elaboration of these central ideas, and of addressing the questions that they raise not only about the origin and treatment of emotional disturbance but also about normal personality development, motivation, thinking and the organization of mental life in general. For he was after a *general* psychology, whose principles would apply equally to the sick and the healthy, to the individual and to society. The early clinical observations had already suggested to him some more fundamental hypotheses about the structure and processes of the mind.

The idea of an emotional "trauma" in (1) and (2) above, which Freud initially identified with sexual interference by a parent-figure (the "seduction hypothesis" which he soon gave up), raised questions about the origins of anxiety, why some anxieties are intolerable, what agency initiates the defense of repression, and whether there are other defenses (see DEFENSE MECHANISM). Again, the assumptions in (3) compel one to ask how the contents of the unconscious are organized, how this evidently active system is energized, and what principle governs its indirect incursions into conscious mental life. Already by the turn of the century Freud was thinking of a motivating force (*libido*) whose aim is the satisfaction of instinctual drives towards survival, pleasure and the avoidance of pain, and whose psychological manifestation is in wish-fullfilment (see INSTINCT). This libido is in constant tension with an adaptive agency, the *ego*, whose function is to regulate our actions according to reason and reality. Since the "reality principle" of the *ego* often requires us to delay impulse-gratification, it may conflict with the "pleasure-principle" of the libido. The frustration of libidinal gratification ultimately underlies anxiety, he argued, only to revise the idea later; and the philosophically uneasy anthropomorphic and hydraulic metaphors in which Freud depicts the psychobiological interaction between bodily instinct and mental energy are characteristic.

By the turn of the century also, the form taken by infantile sexuality in the OEDIPUS AND ELEKTRA COMPLEXES had been sketched, and he was ready to illustrate in *The interpretation of dreams* (1900; *Standard edition*, vols. 4 and 5), how "latent" unconscious feelings, images and desires are symbolically transformed and organized into the "manifest", wish-fulfilling content of normal dream-life in accordance with the "pleasure-principle". The following year saw a further application to normal behavior of his hypotheses about the influence of unconscious processes, for in *The psychopathology of everyday life* (1901; *Standard edition*, vol. 6) Freud claims to trace a great many examples of accidents, mistakes, oversights, verbal slips, memory lapses (known collectively as PARAPRAXES) to the specific generative wishes or anxieties of which they are symptomatic expressions.

Freud generalized his concept of libido-motivation in the theory that, in the normal course of development, the growing child gets instinctual gratification from different zones of the body at different age-levels. At about the time that these views were published in *Three essays* (1905; *Standard edition*, vol. 7), the incipient psychoanalytic movement was joined by JUNG from Zurich, who accompanied Freud on a lecturing invitation to Clark University, in 1909, but broke away for theoretical and personal reasons some five years later. That was three years after Alfred Adler had done the same (see McGuire 1974 and *Standard edition*, vol. 14, pp. 48–66).

The application of his theories to cultural and sociological issues began with *Totem and taboo* (1912–13; *Standard edition*, vol. 13) and was taken up again much later in *The future of an illusion* (1927; *Standard edition*, vol. 21), *Civilisation and its discontents* (1930; *Standard edition*) and *Moses and monotheism* (1934–38; *Standard edition*, vol. 23). Freud was deeply interested in the arts, with the marked exception of music, all his life; and, although originally hostile to the Surrealists' deliberate attempts to evoke unconscious associations by their painting, he changed his mind after meeting Salvador Dali in 1938 (Jones 1961, p. 649). His other relevant passion was archaeology (Graeco-Human and Egyptian), and the collection of antiquities that crowded his desk-top used to astonish his visitors. Freud made the first comprehensive statement of his theories in the *Introductory lectures* (1916–17; *Standard edition*, vols. 15 and 16), but personal tragedies and important theoretical revisions followed soon after the end of the first world war.

The post-war influenza epidemic killed his beautiful, happy and healthy daughter Sophie, mother of two young children, at the age of twenty-six. Three years later he learned of the cancer of the jaw which kept him in constant pain and frequent surgery for his last sixteen years. The first theoretical revision of his work was to some extent also a consequence of the war. The "pleasure-principle" did not allow him to explain *inter alia* why soldiers who had been traumatized in battle and removed from combat retained their recurrent nightmares. He concluded that there must be a fundamental 'compulsion to repeat' which is just as basic as the pleasure-principle, and which is in the service of a more general destructive motive called the "death instinct" or *Thanatos*. A group of constructive motives contend against this. It makes up the "life instinct" or *Eros*. Many of Freud's sympathizers have misgivings about these reformulations in *Beyond the pleasure principle* (1920; *Standard edition*, vol. 18), but are much happier with the "structural" revision of psychoanalytic personality theory in *The ego and the id* (1923; *Standard edition*, vol. 19), which introduce the *id* as the reservoir of instinctual impulses, and the *superego* or *ego ideal* as the source of the evaluative regulation of actions and mental activity in addition to the *ego's* controls. Consequently Freud can now express the goal of psychoanalysis as "where Id was Ego shall be". The theory that anxiety is transformed libido was revised in *Inhibitions, symptoms and anxiety* (1926; *Standard edition*, vol. 20) in favor of a more discriminating view in which it can be an expedient signal which calls up one or more of a range of defense mechanisms.

Freud plainly thought that both his theorizing and his therapeutic investigations were "scientific". Doubting critics, however, stress the lack of objectivity in observation, the difficulty of deriving specific testable hypotheses from the theory, the likelihood that the analyst selectively elicits certain sorts of actions or ideas from the patient, and the at least equal effectiveness of therapy based on other psychological theories (Farrell 1981: Cheshire 1975, chs. 4–7). Others argue that Freud was mistaken to think that he was giving a *causal* account of the origins of our mental life. What he provided, they say, was a way to explore and construct the idiographic meanings of that experience for each individual, as one might come to understand a linguistic text. This is the "hermeneutic" or "semiotic" approach, developed obscurely by LACAN (1973); but see also Ricoeur (1970), Blight (1981). On the other hand, there is now a considerable literature, by no means all unfavorable, about the empirical testing of Freudian theory (Kline 1981). And Einstein, having come across some events that could be explained only, as he believed, by Freud's theory of repression, concluded: "it is always delightful when a great and beautiful conception proves to be consonant with reality" (Jones 1961, p.628). Freud died in London on 23 September 1939.   NMC

Bibliography

Blight, J.G. 1981: Must psychoanalysis retreat to hermeneutics? *Psychoanalysis and contemporary thought* 4, 147–205.

Cheshire, Neil M. 1975: *The nature of psychodynamic interpretation*. London and New York: Wiley.

Farrell, Brian A. 1981: *The standing of psychoanalysis*. Oxford and New York: Oxford University Press.

Freud, Ernst L. ed. 1961: *Letters of Sigmund Freud. 1873–1939*. London: Hogarth.

Freud, J. Martin 1957: *Glory reflected: Sigmund Freud -- man and father*. London: Angus and Robertson.

Freud, Sigmund 1895–1938: *Gesammelte Werke*. Frankfurt am Main: S. Fischer. *Standard edition of the complete psychological works of Sigmund Freud*, 24 vols. London: Hogarth: New York: Norton.

*Jones, Ernest 1961: *The life and work of Sigmund Freud*. New York: Basic Books; London: Penguin (1964).

Kline, Paul 1981: *Fact and fantasy in Freudian theory*. 2nd edn. London and New York: Methuen.

Lacan, Jacques 1973 (1979): *The four fundamental concepts of psychoanalysis*. London: Penguin.

McGuire, William, ed. 1974: *The Freud-Jung letters*. London: Hogarth; Princeton, N.J.: Princeton University Press.

Ricoeur, Paul 1970: *Freud and philosophy*. New Haven and London: Yale University Press.

Schrier, I. 1969: Some unpublished letters of Freud. *International journal of psychoanalysis* 50, 419–27.

Sulloway, Frank J. 1979: *Freud, biologist of the mind*. New York: Basic Books: London: Fontana (1980).

G

GABA (gamma-amino-butyric-acid) A putative inhibitory neurotransmitter found in high concentrations in the mammalian brain and spinal cord. It is synthesized in the body from glutamic acid, a reaction which is dependent on a vitamin B6 cofactor. In humans, GABA is found in relatively high concentrations in neural elements of the EXTRAPYRAMIDAL MOTOR SYSTEM, the HYPOTHALAMUS and certain nuclei of the CEREBELLUM, while the concentration in the CEREBRAL CORTEX is relatively low. The inhibitory effects of GABA are probably due to the hyperpolarization of the postsynaptic neuron, thus making it less likely to initiate an action potential. After release, GABA may be cleared from the synaptic cleft (see SYNAPSE) via reuptake into the presynaptic neuron. It has been suggested that deficiencies of GABA may be associated with nervous system disorders such as epilepsy and Huntington's chorea (Cooper, Bloom and Roth 1978).

GPH

Bibliography

Cooper, Jack R., Bloom, Floyd E. and Roth, Robert H. 1978: *The biochemical basis of neuropharmacology*. 3rd edn. New York: Oxford University Press.

galvanic skin response (GSR) A change in the electrical resistance of the skin, related to sweating. The GSR can be produced by a minute electrical current and as such has been widely used as an unconditional response in classical conditioning paradigms. The GSR also occurs in situations which provoke emotion or anxiety. As a result it has become important in lie detection where it is used together with other measures regulated by the autonomic nervous system such as blood pressure and respiratory rate. The underlying assumption is that the individual may be capable of hiding overt expressions of emotion associated with lying, but not the autonomic responses that are beyond voluntary control. While useful in this respect these measures, including GSR, are not always reliable and are usually not admissible as evidence in a court of law. (See also BEHAVIOR THERAPY.)

GWi

genetic counseling Advice about the risk of recurrence of congenital abnormalities. It may be offered to parents after the birth of an abnormal child, or to anyone who may be a carrier of an inheritable condition such as haemophilia (see CHROMOSOME ABNORMALITIES). Assessment of the risk of recurrence involves an accurate diagnosis of the condition, including a search for chromosome abnormalities; a knowledge of the genetic transmission of the disorder, and a search among other family members for affected individuals or carriers. It is as important to be able to reassure parents that their child's abnormalities are not likely to recur in subsequent pregnancies as it is to warn them of a high risk of recurrence.

GCF

Bibliography

Harper, P.S. 1981: *Practical genetic counselling*. Bristol: John Wright and Sons.

genetics, evolution and behavior Genetic and evolutionary influences on human behavior remain controversial areas of study more than a century after Mendel's discovery of particulate inheritance and Darwin's original exposition of evolutionary theory. In the 1970s and early 1980s acrimonious debate reached new depths following, for example, Jensen's publication (1969) of a review paper combining the topics of genetics, intelligence, and race, and Wilson's treatise (1975) on behavioral evolution. The current debates often involve heavy doses of polemical politics and *ad hominem* attacks. However, at the same time they often represent attempts by practitioners of academic disciplines such as anthropology, biology, genetics, psychology, and sociology to come to grips with a plethora of new information which crosses their traditional disciplinary boundaries.

Two fundamental approaches have been applied in the study of genetics. One is mechanism oriented and involves Mendelian segregation combined with physiological and cellular studies of genetic influences on the development of the phenotype of individuals. The second is a statistical approach, variously labeled biometrical or quantitative genetics, which attempts to understand the influence of genetic variation on phenotypic variation by analyzing the patterns of distribution of characteristics among the members of populations. Both approaches have been applied to the investigation of psychological phenotypes.

That genetic variation can have profound influences on behavioral phenotypes of humans was unequivocally demonstrated by the discovery and subsequent investigations of phenylketonuria (PKU) beginning in the 1930s. This now-treatable form of profound mental retardation is related to a metabolic block of a particular enzymatic pathway which is itself due to homozygosity for a particular genetic allele at a single autosomal locus. The discovery of a specific genetic etiology for a particular set of retardates constituted a true breakthrough in investigations of the causes of retardation. PKU is now a classic model for a large set of genetically distinct "aminoacidurias" and further single-gene causes of retardation. Another "breakthrough" in understanding the genetic underpinnings of human variation was the discovery in 1959 that an extra chromosome was the cause of DOWN'S SYNDROME. It was only in 1956 that the normal diploid human chromosome number was established to be 46 (44 autosomes plus two sex

chromosomes, X and Y). Having 47 chromosomes with the supernumerary being an extra copy of the chromosome labeled number 21, hence "trisomy-21", is the cause of Down's Syndrome. Females having one X chromosome rather than the normal two (45X0) were, also in 1959, discovered to display Turner's syndrome, the symptoms of which include a specific cognitive deficit and failure to mature sexually. Klinefelter's syndrome males (47XXY) have an extra X chromosome, and display sexual and personality disturbances. These and many other chromosomal anomalies associated with behavioral symptoms have been discovered in recent decades. At the present time human chromosome studies (cytogenetics) is one of the fastest expanding areas of genetic investigation with implications for psychology. Literally many hundreds of genetic alleles are now known to influence various aspects of psychological function, ranging from sensory abilities to cognition.

The biometrical approach to understanding hereditary contributions to individual differences in human behavior antedates the discovery of Mendelian genetics, having begun with investigations by Sir Francis Galton. Recent advances in methodological sophistication, especially techniques involving path coefficients and utilizing twin and adoptive family data, continue to contribute to an unraveling of the complexities of genetic and environmental influences on psychological individuality. Bouchard and McGue (1981) reviewed 111 studies, many of them recent, containing an aggregate of 526 familial correlations including 113,942 pairings dealing with genetic involvement in intellectual functioning as assessed by IQ tests. The general interpretation of the outcomes of carefully conducted studies has not changed since the inception of IQ tests early in the century; a substantial proportion of the variation in IQ appears to be mediated genetically. However, numerical estimates of the technical heritability statistic, which indexes the proportion of trait variance which is attributable to genetic variance of the population, has changed. Recent large studies point to an heritability of IQ in the vicinity of 0.5, rather than the 0.75–0.8 values which were widely cited in previous decades. Large scale adoption and twin studies, some utilizing the extensive national records available in some countries (such as Denmark), are being conducted for many psychological variables. An inherited susceptibility or predisposition has been documented for many behavioral dimensions, ranging from smoking and alcoholism to homosexuality and likelihood of criminal activity, as well as diverse psychopathologies and variation in normal-range personality traits. Although specific mechanisms remain undiscovered, the evidence is unequivocal for a strong genetic dimension in the etiology of both SCHIZOPHRENIA and affective psychoses. Somewhat surprisingly to many, Plomin et al. (1980) point out that when genetic background is taken into account there remains no evidence for an important role of any known environmental variables in the development of schizophrenia. Although the details vary, and in most cases are poorly understood at present, it is perhaps not surprising that genetic individual differences appear to play a role in the development of individual differences on every psychological variable that has been investigated (Whitney 1976). At the present time the rapidly accumulating knowledge of genetic influences on behavior has exceeded its incorporation into general psychological theory (see BEHAVIOR GENETICS).

Although data now outstrip general theory in the realm of psychological genetics, in the realm of human behavioral evolution theoretical speculations greatly exceed empirical data. Phenotypic variation influenced to some degree by heritable genetic variation, combined with differential reproductive success (individual Darwinian fitness or inclusive fitness) is the essence of evolution. While it is clear that heritable variation does influence most (perhaps all) dimensions of human behavior it is usually difficult to relate behavioral variation and concomitant genetical variation, at least within the normal range of variation, to differential reproductive success. Bajema (1971) has drawn together a number of papers which attempt to measure ongoing genetic evolution in contemporary societies. Unfortunately virtually every serious study is met with a wide range of criticism, much of it not scientifically grounded. Nevertheless, theoretical speculation and accounts of plausible possibilities abound in both the technical and popular literature.

Most recent accounts of human behavioral evolution remain at the level of comparisons between species and largely restrict their treatments of human behavior to species-general typological concepts. This is the case even though natural selection depends on heritable variation among individuals within the species. It has become impolite and exceedingly controversial even to discuss heritable individual differences which could involve human behavioral evolution, and academics tread lightly. Nevertheless possibilities abound, many based on quite extensive data. As an example, phenotypic intelligence as measured by the controversial IQ tests displays many of the characteristics to be expected of an evolutionarily-relevant phenotype. Phenotypic individual differences are large, measurable, and have substantial genetic influence; extreme individuals, at least at the low end of the trait continuum, are severely depressed in reproductive performance; the trait displays inbreeding depression as do many other fitness relevant traits; and a reproductive difference favoring individuals of above average intelligence is demonstrable even within some modern industralized populations. The latter finding, replicated in various independent studies (e.g. Waller 1971), is surprising to many layman who share the common observation that "less bright" people tend to have larger families. The actual data are consistent with that observation. However, a larger proportion of the "less bright" people also have no children at all. When account is taken of the reproductive performance of all the members of a group, including those that do not reproduce, the general outcome has been that higher intelligence is positively related to reproductive performance.

Racial variation is another taboo topic

that could shed considerable light on human behavioral evolution. Of course existing biological races of humans display considerable overlap of distribution for many behavioral traits and share many of the same genes. Some geneticists and anthropologists have stated that the vast preponderance of genetic variation is among individuals within race and not among races, leading to suggestions that investigations of racial subgroups within the species would not be fruitful with regard to evolutionary interests. However, Neel (1981) points out that from simultaneous consideration of only 8 genetic loci one can be correct about 87 per cent of the time in assignment of an individual to race, and greater accuracy can be obtained when dealing with small groups. Races differ in the frequency of many genes, including many of relevance to behavior. Well known examples include the genes responsible for PKU, which are predominantly found among Caucasians; Tay-Sachs disease which is almost exclusively limited to Jewish populations; and Sickle Cell Anemia which is most common in Blacks. The incidence of many behavioral phenotypes also differs substantially among races. Examples are many: the distribution of IQ scores have been found in studies from the 1920s through the 1980s to differ among races in an ordering of Americans of Asian ancestry, Americans of European Caucasian ancestry, Americans of Black African ancestry; rates of psychologically relevant phenomena such as homicide, schizophrenia, affective psychoses, and suicide differ substantially among races. Although studies of racial variation within other species have shed much light on the processes of evolution in general, the recent social climate has tended to stifle investigations of human behavioral genetics and behavioral evolution from this potentially informative perspective. GW

Bibliography

Bajema, Carl J. 1971: *Natural selection in human populations*. New York and Chichester (W. Sussex):John Wiley and Sons.

Bouchard, T.J. and McGue, M. 1981: Familial studies of intelligence: a review. *Science* 212, 1055–9.

Fuller, J.L. and Simmel, E.C. eds. 1984: *Behavior genetics: principles and applications*. Hillside, N. J.: Erlbaum.

*Lumsden, Charles J., and Wilson, Edward O. 1981: *Genes, mind, and culture*. Cambridge, Mass. and London: Harvard University Press.

Neel, J.V. 1981: The major ethnic groups: diversity in the midst of similarity. *The American naturalist* 117, 83–7.

*Plomin, Robert, DeFries, John C., and McClearn, Gerald E. 1980: *Behavioral genetics, a primer*. San Francisco: W.H. Freeman and Company.

*Vogel, F. and Motulsky, A.G. 1979: *Human genetics*. Berlin and New York: Springer-Verlag.

Waller, J.H. 1971: Differential reproduction: its relation to IQ test scores, education, and occupation. *Social biology* 18, 122–136.

Whitney, G. 1976: Genetic considerations in studies of the evolution of the nervous system and behavior. In *Evolution, brain and behavior: persistent problems*, eds. R. Bruce Masterton, William Hodos and Harry Jerison. Hillsdale, N.J.: Lawrence Erlbaum Associates; London: distrib. by Halsted Press Div., Wiley.

Wilson, Edward O. 1975: *Sociobiology: the new synthesis*. Cambridge, Mass.: Belknap Press of Harvard University Press.

gestalt therapy An holistic approach which is guided by the beliefs that self-support and awareness are desirable therapeutic goals; and that therapy may be most beneficial when the client is viewed as a complex process, who acts out a variety of roles which are not necessarily consistent, but which derive their meanings from their configurations in particular contexts.

Gestalt therapy has been nurtured by a number of diverse sources. On the philosophical level, it is heavily indebted to existentialism, with its emphasis on the here and now, wholeness of experience, freedom and responsibility and its conception of "being-as-process". Phenomenology has also contributed significantly to the gestalt approach via its focus on the immediacy of experience, and its dictum that the world is only as it is lived, perceived, experienced by a particular person, and that meaning is an achievement which results from the unique manner in which persons constitute their world. Zen buddhism has also provided some valuable material for the gestalt therapist with its commentary on the self, intuition and the organization of experience.

On the psychological level the principles and procedures of perceptual organization formulated by gestalt psychologists were transposed into motivational and social descriptions by gestalt therapists. Personal experience is characterized as a continuum of figure-ground relationships in which specific needs receive primary attention. When a need is fulfilled, it fades into the background, and other need-configurations emerge. If a need is not fulfilled i.e. if a gestalt is not completed it may produce a conflict which is distracting and drains psychic energy. Full awareness of the continuous process of the formation-dissolution-reformation of gestalten, and the proper acknowledgment of one's role in that process constitute the cornerstone of healthy being. Elements of PSYCHOANALYSIS and behaviorism have been incorporated into the gestalt position, as well as some of the central insights formulated by both JUNG and Reich.

The actual practice of gestalt therapy varies as much as the sources which have molded its approach. Gestalt therapists have developed novel therapeutic techniques, but are not primarily concerned with the development or application of techniques, *per se*. Each therapeutic encounter provides a unique situation. The therapist attends closely to what the client is *doing* in that situation. The therapist attends to the obvious. In addition to listening to what is being said, emphasis is also put on how the client is saying it. Breathing patterns, voice inflection, emotional tone, repetition, posture, gestures, body tensions etc., are closely monitored by the therapist. These features are pointed out to the client, and the therapist may devise an "experiment" which will clarify what is being symbolized by those patterns of activity. The purpose of the experiment is to induce the client to recognize, accept and take responsibility for certain aspects and conflicts within him- or herself, or attitudes toward others which the therapist believes may be at the root of the client's ANXIETY, DEPRESSION, NEUROSIS or general discomfort. A typical experiment may require the client to act out and experience bodily and emotionally the roles of significant others, or those aspects or features of the client's personality which have been suppressed and are responsible for the bevy of resistances which confront the therapist.   CWB

Bibliography

Fagan, J. and Shepherd, I.L., eds. 1970: *Gestalt therapy now: theory, techniques, applications*. New York and London: Harper Colophon Books.

Loew, C., Grayson, H. and Loew, G.H., eds. 1975: *Three psychotherapies: a clinical comparison*. New York: Brunner/Mazel.

Perls, F. 1973: *The Gestalt approach; an eye witness to therapy*. USA: Science and Behavior Books.

Riet, V. Van De, Korb, M. and Gorrell, J.J. 1980: *Gestalt therapy*. New York and Oxford: Pergamon Press.

Gibson, James Born in 1904, in McConnelsville, Ohio. Gibson's family were strict Presbyterians and, like many Americans of that time, he was brought up in a traditional protestant atmosphere. His education was completed at Princeton University where he took his PhD in 1928. His early academic career was at Smith College, at that time an institution exclusively for women. In 1923 Gibson married Eleanor Jack who was also a psychologist and much of his subsequent work was done in collaboration with her. Perhaps the famous cookie cutters with which he showed the role of active exploration in tactile perception, came from the Gibson kitchen.

After many years at Smith the Gibsons moved to Cornell University, where, apart from interruptions in the war and several extended visits abroad, James Gibson spent the rest of his life. During the second world war he worked with the Air Force on the problem of effective training programs for pilots. He is credited with the discovery that has revolutionized instruction in landing an aircraft. Whatever the angle of descent, the only point ahead which shows no parallax, that is does not change its relation to other things in the environment as the plane descends, is the point at which the aircraft will touch down. It has been said that this was the occasion of his discovery of the important role played by geometrical invariants in the process of human perception.

Gibson's work centred round one main problem: how does a human being succeed in perceiving *things?* It was to the systematic exploration of the conditions under which that feat is achieved that he devoted nearly all of his research effort. As with other great experimenters like Michael Faraday, the direction of the program was determined and its momentum sustained by a profound theoretical idea, that men actively explored a structured world with perceptual systems that had evolved for sustaining life in that world.

According to Gibson perception does not rely on sensation, but on the direct "pick up" of information contained in the higher order invariants in the energy flux that bathes a perceiver. His other original concept was "affordance" – the possibility for action that any surface "affords".

In retirement he remained active, taking part in the beginnings of a new interdisciplinary graduate program in the neighboring campus of the State University of New York. He died in December 1979.

RHa

Bibliography

Gibson, J.J. 1966: *The senses considered as perceptual systems.* Boston, Mass.: Houghton Mifflin.

——— 1980: *The ecological approach to visual perception.* Boston, Mass.: Houghton Mifflin.

Michaels, C.F. and Carello, C. 1980: *Direct perception.* Englewood Cliffs, N.J.: Prentice-Hall.

glia Non-nervous accessory cells with special relationships to NEURONS. In mammals, glial cells occupy half the volume of the nervous system and are up to ten times more numerous than nerve cells. Although glia would seem to perform important functions, and virtually every known or suspected function of the nervous system has been assigned at some time to glia, they are probably the cellular element of the nervous system about which the least is known. Thorough description of the roles of glia in neural function remains an important research goal.

Vertebrates have five distinct types of neuroglia: astrocytes, microglia, oligodendroglia, Schwann cells and ependymal cells. Astroctyes are found in the central nervous system (CNS). They form a zone between walls of blood vessels or the coverings of the brain and spinal cord, and the nervous tissue proper. The BLOOD-BRAIN BARRIER between the circulatory system and the cerebrospinal fluid which bathes the nervous system may be due to a continuous layer of astrocytes in elasmobranch fishes (e.g. sharks), but in mammals it is the endothelial cells of the blood vessels, not the astrocytes, which form the barrier. Microglia are small cells normally uncommon in the CNS. They congregate at sites of trauma, infection, etc., where they act as phagocytes, taking up and digesting fragments of debris. There is evidence that microglia may in part derive from mesoderm, whereas other glial cell types originate from ectoderm. Oligodendroglia are the most numerous glial type, forming the sheaths of myelin around CNS neurons (BRAIN AND CENTRAL NERVOUS SYSTEM: ILLUSTRATIONS, fig. 30). Myelin sheaths permit fast information transfer along thin axons, and were essential to the evolution of the nervous systems of higher animals. Schwann cells form the myelin sheaths around neurons outside the CNS. Ependymal cells line the spinal canal and brain ventricles. They form part of the choroid plexus which participates in producing the cerebrospinal fluid.   SCC

Bibliography

Arenander, A.T. and de Vellis, J. 1983: Frontiers of glial physiology. In *The clinical neurosciences,* vol 5. *Neurobiology,* eds. R.N. Rosenberg and W.D. Willis, Jr. New York and Edinburgh: Churchill Livingstone.

Orkand, Richard K. 1977: Glial cells. In *Handbook of physiology.* Section 1. *The nervous system,* vol. 1. *Cellular biology of neurons.* Part 2, eds. J.M. Brookhart, V.B. Mountcastle and E.R. Kandel. Bethesda. Md.: American Physiological Society.

group therapy A form of PSYCHO-
THERAPY in which the same group of
patients meets together regularly with one
or more therapists for the purpose of
obtaining symptom relief or personal
change. Size varies but six to ten patients is
usual, with one or two therapists. Early
kinds of group therapy took the form of
classroom lectures with group discussion.
This method was first used in 1907 by Pratt
to help tuberculous patients manage their
illness. The first attempt to focus on a
group's interactions was by Burrow in the
1920s. Subsequently several styles of
group therapy have been developed. These
may be divided into the psychoanalytic and
the action-based approaches.

In the United States Slavson developed
the use of PSYCHOANALYSIS in groups, focusing on individual patients in turn. In
postwar England, Bion and Ezriel developed a method in which the group as an
entity was the focus of treatment, and
Foulkes developed the method of "group
analysis" in which the conductor uses the
group as the instrument of treatment for
the individual members.

Action-based techniques were first
developed by Moreno who created PSYCHO-
DRAMA. The leader directs a spontaneous
scene in which the group members may
reconstruct a situation in the lives of one of
them. In the 1960s action-based methods

developed rapidly, influenced both by
psychodrama and by psychoanalytic
approaches.

These new methods included encounter
groups, TRANSACTIONAL ANALYSIS, and GES-
TALT THERAPY. In many cases these and
related techniques were designed for ordinary people interested in personal growth
rather than for people designated as
patients.

During the last decade Yalom's work
(1975) on therapeutic factors in group
therapy has had a major impact on the
practice and training of group therapists,
providing a more empirical basis for the
role of the therapist.

Today group therapy is carried out in
a wide variety of settings, including out-
patient clinics, psychiatric hospital wards,
therapeutic communities and day centers
with both mixed and homogeneous groups
of patients. It is widely used in the
treatment of neurosis, personality disorders, chronic psychosis, and the addic-
tions (see DRUG DEPENDENCE).   DK

Bibliography
*Whiteley J.S. and Gordon J. 1979: *Group
approaches in psychiatry*. London: Routledge and
Kegan Paul.
Yalom I.D. 1975: *The theory and practice of group
psychotherapy*. 2nd edn. New York: Basic Books.

H

habit Though the term is not currently widely used in psychology, the concept of habit as a customary manner of acting is used in various branches of psychology. In social psychology habits are examined in terms of cultural customs or norms, and in clinical psychology habit usually refers to compulsive or often irrational behavior, while in cognitive psychology it may refer to a cognitive style or characteristic of processing information.

However the term "habit" is most often found and used in learning theory. Here the term *general habit* refers to the learned act tendency which results in a person maintaining the same relationship between corresponding stimuli and responses within a specific class of situations. In learning theory many early theorists have referred to *habit strength* which is the tendency for a particular stimulus to evoke a particular response. However there is some disagreement about the origin of habit strengths – one view stated that mere repetition of an act, regardless of the consequences, would increase the habit strength and the performance of an act, while later theorists stated that the habit strength would be increased only when the acts were followed by reinforcement. Research in skill acquisition occasionally mentions the *hierarchy* of habits (or skills) meaning that the learning of one aspect of a skill depends on the degree of mastery achieved in some lower aspect of the same skill.

From these learning principles it is possible to suggest ways in which old habits may be broken and new ones formed. One is to give the stimulus for the undesired response at a time when some incompatible response is taking place which provides a good opportunity for learning the incompatible response in place of the undesired one. Another is to repeat the cue for the habit until fatigue or action decrement prevents its occurrence. A third method is to give the stimulus for the habit with such slight intensity that the act does not occur and gradually the stimulus intensity may be increased until finally it no longer elicits the habit, even at normal tendencies. Finally of course habits may be changed by changing a person's motivation. AF

hallucinations Hallucinations are perceptions occurring in the absence of an external stimulus to the sense organs, but which are experienced as arising through the sense organs. They may occur in any sensory modality. In normal people they are especially likely to occur while falling asleep (hypnagogic) or waking (hypnapompic) or during sensory deprivation. In the mentally ill the nature of the hallucination has some diagnostic significance. Auditory hallucinations vary in complexity from noises to conversations and are particularly associated with SCHIZOPHRENIA, severe depression and mania. Visual hallucinations are characteristic of, but not confined to, ORGANIC MENTAL STATES. Olfactory and tactile hallucinations are less common but the latter are of particular value in the diagnosis and study of schizophrenia. In contrast pseudohallucinations are usually defined as vivid images, perceived with the mind rather than in external space, and are recognized as being unreal. A second meaning is a hallucination which the person recognizes as being unreal. Pseudohallucinations have less serious psychiatric significance than true hallucinations. RAM

Bibliography

Jaspers, K. 1959: *General psychopathology*. Trans.J. Hoenig and M.W. Hamilton. Manchester: Manchester University Press.

hallucinogens A classification of psychoactive agents whose common property is the ability to produce pseudohallucinations and altered states of consciousness. Pseudohallucinations are based on real objects, the perception of which is distorted under the influence of the drug, and awareness that the sensory distortions are drug induced is usually retained. There are several subtypes of hallucinogens which differ, in part, in chemical structure: those which result in cholinergic blockade (e.g. atropine scopolamine), those which are derived from catechols (e.g. mescaline), the indole related hallucinogens (e.g. lysergic acid diethylamide, LSD) and the hallucinogenic anesthetics (e.g. phencyclidine; PCP). Although marijuana and hashish can, in high doses, result in sensory distortions, these agents are not usually classified as hallucinogenic. Continued use of many hallucinogens can lead to tolerance, but no physical dependence has been substantiated. GPH

Bibliography

Bowman, W.C. and Rand, M.J. 1980: *Textbook of pharmacology*. 2nd edn. Oxford: Blackwell Scientific Publications.

hearing impaired and deaf, the: psychology and education Hearing impairment is a term used to encompass and describe all types and conditions of hearing loss, hearing problems or deafness.

Severe to total congenital (at birth) or prelingual (before language develops) hearing impairment or deafness occurs in approximately 1 to 2 per 1,000 children, excluding those who have fluctuating, intermittent or temporary conductive hearing loss caused by problems of the middle ear. The occurrence of severe to total hearing impairment in adults is approximately 3–5 percent. As suggested by these figures, the incidence of hearing loss increases with age.

Hearing impairment or deafness usually takes one, or both, of two forms: conductive or sensory neural/ perceptive hearing impairment.

Conductive hearing loss is due to a disorder in the conduction of sound from the external ear to the inner ear. It is most commonly caused by middle ear problems (Ballantyne 1977, Knight 1981).

Sensory-neural hearing loss is usually due to damage or lesions in the inner ear, i.e.: cochlea, auditory nerve, and/or auditory centers of the brain (see BRAIN AND CENTRAL NERVOUS SYSTEM: ILLUSTRATIONS, figs. 26 and 27). Sensory-neural hearing loss may be caused by a variety of conditions, e.g. postnatal causes including infection, viruses, ototoxic drugs, trauma etc. Prenatal and birth causes include: genetic factors, viral infections via the mother (e.g. maternal rubella, cytomegalovirus), ototoxic drugs taken during pregnancy; jaundice; low birth weight; anoxia, etc. (Ballantyne 1977, Knight 1981).

The degree and nature of hearing loss in childhood is usually assessed and diagnosed by an otologist and/or an audiologist. The degree of hearing loss is commonly shown on an audiogram in decibels (db), i.e. a logarithmic scale on vertical axis over the range of frequencies (horizontal axis) in which speech normally occurs i.e. 1.25–8.0 kilohertz (Ballantyne 1977). Other information about a subject's hearing may be obtained through freefield audiometric techniques or objective measures of hearing e.g. impedance or evoked response audiometry or electrocochleography (Knight 1981).

Categories of hearing loss based on the degree of hearing loss indicated on the audiogram tend to fall into five general categories: mild (up to 40 db); moderate (41–65 db); severe (66–80 db); very severe (81–100 db); and profound (101 db or greater).

Because of the heterogeneity of the population of the hearing impaired, factors which are crucial to the understanding of the psychological, educational, auditory, linguistic, learning and behavioral needs and function of the hearing impaired, include: cause, degree and nature of hearing loss; age at onset; age at diagnosis and fitting of appropriate hearing aids; age at, and appropriateness of, audiological, educational and communicational intervention; non-verbal (practical) and verbal skills, function and abilities; motivation and aptitude; presence of additional handicapping conditions; and either enabling or handicapping nature and conditions imposed by those within the hearing impaired person's environment, or by the environment itself (Levine 1981, Moores 1978).

The psychological, educational, communicational, linguistic and social problems and needs of the prelingually hearing impaired (i.e. those whose hearing loss occurs before language is developed or established) tend to be more complex than the needs and difficulties of those who lose their hearing after language is established (Jackson 1981, Levine 1981).

Additional handicaps tend to occur more frequently in cases of congenital sensory-neural hearing impairment which may include: visual acuity, visual field, peripheral visual and visual perceptual difficulties; mental/intellectual handicap; specific learning disorders; physical and physiological difficulties (Bond 1979, Vernon 1969). Hearing impaired persons tend to have an above-average incidence of significant visual problems. (See BLIND, THE: PSYCHOLOGY AND EDUCATION.)

The first few years of life are critical in communication, speech and aural language development (see Moores 1978). The normally hearing person's verbal and non-verbal or practical abilities tend to show a close positive relationship or correlation. Hearing loss occurring before language develops generally results in retardation of language and aural communicational skills, and consequently significant retardation in verbal-educational skills, in comparison with hearing peers of similar non-verbal or practical ability (Moores 1978, Levine 1981, Myklebust 1964). Even temporary, fluctuating, and intermittent hearing losses may cause retardation of verbal educational attainments and skills.

Some educators of the hearing impaired argue (with supportive evidence) that careful early diagnosis, appropriate amplification of sound through individual hearing aids, intensive enriching exposure to developmentally normative patterns of aural (auditory-oral) language and careful,

consistent, parent and family guidance and training, should assist hearing impaired children to develop intelligible speech, adequate aural communicational and linguistic skills and more normative verbal-educational attainments (Nolan and Tucker 1981, Jackson 1981 section 4). Educators who are aurally (auditorily and orally) biased may suggest that there is no place for signing or natural gesture in the education of the hearing impaired.

Hearing aids (Jackson 1981) do not correct or compensate for hearing problems. The hearing aid amplifies sound to enhance whatever useful residual hearing the hearing impaired person has. Even with hearing aids, the pattern of sound may be distorted, uncomfortable and intermittent. It may not be a pleasure for the hearing impaired child to listen or to use his residual hearing.

Failure in, or inability to cope in, an aural environment usually leads to problems of attainment, adjustment and behavior. Inadequacy or inappropriateness of some environments in which the hearing impaired exist, would appear to be a major factor in the higher incidence of maladaptive or disturbed behavioral and emotional patterns among the hearing impaired (Levine 1981, Mindel and Vernon 1971, Moores 1978, Myklebust 1964).

Among factors which have motivated some educators and psychologists to advocate and support the use of sign "languages" in the education of hearing impaired children are: evidence of higher, but still significantly retarded, verbal-educational attainments of those with hearing impaired parents (Moores 1978); severe retardation of verbal-educational attainments; above average levels of emotionally and behaviorally maladaptive, disturbed and disturbing behaviors (Levine 1981, Mindel and Vernon 1971, Moores 1978, Myklebust 1964); and concern about possible disintegration or deterioration in the "deaf cultural group".

Sign language of the hearing impaired is a language in its own right, and consequently has different linguistic structure from other languages. Some educators of the hearing impaired have extracted the sign vocabulary for "deaf sign language" to incorporate the vocabulary into normative "hearing" aural language patterns which are acoustically amplified (individual hearing aids) and simultaneously supported with signs in normative "hearing" grammatical structure. Systems of signing which follow the above procedure include "Signed English" and "Total Communication" (Jackson 1981 Section 4).

There is a diversity of educational placement and preschool services available to the hearing impaired in Britain and North America. Approximately 10 per cent or less of hearing impaired children in Britain are educated in specialized schools. The remainder are educated through facilities such as special classes, or small tutorial groups in ordinary schools; and many hearing impaired children, some with very severe hearing losses, cope adequately in main-stream classes. North American facilities for the hearing impaired have a similar range of preschool and school services. A few colleges in North America cater specifically for the hearing impaired.

Psychological studies of the hearing impaired appear to have moved from a pathological normative model which appeared to concentrate on features of similarity to or difference from the hearing population (Myklebust 1964), to a model based on organizing the environment and communication system to meet the needs of the hearing impaired (Levine 1981, Moores 1978).

Psychological assessment of hearing impaired children requires a clear understanding of the elements, construction, validity, reliability and purpose etc. of any test which is used, as well as understanding what the test actually measures. Tests which have verbal instructions, questions or content, including language which must be read, place the hearing impaired child at a disadvantage owing to linguistic retardation in comparison with non-verbal abilities. In contrast to significant retardation of verbal skills and attainments the hearing impaired tend to show a normative distribution of non-verbal or practical abilities (Bond 1979, Levine 1981, Moores 1978).

This does not mean that verbal tests should not be used with the hearing impaired as verbal tests may provide useful base-line information for comparison with peers – both hearing and hearing impaired, and for remedial programming in comparison with previous performance etc.

Careful, and appropriate early assessment, diagnosis, intervention, communication and placement, based on the individual's needs, abilities and aptitudes, remain crucial to enabling both the hearing impaired person and his environment to succeed.   DEB

Bibliography

Ballantyne, J. 1977: *Deafness*. 3rd edn. Edinburgh. London and New York: Churchill Livingstone.

Bond, D.E. 1979: Aspects of psycho-educational assessment of hearing impaired children with additional handicaps. *Journal of the British association of teachers of the deaf* 3,3.

English, J. ed. 1978: Usher's syndrome: the personal social and emotional implications. *American annals of the deaf* 123, 3.

*Jackson, Anne ed. 1981: *Ways and means 3: Hearing impairment*. Somerset Education Authority: Globe Education Publications.

Knight, N. 1981: A medical view of hearing loss. In Jackson op. cit.

*Levine, E.S. 1981: *The ecology of early deafness: guides to fashioning environmental and psychological assessments*. New York: Columbia University Press.

Mindel, E.D. and Vernon, McCay 1971: *They grow in silence: the deaf child and his family*. Maryland: National Association of the Deaf.

*Moores, D.F. 1978: *Educating the deaf: psychology, principles and practices*. Boston: Houghton Mifflin.

Myklebust, H.R. 1964: *The psychology of deafness: sensory deprivation, learning and adjustment*. 2nd edn. New York and London: Grune and Stratton.

Nolan, M. and Tucker, I.G. 1981: *The hearing-impaired child and the family*. London: Souvenir Press.

Vernon, McCay. 1969: *Multiply handicapped deaf children: medical, educational, and psychological considerations*. CEC Monograph. Washington D.C.: Council for Exceptional Children Inc.

hippocampus (Greek, seahorse) A large, multi-layered paleocortical structure in the limbic system of the brain (BRAIN AND CENTRAL NERVOUS SYSTEM: ILLUSTRATIONS, figs. 15–17). Composed of two interlocking components, Ammon's Horn and the dentate gyrus, the hippocampus extends from its most dorsal position below the cingulate gyrus, in a lateral and ventral direction, until just near the AMYGDALA in the medial temporal lobe region. Through its connections with the entorhinal cortex, which is linked to a complex system of afferent pathways, the hippocampus receives input from all sensory modalities. The major ouflow from the hippocampus is the fornix which projects antero-ventrally, giving off some fibers to the septum and terminating in the mammillary bodies of the HYPOTHALAMUS, (figs. 20 and 21). Historically identified with olfaction and emotion, recent research involving animals and humans implicates the hippocampus in learning and memory operations. There is considerable controversy concerning the precise role of the hippocampus, but, in broad terms, a cognitively-oriented function involving information processing is indicated. GWi

Bibliography

O'Keefe, J. and Nadel, L. 1979: Précis of O'Keefe and Nadel's "The hippocampus as a cognitive map". *Behavioral and brain sciences* 2, 487–533.

Olton, D.S. Becker, J.T. and Handelmann, G.E. 1979: Hippocampus: space and memory. *Behavioral and brain sciences* 2, 313–65.

Rawlins, J.N.P. 1985: Associations across time: the hippocampus as a temporary memory store. *Behavioral and brain sciences* 8, 479–96.

homeostasis Literally "staying the same". Living organisms and some self-regulating machines (such as thermostatically controlled heating systems, or automatic pilots) have the ability to resist change, and to keep certain properties or variables constant, even when factors are present which would tend to change them. This is most commonly done by means of negative FEEDBACK, an arrangement whereby any small fluctuations of the property in question are detected and messages fed back to an earlier point in the causal chain, where compensatory changes are made to cancel out the original fluctuations; hence the name negative feedback.

Homeostatic mechanisms are responsible for many important aspects of automatic self-regulation in animals, from the stabilization of blood chemistry, to the fine control of motor behavior. DDC

hormones Chemical substances secreted by the endocrine glands and transported in the blood stream to sites of action in various parts of the body. Hormones have profound influences on physiology and behavior and play an important role in the development of certain aspects of behavior.

Hormones are present in the blood in very small quantities and the life of individual molecules is short. To have a sustained effect, therefore, hormones have to be secreted continuously in precisely controlled quantities. In some glands secretion is actuated by the nervous system, in others it is stimulated by other hormones. Control is achieved by FEEDBACK. A high level of circulatory hormone tends to inhibit further secretion, and this inhibition is reduced when the level falls. Hormones are very specific in their actions, affecting only certain parts of the body, called target organs. These may include the adrenal glands and the sex glands, which themselves secrete hormones.

The brain has a considerable influence upon hormonal activity, and this is exercised primarily through the PITUITARY gland, which is situated at the base of the brain just below the HYPOTHALAMUS to which it is neurally connected (see BRAIN AND CENTRAL NERVOUS SYSTEM: ILLUSTRATIONS, figs. 15 and 20). The pituitary gland has an anterior and a posterior part which have different embryonic origins. The anterior pituitary secretes a hormone responsible for growth and a number of trophic hormones, as indicated in the table. The trophic hormones have other endocrine glands as their target organs. The role

The main endocrine glands of man, showing their products and function

Gland	Hormone	Function Target
anterior pituitary	growth hormone	growth
	trophic hormones:	
	ACTH	adrenal cortex
	TSH	thyroid
	FSH	gonads
	LH	gonads
	prolactin	mammary glands
posterior pituitary	vasopressin	kidney, blood pressure
	oxytocin	mammary glands, uterus
thyroid	thyroxine	development, metabolic rate
parathyroid	parathormone	calcium, phosphorus metabolism
adrenal cortex	sex hormones	(see below)
	glucocorticoids	metabolism of carbohydrates, protein, and fat
	mineralocorticoids	electrolyte, water balance
adrenal medulla	norepinephrine	circulatory systems,
	epinephrine	glucose release
pancreas:	glucagon	glucose release
cells	insulin	glucose transfer, utilization
cells		
ovaries:	estrogen	development and
follicles	progesterone	maintenance of sexual
corpus luteum		anatomy, physiology, and
	testosterone	behavior
testes		

ACTH	adrenocorticotrophic hormone
TSH	thyroid stimulating hormone
FSH	follicle stimulating hormone
LH	luteinizing hormone

of the brain in controlling the activity of the anterior pituitary is essentially regulatory. For example, some trophic hormones are first secreted at puberty and influence the growth and development of the sex glands. Thereafter the level of circulating sex hormones is regulated by feedback via the anterior pituitary.

The brain has a more direct influence upon the posterior pituitary and the adrenal medulla. The posterior pituitary produces two hormones in mammals, vasopressin and oxytocin, which can be released very quickly in response to circumstances. For example when a young animal attempts to suckle, messages from the mammary glands are received by the brain which instructs the posterior pituitary gland to release oxytocin. This hormone is responsible for milk let-down, and the young animal must stimulate this chain of events in order to obtain milk from its mother.

The hormone vasopressin has a similar quick-acting role in inducing changes in blood pressure. The adrenal medulla secretes adrenalin hormones which play a role similar to that of the AUTONOMIC NERVOUS SYSTEM and are released during fear and in other situations involving emotion.

Hormones affect behavior in a variety of ways. The most important is that they alter the animal's predisposition to indulge in certain types of behavior such as sexual behavior and migration. For example, females of many species have periods of heat during which they are capable of ovulation and are receptive to advances from males, or may actively seek out males. During this period there is a peak in the blood concentrations of estrogen and progesterone, two hormones produced by the ovary under the influence of the pituitary gland. This cycle of hormonal activity, called the estrus cycle, corresponds with the development of eggs in the ovary. The females become receptive when the eggs are ready for fertilization.

In some primates, including humans, all apes and some monkeys, the estrus cycle is replaced by a different type of cycle, called the menstrual cycle. This is characterized by periodic bleeding, called menstruation, from the uterus and vagina of sexually mature females. Menstruation occurs as a result of complex interactions among the circulating hormones. The ovarian follicles (incipient eggs) develop under the influence of follicle stimulating hormone (FSH) released by the anterior pituitary gland. Under the influence of FSH the uterus develops a rich blood supply in readiness for the implantation of the fertilized egg. The ovary also produces estrogen (or estradiol) which has a feedback effect on the pituitary gland, causing it to release more FSH. After about fourteen days the follicle ruptures under the influence of a surge of luteinizing hormone (LH) pro-

duced by the anterior pituitary gland. The rupture of the follicle releases the egg and the remaining follicular cells develop into the corpus luteum, which secretes the hormone progesterone. This has a negative feedback effect on the pituitary gland and leads to a reduction in FSH secretion. Fertilization may occur at this stage of the menstrual cycle, in which case the egg becomes implanted in the wall of the uterus and the hormonal changes characteristic of pregnancy are initiated. If fertilization does not occur, the rich blood supply of the uterine wall disintegrates and is shed into the vagina, resulting in the characteristic menstrual flow.

The hormonal balance of female Barbary doves is strongly influenced by participation in courtship and this form of communication is important in establishing cooperation between the mated pair. In the early stages of courtship the male shows aggression towards the female and this has the effect of inhibiting her reproductive cycle until the male's hormonal condition has time to change. Another aspect of behavior in which social relationships are important is dominance. Males with high levels of testosterone tend to be socially dominant and their aggressiveness towards inferiors may result in hormonal changes due to stress. In this way the reproductive potential of subordinate animals may be suppressed as a result of the action of hormones from the adrenal cortex, secretion of which is characteristic of stress. DJM

Bibliography
Muller, E.E. and MacLeod, R.M. eds. 1984: *Neuroendocrine perspectives*. New York: Elsevier.

hunger and thirst: physiological determinants *Hunger and thirst* are terms representing the intervening variables that have been posited to account for the discontinuous, episodic occurrence of feeding and drinking. Many workers have postulated complementary sets of stimuli of *satiety* that must work to inhibit or curtail the processes of hunger and thirst before the relevant imbalances are fully redressed.

At another level of analysis the three terms are also used to refer to the reportable experiences or sensations of an individual inclined to eat or drink in the case of hunger or thirst and inclined not to eat or drink in the case of the respective satieties. Failure to distinguish clearly these levels of discourse has produced considerable confusion on occasion. Little physiological information is available on the determinants of the experiential dimension, and therefore the present analysis is restricted to identification of the physiological determinants responsible for the postulated intervening variables.

In the case of *hunger* the physiological determinants include the visceral and metabolic events associated with insufficient energy within the body. The organism clearly needs a variety of nutrients and, consistent with these requirements, the specific dimensions of the types of utilization that are monitored by the body are multiple. Several of these visceral and metabolic consequences of energy have been shown to operate as determinants of hunger under at least some conditions. Their relative contributions to the control of feeding in an intact animal are the subject of controversy still. Rather than list them in the order of their importance, most accounts follow the strategy used herein of listing them arbitrarily by hierarchies of class of action or site of receptors.

Both practically and conceptually, the determinants of feeding behavior fall into two categories depending on whether they serve to accomplish *short term control* of feeding or to affect the *long term control* of intake. The former mechanisms include those that operate to influence the hour-by-hour pattern of feeding or the meal-to-meal episodes of hunger, whereas the latter controls correct day-to-day or even week-to-week deviations in energy balance. In the case of the short term controls of hunger, one of the first stimuli recognized was blood sugar. Jean Mayer (1955) suggested that meal-to-meal feeding was determined by a *glucostatic mechanism*. According to this widely cited view, falling glucose utilization (as measured by the difference in glucose levels between arterial and venous blood) of an area of the HYPOTHALAMUS in the brain is a signal that stimulates feeding. Numerous variations of this theory, many of them emphasizing other alternative or additional sites (such as the liver) for the detectors, have been developed. The theory has the attractive features that (1) blood glucose is the major source of energy utilized by the brain and (2) specific cells within the brain and the body have been shown to respond to glucose.

Another mechanism thought to influence short term control of hunger is a *thermostatic mechanism* proposed by Brobeck (1960). Recognizing that different types of food seem to have different satiating capacities roughly correlated with the heat produced in their metabolism, Brobeck suggested that the thermic effects of nutrient metabolism, or specifically the "specific dynamic actions" of foods were sensed and modified feeding in order to regulate the energy supply. Since the glucostatic theory and the thermostatic hypothesis do not readily account for all feeding behavior in all short term situations, some scientists have recently proposed different variants of an energy sensing model in which some universal factor in energy metabolism (e.g. pyruvate production) is the adequate stimulus for a hypothetical receptor that controls hunger.

Feeding is also promoted by gustatory and olfactory stimuli. Although it has been traditionally recognized that taste and smell are important in identifying and selecting foods, recent research has served to identify another role – one of motivation – of taste and smell in feeding. Sensory contact with appropriate and palatable food serves to elicit and energize feeding behavior, and in that manner gustatory and olfactory stimuli may be considered signals of hunger. At the end of a meal, taste and smell may also participate in an "oral metering" process which may promote the termination of feeding.

Another analysis of the short term determinants of hunger has been the attempt to identify those controls of *satiety* which serve to limit or eliminate hunger. It has been shown that distension of the stomach as well as nutrient stimulation of gastric chemoreceptors can inhibit food intake or limit hunger. It has also been demonstrated that cholecystokinin, a hormone secreted by the small intestine when it is stimulated by food, reduces the size of a meal. Other hormones of the gastrointestinal tract may also have satiating consequences. Although the loci for the effects are controversial, food also has other satiating effects after it is absorbed from the gastrointestinal tract and enters the circulation.

In terms of long term determinants of hunger, the most widely discussed mechanism is the *lipostatic control* first hypothesized by Kennedy (1953). This view argues that some form of lipids or a related metabolite is monitored and that hunger and feeding are responses mobilized by a lipostatic control in order to correct a deficit in the level of fat stores (over 90 per cent of the total energy stored in the body is in the form of fat). Long term control exercised by this mechanism is taken to be responsible for the striking day-to-day constancy in body weight and fat stores maintained by most adult animals, including those individuals with extremely high (obese) or low (thin) but stable values.

Recent analyses, stimulated by some of the inadequacies of the traditionally recognized determinants of hunger to account for the bulk of feeding, have suggested that there are important *nonhomeostatic* determinants of hunger as well. This view suggests that hunger, except in emergency cases, is in considerable part the result of learned strategies and of endogenous "programs" that have been selected for in the process of evolution to a given ecological niche and that produce feeding behavior in cycles or patterns that anticipate and avoid the onset of homeostatic imbalances. According to some investigators, the factors of taste and smell mentioned above are not under tight homeostatic control, and this situation accounts for why exposure to a surfeit of palatable foods can lead to overeating or hyperphagia and obesity.

Several brain systems are responsible for the control of feeding. The medulla oblongata (see BRAIN AND CENTRAL NERVOUS SYSTEM: ILLUSTRATIONS, fig. 6) contains the circuitry necessary to make ingestion and rejection responses to taste stimuli and to make simple adjustments in these responses on the basis of the presence of food in the gastrointestinal tract. The HYPOTHALAMUS contains neural circuitry important to the normal operation of hunger. This circuitry includes one system or set of systems in the *ventromedial hypothalamus* (fig. 20). Destruction of this region by brain lesions leads to the classical ventromedial hypothalamic syndrome characterized by excessive eating, OBESITY and finickiness with respect to the taste qualities of nutrients. The hypothalamus also includes a second system in and traversing the *lateral hypothalamus*. Damage to this system leads to a constellation of deficits in feeding including aphagia, ANOREXIA, finickiness, permanent reductions in the maintained level of body weight and deficits in arousal or the sensorimotor integration necessary for feeding. Electrical recording from neurons in these hypothalamic regions indicates that neural activity there is influenced by several metabolites and visceral events already mentioned. Other mechanisms including the LIMBIC SYSTEM and particularly the AMYGDALA (figs. 15 and 21) play key roles in the analysis and integration of sensory inputs and experience in the control of hunger.

Thirst, meaning the condition that accounts for drinking or the consumption of water, has a reasonably well defined set of controls analogous to those outlined for hunger. Water debt has impact on two dimensions of the body fluid compartments that are sensed by strategically located receptors and that are ultimately translated into thirst. This dual compartment/dual stimulus or "double depletion" hypothesis has been recently articulated by Fitzsimons (1979), Epstein (1982) and a number of others. In its basic form, this double depletion hypothesis postulates that osmotic and volemic changes in water balance within the body generate thirst.

Osmotic stimulation to drink occurs

when the water intake lags behind the rate of loss that occurs because of respiration, sweating and excretion. As this happens, a relative increase in electrolyte concentration or osmolarity occurs in the cells of the body, the extracellular space, and the blood as well. Hypovolemic stimulation results when body water and electrolytes are lost simultaneously or at corresponding rates (such as when body fluids move into the digestive tract or the individual loses fluids by diarrhea or hemorrhage). Hypovolemia means a lowering of blood volume.

The osmotic stimuli for thirst operate on *osmoreceptors* found in both the brain and the periphery. One of the first identified concentrations of these osmoreceptors is located in the lateral preoptic area of the hypothalamus (fig. 20), an area adjacent to the supraoptic nucleus and the nucleus circularis, both of which have been implicated in the osmotic controls of antidiuretic hormone release for conserving water. Other areas of the body including sites in the liver may also contain osmoreceptors. The lateral preoptic area of the hypothalamus is particularly central to osmotic drinking insofar as lesions of this region produce a profound adipsia or lack of drinking to osmotic stimulation.

The receptors monitoring hypovolemia are located in the circulatory system, particularly on the venous side where they serve as *baroreceptors* by continuously monitoring the stretch produced on tissues by the blood volume. Activation of these stretch receptors leads to a cascade of neuroendocrine events that liberates the active form of the hormone angiotensin in the blood stream. Angiotensin, sometimes called the hormone of thirst, serves not only to mobilize physiological adjustments which tend to offset the decrease of blood volume but also to activate directly brain mechanisms of volemic thirst. In the brain, angiotensin acts at specialized receptor tissues found adjacent to the ventricles. The subfornical organ and the organum vasculosum of the lamina terminalis are the two best studied of these receptor sites. These circumventricular sites are interconnected, and they apparently project to the lateral hypothalamus.

Lesions of the receptor tissues or the lateral hypothalamus can produce profound volemic adipsia. Current evidence suggests that osmotic thirst and volemic thirst mechanisms work in an additive fashion to determine the amount of water consumed.

Satiety signals separate from simple repletion of the water deficit seem to play less of a role for thirst than the analogous signals do in the case of feeding. This situation presumably stems from the fact that, unlike complex macronutrients, ingested water is rapidly absorbed from the gastrointestinal tract and rapidly equilibrates in the body water compartments. Still, research has suggested that some water satiety may involve factors other than elimination of the stimulus of thirst. Oral metering and gastric metering, the latter by distension and osmoreceptors in the stomach, seem to inhibit drinking in some situations before water is absorbed from the gastrointestinal tract.

Some determinants of thirst are considered nonhomeostatic. Some drinking appears to occur from habit or rhythmic patterns of behavior and may operate so as to stave off the development of water deficits that might activate osmotic and volemic controls. Similarly, meal-associated (*prandial drinking*) may result from the local stimulus of a dry mouth or the need to moisten food for swallowing, rather than from a deficit signal. Some researchers in the field argue that these nonhomeostatic determinants may serve to operate as anticipatory mechanisms and may account for a large percentage of ad libitum drinking.   TLP

Bibliography

Brobeck, J.R. 1960: Food and temperature. *Recent progress in hormone research* 16, 439–66.

Code, C.F. ed. 1967: Control of food and water intake, vol. 1, sect. 6. In *Handbook of physiology*. Washington. D.C.: American Physiological Society.

Epstein, A.N. 1982: The physiology of thirst. In *The physiological mechanisms of motivation*, ed. D.W. Pfaff. Heidelberg. Berlin and New York: Springer-Verlag.

———— , Kissileff, H.R. and Stellar, E. eds.

1973: *The neuropsychology of thirst: new findings and advances in concepts*. Washington, D.C.: V.H. Winston and Sons.

Fitzsimons, J.T. 1979: *The physiology of thirst and sodium appetite*. Cambridge and New York: Cambridge University Press.

Kennedy, G.C. 1953: The role of depot fat in the hypothalamic control of food intake in the rat. *Proceedings of the Royal Society. London. Series B* 140, 578–92.

Mayer, J. 1955: Regulation of energy intake and the body weight: the glucostatic theory and the lipostatic hypothesis. *Annals of the New York Academy of Science* 63, 15–42.

Morgane, P.J. and Panksepp. J. eds. 1980: *Handbook of the hypothalamus, Volume 3-Part A*. New York and Basel: Marcel Dekker, Inc.

Silverstone, T. ed. 1976: *Appetite and food intake*. Berlin: Abakon Verlagsgesellschaft.

hyperkinetic states These childhood states are characterized by motor restlessness, fidgetiness, poor attention, distractibility, impulsiveness and excitability. They occur more often in boys than in girls, and may be accompanied by clumsiness, learning difficulties, emotional disturbance and anti-social behavior. They are diagnosed much more frequently in North America than in Britain, possibly owing to some overlap in the diagnostic criteria used for hyperkinetic states and conduct disorder. Research into etiology has indicated a number of relevant factors, including genetic, structural or physiological brain abnormalities, toxic or allergic reactions, and family factors (maternal depression, early deprivation and poor family organization). Treatment with stimulant drugs and BEHAVIOR THERAPY produces improvements in many children. Diets low in allergens or food additives (e.g. the Feingold diet) are also used, but are still at an experimental stage. The outlook for hyperkinetic children with associated behavior problems and learning difficulties is not good; although overactivity itself decreases in adolescence.   GCF

Bibliography

Black, D. 1982: The hyperkinetic child: two views. *British medical journal* 284, 533–34.

hypnosis and hypnotism The word hypnosis is a shortened form of neurohypnosis or "nervous sleep" first used by James Braid (1795–1860) to refer to a trance-like state which could be observed in patients who had undergone certain verbal or non-verbal procedures aimed at inducing such a state. The act of carrying out these procedures is known as hypnotism.

The notion that an individual can be placed in a state somewhat different from normal awareness in which he or she becomes vulnerable to suggestion probably dates back as far as the cult of Aesculapius in the fourth century BC. However, the popularity of hypnosis in Europe stemmed from the practices of Franz Anton Mesmer (1734–1815) who claimed to be able to cure a variety of ailments by redistributing body fluids by the use of "animal magnetism". Mesmer's action of passing a magnet over the patient's body and the atmosphere in which he held his healing sessions influenced some individuals to have "fits", to behave in a somnambulistic way, to experience hallucinations and apparently to become impervious to pain.

Although, upon careful investigation, these phenomena were found to be attributable to the imagination and gullibility of the patients, Mesmer's results impressed later, more respectable, practitioners such as Braid and Esdaile (1808–59) who used hypnosis for surgical operations, and CHARCOT (1825–93), FREUD (1856–1939) and others who used it in the treatment of emotional disorders.

Before the beginning of experimental research on the topic in the 1920s it was generally believed that hypnosis could bring about certain conditions in the patient not otherwise attainable. Examples are analgesia, age regression, posthypnotic amnesia, sensory changes like blindness, an increase in physical strength, and willingness to commit anti-social acts.

The results of sixty years of carefully controlled experiments suggest that these effects and others result not from some alteration in the hypnotized persons' capacities, but from a number of interacting factors influencing them. These include prior knowledge of how hypnotized persons behave, expectations, willingness to volunteer and eagerness to experience something unusual, the "demand characteristics" of the situation (Orne 1962) such as the behavior of the hypnotist and the instructions given, and individual motives and beliefs. Physiological tests have so far failed to produce any consistent criteria of hypnosis, and brain patterns are those of relaxation rather than sleep.

Current theories of hypnosis tend to fall into two groups; those emanating from the psychodynamic and clinically orientated therapists who still maintain that hypnosis represents an altered state of consciousness with special and unique effects, and those put forward by experimentally oriented social psychologists who see hypnosis as a consequence of "role playing" and/or the influence of a number of social variables. One member of this group, T.X. Barber writes "hypnosis" in parentheses to indicate his conviction that the word is unnecessary, since the associated phenomena can be more easily explained in other terms (Barber 1969).

Some of the discrepancies in research findings from these two groups may stem from the very different subjects they use and the settings in which they work.

Hypnosis is still widely and successfully used by practitioners, especially in dentistry, obstetrics and PSYCHOTHERAPY. The patient's belief in the efficacy of hypnosis and trust in the hypnotist seems to exert a powerful influence, probably as a variant of the placebo effect.   SMH

Bibliography
Barber, T.X. 1969: *Hypnosis: a scientific approach.* New York: Van Nostrand.
Gordon, Jesse. E. ed. 1967: *Handbook of clinical and experimental hypnosis.* London: Collier-Macmillan.
Orne, M.T. 1962: On the social psychology of the psychological experiment with particular reference to demand characteristics and their implications. *American psychologist* 17, 776–83.

hypochondriasis An excessive preoccupation with bodily symptoms (especially pain) often accompanied by fears of a serious physical illness, such as cancer and heart disease. It may be a feature of a wide variety of psychiatric disorders including depression, hypochondriacal PERSONALITY DISORDER, ANXIETY, HYSTERIA and SCHIZOPHRENIA. It has been argued that there is a primary hypochondriacal neurosis but investigation suggests that most of such patients are suffering depressive illness and the remainder from some other primary disorder (Kenyon 1964). In treatment, once a physical illness has been excluded, the main aims are to control the demands for excessive medical investigation and at the same time treat the underlying psychological disorder appropriately. Minor problems can be satisfactorily managed by reassurance and simple counseling.   RAM

Bibliography
Kenyon, F.E. 1964: Hypochondriasis: a clinical study. *British journal of psychiatry* 110, 478–88.

hypomania This commonly designates a mild state of mania, the latter term being avoided in some contexts because of its alternative meanings (that is, mania as an undifferentiated madness with disturbed behavior, or a morbid compulsion). The hypomanic state comprises restlessness and overactivity, disinhibited and extravagant behavior, racing thoughts and elated mood, often with irritability. It is usually seen within the context of an AFFECTIVE DISORDER, in most cases alternating with depression (see DEPRESSION, BIPOLAR). More rarely a brief episode may be understandable as a reaction to an emotional upset; psychoanalysts use the term manic or hypomanic defense where they speculate that the ego breaks free temporarily from the inhibiting effect of the superego.

A hypomanic illness usually remits spontaneously after a few weeks, but recurrence is likely.   DLJ

Bibliography
Paykel, E.S. ed. 1982: *Handbook of affective disorders.* London and New York: Churchill Livingstone.

hypothalamus (See BRAIN AND CENTRAL NERVOUS SYSTEM: ILLUSTRATIONS, figs. 5 – 6.)

A small but vital brain structure located at the base of the diencephalon. It maintains widespread connections with other brain areas through such principal afferent pathways as the fornix which originates in the HIPPOCAMPUS, the medial forebrain bundle from the anterior forebrain and the stria terminalis from the AMYGDALA (figs. 15–18, 20 and 21). Major efferent projections are to the THALAMUS (mammillothalamic tract) and the BRAIN STEM (mammillotegmental tract). The hypothalamus, consisting of a densely packed collection of nuclei, acts as the control center for the AUTONOMIC NERVOUS SYSTEM (fig. 11). Posterior and lateral hypothalamic nuclei regulate sympathetic functions while anterior and medial nuclei are concerned with parasympathetic discharge. The hypothalamus has important links with the endocrine system and influences the secretion of hormones which affect metabolism, growth, electrolyte balance and secondary sex characteristics (e.g. fig. 22). Areas of the hypothalamus also control a wide range of vegetative or life sustaining functions which include feeding and drinking, temperature control and sexual behavior. Damage to these areas produces growth abnormalities. The hypothalamus is also involved in emotionality. Animals with hypothalamic lesions often show only fragmentary emotional responses and appear incapable of integrated reactions of fear or anger.   GWi

Bibliography

Krieger, D.T. and Hughes, J.C. eds. 1981: *Neuroendocrinology*. Sunderland, MA: Sinauer.

Martini, L., Molta, M. and Fraxlin, F. eds. 1970: *Proceedings of the workshop conference on integration of endocrine and nonendocrine mechanisms in the hypothalamus*. New York: New York and Co.

O'Riordan, J.L.H., Malan, P.G. and Gould, R.P. 1982: *Essentials of endocrinology*. Oxford: Blackwell Scientific Publications.

Rolls, E.T. 1975: *The brain and reward*. London: Pergamon Press.

hysteria Neurotic disorder in which psychological and/or physical functioning is disturbed (e.g. in respect of emotional control, movement-coordination, sensory reactions or state of consciousness) without any evidence of physical pathology, and with some indication of psychological motivation. The term derives from the Greek word for womb (*hysteron*) because in antiquity the complaint was thought to be an exclusively female one related to the functioning of that organ. Towards the end of the last century interest developed in the susceptibility of hysterics to HYPNOSIS as a means of removing their symptoms and even of discovering their cause. See Veith (1965) for an account of changing medical concepts of the disorder. Freud's first psychotherapeutic investigations were into cases of hysteria, whose symptoms he regarded as the symbolic expression of wishes that had been subjected to repression because of their connection with sexual guilt (see FREUD, SIGMUND). For Eysenck (1957), as for Jung, the "dimensions" of hysteria are associated with unstable extraversion.   NMC

Bibliography

Breuer, Joseph and Freud, Sigmund 1895: *Studies on hysteria. Standard edition of the complete psychological works of Sigmund Freud*, vol. 2. London: Hogarth Press; New York: Norton.

Eysenck, Hans J. 1957: *Dimensions of anxiety and hysteria*. London: Routledge and Kegan Paul.

Roy, A. 1982: *Hysteria*. Chichester: John Wiley and Sons.

Veith, Ilza 1965: *Hysteria: the history of a disease*. London and Chicago: Chicago University Press.

I

ideal self An image or representation of oneself as one would like to be. Derived from societal values and significant others, the ideal self is composed of wished for (but possibly unattainable) modes of behavior, values, traits, aspects of personal appearance etc. A disparity between the ideal self and self-concept (i.e. image of oneself as one really is) is taken to be a sign of poor mental health, and its reduction a primary goal of psychotherapy (see Rogerian therapy in RADICAL THERAPY). The self-ideal disparity has consequences for the regulation of behavior since it is intrinsically anxiety producing. Recent work in experimental social psychology has sought to explicate these regulative processes by studying the conditions under which a self-ideal comparison is likely to be induced and then subsequently dealt with by the individual.   BRS

inhibition: general A demonstrable nervous activity or a hypothetical process which holds in abeyance some neural and/or behavioral activity which might otherwise occur. At the interneuronal level in the central nervous system inhibition as an accompaniment to excitation clearly expands the logical possibilities of neural functioning in "computer circuit" terms, and some of its roles, e.g. in sharpening sensory input (Hartline and Ratliff 1957) and in feedback control of muscles, have been elegantly analyzed (Eccles 1969).

It has long been clear (Sherrington 1906) that the contractions of particular sets of muscles must entail the suppression of activity in other muscles for coordinated individual movements to emerge. The same notion has been applied to the motivational problem of how a specific sequence of action is selected by an animal at any one time from its total behavioral repertoire. The ethological concept of conflict entails inhibitory relations between behavior tendencies; Andrew (1956), van Iersel and Bol (1958) postulated that it was the balanced mutual inhibition between powerful drives such as flight, fight or sexual attraction (e.g. in courtship or agonistic situations) which cleared the stage for the occurrence of the more mundane displacement activities (the "disinhibition hypothesis"). Incomplete inhibition might result in alternation between one behavior and another ambivalent behavior, or the truncated intention movements.

With qualifiers such as "internal", "external" or "conditioned" inhibition, and inhibition "of delay" (Pavlov) "reactive" inhibition and "latent" inhibition (Lubow and Moore 1959), learning theorists and comparative psychologists have used the term inhibition in a plethora of ways (see e.g. Boakes and Halliday 1972). Indeed, several kinds of "neuropsychological" (Hebb 1949) inhibition had been postulated on largely behavioral grounds before the demonstration by physiologists of inhibitory SYNAPSES and presynaptic inhibition in the brain. Although clear links may sometimes be demonstrable, it is important not to assume that there is necessarily any direct correspondence between inhibitory processes at synaptic or ganglionic levels and those postulated at behavioral levels of explanation.   DWD

Bibliography

Andrew, R.J. 1956: Some remarks on behavior in conflict situations, with special reference to *Emberiza* spp. *British journal of animal behaviour* 4, 41–5.

*Boakes, Robert A. and Halliday, Michael S., eds., 1972: *Inhibition and learning*. New York: Academic Press.

Eccles, John C. 1969: *The inhibitory pathways of*

the central nervous system. Sherrington Lectures. Liverpool: Liverpool University Press; Springfield, Ill.: Thomas.

Hartline, H.K. and Ratliff, S. 1957: Inhibitory interaction of receptor units in the eye of *limulus*. *Journal of general physiology* 40, 357–76.

Hebb, D.O. 1949: *The organization of behavior*. New York: Wiley.

Iersel, J.J. van and Bol, A.C.A. 1958: Preening of two tern species. A study on displacement activities. *Behaviour* 13, 1–88.

Lubow, R.E. and Moore, A.U. 1959: Latent inhibitions: the effect of non-reinforced preexposure to the conditioned stimulus. *Journal of comparative and physiological psychology* 52, 415–19.

Roeder, K.D. 1967: *Nerve cells and insect behavior*. 2nd edn. Cambridge. Mass.: Harvard University Press.

Sherrington, C.S. 1906: *Integrative action of the nervous system*. Cambridge: Cambridge University Press.

insanity A condition, usually of persons or of minds, in which the capacity for rational thought and/or behavior is seriously impaired. By long tradition, certain kinds of insanity are important both in medicine and in law, though the term insanity (like its close synonyms madness and lunacy) signifies so wide a range of conditions that its use as a technical term has been largely discontinued. In this article insanity will be considered first in medicine, then in law, and then in the common ground between these two disciplines.

Since classical times, and in most cultures, at least some forms of insanity have been regarded as, or as a product of, disease. Just which forms of insanity are properly so regarded has, however, been variously interpreted. Historically, the "disease theory" has had to compete with religious or spiritual theories, usually of demonic influence as in medieval Europe, sometimes of divine. Nowadays, although such theories persist in some parts of the world, opposition to the "disease theory" has come mainly from such disciplines as sociology, psychoanalysis, psychology and political science (Caplan, Engelhardt and McCartney 1981). These disciplines, indeed, have produced a spate of alternatives to the "disease theory" which, notwithstanding the many successes of modern medicine, shows no signs of abating.

It is of course the "disease theory" that has been most influential in medicine, doctors on the whole having confined their interest to those insane conditions that are most generally, and least contentiously, regarded as disease. In recent years the study of these conditions has been pursued largely along empirical lines: by clarifying their description and classification; by developing reliable methods for their identification; and by exploring their causes and effects (Wing 1978). It is in the context of work of this kind that the term "insanity" has now been abandoned as too emotive and too imprecise for technical use in medicine. In the International Classification of Disease (WHO 1978), for example, the nearest approximation to "insanity" is PSYCHOSIS. But this term here designates a carefully defined group of conditions characterized by the presence of DELUSIONS and/or HALLUCINATIONS, and distinguished one from another by differences in the form and content of these phenomena, and by the presence or absence of various associated symptoms and signs.

The importance of insanity in law rests on the idea that the insane, being irrational, are not always fully responsible for what they do. It follows from this idea, as a principle of natural justice, that while it may sometimes be necessary to restrict the rights of the insane (for their own protection or for the protection of others), they should not normally be held liable under the law to the same extent, or in the same way, as those who are sane. This principle, however, although acknowledged by as early a writer as Aristotle (*Nicomachean Ethics*, Bk. III), has been subject to considerable difficulties of interpretation, and, in consequence, the details of its application, and the legal terminology employed, have varied widely (Walker 1968).

These difficulties of interpretation are well illustrated by the treatment of the insane in law in England and Wales at the present time. This is governed by a complex body of legislation and precept, the more important statutory provisions being contained in no fewer than four Acts of Parliament: the Criminal Justice Bill 1948, the Homicide Act 1957, the Mental Health Act 1983, and the Criminal Procedure (Insanity) Act 1964. In this legislation, the insane are variously identified and, for different legal purposes, differently defined. Several distinct legal species of insanity have therefore to be carefully distinguished, though the legislation, taken as a whole, is extremely comprehensive. Thus, it provides, inter alia, for remand, on bail or in custody, for psychiatric reports; for (possibly indefinite) admission to hospital without trial if an accused person is found to be "unfit to plead" by reason of mental disorder; for complete acquittal by the "special verdict" of "not guilty by reason of insanity", where the accused is found to be not responsible for his actions according to law (the test of which remains the McNaghten rules); for a reduction in the charge from murder to manslaughter in cases of unlawful homicide, if the responsibility of the accused is found to be "substantially reduced" by "abnormality of mind" (so called "diminished responsibility"); and for wide discretionary powers in sentencing, including orders for admission to hospital and for guardianship under the care of a local authority. Similarly, in civil law, insanity remains a sufficient ground for divorce, and is generally accepted as good evidence for testamentary and for contractual incapacity.

The difficulties presented by insanity are nowhere more evident than in the area of overlap between medicine and law, and it is in this area in particular that, notwithstanding the success of empirical methods in medicine, problems arise in medical practice in relation to insanity that are not, or not primarily, empirical in nature. Some of these may be circumvented: in regard to the establishment of criminal responsibility, for example, and the closely related question of civil capacity, doctors may seek to restrict their witness as experts to matters of fact – a policy which is endorsed by the recent Report of the Committee on Mentally Abnormal Offenders (Butler 1975). But others, as in the case of involuntary or compulsory treatment, may not be: the justification for such treatment is similar to the justification for the special treatment of the insane in law (that, being irrational, they are not always fully responsible); and it is indeed commonly given statutory legal authority (as in the Mental Health Act 1983); but its proper use is a matter of ethics not of science, and of specifically medical ethics at that. In relation to such issues, therefore, the "disease theory" of insanity, at least in its modern highly empirical form, is insufficient even for the particular and special purposes of medical practice. The growing recognition of this, together with the increasing importance of non-empirical problems in medicine generally, provides perhaps one important reason for the appearance in recent years of so many proposed alternatives to the "disease theory", however adequate or inadequate these may yet prove to be. (See MEDICAL MODELS.)   KWMF

Bibliography

Butler, Rt. Hon., the Lord. (Chairman) 1975: *Report of the Committee on Mentally Abnormal Offenders*. London, Cmnd., 6244, HMSO.

*Caplan, A.L., Engelhardt, H.T. and McCartney, J.J. 1981: *Concepts of health and disease*. Reading, Mass. London and Amsterdam: Addison-Wesley.

*Walker, N. 1968: *Crime and insanity in England*. Edinburgh: Edinburgh University Press.

*Wing, J.K. 1978: *Reasoning about madness*. Oxford and New York: Oxford University Press.

World Health Organisation 1978: *Ninth revision of the international classification of diseases*. Geneva: WHO.

instinct: psychodynamics A term which refers both to innate and fixed behavior patterns common to most members of a species and to a motivational force usually distinguished by its goal. In his writing Freud used the German word *Instinkt* for the former and *Trieb*, sometimes translated as drive, for the

127

latter. He developed his theory of instinct (*Trieb*) in the context of his psychoanalytic investigations of sexuality. Freud described an instinct as having a source within the body and a pressure or quantity of energy which was seeking release, related both to its somatic source and to its object. A subject's choice of object and method of gaining satisfaction or aim are constructed in the course of development and represented psychologically. Freud viewed instinct as 'a borderline concept between the mental and the physical' (Freud 1915). In a wider sense Freud was a dualist, initially placing ego or self-preserving, and sexual or species perpetuating, instincts in competition, but in his final formulations opposing eros (love, both self and sexual instincts) and thanatos (instinct of death and disorder).   BBL

Bibliography

Freud, S. 1915 (1957): *Instincts and their vicissitudes. Standard edition of the complete psychological works of Sigmund Freud*, vol. 14, London: Hogarth Press; New York: Norton.

institutionalization A syndrome of apathy, social withdrawal and lack of initiative which is associated with long periods in any unstimulating institution, including prisons, children's homes, mental retardation hospitals and psychiatric hospitals (Goffman 1961). In chronic SCHIZOPHRENIA (which is characterized by negative symptoms of withdrawal and lack of volition) there is a particular vulnerability to institutionalization. Patients may become mute, and suffer considerable social deterioration. This used to be common in the large asylums and still occurs to a less severe extent in hospital and residential care and in schizophrenics at home. Prevention and treatment require individually planned rehabilitation aiming at slow improvement to the optimal level of function.   RAM

Bibliography

Goffman, E. 1961: *Asylums*. New York: Doubleday.

Wing, J.K. and Brown, G.W. 1970: *Institutionalization and schizophrenia*. Cambridge and New York: Cambridge University Press.

intracellular chemistry *See* MEMORY AND LEARNING: SYNAPTIC STRUCTURE THEORIES AND INTRACELLULAR CHEMICAL THEORIES.

J

Janet, Pierre (1859–1947) Neurologist, philosopher and professor of experimental psychology at the Collège de France, Janet was a pioneer of psychodynamic psychiatry. He is best known for his descriptions of the clinical features of hysteria and his use of cathartic treatment (1965). Influenced by the teaching of CHARCOT, the fundamental concept of his psychopathology was "psychasthenia" a weakness of the highest integrative function of the brain which predisposes to NEUROSIS. He believed that treatment should provide stimulation and among the methods he investigated were hypnosis, suggestion and discussion and guidance aimed at "re-education".   RAM

Bibliography
Janet, Pierre 1965: *The major symptoms of hysteria*. New York: Hafner.

Jaspers, Karl (1883–1969) Philosopher and psychiatrist, Karl Jaspers was a member – together with Gruhle, Schneider and Mayer-Gross – of the Heidelberg School, renowned for its studies of mental phenomena. His work on morbid jealousy in 1910 revealed his astonishing powers of observation and description. In 1913 he published the first edition of his *General psychopathology* which remains unsurpassed in its objective analysis and categorization of psychic events, their evolution and their consequences. He also defined the scope and limitations of various methods of exploring the psyche; in particular he distinguished those disorders whose development can be understood through empathic understanding from those where causal connexions must be inferred.

He has come to be seen as one of the founders of existential psychology.   DLJ

Bibliography
Jaspers, Karl 1962: *General psychopathology*. Trans J. Hoenig and M.W. Hamilton. Manchester: Manchester University Press; Chicago: University of Chicago Press.

Jung, Carl (1875–1961) The contributions to personality theory of the Swiss psychiatrist Carl Jung were developed over a period of more than fifty productive years and now reside in the twenty volumes of his collected works (ed. Read et al., 1953–79). None of these, however, is devoted to a systematic discussion of what has come to be known as Jungian theory, nor do any of these volumes present an entire theory in brief outline. The task of systematizing the work was left to others. The better-known attempts have been offered by Jacobi (1962), F. Fordham (1966) and Hall and Nordby (1973).

Jung's earliest interest in the study of personality stemmed from his attempt to understand the dynamic relationship between conscious and unconscious processes Read et al. vols. 1 and 2). This work led to an alliance with Sigmund FREUD in the early development of psychoanalysis as a theory of personality and as a method of therapy. His defection from the psychoanalytic school founded by Freud, after five years of intense participation, was occasioned by his dissatisfaction with Freud's pansexual explanation of the origins of personality development and Freud's reluctance to approach the deeper layers of the unconscious which he feared would be associated with mysticism.

The publication in 1912 of Jung's book, *Symbols of transformation*, heralded his departure from the psychoanalytic ranks and he began a lonely, tortuous path, largely unaided by others until later life, to understand the nature of personality. In this book, in which the spontaneous fantasy productions of a single individual are analyzed, much of the material that constituted the basis for a lifetime of original work are to be found in nascent form.

In general outlines Jung thought of the personality as a series of interacting bipolar energic subsystems whose undifferentiated potentialities existed at birth in a vast realm he labeled the "collective unconscious". The encounter with life forced a differentiation of the inherently dominant poles into consciousness to shape and form conscious experience. The path through life was guided by the ultimate pull to make the potential actual, to reconcile or balance the opposites, to make available to consciousness the implicit potential latent in the original structure. This life-long process he designated as "individuation". Energy was inferred from change created by the tension of opposites.

From a structural point of view Jung described personality as consisting of two dynamic, interacting realms, consciousness and the unconscious. Within consciousness he delineated two structures, the ego and the persona. The ego he designated as the center of the conscious field, the experiencing "I" or "me", the source of the individual feeling of identity and continuity. Surrounding the ego is the persona, the individual's "face to the world", the constellation of roles, attitudes and behavior by which a person presents who he or she is to the world in response to societal demands. The ego, of necessity allied with the persona, must guard against an overidentification with this public mask to the exclusion of the expression of inner promptings from unconscious sources. Such an imbalance leads to tension resulting in psychological distress.

Jung divided the unconscious into its personal and collective aspects. The personal unconscious consists largely of experiences that were once either dimly conscious or too painfully salient to maintain a consistent persona image. Through repressive kinds of mechanisms they are kept from easy access to consciousness. Some semblance of order is postulated to exist in the personal unconscious through the formation of complexes, an adherence of relevant experiences around an attracting nucleus. Thus all repressed thoughts, feelings, memories and wishes relating to experience with one's mother are described as part of a "mother complex".

The deeper layers containing the primal, universal material without which the ultimate aspects of personality cannot be forged are thought to reside in the collective unconscious, a concept unique to Jungian psychology. He conceived of mind as being capable of generating images prior to and independent of conscious experience, similar in form in all people, prototypical or archetypal in nature. In and of themselves they are the raw materials which often appear in dreams, fantasies and other creative human products, usually called forth by the imbalances caused by the demands of conscious existence. When intuitively factored they reflect the central themes with which human beings have struggled throughout history. These include good and evil, gender, power and mortality among many others. Jung personified these clustered images by giving them various names. The gender archetypes Anima and Animus referred to the hidden opposite side of the male and female, respectively. The Wise Old Man and the Great Mother were names assigned to the authoritative power figures appearing in unconsciously derived imagery. Archetypal figures or structures are all collective but not necessarily unconscious. The ego and the persona are archetypal in structure yet largely conscious in content while the shadow, a collective term which includes all that is primitive and all that is hidden about personality, contains a large segment of material that was once conscious. The flow of psychological life is conceived as a continuous engagement between consciousness and the unconscious within the confines of a relatively closed system. The development of personality, although influenced by the outside world, is pictured basically as an internal struggle.

In the search for an operating framework in which to describe the manifestations of personality, Jung settled on a typological schema which because of its empirical possibilities has had more impact in academic psychological circles than any other aspect of his theoretical work. In his classic volume *Psychological types* (1933), Jung attempted to bring order into the diversity presented by individual differences in personality through the delineation of a conceptual model which included two basic attitudes and four essential psychological functions common to humankind. The attitudes were termed "introversion" and "extraversion," probably biologically determined, which influenced the direction of energy, or interest, in the psyche. In introversion the focus of interest was centered on the internal, subjective, intrapersonal aspects of psychic life, in extraversion, on the external objective, interpersonal side. As in all major Jungian concepts, a bipolarity is intended. The functions were described as thinking and feeling, a rational pair, and sensation and intuition, a perceptual pair. Thinking and feeling are evaluative or judgmental functions, the former emphasizing the use of cognitive and intellectual information, the latter relying upon affective cues. The data they utilize are in the service of settling value issues, such as whether something is good or bad, liked or disliked. The perceptual functions are concerned with the processes related to the identity of things rather than their value. Sensation operates as the function concerned with facts or the apparent, concrete nature of the world. Intuition is directed toward the elaboration of the possibilities or relational aspects of perceptual data.

In describing personality Jung assumes that both attitudes and all four functions are part of the inherent endowment of all human beings. During the course of development, as a result of the mix of individual propensities, familial and more general cultural pressures, one of the attitudes and one of the functions are most clearly differentiated and become the conscious, operating framework of the personality. Thus, as a first approximation, personality may be described by the combination of the dominant attitude and the first function. For any person this would result

in one of eight possibilities, either introversion or extraversion in tandem with one of thinking, feeling, sensation and intuition. Further complexity is added by the differentiation into consciousness of an auxiliary function, one of the pair of functions orthogonal to the first function. An individual would then have as descriptors of personality three identifying features, a dominant attitude, a first function and an auxiliary function. The general schema that emerges is a sixteen category typology. The behavioral and imaginal characteristics of each type are elaborated in the work of Isabel Briggs-Meyers (1962) whose Type-Indicator represents the most sophisticated attempt to measure individual type structure.

The concept of development, although central to Jung's teleological view of personality, focused little on the problems of early childhood and socialization. Initially he was content to adopt the Freudian view. In later years the contributions of Frances Wickes (1966) and Michael Fordham (1947) related Jung's ideas to the experiences of childhood. Jung's picture of development remained at a much more global level. He conceived of the progression of life as basically divided into two parts. The first half, roughly marked by the end of the fourth decade, was directed toward the adaptational problem of establishing one's position or place in the world. This he saw proceeding through the development of the dominant attitude and the first function and all that such development intended in the essential choices of occupation, object attraction, mate selection, values and more general interests. As a result of this necessarily one-sided emphasis, there grows over time a pressure for expression of the neglected, more unconscious aspects of the personality contained in the opposite attitude and the fourth function, the polar opposite of the first. The occurrence of this psychological unrest may be related phenomenologically to what is commonly termed the mid-life crisis, a mark of entry into the period Jung called the second half of life. During this stage the adaptational problem shifts from finding one's way into the world to that of finding one's way out, the ultimate confrontation with mortality. In a poetic vein Jung described the entire process as an exploratory trek of traversing a mountain in which the initial energy is devoted to reaching the summit with limited concern for what lies beyond. When the peak is reached, a set of new problems is revealed in how to descend and negotiate all that is involved in concluding the task.

Thus the path of personality development is directed toward an ultimate outcome which Jung called "individuation". In its most general sense the process of individuation mirrors the sequential progression of physical existence. The templates of the physical structures are given at conception, differentiate at different rates, are strengthened or impeded by different experiences and form different integrations with each other at various times in the life history. The ultimate outcome under positive circumstances is a well-articulated, smooth-functioning physical system equipped to do in the species sense what it is capable of doing. This model Jung basically used for psychological individuation. He delineated the essential system parts (consciousness and the unconscious), the structural units within those parts (the archetypes), the stylistic framework in which these structural units operated (the attitudes and functions), and provided a dynamic rule of order by which the system and its parts were governed (the law of opposites). The energic aspects of the interaction of the system parts were guided by the principles of equivalence and entropy borrowed from the laws of thermodynamics.

In yet another vein Jung described the individuation process as directed toward the achieving of selfhood. Since the self in Jungian thought represents the totality of psychic life, we must interpret that statement as meaning the achievement of the most differentiated and integrated state of psychological development. In a metaphoric sense, as in alchemy, when the primal ingredients are put together in an appropriate mix, there will emerge an ultimate substance which will be greater than the sum of its parts. For Jung the press toward individuation is accelerated in the second half of life largely as a result of the imbalances created by the necessary adaptations during the first half of life. He identified the essential steps in the achieving of selfhood. These included relinquishing an absolute identification with the ego, accepting the power of the collective unconscious aspects of the psyche, making all the functions and the non-dominant attitude conscious and thus available for use, and similarly integrating the archetypes of the collective unconscious into conscious experience. The successful result of such a continuing set of efforts is largely ideal and hardly permanent. It creates a state of internal harmony through which both the immediate problems of living and the larger problems of life may be filtered.

While Jung thought of individuation as a universal human process, he also pointed out that the path did not necessarily resolve into an individual human struggle. Institutionalized, symbolic, non-conscious forms have emerged in the development of culture to deal with these very problems. Religious systems and their ritual practices may speak directly to these issues. Jung saw the individual need to "know oneself" as both an affliction and a blessing in that the progress of humankind is reflected in the expansion of consciousness which involves pain as part of the price of achievement.

IEA

Bibliography

Fordham, F. 1966: *An introduction to Jung's psychology*. Harmondsworth: Penguin.

Fordham, M. 1947: *The life of childhood*. London: Routledge and Kegan Paul.

Hall, C.S. and Nordby, V.J. 1973: *A primer of Jungian psychology*. New York: New American Library.

Jacobi, J. 1962: *The psychology of C. G. Jung*. New Haven, Yale University Press.

Jung, C.G. 1933: *Psychological types*. New York: Harcourt.

—— 1961: *Memories, dreams. recollections*. (Recorded and edited by Aniela Jaffé) New York: Pantheon.

Meyers, I.B. 1962: *The Meyers-Briggs type indicator*. Princeton: Educational Testing Service.

Read, H. et al. eds. 1953–79: *The collected works of C.G. Jung*. Princeton: Princeton University Press.

Storr, A. 1983: *Jung: selected writings*. London: Fontana.

Wickes, F. 1966: *The inner world of childhood*, rev. edn. New York: Appleton-Century.

K

Klein, Melanie (1882–1960) In extending psychoanalytic techniques to study the inner worlds of two and three year olds Klein provided one of the earliest detailed accounts of pre-Oedipal development and a clinically fruitful description of primitive thought processes. She created a method to treat severely disturbed young children and to gain access to their fantasies through the use of carefully chosen play material.

Klein worked within FREUD's final theory of sexual and aggressive instincts. Although she employed concepts derived from the theory of psychosexual development and the stages of oral, anal and phallic-genital organizations these erotogenic zones achieved psychic importance earlier and often, according to her developmental timetable, simultaneously. Her identification of the Oedipus complex in primitive form in the first year was a major departure from classic psychoanalytic theory.

Her introduction of the concept of *position*, an organized constellation of mental processes, provided a new way of describing mental structures and objects. The *paranoid-schizoid position* characterized development in the first few months of life. The fantasy world of the infant was described as being unstable and made up of *part-objects*, fragmentary perceptions, e.g. breasts, penises, but not the whole persons of either parent. Denial, splitting into affectively good (satisfying) and bad, projection of the bad outward and introjection of the good, were seen as dominant thought processes of the paranoid-schizoid position. These mental functions are metaphorically linked with the infant's bodily processes, such as defecation, ingestion. Klein used terms such as good and bad breasts to characterize the unconscious fantasies of the very young infant. That objects are not yet constituted as the symbolic wholes of the second year is an important aspect of early development and of paranoid-schizoid thinking. The identification and description of the thought processes of this psychic constellation proved fruitful in later extensions of psychoanalytic techniques to treatment of severely disturbed adults (Rosenfeld 1965).

Klein held that by the middle of the first year the infant became aware that the good breast which it loved, and the bad persecutory breast which was the repository of its hate and which it feared, were one. Sadness thus accompanied thoughts of the destruction wrought by aggressive impulses and from its love of the object a need to make reparations developed. This achievement, which she described as the beginning of the *depressive position*, marked the infant's creation of whole objects and its ambivalence about the consequences of its desires in relation to these objects. The precarious nature of this achievement and a return to the more primitive mental processes of splitting, projection and introjection is evidenced in the everyday life of individuals and groups (Bion 1961).

Klein's later theories of the importance of *primitive envy* in mental life were as controversial as her description of infantile mental life in terms of unconscious fantasies. She postulated that primitive envy arose with early deprivation; the part object was viewed as possessing and enjoying something desirable but unobtainable. This primitive envy resulted in a wish to destroy the part object. Thus jealousy was seen as a developmental achievement for it allowed a desired object continued existence even though it was unobtainable.

BBL

Bibliography

Bion, W.R. 1961: *Experiences in groups and other papers*. London: Tavistock Publications.

Rosenfeld, Harold 1965: *Psychotic states: a psychoanalytic approach*. London: Hogarth Press.

Segal, Hanna 1979: *Klein*. London: Fontana/Collins.

Korsakov's syndrome (or Korsakov's psychosis) In 1889 the Russian neuropsychiatrist Korsakov described a chronic syndrome in which memory deficit was accompanied by confabulation and irritability. Nowadays the term is used in various ways. Some psychiatrists and psychologists apply it to any amnesic syndrome; that is, profound and lasting impairments of recent memory and of time-sense, with relative preservation of remote memory and good preservation of other cognitive functions. Others apply it only to a combination of the amnesic syndrome and confabulation (giving an elaborate account of events that never occurred in order to fill gaps in the memory). Others do not find the term useful.

Disorders of this type are often due to thiamine deficiency, which usually results from many years' abuse of alcohol but also from other causes such as persistent vomiting. The syndrome often follows WERNICKE'S SYNDROME. At post mortem examination of the brain, hemorrhagic lesions are found in the gray matter around the third and fourth ventricles and the aqueduct.   DG

Kraepelin, Emil (1856–1926), an influential psychiatrist, teacher and writer (his textbook first appeared in 1883). Kraepelin is generally regarded as one of the founders of modern psychiatry, largely by virtue of his work on the classification of disorders (see NOSOLOGY). He described manic-depressive insanity, and in 1896 gave the name "dementia praecox" to the group of illnesses which Bleuler in 1911 was to call the schizophrenias (see SCHIZOPHRENIA). He considered that this illness resulted from some irreversible happening in the brain, the natural outcome being dementia; he nevertheless documented some spontaneous remissions. He also pointed the way to several techniques of investigation, notably by studying whole-life case histories and family histories, so that he was able to explore the interplay of genetic and environmental factors.   DLJ

Bibliography

Kraepelin, E. 1906: *Lectures on clinical psychiatry*. Trans. T. Johnstone. London: Baillière, Tindall and Cox.

Slater, E. and Roth, M. 1969: *Clinical psychiatry*. London: Baillière, Tindall and Cassell.

L

Lacan, Jacques (1901–81) Flamboyantly and stylistically baroque French psychoanalyst and psychiatrist, whose own history is that of the schisms and divisions of French psychoanalytical societies in 1953, 1964 and 1980. Lacan trained as a psychiatrist in the French clinical tradition in the 1920s in Paris and as a psychoanalyst in the 1930s, and was a member of surrealist and philosophically avant-garde circles of the period. He was an early champion of Heidegger and much influenced by Kojève's lectures on Hegel, infusing PSYCHOANALYSIS with philosophy and poetry. In 1936 he outlined his notion of the MIRROR-PHASE. His approach was always marked by an extraordinary fidelity to FREUD, an immense erudition, an emphasis on psychic structure rather than development, and a recognition of the privileged place of language in accounting for the Freudian discoveries and the nature of the psychoanalytic dialogue.

The main lines of his theory were laid out on the occasion of the first institutional schism in 1953, in his famous Discours de Rome (see Wilden 1968): the focus was always to be on the functions and theory of language and speech in psychoanalysis. One aphorism, 'the unconscious is structured like a language', offers a clear sense of Lacan's project. Firstly, he wished to indicate that the working material of psychoanalysis, speech, is what allows a conceptualization of the processes discovered by Freud in the dream, in slips of the tongue and in jokes – Freud's condensation and displacement are alternative names for the processes of metaphor and metonymy at work in language. Second, Freud's discovery that symptoms are symbolic, representing repressed thoughts, indicates that symptoms (and by inference, the unconscious) are structured linguistically. The key to the unraveling of

their meaning is found, as all analysts agree, in the process of transference, during which the patient's discourse slowly translates the symptoms, phobias, patterns of behavior and character traits into speech offered to the analyst. The analyst is thus cast as the witness to the patient's revelation, or as the other conjured into existence through the mediation of speech.

Employing a theory of language derived in part from Hegel and Heidegger, but equally from the structuralism of Saussure, Jakobson and Lévi-Strauss, Lacan emphasized the structure of linguistic elements which determine the material offered by patients in analysis, so that interpretation and analysis are to be viewed as working synchronically on the linguistic elements unique to each patient – in other words, the linguistic elements which are lost, distorted and transformed in constructing both symptoms on the one side, and the patient's distinctive subjectivity, on the other. Lacan questioned the parallelism of the two systems of signifier and signified which, according to Saussure, make up language. He stressed instead the priority of the signifier in determining meaning. But he emphasized less the formal systemic features of language than the dynamic relation between the subject and his speech. Starting from his theory of the mirror-phase, with its accompanying concept of the Imaginary, he distinguished between the ego, an imaginary constructed unity, and the subject, diversified as it is in complex relations with the ego, the other (the ego's imaginary counterpart) and the Other. This last, or "big Other", is the locus of the linguistic code, the guarantor of meaning, the third party in any dual relationship such as that of analysis or of love. The subject's speech is vouched for by this Other, yet is distorted and transformed in having to pass via the fantasy structure in which figure the ego and its relations to its objects. The relation of the subject to the Other is thus the mainline of the unconscious, for which analysis aims to clear the way.

Lacan's remarkably close readings of Freud's texts supported and illuminated each turn in his theory's development. The theory of the mirror-phase is linked closely to Freud's concept of narcissism and to the notion that both the ego and love are fundamentally narcissistic in character. He highlighted the concept *nachträglich* (deferred action), the retrospective mode of causality proper to the unconscious, a formal consequence of the battery of signifiers that make it up. Similarly Freud's account of the origin of society and law in *Totem and taboo* is read as a myth that highlights the essential function of the father in the constitution of the human subject. In contrast to other recent psychoanalytic theories, which stress the pre-eminence of the mother-child relation (pre-Oedipal, pre-genital), Lacan affirms the centrality for the subject's history of the triadic Oedipus complex, in which the function of the father is both essential and mythical. Essential, since the father is the representative of the law, in the last instance the law of language, and supplies the third term or mediating function that allows the child to find a place in the symbolic order (language) and escape from the murderous fascination of the image (other) of the mirror-phase, experienced in fantasy as fascination with the mother. Mythical, because the father's function is strictly metaphorical – he functions neither as real father (flesh and blood), nor as imaginary father (though the latter figures in fantasy as an ideal and punitive agency), but as the Name of the Father, with his name assigning the child a place in the social world and allowing the child to become a sexed being through the phallic function to which the Name of the Father refers. Lacan's account of the entry of the child into the Symbolic, by courtesy of the father's mythical function, is thus a revised version of Freud's Oedipus complex. The OEDIPUS COMPLEX represents the way in which infants become sexed (through their various responses to being deprived of the phallus), and become human (in escaping from the mother of the mirror-phase, whose own incompleteness renders the child's sense of wanting insupportable, into the Symbolic, in which lack is symbolizable through the generation of desire). With the triad of concepts appropriate to each sector (need/Real, demand/Imaginary, desire/Symbolic), Lacan continues his criticism of those versions of psychoanalytic theory which equate Freud's instincts (*Triebe*) with biologically determined need, arguing instead that the true realm of psychoanalytic action is the world of desire, which is created by language transforming need into desire in answer to the unsatisfiable demands of the other (mother) for love. Desire, like the Freudian instinct, is never fulfilled, always there, continually displaced and transformed.

Lacan's later theories (from the mid-1960s on) concentrated on the relation between the signifier, the Other and the object *a* (a concept linked, on the one hand, with the other of the mirror-phase and, on the other hand, with the privileged objects of Freudian instincts – the breast, feces, urine, penis, to which Lacan adds the voice and the gaze). His concern was to specify the formal characteristics of psychoanalytic discourse – an extension of his emphasis on speech as the uniquely efficacious medium of psychoanalysis. The linguistic aspect of the teaching was replaced by a more formal mathematical approach, including an attempt to define the properties of the various "spaces" postulated by psychoanalytic theory (e.g. inside/outside) – not only the space of the unconscious, distinct and yet continuous with consciousness (and thus well represented by a Möbius strip), but also the Borromean knots in which the signifying chains of demands and desires are linked together by the subject. The close alliance with mathematics (topology and number theory) and philosophy (epistemology and logic) further his attack on "psychologism". For him, psychoanalysis, rather than being a psychology of the individual or a quasi-biological account of adaptation to the environment, is more akin to the Socratic dialogue, whose aim is truth. The Freudian discovery consists in showing how desire is necessarily implicated in the truth sought by the subject along the paths opened up by the signifier.

JF

Bibliography

Bowiek, M. 1979: Jacques Lacan. In *Structuralism and since*, ed. J. Sturrock. Oxford: Oxford University Press.

Lacan, J. 1966: *Écrits*. Paris: Seuil.

———— 1977: *Écrits: a selection*. London: Tavistock; New York: Norton.

———— 1977: *The four fundamental concepts of psychoanalysis*. London: Hogarth Press; New York: Norton.

Lemaire, A. 1978: *Jacques Lacan*. London and Boston: Routledge and Kegan Paul.

Wilden, A. 1968: *The language of the self*. Baltimore: Johns Hopkins University Press.

Laing, R.D. Scottish psychiatrist, born 1927. He has been instrumental in demonstrating the degree to which we are alienated from our own experience; how we have come to rely upon external criteria and appearances for our understanding of ourselves. 'No-one can begin to think, feel or act now except from the starting point of his or her own alienation.' In his emphasis on therapy viewed as a social and political activity Laing calls into question the foundations of our popular cultural awareness, especially our notion of sanity, or what constitutes the accepted continuum between the poles of "normal" and "abnormal", "sane" and "insane", "appropriate" and "deviant". According to Laing, in *The politics of experience*, 'the "normally" alienated person, by reason of the fact that he acts more or less like everyone else, is taken to be sane'. And, 'our collusive madness is what we call sanity'. Laing has also set the tone for this "radical" therapy by stating: 'Psychotherapy must remain an obstinate attempt of two (or more) people to recover the wholeness of being human through the relationship between them.' The popular shift towards the various alternative psychologies represents the search for such wholeness. (See RADICAL THERAPY.)

DAL

Bibliography

Laing, R.D. 1967: *The politics of experience*. New York: Pantheon Books.

Language Assessment, Remediation and Screening Procedure (LARSP) is a linguistically based method for the analysis and remediation of the grammatical disorders of adults and children. Conceived by D. Crystal, P. Fletcher, and M. Garman at the University of Reading, LARSP was developed with the pragmatic aim of providing the speech therapist with a systematic procedure by which an individual's grammatical disability could be assessed in terms which facilitate subsequent remedy.

The procedure, as described by Crystal et al. (1976), consists of three stages. First, a sample of the patient's speech is recorded, transcribed, and grammatically analyzed. This analysis is then entered onto the LARSP profile chart where it is interpreted according to a developmental metric. Finally the interpretation is used to determine strategies for attaining remedial goals. The transition from assessment to remediation is helped by the developmental framework of the major part of the profile. The order in which grammatical structures are presented in the chart reflects the order in which children normally acquire them. Because grammatical disorders are pictured in terms of acquisitional delay, the LARSP therapist, working either with adults or children, is able to plot the progress of the patient according to a consistent metric, and to answer, at each stage in the treatment, the essential remedial question: "Which structure to teach next?" In addition to its widespread use in speech clinics, LARSP has been adapted for use by school teachers in an assessment and remediation model entitled "Structural Analysis of the Language of School-Age Children" (SALSAC).

(See also SPEECH DISORDERS.)

TJT

Bibliography

Crystal, D., Fletcher, P. and Garman, M. 1976: *The grammatical analysis of language disability*. London: Edward Arnold.

lateralization The organization of brain function such that the two hemispheres are specialized to control different psychological operations. In contrast to sensory, perceptual, and motor functions which are represented in both cerebral hemispheres, mechanisms for certain sophisticated verbal and nonverbal skills are usually found in only one hemisphere. For example, speech and language functions, at least in right-handed people, are exclusively lateralized in the left hemisphere. This has been determined by observing the effect of electrical stimulation of the brain, studying individuals with cerebral damage, and by using sodium amytal, a drug that selectively anesthetizes speech areas in the fully conscious patient. The right hemisphere, on the other hand, is dominant for nonverbal activities related, for example, to imagery, artistic expression, and performance on tasks requiring spatial skills. There is some evidence that lateralized functions affected by unilateral brain damage are taken over by the opposite hemisphere. This, along with the fact that children show less hemispheric specialization than adults, suggests that cerebral dominance may be a part of a development pattern involving differential suppression of function in each hemisphere. It has been suggested that since the two hemispheres process information in quite different ways, relative differences in cerebral dominance could affect the nature of human consciousness both between individuals and across cultures.   GWi

Bibliography

Levy, J. 1981: Lateralization and its implications for variations in development. In *Developmental plasticity*, ed. E. Gollin. New York: Academic Press.

learned helplessness This term was introduced by Martin Seligman (1975) to denote a state of apathy which may be induced experimentally in animals and which is similar to some states of depression occurring naturally in humans. He described experiments in which dogs were subjected to electric shocks without the possibility of escaping from them. After a time the animals became inactive and submissive, lost appetite and failed to escape from shocks which they had previously known how to avoid.

Seligman suggested that depression in humans could be caused by the repeated experience of being unable to act in such a way as to achieve a desired outcome or to avoid emotional trauma. Such experiences in childhood may predispose an individual to depression, whereas the development of a sense of control over the environment may render him immune. The theory thus has etiological (see AFFECTIVE DISORDERS), preventive and also therapeutic implications, forming the basis of one type of cognitive therapy. Seligman also suggests that "unmerited" reward may have similar effects.   DLJ

Bibliography

Seligman, Martin E.P. 1975: *Helplessness*. San Francisco: Freeman.

Abramson, L.Y., Seligman, M.E.P. and Teasdale, J.D. 1978: Learnt helplessness in humans, critique and reformulation. *Journal of abnormal psychology* 87, 49–74.

learning difficulties (Note: For the sake of brevity the word "child" includes "young person".)

The term "learning difficulties" may be used either to refer to particular aspects of learning, in which a child may have difficulty, or in a more general way, to the fact that a child has difficulty in learning. This latter use of the term was introduced in the British Report of the Committee of Enquiry into the Education of Handicapped Children and Young People (Warnock Report, DES 1978). In this Report it was recommended that the previously used categories of handicap should be discarded and that children should be considered in terms of their special educational needs. Consequently it was suggested that the term "educationally subnormal" should be replaced by "children with learning difficulties", and qualified by the terms "severe", "moderate" and "specific". "Severe" and "moderate" learning difficulties were intended to refer respectively to severe and moderate levels of subnormality. The term "learning difficulty" was subsequently incorporated into the wording of the British 1981 Act on Special Education, where a child with special educational needs was described as one who had a 'learning difficulty which calls for special educational provision to be made for him'. Furthermore, a child with learning difficulty was defined as one who 'has a significantly greater difficulty in learning than the majority of children of his age' or who 'has a disability which either prevents or hinders him from making use of educational facilities of a kind generally provided in schools'.

The concept of learning difficulty adopted in the Act's definitions is not elaborated further, but would appear to include the level and nature of curricular content which would be regarded as appropriate for the children concerned, in line with the administrative connotation of the definition of "special educational need".

In the USA the term "learning disability" has been incorporated into the Education for all Handicapped Children Act of 1975 (PL 94–142). The Act includes a definition of the term indicating that it refers to deficiencies in processes underlying educational performance but excluding other forms of primary causation (e.g. environmental deprivation). This "definition by exclusion" has been criticized by Hallahan and Bryan (1981) among others.

"Learning difficulties" in the sense of a term referring to difficulties in particular aspects of learning has been used in a number of ways. One of the most common themes in its definition has been concerned with discrepancies in the levels of a child's performance. It has been noted that a child's level of performance in certain aspects of educational attainment, of communication, or of behavioral adequacy, may be lower than in other aspects of his performance or functioning, and that in certain instances these are assumed to be the result of *specific* difficulties in learning which are primary, and not the consequence of emotional disturbances, of deprivation of experience, or of sensory or motor impairment. In so far as the difficulties represent *discrepancies* in levels of performance, it is also assumed that they are not a concomitant of a generally low level of intelligence (Wedell 1975). These considerations involve two sets of assumptions – those concerned with the nature of the difficulties, and those concerned with their causes.

The account of the nature of learning difficulties outlined above has to be seen in the context of a growing doubt about intelligence as a unitary concept. Historically, learning difficulties had been defined in terms of "backwardness" and of "retardation" (Tansley and Panckhurst 1981). These terms tended to be defined in terms of the discrepancy between a child's educational attainment and either his chronological age (backwardness) or his level of "intelligence" (specific retardation: in this sense should be clearly distinguished from "mental retardation"). Specific retardation, therefore, contrasted a child's attainment with his "potential" (intelligence) and these children were therefore called "under achievers". Experts in psychometrics have questioned the validity of the concept of under achievement and of the discrepancy model in general (Thorndike 1963). Learning difficulty as defined in terms of a discrepancy between actual and expected performance is an uncertain concept.

Children's difficulties in learning have been manifested and described in a variety of ways. A common description has been in terms of syndromes of difficulties, such as DYSLEXIA. These syndrome names are derived from clinical neurological studies of adults, who have lost the capacity to perform in particular ways as the result of various forms of neurological impairment. The extension of the use of these terms to children is questionable since in these cases they refer not to a loss of a capacity, but to a failure to develop or acquire it (Wedell 1975). Furthermore, in clinical neurology, syndromes are established on the basis of the demonstrated co-occurrence of symptoms, and the evidence for this, for example, in children described as dyslexic, is contradictory (e.g. DES

1972). Doubt also applies to syndrome terms such as "hyperactivity", used to describe restlessness and short attention-span in children. Schacher, Rutter and Smith (1981) have pointed out that hyper-activity in many children is situation or task specific and cannot be used to describe a child in a general way.

The above accounts of learning difficulties also have associations with assumptions about their cause, and much of the literature refers to learning "disabilities". This is already often implicit in the discrepancy model of learning difficulty. Accounts of the syndrome models almost invariably also refer to disabilities underlying the symptomology. These disabilities are described in terms of the dysfunction of psychological processes which is thought to cause the impaired performance, such as defects in perceptuo-motor functions, in language and in memory. Difficulties in reading and spelling are ascribed, for example, to defects in intermodal association, and attention difficulties to defects in perception. Much research has been devoted to investigating these associations, but the evidence, while supporting many of these hypotheses, has not proved conclusive. Wedell (1973) pointed out that the causal relationship between the hypothesized underlying processes and performance on the target tasks was likely to be more complex than had been acknowledged. For example, any particular performance might be subserved by different combinations of processes and the ways in which a child had been taught the task was also likely to exert an important influence.

Much research has been devoted to attempts to discover the organic bases of learning difficulties, and some of the early studies were particularly concerned with this. In the face of insufficient evidence for associations with demonstrable neurological impairment, some have put forward the notion of "minimal cerebral dysfunction"; a hypothesis that some forms of learning difficulty might be caused by subclinical forms of neurological impairment.

Approaches to the assessment and treatment of learning difficulties have been derived from the various conceptualizations mentioned above. Delacato (1966), for example, devised means of assessing delayed and impaired neurological function, and also training procedures aimed at rectifying these. However, doubt has been expressed about these approaches by the American Academy of Cerebral Palsy. Many batteries of tests to assess the psychological processes thought to underlie learning difficulties have been produced, for example the Illinois Test of Psycholinguistic Abilities and the Frostig Developmental Test of Visual Perception. These batteries have been linked with remedial programs for the particular functions assessed. However, studies designed to investigate the effectiveness of these programs have only partly substantiated their effectiveness in improving children's performances on the test batteries, and only rarely shown the children to improve significantly more in the target educational performances (e.g. Hammill and Larsen 1974). Similarly, attempts by means of early identification procedures to assess these functions in children at the early stages of schooling, in order to predict which children would later have difficulties in learning, have had little success (Lindsay and Wedell 1982).

The above findings have contributed to the conclusion already mentioned above, that the causation of learning difficulties is very complex and this, in turn, has led to attempts to help children with learning difficulties through "direct instruction". These approaches involve the specification of the target task which the child is required to learn in terms of "behavioral" objectives. The sequence of instruction is based on task-analysis aimed at identifying the successive steps necessary for the child to master the target task. The methods employed in teaching are derived from operant learning theory, but many of the approaches to task analysis are based on notions similar to those underlying the "process" approach to learning difficulties (Wedell 1973). An important feature of this teaching approach is the detailed recording of the child's progress towards each objective, by means of "precision teaching"

(Haring et al 1978). This teaching approach is still at the early stages of development, but has the advantages that the evaluation of its effectiveness is integral to it.

This brief account of learning difficulties has indicated that the phenomenon to which the term refers is well demonstrated, but that the understanding about how the difficulties are caused and how they should best be remedied is still a matter of controversy. The issues involved represent an interesting aspect of the meeting of psychology and education.

DMG

Bibliography

Delacato, C.H. et al. 1966: *Neurological organisation and reading*. Springfield Ill.: Thomas.

Department of Education and Science 1972: *Children with specific reading difficulties*. London: HMSO.

———— 1978: *Special educational needs (The Warnock Report)*. London: HMSO.

Hallahan, D.P. and Bryan, I.H. 1981: Learning difficulties. In *Handbook of special education*, eds. J.M. Kaufman and D.P. Hall. Englewood Cliffs. N.J.: Prentice Hall.

Hammill, D.D. and Larsen, S.C. 1974: The effectiveness of psycho-linguistic training. *Exceptional children* 41, 5–14.

Haring N.G. et al. 1978: *The fourth R: research in the classroom*. C.E. Merrill.

Lindsay, G.A. and Wedell, K. 1982: The early identification of educationally "At Risk" children revisited. *Journal of learning disabilities* 15, 212–17.

Schacher, R., Rutter, M. and Smith, A. 1981: The characteristics of situationally and pervasively hyperactive children: implications for syndrome definition. *Journal of child psychology and psychiatry* 22, 375–420.

Tansley, P. and Panckhurst, J. 1981: *Children with specific learning difficulties*. National Foundation for Educational Research.

Thorndike, R.L. 1963: *The concepts of over and under achievement*. New York: Columbia University Teachers' College.

Wedell, K. 1973: *Learning and perceptuo-motor disabilities in children*. New York and London: Wiley.

———— 1975: Specific learning difficulties. In *Orientations in special education*. New York and London: Wiley.

life events The jargon term "life events" covers all significant social changes and sudden adversities which people may experience. Rigorous standards of assessment are necessary to test the hypothesis that change, particularly if stressful, can lead to various physical and mental conditions. Two methods have been developed, the inventory (Holmes and Rahe 1967) and the interview schedule (Brown 1974). Each method has its particular problems (Bebbington 1985).

In general, an excess of life events is reported before the onset of many physical diseases (Birley and Connolly 1976) and mental conditions such as SCHIZOPHRENIA and DEPRESSION and especially before SUICIDE attempts.

However, the association is fairly weak. Modifying factors and, in particular the mediating mechanisms are unclear. Moreover, the association may not arise because events cause the disorder in question. Insidious illness can itself generate such events. The subject and the researcher may share the bias that stress has important effects. Finally psychiatric disorders, particularly depression, have a significant bearing on the way in which we view and report our experiences.   PBe

Bibliography

Bebbington, P.E. 1985: Psychosocial etiology of schizophrenia and affective disorders. In *Psychiatry*, ed. R. Michels. Philadelphia: Lippincott.

Brown, G.W. 1974: Meaning, measurement and stress of life events. In *Stressful life events: their nature and effects*, eds. B.S. and B.P. Dohrenwend. New York: John Wiley.

Holmes, T.H. and Rahe, R.H. 1967: The social readjustment rating scale. *Journal of psychosomatic research* 11, 213–18.

limbic system A group of interconnected structures located primarily in the telencephalon of the brain (BRAIN AND CENTRAL NERVOUS SYSTEM: ILLUSTRATIONS, figs. 15–18). Areas most often included in the limbic system are the cingulate gyrus, HIPPOCAMPUS, entorhinal cortex, septum, and AMYGDALA. The anterior THALAMUS and mammillary bodies of the diencephalon (fig. 5), because of their anatomical and functional connections with limbic structures, are often considered part of this system. Historically designated rhinencephalon or "smell brain", the term limbic system was adopted when it became apparent that this part of the brain played a smaller role in olfaction than had originally been thought. The limbic system is frequently referred to as the visceral brain, implying a collective role in emotionality. In practice attempts to characterize the limbic system as a single functional entity seem inappropriate. Through its various structures the limbic system is involved in a range of specific operations bearing on emotional and motivational behavior as well as learning and memory processes.   GWi

Bibliography

Gray, J.A. 1982: *The neuropsychology of anxiety. An enquiry into the functions of the septohippocampal system.* Oxford: Oxford University Press.

loneliness The unpleasant experience of a discrepancy between the social relationships a person wishes or expects to have, and the kind of relationships he or she actually has. Relationships may be deficient in quantity, quality or both, but it is the person's own subjective view which is involved. Loneliness is not the same as objective physical or social isolation, although it may sometimes be associated with isolation.

Loneliness is most frequently thought of as a mood, emotion or feeling, but it may also refer to an attitude towards social relationships, to a life style, or to a condition of life (e.g. that of an elderly widower living alone). Experiences of loneliness are probably more frequent among younger than among older people, but equally frequent among men and women. However, there are likely to be group differences in the type of loneliness experienced and in the willingness to admit to loneliness.

There are many possible sources of loneliness, both situational or circumstantial (e.g. death of a loved one, unemployment, moving) and personal or psychological (e.g. shyness, poor health, poor social skills). Experiences of lone-

liness and their intensity will usually reflect some combination of these factors.   LAW

Bibliography

Peplau, L.A. and Perlman, D. eds. 1982: *Loneliness: a sourcebook of current theory, research and therapy.* New York: Wiley.

Luria, Aleksandr Romanovič (1902–1977) A Soviet psychologist and founder of neuropsychology, Luria was born at Kazan in a family of physicians. At the turn of the century Kazan had become the scientific center of south-eastern Russia; in 1885–6 Bekhterev had founded there the first Russian psychological laboratory.

During his studies at the University of Kazan (1918–21), Luria considered the need for establishing a new, "real" psychology which would neither discard the descriptive approach nor ignore the potentialities inherent in the application of natural-scientific (nomothetic) methods.

After a brief diversion into both the psychoanalysis of FREUD and the reflexology of Bekhterev (see Luria 1982, ch. 1), the young psychologist began to investigate the impact of the affective connotations of linguistic tokens upon the latent time of word associations. The research was carried out at the Psychological Institute of the University of Moscow, where he had been invited to head the Section of General Psychology and to join Aleksei N. Leontiev (1903–1979), a man who paired a great talent for theoretical thinking with ingenuity in experimental design, in the effort to build up a truly materialistic psychology. The results of Luria's early Moscow research had some relevance for the diagnosis of emotions and were first published in English (1932).

In 1924 Luria met the speech theorist and psychologist Lev S. Vygotsky (1896–1934), who was elaborating the cultural-historical approach to higher (i.e. specifically human) mental functions (on Vygotsky and his conceptions see Wertsch 1985). Toward the end of his life, Luria repeatedly affirmed his admiration for Vygotsky and the psychophysiologist Nikolai A. Bernštein (1896–1966), and that the work of the former had determined his own scientific career. A man of many gifts and of wide scholarly interests, Vygotsky became the leading figure of the *"troika"*, the group constituted by Vygotsky, Luria, and Leontiev.

The main idea of the cultural-historical approach is that any human mental function is socially mediated by linguistic and other signs which become operative in the organization of action. Until 1934 the *"troika"* followed three lines of research:
1. It studied the development of higher mental functions mediated by signs (perception, memory, attention, and thought). These studies were presented in Leontiev's monograph *The development of memory* (1935).
2. The second domain of investigation concerned the dynamic relationship between the biological and the social factors in the ontogeny of the child. By closely observing the development of twins, Luria showed that the role of biological factors varies for each mental function: their impact is strong in sensory-motor functions, less strong in what could be called "natural" functions (such as visual memory), and nearly absent in higher mental functions.
3. Finally, the research program of the cultural-historical approach also had to address the nature of intercultural difference in mental functions.

Luria began to plan an expedition either to Siberia or to South-East Asia. Two expeditions, both to Uzbekistan, were finally organized in 1931 and 1932 with Kurt Koffka as the only non-Soviet participant (see Luria 1934).

The results of the expeditions were published more than forty years later (Luria 1974a). Despite certain difficulties in interpretating the field data, it was shown that cultural factors impinge upon a great variety of higher mental processes (ranging from optical illusions to semantic categorization and syllogistic thinking), and that these differences tend to vanish as soon as subjects are exposed to industrial forms of life (introduced into Uzbekistan after 1920).

With his increasing scientific reputation, Luria's international recognition also grew.

In 1927, the young professor was already traveling to Germany where he established personal contacts mostly with the Gestaltists of the Berlin School, and to the United States of America. Here he had the opportunity to meet PAVLOV, and discuss their methodological differences. In the early 1930s a doctoral student of Lewin, Bluma V. Zeigarnik, became one of his closest collaborators and remained so throughout his life.

After Vygotsky's death in 1934 Luria began to delimit a new field of investigation at the cross-roads of psychology, medicine, physiology, and linguistics. He took advanced courses in medicine and subsequently worked as an assistant of the well known neurosurgeon N.N. Burdenko. The aim of his endeavor was to understand the cerebral organization of speech mechanisms, and to describe the effects of aphasic disorders upon voluntary action. A vast number of clinical observations enabled Luria to uncover the conditions determining various forms of aphasia.

At the beginning of the war in 1941, Burdenko was made Chief Surgeon of the Red Army, and Luria, like many other psychologists (see for example Zaporožets and Leontiev 1945), started to work in the field of reeducation. He was employed on a ward in a neuropsychiatric hospital near Čeljabinsk in the Urals. Following a multitude of observations and experiments, he finally succeeded in explaining many pure and mixed types of aphasic disorders resulting from localized lesions. These were published after the war in a seminal work *Traumatic aphasia* (1947).

The cerebral mechanisms subserving linguistic activity turn out to be complex functional systems made up of numerous interrelated parts, each one playing a specific role. Among these systems, Luria described two regions: T_1 the superior temporal region of the dominant (left) hemisphere and T_2 the middle segment of the convex portion of the dominant (left) hemisphere. Lesions in each cause distinct syndromes of linguistic impairment. In lesions of T_1, phonemic hearing breaks down, which leads to acoustic (sensory) aphasia. In lesions of T_2 however, phonemic hearing remains intact, but other more complex aspects of linguistic activity suffer from breakdown in the understanding of grammatical construction and lexical semantics. The idea of construing cerebral mechanisms as functional systems in accordance with the Vygotsky School was indeed fundamental in the elaboration of specific reeducational methods.

But the relation between speech and intention also turned out to be less simple than Luria and Vygotsky had first believed. According to their early assumption, if meanings of words are means in the realization of intentional, conscious acts, then aphasic disturbances had to be explained in terms of the disintegration of intentionality. Yet, this hypothesis was false in most cases. Luria therefore began to analyze in greater detail the ontogeny of both speech and activity. Research was carried out with some of his students between 1950 and 1956 at the Institute of Defectology of the Academy of the Pedagogical Sciences. It made use of a large battery of methods using "critical" or "conflictual" visual and verbal stimuli. The studies show that, although speech obviously plays a key-role in the programing of acts, the realization of such acts may occur on the grounds of other mechanisms, too. To explain these phenomena observed under stable circumstances, Luria resorted to Pavlov's theory of higher neural functions, and even to a larger degree to P.K. Anokhin's conception of FEEDBACK mechanisms and Bernštein's model of comparison between program and performance via the detection of signals of success or failure.

The most productive period of Luria's scientific career began in the late 1950s. He was then associated with the Burdenko Neurosurgical Institute, and from 1966 with the newly established Faculty of Psychology of the University of Moscow. Leontiev was to be the Faculty's dean for many years.

Luria's generalized conception is to be found in the handbook *Higher cortical functions in man* (Luria 1962). This text argues for a systems approach to higher mental functions, explains the dynamic localization of cerebral mechanisms, and presents for the first time the tools of neuro-psychological investigation, the method of syndrome analysis (on this aspect of Luria's work, see Christensen 1974). Luria further undertook studies together with Khomskaja and Tsvetkova on the intentional monitoring of motor action, which gave rise to the functional theory of each part of the brain. Contributions of that period reveal the role of the prefrontal lobe in the performance of intentional movements on the one hand, and of the constructive activity in complex cognitive processes on the other. Furthermore, they emphasize subcortical functions which maintain the tonus of cortical activity at the optimal level.

According to the theory of dynamic localization of higher mental functions, the human brain can be divided into three functional blocks:

(a) the energizing block, located at the base of the brain and responsible for the regulation of wakefulness and the response to stimuli;

(b) the information-processing block, located at the posterior sections of the large hemispheres, and responsible for the analysis, the coding, and the storage of information;

(c) the program-designing block, located in the anterior sectors of the brain (including the frontal lobes), and responsible for the formation of intentions and programs of movements.

The whole brain participates in the realization of each mental process, whereby each block makes a specific contribution to this realization. On the other hand, functional disorders may be restored by a variety of neurophysiological structures.

In the last years of his life, Luria published two books dealing with special problems: *Neuropsychology of memory* (Luria 1974–76) and *Basic problems of neurolinguistics* (Luria 1974b). In these monographs, the applicability of the theory of dynamic localization was successfully tested in the analysis of speech and memory disturbances. With respect to aphasia, Luria pointed out that clearly distinguishable functional losses are caused by lesions in each cerebral block. In block (a) lesions lead to speech disturbances of a more or less global, yet unspecific character. In block (b), patients suffer either from the loss of what, following Roman Jacobson, may be called the operational construction of grammatical and syntactical relations, or from a breakdown of the formation of units necessary in phonetic articulation. Finally, lesions in block (c) cause destruction in the formation of meaning schemata and of the motor program for syntagmatic constructions. Luria's views on the goal-directedness or intentionality of acts in general, and of speech acts in particular, were once again systematized in the post-humously published *Language and consciousness* (Luria 1979a).

Another domain of creativity in the last years of Luria's life relates to the topic of personality or personhood, a topic already present in his early conception of a new, "real" psychology. It should be noted that the cultural-historical school argued for the idea that the viewpoint of consciously acting persons be introduced into psychology and that it constitute the unit of analysis. As Vygotsky used to remark: 'something is being remembered or thought of in "natural" mental functions, but man remembers or thinks of something when higher mental functions are at stake'. The case studies written in this vein on the mind of a mnemonist (Luria 1968) and on the man with a shattered world (Luria 1971) won international reputation. To the same type of texts also belongs the scientific autobiography, first edited in English with great care by Michael and Sheila Cole (Luria 1979b). Furthermore, Luria followed with passionate attention the neurological research done on psychological troubles due to peripheral neurological traumata, a field towards which scientists could hardly offer more than a boring "veterinary approach" (as he wrote in a letter to Oliver Sacks, see Sacks 1984). Before he died, he had definite plans to write other case-studies, and the obituary of the journal *Voprosy psikhologii* (Problems of psychology) mentions two yet unpublished manuscripts.

Aleksandr Romanovic Luria thought of himself as an heir of the European tradition of "Romantic Science", and he felt that in the end it is better to give an approximately correct answer to an adequately formulated problem rather than to answer with ultimate rigor to a badly phrased question. (For an assessment of Luria's work, see Khomskaja et al. 1982)   BMV/AM

Bibliography

Christensen, A.L. 1974: *Luria's neuropsychological investigation*. Copenhagen.

Khomskaja, E.D., Tsvetkova, L.S. and Zeigarnik, B.V. eds. 1982: *A.R. Luria i sovremennaja psikhologija*. Moskva: Izdatel'stvo Moskovskogo universiteta.

Leontiev, A.N. *Razvitie pamjati*. Moskva: Ucpedgiz.

Luria, A.R. 1932: *The nature of human conflicts*. New York: Liveright.

——— 1934: The second psychological expedition to Central Asia. *Journal of genetic psychology* 44, 255–59.

——— 1947 (1968): *Traumatic aphasia*. The Hague: Mouton.

——— 1962 (1966): *Higher cortical functions in man*. New York: Basic Books (2nd rev. edn. 1980).

——— 1968: *Malen'kaja knižka o bol'šoj pamjati*. Moskva.

——— 1971: *Poterjannyj i vosvraščennyj mir*. Moskva.

——— 1974a (1976): *Cognitive development: its cultural and social foundations*. Cambridge, Mass.: Harvard University Press.

——— 1974b: *Basic problems of neurolinguistics*. The Hague: Mouton.

——— 1974–76: *Nejropsikhologija pamjati*. Vols. 1 and 2. Moskva: Izdatel'stvo Nauka.

——— 1979a: *Jazyk i soznanie*. Moskva: Izdatel'stvo Moskovskogo Universiteta.

——— 1979b: *The making of mind: a personal account of soviet psychology*. Cambridge, Mass: Harvard University Press.

——— 1982: *Etapy projdennogo puti*. Moskva: Izdatel'stvo Moskovskogo Universiteta.

Sacks, O. 1984: *A leg to stand on*. New York: Summit Books.

Wertsch, J. 1985: *Vygotsky and the social formation of mind*. New York: Harvard University Press.

Zaporozets, A.V. and Leontiev A.N. 1945: *Vosstanovlenie dviženija*. Moskva: Sovetskaja Nauka.

M

medial forebrain bundle A large ascending and descending fiber tract that connects the septal regions in the anterior forebrain and the ventral tegmentum in the midbrain (BRAIN AND CENTRAL NERVOUS SYSTEM: ILLUSTRATIONS, figs. 5, 6, 16 and 18). The medial forebrain bundle passes through the HYPOTHALAMUS and gives off important collaterals to the lateral hypothalamic areas (fig. 20). Mild electrical stimulation at all points throughout the medial forebrain bundle produces pleasurable or rewarding effects as evidenced by animals' readiness to respond for such stimulation. Other brain areas also support self-stimulation but the effect is most reliable and dramatic for the medial forebrain bundle which can yield response rates in a Skinner box of up to 10,000 per hour. Stimulation-produced reward has been compared to the effects of natural reinforcers (e.g. food, water) but differences in animals' behavior in relation to the two types of reinforcers suggest that different mechanisms may be activated. For example, responding for brain stimulation extinguishes more rapidly, is optimal at short inter-response intervals, and requires considerably more prodding to re-establish after the delay. This pattern suggests that electrical stimulation of the medial forebrain bundle and related structures may activate, in addition to a reward system, a drive system to sustain motivation for continued behavior. By contrast natural reinforcers produce only the rewards since motivation is provided by the animal's deprived state. GWi

Bibliography

Rolls, E.T. 1975: *The brain and reward*. London: Pergamon Press. pp. 38–42.

medical models The classical medical model of diagnosis consists of a sequence of history taking, physical examination and laboratory investigations. This model represents an orientation towards "disease" which is defined as a named medical entity, generally without definition of the cause. The medical model has been strongly criticized for being incomplete and omitting such areas as the exploration of patients' ideas, concerns and expectations, non-verbal communication and other aspects of the doctor-patient relationship. These areas are compatible with an alternative "holistic" approach to medical care in which any problem is defined simultaneously in terms of its physical, psychological and social components (Pendleton et al. 1984). This is related, in turn, to the suggestion that medical care should pay greater attention to "illness" than to "disease". Illness is seen as a social phenomenon rather than a medical entity and takes account of the meaning attached to a problem by the patient. This subjective interpretation can strongly affect the patient's decision to seek medical help and to comply with medical advice.

Psychological models of medical care focus upon this "patient-centered" perspective. Research suggests that the behavior of people who consider themselves ill is influenced by the way in which they perceive their symptoms as well as by many social and cultural factors which affect attitudes to pain, health, illness and health services. The most popular approach is the Health Belief Model (Becker 1974) which states that the likelihood that an individual will take action with regard to an illness will depend upon certain health beliefs: general concern about health, perceived susceptibility to and severity of the illness, and the benefits weighed against the disadvantages of the recommended action or treatment. Other research suggests, in addition, that patients' *causal explanations* of their illness significantly affect their ability to cope and to seek medical help. "Folk models" of infection often affect the management of minor illness (Helman 1978).

The traditional medical model is therefore limited in scope and has been extended towards a broader view of diagnosis which takes account of both the scientific discipline of the disease perspective and the psychological and social characteristics of the patient. In psychiatry the medical model of mental disorder has frequently been criticized both from a behaviorist and from a more humanistic perspective (e.g. Laing and Esterson 1964). Both schools think that learning and adaptation are the mechanisms which produce the behavior regarded by psychiatrists as symptoms. The current criticisms being leveled at medical models in general medical practice clearly cast greater doubt upon the always questionable derivative usage in psychiatry.   JK

Bibliography

Becker, M.H. 1974: *The health belief model and personal health behavior*. Health education monographs, 2.

Helman, C. 1978: Folk models of infection in an English suburban community and their relation to medical treatment. *Culture, medicine and psychiatry* 2, 107–438.

Laing, R.D. and Esterton, A. 1964: *Sanity, madness and the family*. London: Tavistock.

Pendleton, D.A. et al. 1984: *The consultation: an approach to learning and teaching*. Oxford and New York: Oxford University Press.

meditation The practice of mind, thought, attitude or psychophysiological transformation generally in the context of some spiritual tradition; technique for inducing altered states of consciousness often called "mystical". Knowledge that consciousness may be experienced in different ways is extremely ancient. Natural mysticism among primitive peoples, arising from both solitary and group practices often involving repetitive dance and chant rhythms, seems to be the original basis for the institutionalization of consciousness changing practices in the major world religions. Hindus, Buddhists, Sufis, Jews and Christians all have literatures containing manuals of meditative techniques. The prime characteristic of all of them is the loss of self-identifying awareness and a sense of absorption in a wider consciousness however that may be defined (Coleman 1977). There may well be a universal need for such experience which twentieth-century western culture with its emphasis on rationality has denied (Crook 1980). Contemporary movements promoting meditation spring from the urge to meet that need outside conventional religion and its consequent commercialization in a consumer economy.

The prime feature of the mind in its normal consciousness is that sensory experience is edited or filtered by a system of mental categorization so that the world is experienced primarily as represented by the categories by which it is mapped. All such conceptual systems are the result of social conditioning from babyhood and are closely related to the human capacity for language. In particular, an association between bodily experiences and contingent effects of behavior in an environment leads to the inference that the self exists as an agent or "me" (ego). This waking state of "objective self-awareness" (Duval and Wicklund 1972) is characterized by classification of self versus others and comparative evaluations of experience in the continuum of time past, present and future. Problems of self-esteem and its maintenance in a world of comparative social evaluations lie at the root of social anxiety or disquiet. Meditational techniques that induce (a) calming, (b) catharsis of tension, (c) insight into the nature of the personal process, are often of considerable therapeutic value. Further, a training in meditation can lead to selfless experiences of being, bliss and love held to be of the highest value in world religions and which lead to a more altruistic attitude towards fellow sentient beings (Naranjo and Ornstein 1971).

Most traditional meditation techniques utilize a combination of exercises concerned with one or more of the following: control or regulation of breathing, focused attention, relative perceptual deprivation,

e
ss
he
ked
soci-
a part
rsa and
d within

became
nshrined in
eud's *Inter-*
in which an
el of the mind
sciousness was
f the mind and of
ssumed to be the
the "system con-
houghts and memo-
cious by receiving
cathexis". A subjacent
, the "system precon-
thoughts and memories
ecalled relatively easily by
ion cathexis. Within this
ts proceeded according to
processes, that is to say they
y rational and could be
ublicly without being regarded
e or disordered. The "system
ious" was considered to be sepa-
m yet a deeper layer of the mind,
stem unconscious". Here thoughts
marked by the imprint of intense
ionally charged sexual energies. Con-
ions between trains of thought in this
tem were marked by the primary process
at characterizes the thinking of dreams,
he formation of myths, poetic and artistic
images, and which underlie the meaningfulness that psychoanalytic clinicians see in
slips of the tongue, symptomatic acts and
neurotic and psychotic forms of disturbed
thinking. Memories within the "system
unconscious" are forcibly kept out of
consciousness and are said to be, thereby,
dynamically unconscious.

Because of the intensity of the instinctual drive derived from energies attached to the memories and wishes within the "system unconscious" they are considered to be seeking expression ("discharge") in the form of actions or conscious representation and recall. Such expression is prevented by a hypothetical "censor" located between the two deepest "censor" located between the two deepest layers of the mind that serves as an agency of defense. At the censor, unconscious memories are processed by disguise and distortion until they can be expressed in the more conscious layers of the mind without threatening the survival of the person or giving offense to social constraints.

This model of the mind ("the topographical model") remains in clinical use by psychoanalysts although many contemporary theorists have abandoned the notions of mental energies or have retained them only as metaphorically useful. The notion that forgetting can be seen as a forceful expulsion of unwelcome, disruptive or socially unacceptable thoughts, is completely retained and is ascribed, to this day, to a variety of defensive activities (see DEFENSE MECHANISM).

The distortion and control of memories by primary process thinking whereby recall is inhibited or modified by reason of the meaning attached to the thoughts, is a fundamental aspect of contemporary psychoanalytic thinking. Moreover, it was postulated by Freud, in the early years of this century (Freud 1905) that early childhood memories were all subject to massive repression constituting the "amnesia of childhood". Freud himself thought that the large scale suppression of childhood memories was due to their being linked to the intense and forbidden sexual wishes of the child. Later Freud and other psychoanalysts added the intensity of sadistic, aggressive childhood wishes to the reasons for this repression. Yet other analysts have suggested that the strong anxieties and envy proposed as dominating childhood mental life may also account for the infantile amnesia.

Other psychoanalysts have put forward the notion that the amnesia is mainly the consequence of the shedding of redundant wishes and patterns of activity and expression. Whatever the reasons thought to account for the paucity and distortion of early childhood memories, the fact of childhood amnesia is important in psychoanalytic theory and clinical practice: the

"yogic" body postures, and the mental visualization of scenes or symbols representing desired goal states or stages. All practices induce shifts in the electrophysiological condition of the psychosomatic system in ways that are still little understood or researched. Among the known effects of one recently researched tradition (Transcendental Meditation or TM) the following have been established: the induction of alpha brain waves and, in deeper meditation, theta waves together with a synchronization of waves at the front and back of the brain during a session and synchrony in the two hemispheres, changes in *galvanic skin responses*, lowered respiration rate and oxygen consumption and other biochemical changes (see BIOFEEDBACK; ELECTROENCEPHALOGRAM).

TM consists of quiet relaxed breathing and the mental repetition of a mantra especially chosen for the subject. It is an easily acquired technique nowadays carefully taught by a multitude of trained instructors all over the world. It is based upon an ancient Hindu technique popularized by the Maharishi Mahesh. Much of its scientific evaluation has been suspect especially where it has been conducted by advocates of the system by which it is promoted commercially (Bloomfield et al. 1976). Where independent evaluation has been attempted some of the positive effects have however been confirmed (West 1979). TM does reduce arousal especially in easily stressed individuals and this is valuable for those suffering from ANXIETY, tension and their concomitant effects. Some long term effects have been reported and are likely to be dependent upon persistence in practice.

TM and other calming meditations have close resemblances to the AUTOGENIC TRAINING of J.H. Schultz, a German doctor concerned with stress relief and self-control of bodily conditions early in this century. In this procedure the subject is told to hold his attention firmly on some bodily condition – the weight of an arm, coolness of the forehead, warmth in the hands or an assertion "I am at peace". There is a similarity here with the firm body posture and mental repetition of

mantras found in TM and Buddhist meditations and especially with the "mindfulness" of the body found in Vipassana and described in one of the earliest sutras of the Buddha. Holding the attention firmly upon an inner condition seems to reduce the tendency of the mind to wander in a reverie of anxiety-producing themes.

In Zen meditation the main intention is the establishment of an alert awareness both of environment and of one's own body and mental processes rather than the induction of quiescent trance. This awareness can break open the narrow categories by which self's action as an agent and respondent are cognitively confined, and experiences of oneness with the world may arise.

Close observation of the functioning of the mind (as in the Samatha meditation of the Theravada or in the similar Zazen of the Soto Zen school) is clearly the experiential basis for the models of mind found in Buddhist psycho-philosophical texts. The experience of "sitting" shows that after some hours of repetitive practice the calming effect reaches a more or less stabilized condition in which subtle shifts in the mental condition are easily observed. As the environmental stimuli change so the conscious concomitants of the auditory, visual or other senses vary in prominence as attention increases or decreases its focus on particular sources of stimulation. As memories arise and concomitant emotional conditions are produced, the way in which the "inherent ego" appears and disappears with its hopes, fears, rationalizations and vanity becomes very clear and the whole "script" of one's life may be observed with an insight which can have markedly therapeutic effects.

In Rinzai Zen a deliberate effort is made to press the rationalizing mind and its ego-defensive operations beyond the realm of words and ideas. To this end the meditator is given a Koan or paradoxical question to solve and is forced at intervals in a retreat to bring his answers to an alertly critical master (Sekida 1975; Kapleau 1965). When the meditator reaches a point of desperation, struggling with the meaning of "What is the sound of one hand clapping" for example, he may break out into an intuitive realization that beyond words is the world itself, directly apprehensible and *there* in its own nature, with which the meditator senses his own belonging. The "emptiness" of thought which is the essence of these "enlightenment experiences" is the key to the understanding of the vast Mahayana literature upon which the concept rejecting practices of Zen are based (Kapleau 1965). Such training leads to the development of the "renouncing mind" of the Bodhisattva in which selfish egoism gives way to the use of the ego in the service of others. Such "opening" experiences seem particularly to involve a process of disidentification from habitual concepts of "me" and "mine".

Meditation training in the Gelugpa order of Tibetan monks is based on the discursive intellectual presentation of Buddhist psychology rather than on intuition. Extensive study of texts is linked to "checking meditation" in which the ideas are matched against experience in the subjects' own life in a test of their personal validity. All teachings are treated in this way and if the course is a long one it is at least extremely thorough. Mistakes that can arise in following the short-cuts of Zen are thus avoided.

Tibetans have also developed the tantric meditations of Hindus within a Buddhist framework. Tantra involves extensive visualization and the deliberate identification of the subject with the internalized icons. These pictures of Buddhas and the like, in both their benign and horrific forms, represent psychological forces which the adept can learn to manipulate. The practice is often associated with visualizations of bodily processes using the categories of ancient Hindu physiology. Breathing exercises and advanced yogic practices combine to produce powerful effects. No novice should attempt such practice without an appropriate teacher who will ask for preliminary preparation and initiation before advanced practice can begin. Textual research suggests strongly that the sexual imagery in much of tantric practice refers to the origin of these exercises in group rites in which sexual interaction was

normal. With a suitable partner this may sometimes be the case today. The mutual endeavor is, however, on a plane of sublimation that requires subtle control of sexual physiology if it is not to degenerate into mere indulgence. It is not surprising therefore that these powerful exercises are rarely taught outside the circle of carefully prepared initiates.

Powerful psychophysiological changes referred to as "raising the Kundalini" (Gopi-Krishna 1976) etc. are unlikely to be fictitious but as with Tantra none of them have yet been researched by accredited scientists. There are similarities to the bioenergetic therapies based upon the work of Wilhelm Reich (Lowen 1975; Boadella 1975). Research on the relations between advanced yoga of this type and bioenergetics may have great value for the future.

The value of meditating for an individual depends on attitude and context. In the spiritual market place many contemporary cults of meditation, with their emphasis on gurus and membership of self-defining elitist institutions, may perhaps be seen as an expression of the disintegration of the family system in the modern West and attendant uncertainty regarding parental and sexual roles and mores. Young people, often desperate for guidance, find parental substitutes in strange places and are liable to become brain-washed practitioners of powerful psychosomatic exercises, access to which is made dependent on cult membership and financial contribution. Only where meditation is used as a means to personal development, insight and above all autonomy can its true potential be realized.   JHC

Bibliography

Bloomfield, H.H. et al. 1976: *TM: how meditation can reduce stress*. London: Unwin.

Boadella, D. 1975: Between coma and convulsion. *Energy and character* 6.1, 4–24; 6.2, 18–27; 6.3, 27–38.

Coleman, D. 1977: *The varieties of meditative experience*. London: Ryder.

*Crook, J.H. 1980: *The evolution of human consciousness*. Oxford and New York: Oxford University Press.

Duval, S. and Wicklund, P. [. . .] *objective self-awareness*. [. . .] Press.

Gopi-Krishna, P. 1976: [. . .] *consciousness*. New Delhi: [. . .]

*Kapleau, P. 1965: *The th[. . .] Boston: Beacon Press.

Lowen, A. 1979: *Bioenergetics*. Lo[. . .]

*Naranjo, C. and Ornstein, R. [. . .] *psychology of meditation*. New York: V[. . .]

Sekida, K. 1975: *Zen training: me[. . .] philosophy*. New York: Weatherhill.

West, M. 1979: Meditation. *British jour[. . .] psychiatry* 135, 457–67.

memory and forgetting: psychoanalytic theories

As with all theoretical and clinical systems, evolution over time has allowed some features of PSYCHOANALYSIS to be changed and others to remain unaltered and the nature of memory and the process of forgetting as understood within psychoanalysis can be portrayed by describing the historical developments.

Psychoanalysis began with Breuer and FREUD'S clinical observations (see Freud 1893–95) that the symptoms of HYSTERIA could be interpreted as symbolic representations of traumatic memories that could not be recalled because of the meaning, for the subject, of the content of the memories. Therapeutic help consisted, in the early days of Freud's psychotherapeutic work, of pressurizing the patient to rediscover the covered up memories. Freud noted that, in fortunate circumstances, recovering lost memories produced apparent cure; the symptom as a disguised form of remembrance was replaced by a direct memory, accompanied by some of the feelings appropriate to the originating traumatic experience. The events of the traumatic experience were, according to Freud's observations, sexual in nature and not available for conscious recall because social conventions forbade the sexual arousal in the (usually) young person. The event was commonly thought to have been a seduction by a household member or the witnessing of sexuality between family members. Hysterical patients were said to be suffering from "reminiscence" and "yogic" body postures, and the mental visualization of scenes or symbols representing desired goal states or stages. All practices induce shifts in the electrophysiological condition of the psychosomatic system in ways that are still little understood or researched. Among the known effects of one recently researched tradition (Transcendental Meditation or TM) the following have been established: the induction of alpha brain waves and, in deeper meditation, theta waves together with a synchronization of waves at the front and back of the brain during a session and synchrony in the two hemispheres, changes in *galvanic skin responses*, lowered respiration rate and oxygen consumption and other biochemical changes (see BIOFEEDBACK; ELECTROENCEPHALOGRAM).

TM consists of quiet relaxed breathing and the mental repetition of a mantra especially chosen for the subject. It is an easily acquired technique nowadays carefully taught by a multitude of trained instructors all over the world. It is based upon an ancient Hindu technique popularized by the Maharishi Mahesh. Much of its scientific evaluation has been suspect especially where it has been conducted by advocates of the system by which it is promoted commercially (Bloomfield et al. 1976). Where independent evaluation has been attempted some of the positive effects have however been confirmed (West 1979). TM does reduce arousal especially in easily stressed individuals and this is valuable for those suffering from ANXIETY, tension and their concomitant effects. Some long term effects have been reported and are likely to be dependent upon persistence in practice.

TM and other calming meditations have close resemblances to the AUTOGENIC TRAINING of J.H. Schultz, a German doctor concerned with stress relief and self-control of bodily conditions early in this century. In this procedure the subject is told to hold his attention firmly on some bodily condition – the weight of an arm, coolness of the forehead, warmth in the hands or an assertion "I am at peace". There is a similarity here with the firm body posture and mental repetition of mantras found in TM and Buddhist meditations and especially with the "mindfulness" of the body found in Vipassana and described in one of the earliest sutras of the Buddha. Holding the attention firmly upon an inner condition seems to reduce the tendency of the mind to wander in a reverie of anxiety-producing themes.

In Zen meditation the main intention is the establishment of an alert awareness both of environment and of one's own body and mental processes rather than the induction of quiescent trance. This awareness can break open the narrow categories by which self's action as an agent and respondent are cognitively confined, and experiences of oneness with the world may arise.

Close observation of the functioning of the mind (as in the Samatha meditation of the Theravada or in the similar Zazen of the Soto Zen school) is clearly the experiential basis for the models of mind found in Buddhist psycho-philosophical texts. The experience of "sitting" shows that after some hours of repetitive practice the calming effect reaches a more or less stabilized condition in which subtle shifts in the mental condition are easily observed. As the environmental stimuli change so the conscious concomitants of the auditory, visual or other senses vary in prominence as attention increases or decreases its focus on particular sources of stimulation. As memories arise and concomitant emotional conditions are produced, the way in which the "inherent ego" appears and disappears with its hopes, fears, rationalizations and vanity becomes very clear and the whole "script" of one's life may be observed with an insight which can have markedly therapeutic effects.

In Rinzai Zen a deliberate effort is made to press the rationalizing mind and its ego-defensive operations beyond the realm of words and ideas. To this end the meditator is given a Koan or paradoxical question to solve and is forced at intervals in a retreat to bring his answers to an alertly critical master (Sekida 1975; Kapleau 1965). When the meditator reaches a point of desperation, struggling with the meaning of "What is the sound of one hand clapping" for example, he may break out into an intuitive realization that beyond words is the world itself, directly apprehensible and *there* in its own nature, with which the meditator senses his own belonging. The "emptiness" of thought which is the essence of these "enlightenment experiences" is the key to the understanding of the vast Mahayana literature upon which the concept rejecting practices of Zen are based (Kapleau 1965). Such training leads to the development of the "renouncing mind" of the Bodhisattva in which selfish egoism gives way to the use of the ego in the service of others. Such "opening" experiences seem particularly to involve a process of disidentification from habitual concepts of "me" and "mine".

Meditation training in the Gelugpa order of Tibetan monks is based on the discursive intellectual presentation of Buddhist psychology rather than on intuition. Extensive study of texts is linked to "checking meditation" in which the ideas are matched against experience in the subjects' own life in a test of their personal validity. All teachings are treated in this way and if the course is a long one it is at least extremely thorough. Mistakes that can arise in following the short-cuts of Zen are thus avoided.

Tibetans have also developed the tantric meditations of Hindus within a Buddhist framework. Tantra involves extensive visualization and the deliberate identification of the subject with the internalized icons. These pictures of Buddhas and the like, in both their benign and horrific forms, represent psychological forces which the adept can learn to manipulate. The practice is often associated with visualizations of bodily processes using the categories of ancient Hindu physiology. Breathing exercises and advanced yogic practices combine to produce powerful effects. No novice should attempt such practice without an appropriate teacher who will ask for preliminary preparation and initiation before advanced practice can begin. Textual research suggests strongly that the sexual imagery in much of tantric practice refers to the origin of these exercises in group rites in which sexual interaction was

normal. With a suitable partner this may sometimes be the case today. The mutual endeavor is, however, on a plane of sublimation that requires subtle control of sexual physiology if it is not to degenerate into mere indulgence. It is not surprising therefore that these powerful exercises are rarely taught outside the circle of carefully prepared initiates.

Powerful psychophysiological changes referred to as "raising the Kundalini" (Gopi-Krishna 1976) etc. are unlikely to be fictitious but as with Tantra none of them have yet been researched by accredited scientists. There are similarities to the bioenergetic therapies based upon the work of Wilhelm Reich (Lowen 1975; Boadella 1975). Research on the relations between advanced yoga of this type and bioenergetics may have great value for the future.

The value of meditating for an individual depends on attitude and context. In the spiritual market place many contemporary cults of meditation, with their emphasis on gurus and membership of self-defining elitist institutions, may perhaps be seen as an expression of the disintegration of the family system in the modern West and attendant uncertainty regarding parental and sexual roles and mores. Young people, often desperate for guidance, find parental substitutes in strange places and are liable to become brain-washed practitioners of powerful psychosomatic exercises, access to which is made dependent on cult membership and financial contribution. Only where meditation is used as a means to personal development, insight and above all autonomy can its true potential be realized.   JHC

Bibliography

Bloomfield, H.H. et al. 1976: *TM: how meditation can reduce stress*. London: Unwin.

Boadella, D. 1975: Between coma and convulsion. *Energy and character* 6.1, 4–24; 6.2, 18–27; 6.3, 27–38.

Coleman, D. 1977: *The varieties of meditative experience*. London: Ryder.

*Crook, J.H. 1980: *The evolution of human consciousness*. Oxford and New York: Oxford University Press.

Duval, S. and Wicklund, R.A. 1972: *A theory of objective self-awareness*. New York: Academic Press.

Gopi-Krishna, P. 1976: *Kundalini: path to higher consciousness*. New Delhi: Orient.

*Kapleau, P. 1965: *The three pillars of Zen*. Boston: Beacon Press.

Lowen, A. 1979: *Bioenergetics*. London: Penguin.

*Naranjo, C. and Ornstein, R. 1971: *On the psychology of meditation*. New York: Viking.

Sekida, K. 1975: *Zen training: methods and philosophy*. New York: Weatherhill.

West, M. 1979: Meditation. *British journal of psychiatry* 135, 457–67.

memory and forgetting: psycho-analytic theories

As with all theoretical and clinical systems, evolution over time has allowed some features of PSYCHOANALY-SIS to be changed and others to remain unaltered and the nature of memory and the process of forgetting as understood within psychoanalysis can be portrayed by describing the historical developments.

Psychoanalysis began with Breuer and FREUD'S clinical observations (see Freud 1893–95) that the symptoms of HYSTERIA could be interpreted as symbolic represen-tations of traumatic memories that could not be recalled because of the meaning, for the subject, of the content of the memories. Therapeutic help consisted, in the early days of Freud's psychotherapeutic work, of pressurizing the patient to rediscover the covered up memories. Freud noted that, in fortunate circumstances, recovering lost memories produced apparent cure; the symptom as a disguised form of remem-brance was replaced by a direct memory, accompanied by some of the feelings appropriate to the originating traumatic experience. The events of the traumatic experience were, according to Freud's observations, sexual in nature and not available for conscious recall because social conventions forbade the sexual arousal in the (usually) young person. The event was commonly thought to have been a seduction by a household member or the witnessing of sexuality between family members. Hysterical patients were said to be suffering from "reminiscence" and

psychotherapy consisted of the devel-opment of actual recall so that what had before been unconscious would now become conscious. Memory and forgetting became, thereby, central preoccupations of psychoanalysis, and have remained so to this day despite the fact that there have been vast changes in the formulation of psychoanalytic theories, and the tech-niques and subject matter of psychoanaly-tic therapies.

In his earliest psychoanalytic writings Freud considered that recall of the trau-matic circumstances underlying the devel-opment of neurotic symptoms was prevented by the quantity of emotion tied up in the original experience, or evoked by the events of the trauma somehow being on the threshold of recall. The prevention of access of uncomfortable or disturbing memories to consciousness was described as *defense* and this notion, so relevant to the psychoanalytic theory of memory and for-getting, remains central to this day.

The next step in the development of the subject came in a series of unpublished letters from Freud to Wilhelm Fliess which are known as a "Project for a Scientific Psychology" (Freud 1950) written in 1895. In this document perception and memory were ascribed to separate systems of the nervous system, an idea that has been retained within contemporary psychoana-lytic thinking. Moreover Freud empha-sized in these writings the importance of motivation affecting memory and recall, and he differentiated between conscious logical rational thinking (known as "secon-dary process thinking") which utilized memories in ways acceptable to the waking, public aspects of thinking and those forms of thought observable in dreams and in neurotic symptom formation. In this form of thinking ("primary process thinking") memories are laid down according to the pressure of strong instinctual forces e.g. the sex drives ("libido") whose "energies" (hypothesized as having potentially measurable qualitative and quantitative aspects) distort the form of the memories and, above all, determine the pressure with which such memories seek access to consciousness and are substantially opposed by the forces mobilized by the waking, conscious mind: primary process thinking shows an absence of control by the rational waking mind. Memories are linked by emotional association, by chance associations, by processes of symbolization, a part can stand for a whole and vice versa and several memories may be contained within one thought ("condensation").

These conceptualizations became greatly elaborated and firmly enshrined in psychoanalytic theory in Freud's *Interpretation of dreams* (1900) in which an extensive account of a model of the mind was given. In this, consciousness was ascribed to a small area of the mind and of mental activity. It was assumed to be the quality of thinking in the "system conscious" within which thoughts and memories became conscious by receiving sufficient "attention cathexis". A subjacent layer of the mind, the "system preconscious" contained thoughts and memories which could be recalled relatively easily by receiving attention cathexis. Within this system thoughts proceeded according to the secondary processes, that is to say they were largely rational and could be expressed publicly without being regarded as strange or disordered. The "system preconscious" was considered to be separated from yet a deeper layer of the mind, the "system unconscious". Here thoughts were marked by the imprint of intense emotionally charged sexual energies. Connections between trains of thought in this system were marked by the primary process that characterizes the thinking of dreams, the formation of myths, poetic and artistic images, and which underlie the meaningfulness that psychoanalytic clinicians see in slips of the tongue, symptomatic acts and neurotic and psychotic forms of disturbed thinking. Memories within the "system unconscious" are forcibly kept out of consciousness and are said to be, thereby, dynamically unconscious.

Because of the intensity of the instinctual drive derived from energies attached to the memories and wishes within the "system unconscious" they are considered to be seeking expression ("discharge") in the form of actions or conscious representation and recall. Such expression is prevented by a hypothetical "censor" located between the two deepest layers of the mind that serves as an agency of defense. At the censor, unconscious memories are processed by disguise and distortion until they can be expressed in the more conscious layers of the mind without threatening the survival of the person or giving offense to social constraints.

This model of the mind ("the topographical model") remains in clinical use by psychoanalysts although many contemporary theorists have abandoned the notions of mental energies or have retained them only as metaphorically useful. The notion that forgetting can be seen as a forceful expulsion of unwelcome, disruptive or socially unacceptable thoughts, is completely retained and is ascribed, to this day, to a variety of defensive activities (see DEFENSE MECHANISM).

The distortion and control of memories by primary process thinking whereby recall is inhibited or modified by reason of the meaning attached to the thoughts, is a fundamental aspect of contemporary psychoanalytic thinking. Moreover, it was postulated by Freud, in the early years of this century (Freud 1905) that early childhood memories were all subject to massive repression constituting the "amnesia of childhood". Freud himself thought that the large scale suppression of childhood memories was due to their being linked to the intense and forbidden sexual wishes of the child. Later Freud and other psychoanalysts added the intensity of sadistic, aggressive childhood wishes to the reasons for this repression. Yet other analysts have suggested that the strong anxieties and envy proposed as dominating childhood mental life may also account for the infantile amnesia.

Other psychoanalysts have put forward the notion that the amnesia is mainly the consequence of the shedding of redundant wishes and patterns of activity and expression. Whatever the reasons thought to account for the paucity and distortion of early childhood memories, the fact of childhood amnesia is important in psychoanalytic theory and clinical practice: the reconstruction of an outline knowledge of a patient's childhood experiences is a regular part of psychoanalytic psychotherapy.

In the third decade of this century Freud revised his model of the mind (Freud 1923 and 1926) by proposing a tripartite division into the ego, the superego and the id (the "structural model") (see FREUD). Memory was given as a function of the ego which was also conceived as having control of recall, conscious logical thinking, of carrying out defensive functions and of synthesizing and integrating the overall activity of the mental apparatus. This reorganization of the psychoanalytic model of the mind was thought necessary in order to express the fact that defensive operations causing memory lapses, for example, were directed against unconscious impulses affecting the content of the memories but the operations were themselves also unconscious and inaccessible to recall (except during and by means of the process of psychoanalysis).

The major innovation of the model was the idea of the superego. This was put forward as an agency of the mind in which the rules for behavior, parents' prohibitions and aspirations for their children, become incorporated within the mind of the growing child and become, in the end, rules, ideals and requirements which consciously and unconsciously govern not only behavior but also attitudes towards the self.

In the structural model personal expression, symptom formation and identity are considered to be the outcome of the pressures of the instinctual drives coming from the id, which are controlled and shaped in their expression by the balance of ego and superego activities.

The memories of the relationship with the parents and other significant adults, are enshrined within the mind as having major effects on personality. Increasingly, contemporary psychoanalytic theory is concerned with the way in which internalizations of personal experiences in relation to significant others are the dominating memory systems, built up into a representational world structuring large aspects of experience including processes of memory and forgetting.   CD

Bibliography
Freud, S. 1893–95: Studies on hysteria, vol. 2;
——— 1895: Project for a scientific psychology, vol. 1;
——— 1900: Interpretation of dreams, vols. 4 and 5;
——— 1905: Three essays on sexuality. vol. 7;
——— 1923: The ego and the id, vol. 19;
——— 1926: Inhibitions, symptoms and anxiety, vol. 20;
In *Standard edition of the complete psychological works of Sigmund Freud*, vols as shown. London: Hogarth Press; New York: Norton.

memory and learning: physiological bases This is concerned with (a) the neurophysiological, neurochemical and neuroanatomical foundations of the structural organization of memory, and (b) the neurobiological mechanisms associated with alterations of memory (plasticity) as a function of experience (learning).

On a conceptual level the structure of longterm memory (LTM) is assumed to be the repository of most of our knowledge and skills. Information within LTM has been divided into episodic and semantic memory components. Episodic memory records information about spatio-temporal dated events which have autobiographical reference (context). The context consists of the external environment and the internal states of the organism, including affect. Semantic or reference memory concerns our permanent knowledge of the world and primarily concerns concepts and rules. It can be subdivided into (1) sensory-perceptual knowledge, which concerns the processing of sensory information, the generation of images and the storage of cognitive maps, (2) procedural-motoric knowledge, which concerns the processing of motor skills (e.g., skiing or speech production), and (3) declarative or propositional knowledge which includes our knowledge of general facts.

Contemporary views assume that these function systems are organized as a network of interconnected nodes. The connections, links or associations between and within nodes are assumed to be organized in a multi-level heterarchical fashion, that is components at one level subsume a structured set of components at a lower level, and are themselves subsumed within yet higher level units. Each node is subdivided into levels and each level is composed of attributes.

The LTM system can be in either an inactive or active state. To be in an active state the LTM system has to be triggered by sensory or data-driven input and/or by conceptual or memory-driven input. Once a subset of nodes is activated in LTM, activation will spread to other interconnected nodes (spreading activation) and will last for a short time (short-term memory) or a somewhat longer time (working memory), depending upon the degree of attention, rehearsal or consolidation (controlled processing). The greater the amount of controlled processing the longer the duration of activation, and the greater the probability of change within the LTM network of nodes.

On a neurobiological level it is thought that the anatomical structure subserving LTM is either distributed, that is the whole central nervous system codes every memory (mass action) or is relatively localized, that is specific neural "units" participate in mediation of specific memories. Even though there is a problem in defining the critical neural unit of analysis (e.g., SYNAPSE, synaptic conglomerate, synaptic assembly, NEURON, neural assembly, junctional thicket, simple circuit, neural region, system or complex system) the contemporary view is that specific neural regions, though overlapping and interacting to a great extent, contribute to a subset of nodes which comprise the structure of LTM. Many neural regions contribute to LTM structure, but at the highest level of organization there are a few regions that appear to be of critical importance. These include the CEREBRAL CORTEX, hippocampal formation, amygdaloid complex and caudate nucleus. The cerebral cortex subserves all the functional systems involved with semantic memory; the HIPPOCAMPUS is involved in processing the environmental contextual component of episodic memory; the amygdaloid complex contributes to the coding of internal states including affect; and the caudate nucleus

processes additional information involved in procedural knowledge.

The cerebral cortex can be divided into major interconnected regions such as frontal, temporal, parietal, and occipital lobes which include primary sensory and motor areas as well as association areas. It has been suggested that the functional unit that corresponds to lower-level nodes might be the small cortical columns within the sensory and motor cortical areas. The functional unit that mediates higher-order level nodes might be the larger cortical columns within the association cortical areas (Eccles 1980).

Based on lesion, electrical stimulation, and electrical recording techniques as well as brain pathology in both animals and humans, it has been possible to uncover dissociations which imply specificity of function of the cortical columnar organization subserving the semantic node network.

For example, language (verbal) information is mainly, but not exclusively, stored on one side of the cerebral cortex (usually the left in humans), while visuo-spatial (nonverbal) information is stored mainly on the right side of the cortex (see LATERALIZATION). Support for this verbal-nonverbal dissociation is derived from observation that brain damage to the left cerebral cortex produces primarily language problems, while brain damage to the right cerebral cortex produces primarily visuo-spatial problems, and that a cut of the corpus callosum which disconnects the two sides of the cerebral cortex results in patients who can process and store primarily language information with the left side and primarily visuo-spatial information with the right (Gazzaniga and LeDoux 1978; Geschwind 1970).

Within the language semantic memory network a neural region within the left frontal lobe known as Broca's area mediates motoric aspects of language knowledge, while a neural region within the left temporal lobe known as Wernicke's area mediates propositional aspects of language knowledge.

Within the visuo-spatial semantic memory network the frontal lobe mediates egocentric or personal space (based on perspective), while the parietal lobe mediates allocentric or absolute space (space based on invariance, i.e., cognitive map) (Semmes et al. 1963).

In contrast to the cerebral cortex involvement with semantic memory the hippocampal formation is a critical neural region involved in the mediation of the environmental contextual component of episodic memory. This conclusion is based on the observation that bilateral medial temporal lobe damage including the hippocampal formation in animals and humans produces an extensive and durable memory loss for new episodic information (Kesner 1983; Milner 1974). Patients with hippocampal damage appear to forget rather quickly events that occur in their daily life: they are usually unable to tell you where they are, what they had for breakfast or when they met you previously. In contrast they are able to converse normally at least about events that occurred before their brain damage, their verbal skills are intact and they can carry out mental arithmetic. Furthermore they can reasonably well learn and retain a variety of rules of specific procedural-motoric knowledge skills (tracking, mirror tracing, eye-lid conditioning) and declarative knowledge skills (mirror reading, rule-based verbal paired-associate learning, rules of card games) while not remembering having previously performed the task, the specific contingencies of the task, or when and where they learned the task (see MEMORY AND LEARNING DISORDERS).

Changes from an inactive to an active state in critical neural regions that comprise LTM can be indexed by dynamic changes in electrical firing patterns and biochemical functions. The duration of this active state is influenced by a large number of parameters. One neural mechanism that could mediate and maintain an active state for a long time is known as long-term potentiation. It can be measured readily in the hippocampal formation. Long-term activation (consolidation) increases the probability that relatively permanent changes (learning) might occur within the structure of LTM. Support for the idea that long-term activation might be necessary for new learning comes from the observation that pharmacological and electrical brain stimulation treatments can modify the storage and subsequent retrieval of new information within LTM (McGaugh and Herz 1972); on a time-dependent basis (that is, treatments are effective in altering information for only a limited duration after exposure to a new learning experience).

A number of neurophysiological, neurochemical and neuroanatomical mechanisms have been proposed as capable of mediating the structure of LTM. They include changes in neuronal firing, phosphorylation of membranes, synaptic efficacy, the formation of new peptides, proteins and synapses or dendritic differentiation.

The goal is to understand the mechanisms of plasticity within specific neuronal "units" in order to characterize and describe further the dynamic and structural aspects of long-term memory.   RPK

Bibliography

Eccles, John C. 1980: *The human psyche.* Heidelberg: Springer Verlag.

Gazzaniga, M.S., and LeDoux, J.F. 1978: *The integrated mind.* New York: Plenum Press.

Geschwind, N. 1970: The organization of language and the brain. *Science* 170, 940–44.

Kesner, R.P. 1985: Neurobiological views of memory. In *Learning and memory: a biological view,* eds. J.L. Martinez and R.P. Kesner. New York: Academic Press.

Lachman, R., Lachman, J.L. and Sutterfield, E.C. eds. 1979: *Cognitive psychology and information processing: introduction.* Hillsdale, N.J.: Lawrence Erlbaum Associates.

McGaugh, J.L., and Herz, M.M. 1972: *Memory consolidation.* San Franciso: Freeman.

Milner, B. 1974: Hemisphere specialisation: scope and limits. In *The neurosciences: third research program,* eds. F.O. Schmitt and F.G. Warden. Cambridge, Mass.: MIT Press.

Rosenzweig, M.R. and Bennett, E.L. eds. 1976: *Neural mechanisms of learning and memory.* Cambridge, Mass.: MIT Press.

Semmes, J. et al. 1963: Correlates of impaired orientation in personal and extrapersonal space. *Brain* 86, 747–72.

Teyler, T. ed. 1978: *Brain and learning.* Stamford, Connecticut: Greylock Inc.

Whitty, C.W.M., and Zangwill, O.L. eds. 1977: *Amnesia: clinical, psychological and medicolegal aspects.* London and Boston: Butterworth.

memory and learning: synaptic structure theories and intracellular chemical theories These theories postulate that the changes in nervous tissue underlying learning and the formation of memory involve either the growth of new synapses or the alteration of the properties of existing synapses. A SYNAPSE is the area of communication between one nerve cell and another. The communication usually occurs when a signal (ACTION POTENTIAL) in one NEURON leads to the release of a chemical transmitter from its terminals. The transmitter diffuses across the synaptic gap and combines with a receptor molecule in the membrane of the postsynaptic cell. This combination then leads either to activation (excitation) or depression (inhibition) of activity in the postsynaptic cell. Synapses may occur on the cell body (soma and dendrites) or on the initial segment of the axon of a neuron, in which case they can either excite or inhibit the generation of the action potential. Synapses may also be present on the axon terminals, in which case their action is to modulate the release of transmitter from the terminals when a nerve action potential arrives down the axon.

Before much was known about the nature of synaptic transmission Hebb (1949) suggested that the formation of long-term memories could occur via the development of new synaptic knobs which would thus increase the area of contact between the axon of one neuron and the cell body of another. As more information became available, he also included the possibility that an existing synapse might become more effective perhaps through an increase in the amount of transmitter in the presynaptic terminal. There is some evidence that large changes in environmental conditions (such as a change from dark to light in previously dark-reared young animals (Rose 1980)) lead to changes in the number of synapses detectable by anatomical methods. However, the majority of present theories of the physical basis of learning and memory propose modification of existing synapses. The types of changes which have been proposed include: altering the width of the synaptic gap (Hyden 1974); altering the effectiveness of the presynaptic action potential in activating transmitter release (Kandel 1978; Mark 1979); altering the affinity or number of postsynaptic receptors for the *neurotransmitter* (Rose 1980). Such modification could lead to either an increase or a decrease in the efficacy of transmission at a synapse. Any particular memory would presumably involve modification of a large number of synapses. The memory would then be coded in terms of which synapses were modified and in each case whether the modification involved depression or activation. This point of view concerning how a memory is coded need, in principle, require only one species of synaptic molecule, which would be either increased or decreased in number or activity. There might be a number of ways in which the modification of this molecule could be brought about, but the hypothesis does not require a vast range of different molecules to code for different memories.

In the late 1950s and 1960s the climate of scientific opinion was different and there was a surprisingly wide acceptance of the idea that memories should be coded molecularly – one memory, one molecule. This led to the search for such memory molecules. The major strategy in this search was to train animals on a task and then kill them and administer homogenates or extracts of their brain (or even of their whole bodies in the case of planaria) to naive animals and see whether the memory was transferred. A number of positive results were reported. However, they were difficult or impossible to replicate, and in the case of the transfer of information between planaria by cannibalism it was found that the animals had not learnt the task but had merely been pseudoconditioned (Jensen 1965). Another problem with the early transfer experiments was that they purported to show transfer of an RNA code from one animal to another via oral ingestion or by injection, and yet the RNA would have been most unlikely to have remained intact or if it had to have been able to gain access to brain cells. For these reasons, the idea of memories being coded individually by RNA has fallen into disrepute.

However, one sort of transfer experiment has been replicated in some laboratories. This is the ability of a peptide (named scotaphobin) apparently formed in the brain of rats during training in a one-trial dark avoidance situation to cause dark avoidance in mice injected with it (Ungar, Desiderio and Parr 1972). While the significance of this finding is not understood it is probably related to the finding that a number of other peptides which are found in the brain and elsewhere, which are whole or are parts of neurohormones (viz. vasopressin, oxytocin, the 4–10 part of ACTH, encephalins, etc.) can have profound and fairly specific effects on behavior including learning and memory (de Wied and Jolles 1982). It is perfectly possible that the synthesis, release and action of these and other peptides is involved in the modulation of synaptic activity underlying learning and memory.

Research into the biochemical basis of learning and memory has involved experiments both on complex animals learning complex tasks and also on simpler "models of learning". In both cases two main approaches have been used: the interventional and the correlational. In the first the strategy is to look for drugs which have a well-defined action at the molecular level and see whether they interfere with learning and memory storage and/or retrieval. In the second approach, animals are taught a task and then a search is made for biochemical/physiological changes in the nervous system correlated with the acquisition of the memory. A major problem in this latter sort of experiment is what controls should be used since even "rested" controls may be learning something and "yoked" controls (which for example receive matched non-contingent shocks every time an experimental animal receives a contingent shock) undoubtedly

learn something (e.g. "whatever I do I can't get away from the shock").

Simple models of learning include single synapses such as the neuromuscular junction of vertebrates. Here it is well known that synaptic efficacy can be increased for periods as long as an hour if the nerve is stimulated tetanically, that is by a rapid repetition of the stimulus, (say 30 shocks/second for 60 seconds) – post-tetanic potentiation. The molecular basis of this process is not fully understood, but it is likely to involve increased effectiveness of an action potential in the presynaptic terminal in opening the calcium channels of the presynaptic membrane. (These channels allow calcium to enter and activate, by an as yet unknown mechanism, the release of transmitters from presynaptic vesicles probably by exocytosis.)

Changes in the presynaptic release mechanism have been postulated to occur in another model of learning, that is long-term facilitation of synaptically-generated field potentials in the mammalian HIPPOCAMPUS (Bliss 1979). The hippocampus is an area of the brain which is widely believed to have a role in learning and memory in man and other mammals. It has been shown that infrequent repetition of tetanic stimulation of inputs such as the perforant path (which runs from the entorhinal cortex to the granule cells of the dentate gyrus) leads to potentiation of the granule cells' responses to single stimuli to the perforant path. This potentiation can last for many weeks and may well be a component of memory systems.

Another example of presynaptic changes underlying long-term alteration of synaptic efficacy has been elegantly demonstrated by Kandel (1978) in the marine snail, *Aplysia*. The gill withdrawal reflex of this animal in response to stimulation of the siphon or the mantle has been shown to habituate or under different circumstances to become sensitized. Such habituation and sensitization while not falling within a classical definition of learning has been used as a simple model of learning (and more recently, associative learning has also been demonstrated in this animal). Long-term habituation, lasting days or even weeks, is produced if four training sessions, of ten stimuli each, are given on consecutive days. The habituation of responses has been postulated to involve a decrease in the number of calcium channels in the axon terminals of the sensory nerve cell in consequence of its own prolonged activity. Such a change could be brought about via presynaptic autoreceptors for the transmitter being released, or via changes in intraterminal ion content or might be more directly related to the presynaptic action potential. Similarly, the contrasting sensitization to noxious stimuli can also last for periods of weeks if the pattern of training is suitably chosen. In this case the mechanism is heterosynaptic, involving facilitation of the synaptic release of transmitter from the sensory nerve terminal by the terminal of an axon originating in the head of the animal, which synapses upon the sensory presynaptic terminal. It appears that the transmitter released from this presynaptically facilitating neuron may be 5-hydroxytryptamine (5HT) and there is some evidence that its effect may be exerted via an increase in the intracellular level of cyclic AMP which somehow increases the effectiveness of the voltage-dependent calcium channels in the sensory neuron terminal. Such an effect means that each nerve impulse in the sensitized sensory neuron would release more transmitter than before sensitization. This work of Kandel and his associates is the nearest that research has got to a molecular and physiological understanding of any learning process. Such work has become increasingly relevant to learning in "higher" animals as it has been extended into the study of associative learning (Kandel and Schwarz 1982).

It is of importance to emphasize that in all those cases where changes in synaptic efficacy have been demonstrated as an integral part of a model learning system, the changes have occurred presynaptically. It is also of considerable interest that the changes observed were qualitatively similar in *Aplysia* for both short-lived (up to a day) and long-lasting (weeks) habituation and sensitization.

These hypotheses which propose that modulation of presynaptic efficacy underlies learning and memory do not in themselves explain the long-lasting nature of the changes. Any theory of the biochemical basis of memory must take into account the remarkable durability of some memories – for example, childhood memories can persist into extreme old age in humans. The synaptic growth theory of course would appear to account for this durability of memory. If, however, memory involves near-permanent activation or inactivation of specific existing synapses, then we need to assume that there are new molecules synthesized as a correlate of learning which are involved in this modification. For example, if we consider the long-term sensitization of the *Aplysia* reflex, activation of a 5 HT-mediated synapse leads to activation of the enzyme adenylate cyclase which leads to an increase in cyclic AMP which acts via activation of another enzyme (probably a protein kinase) to depress activity in a membrane potassium channel. (Potassium current in this channel is required in the repolarization of the presynaptic membrane and hence in closing the calcium channels.) Long-term changes in the effectiveness of transmitter release could involve long-term changes in the properties of the protein kinase or the potassium channel itself. Such long-term effects would probably require a change in the nature of the protein synthesized (perhaps production of different subunits). For this to occur, a signal must pass from the nerve terminals back to the cell body of the sensory neuron. This signal would then (say) switch on, either at the level of transcription of DNA in the nucleus, or at the level of translation in the cytoplasm, the synthesis of the new protein. The new protein would then be transported down the axon to be incorporated into the nerve terminal membrane. (Kandel and Schwarz, 1982, have hypothesized that the signal is cyclic AMP and that the new protein is a high affinity regulatory subunit of a protein kinase which is activated by cyclic AMP and interacts with the potassium channel. This theory would explain the permanence of long-term sensitization in *Aplysia* and proposes that cyclic AMP has the role both of the short-term sensitizing agent and the long-term signal.)

It has often been suggested that memory involves the synthesis of new proteins. As mentioned earlier, these proteins do not need to be specific to any particular memory. There is ample evidence from correlational experiments that both learning of tasks such as a Y-maze discrimination task in rats, and models for learning including imprinting in chicks, are associated with increased incorporation of radioactive precursor into RNA, simple proteins and glycoproteins (Matthies 1979; Rose 1980; Routtenberg 1979). Furthermore, interventional studies, using drugs which inhibit protein synthesis have shown that it is possible to block either long term storage or long term retrieval processes by massively blocking protein synthesis (e.g. Squire and Barondes 1973). Such inhibition does not necessarily interfere with learning, although it can do where the learning procedure involves many trials.

Time-dependent changes in the susceptibility of memories to disruption are well known and have been built into a number of theories of memory formation. Mark (1979) studying one-trial aversion learning in the chick (they learnt not to peck an attractive object painted with nasty-tasting methyl-anthranilate) used ouabain to block the sodium pump (which normally pumps potassium ions into and sodium ions out of cells, and is responsible for keeping intracellular concentration of these ions constant). If the ouabain was given at the time of exposure to the aversive situation it blocked subsequent memory, but ouabain had no effect if administered after learning. In contrast, inhibition of protein synthesis with cycloheximide at the time of learning left memory unaffected for about half an hour, but later caused amnesia. Mark interpreted these findings by suggesting that activity at the "learning" synapses led to a small increase in intracellular sodium which activates the sodium-pump. He suggested that the increased flow of sodium out of the cell is an essential component of the memory formation and is coupled to an increase in the rate of entry of amino acids which would then stimulate protein synthesis (presumably at the cell body). This protein synthesis is necessary for the formation of the long-term memory. While there is no evidence either for or against such a suggestion, the protein concerned could of course be involved in the calcium channel as was proposed for the *Aplysia* synapse.

Another hypothesis which incorporates time-dependent changes in memory is the cholinergic theory of Deutsch (1973, ch. 3, pp. 59–76). There is a wealth of information, including clinical data, that cholinergic systems are involved in memory. Deutsch apparently showed that the susceptibility of memory (for a light-discrimination task) in rats to drugs which interact with cholinergic synapses, varied in a time-dependent way. He suggested that the formation of memory (and/or its retrieval system) involved a gradual increase in the efficacy of the nerve action potential in causing acetylcholine release in the hippocampus. He further proposed that forgetting involved a decrease in this efficacy. While not all Deutsch's findings are readily reproducible the theory has been of value in providing readily testable predictions and in the discussion of clinical findings, including the memory deterioration found in old age and more dramatically in Alzheimer's disease.

In conclusion, it appears likely that the long-term changes underlying learning and memory involve presynaptic transmitter release mechanisms modulated via changes in the amounts or activity of membrane proteins.   JHM

Bibliography

Bliss, T.V.P. 1979: Synaptic plasticity in the hippocampus. *Trends in neuroscience* 2, 42–5.

Deutsch, J.A. 1973: *The physiological basis of memory.* New York and London: Academic Press.

de Wied, D. and Jolles, J. 1982: Neuropeptides derived from pro-opiocortin: behavioral, physiological, and neurochemical effects. *Physiological review* 62, 976–1043.

Farley, J. and Alkon, D. 1985: Cellular mechanisms of learning, memory and information storage. *Annual review of psychology* 36, 419–93.

Hebb, D.O. 1949: *The organization of behavior.* New York: John Wiley and Son; London: Chapman and Hall.

Hyden, H. 1974: A calcium-dependent mechanism for synapse and nerve cell membrane modulation. *Proceedings of the National Academy of Sciences.* New York 71, 2965–8.

Jensen, D.D. 1965: Paramecium, planaria and pseudolearning. *Animal behaviour.* Supplement 1, 9–20.

Kandel, F.R. 1978: *A cell-biological approach to learning.* Grass Lecture Monograph 1. Bethesda, Maryland: Society for Neuroscience.

——— and Schwarz, J.H. 1982: Molecular biology of learning: Modulation of transmitter release. *Science* 218, 433–43.

Mark, R. 1979: Sequential biochemical steps in memory formation: evidence from the use of metabolic inhibitors. In *Brain mechanisms in memory and learning*, ed. M.A.B. Brazier. New York: Raven Press.

Matthies, H. 1979: Biochemical, electrophysiological and morphological correlates of brightness discrimination in rats. In *Brain mechanisms in memory and learning*, ed. M.A.B. Brazier. New York: Raven Press.

Rose, S.P.R. 1980: Neurochemical correlates of early learning in the chick. In *Neurobiological basis of learning and memory*, eds. Y. Tsukada and B.W. Agranoff. New York: John Wiley and Sons.

Routtenberg, A. 1979: Anatomical localization of phosphoprotein and glycoprotein substrates of memory. *Progress in neurobiology* 12, 85–113.

Squire, L.R. and Barondes, B.H. 1973: Memory impairment during prolonged training in mice given inhibitors of cerebral protein synthesis. *Brain research* 56, 215.

Ungar, G., Desiderio, D. and Parr, W. 1972: Scotophobia. *Nature* 238, 198.

memory and learning disorders

Difficulties in acquiring new information and/or in remembering past events. These disorders have many causes and can take a variety of forms. An initial classification can be made by distinguishing disorders of functional, or psychogenic, origin from disorders that result from neurological injury or disease. The former are relevant to psychiatry in that the nature of the disorder in any individual is believed to be related to conflict, repression and persona-lity structure, the latter are relevant to neurology and neuroscience in that the nature of the disorder is related to the organization of memory in the normal brain.

Functional disorders of memory typically involve the loss of personal, autobiographic memory from part of a person's past, sometimes including his or her own identity. While the disorder persists, the ability to establish a record in memory of daily events can be normal, as can be the ability to remember external events (such as news items) that occurred during the affected time period.

This type of amnesia may be the best known, having been the subject of considerable dramatic treatment in films and literature. It is not, however, so common as the disorders of learning and memory that result from brain injury, disease or certain other agents having known effects on the central nervous system. These disorders mostly occur in the context of other neurological problems such as dementia, loss of vigilance, APHASIA, or inattention. To some extent of course memory cannot be considered in isolation from other functions. If attention is poor acquisition of memory will be impaired. If language dysfunction occurs it may be difficult to remember or to recall words with the usual facility. One reason why memory complaints are so common in neurological and psychiatric clinics is that many kinds of neurological disorders affecting higher cortical functions have some impact on memory, even if the disorder does not primarily affect it.

These facts notwithstanding, neurological disorders of memory can also occur as a strikingly circumscribed deficit in which learning and memory are affected out of proportion to any other deficit of higher function. AMNESIA can occur for a variety of reasons, e.g. after temporal lobe surgery, chronic alcohol abuse, head injury, anoxia, encephalitis, tumor or vascular accident. It has been known for almost 100 years that this disorder depends on disruption of normal function in one of two areas of the brain, the medial surface of the temporal lobes and the diencephalic midline of the brain in the region of the THALAMUS and HYPOTHALAMUS.

The amnesic patient who has sustained damage to one of these brain regions can appear normal to casual observation. Such a patient may have normal intellectual capacity, normal ability to hold information in immediate memory (digit span is normal), intact social skills and may retain knowledge acquired earlier in life. The defect lies in acquiring new memories and in recalling some recently acquired ones. Memory for the pre-morbid period is affected in a lawful way, so that recent memories are most, and old memories least, affected. Amnesia often occurs in the absence of confabulation or confusion and with awareness by the patient of his condition. The memory deficit is non-selective, that is it affects all sorts of information regardless of its importance and regardless of the sensory modality (visual, auditory, olfactory) through which information is presented.

This generalization holds when the involvement of the critical areas of the nervous system is bilateral. When involvement is unilateral, however, the amnesic disorder is material-specific, rather than global, i.e. the deficit in learning and memory involves either verbal material, in the case of left-sided injury or disease, or non-verbal material, in the case of right-sided injury or disease (see LATERALIZATION).

In the case of transient memory disorders, which can occur after head trauma, transient ischemic episodes, or electroconvulsive therapy, there are lawful features to the course of recovery. Anterograde amnesia, or loss of new learning capacity, gradually diminishes while retrograde amnesia, or loss of pre-morbid memory, gradually shrinks in a spontaneous fashion. During shrinkage of retrograde amnesia oldest memories tend to recover first and most recent memories last. This order is not absolute, however, and recovery often occurs by the emergence of islands of memory which join up to form a continuous record of past experience. Retrograde amnesia can continue to shrink after anterograde amnesia has subsided,

but all patients are left with some lacuna in memory, consisting of the time during which anterograde amnesia was present together with some retrograde amnesia. The persisting retrograde amnesia is usually brief, perhaps just a few seconds, but it can sometimes cover several weeks or months prior to the onset of amnesia.

Another feature of memory that is spared in amnesia is the phenomenon of priming. Priming refers to a transient biasing of behavior as the result of prior experience, which can occur in the absence of conscious awareness. For example, subjects are shown a list of words (e.g. *MOTEL, DEFINE*) and are then shown word stems (e.g. *MOT, DEF*) and asked to say the first word that comes to mind. Amnesic patients exhibit as strong a tendency as normal subjects to produce the previously presented words despite the fact that they will not recognize these words as familiar when asked to pick them out from a group of words.

Although amnesia can be severely disabling the deficit is narrower than was once thought. Amnesia does not affect all domains of learning and memory. Amnesic patients can exhibit learning of motor skills, as well as perceptual skills such as mirror-reading, and cognitive skills such as puzzle solving. Day-to-day learning of these skills can proceed normally in amnesia, despite the fact that patients may deny having performed such tasks before. The preservation of skills in amnesia has suggested a distinction between what has been termed procedural and declarative knowledge. Procedural learning, which is spared, is thought to result in the modification of tuning of existing schemata, and in knowledge that is implicit, i.e. accessible only by engaging in or applying the procedures in which the knowledge is contained. Declarative learning, which is not spared, refers to all the specific-item information that is the subject of conventional memory experiments such as faces, words and places. Memory for these facts is dependent on the brain regions damaged in amnesia. Thus amnesia involves a specific disorder in establishing and using declarative representations about past events.

161

The existence of severe disorders of learning and memory inevitably raises questions of treatment and rehabilitation. The memory disorder itself cannot be reversed because the disorder derives from damage to brain cells, which cannot be replaced. In general, conditions that help normal memory also help impaired memory. Thus improved concentration, the use of imagery and repetition may all be useful to patients with disorders of learning and memory except in the most severe cases. Patients with left unilateral brain damage can benefit particularly from the use of imagery, because this strategy seems to engage right hemispheric brain systems to some degree and compensates in part for the effects of brain damage. There has also been considerable recent interest in the theory that memory disorders might be responsive to drug treatment. This hope springs from the discovery of the special role of dopaminergic neurons in Parkinson's disease and from the development of Levodopa for its treatment. Might some memory disorders reflect the disproportionate loss of one brain neurotransmitter system (see NEUROTRANSMITTER SYSTEMS) that could respond to treatment with appropriate agonists? Despite a large body of experimental work, especially with drugs that influence the activity of cholinergic neurons (e.g. physostigmine, choline, lecithin) and with hormones (e.g. vasopressin), pharmacological treatments with clinical promise are not yet available.

Meanwhile the study of learning and memory disorders continues. It is of considerable scientific interest, both because of the frequency of memory problems in clinical patients and because analysis of these disorders can reveal so much about the neurological foundations of normal memory.

(See also MEMORY AND LEARNING: PHYSIO-LOGICAL BASES.) LRS

Bibliography

Squire, L.R., 1982: The neuropsychology of human memory. *Annual review of neuroscience* 5, 241–73.

Squire, L.R., and Davis, H.P. 1981: The pharmacology of memory: a neurobiological perspective. *Annual review of pharmacology and toxicology* 21, 323–56.

Whitty, C.W.M. and Zangwill, O.L. eds. 1977: *Amnesia: clinical, psychological and medicolegal aspects*. London: Butterworth.

memory and mood Recent research has demonstrated that mood influences the type of material retrieved from memory. Past, positive personal experiences and certain positive words are more likely to be recalled when a person is in a happy mood than when he or she is in a depressed mood. Conversely, past, negative personal experiences and certain negative words are more likely to be recalled in a depressed mood than in a happy mood. State-dependent learning provides a plausible explanation of these findings. Clinically the effects of mood on memory are important because they may give us insight into the processes that control mood states. Cognitive theories of depression propose that certain negative thoughts produce depressed mood and many of the other symptoms of depression. Studies of the effects of mood on memory suggest that once an individual becomes depressed there is an increase in the frequency of just those cognitions that might maintain depression and a decrease in the frequency of those cognitions which might alleviate it. This reciprocal relationship between depressed mood and cognition could form the basis of a vicious circle that would serve to perpetuate depression. MM

Bibliography

Bower, G.H. 1981: Mood and memory. *American psychologist* 36, 129–48.

Clark, D.M. and Teasdale, J.D. 1985: Constraints in the effects of mood on memory. *Journal of personality and social psychology* 48, 1595–1608.

menarche The onset of menstruation in adolescence. It takes place relatively late in the developmental sequence of puberty, always after the peak growth velocities have been reached. On average, it occurs at 12.9 years, 3.3 years after the onset of the adolescent growth spurt and 1.1 years after peak height velocity is attained (see Frisch and Revelle 1970). Timing is influenced by genetic factors, nutrition, illness and geographical location. There is evidence that the age of menarche has been decreasing during the last century by a few months each decade although the trend may have slowed down (see Tanner 1978). The causation of this secular trend remains controversial but it has been linked with improved nutrition, general health and standards of living. The age of onset has different psychological consequences. Early menarche associated with precocious puberty may generate a negative self-image stemming from feelings of isolation and difference from peers but generally delayed menstruation is not a source of distress. WLIP-J

Bibliography

Frisch, R.E. and Revelle, R. 1970: Height and weight at menarche and a hypothesis of critical body weights and adolescent events. *Science* 169, 397.

Tanner, J.M. 1978: *Foetus into man*. London: Open Books; Cambridge, Mass.: Harvard University Press.

menopause The permanent cessation of menstruation occurring during the middle period of life. It is associated with the end of ovulation and with atrophy of the female reproductive organs. It is not known to occur in other mammals, and its evolutionary origin is probably associated with the prolonged period of infant care in humans.

Symptoms specific to the menopausal period include vasomotor, genital and psychological changes. Some normal aspects of ageing (e.g. dryness of the skin, loss of proteins from the bones, leading to brittleness, or osteoporosis) are exaggerated by aspects of the postmenopausal bodily state, such as lack of estrogen.

The most common and well known vasomotor symptom is the hot flush, produced by impairment of the neural mechanism controlling the blood vessels, and this may be further exaggerated by emotional factors. The principal symptoms affecting urinary and sexual functioning are dryness of the vagina and the urethra. Psychological symptoms such as irritability, depression, insomnia and feelings of nervousness, as well as general somatic symptoms such as headaches and giddiness, are also reported.

While the main physical changes (hot flushes, genital symptoms), probably result from declining estrogen levels, the cause of the psychological changes is controversial. One view is that they derive directly from a change in hormone balance, specifically from the decline in estrogen levels. Another is that they result from the physical consequences of hormonal changes, e.g. sweating or incontinence may lead to insomnia, and hence to tiredness and irritability, which produces further interpersonal conflicts and stresses, and eventually depression. A third view is that any symptoms of a decline in general health, or signs of depression or emotional problems occurring around the time of menopause will be attributed (generally incorrectly) to it. Major stresses, mostly involving the death of close friends and relatives, or children leaving home, often coincide with the time of the menopause. These stresses could be responsible for many of the general health and psychological symptoms. JA

Bibliography

Weideger, Paula 1975: *Menstruation and menopause*. New York: Knopf; London: Women's Press (*Female cycles*) 1978.

Bart, P.B. 1971: Depression in middle-aged women. In *Women in sexist society*, eds. V. Cornick and B.K. Moran. New York: Basic Books.

mental handicap Can be defined as 'that condition where intellectual deficit is associated with social, physical or psychiatric handicap, and requires special services or treatment' (Corbett 1977). (Mental handicap is also sometimes used to describe conditions where intellectual deficit appears to be present because of social inadequacy resulting from chronic psychiatric disorder. This has led to much confusion, and the term is not used in this sense here.)

Intellectual deficit is assessed by standardized tests of intelligence, such us the Wechsler Adult Intelligence Scale (WAIS). An intelligence quotient lower than two standard deviations below the mean (i.e. an IQ of less than 70) is usually taken as the cut off point for legal and administrative purposes. There are two main categories of mental handicap, mild (IQ 50–70) and severe (IQ below 50). Most severe mental handicap is associated with organic brain disease.

A number of epidemiological surveys in various countries have reported the incidence of mild mental handicap to be 20–30 per 1,000 population, and the incidence of severe mental handicap between 3 and 4 per 1,000 population aged 15–19. Variations in findings are related to differences in the concepts of mental handicap used – some studies base their findings on measures of IQ alone; others use a combination of IQ and social criteria. There is a strong association between mild mental handicap and low socioeconomic status: poor housing, overcrowding, poverty, poor nutrition, inadequate stimulation and education.

The commonest genetic cause of mental retardation is DOWN'S SYNDROME (mongolism) – a chromosome abnormality accounting for 25 per cent of severely retarded hospitalized patients. Other genetic conditions include the inherited metabolic disorders (e.g. phenylketonuria); tuberose sclerosis; neural tube defects. Clinically, these disorders are recognized by the presence of various physical abnormalities with intellectual deficit. Some conditions (e.g. the CHROMOSOME ABNORMALITIES) can be diagnosed antenatally if amniocentesis is undertaken. Although genetic defects cannot be corrected, there are some genetic conditions where treatment is possible to prevent further intellectual impairment (e.g. a special diet for phenylketonuria; surgical treatment of hydrocephalus associated with spina bifida). In mild mental handicap, it is believed that polygenic inheritance plays an important part, in association with the adverse social circumstances already described. Incidentally, there is some evidence that children of mentally handicapped parents tend to have higher IQs than their parents ("regression to the mean"). (See GENETICS, EVOLUTION AND BEHAVIOR.)

The distribution of intelligence in the population means that a certain proportion of mentally handicapped people are to be expected as a result of normal variation. During pregnancy, the growth and development of the fetus's brain and nervous system can be harmed in a variety of ways: e.g. by maternal infections such as rubella (german measles); high blood pressure or toxemia which affects placental function; antenatal hemorrhage; rhesus incompatibility; drugs such as thalidomide; poisons such as coal gas; alcohol and smoking. During birth, damage may occur from birth trauma, lack of oxygen or low blood pressure. In the immediate postnatal period, the damaging factors include neonatal seizures, infection, hypoglycemia (low blood sugar), hypothermia, severe jaundice, intraventricular hemorrhage, and the other complications of prematurity, such as the respiratory distress syndrome. Trauma to the skull and underlying brain may be caused accidentally during this period, or as a result of non accidental injury (child abuse). Brain infections (meningitis, encephalitis); prolonged hypoxia due to respiratory or cardiac arrest, poisoning by carbon monoxide or lead may all cause mental handicap in a previously normal child. Infantile spasms, a form of epilepsy which develops during the first year of life, may also be accompanied by mental handicap.

Children with severe mental handicap present early in childhood with delay in attaining their developmental milestones, together with the signs of any accompanying physical disorder (e.g. cerebral palsy). Most of these children will be recognized during their first year of life. Some, such as those with Down's syndrome, will be recognized at birth, and their parents given a prediction of the degree of mental handicap to be expected.

Mild mental handicap may go unnoticed

until the child starts school, or even later if little attention is paid to educational achievement. Learning problems or behavior disturbance in the school setting will then alert the teacher to the need for psychometric assessment by a psychologist. The finding of low scores on all subtests of intelligence will confirm intellectual deficit and the child will then be placed in an appropriate educational environment, such as a special unit or school. Occasionally, previously unrecognized mentally handicapped adults present with behavior disturbance when faced with a life stress such as the death of their parents, or a change in management of the firm where they have been happily carrying out a simple job for years.

In addition to general intellectual deficit a full assessment of individual difficulties may then reveal handicap in any (or all) of the following areas: Physical: defects of motor coordination and movement, hearing, vision or speech; EPILEPSY occurs in 30 per cent of severely retarded children. Social: problems may range from social incompetence (inability to ask for and follow directions, handle money, use a telephone, etc.) to antisocial behavior (masturbating or urinating in public, taking other people's possessions, making overt sexual advances in public). Psychiatric: children and adults with intellectual deficit have an increased risk of psychiatric disorder. This is accounted for by many factors, including brain malfunction, temperament, immaturity, the effects of social rejection, and institutional care. The types of psychiatric disorder seen are the same as those occurring in people of normal intelligence; i.e. conduct and emotional disorders in children; SCHIZOPHRENIA, AFFECTIVE DISORDERS, NEUROSES and PERSONALITY DISORDERS in adults. The following are more commonly associated with mental handicap: infantile AUTISM, HYPERKINETIC STATES, sterotyped repetitive movements and pica.

Prevention and treatment. It is now possible to prevent mental handicap in a number of ways such as: GENETIC COUNSELING for prospective parents in cases where there is a high risk of the occurrence of an abnormal fetus; amniocentesis in pregnancy, detecting fetuses with genetic abnormalities such as Down's syndrome at a stage when termination of pregnancy can be considered; ultrasonic scanning in pregnancy to detect abnormalities such as spina bifida; careful antenatal and obstetric care; good neonatal care of the newborn baby, reducing brain damage caused by treatable conditions such as hypoglycemia, phenylketonuria and congenital hypothyroidism; rubella immunization of all schoolgirls, to prevent congenital rubella; enriching the child's environment in deprived areas, as was done in the Milwaukee early intervention program. Additional social and psychiatric handicaps may be preventable by early recognition of mental handicap through developmental screening. The family can then be supported from an early stage, and helped to develop the child's skills and counter any behavior problems before they become established. Later, appropriate school and occupational placement; training in social skills; improving the quality of institutional care; and changing society's attitude toward the mentally handicapped from rejection to acceptance may all contribute to the prevention of other difficulties.

A number of research studies have now shown that mentally handicapped adults and children in long-stay hospitals have fewer skills, more disturbed behavior and a lower level of functioning than those living at home or in small "family" units. This has led to a reappraisal of the role of hospitals in the care of the mentally handicapped. There is growing acceptance of the view that this should be limited to the short-term treatment of problems such as disturbed behavior, seizure control or psychiatric illness, except for the most severely mentally and physically handicapped who need continuous nursing care. Most others can be cared for much more appropriately in the community, in small group homes, foster homes, hostels, etc. Special secure facilities may be necessary for adolescents and adults whose aggressive or antisocial behavior cannot be contained in any other setting.

The mentally handicapped living in the

community need education, occupation, recreation and opportunities to take part in as many everyday activities as possible. Their families need support – financial, practical and emotional – and opportunities for relief from the stresses of coping with a handicapped child or adult for shorter or longer periods. Children and their families can often attend a pediatric department or assessment center, which provides a range of assessment and treatment facilities. In some areas preschool counselors or specially trained health workers visit at home to provide stimulation for the child and guidance for the parents. Attendance at the nursery class of a special school can start when the child is two and continue to sixteen, or even longer in some cases. Short-term care is usually provided through foster parents or children's homes. Resources for adults are often scarce. They should include different types of living accommodation to meet their varying levels of dependency, provide short and long-term care, and a range of occupational activities, e.g. Adult Training Centers, sheltered workshops or sheltered employment. Community based multi-disciplinary teams of professionals (psychologists, nurses, social workers, etc.) are available in many areas to offer expert help with specific problems and to support families. Voluntary organizations also form an important part of the network of community support and often provide valuable resources through fund raising activities.

The life expectancy for the mentally handicapped is now greater than ever before, and many are reaching their sixties and seventies. Where there is an underlying physical condition the severity of this, and its treatability, will affect life expectancy. The prognosis for associated behavioral and psychiatric difficulties depends on a number of factors including the family background, placement in an institutional environment, and the availability of occupation and training facilities.

GCF

Bibliography

Caldwell, B.M., Bradley, R.H. and Elardo, R. 1975: Early intervention. In *Mental retardation and developmental disabilities*, vol. 7, ed. E.J. Wortis. New York: Brunner Mazel.

Corbett, J. 1977. Mental handicap — psychiatric aspects. In *Child psychiatry, modern approaches*, ed. M. Rutter. Oxford: Blackwell Scientific Publications; Philadelphia: Lippincott.

Tizard, J. 1960: Residential core of mentally handicapped children. *British medical journal* 1041–46.

mid-life crisis A term denoting any of several types of behavior in the middle years, from the private awareness of the finitude of the life span to the life style rearrangements of career change or divorce and remarriage. The term was introduced to describe phenomena which arise as a consequence of demographic changes – increased longevity and the quickening of the life cycle of the family, producing a normative expectation of an extended post-parental period. Increased scientific attention to the middle years has shown that this middle phase of life is not a plateau but a time of changes, and has given rise to the popular term "mid-life crisis". The awareness of biological decline, the irrevocability of decisions made earlier in the life cycle, possible stagnation in marriage and career, declining opportunities with advancing age: in brief, intrinsic and extrinsic causes, maturational, social and existential, contribute to change as well as to the sense of crisis in middle life.   ND

Bibliography

Norman, William H. and Scaramella, Thomas J. eds. 1980: *Mid-life: developmental and clinical issues*. New York: Brunner/Mazel.

mirror-phase A moment in infant development postulated by LACAN (1936), based on infant observation, animal ethology and psychoanalysis of adults. Between six and eighteen months, infants exhibit a characteristic fascination with their image in a mirror – or similar surface such as the mother's eyes – a moment of watchful jubilation, often punctuated by an inquiring look to an accompanying adult. Lacan sees in this moment the foundation of the ego; the mirror-image is taken as the ideal ego, representing a self-sufficient unity in contrast with the child's sense of its own powerlessness and incoordination; it finds itself in this first "other", its own image. In seizing on its image as its self, this initial alienating identification is typical of the ego's primary function: misunderstanding, misrecognition and, more broadly, fantasy. Language (the Symbolic) allows the child to find a way out of the aggressive dyadic mirror-relation to the other (Imaginary), leaving as a residue the Real (that which cannot be symbolized). JF

Bibliography

Lacan, J. 1936, 1977: The mirror stage as formative of the function of the I as revealed in psychoanalytic experience. In *Écrits: a selection.* Trans. A. Sheridan. London: Tavistock; New York: Norton.

MMPI, the The Minnesota Multiphasic Personality Inventory is an objective personality inventory developed as an aid in assessing clinical problems. It is the most widely researched personality measure with substantial validity studies supporting its use. The information available on its scales has encouraged the broad use of automated (computer based) interpretation. the MMPI clinical scales were devised according to a strategy of empirical scale construction. Items which validly discriminated the clinical group from normals were included in the scale. Scales were devised to assess hypochondria, depression, hysteria, psychopathic deviation, psychasthenia (obsessive-compulsive behavior), schizophrenia, and mania. In addition, there are several validity scales to alert the clinician to deviant response attitudes such as lying (L Scale), faking (F Scale) and general defensiveness (K Scale).   JNB

models: role in theories Analogical (and idealized) representations of things, processes, etc., and more recently of formal systems. A specialized use for the term has appeared in psychology, as a synonym for "theory". In most scientific contexts a model is distinguished from a theory, in that a theory is taken to be a discourse about a model.

In engineering and the physical sciences models play a very large part both in the design of experiments and in the construction of theories. The uses of models can best be understood through the distinctions between a model, its subject and its source. A doll is both a model *of* a human infant (subject) and modeled *on* a human infant (source). Source and subject are identical. Such models are homeomorphs. Natural selection is modeled *on* domestic selection but it is a model *of* the unobservable real process of speciation. Source and subject are different. These are paramorphs.

Homeomorphic models are used to bring out features of systems we already know about. For example, a hydraulic network can be used as a model of an electric circuit, suggesting certain otherwise unnoticed features of the circuit. Models are also used creatively when the behavior is unobservable. Paramorphic models are used to represent the unknown productive mechanisms. Such models must be functionally equivalent to the unobservable productive process, that is the imagined model must behave like the real process. For example, a machine computational process which produces results like those produced by people who are thinking about a particular type of problem may be used as a paramorphic model of the unknown cognitive process by which the real thinker solves a problem. The success of a paramorphic model in modeling the behavior of the real system it represents is not enough to guarantee that it is a true representation of that system, but it will be seen as a probable representation if it continues successfully to simulate the thinker's cognitive processes and has no equally plausible rival.

If explanations were merely formal discourses, deductively related to that which they purported to explain, there would be indefinite numbers of explanations for any given set of phenomena. The use of a paramorphic model not only allows for a plausible interpretation of the theoretical terms in a favored formal theory, but serves to eliminate all those others which are incompatible with it. There is no known formal criterion which will serve the same purpose. Models, then, are indispensable for developing theoretical explanations to the point at which their plausibility as representations of the real processes productive of the phenomena of interest can be tested.

Models are analogues of whatever they represent. The principles by which models are used in scientific reasoning are part of the "logic of analogy". An analogue has three comparative relations with its subject, a positive analogy (likenesses), a negative analogy (differences), and a neutral analogy (those properties of the model and its subject which have not been tested for likeness or difference one with another). The assessment of the plausibility of a model can be made fairly rigorous in terms of the balance between positive, negative and neutral analogies. For instance, if there are many likenesses, few differences and not much unexplored, a model is likely to be found acceptable by its users as a true representation of the process it simulates.

Discussion of the use of models in the sciences has centered on two issues: (1) Under what conditions are models to be taken as good guides to hypotheses about unobserved processes and structures? Commentators who have concentrated only on examples of homeomorphic or heuristic models have tended to argue that models are dispensable and should be treated as part of the psychology of scientific thinking. Those who have studied the creative uses of paramorphic models have tended to argue that novel representations of previously unknown processes could not have been achieved without the use of a model. (2) A corresponding argument has developed around the issue of the role of metaphor and simile in scientific discourse. The two issues are closely related since a system of metaphors (say the role-rule theory in social psychology) may be introduced into a scientific discourse on the basis of a model-source (say "man as actor"). On the basis of the actor analogy the unobservable determinants of regularities in behavior are likened to rules and conventions, and the process of the regulation of behavior to rule-following.   RHa

Bibliography

Black, M. 1962: *Models and metaphors*. Ithaca, N.Y.: Cornell University Press.

Bunge, M. 1973: *Model, matter and method*. Dordrecht: Reidel.

Collins, L. ed. 1976: *The use of models in the social sciences*. London: Tavistock.

Harré, R. 1972: *The principles of scientific thinking*. London: Macmillan; Chicago: Chicago University Press (1973).

Hesse, M.B. 1963: *Models and analogies in science*. London and New York: Sheed and Ward.

morbid jealousy The essential feature of morbid jealousy (pathological jealousy, Othello syndrome) is a delusion that the marital partner is unfaithful. The belief is held on inadequate grounds and is unaffected by argument. Characteristic behavior includes intense seeking for evidence of infidelity, with repeated cross questioning of the partner and allegations which may lead to violent quarrels. The frequency of the condition is unknown but it is not uncommon in psychiatric practice and is a major cause of murder and other violence. Morbid jealousy is associated with many types of psychiatric disorder, most commonly SCHIZOPHRENIA, DEPRESSION, ALCOHOLISM and PERSONALITY DISORDER. There is a considerable risk of violence and once this has occurred there is a high risk of repetition.   RAM

Bibliography

Sheperd, M. 1961: Morbid jealousy: some clinical and social aspects of a psychiatric symptom. *Journal of mental science* 107, 687–704.

N

narcotics A name given to the natural or synthetic derivatives of opium which have the ability to produce both sleep and analgesia (Julien 1978). Narcotic opiates can be classified as those which occur naturally in the exudate of the opium poppy (e.g. morphine), semisynthetic derivatives (e.g. heroin) and synthetic opiates (e.g. methadone). The primary medical uses of opiates in general are in the treatment of persistent coughing, in diarrhea and for relief of moderate to severe pain. The more potent opiates such as heroin or morphine can also produce euphoria, or a sense of well-being, which contributes significantly to their recreational abuse. Continued use of virtually all the opiates can lead to tolerance and physical dependence. Their mechanisms of action are complex and not fully understood, but appear to be mediated via interactions with endogenous opiate receptors (see ENCEPHALINS/ ENDORPHINS).   GPH

Bibliography

Julien, R.M. 1978: *A primer of drug action.* 2nd edn. San Francisco: Freeman.

neo-Freudian theory A term used of the approach of psychoanalytic theorists who have rejected, added to, or modified significant portions of FREUD's original theory. The term is used by different writers with varying levels of specificity. In its most general sense it can apply to a wide range of psychoanalytically-orientated psychologists whose theories diverge from Freud's in greater or lesser degrees: in this sense for example, JUNG, Erikson, Rank and object relations theorists (see KLEIN) could all be considered neo-Freudians, even though Erikson accepts the basic premises of Freudian analysis while Jung rejects many of them. Usually, however, the term

neo-Freudian is reserved for a smaller group of psychoanalysts whose theories share two core features: (1) they reject Freud's "libido theory", his view that the primary motivators in personality are innate biological instincts of sexuality and aggression which are specific to childhood; and (2) they correspondingly emphasize the importance of social needs, the influence of cultural and interpersonal factors and the role of the self in personality development.

The four theorists most frequently described as neo-Freudians in this more restrictive sense are Alfred Adler, Karen Horney, Erich Fromm and Harry Stack Sullivan. The following brief discussion first describes the major contributions of these thinkers and then summarizes what their theories have in common.

Alfred Adler was born in Vienna in 1870. He was a member of the original small group of psychoanalysts which met at Freud's house to discuss analytic theory, and was the first president of the Vienna branch of the Psychoanalytic Society. He came to reject some basic tenets of Freud's theory, however, including the notion that sexual trauma is the basis for neurosis, and resigned from the society in 1911 to form his own school which he named Individual Psychology. Adler sees the person as a united whole, indivisible, responsible for his actions, free and striving towards conscious goals. The major tenets of his theory are contained in six key concepts:
(1) *fictional finalism*, the notion that people are motivated not primarily by past events, but by their images and expectations for future possibilities;
(2) *striving for superiority*, the individual's innate tendency to develop his capacities to the full and to strive for perfection;
(3) *inferiority feelings*, which Adler sees as the normal response to the realization of

being less than perfect and which motivate all efforts towards self-actualization;

(4) *social interest*, the innate tendency to be interested in other people and in the social group, manifested in cooperation, empathy, altruism and, ultimately, the desire for a perfect society;

(5) *style of life*, the different unique forms in which individuals strive for perfection; and

(6) the *creative self*, the active, constructive center of personality which interprets experience and chooses a response to it.

Karen Horney was born in Germany in 1885. She was associated with the Berlin Psychoanalytic Institute from 1918 to 1932, then emigrated to the USA where she founded an association and a training institute. Horney saw herself as remaining within the Freudian tradition, though she tried to correct what she saw as the limitations of Freud's approach: his biological and mechanistic orientation. She accepted Freud's notions of psychic determinism, unconscious motivation and the importance of irrational emotional experience. The root of neurosis for Horney is the childhood experience of basic anxiety and the strategies adopted in response to it. The helpless, totally dependent child encountering rejection, inconsistency or harsh treatment from its parents, feels that its safety and fundamental security are threatened. The child can adopt various strategies to cope with this, and these can become permanent features of personality and eventually take on the status of needs in their own right. Horney catalogues ten of these neurotic needs; they all mirror needs of normal people, but in an unrealistic, exaggerated and insatiable form: for example, the need for perfection, for total love, for complete control. Horney does not believe that the experience of basic anxiety is an inevitable part of development; it can be avoided if the child is treated with love, respect and consistency.

Like Horney, Erich Fromm was born in Germany and emigrated to the United States in the early 1930s. Fromm's work was influenced by the writings of Karl Marx and by existentialism as well as by psychoanalytic theory. He calls himself a "dialectical humanist". The central notion in Fromm's theory is his description of the human condition. Humans, he says, are animals and thus part of nature; however, because of their distinctively human nature they are also more than an animal and experience a separation between themselves and the natural world and between themselves and other people. This separateness from the natural order gives human beings the freedom to choose their lives; this freedom gives human life its meaning and potential, but it also gives rise to anxiety. As a result, people often try to relinquish their freedom through conformity or submission to authorities. Like Freud and Adler, Fromm believes that there is a species-specific, innate human nature which is independent of culture. However he has also emphasized the role that social context plays in determining the way in which the individual deals with basic human needs. Different societies and different groups within society create particular types of "character". Moreover Fromm judges societies on the basis of how well they meet the basic human needs of their members; he argues that no present society makes an adequate job of this task, and calls the form of society that he believes would do so "Humanistic Communitarian Socialism".

More than any of the other neo-Freudians, Harry Stack Sullivan moved away from Freudian theory and articulated a model of personality that is thoroughly social and interpersonal. In fact Sullivan claims that the notion of personality, conceived in terms of the single individual, is hypothetical, an illusion. Personality, he argues, consists in the relatively enduring patterns of interpersonal relations which are manifested in our lives – our relations both with real others and with the imagined others which make up the content of our thoughts, feelings and fantasies. He was strongly influenced by social psychology and anthropology, particularly by George Herbert Mead and other theorists at the Chicago School of Sociology. He was born in 1892 in New York and trained as an analyst. Sullivan described six stages in personality development, each of which represents a new interpersonal constellation. In *infancy* the child relates to the mother via its oral activity towards the nipple and develops notions of the good and bad other, and the correct and the wrong other. In *childhood* with the beginning of language, the child begins to relate to playmates and to form more cognitive representations of others. In the *juvenile* period (first school) the child learns to relate to the peer group and to authorities outside the home. In *pre-adolescence* "chum" relations with same sex peers are central for learning cooperation, mutuality, reciprocity and intimacy. The development of patterns of heterosexual relationships become the focus in *early adolescence*, as puberty brings the beginning of the lust dynamism and this becomes differentiated from companionship and intimacy. Finally, in *late adolescence*, a long period of education in varying social roles and relations brings about the transition to the complexity of adult social living and citizenship.

All four theorists share several core orientations which characterize the neo-Freudian approach. First, they all take a more positive and optimistic view of human nature than does classical psychoanalysis; they stress the striving for self-actualization, for active adaptation to the environment and for social relatedness and harmony, in contrast to Freud's emphasis on antisocial impulses of sexuality and aggression. Where Freud sees the individual as in inevitable conflict with the society which demands restriction of his impulsive acts, the neo-Freudians propose a more harmonious relationship between the individual and society. They see social life as a fulfilment of basic human nature, not a repression of it. In addition, these writers pay as much attention to the role of conscious conflicts and experiences in adolescence and adulthood as to unconscious conflicts in early childhood. Finally, they stress the effects of the social milieu in determining personality.   SB

Bibliography

Adler, A. 1927: *The practice and theory of individual psychology*. New York: Harcourt, Brace and World.

Ansbacher, H.L. and R.R. eds. 1956: *The individual-psychology of Alfred Adler*. New York: Basic Books.

Fromm, Erich 1941: *Escape from freedom*. New York: Rinehart.
—— 1947: *Man for himself*. New York: Rinehart.
—— 1955: *The sane society*. New York: Rinehart.

Hall, Calvin S. and Gardner, Lindzey 1978: *Theories of personality*, 3rd ed. New York and Chichester: John Wiley.

Horney, Karen 1942: *Self-analysis*. New York: Norton.
—— 1950: *Neurosis and human growth*. New York: Norton.

Munroe, Ruth L. 1955: *Schools of psychoanalytic thought*. New York: Dryden Press.

Sullivan, H.S. 1953: *The interpersonal theory of psychiatry*. New York: Norton.

neural control of higher mental processes Certain neural systems in the brain are specialized to regulate higher mental functions. The study of these systems in relation to the behavior they control is called neuropsychology. Although any organism with a central nervous system may be the object of neuropsychological inquiry, most of what we know derives from the study of brain damaged and normal humans. Four methods are applicable: (1) the identification of the particular behavioral changes that occur when the brain is damaged; (2) the relation of each behavioral change to a particular site of damage using neurological evidence of the location and extent of the lesion; (3) the description of behavior in normal people that reflects the way in which their brains are organized; and (4) the monitoring of patterns of activity in the brain while people are engaged in particular tasks.

When a restricted area of brain is damaged by naturally occurring disease (stroke, brain tumors, trauma etc.), is surgically removed or is temporarily anesthetized, certain skills become unavailable. The patient may lose the ability to understand speech or speak intelligibly (receptive and expressive APHASIA respectively), to recognize objects or patterns in sight, hearing or touch (agnosia), to perform skilled actions (apraxia), to recognize and use spatial relationships (visuospatial disorientation), or to remember events (AMNESIA). But the way in which the patient behaves does not simply reflect the loss of an ability because other systems readjust in order to minimize the impact of the deficit on adaptive living. Nor are the effects of brain damage always negative. Foci of irritable nerve cell discharge may be established, resulting in paroxysms involving behavioral fragments out of context, such as paroxysmal speech or arrest of speech, laughing or crying. Or the lesion may disinhibit a lower level system, causing behavioral exaggerations such as hallucinations and perceptual distortions. Still other systems work in terms of shifting balance between opponent processes. Damage may skew such a balance so that one process is permanently in the ascendant, such as turning right versus turning left, concluding a task prematurely versus unduly persevering in it, or attending over a wide or within a narrow focus. In this way, the behavioral repertoire falls apart, revealing its components (Lashley 1931).

Relating these components to different sections of brain (localization of function) is not straightforward either, as the damaged area may be central to the lost activity, or may merely incorporate an input or output communication channel. It is therefore necessary to let multiple sources of evidence converge in support of a particular localization before accepting it as definitive. One source of corroboration is obtained through monitoring the brain by objective methods capable of determining which of its parts are active when people think or act in certain ways. The active areas generate identifiable electrical phenomena detectable on the ELECTROENCEPHALOGRAM, measurable increases in regional cerebral blood supply, and metabolic rate increase which is demonstrable by positron emission tomography. These methods can be applied both to brain damaged and to normal people.

Normal people have been found to behave in ways that reveal the effects of brain organization. Because in most people language is represented on the left side of the brain and because each half brain is responsive to the opposite side of space, they exhibit perceptual asymmetry in that they are quicker and more accurate in identifying verbal messages, by ear and by eye from the right rather than from the left. Converse asymmetry is found for certain tasks involving relationships in space, which tap the specialization of the right half brain. Also, when one half brain is active, while performing its specialized function, bodily movements towards the opposite side of space may occur. While thinking in words or speaking, people may look to the right (Kinsbourne 1972) or gesture with the right hand (Kimura 1973). Finally, it is possibly to determine the interconnection in the brain of the areas subserving two activities by seeing how well people can do both at the same time (Kinsbourne and Hicks 1978). For example people whose speech is left sided in the brain are better able to perform unrelated finger movements of the left hand than of the right hand while speaking: the control areas for speech and right finger movement share the same (left hemispheric) space and interfere with each other. This "cross talk" interference occurs because, although different parts of the brain are differently specialized, they are all, to a varying degree, interconnected within the neural network. It therefore becomes possible to construct two separate but parallel maps of the brain, one derived from specific lesion effects, and another charting a brain behavioral space based on task interactions in normal people.

Findings from these sources support certain general conclusions. Input analysis is represented in a posterior location in the CEREBRAL CORTEX relative to the first cortical relays of information flow in the various sensory modalities. Output functions are represented in an anterior location relative to the cortical final common pathways for movement control. In almost all right-handers, language is left-lateralized with speech reception posterior to speech expression. Other left-lateralized functions include the recognition and production of items in proper sequence, the identification of objects, letters and colors, and the programming of individual acts in proper sequence. Overall, the specialized contribution of the left hemisphere is reasonably well summarized as the extracting of item information from incoming messages, and the programming of the specifics of response. The right hemisphere establishes the context within which those specifics are extracted and encoded. It provides a spatial framework into which sequentially processed items can be entered, to establish and conserve their relationship to each other in space. Its role in temporal organization is less well established, but it does appear to be involved in perception of melody. Syndromes of deficit that result from right hemisphere damage include inability to orient in space (visuospatial agnosia), to read maps (topographical aphasia) and to recognize faces (topographical apraxia).

A skill that is embarrassed by lesions on either side is the ability to copy designs, but the type of "constructional apraxia" differs depending on the side of lesion. Left damage results in roughly adequate but simplified renderings, whereas right damage results in a copy in which the individual components are identifiable, but their relationships in space are grotesquely distorted. This is a particularly clear demonstration of the way in which the specialized functions of each hemisphere make simultaneous complementary contributions to the overall mental effort.

Also, each hemisphere controls the ability to shift attention toward the opposite side; hemisphere damage may result in unilateral "neglect" of the opposite side of the person and of space. When the hemispheres are disconnected (by surgical section of the interconnecting corpus callosum) each hemisphere remains uninformed of specific information made available only to the other side (Sperry 1966). However, the person remains able to orient himself within ambient space (Trevarthen 1974). It appears that the "disconnection syndrome" applies only to those functions which are unilaterally represented in the brain. The attempts that

have been made to attribute to each hemisphere a separate consciousness, or even merely a distinct cognitive style, (Bogen 1969) are misconceived. In "split-brain" man higher mental function is controlled by one hemisphere at a time, control shifting from hemisphere to hemisphere depending on the nature of the task.

When one hemisphere is surgically removed (by "hemispherectomy") the other over time exhibits compensatory ability (particularly, but not only, when the operation is performed early in life, when the neural network remains relatively "plastic"). Virtually all the specialized functions of each hemisphere are also potentially represented in the other, and this compensatory potential is present to some degree at any age. Paradoxically, many unilateral hemisphere syndromes appear only in minor form when much or all of the other hemisphere is lost. This suggests that in normal functioning, each hemisphere inhibits tendencies on the other side of the brain with similar cognitive potential. Extensive damage releases such territories from inhibition, whereupon they assume a compensatory role.

The variation of brain organizations between individuals and between different gender groups is controversial, but it is clear that in non-right-handers (about 11 per cent of the general population) LATERALIZATION may deviate from that outlined above (Milner 1974). Specifically, there may be a high degree of bilateral representation of customarily lateralized processes, or there may be a mirror reversal, with language right-lateralized and spatial relationships represented on the left. It appears, however, that these deviations from the dextral carry no penalty in efficiency of function. Non-right-handers in the general population are no less intelligent in any respect than right-handers (Hardyck, Petrinovich, and Goldman 1976).

Neuropsychological study has shown that different brain mechanisms communicate with each other to excite or inhibit. Our present model of brain control of behavior, therefore, includes communication channels and positive and negative

FEEDBACK mechanisms. The efforts of behavioral scientists to generate models of the brain and to design simulations of aspects of human behavior, are relevant to how the brain actually works only if they too incorporate communication channels and feedback loops in their design. Neuropsychological findings are useful in testing the validity of psychological inferences. Behavior that is dissociable by focal brain damage cannot be modeled as unitary, and behavior that is regularly comparably implicated by focal damage should be incorporated within the same hypothetical system. This use of neuropsychological information is a recent, but constructive, development in behavioral science.   MK

Bibliography

Bogen, J.E. 1969: The other side of the brain 2. An appositional mind. *Bulletin Los Angeles neurological society* 34, 135–62.

Hardyck, C., Petrinovich, L.F. and Goldman, Roy D. 1976: Left-handedness and cognitive deficit. *Cortex* 12, 266–79.

Kimura, D. 1971: Manual activity during speaking 1. Right Handers. *Neuropsychologia* 11, 45–50.

Kinsbourne, M. 1972: Eye and head turning indicate cerebral lateralization. *Science* 176, 539–41.

—— and Hicks, R.E. 1978: Functional cerebral space: a model for overflow, transfer and interference effects in human performance. In *Attention and performance 7*, ed. J. Requin. Hillsdale, N.J.: Lawrence Erlbaum.

Lashley, K.S. 1931: Mass action in cerebral function. *Science* 73, 245–54.

Marshall, J.F. 1984: Brain function: neural adaptations and recovery from injury. *Annual review of psychology* 35, 277–308.

Milner, B. 1974. Hemispheric specialisation: scope and limits. In *The neurosciences*, eds. F.O. Schmitt and F.G. Worden, Third study program. Cambridge, Mass.: MIT Press.

Sperry, R.W. 1966: Brain bisection and consciousness. In *Brain and conscious experience*, ed. J.C. Eccles. New York: Springer.

Trevarthen, C. 1974: Functional relations of disconnected hemispheres in the brain stem and with each other: Monkey and man. In *Hemispheric disconnection and cerebral function*, eds. M. Kinsbourne and W.L. Smith. Springfield. Ill.: Thomas.

neurochemistry and behavior The study of neurochemistry in relation to behavior is an attempt to understand the chemical processes occurring in the brain that underlie the expression of behavior. Research in this area has focused on two rather distinct problems: the chemical mechanisms of learning and the molecular nature of memory; and a "chemical coding" of behavior which occurs because specific aspects of behavior are frequently associated with the use of specific brain pathways which use specific chemical NEUROTRANSMITTERS.

Much of the chemistry of the brain cells is not distinct from that of other cells in the body. However, the human brain uses 20–25 per cent of the oxygen consumed by the body in the resting state, and more than half the energy produced is used to maintain the electrical activity of the brain. For this reason the use of specific brain pathways is associated with local changes in energy consumption. Measurement of changes in CEREBRAL BLOOD FLOW and glucose uptake (Sokoloff 1977) can be used to indicate changes in electrical activity, and hence the involvement of particular brain structures or pathways with particular behavior.

The chemicals most often implicated in memory are RNA and proteins. Inhibitors of protein synthesis impair the formation of long-term memory and, on the basis of substantial evidence of this type, most investigators now believe that protein synthesis is necessary for the formation of permanent memory (Dunn 1980). Nevertheless the specific proteins involved have not been identified. The earlier idea that the proteins might be specific to the memories has now largely been discarded, and current thinking is that changes may occur in proteins normally found in the brain. Similar but more equivocal evidence has implicated RNA in memory. Studies initiated by Hydén in the 1940s indicated that the metabolism of RNA in nerve cells (neurons) was unusually sensitive to changes in nervous system activity. With the discovery by Watson and Crick that the sequence of bases in DNA was the genetic code, the possibility that memories might be coded in the base sequences of RNA molecules was entertained. Work from a number of groups in the 1960s indicated that increases in the synthesis of RNA occurred during learning in animals. However, no specific RNA molecules were found, nor any evidence for any functions of RNA in the brain that do not occur in other tissues. Both the biochemical and behavioral analyses used in the studies of RNA in relation to learning have been severely criticized (Dunn 1980). The relationship of RNA to brain function is still an enigma, but few scientists believe that RNA is specifically related to memory. More recent evidence indicates that changes in certain protein derivatives, such as glyco-proteins and phosphoproteins occur during learning and may be related to memory (Routtenberg 1979, Matthies 1979).

Each NEURON in the brain is character-ized by its *neurotransmitter*. The distri-bution of neurotransmitters among neurons is not random, but such that particular neurotransmitters may be associated with specific functions. Most psychoactive drugs have highly specific effects on a particular neurotransmitter, so that the effect of a drug is a chemical coding of behavior on particular nerve cells.

Particularly good examples of this are the effects of drugs active on DOPAMINE. Parkinson's disease is relatively common in elderly humans and affects the control of movement so that sufferers exhibit tremor and slowness of movement. Pathological studies have established that the disease is associated with the death of dopamine-containing cells in the brain. Drugs that antagonize dopamine functions in the brain can produce Parkinsonian symptoms. On the other hand, drugs that promote dopa-mine's actions can ameliorate the symp-toms of Parkinsonian patients; Levodopa, the drug most frequently used, is highly effective in the treatment of Parkinson's disease.

Another example is the anti-psychotic drugs used to treat SCHIZOPHRENIA. These drugs all appear to antagonize dopamine's actions in the brain. It is therefore believed that the expression of the psychotic behav-ior is produced via dopaminergic neurons. It should not be assumed that the psychosis is *caused* by a disorder of these neurons; extensive investigations have failed to produce good evidence that this is the case. Psychotic behavior probably involves a different set of dopamine neurons from those involved in the symptoms of Parkin-son's disease.

Drugs specific for particular neuro-transmitters have proved extremely useful for elucidating brain mechanisms, and particularly for identifying the brain circuits underlying particular behavior. Current evidence suggests that important controls can be exerted by the receptors for the neurotransmitters on the receiving cells. These receptors are proteins that recognize the neurotransmitters and are located on the external surface of the membranes that enclose receptive cells. Many drugs can bind to these receptors either to mimic or to antagonize the actions of the neurotransmitter. There is often more than one receptor type for each neurotransmitter, permitting even more specificity in the use of drugs with selective actions on the different receptor types. It now appears that regulation of these receptors may be an important mechanism for behavioral regulation. Increased num-bers of receptors can produce an increased sensitivity to the neurotransmitter, and decreased numbers of receptors, decreased sensitivity. Such changes have been documented following chronic treatment with drugs active on neurotrans-mitter receptors. There is now speculation that changes in the sensitivity of receptors may underlie behavioral adaptation and even certain disease states. Certainly, chronic treatment with anti-psychotic or antidepressant drugs result in changes of receptor sensitivity in the brain, and these changes may parallel the therapeutic effects of the drugs (Burt et al. 1977).

The neuropeptides form a new class of neurotransmitters in the brain. The ENDOR-PHINS are the most well known of these neuropeptides, but more than twenty have been discovered. The neuropeptides can violate Dale's principle (see NEURO-

MODULATORS) and may appear in the same cells as other neurotransmitters, but not in any consistent pattern. The neuropeptides appear to be even more specific than the other neurotransmitters for particular types of behavior: the endorphins may be involved in the suppression of pain, while *substance P* may accentuate it. *Angiotensin II* can specifically induce drinking, and *cholecystokinin* causes cessation of eating. The neuropeptides are different from the other neurotransmitters in a number of respects. Minute quantities are necessary to elicit specific types of behavior and they may act as long-distance messengers within the brain, communicating between cells located in different parts of the brain via the extracellular or cerebrospinal fluid.   AJD

Bibliography

Burt, D.R., Creese, I. and Snyder, S.H. 1977: Antischizophrenic drugs: chronic treatment elevates dopamine receptor binding in brain. *Science* 196, 126–28.

Dunn, A.J. 1980. Neurochemistry of learning and memory: an evaluation of recent data. *Annual reviews of psychology* 31, 343–90.

Feldman, R.S. and Quenzer, L.F. 1984: *Fundamentals of neuropsychopharmacology.* Sunderland, Mass.: Sinaver.

Iversen, L.L., Iversen, S.D. and Snyder, S.H. eds. 1975–84: *Handbook of psychopharmacology.* vols. 1–18. New York: Plenum Press.

Matthies, H. 1979. Biochemical, electrophysiological, and morphological correlates of brightness discrimination in rats. In *Brain mechanisms in memory and learning: from the single neuron to man*, ed. Mary A.B. Brazier. New York: Raven Press.

Routtenberg, A. 1979: Anatomical localization of phosphoprotein and glycoprotein substrates of memory. *Progress in neurobiology* 12, 85–113.

Sokoloff, L. 1977: Relations between physiological function and energy metabolism in the central nervous system, *Journal of neurochemistry* 29, 13–26.

neurolinguistics The application of the methods and models of linguistics, particularly psycholinguistics, to the study at the neurological level of language production, reception, processing and acquisition as well as the disturbance of each of these (Lebrun 1976). Neurolinguistics encompasses aspects of linguistics, psychology and the brain sciences and consequently research in this area is often carried out by interdisciplinary teams working in conjunction with medical facilities.

The problems most typically studied under this discipline have been primarily in two areas: language pathology and the underlying neural mechanisms of normal speech, but not every facet of disturbed verbal behavior has received equal attention. In practice neurolinguistics usually limits itself to examining organically caused impairments of language competence or language acquisition, and especially to the linguistic implications of aphasic speech and language. Stuttering, SCHIZOPHRENIA, mutism, DOWN'S SYNDROME, the special needs of the deaf and of laryngectomy victims have not occupied a place in the center of research. Even studies of normals have frequently grown out of their use as control groups or background studies in conjunction with disturbed speech.

With respect to research methods, neurolinguistics relies on traditional case studies, particularly in older accounts of language impairment and linguistics. But more recent investigations have increasingly emphasized experiments rather than compilations of symptomatology, lesion site, cause, prognosis, and so on. Indeed some feel that it is in experimental findings that neurolinguistics has the best chance to make its mark on linguistics as a whole and to contribute to overlapping disciplines. The need to elicit data from test subjects here, as in linguistics and psychology generally, is often crucial, since the phenomena under study may not occur sufficiently frequently in spontaneous speech for the testing of hypotheses.

With respect to the kinds of language functions investigated, neurolinguistics follows linguistics in preferentially focusing on the production and reception of spoken language. As a consequence, neurolinguistic studies of deficits in reading (dyslexia) or writing (agraphia) tend to be in a minority. The study of aphasic language usually begins by selecting groups of subjects who have been classified into impairment types by means of clinical diagnoses and psychological testing, e.g. the Boston Diagnostic Aphasia Examination. Though there are many different classificatory systems for aphasics the nineteenth-century dichotomy identified by the Frenchman Paul Broca and the German Carl Wernicke is still the most commonly employed. Broca's (or motor) aphasia is linked to damage to the anterior language area (the third frontal convolution of the dominant hemisphere), while Wernicke's (or semantic) aphasia is associated with lesions in the posterior language area (angular, supramarginal and superior temporal gyri of the dominant hemisphere). Once selected the groups are asked to demonstrate their performance on some subpart of the language system. These subparts are: semantics (meaning) and lexicon (vocabulary), syntax and grammar, phonology (sound systems) and prosody (intonation, loudness, word accent). Results can then be compared as a function of aphasia type. There has also been considerable research attempting to uncover the relationship between language acquisition in children and language dissolution due to stroke, tumor, EPILEPSY, wounds, traffic accidents or other causes of aphasia. Still other investigators have examined the sequence of recovery from aphasia in bi- or multi-linguals.

Some recent studies indicate that lesions of the subdominant (right) hemisphere result in deficits to affect on the emotional coloring of language. Ross (1981) calls these syndromes aprosodia. (See also SPEECH DISORDERS.)

Work on word-semantics and lexicon looks at the psychological reality of organizational patterns and strategies of word retrieval. The simplest experiment of lexical organization is word association (see WORD ASSOCIATION TESTS). The behavior of normals indicates the existence of a system of direct and indirect associations that can be quite dense with common words such as *man* but becomes more diffuse with less frequently employed words (Lesser 1978:79). According to Schuell (1950) and Rinnert and Whitaker (1973) aphasics have

word finding or naming difficulties (*anomia*) that resemble the kind of retrieval problem that normals have, but their degree of difficulty is much more acute. At least, the parallel holds for Broca's patients. It does not extend to Wernicke's aphasics, however, who were found by Howes (1964) to produce inappropriate or even no associations.

Simple word association tests fail to consider the effect of one word clues on subsequent associations. This factor turns out to be quite significant. LURIA and his associates in the Soviet Union emphasized the influence of a concept known as semantic fields which seems to represent a combination of sound and meaning units. Weigl (1970) makes crucial use of semantic fields, for example, in his work on deblocking. Deblocking of anomia can be effected by means of word clues in the same semantic field. Interestingly, a polysemous word given as a clue will deblock all semantic fields in which it partakes, e.g. *spring* would presumably deblock names of seasons as well as names of machine parts.

Another concept from linguistic analysis that has been tested among aphasics is the semantic feature. In order to account for the apparent cross-classificatory nature of verbs and accompanying nouns Chomsky (1965) proposed a scheme of restrictions based on binary features such as [+ human]. This feature can, for example, become active in determining the choice in English between the relative pronouns *who* and *which*. Zurif et al. (1974) tested Broca's patients and normals to discover whether they could abstract out a feature [+ human] from a list of words. The patients were asked to identify associated groups of words such as *mother, wife, husband* from a list containing the names of animals, fish and reptiles. Generally, Broca's aphasics were capable of abstracting this feature. Wernicke's patients, however, could not, but produced bizarre and inappropriate combinations and groupings.

One final study of the disruption of the lexicon (and also phonology) is especially interesting and relevant for neurolinguistics. Kehoe and Whitaker (in Goodglass and Blumstein 1973) reported on a twenty-three-year-old female who suffered a subdural hematoma in the left hemisphere that produced lesions in the posterior language area (a small area in the supra-marginal gyrus as determined at autopsy). No other damage was found. This patient had been tested by a speech pathologist who indicated 'no systematic aphasic symptoms'. Yet upon close detailed examination the patient showed very specific unsuspected deficits. Reading and oral manipulation (spelling and defining) of words of Latin origin with two or more syllables resulted in consistent breakdown of some English compounding rules. Words such as *constitutionality* were repeated with an 80 per cent error rate. The authors hypothesized that the patient had lost the ability to derive morpho-phonologically and semantically a form from the stored base. Latinate vocabulary items such as: *degradation, feminity, secessionist, citizenry, practicality*, were totally blocked. The following items, many of which are post-medieval neo-Latin coinings: *vehicular, pathological, siberian, revolutionary* could be repeated only after several false starts. And finally the following non-Latinate words of equal length and complexity caused no problems: *Mesopotamia, Mississippi, glamorousness*. Made-up words were also reproduced perfectly. This kind of very specific deficit affecting only derivationally complex words would seem to support the view that real words are listed individually and subsequently subject to derivational rules.

In addition to the abnormality shown at the semantic level, aphasics also show syntactic anomalies in their speech. The grammatical disturbance associated with anterior damage, Broca's aphasia, is known as agrammatism; that associated with Wernicke's area, paragrammatism. The first, according to Goodglass (in Goodglass and Blumstein 1973), is typified by: loss of articles, prepositions and personal pronouns; incorrect substitutions of these categories; substitution of the infinitive for inflected forms of the verb (in German and French); loss of coordinating and subordinating conjunctions so that sentences resemble the telegraphic style. There is also disturbance of sentence intonation as it reflects the breaking of a sentence into its syntactic constituents, i.e. phrasing. Fluent Wernicke's aphasics, on the other hand, may have considerable subordinate structure remaining. At first encounter this latter group might even seem not to be impaired, but their sentences have a characteristic meaninglessness, resulting from transpositional errors and word finding difficulties. Jakobson (1956) was one of the first to apply linguistic descriptions to these error patterns. Broca's aphasics suffered, in his view, from paradigmatic disturbances (e.g. different realizations of a form in an inflectional paradigm) while Wernicke's aphasics had *syntagmatic* disturbances (problems in sequencing). Jakobson also predicted that *government* (the *s* in *father's hat*) should be more fragile than *agreement* (the *s* in *he grows tomatoes*), and that an *s* marking a semantic category such as plurality (*house/houses*) would be most stable. The predicted hierarchy of difficulty was, however, not confirmed in Goodglass's experiments. On reception tests both types of aphasics found it more difficult to discover missing *agreement* inflection, than *government* inflection. A missing plural *s* was the easiest to ascertain. Wh-questions (with *who, which, when, where*, etc.) and imperatives caused less difficulty than simple declaratives, which in turn were easier than yes-no questions (those beginning with *do, can*, etc.), conditionals (beginning with *if*) and subordinate clauses. Some specific errors found in Broca's patients were over-use, correct and incorrect, of the present progressive, and considerable difficulty with the passive. Broca's sufferers omitted unstressed utterance-initial words (i.e. words which are both phonologically and psychologically less prominent than stressed ones) more often than Wernicke's patients.

Work by Zurif and Caramazza (1976, 1978) has indicated that some aphasics exploit plausibility and knowledge of the world to compensate for their syntactic deficits. They can thereby mask debilities that are ascertainable only in specifically designed tests. Zurif and Caramazza report

that Broca's patients, when confronted with center-embedded sentences, i.e. noun phrase–relative clause–verb phrase, depended on semantic as well as on syntactic information in their processing. Four sub-types of this structure were tested:
(1) syntactically well-formed and semantically meaningful and plausible sentences, e.g. *the apple that the boy is eating is red*;
(2) relative clauses containing reversible verbs, which means that purely syntactic information is crucial to understanding, e.g. *the boy that the girl is chasing is fat*;
(3) syntactically well-formed but semantically implausible sentences, e.g. *the boy that the dog is petting is fat*; and
(4) declarative sentences without relative clauses.

Type (4) sentences were generally comprehended best and type (3) sentences least well. It was significantly easier for aphasics to recognize semantic deviance than to understand clues that depend on syntactic encoding. Zurif and Caramazza conclude that if a patient cannot rely on word order, semantic information or lexical constraints, his comprehension is markedly reduced. This kind of study has found, quite surprisingly, that even Broca's aphasics show well-profiled syntactic deficits, even though most previous investigations suggested that Broca's aphasia results only in output disturbance leaving the representation of language itself intact.

Phonological studies of aphasic speech are also being used to test linguistic hypotheses. Blumstein (in Goodglass and Blumstein 1973), for example, took as a starting point two concepts from phonological theory: markedness and distinctive features. She tried to find support for these ideas in the performance of a variety of aphasic patients. By markedness she understood the relative frequency or infrequency with which a particular sound occurs in the languages of the world or its ability to enter into phonological processes such as assimilations, metathesis, etc. The English sounds [þ] and [ð], corresponding to the *th* in *breath* and *breathe*, are not often encountered. Further they are acquired late by children and disappear in some

varieties of English. They are therefore held to be more marked than say [t]. Blumstein defined distinctive features as linguistic elements needed to state phonological rules, which break sounds down into units of analysis finer than the structuralist phonemes. Distinctive features offer the advantage of enabling an error to be regarded as incorrect feature selection instead of its having to be assumed that one entire phoneme has been substituted for another. On the basis of the theory of markedness and distinctive features one would predict that paraphasias would tend to result from a phonological segment's becoming less marked, and from substituting one single feature. Missing a targeted segment by two distinctive features or more should be rarer. Blumstein's results did indeed show that substitutions of one feature were most common and that there is a tendency towards unmarking regardless of lesion site. Particularly prone to disintegration was the *s* sound and the other fricatives [f], [v]. A careful study of the error types indicates that the following disruptions can occur: devoicing of final consonants, lack of control of aspiration, mistargeting (i.e. unsystematic changes in the place of articulation) of vowels and inappropriate nasalization.

Finally, neurolinguistics and language pathology has investigated the so called regression hypothesis (Jakobson 1968). It was speculated that language acquisition and language breakdown in aphasia represent inverse processes of one another. Those elements of grammar last acquired are most susceptible to disturbance, those first acquired are most stable. Zurif and Caramazza (1978) entertain this hypothesis and conclude on the basis of tests such as those discussed above that the regression hypothesis as it stands is untenable. While there are some similarities between children's speech and that of Broca's patients there are also some points of irreconcilable difference. Furthermore Wernicke's patients do not correspond to any stage in the language acquisition process. In a sense this result is not too surprising, despite outward and misleading similarities: a brain exposed to language for years or decades could hardly perform after injury in the same way as an uninjured brain only first encountering language.

A series of other techniques has also been used to obtain information about language manipulation in normals or in aphasics. These include: brain wave studies with the ELECTROENCEPHALOGRAPH or electrocorticograph; direct electrical stimulation of the language area during neurosurgery, which may result in an aphasia during the stimulation; studies of evoked potential, which results when cortical neurons are stimulated; language behavior during the Wada Test, (the injection of sodium amytal into the blood supply of one hemisphere); *brain scans* for tumors or other irregularities; radiological studies of *blood flow* to various parts of the brain during speech; *dichotic hearing* or *tachistoscopic vision* studies (which are based on the neurological property that the right ear or eye, which directly connects to the dominant (usually left) hemisphere, can process speech and language slightly better than the other ear or eye) and work with split brain patients.   JAE

Bibliography

Chomsky, N. 1965: *Aspects of the theory of syntax*. Cambridge, Mass.: MIT Press.

*Goodglass, H. and Blumstein, S. eds. 1973: *Psycholinguistics and aphasia*. Baltimore and London: Johns Hopkins University Press.

Howes, D. 1964: Application of the word frequency concept to aphasia. In *Disorders of language*, eds. A.V.S. DeReuck and M. O'Conner. London: Churchill.

Jakobson, R. 1956: Two aspects of language and two types of aphasic disturbances. In *Fundamentals of language*, eds. R. Jakobson and M. Halle. The Hague: Mouton.

——— 1968: *Child language, aphasia and phonological universals*. Janua Linguarum Series Minor 72. The Hague: Mouton.

Lebrun, Y. 1976: Neurolinguistic models of language and speech. In H. and H. Whitaker, eds, vol. 1, op. cit.

Lesser, R. 1978: *Linguistic investigations of aphasia*. London: Edward Arnold.

Rinnert, C. and Whitaker, H. 1973: Semantic confusions by aphasic patients. *Cortex* 9, 56–81.

Ross, E.D. 1981: The aprosodias: functional-anatomic organization of the affective components of language in the right hemisphere. *Archives of neurology* 38, 561.

Schuell, H. 1950: Paraphasia and paralexia. *Journal of speech and hearing disorder* 15, 291–306.

Weigl, E. 1970: Neuropsychological studies of the structure and dynamics of semantic fields with the deblocking method. In *Sign, language, culture*, ed. A. Greimas. Janua Linguarum Series Major 1. The Hague: Mouton.

Whitaker, H. and H. eds. 1976–1980: *Studies in neurolinguistics*, vols. 1–4. New York, San Francisco, London: Academic Press.

Zurif, E. and Caramazza, A. 1976: Psycholinguistic structures in aphasia. In H. and H. Whitaker, eds, op. cit.

——— eds. 1978: *Language acquisition and language breakdown: parallels and divergencies*. Baltimore and London: Johns Hopkins University Press.

———, Myerson, R. and Galvin, J. 1974: Semantic feature representations for normal and aphasic language. *Brain and language* 1, 167–187.

neurometrics It has long been known that small, variable electrical voltages, of the order of tens of microvolts, can be recorded from large (5 mn) electrodes attached with conductive paste to the surface of the human scalp. At first, these slowly fluctuating voltages were thought to reflect the summated electrical fields produced by the discharge of large numbers of nerve cells, or NEURONS. With the advent of microelectrode techniques, which permitted observation of the discharge of single neurons in the brains of experimental animals and their correlation with slow potentials, this view changed. It is now believed that these fluctuating voltages largely reflect the integrated, post-synaptic potentials of large populations of neurons. Since post-synaptic potentials alter the excitability of the cell, slow waves recorded from the scalp can be considered to be proportional to the probability of synchronous or coherent discharge in large ensembles of neurons.

Two classes of slow waves can be recorded from the human scalp: (1) spontaneous fluctuations of voltage, referred to as the ELECTROENCEPHALOGRAM, or EEG; and (2) transient sequences of voltage oscillations which are time-locked to environmental stimuli, referred to as evoked potentials (EPs) or event-related potentials (ERPs). ERPs can be extracted from the EEG by computer averaging methods. A special class of EPs is the so-called "far-field" or brainstem evoked potential (BSEP), which is recorded from the vertex of the scalp and reflects volume conduction of potentials from the brainstem in response to auditory or somatosensory stimuli.

Reflection of brain functions in EEG or ERP features

Voluminous evidence demonstrated that a wide variety of important aspects of brain functions are reflected in the EEG and ERPs. Many neurological diseases cause changes in the amplitude frequency spectrum, bilateral synchrony or symmetry of the EEG, or produce waveshapes with a morphology characteristic of certain disorders.

ERPs elicited by sensory stimuli of different modalities display waveshapes more or less typical for each modality. These waveshapes tend to be of maximal amplitude over the corresponding sensory cortical projection areas (BRAIN AND CENTRAL NERVOUS SYSTEM: ILLUSTRATIONS, fig. 3), but are also detected over other cortical regions, usually with different waveshapes. An important feature of ERPs is that their morphology changes as a function of a number of different parameters: the focus of attention of the subject, the information content of the stimulus, whether or not a priori expectancies about the stimulus have been engendered in the subject by the context in which the stimuli occur, and the semantic or symbolic significance of the stimuli.

It is useful to consider the morphology of the ERP as consisting of a succession of waves, each primarily reflecting a step in sequential processing of the information contained in the stimulus as it is evaluated by the subject in terms of prior experience and the immediate context in which the stimulus is received. Since these steps are necessarily sequential, wave components of increasing latency (time elapsed after stimulus delivery) correspond to later stages of information processing.

Unfortunately substantial differences exist across individuals with respect to the morphology of the ERP, the latency of particular components elicited by a particular stimulus, and the clarity with which particular components can be identified. It is not known whether this variability primarily reflects inherent differences in anatomical organization of functional systems mediating various processes, differences in the functional state of different subjects, or differences in the time required by different subjects to perform the sequence of functions involved in processing sensory input. For these reasons it is difficult to specify the precise latencies and amplitudes of ERP components expected in an individual subject under specified stimulus conditions. The simplest solution to this problem is achieved by using each subject as his own control. A more complex statistical approach is discussed below.

Correspondence between steps in information processing and latency of ERP components

Nonetheless, bearing these reservations in mind, a temporal schema can be constructed giving the approximate latencies of the sequences of steps involved in processing information about a sensory stimulus. Such a schema, for visual stimuli, is as follows:

Receptor activation
↓
Afferent input
↓
Cortical registration (50–100ms)
↓
Analysis of contrast (100–150ms)
↓
Attentional processes (100–200ms) (reflects both internal state and prior experience)
↓
Perception (200–240ms) (Classification of input requiring memory access)
↓
Expectancy (300–360ms) (Evaluation of stimulus probability in prior context)
↓

$\downarrow$

Match from memory of prior event(s) (420–450ms)

$\downarrow$

Semantic significance (450–500ms)

(For more detailed information about the experimental evidence supporting this proposed sequence of processes, encompassing aspects of sensation, perception and cognition as reflected in the ERP, see Thatcher and John 1977.)

Exogenous versus endogenous processes

Consideration of this schema reveals that, on purely logical grounds, it is possible to distinguish between aspects of the ERP determined by the physical stimulus and the state of the afferent pathways ("exogenous" processes) and those influenced by the prior experience, expectation or semantic processes of the subject ("endogenous" processes). In this framework, what psychologists call "sensation" represents an exogenous process, "attention" is partly exogenous and partly endogenous, in that centrifugal outputs due to fatigue, habituation or arousal can inhibit afferent input and "perception" and "cognition" are primarily endogenous. Microelectrode studies, using microelectrodes chronically implanted in unrestrained animals, have revealed that two types of neurons can be indentified in many brain regions. So called "stable cells", which respond to physical features of the stimuli independent of their meaning, are believed to participate in exogenous processes. "Plastic cells", which show firing patterns correlated with subsequent behavioral responses independent of the physical features of the stimulus, are believed to participate in endogenous processes (Ramos, Schwartz and John 1976).

"Readout" or "emitted" potentials

In studies of differential generalization in differentially conditioned animals, it has been reported that the presentation of ambiguous stimuli with parameters midway between those of differential conditioned stimuli elicits ERPs with different morphologies, reliably predictive of subsequent differential behavioral responses.

Since the different ERP morphologies cannot plausibly be attributed to the neutral physical stimulus, which is identical and ambiguous whenever presented, and since the different ERP morphologies elicited closely correspond to the morphologies of the ERPs elicited by the differential stimuli used in establishing the different conditioned responses, these findings have been interpreted to reflect readout from memory of temporal patterns of coherent firing in neuronal ensembles (Ramos, Schwartz and John 1976).

Analogous reports have been published on human subjects, either in differential generalization (Begleiter and Platz 1969) or in production of so called "emitted potentials" when expected stimuli fail to occur (Sutton et al 1967).

A number of other obviously endogenous processes have been repeatedly reported in the ERP literature. The best known of these is the so called $P_{\overline{300}}$, which is a late positive component in the ERP with an amplitude which increases the *less* predictable or *more* significant the eliciting stimulus (Sutton et al. 1965). In information theoretical terms, the more unlikely a stimulus, the larger will be $P_{\overline{300}}$.

Another important endogenous process is revealed in match-mismatch procedures, in which the second member of a pair of events is compared to the first member for adherence to any of a variety of logical rules, i.e. same-different, true-false or semantic equivalence. Conformity of the second stimulus to the first with respect to the particular logical rule imposed on the subject is reflected by a late positive component at about 450 ms (Thatcher and John 1977).

A particularly interesting endogenous process has been described (Kutas and Hillyard 1980). When a word is presented in a context which is semantically improbable, such as "I drink my coffee with sugar and *cement*", the unexpected word elicits a large, negative component in the ERP at about 480 ms.

These various types of evidence demonstrate unequivocally that analysis of the ERPs elicited in carefully controlled experimental situations can provide access to reflections of brain mechanisms related to *mental activity*. For this reason, ERP research is of unique importance in psychology and has philosophical implications perhaps transcending any other phenomena for an understanding of the physical and physiological basis of mind.

Brain stem or "far-field" potentials

A special class of ERPs, perhaps totally exogenous in origin (although the contributions of fatigue, habituation and attention have not yet been totally ruled out), is the so-called brain stem evoked potential. This waveshape, sometimes referred to as the "far-field" evoked potential, arises in the brain stem and can be detected at the vertex because of volume conduction. Since it is extremely small, on the order of 0.25 microvolts, very low noise amplifiers and averages of as much as 2,000 responses are required to extract the BSEP from the ongoing EEG, which is 2–4 orders of magnitude larger in amplitude. The auditory BSEP characteristically displays 7 peaks in an epoch of about 12 ms poststimulus. The latency of each peak corresponds to the depolarization of ensembles of neurons at successive relay nuclei in the lateral lemniscal pathways of the auditory system between the auditory nerve entry to the brain stem and the inferior colliculus. Since the variability of latency in normal subjects for each peak is in the order of 1200 microseconds, and relative amplitudes fall within predictable ranges, the auditory BSEP provides an exquisitely sensitive technique for evaluation of the functional status of lateral lemniscal pathways. Although less widely used, the somatosensory BSEP provides comparable information about the medial lemniscus.

It should be obvious from the cursory summary above that the EEG and ERP not only afford a unique insight into a variety of brain functions of considerable importance for the resolution of basic research issues in neurophysiology and physiological psychology, with substantial philosophical implications, but can be of great value in diagnosis and treatment of a wide variety of disorders and dysfunctions of the brain. A major obstacle in the practical application of these electrophysiological methods has been the qualitative nature of subjective evaluations of EEG and ERP phenomena, as well as the wide variability of such phenomena across samples of healthy, normally functioning individuals.

With the advent of powerful minicomputers and economical microprocessors, a radically different approach to evaluation of EEG and ERP data has become possible. This approach is called "neurometrics" (John et al. 1977, John 1977). Neurometric technology has several distinctive and essential aspects:
(1) Precise specification of the environment of the subject and the physical characteristics of all stimuli;
(2) Automatic computer controlled rejection of artifacts and presentation of stimuli, to ensure standardization of data;
(3) Objective computer extraction of quantitative EEG and ERP features of clinical utility, based upon automatic algorithms of demonstrated concordance with clinical judgments;
(4) Transformation of all extracted diagnostic features to relative probability, by use of the Z transform based upon the mean and standard deviation of identical features extracted from a large sample of healthy, normally functioning individuals the same age as the subject;
(5) Construction of *abnormality vectors* representing each subject as a vector in an n-dimensional space of electrophysiological features, each dimension scaled according to the common metric of relative probability. The direction of the abnormality vector in the measure space defines the *quality* or nature of the abnormality, and the length of the abnormality vector defines the *quantity* or severity of the abnormality.

Clinical applications

Perhaps the most important single finding from the application of neurometric techniques has been the discovery that the relative (percent) power in the delta (1.5–3.5 Hz), theta (3.5–7.5 Hz), alpha (7.5–12.5 Hz) and beta (12.5–25 Hz) band of the resting, eyes closed EEG shows a systematic alteration with age (see EEG and fig. 33). This alteration is character-

183

istically different for fronto-temporal, temporal, central and parieto-occipital electrode derivations. Regression equations have been derived which describe this systematic change in the relative power frequency spectrum as a function of age. These regression equations accurately describe the distribution of EEG relative power in these different frequency bands in large samples of healthy, normally functioning children from a wide variety of cultural and ethnic backgrounds. The incidence of standard scores, or z-values, beyond the 0.05 probability level was equal or less than expected by chance in healthy children from the US, Sweden and Barbados. Healthy children from different socioeconomic strata, of different ethnic backgrounds, or of different sexes were not discriminable from each other. Thus, these descriptors of the resting EEG seem to provide a culture-fair estimate of brain maturation independent of cultural, ethnic, socioeconomic or sexual factors. In contrast, children at risk for a wide variety of neurological diseases or with learning disabilities of unknown origin displayed 40–64 per cent of abnormal values for these EEG parameters (John et al. 1980). Multivariate, independently replicated discriminant functions indicate that the discriminability of normal from learning-dysfunctional children based on neurometric EEG features is of the order of 75 per cent.

Space precludes a detailed review of further clinical findings. Neurometric features of a wide variety of neurological diseases have been reviewed by Harmony (1981). Significant and consistent features of neurometric abnormality have been found in children of normal intelligence disabled in verbal vs. arithmetical learning, in normally functioning vs. dysfunctional elderly patients (John et al. 1977), in patients after traumatic head injury, in chronic alcoholics, in manic-depressive psychosis and in a variety of other diseases.

Conclusion

Electrophysiological evaluations of brain functions, in general, and neurometric evaluations, in particular, provide a power-ful, unique and relatively new window into psychological processes of basic and practical interest. With the increasing focus of attention on computer evaluation of electrophysiological processes, and with the rapidly decreasing cost of microprocessors whose computational capability is escalating at an exponentially increasing rate, the information available from quantitative evaluation of electrical correlates of brain functions can be expected to become increasingly important in our understanding of the relationship between brain and behavior. ERJ

Bibliography

Begleiter, H. and Platz, P. 1969: Cortical evoked potentials to semantic stimuli. *Psychophysiology* 6, 91–100.

Harmony, T. 1981: *Functional neuroscience*, vol. 3: *Neurometric diagnosis of neuropathogy*. Hillsdale, N.J.: Lawrence Erlbaum.

John, E.R. 1977: *Functional neuroscience*, vol. 2. *Neurometrics: clinical applications of quantitative electrophysiology*. Hillsdale, N.J.: Lawrence Erlbaum.

—— and Alter, I. 1981: Evaluation of coma patients with the brain state analyzer. In *Seminars in neurological surgery*, eds. R.G. Grossman and P.L. Gildenberg, New York: Raven Press.

—— et al. 1977: Neurometrics: numerical taxonomy identifies different profiles of brain functions within groups of behaviorally similar people. *Science* 196, 1393–410.

—— et al. 1980: Developmental equations for the electroencephalogram. *Science* 210, 1255–8.

Kutas, M. and Hillyard, S.A. 1980: Reading senseless sentences – brain potentials reflect semantic incongruity. *Science* 207, 203–5.

Ramos, A., Schwartz, E. and John, E.R. 1976: Stable and plastic unit discharge patterns during behavioral generalization. *Science* 192, 392–6.

Sutton, S. et al. 1965: Evoked potential correlates of stimulus uncertainty. *Science* 153, 1187–8.

—— 1967: Information delivery and the sensory evoked potential. *Science* 155, 1436–9.

Thatcher, R.W. and John, E.R. 1977: *Functional neuroscience*, vol. 1. *Foundations of cognitive processes*. Hillsdale, N.J.: Lawrence Erlbaum.

neuromodulators Substances that convey information to nerve cells through mechanisms other than neurotransmission. The concept of neuromodulation is relatively new and not yet fully established. It was introduced and further developed as the result of increasingly numerous demonstrations of the existence of endogenous substances which do not change neuronal membrane potential directly as do neurotransmitters (see SYNAPSE AND SYNAPTIC TRANSMISSION), but still affect the efficiency of the neurotransmission process. The term "synaptic modulator" was originally introduced by Krivoy et al. (1963) to describe the action of Substance P and other so called neurotropic peptides on synaptic excitability in the spinal cord. Krivoy and co-workers defined a synaptic modulator as 'a substance that alters (increases or decreases) the efficiency of the neurotransmission process without per se producing a propagated response associated with a reversal of the membrane potential'. This, like the definition which opens the paragraph, is a *definitio per exclusionem*, and it does not include a statement of either site or mechanism of action. It is now clear that neuromodulating substances form a very heterogeneous class from the viewpoint of both chemical structure, and sites and mechanism of action. Substances traditionally classified as *hormones* or *neurotransmitters* may be neuromodulators or have neuromodulator functions as well. Neuromodulators are thought to be of importance in the regulation of a wide variety of behavioral, neuroendocrine and autonomic processes.

Peptides predominate among the newly discovered endogenous compounds which have been added to the list of substances involved in communication between nerve cells in the central and the peripheral nervous system. This emphasis on peptides is partly the result of new techniques being available. Sophisticated immunohistochemical methods developed in recent years have enabled these neuropeptides to be visualized in neuronal systems and the various neuronal networks to be traced. Double-staining techniques allow more than one substance to be visualized in a single tissue section. This allows the localization of possible interaction between

networks. Double-staining has also led to the surprising and intriguing discovery of the coexistence, in single neurons, of neuropeptides and representatives of classical neurotransmitters in apparent violation of Dale's Principle ("one neuron, one neurotransmitter"). Among the neuropeptides are many substances previously known as pituitary or intestinal hormones so that the list of neuropeptides now includes: thyrotopia releasing hormone (TRH), luteinizing hormone releasing hormone (LHRH), somatostatin (growth hormone release-inhibiting hormone), vasopressin, oxytocin, ACTH (see also ACTH), encephalins, endorphins (see also ENCEPHALINS/ENDORPHINS), growth hormone, prolactin, insulin, glucagon, angiotensin, secretin, gastrin, substance P, neurotensin, cholecystokinin, vasoactive intestinal peptide (VIP), carnosine and bombesin (see Hökfelt et al. 1980). Specific binding sites for the neuropeptides have been found in the central and peripheral nervous systems. This was achieved by measuring the specific *in vitro* binding of radiolabeled ligands and their displacement by non-labeled compounds and by using autoradiography for microscopic visualization of many of the neuropeptides. Although a neurotransmitter role has been suggested in various cases, many of the neuropeptides are presently thought to function as neuromodulators. This role is postulated not only from the results of behavioral, electrophysiological and neurochemical studies, but also from the notion that the dynamics of synthesis, storage and bio-inactivation of neuropeptides differ markedly from those of the classical neurotransmitters. This aspect of neuropeptides suggests the existence of slow-reacting regulatory mechanisms in peptide-containing neurons (see Hökfelt et al. 1980; Barker and Smith 1980). In contrast, the synapse in neurotransmitter-containing neurons must be capable of immediate recovery and return to the pre-activation condition; rapidly operating mechanisms for the adaptation of synthesis and release processes are essential.

As it is still difficult to make a rigid classification of substances with neuromodulatory effects, there are conflicts between the classifications so far proposed. Functional criteria suggest three subclasses (see Elliott and Barchas 1980; Barker and Smith 1980):

1. Synaptic neuromodulators act between nerve cells in synaptic contact. The effect of a synaptic neuromodulator is local and restricted to one cell postsynaptic to the one from which the neuromodulator is released.

2. Hormonal neuromodulators affect the neuronal activity of neurons at a relatively great distance from their site of release. In principle hormonal neuromodulators can act on a large population of nerve cells, viz. on those cells that possess neuro-modulator-specific recognition sites whether membrane-bound or cytoplasmic. Substances considered as classical hormones and which are released from peripheral sources (e.g. adrenal steroids) can also have modulating effects on specific populations of neurons in the central nervous system (see also STEROIDS). There are neurons, both in the peripheral autonomic nervous system and in the hypothalamic neurosecretory systems, with axons which do not make synaptic contacts with target cells or other neurons. There is recent morphological evidence that there occur noradrenaline-containing terminals in the cortex and dopamine-containing terminals in the caudate nucleus which also appear to be devoid of synaptic contacts. Such evidence suggests that NOREPINE-PHRINE and DOPAMINE released from these terminals function as hormonal neuromodulators rather than as neurotransmitters (for references see Vizi 1980).

3. The third subclass of neuromodulators is formed by substances that act postsynaptically to their site of release as neurotransmitters by evoking a propagated response, and that simultaneously modulate their own release or synthesis via presynaptic mechanisms. Since this modulation leads in all cases to decreased neuronal activity, it is called auto-inhibition. Auto-inhibition mediated by presynaptic autoreceptors is a feature of many neurotransmitter systems in both the central nervous system and the periphery (see Vizi 1980).

The exact mechanism of action of most of the putative neuromodulators has not yet been found. The definitions given above, however, allow the prediction that any of the processes involved in neurotransmission and neurotransmitter metabolism in the "target-synapse" of a neuromodulator are potential sites for its amplifying or damping effect on neuronal activity. Neuromodulators can elicit their effects through specific membrane receptors, via membrane-bound enzymes or other proteins or via cytoplasmic or soluble recognition sites. Neuromodulators can act on processes preceding or following the membrane depolarization or hyperpolarization induced by transmitters. For example, through their effects on ion transport systems neuromodulators can elevate or depress thresholds for de- or hyperpolarization, thereby attenuating or facilitating neurotransmission. Intracellular processes can be influenced directly or via the activation of membrane receptors and the consequent activation of receptor-linked adenylate or guanylate cyclase systems. The latter possibility holds for both pre- and post-synaptic neuromodulator-specific receptors. The effects can be exerted on synthesis, uptake, storage or metabolism of the substance which acts as a neurotransmitter in the "target-synapse" of the neuromodulator. Neuromodulators can also act by influencing the affinity of neurotransmitter receptors for their endogenous agonists by exerting allosteric effects on these receptors, thereby increasing or decreasing receptor efficiency.

Substances with neuromodulating actions do not necessarily originate from nerve terminals or even from neuronal cells. Evidence has been presented for a modulating role of prostaglandins in synaptic transmission. Prostaglandins of the E-type, which are released from the postsynaptic cell as a consequence of its activation by the transmitter, reduce neurotransmitter release through presynaptic effects on Ca^{2+} ion fluxes. A similar action has been suggested for adenosine (trans-synaptic modulation). DHGV

Bibliography

*Barker, J.L. and Smith, T.G. 1980: Three modes of intercellular neuronal communication. In *Adaptive capabilities of the nervous system. Progress in brain research*, vol. 53, eds. P.S. McConnell et al. Amsterdam and New York: Elsevier/North-Holland Biomedical Press.

Boosfield, D. 1985: *Neurotransmitters in action*. New York: Elsevier.

Feldman, R. and Quenzer, L. 1984: *Fundamentals of neuropsychopharmacology*. Sunderland, Mass.: Sinauer.

*Hökfelt, T. et al. 1980: Peptidergic neurons. *Nature* 284, 515–21.

Krivoy, W.A. et al. 1963: Synaptic modulation by substance P. *Federation proceedings* 38, 2344–47.

Vizi, E.S. 1980: Non-synaptic interaction of neurotransmitters: presynaptic inhibition and disinhibition, In *Modulation of neurochemical transmission: advances in pharmacological research and practice*, vol. 2, ed. E.S. Vizi. Proceedings of the 3rd Congress of the Hungarian Pharmacological Society, 1979. Budapest: Pergamon Press/ Akadémiai Kiadó.

neuron (See BRAIN AND CENTRAL NERVOUS SYSTEM: ILLUSTRATIONS, figs. 30–32.) A nerve cell with all its processes. Neurons are specialized to receive signals, process them and pass them on to other neurons or effector organs such as muscles or glands. The neuron doctrine, as originally proposed, holds that neurons form the basic developmental, structural and functional units of the nervous system. Classically, each neuron possesses DENDRITES which receive inputs and integrate them, an axon which conducts a nerve impulse to the synaptic terminals where the signal is passed to another cell and a cell body which carries on the metabolic activities of the cell. Recently it has become clear that the neuron is not always the functional unit of the nervous system. Rather, localized portions of several neurons may be connected to perform a task relatively independently of other parts of the neurons involved (Shepard 1979).

Generally the dendrites of a neuron receive connections, often from many other neurons. These connections, or SYNAPSES, (fig. 32) may provide either excitatory or inhibitory input which is mediated electrically or chemically. In an electrical synapse, an electrical signal in one neuron is relayed to a second neuron via a low resistance pathway. In a chemical synapse a substance is released from one neuron which causes currents to flow through the cell membrane of another neuron. In either case, all the inputs onto the dendrites are integrated in space and time to produce a single voltage at the spike initiation zone (axon hillock). Here analog signals are converted to digital signals as nerve impulses (ACTION POTENTIALS) are triggered when the membrane voltage exceeds threshold. Nerve impulses are unitary events which propagate from the axon hillock toward the synaptic terminals. At the terminals electrical or chemical transmission proceeds to other cells. Chemical transmitters released by neurons at synapses include ACETYLCHOLINE, DOPAMINE, SEROTONIN, and GAMMA-AMINOBUTYRIC ACID. Special proteins, called neuropeptides, such as substance P and ENCEPHALINS may also be released by neurons. The cell body may not participate directly in the electrical activities of the neuron, but performs the metabolic activities characteristic of all cells. Since the axons of neurons may be as long as several meters, mechanisms exist for the rapid transport of materials from the cell body to the synaptic terminals and back (axonal transport).

Neurons show great diversity in structure and function. Not all cells generally regarded as neurons have all the normal properties associated with neurons. For example, cells which are connected to neurons, but which have only some of the characteristic features of neurons include those specialized for nonspecific secretion (neurosecretory cells) and sensory receptors (hair cells, rods and cones, etc.). Similarly, although propagated action potentials are characteristic of neurons, not all nerve cells conduct them. SCC

Bibliography

Bullock, T.H., Orkand, R. and Grinnell, A. 1977: *Introduction to nervous systems*. San Francisco: W.H. Freeman.

Kuffler, S.W. Nicholls, J.G. and Martin, A.R. 1984: *From neuron to brain.* 2nd edn. Sunderland, MA: Sinauer Associates Inc.

Kandel, E.R. and Schwartz, J.H. 1981: *Principles of neural science.* Oxford and New York: Elsevier/North-Holland.

—— 1983: *Neurobiology.* New York and Oxford: Oxford University Press.

Shepard, G.M. 1979: *The synaptic organization of the brain.* 2nd edn. Oxford and New York: Oxford University Press.

neurons: alpha and gamma motor

Alpha and gamma motor neurons are nerve cells in the ventral horn of the SPINAL CORD whose activity controls the state of contraction of extrafusal and intrafusal muscle fibers respectively. *Skeletal muscle* fibers are of two types. Extrafusal muscle fibers are innervated by alpha motor neurons and are responsible for the work performed by muscles. The whole set of muscle fibers innervated by a single alpha motor neuron is called a *motor unit.* Motor units range in size from only a few to a thousand or more muscle fibers. Small motor units provide fine control of movements. The force that muscles generate can be graded in two ways. First, the rate of firing of a given alpha motor neuron can be changed. Second, the number of motor units activated can be varied. Smooth movements that result from the progressive activation of motor units start with the smallest units and recruit progressively larger motor units as the force generated increases.

Intrafusal muscle fibers (nuclear bag fibers and nuclear chain fibers) form *muscle spindles* which signal the length of muscles to the central nervous system. Primary spindle afferents (Ia) innervate all intrafusal fibers, whereas secondary spindle (II) afferents innervate only nuclear chain fibers. The length of muscle spindle fibers is controlled by gamma motor neurons. Nuclear bag fibers are innervated by dynamic gamma motor neurons and nuclear chain fibers, by static gamma motor neurons. Gamma motor neurons are necessary to maintain the loading of the muscle spindle as the length of the muscle as a whole changes. Otherwise sudden contraction of the muscle, for example, would unload the muscle spindles and inactivate them. Another simpler innervation pattern in which one motor neuron innervates both intra- and extrafusal muscle fibers is used in simpler vertebrates and persists, in part, through carnivores and possibly to man. Exactly why two separate motor innervations have evolved is problematic, since it appears that alpha and gamma motor neurons are usually coactivated.

Motor neurons are activated or inhibited directly by muscle spindle and *Golgi tendon organ* afferents (Ib) (e.g. myotactic and inverse myotactic reflexes) and by descending inputs from the CEREBRAL CORTEX, reticular formation, and vestibular system. Motor activities such as locomotion, for example, appear to involve the expression of a motor program embodied in the spinal circuitry including the reflexive effects of afferents, modulated by descending inputs from supraspinal centers.   SCC

Bibliography

Harris, D.A. and Henneman, E. 1980: Feedback signals from muscle and their efferent control. In *Medical physiology*, vol. 1, ed. V.B. Mountcastle. St. Louis and London: C.V. Mosby. pp. 703–717.

Henneman, E. 1980: Organization of the spinal cord and its reflexes. In *Medical physiology*, vol. 1, ed. V.B. Mountcastle. St. Louis and London: C.V. Mosby. pp. 762–56.

Stuart, D.G. and Enoka, R.M. 1983: Motorneurons, motor units, and the size principle. In *The clinical neurosciences*, vol. 5. *Neurobiology*, eds. R.N. Rosenberg and W.D. Willis, Jr. New York and Edinburgh: Churchill Livingstone.

neurons: local circuit

Nerve cells concerned with processing only within a local region of the nervous system. The nervous system may be structurally and functionally divided into regions or centers such as the HIPPOCAMPUS, the THALAMUS, the CEREBRAL CORTEX, etc. Neurons whose cell bodies lie within a given center are usually of two types. Some cells, termed principal, projection, relay or Golgi Type I neurons, have DENDRITES within the center, but project their axons to other centers. Such neurons relay information between neural centers. Other cells, called local circuit neurons, interneurons, intrinsic neurons, or Golgi Type II neurons, have all of their processes within the neural center and are involved only in the activity of that local region. Often local circuit neurons make complex synaptic connections with each other and processes of principal cells that include reciprocal dendro-dendritic synapses (see DENDRITES AND DENDRITIC SPINES). SCC

Bibliography

Kandel, E.R. and Schwartz, J.H. 1981: *Principles of neural science*. New York and Oxford: Elsevier/North-Holland.

Rakic, P. 1976: *Local circuit neurons*. Cambridge, Mass. and London: MIT Press.

Roberts, A. and Bush, B.M.H. 1981: *Neurones without impulses*. Cambridge and New York: Cambridge University Press.

Shepard, G.M. 1979: *The synaptic organization of the brain*. 2nd edn. Oxford and New York: Oxford University Press.

neuropsychiatry Usually refers to the branch of psychiatry concerned with the cognitive, emotional and behavioral effects of manifest brain disorder (that is, excluding those disturbances where coarse brain disease is absent or is not currently demonstrable). The neuropsychiatrist concerns him- or herself with such illnesses as epilepsy, dementia, endocrine and cerebral-vascular abnormalities, and infections and tumors of the brain.

The term may also be used to designate the combined disciplines of neurology and psychiatry which in some countries constitute a single specialization. DLJ

Bibliography

Lishman, W.A. 1978: *Organic psychiatry, the psychological consequence of social disorders*. Oxford: Blackwell Scientific Publications; St Louis, Missouri: C.V. Mosby.

neurosis Neuroses are exaggerated forms of normal reactions to stressful events. There is no evidence of any kind of organic brain disorder, patients do not lose touch with external reality, and, although often associated with a degree of PERSONALITY DISORDER, the personality is not grossly abnormal. They may occur acutely at times of stress or may be chronic and associated with longstanding social difficulties. The term "neurosis" originated in the eighteenth century and was used with a variety of meanings during the nineteenth century. The present meaning is largely attributable to FREUD who defined a group of psychoneuroses of psychological etiology.

There is a distinction between the various neurotic syndromes described below and individual neurotic symptoms (for example anxiety and depression) which are extremely common in the general population and may be associated with many psychiatric disorders. Estimates of prevalence of neurotic disorder vary according to the strictness of the criteria used (see Goldberg and Huxley 1980). They make up the majority of the psychiatric cases seen in general practice, where they usually present with an undifferentiated clinical picture. The more severe neuroses can be divided into the specific syndromes, even though in clinical practice there is considerable overlap between them. Other categories listed in the current ninth edition of the International Classification of Disease (WHO 1978) and the American classification, DSM III (American Psychiatric Association 1980) are *acute reactions to stress* and *adjustment reactions*. These are used for the acute and the more prolonged emotional reactions occurring following severe stress in those with no evidence of previous psychiatric abnormality. It is difficult to distinguish between these normal (i.e. appropriate reactions) and neurosis. The traditional diagnoses of HYPOCHONDRIASIS and neurasthenia are now not normally regarded as primary psychiatric syndromes.

The neuroses have a very variable prognosis (see Goldberg and Huxley 1980). The majority of recent onset cases seen by doctors improve within a few months but a minority have a much more prolonged course. This is more likely if the initial problems are severe, if there are severe social difficulties and if the patient lacks social support and friendships. Prolonged psychological symptoms are usually associated with severe social handicaps.

Etiology Etiological factors can be considered in two groups, predisposing and precipitating. Predisposing factors include general social conditions, family difficulties or support, and to a limited extent genetic factors. Abnormalities and vulnerability of personality have frequently been described but there is no close relationship between the type of personality and the type of neurosis. Epidemiological research has described the role of protective (e.g. intimate marriage) and vulnerability factors (e.g. young children, poor marriage, lack of a job) in the patient's social circumstances (Brown and Harris 1978). Precipitating factors are stressful events such as childbirth, marriage, retirement and moving home. The principal theoretical approaches to explaining the interaction between stress and personality have been psychoanalytic (see Kaplan et al., 1980). Very different are learning theories which attempt to explain neuroses in terms of early experience and make use of learning mechanisms identified in the study of animal behavior (see Kaplan et al, 1980).

Treatment There are three main approaches to treatment: the relief of symptoms, help to solve the patient's problems, and treatment to alter vulnerability to neurosis. When the symptoms are mild and seem to be a temporary response to a stress that is likely to resolve quickly, support is all that is required. There is only a limited role for symptomatic relief by using anxiolytic drugs for a short period. Longer term drug treatment is ineffective and may lead to drug dependence. Frequently, however, it is necessary to help the patient with active steps to deal with problems in his or her life. As far as possible the patient is encouraged to make their own plans to solve their difficulties but practical help from a doctor or social worker may also be needed. More fundamental treatment by psychotherapy should be considered when it seems that neurosis has resulted from persistent maladaptive behavior and difficulties in personal relationships. In practice this varies between brief counseling and prolonged psychoanalytic treatment.

Clinical Features

Anxiety neurosis (or anxiety state) is a syndrome in which there are various combinations of physical and mental symptoms of anxiety, which are not attributable to real danger, and which occur either in attacks or as a persistent state. Apart from anxiety itself, psychological symptoms include irritability, difficulty in concentration and restlessness. Physical symptoms include signs of arousal of the autonomic nervous system including palpitations, sweating, nausea and diarrhea. In addition there may be tremor, difficulty in breathing or overbreathing, dizziness and headache. In some patients the physical symptoms predominate and physical disorder must be carefully considered in differential diagnosis. In treatment, short term anxiolytic drugs can be useful and specific medication can also have a limited use in the treatment of palpitations and other autonomic symptoms. Relaxation training is often as effective as medication in less severe cases. A more elaborate and varied form of BEHAVIOR THERAPY, anxiety management training, is even more effective.

In *phobic anxiety neuroses* there is an abnormal fear of certain objects or specific situations together with a strong wish to avoid them. There are three main groups: simple phobias, agoraphobia and social phobias (Marks 1969). Simple phobias are specific fears of objects or situations such as heights, thunder storms, spiders and mice. They are common in children and most adults have minor unreasonable fears. More severe phobias can cause considerable suffering and social limitations. Agoraphobia is anxiety when traveling from home, mixing with crowds or in any situation which a sufferer cannot easily leave. The fear, panic attacks and avoidance cause those with the most severe symptoms to be very restricted and perhaps housebound (Mathews et al., 1981). Sudden onset or worsening of agoraphobia or other phobic symptoms can be secondary to an AFFECTIVE DISORDER. The first step in treatment is, therefore, to look for, and if necessary treat, underlying depressive illness. Anxiolytic drugs may provide temporary relief but lasting improvement requires behavioral treatment to overcome the avoidance. DESENSITIZATION and other forms of behavior therapy are appropriate.

Depressive neurosis is a less severe form of affective disorder in which disproportionate depression has followed on upsetting events, meeting the definition of neurosis. It is, however, difficult to differentiate from affective disorder and there is considerable controversy about the classification of depression. Even so it is evident that depression and related symptoms, such as poor concentration, fatigue, poor sleep and irritability, are common neurotic symptoms both as a depressive syndrome or as part of the other syndromes.

The main feature of HYSTERIA is evidence of physical symptoms in the absence of organic pathology, which have been produced unconsciously and are not caused by overactivity of the autonomic nervous system. The very long history of varying usage and the great variability in the clinical picture have led to severe problems in clear definition. It is usual to separate two groups of symptoms:

1. *conversion symptoms*, which derive from Freud's original formulation (Freud and Breuer (1955)) and include the physical symptoms such as paralysis, disorder of coordination, sensory disturbances, and a variety of pain syndromes;

2. *dissociative symptoms*, in which there is an apparent dissociation between different types of mental activity. These include amnesia, hysterical fits, somnambulism and multiple personality.

In addition there are more general clinical features which include symbolic meaning, secondary gain and belle indifference. Although usually stressed in the literature they are not always present. Apart from these two groups clinical variants include epidemic hysteria (particularly among young girls in schools or other groups) and Briquet's syndrome, a name that has been used to describe a group of patients with chronic multiple symptoms including both hysterical and other neurotic symptoms.

Careful physical assessment is always necessary before making the diagnosis of hysteria. Apart from treatment of the underlying neurotic problem, management is concerned to relieve the presenting symptoms. This is best achieved by a firm and optimistic yet sympathetic approach which avoids reinforcing the symptoms and also provides the patient with a face-saving opportunity for recovery. The prognosis is good in recent onset cases but when there is a long history symptomatic improvement is less likely.

The principal symptom in *obsessive compulsive neurosis* is a feeling of subjective compulsion to carry out an action or to dwell on an idea to an extent that is regarded as inappropriate or not sensible. The compulsion is accompanied by a subjective resistance with ideas that are regarded as inappropriate and absurd. Obsessional neuroses are uncommon. Their main symptoms are obsessional thoughts, images, ruminations, impulses and rituals. Although most episodes improve over a period of months the more severe disorders can be extremely persistent. It is necessary to exclude other primary disorders such as depression as the cause of obsessional symptoms.

In *depersonalizaton* perception is disturbed and external objects or parts of the body are experienced as having changed in quality, being unreal, remote or automatized. The symptom is common as a feature of other syndromes but primary depersonalization neurosis is rare. (See also ANOREXIA NERVOSA; BULIMIA NERVOSA.) RAM

Bibliography

American Psychiatric Association 1980: *Diagnostic and statistical manual* 3.

Brown, G.W. and Harris, T. 1978: *Social origins of depression*. London: Tavistock.

Freud, S. and Breuer, J. 1955: Studies on hysteria. *Standard edition of the works of Sigmund Freud*, vol. 2. London: Hogarth; New York: Norton.

Goldberg, D. and Huxley, P. 1980: *Mental illness in the community*. London: Tavistock.

Kaplan, H.I., Freedman, L. and Sadock, B.J. 1980: *Comprehensive textbook of psychiatry*. 3rd edn. Baltimore: Williams and Wilkins.

Marks, I.M. 1969: *Fears and phobias*. London: Heinemann; New York: Academic Press.

Mathews, A.M., Gelder, M.G. and Johnston, D.W. 1981: *Agoraphobia, nature and treatment*. New York: Guildford Press.

World Health Organisation 1978: *Mental disorders: glossary and guide to their classification in accordance with the ninth revision of the International Classification of Diseases*. Geneva: WHO.

neurotransmitter system A group of neurons which synthesize and release the same neurotransmitter is called a neurotransmitter system. Since each neurotransmitter system now known is distributed throughout more than one part of the nervous system, much of the current research in this area is focused on determining whether a neurotransmitter system functions as a single unit in regulating physiology and behavior, or whether there are subsystems with different functions. The answer to this question is important not only for understanding normal human brain processes, but also for treating the consequences of abnormal brain function. Considerable effort has been made to determine the neuroanatomy of each known neurotransmitter system, and its possible role or roles in physiology and behavior.

The neuroanatomical analysis of neurotransmitter systems includes locating the cell bodies of NEURONS which produce a particular transmitter, determining where the input to them originates, and finding where their output goes. This is an extremely active research area due to the frequent exciting discoveries of new chemical substances in the brain, and the technological advances in methods for locating and identifying them. The results of these studies have shown that there is a wide range in the extent to which the different neurotransmitter substances are distributed throughout the brain and spinal cord. Some neurotransmitters such as ACETYLCHOLINE are found in neurons in many brain regions, each with its own unique set of inputs and outputs. Other neurotransmitters such as DOPAMINE are located in neurons whose cell bodies are found in relatively restricted parts of the brain, yet their outputs may still go to several different brain regions. for example, some dopamine-containing neurons communicate with the BASAL GANGLIA, while others send information to the LIMBIC SYSTEM (e.g., Cooper, Bloom and Roth 1978). These neuroanatomical findings suggest that each neurotransmitter system may have more than one behavioral or physiological function.

Long before neurons producing specific neuro-transmitters could be precisely localized there was widespread interest in the possible behavioral functions of these substances. Most drugs which act to change mood or behavior affect some aspect of SYNAPTIC TRANSMISSION, and thus involve neurotransmitters. As the mechanisms of action of the drugs have been discovered, their behavioral effects have been associated with the neurotransmitter system upon which they act. However, even drugs thought to be specific to one neurotransmitter system often affect several different aspects of behavior, which may represent the effects of the drug at different neuroanatomical sites. In order to discover which subsets of a single neurotransmitter system are responsible for the different behavioral effects of a drug, special experimental techniques have been employed. Injection of drugs with known mechanisms of action into various brain regions in animals has revealed several important facts. First, different drugs injected into the same region of the brain may elicit different types of behavior; this is known as the chemical coding of behavior (Miller 1965). Second, more than one neurotransmitter is involved in any complex behavior. Finally, the same drug injected into different brain regions may elicit either the same or widely differing types of behavior. For example, acetylcholine injected into many parts of the limbic system will elicit drinking, but when injected into other limbic system sites it elicits aggression, and when injected into the basal ganglia it induces tremor. These principles suggest that when referring to a neurotransmitter system in a functional or behavioral sense, a subset of the entire system must be defined.

The current interest in the roles of neurotransmitter systems in behavior stems both from recent discoveries regarding certain degenerative disorders of the nervous system, and from the tremendous success of drug therapy in treating some psychiatric disorders. More than twenty years ago it was discovered that persons with Parkinson's disease, who have symptoms such as tremor, rigidity of the limbs, and a decrease in spontaneous motor movements, also have degeneration of the dopamine-containing neurons which communicate with the basal ganglia. The behavioral symptoms can be improved remarkably by replacing the missing dopamine either by giving drugs which act like dopamine, or drugs which the brain can convert into dopamine (Hornykiewicz 1975). Parkinson's disease has become a model for studying the roles of neurotransmitters in a variety of neurological disorders in order to discover rational drug therapies. Another neurological disorder, Huntington's chorea, involves abnormal involuntary movements and a gradual deterioration of cognitive function. In this hereditary disease there is degeneration of neurons which produce acetylcholine and GABA in the basal ganglia and neocortex (Wu et al. 1979). New therapies currently being tested include drugs and diets which enhance the actions of these diminished neurotransmitters. Finally, at least one form of senile dementia (Alzheimer's disease) is marked by the degeneration of some of the neurons which produce acetylcholine and communicate with the neocortex (Whitehouse et al. 1981). Since blockage of acetylcholine interferes with memory formation in normal people, it is possible that the loss of acetylcholine-containing neurons underlies the memory deficit in Alzheimer's disease. Again, new experimental therapies include drugs which act in place of the missing neurotransmitter.

The second source of interest in the behavioral roles of neurotransmitter systems in people stems from the remarkable success of drug treatment for certain psychiatric disorders. When behavioral symptoms can be relieved by a drug which acts to block or enhance a particular neurotransmitter it is possible that some disorder involving this substance may have been the cause of the symptoms. For example, drugs effective in treating SCHIZOPHRENIA block dopamine. It has therefore been suggested that some schizophrenics may have hyperactivity of one of the dopamine subsystems (Carlsson 1978). Similarly, DEPRESSION can be treated with drugs which enhance the effectiveness of neurons which utilize NOREPINEPHRINE, dopamine, and possibly SEROTONIN. Depression has therefore been viewed as a disorder in which there may be a deficiency of one or all of these chemicals in the brain (Maas 1975).

While these hypotheses are attractive in that they provide a possible biological mechanism for emotional disorders which is consistent with the effects of the drugs used to treat them, it has been difficult to obtain direct evidence of the hypothesized differences in the brains of persons with these disorders. Unlike the known pathological changes in Parkinson's disease, Huntington's chorea, or senile dementia, there is no documented loss of neurons associated with a specific neurotransmitter substance in either schizophrenia or depression. Investigators must search for changes in the level of activity in the suspect neurons, rather than for degeneration. It is difficult, if not unethical, to assay the brains of living patients for increases or decreases in the activities of specific neurons; the researcher must settle for measures of neurotransmitter function in the cerebrospinal fluid, blood, or urine, none of which give accurate or uncontaminated measures of neurotransmitter activity in the brain. Differences in enzymes and hormone levels have been discovered in the blood of both schizophrenics and depressive persons, but none of these changes points unequivocally to a disorder of a single neurotransmitter system (e.g. Orsulak et al. 1978).

Postmortem examinations of the brains of schizophrenics and depressives provide a more direct way of testing neurotransmitter theories of emotional disorders. Workers studying schizophrenia are searching for changes in dopamine activity in the limbic system and basal ganglia, and some recent results support these expectations (Mackay et al. 1980). However, the interpretation of these findings is complicated by the fact that many of the patients had been prescribed drugs which affect dopamine. In addition, many other factors such as diet, general state of health before death, and agonal state may affect brain chemistry.

Because the blockage of dopamine in the basal ganglia may lead to motor symptoms resembling those of Parkinson's disease, it would be preferable to design a drug for schizophrenia which would act more selectively at limbic system sites. This now seems possible due to biochemical differences in the various dopamine subsystems. Knowledge of the neuroanatomy, biochemistry, and behavioral aspects of a neurotransmitter system can help in the design of drugs which are not only effective, but are also selective in their effects. As additional neurotransmitter systems are identified, further progresss can be made in understanding normal brain function, and in designing treatments for behavioral disorders.   CVanH

Bibliography

Carlsson, A. 1978: Antipsychotic drugs, neurotransmitters, and schizophrenia. *American journal of psychiatry* 135, 164–73.

*Cooper, Jack R., Bloom, F.E., and Roth, Robert H. 1978: *The biochemical basis of neuropharmacology*. 3rd edn. New York: Oxford University Press.

Hornykiewicz, O. 1975: Parkinson's disease and its chemotherapy. *Biochemical pharmacology* 24, 1061–65.

Maas, J. 1975: Biogenic amines and depression. *Archives of general psychiatry* 32, 1357–61.

Mackay, A.V.P. et al. 1980: Dopaminergic abnormalities in postmortem schizophrenic brain. *Advances in biochemical pharmacology* 24, 325–33.

Miller, N.E. 1965: Chemical coding of behavior in the brain. *Science* 148, 328–38.

Orsulak, P.J. et al. 1978: Differences in platelet monoamine oxidase activity in subgroups of schizophrenic and depressive disorders. *Biological psychiatry* 13, 637–47.

Panksepp, J. 1986: The neurochemistry of behavior. *Annual review of psychology* 37, 77–107.

Snyder, Solomon H. 1980: *Biological aspects of mental disorder*. New York and Oxford: Oxford University Press.

Whitehouse et al. 1981: Alzheimer disease: evidence for selective loss of cholinergic neurons in the nucleus basalis. *Annals of neurology* 10, 122–26.

Wu, J-Y. et al. 1979: Abnormalities of neurotransmitter enzymes in Huntington's chorea. *Neurochemical research* 4, 575–85.

neurotropism The tendency displayed by developing or regenerating axons for growth in a particular direction in the nervous system. The determinants of this attractive influence are unknown, but the presence of chemical signals as neurotropic "lures" has been postulated. An alternative, though not necessarily mutually exclusive hypothesis proposes that the formation of appropriate connectivity in the nervous system is simply a function of temporally constrained mechanical factors that guide and direct growth.   BER/RCS

Bibliography

Ebendal, T., Olson, L., Seiger, A. and Hedlund, K-O. 1980: Nerve growth factors in the rat iris. *Nature* 286, 25–8.

Sperry, R.W. 1963: Chemoaffinity in the orderly growth of nerve fiber patterns and connections. *Proceedings of the National Academy of Science* USA 50, 703–10.

norepinephrine   (noradrenaline) One of the catecholamine NEUROTRANSMITTERS found in the peripheral and central nervous system. Norepinephrine is synthesized from DOPAMINE by dopamine β-hydroxylase, an enzyme that serves as a marker for norepinephrine (noradrenergic) neurons. Peripherally, norepinephrine is an important neurotransmitter in the sympathetic nervous system. Centrally, a major site for the cell bodies of noradrenergic neurons is the locus ceruleus of the BRAIN STEM. Noradrenergic projections descending from this region synapse at lower brain stem nuclei and in the spinal cord. Ascending noradrenergic pathways, including the MEDIAL FOREBRAIN BUNDLE and the dorsal bundle, project to various brain regions, including the cerebral cortex, and nuclei in the THALAMUS, HYPOTHALAMUS, HIPPOCAMPUS and RETICULAR ACTIVATING SYSTEM. Other noradrenergic neurons project from locus ceruleus to the CEREBELLUM. Norepinephrine synapses can be either excitatory or inhibitory. Behavior associated with increased noradrenergic functioning includes behavioral arousal, alertness, mood elevation, and responses to stimulants. Decreases in norepinephrine levels have been associated with the initiation of paradoxical sleep.   GPH

Bibliography

Jones, L.S., Gauger, L.L. and Davis, J.W. 1985: Anatomy of brain α-adrenergic receptors. *Journal of comparative neurology* 231, 190–208.

Zukerman, M. 1984: Sensation-seeking: a comparative approach to a human trait. *Behavioral and brain sciences* 7, 413–71.

nosology The science of the definition of disease entities. It is concerned with the principles by which illnesses can be differentiated from one another and with the classification of illnesses as a basis for the making of diagnoses. A satisfactory nosological system would describe for each discrete disease a specific cause, presenting picture, time course and outcome, and in addition would ideally provide confirmatory objective tests and specific treatments. In psychiatry we are far from the ideal. Until a century ago mental illness was conceptualized as a unitary psychosis, with stages from melancholia to furor, delusional madness and finally dementia. With KRAEPELIN, JASPERS and BLEULER, studies of genetics, phenomenology and life histories led to the current classification into the broad categories of organic and functional PSYCHOSIS, NEUROSIS, PERSONALITY DISORDERS and MENTAL HANDICAP.   DLJ

Bibliography

Clare, A. 1979: The disease concept in psychiatry. In *Essentials of postgraduate psychiatry*, eds. P. Hill, R. Murray and A. Thorely. London: Academic Press; New York: Grune and Stratton.

nutrition and the nervous system

Since the human body cannot manufacture everything it needs for its development and maintenance it is not surprising that abnormal states of nutrition can have dramatic effects on the developing nervous system. General malnourishment or specific vitamin deficiencies due to poor diet during the early stages of life can have pronounced effects on intellectual functioning. In adults much of the nervous system pathology that results from chronic alcoholism may be secondary to poor nutrition. Wurtman and Fernstrom (1976) have shown that variations in normal dietary intake are reflected in the synthesis, and perhaps release, of various neurotransmitters. In rats fed a meal comprised primarily of carbohydrates, concentrations of SEROTONIN in the brain are subsequently increased. Meals high in protein content result in increased brain levels of DOPAMINE and NOREPINEPHRINE. Brain levels of ACETYLCHOLINE can similarly be modified by the ingestion of foods rich in its precursor, choline. Changes in levels of neurotransmitters may be reflected in behaviors mediated by them, and the alteration of NEUROTRANSMITTER SYSTEMS by the manipulation of diet may have important therapeutic applications.   GPH

Bibliography

Wurtman, R.J. and Fernstrom, J.D. 1976: Control of brain neurotransmitter synthesis by precursor availability and nutritional state. *Biochemical pharmacology* 25, 1691–96.

O

obesity Refers to the presence of an abnormally high proportion of body fat. "Overweight" refers to a body weight which is above an arbitrary standard. These words are often used interchangeably. Obesity is associated with many disorders which increase morbidity and mortality. Its prevalence is increasing in developed countries. Since the majority of obese people eat no more than their normal weight counterparts, obese people as a group are deficient in their utilization of energy. Psychological and social factors are also of etiological importance. Treatment aims to establish an energy deficit with energy expenditure exceeding energy intake. In general, emphasis is placed on the reduction of energy using dietary advice, behavioral intervention, anorectic drugs, or surgery. The long-term results are disappointing.   CGF

Bibliography

Garrow, J.S. 1981: *Treat obesity seriously*. Edinburgh: Churchill Livingstone.

Schachter, S. 1971: *Emotion, obesity and crime*. New York: Academic Press.

object relations A term used frequently by contemporary psychoanalytic writers (see KLEIN). Its meaning reflects a theoretical movement away from a model of the subject as isolated and biologically (instinctually) motivated toward a view which encompasses the subject's interactions with its surroundings — its interpersonal relations. Use of the word *object* to refer to persons derives from the commitment of psychoanalysts to an instinct theory. The object through which instinctual gratification is held to be achieved is usually a person, an aspect of a person or a symbolic representation of a person toward which the subject directs its actions or desires. Technically "object relations" refers to the mental representations of the self and other (the object) which are an aspect of ego organization and not to external interpersonal relationships.   BBL

Oedipus and Elektra complexes

After the Greek legends in which, respectively, King Oedipus inadvertently killed his father, and Elektra avenged the murder of her father by assisting in the murder of her mother, these terms refer in psychoanalytic personality theory (see FREUD) to two clusters of mainly unconscious feelings and ideas which set in at the "phallic" stage of psychosexual development. The child's attachment to the opposite-sex parent becomes sexualized, so that the child wishes to possess him or her and get rid of the other parent. The boy's rivalry with the father produces "castration anxiety", the female parallel of which is "penis envy". The child deals with the associated anxieties by eventually "identifying" with the same-sex parent (see DEFENSE MECHANISM) and "introjecting" his or her prohibitions as a basis for the primitive superego, and his or her positive values as ego ideal (Freud 1917, ch. 21). Some non-clinical studies of dreams and PROJECTIVE TESTS do seem to support some of the constituent hypotheses of these complexes (see Kline 1981, ch. 6).   NMC

Bibliography

Freud, Sigmund 1917: *Introductory lectures*. Part 3. *Standard edition of the complete psychological works of Sigmund Freud*, vol. 16. London: Hogarth Press; New York: Norton.

Kline, Paul 1981: *Fact and fiction in Freudian theory*, 2nd edn. London and New York: Methuen.

organic mental states Abnormalities of psychological functions (consciousness, memory, perception, thinking or mood) and behavior, which result from disorders of the brain. Organic mental states are usually accompanied by physical symptoms which are characteristic of the underlying condition. Many alternative terms have been used, among them: organic psychoses, exogenous reactions, symptomatic psychoses, psycho-organic syndromes, brain syndromes and organic reactions. Such terms suggest, with variable degree of success, the presence of psychological and physical manifestations in these conditions. Physical diseases of the brain tend to produce similar patterns of psychological disturbance, irrespective of the actual cause (Bonhoeffer 1909, Bleuler 1951). However, psychological symptoms taken together with physical signs, especially the neurological manifestations, can be of considerable help in locating the site of the lesion.

Organic mental states can be classified by reference to their clinical picture into two principal types: acute and chronic organic mental states.

Acute organic mental states
These are usually self-limited and reversible conditions, of sudden onset, and presenting a characteristic picture and course. The main symptom at the outset is clouding of consciousness (see CONSCIOUSNESS DISORDERS). The individual's attention is impaired and concentration is poor, with a tendency to lose track during conversation. The person may appear drowsy, and time sense (e.g. time of day, estimation of time) may be lost. Clouding of consciousness tends to fluctuate, and it is usually worse in the evening. Motor activity can be considerably reduced, especially with severe clouding of consciousness. In other cases, the individual may be restless, showing intermittent agitation and repetitive behavior involving stereotyped movements, as in delirium. Here the individual may suffer perceptual abnormalities involving the visual and auditory fields, as well as bodily sensations. There are frequent and short-lived *misinterpre-*

tations and *illusions*, and HALLUCINATIONS, usually visual, are a prominent feature of the clinical picture. *Thinking* is commonly slow, with failure to grasp, and is often disconnected and incoherent. *Delusional ideas*, especially involving persecution or threat, are very common, and their content tends to be colored by the individual's personality and background (Wolff and Curran 1935). *Memory functions* are severely affected, and the individual has difficulty registering new information, storing data or recalling material. Memory for recent events is poor, and disorientation in time and place is common (see MEMORY AND LEARNING DISORDERS). The patient's *mood* is also affected, anxiety and fear being frequent features. Anger and suspiciousness can be present, especially in association with delusional ideas or hallucinations. As the acute organic state improves, sleep becomes restful and prolonged, and recovery follows although memories surrounding the event remain hazy. A deteriorating course would usually progress toward coma, and in some cases, the individual may lapse into a chronic organic state.

Chronic organic mental states
These present a characteristic picture, usually with a progressive course. They may develop after an acute organic state, or they may have a gradual onset, with evidence of general intellectual decay, especially in memory and thinking, and showing personality changes with suspiciousness, uninhibited behavior or affective changes such as depression. As the condition progresses, the individual may show lack of interest and activity, social withdrawal and neglect in personal appearance and standards. The person's *memory* suffers global deterioration with forgetfulness at first, and then with more definite lapses of memory, and disorientation in time is usually present. Registration of new information is reduced and retention and recall are also affected. Confabulation may be present. Poverty of *thinking* is characteristic, and the patient's thoughts are slow and muddled, with difficulty thinking in abstract terms. Delusional ideas, usually

197

involving persecution or threat, can develop and contribute to suspicion and abnormalities of *mood*. The latter may include ANXIETY and hostility. Inappropriate or superficial emotional responses may be present.

When the organic mental state is the result of localized rather than generalized brain damage the clinical picture may have characteristic psychological and neurological symptoms, in addition to those associated with an acute or chronic course. The main psychological features of focal brain damage are as follows (see also BRAIN AND CENTRAL NERVOUS SYSTEM: ILLUSTRATIONS, figs. 1,2 and 3).

Frontal lobe: cognitive impairment in chronic disorder is similar to that seen in generalized disorders, but there may be prominent personality changes with disinhibition, impulsivity and euphoria, or with lack of drive and psychomotor retardation.

Parietal lobe: damage to the dominant parietal lobe is associated with specific language difficulties involving the production or understanding of words (see SPEECH DISORDERS). Non-dominant hemisphere lesions may lead to problems recognizing the body image, so that parts of the body may be perceived as missing. The outside space may also be misperceived. Visuospatial difficulties may be present with lesions of either parietal lobe, so that the person has difficulties placing objects in space or finding the way about.

Temporal lobe: memory disturbances are characteristic of bilateral damage to the temporal lobes (see MEMORY DISORDERS). Language difficulties may follow lesions to the dominant temporal lobe, while non-dominant lesions may be associated with visuospatial symptoms. Personality changes, with aggressive outbursts may be present.

Occipital lobe: visual symptoms are prominent here, with difficulties in recognizing written material, color or objects. Visual hallucinations may also occur.

Organic mental states can be caused by a great variety of agents, some producing damage to the brain itself and some resulting from disorders in other parts of the body which have indirect effects on the central nervous system (Lishman 1978). Acute organic reactions can result from the following disorders, among others:

(a) Brain lesions caused by:

trauma: head injury can lead to concussion, with a period of unconsciousness or clouding, and this can be followed by an *acute* post-traumatic delirium or other disorders.

tumors: in addition to the general feature of the acute reaction, the individual may have symptoms which suggest the location of the tumor.

infection of the central nervous system or the meninges, as in viral conditions or syphilis.

vascular disorders, such as cerebral hemorrhage or thrombosis.

degenerative conditions such as dementia, complicated by other disorders such as infections or vascular accidents.

epileptic disorders, especially psychomotor seizures (see EPILEPSY).

(b) Conditions affecting other systems which have effects on brain function:

metabolic disorders: e.g. acute disease of the liver or kidney.

endocrine disorder: e.g. of the thyroid, parathyroid, adrenal glands (see ENDOCRINE DISORDERS).

nutritional disorders: such as vitamin deficiencies.

lack of cerebral oxygen: as in cardiovascular and respiratory disorders.

infection: e.g. pneumonia and septicemia.

toxic conditions: e.g. effect of drugs (alcohol, barbiturates) or their withdrawal, or of poisons such as lead or mercury.

Chronic organic states can be caused by similar agents to those producing acute reactions, but here the structural damage is more persistent and the condition is less likely to be reversible. They often follow on from acute organic states. Chronic organic states can be the result of brain lesions or generalized disorders:

(a) Brain lesions:

trauma: post-concussional syndrome, post-traumatic dementia and psychotic states may follow severe head injury.

infections: e.g. syphilis (general paralysis of the insane) (Hare 1959), viral encephalitis.

degenerative conditions: the dementias: senile, arteriosclerotic, Alzheimer's,

Huntington's, and the rare dementia due to abnormal pressure hydrocephalus which is important because of its potential reversibility (Lishman 1978).

tumors: the symptoms have localized significance.

(b) Conditions affecting other systems, among them:

metabolic diseases: e.g. chronic and severe liver and kidney conditions.

endrocrine disorders as in acute reactions.

nutritional as in thiamine deficiency (WERNICKE'S SYNDROME).

toxic conditions: e.g. damage from alcohol (KORSAKOV'S SYNDROME), barbiturates or poisons.

lack of cerebral oxygen: e.g. cardiovascular and respiratory diseases.   JC

Bibliography

Bleuler, M. 1951: Psychiatry of cerebral diseases. *British medical journal* 2, 1233–8.

Bonhoeffer, K. 1909: Exogenous psychoses. In *Themes and variations in European psychiatry*, eds. S.R. Hirsch and M. Shepherd. Bristol: John Wright.

Hare, E.H. 1959: The origin and spread of dementia paralytica. *Journal of mental science* 105, 594–626.

*Lishman, W.A. 1978: *Organic psychiatry: the psychological consequences of cerebral disorder*. Oxford: Blackwell Scientific Publications; St Louis, Missouri: C.V. Mosby.

Slater, E. and Roth, M. 1969: *Clinical psychiatry*. London: Baillière, Tindall and Cassell.

Wolff, H. and Curran, D. 1935: Nature of delirium and allied states. *Archives of neurology and psychiatry* 35, 1175–215.

P

pain Probably the least understood and most ineptly treated subject in medicine today. Perhaps for these reasons alone it has little difficulty in retaining its position as the most complex and certainly the most fascinating of medical problems.

It must be significant that opium, first used in the third century BC, is still the most commonly used systemic analgesic.

The existence of an adequate theory of the mechanism of pain would do much to reduce our ignorance and an attempt to achieve this end was made by Melzack and Wall (1965) who introduced the gate theory (see PAIN; GATE CONTROL SYSTEM). This postulated the existence of a filter or gate in the substantia gelatinosa of the SPINAL CORD where susceptive stimuli were modified in the light of previous experience and emotional state at the time. If, as a result of these modifying factors, the critical threshold for firing-off was not reached, then pain would not be felt. This theory has been used to explain the fact that soldiers who were shot in battle felt no pain at all. As with other theories the gate theory is no longer acceptable in its original form and has been extensively modified to provide a role for the endogenous opioid peptides and ENCEPHALINS which have been recently isolated and provide an exciting prospect for the future.

There are many gaps in our knowledge regarding mechanism but some of these have been filled in by experience gained largely from pain clinics. These are excellent but have limited scope as most have no beds and many workers believe that it is not possible even to skim the surface of the problem in a twenty-minute out-patient interview. It should be remembered that these patients have all been treated before, unsuccessfully, and look upon the pain clinic as their last hope. It is small wonder that success in this field, if achieved, is always hard earned.

The patients have intractable pain, i.e. pain that has been present for over a month and is unremitting, despite treatment. It is usually associated with malignancy, but that need not be the cause. Despite the undeniable fact that cancer pain can be intractable, it is surely no more so than the pain in a patient who has had three laminectomies, two spinal fusions and is still in pain.

Hospices have made an immense contribution to the management of the terminally ill cancer patient (see Saunders 1967). The very word "cancer" tends to be emotive but this should not be allowed to obscure the abject misery to which many patients with non-malignant pain are condemned for many years. It can be extremely damaging both physically and mentally, not only to the patient, but also to his family.

Today the existence of pain centers, or units, which are virtually autonomous, having their own beds, nursing staff and treatment rooms, has allowed the practice of a multi-disciplinary approach to the problem (Bonica 1974). Patients can be admitted directly from general practitioners or from other hospitals and a thorough assessment can be made at leisure. Problem cases can be seen by attending consultants from other specialities if necessary.

Many patients will take two or three days to relax and appreciate the aims of the unit, which is to understand their problem and help their pain. Because of their previous shuttling from doctor to doctor with no improvement there are some who think nobody believes that they are in pain. This leads to an inevitable depression and lack of confidence in themselves and their medical attendants. Management of these patients is time-consuming and often unrewarding. The placebo effect is very much in evidence in pain centres but the "negative placebo" effect also lurks just beneath the surface if a patient's equilibrium is upset.

The standard methods of treatment available are interruption of pain transmission by nerve blocks or by drug therapy. Both of these need to be bolstered by supportive counseling.

All patients attending pain clinics will have been on drugs at some stage, but their use tends to be disappointing in chronic pain. Perhaps their most effective role is in the management of terminal cancer. The final breakthrough will almost certainly be achieved in the pharmacological field, but until that time nerve blocks, by various means, serve a very important function.

JWL

Bibliography

Bonica, J.J. 1974: Organisation and function of a pain clinic. In *Advances in neurology*, vol. 4, ed. J.J. Bonica.

Melzack, R. and Wall, P.D. 1965: Pain mechanisms: a new theory. *Science* 150, 971–9.

Saunders, C.M. 1967: *The management of terminal illness*. London Hospital Medicine Publications.

pain: gate control system Pain is a sensory experience associated with injury or spoken of in terms of injury. To separate physiological mechanisms from a sensory experience smacks of dualism (Melzack and Wall 1982). Nociceptive nerve fibers in peripheral nerves detect injury. Impulses in these fibers enter the spinal cord from the body. At the first central synapses these impulses enter a gate control system (Melzack and Wall 1965). Their further progress to trigger pain reactions depends on the convergence of other impulses from the periphery which may be of innocuous origin. This convergence can inhibit or exaggerate the transmitted message and forms the basis of many folk and modern therapies. The gate control is also strongly affected by control systems descending from the brain and this may form the basis for the marked effect of attitude, experience etc., on pain. The entry control region includes the substantia gelatinosa which is the site of action of opiates as analgesics and contains an elaborate selection mechanism which is rapidly controlled by the gate control and slowly by connectivity control mechanisms. In their further course, impulses signaling the presence of injury are subject to detailed control at each stage. The relationship of injury to pain is contingent and variable (Wall 1979).   PDW

Bibliography

Melzack, R. and Wall, P.D. 1965: Pain mechanisms: a new theory. *Science* 150, 971–9.

—— 1982: *The challenge of pain*. Harmondsworth: Penguin.

Wall, P.D. 1979: *Pain* 6, 253–4.

pain and the nervous system (see BRAIN AND CENTRAL NERVOUS SYSTEM, fig. 29). Sensation of pain is a submodality of the SOMATOSENSORY system and usually results from noxious stimuli. Pain is mediated by nociceptors (receptors responding to noxious stimuli). Mechanical nociceptors are activated by strong mechanical stimulation such as that inflicted by sharp objects. Heat nociceptors respond to temperatures above about 45°C. Mixed nociceptors respond to a variety of noxious stimuli. Nociceptive axons form two groups: small, myelinated Aδ fibers which mediate fast pain, a sudden, sharp sensation; and small, unmyelinated C fibers which mediate slow pain, a sickening, burning sensation. Pain afferents from the body have synapses in the dorsal horn of the spinal cord. Second-order NEURONS send fibers carrying information about painful stimuli in the anterolateral tracts (spinoreticular and spinothalamic fibers) to large regions of the BRAIN STEM and to the THALAMUS (see BRAIN AND CENTRAL NERVOUS SYSTEM: ILLUSTRATIONS, figs. 6, 7 and 19). Fibers from the head and neck innervate these regions via the trigeminal system. In the thalamus two different regions receive pain fibers from the anterolateral tracts and project to CEREBRAL CORTEX. Blunt stimulation of neurons in the thalamus, however, does not mimic the sensory quality of pain, suggesting that spatio-temporal patterning of pain and touch inputs may be as important a determinant of pain sensation at this level as the specific pathway over which excitation arrives. Thalamic-cortical connections may be more useful for localizing painful stimuli to body sites than in the perception of pain itself. Cortical ablation rarely relieves the sensation of pain but commonly increases tolerance of the sensation.

Neural connections exist which modify the information in ascending pain pathways and reduce the sensation of pain (analgesia). Electrical stimulation of portions of the brainstem (e.g. region of the dorsal raphé nucleus) produces analgesia. A lessening of pain can also be produced by opiates (ENCEPHALINS/ENDORPHINS) and neural opiate receptors have been identified in the brain. Converging lines of evidence suggest that encephalin/endorphin-containing interneurons may serve to inhibit the transmission of pain information in the dorsal horn of the spinal cord itself. These interneurons may be driven by descending fibers from those very regions of the brainstem where electrical stimulation produces analgesia. Other kinds of analgesia, such as that introduced by novel STRESS, do not appear to involve opiates alone in their mode of action, suggesting multiple mechanisms for modifying incoming sensory information about pain-producing stimuli.   SCC

Bibliography

Basbaum, A.I. 1983: The generation and control of pain. In *The clinical neurosciences*, vol 5. *Neurobiology* eds. R.N. Rosenberg and W.D. Willis, Jr. New York and Edinburgh: Churchill Livingstone.

Bonica, J.J., ed 1980: *Pain. Research publications: association for research in nervous and mental disease.* New York: Raven Press.

Burgess, P.R. and Perl, E.R. 1973: Cutaneous mechanoreceptors and nociceptors. In *Handbook of sensory physiology*, vol. 2, *Somatosensory system*, ed. A. Iggo. Berlin and New York: Springer-Verlag.

Terman, G.W. et al. 1984: Intrinsic mechanisms of pain inhibition. *Science* 226, 1270–7.

Papez's circuit A neural circuit identified in 1937 by the neuroanatomist J.W.

Papez. It consists of the mamillary bodies in the HYPOTHALAMUS, anterior THALAMUS, cingulate gyrus, entorhinal cortex, HIPPOCAMPUS, and their interconnecting fibers (see BRAIN AND CENTRAL NERVOUS SYSTEM: ILLUSTRATIONS, figs. 16 and 17). Papez suggested that these structures comprise a closed reverberatory system mediating emotional experience and behavior. Emotional reactions are seen as developing on the basis of central and peripheral input. The central signals originate in the cerebral cortex and are conveyed to the hippocampus. From the hippocampus, they are transmitted to the mamillary bodies where they combine with visceral and sensory impressions from the hypothalamus. The information is then projected to the anterior thalamus, up to the cingulate gyrus where emotions are experienced, and finally, via the entorhinal cortex and hippocampus, back to the hypothalamus where expression is regulated. Although influential for some time, it is now apparent that Papez's formulations were based on questionable anatomical and clinical data. While parts of the circuit (e.g. the hypothalamus), can be linked to emotion, in recent years various structures have also become associated with other functions, particularly those related to learning and memory processes. (See EMOTION: NEUROBIOLOGICAL APPROACH TO.)   GWi

paranoid states A group of psychotic disorders in which paranoid DELUSIONS are prominent but HALLUCINATIONS and deterioration of personality are uncommon. They are distinguished from paranoid syndromes secondary to other psychiatric disorders such as ORGANIC STATES, AFFECTIVE DISORDERS and paranoid SCHIZOPHRENIA. The category of paranoid states is to some extent a temporary diagnostic grouping for cases whose classification in relation to other psychiatric disorders is uncertain. The diagnosis of a paranoid state is therefore used for acute and chronic paranoid states which are closely similar to schizophrenia but lack the generally accepted diagnostic features. KRAEPELIN distinguished two principal forms, paraphrenia and paranoia. The former was a paranoid PSYCHOSIS with conspicuous hallucinations in middle life, which is now normally regarded as being indistinguishable from paranoid schizophrenia. Paranoia was described as a chronic psychosis with systematized delusions but without developed evidence of hallucination or thought disorder. This syndrome is extremely rare and it is doubtful whether it can be distinguished as a separate category. In current psychiatric practice the terms paraphrenia and paranoia are probably best avoided, although the diagnosis "late paraphrenia" is widely used for the schizophrenia-like paranoid illnesses of old age. Paranoid states are among the causes of a number of uncommon paranoid psychiatric syndromes, such as MORBID JEALOUSY.   RAM

Bibliography

Kendler, K.S. and Tsuang, H.T. 1981: Nosology of paranoid schizophrenia and other paranoid psychoses. *Schizophrenia bulletin* 7, 594–610.
Lewis, A. 1970: Paranoia and paranoid: a historical perspective. *Psychological medicine* 1, 2–12.

parapraxis In psychoanalytic theory the disruption of a specific action or mental process by a determinant, such as a wish or anxiety, which has become unconscious as the result of REPRESSION. Disruption takes the form of omission, as in forgetting, or substitution, as in speech-error (known popularly as the "Freudian slip"). FREUD discussed such errors extensively in *Psychopathology of everyday life* (Freud 1901) in order to demonstrate that healthy people also have the unconscious processes which produce neurotic symptoms. The particular action which is disrupted may be only rather indirectly or symbolically associated with the repressed material, but Freud distinguishes degrees of awareness of the source of the error. One may be aware of the "disturbing intention" but not have seen its connection with the "disturbed intention", or one may be quite unaware of the former intention and vigorously resist acknowledging it (Freud 1916, ch. 4).

Various attempts have been made to explain away Freud's and others' examples by means of "simpler" hypotheses (e.g. Timpanaro 1976).   NMC

Bibliography

Freud, Sigmund 1901, 1916: *Psychopathology of everyday life* (vol.16); *Introductory lectures* (vol.15), *Standard edition of the complete psychological works of Sigmund Freud*. London: Hogarth Press; New York: Norton.
Timpanaro, Sebastiano 1976: *The Freudian slip*, trans. Kate Soper, London: New Left.

passive-aggression Behavior characterized by indirect resistance to demands for adequate performance in either social or work settings. This is accomplished by such tactics as forgetting appointments, procrastination and misplacing important materials. The term is derived from the assumption that the individual is expressing resentment and aggression in a non-assertive fashion. Passive-aggression is often used to resist the demands of authority; children often use this tactic on their parents. Passive-aggressive behavior in several aspects of an individual's life, particularly when more adaptive behavior is possible, results in general ineffectiveness. This condition, along with other factors, may lead to a diagnosis of passive-aggressive personality disorder according to criteria set out in the *Diagnostic and statistical manual 3*. (American Psychiatric Association 1980.)   RHo

Bibliography

American Psychiatric Association 1980: *Diagnostic and statistical manual 3*.

Pavlov, Ivan Petrovich (1849–1936) Physiologist and pioneer of the study of conditioning. Pavlov was born in Ryazan, Russia and entered the University of St Petersburg in 1870. He graduated in natural science in 1875 and entered the Military Medical Academy. He obtained his doctorate in 1883 and then spent a few years in Germany, studying with Carl Ludwig in Leipzig. He became professor of pharmacology at the Military Medical

Academy in 1890 and professor of physiology in 1895. He received the Nobel Prize for Medicine in 1904 for his work on the physiology of digestion.

An opponent of simplistic experimentation in physiology, Pavlov developed a range of new methods for the empirical study of processes in the normal, living animal. His earliest work was on the physiology of the circulation of the blood. By an ingenious surgical technique he was able to isolate different parts of the digestive system to study the relationship between digestive processes and venous and arterial activity. Out of this came his theory of specific irritability, that is the idea that particular organic systems are sensitive to specific stimulants and repressants.

During the course of his digestive studies Pavlov noticed that dogs sometimes salivated in anticipation of receiving food. This led him to the discovery of the conditioned reflex, now regarded as a fundamental aspect of learning. He distinguished between unconditioned reflexes, internally stimulated and inbuilt so to speak, and conditioned reflexes, the effect of environmental and external agencies, or built up to continue the metaphor. It is the conditioned reflex that makes possible the fine adaptation of individual systems to their particular environments. From 1902 until his death Pavlov more or less concentrated his researches on this phenomenon of CONDITIONING, and he is responsible for many of the basic concepts current in this field of study today. In particular he extended his researches to the creation and dissipation of artificial neuroses. The connection with human psychology did not escape him, and many of his later studies had a human slant; for instance his attempt to find a physiological basis for the traditional classifications of the human temperament. Pavlov died in 1936.   DJM/RHa

Bibliography
Pavlov, I.R. 1927: *Conditioned reflexes*. London: Oxford University Press.

Penfield, Wilder G. Born in Spokane, Washington in 1891, Penfield was edu-
cated at Princeton, Johns Hopkins and with the help of a Rhodes Scholarship (1914) at Oxford. During the First World War he served in the medical services in France, in various capacities. In 1917 he married Helen Kermott. After the war he spent some time as a postgraduate student in London and in continental Europe. He returned to North America in 1921 and held various neurosurgical appointments in New York until 1928. In that year he took up the post of Neurosurgeon to the Royal Victoria Hospital in Montreal and remained there until 1934 when he became the first Director of the Montreal Neurological Institute. Most of Wilder Penfield's working life was spent as a neurosurgeon, specializing in the treatment of EPILEPSY. It was out of this work that his contributions to neuro-psychology developed. His scientific studies were directed to two problems, the nature of memory and the relationship between consciousness and brain physiology. In effect these studies were an ingenious exploitation of a truly vast repertoire of observations (1132 patients in all) accumulated in the course of his daily medical work.

As his experience grew Penfield seems to have become more and more convinced of the utility and perhaps the ultimate truth of a dualistic theory of mind and brain. In the light of this theory he painstakingly and systematically collected a great many reports from patients, as to their conscious experiences when different parts of their brains were being stimulated, particularly by electric currents. Electrical stimulation at precisely identified locations was made possible by the insertion of electrodes under local anesthetics.

Penfield made two main discoveries. In following up the spread of an epileptic disturbance he found that stimulation of a local area lead to the suspension of normal functioning in that area, but to the activation of appropriate normal performance in a quite specific distant area. The brain was organized as specific pathways through which neural impulses passed, activating first the proximal and then the distal area. This discovery effectively put paid to the generalized network model, in which the stimulation of some local area was thought to spread through a web of interconnections.

But the major contribution of this work was the discovery of the "interpretative cortex". It was this discovery that lay behind Penfield's theories of consciousness and memory. He found that the gray matter of the right temporal lobe of the brain, adjacent to the main speech area, seemed to be the seat of immediate conscious awareness. Stimulation of that region produced clear and distinct states of awareness. He also showed that this area was linked to a distant activation area in the diencephalon, the brain stem. The interpretative cortex is implicated in two related processes. There is an automatic and unconscious process by which current experience is checked against the records of past experience. The conscious result of this checking is the experiencing of some among a range of generalized feelings, such as threat, familiarity and so on. But there is another process, by which there occurs a conscious presentation of a detailed record of past "strips" of the stream of consciousness. These presentations are evoked by electrical stimulation of the temporal lobe with an implanted electrode, and they are of great clarity, detail and endurance. It is the existence of these phenomena which have become known outside academic neurophysiology and are usually linked with Penfield's name.

Penfield interprets his results as showing that there is one memory file (supposedly in the diencephalon) but two modes of access; one automatic and leading only to generalized conscious awareness, and the other intentional leading to specific and detailed representations. The "keys" to the memory file are somehow maintained in the hippocampus but that organ does not contain any memory content. The Penfield theory not only bears upon the nature of memory and its relation to consciousness but also serves to explain the difference between petit mal and grand mal epileptic seizures. A petit mal seizure interferes with the process by which detailed memory records are created and recovered, hence the characteristic

lack of awareness of the sufferer. But all automatic processes are unaffected. A grand mal seizure however affects the unconscious and automatic mechanisms, hence the distinctive massive disturbances to motor functioning as well as unconsciousness.

The merit of Penfield's work has been widely recognized with a Fellowship of the Royal Society and the Order of Merit. (See also BRAIN STIMULATION AND MEMORY.)   RHa

Bibliography

Penfield, W.G. 1958: *The excitable cortex in conscious man.* (The Sherrington lectures.) Springfield, Ill.: Thomas.

Penfield, W.G. and Perot, P. 1963: The brain's record of auditory and visual experience. *Brain* 86, 595–696.

Worden, F.G., Swazey, J.P. and Adelman, G. eds. 1975: *The neurosciences: paths of discovery.* Cambridge, Mass. and London: MIT Press, chapter 25.

perception: philosophical issues

Perception, understood as awareness of the world about us by means of the senses, is a philosophical problem because certain facts about the nature of perception and certain theories about how it takes place appear to show that what we are aware of is not an objective world of physical objects but certain ideas, impressions, images or sense-data which are distinct from such a world. The question then arises how we can have knowledge of such a world or even have reason to believe in its existence. Because of such familiar facts as perspective, refraction and dependence of color on lighting, an accurate description of what appears to us could not be a description of the world as we ordinarily take it to be; still less could it be a description of the world as presented by any scientific theory. Moreover, sense-perception appears to be the end result of a long causal chain of which the object we claim to see is at best a distant and theoretically dispensable link.

Faced with this problem, philosophers have disagreed about its solution. Some have adopted some form of causal theory, according to which our ideas or sense-data are caused by an inferred physical reality. The simplest version of such a theory is probably representationalism in which what we perceive is taken to resemble the physical objects which cause it. No great philosopher has been a pure representationalist; but the overwhelming majority of philosophers and scientists at least from the time of Democritus have held a semi-representationalist theory; thus atomists, including Locke and Newton, held that mechanically relevant, measurable primary qualities such as shape, size and motion are the same in both atoms and the ideas they cause, whereas smell, taste, color, heat, and the like are taken to be caused by atoms which are odorless, tasteless, colorless and neither warm nor cold.

But this notion of the physical world as essentially inaccessible to perception has not satisfied empirically-minded philosophers, who have agreed with Kant that we can know nothing of a transcendent world of things in themselves or even, like those who accept the verification principle, declare that talk of such a world must be meaningless. Many of these philosophers have accepted either subjective idealism, according to which the world is composed of essentially mental ideas, or a phenomenalism which substitutes neutral sense-data for these mental entities. Anticipating Russell's principle of replacing inferred entities by logical constructions, Berkeley declared that physical objects were mere 'bundles of ideas' whilst Mill said that they were 'permanent possibilities of sensation'. In a similar vein modern phenomenalists said that they were 'logical constructions out of sense-data'. To talk of the physical world is therefore merely a compendious way of describing and predicting the course of our sense-experience, while science should not be regarded as telling us of a world beyond our senses but as constructing models and theories the whole function of which is to explain and predict the course of our sense-experience. Berkeley clearly adumbrated this view, of which Mach is a classical exponent.

Both the traditional causal theorist and the phenomenalist accept the arguments which claim to show that we cannot be aware of physical objects directly but must either infer them or regard talk about them as merely a commodious and compressed way of talking about ideas or sense-data. The view that we are sensibly aware of physical bodies was disparagingly known as "naive realism", but a minority of philosophers has always been dissatisfied with the arguments outlined at the beginning of this article. The description of how things appear, our everyday description of the physical world and the account of that world given by scientists should not be regarded as descriptions of a veil of appearance and of two worlds lurking behind it but as three equally legitimate descriptions of one and the same world. Similarly the physiologist does not tell us what happens instead of our seeing objects but how we see an object. No doubt physical objects cause a long chain of events in the central nervous system, but what we perceive is not, for example, an elliptical sense-datum caused by a round coin, but a round coin that looks elliptical. Or again, this minority holds, when we say that a tomato is red we are expressing no view whatsoever about the nature of the ultimate particles of matter; it is a gross error to suppose that because science assigns no color to the particles it is a mistake to speak of ordinary bodies as colored. Perhaps the most powerful argument that can be put for this view is the following: if the empirical facts about perceptual illusion and the empirical findings of the sciences are held to constitute an empirical refutation of the view that we perceive physical objects directly it must be possible to conceive of a world in which the empirical facts were compatible with "naive realism". How would objects look in such a world? Would coins look round from all angles, for example? The difficulty of answering such questions might suggest that the theory which generates them is confused. The best known exponent of this minority position is J. L. Austin.   JOU

Bibliography

Austin, J.L. 1962: *Sense and sensibilia*. Oxford:

Clarendon Press; Cambridge, Mass.: Harvard University Press.

Berkeley, George 1710: *A treatise concerning the principles of human knowledge* (many editions).

Locke, John 1690: *An essay concerning human understanding*. Bk 2, ch. 8 (many editions).

perception: psychological issues

As a term in psychology perception refers to the apparently direct and immediate knowledge of the world, and also of our own bodies, by neural signals from the eyes, the ears, the nose, the tongue, and the many other sense organs which include the skin senses of touch and hot and cold and pain; and also organs of balance in the inner ear, and the unconscious monitoring of forces on the muscles and joints to signal the positions of the limbs. We usually think of our own perceptions as our consciousness of the world around us, and of ourselves; but much of the perception by which behavior is initiated and controled is totally unconscious, and awareness of the perception of things and states of affairs, by which we act, is never more than fragmentary. We are never fully aware of what features of sensory signals are being used for the perceptions by which we survive in a hostile world, and are intelligent. This has several important implications: that we cannot be altogether responsible for what we do if "responsibility" requires awareness; and it shows that experiments are essential for discovering not only processes of perception but even what it is we perceive to recognize things, walk around without bumping into things, drive a car, or read a book. It also throws severe doubts on the notion that consciousness is causally significant for behavior. However this may be, we do talk about perception in animals, even though we may doubt whether they have consciousness at all like ours. The simple animals are however not generally thought to have perception at all as we do, but only more or less rigid and predictable tropisms and reflexes, by which behavior is more or less stimulus-determined. This distinction between behavior controlled rather directly by stimuli and far less directly by perception is

important, for although there is no general agreement on how best to think about, or explain perception yet it at least seems clear to most psychologists and physiologists working on these problems that perception is essentially the reading of meanings from sensory signals; so that behavior is, generally, appropriate to all manner of hidden characteristics of objects, and situations, and is not merely triggered and guided by the stimuli that happen to be available. Perception is more than a matter of reflexes and tropisms, for it uses subtle "cues" of many kinds to make inferences to what the objects around us are like; and it is predictive. To be predictive in unusual situations, it has to draw intelligent analogies from a rich store of generalized knowledge of the world. This cognitive, knowledge-based, aspect of perception allows appropriate intelligent behavior even when there is very little available information from the senses; and even our eyes, which probably command more of the brain than all the other senses, cannot transmit anything like so much information in "real time" as they seem to do. When we open our eyes and immediately, without any apparent effort, see a room or a view all at once like a superb photograph; the perception is not at all like a photograph, but is created essentially from guesses as suggested by cues from sensed shapes of contours and textures which are essentially inferred as objects, and shadows and so on.

This view of perception as brain-descriptions based on inferences from sensory data is quite a new idea. It is associated especially with the modern founder of Physiological Optics, as it is sometimes called, the German physiologist and physicist, Hermann von Helmholtz (1821–94) who described perception as being given by Unconscious Inference. A much earlier and very different view (which was held by the Greeks including the great geometer Euclid who wrote a book on optics) and which is still in various forms accepted by some psychologists today, especially the distinguished writer on perception the late James J. GIBSON, is that visual perception is not derived by inferences from sensed data: but is given directly from the world, or at least from surrounding patterns of light. In Gibson's well known phrase, this is direct 'Pick up of information from the ambient array'. This approach has revealed a great deal about which features, textures, and so on are accepted and used for perception. So, even if one feels this philosophy to be inadequate or even ultimately misleading there is no doubt that the experiments inspired by it are extremely useful. Here though we will take a more Helmholtzian approach, based not so much on Gibson's ambient array, but rather on the reading of neural signals from the image forming eye. Retinal images and selection of visual features by eye movements are, rather curiously, hardly mentioned and even rejected altogether by the stricter Gibsonians; so, the reader will appreciate that we are in a somewhat stormy sea of controversy from the very outset.

There are, as can be seen by looking into an eye with a suitable ophthalmoscope, photograph-like optical images in the eyes. These are upside down and laterally reversed, as cast onto the retinas at the back of the eyes by the curved corneas and the internal crystalline lens. However, the retinas are more than mere screens for the ever changing optical images from the world: for they are mini computers, performing the first stages of processing of the electrical signals of the incoming ("afferent") nervous system for vision. All the information that we receive from any of the senses is coded by electrical impulses running in nerve fibers at about the speed of sound, and increasing in frequency from about 5–800 impulses per second, as the intensity of the light (or the pressure on the skin, or whatever) increases. It is a remarkable fact that all we know and experience of the world is provided by patterns of these electrical impulses – ACTION POTENTIALS – running in bundles of fibers into the dark silent brain. The action potentials from all the senses are, physically, essentially the same; and the action potentials sending (efferent) signals to the muscles are also essentially the same. The fact that some provide sensations of color, and others of sound or touch or pain, is dependent on which parts of the brain receive the action potentials. If nerves from one sense were transposed to the region of brain normally fed from another sense, then the sensations would be reversed. We might then hear light and see sounds!

The organs of sense, such as the eyes and the ears, are in engineering terms transducers; as they detect patterns of energy from the external world (and in some cases from the body) and convert the received physical energy patterns into the coded messages, transmitted by action potentials. They are incredibly sensitive, so that the light receptors of the retina (the rods, for black-white vision, and the "cones" for color) respond to a single photon, which is the physically smallest possible packet of energy. If the ears were any more sensitive, we would hear the random movement of the molecules of the air banging against the ear drum.

How are the signals from the senses read by the brain? This is the big question (at least for a Helmholtzian approach) for understanding perception, and it can at present only be partially answered. As by far the most is known about VISUAL PERCEPTION – though of course the other senses are extremely important and in their own ways perhaps as interesting – we shall consider only visual perception here but many of the same principles apply to other senses. It is now known that the signals arriving from the million or so fibers of the optic nerves are processed in many successive stages, and that an important early stage (taking place in the striate cortex, at the back of the brain where, somewhat curiously the signals go, to work forwards as they are analyzed and read for their meanings) is selection of a few simple features – such as orientations of contours or edges, and movements. Thus single cells in the striate cortex fire to particular features. This was discovered by two American physiologists, David Hubel and Torsten Wiesel, and was a key discovery to how the brain reads sensory signals. The point is that the initial picture at the eye is soon lost, as features are selected and represented by combinations of firing brain cells. These patterns of electrical activity are essentially *descriptions* of the scene; and this description depends very much upon stored knowledge of objects which is given by later stages of processing which are not understood in detail. This is obvious, when one comes to realize that we act upon all manner of features of things which cannot be sensed, at least when we perceive them. Thus we perceive an ice cream as cold before we touch it; and far more subtly, we see that a person is angry or pleased from his expression or a gesture. Actually we may not be able to say just how we can see the mood of a person – or the distances or sizes or shapes of objects, or what they are made of or what they are doing or likely to do next. As we have said, but little of this complex richness or perception is available to consciousness.

Partly because consciousness is really rather unimportant for perception as a whole – even if it does dominate how we think of the visual and musical arts – it is a useful step to consider and investigate perception in animals, and perhaps more surprisingly also in machines designed to accept and make sense of signals. The new science of artificial intelligence is extremely important for making explicit, and for testing, theoretical ideas of how the brain may function to confer perception and intelligence, and these are closely linked. It is now known that computers can be fed with visual signals from TV camera "eyes", and programmed to read the video signals, so that they can describe and respond appropriately to external objects. It is important to allow the computer to accept as little as possible, to prevent it being overloaded with unimportant detail: what is accepted must convey a lot of information. It turns out that corners and edges of objects are extremely important features and textures of surfaces considerably less so. It is very likely that we, also, derive most of our useful visual information from edges and from shapes such as converging lines indicating depth and orientation in depth of objects; as converging lines in the retinal image is often due to shrinking of the image (exactly as for a camera) with increasing distance – to generate perspective shapes, which may be accepted as usually reliable

evidence of distances, for things such as tables, rooms and roads which are usually rectangular. It follows though that when objects are queer shapes – such as actually converging to one end – then powerful illusory distortions can be generated; as the signals from the eye are misread by assumptions of rectangularity, or other common shapes. Illusions of many kinds can also be caused by adaptation of neural mechanisms, as occurs with after-images to bright lights, or to continuous motion which produces illusory, apparent, motion in the opposite direction.

Adaptations of the channels of the senses can be used to reveal what the channels are, and their characteristics, so adaptations of this kind are important as research tools for relating physiological processes and mechanisms with perception. Other kinds of illusions, such as those of perspective misapplied, reveal how and what kinds of knowledge or assumptions are accepted for reading sensory signals; for they can be read with inappropriate assumptions, to generate cognitive illusions which are a give away to how we use, and in some situations misuse, stored knowledge for seeing the world and ourselves – in terms of the past, for predicting and so surviving into the immediate future where all threats and promises wait upon our intelligent perception.   RLG

Bibliography

Barlow, H.B. and Mollon, J.D. 1982: *The senses*. Cambridge and New York: Cambridge University Press.

Frisby, John P. 1979: *Seeing: illusion, brain and mind*. Oxford and New York: Oxford University Press.

Gibson, J.J. 1950: *Perception of the visual world*. London: Allen and Unwin.

────── 1980: *The ecological approaches to visual perception*. Boston: Houghton Mifflin.

Gombrich, E.H. 1960. *Art and illusion*. Phaidon.

Gregory, R.L. 1966. *Eye and brain*. London: Weidenfeld.

────── 1970: *The intelligent eye*. London: Weidenfeld.

Helmholtz, H. von. 1867 (1963): *Handbook of physiological optics*, ed. J.P.C.S. Southall. New York: Dover.

personality disorders The term implies a variation from the average in the enduring characteristics of personality to an extent that causes the patient or other people distress or difficulty. It is usually recognizable by adolescence but may become less obvious in middle or old age. The disorder may affect all aspects of personality in one or more of its components. It is essential to distinguish this psychiatric category from mere abnormality of personality in the sense of any variation, favorable or unfavorable, from the average (see Schneider 1950). Just as it is difficult to make a distinction between normal and abnormal it is difficult to classify types of personality disorder in terms of a restricted number of categories. Two main approaches have been used. The first is a purely descriptive typology using terms such as aggressive or inadequate. The second also implies etiology for it defines the abnormal personality by reference to a syndrome of illness which it partially resembles. For example, schizoid personalities (who are eccentric, socially withdrawn and lack emotional rapport) are so called because of a supposed relationship to SCHIZOPHRENIA. In clinical practice it is often preferable to describe personality traits in a sentence or two rather than to attempt to fit patients in to a limited series of personality types.

The most useful descriptions of the most generally recognized types of personality disorder are those in the ninth edition of the International Classification of Disease (WHO 1978). Unfortunately, however, these incorporate both the descriptive and the etiological approach in its nomenclature and descriptions. There are eight main categories.

Paranoid: in which there is excessive sensitiveness to setbacks or to what are taken to be humiliations and rebuffs, a tendency to distort experience by misconstruing the neutral or friendly actions of others as hostile or contemptuous, and a combative and tenacious sense of personal rights. There may be a proneness to jealousy or excessive self-importance. Such persons may feel helplessly humiliated and put upon; others, likewise excessively sensitive, are aggressive and insistent. In all cases there is excessive self-reference. (See PARANOID STATES.)

Affective: characterized by lifelong predominance of a pronounced mood which may be persistently depressive, persistently elated, or alternately one then the other. During periods of elation there is unshakeable optimism and an enhanced zest for life and activity, whereas periods of depression are marked by worry, pessimism, low output of energy and a sense of futility. (See AFFECTIVE DISORDERS.)

Schizoid: in which there is withdrawal from affectional, social and other contacts with autistic preference for fantasy and introspective reserve. Behavior may be slightly eccentric or indicate avoidance of competitive situations. Apparent coolness and detachment may mask an incapacity to express feeling. (See SCHIZOPHRENIA.)

Anankastic (obsessional): characterized by feelings of personal insecurity, doubt and incompleteness leading to excessive conscientiousness, checking, stubbornness and caution. There may be insistent and unwelcome thoughts or impulses which do not attain the severity of an obsessional neurosis. There is perfectionism and meticulous accuracy and a need to check repeatedly in an attempt to ensure this. Rigidity and excessive doubt may be conspicuous. (See NEUROSIS.)

Hysterical (histrionic): characterized by shallow, labile affect, dependence on others, craving for appreciation and attention, suggestibility and theatricality. There is often sexual immaturity, e.g. frigidity and over-responsiveness to stimuli. Under stress hysterical symptoms (neurosis) may develop. (See HYSTERIA.)

Asthenic (dependent, inadequate): characterized by passive compliance with the wishes of elders and others and a weak inadequate response to the demands of daily life. Lack of vigor may show itself in the intellectual or emotional spheres; there is little capacity for enjoyment.

Personality disorder with predominantly sociopathic or asocial manifestation: characterized by disregard for social obligations, lack of feeling for others, and impetuous violence or callous unconcern. There is a gross disparity between behavior and the prevailing social norms. Behavior is not readily modifiable by experience, including punishment. People with this personality are often affectively cold and may be abnormally aggressive or irresponsible. Their tolerance of frustration is low. They blame others or offer plausible rationalizations for the behavior which brings them into conflict with society (see PSYCHOPATHIC PERSONALITY; SOCIOPATHIC PERSONALITY).

Explosive: characterized by lability of mood with liability to outbursts of anger, hate, violence or affection. Aggression may be expressed in words or in physical violence. The outbursts cannot be readily controlled by the affected person, who is not otherwise prone to antisocial behavior.

The current American classification, Diagnostic and Statistic Manual 3 (American Psychiatric Association, 1980) includes further categories, such as the schizotypical, borderline, narcissistic, avoidant and passive aggressive. The first two of these are derived from the various descriptions of the so called borderline syndrome (see BORDERLINE STATES).

Since rather little is known about factors accounting for normal variations in personality it is unsurprising that the causes of personality disorder are poorly understood. Psychopathic personality has been studied in greater detail than any other sub-type. Adequate prospective research is made difficult by the need for a very prolonged follow-up after the events in early life that are potentially relevant. There is some evidence both that genetic influences are determinants of childhood temperament and adult traits; also that the quality of adult social relationships depends upon early experience (Rutter 1981). Psychoanalytic and other psychodynamic theories have proposed detailed explanations of the development of personality (see Neal 1971).

The definition of personality disorder implies that they are life long. However, clinical impression suggests that abnormalities may become rather less severe with age. Aggressive behavior, for instance, is much less common after the age of forty years but other difficulties in relationships are more persistent. Although potential for personality change is small, after early adult life many people are able to modify their social circumstances so as to find a way of life to which they suited and in which there is less likelihood of distress for themselves and other people.

There are two main approaches to treatment. First an attempt to change personality, secondly a more modest attempt to help people to adjust their lives in ways which would provide greater satisfaction and fewer conflicts and problems. The former aim usually requires PSYCHOTHERAPY and is easier in those who are younger and whose personalities are less clearly fixed. Success depends upon motivation and an adequate degree of insight and may require prolonged treatment. It is usually much easier and also more appropriate to concentrate on helping the patient to decide how to improve his or her social circumstances. The most severely handicapped may require support and encouragement over a very prolonged period.   RAM

Bibliography

American Psychiatric Association 1980: *Diagnostic and statistical manual 3*.

*Kaplan, H.I., Freedman, L. and Sadock, B.J. 1984: *Comprehensive textbook of psychiatry*, 4th edn. Baltimore: Williams and Wilkins.

Neal, A. 1971: *Theories of psychology: a handbook*. London: University of London Press.

Rutter, M. 1981: *Maternal deprivation reassessed*. 2nd edn. Harmondsworth and New York: Penguin.

Schneider 1950: *Psychopathic personality*. 9th edn. Vienna: F. Derlicke.

World Health Organisation 1975: *Mental disorders: glossary and guide to their classification in accordance with the Ninth Revision of the International Classification of Diseases*. Geneva: WHO.

phenomenology: in psychiatry This term may be used to refer to the ensemble of mental symptoms and signs in an individual case or group of cases or in a disorder. In its stricter usage it is the study, description and classification of the evidence of mental activity. Jaspers (1962, pp.

55–60) considers four groups of phenomena.
1. The individual's subjective experiences, perceptions, thoughts, impulses and self-awareness.
2. Objective mental performances, such as measurable evidence of memory and intelligence.
3. Somatic accompaniments of mental events, such as autonomic nervous system activity.
4. Meaningful objective phenomena which can be seen as evidence of the individual's intentions.

Subjective phenomenology forms the cornerstone of existential psychology and of existential analysis in which mental disorders are seen as the individual's attempt to reconcile various aspects of his experience.   DLJ

Bibliography

Jaspers, Karl 1962: *General psychopathology*. Trans. J. Hoenig and M.W. Hamilton. Manchester: Manchester University Press; Chicago: University of Chicago Press.

pheromone A chemical smell substance released by one member of a species that has a highly specific effect on a conspecific. Pheromones are most highly developed in insects. For instance it has been shown experimentally that the antennae of the male silk moth are exceptionally receptive to just one chemical substance, bombykol, and are able to respond to a single molecule of it. Female silk moths release minute amounts of bombykol, and are located by males who fly upwind along the scent trail. Pheromones are used extensively by social insects such as bees, and ants. In bees there is a "queen substance" pheromone that actually controls the sexual development of colony females, rendering them infertile workers. Ants find their way to food along trail pheromones, and give up the food they bring back to the nest only to others emitting the correct pheromone.

Among mammals scent-signals are often implicated in sexual arousal, being most often given when a female is in estrus, i.e. sexually receptive. They have the effect of stimulating male sexual activity. This is true of primates such as the rhesus monkey. In humans, research has shown the ability of men to detect and be aroused by what may be pheromones emitted by women; in general, however, human sexual approach is characteristic of both women and men, and is made up of a vast complex of non-olfactory signals.   VR

phobia An unrealistic and disproportionate fear of an object or situation. Characteristically a phobia cannot be reasoned away and is beyond voluntary control; intense ANXIETY or panic is evoked by the prospect or actuality of exposure to the feared situation which tends to be avoided. Phobias constitute a form of NEUROSIS, and may be sub-divided into agoraphobia, social phobias, animal phobias, various other specific phobias (for example of thunder or heights) and illness phobia.

There are two main approaches to the understanding and treatment of phobias. Psychodynamic theories regard the fear as the displacement onto an external object of anxiety aroused by unacceptable impulses from the unconscious; resolution is through PSYCHOANALYSIS or PSYCHOTHERAPY. By contrast behaviorists emphasize the learning of associations between the object and anxiety responses in the formation of a phobia; treatment is directed at learning to confront the object without anxiety (see BEHAVIOR THERAPY).   DLJ

Bibliography

Marks, I.M. 1969: *Fears and phobias*. London: Heinemann; New York: Academic Press.
Ost, L.G. 1985: Ways of acquiring phobias and outcome of behavioral treatments. *Behaviour research and therapy* 23, 683–9.

physical disability, psychological aspects of The World Health Organisation defines disability as 'the loss of physical or intellectual function as a consequence of impairment' which, in turn, is defined as 'the loss or reduction of certain anatomical or physiological properties of an individual'. Handicap is defined as 'the social and environmental disadvantage experienced by an individual as the result of a disability'.

Physical disability may result from neurological dysfunction or a disorder of other systems. In the former, loss of function follows an impairment of the central nervous system. In the latter, resulting problems are caused directly by disorders of muscles, bones, or other systems.

Sometimes people with such problems do not appreciate the difference. For example, a person with hemiplegia following a head injury may believe the affected limbs themselves are damaged, rather than that part of the brain which controls them. It is possible to have disabilities from both causes, for example, a person with advanced arterial disease might, having had a stroke causing paralysis, also develop vascular insufficiency of the legs causing gangrene which results in amputation.

Some common causes of physical disability of neurological origin are: head and spinal injury; cerebral vascular accident (stroke); degenerative disease, e.g. multiple sclerosis, motor neuron disease and Parkinson's disease; tumors; infection, e.g. meningitis and encephalitis; anoxia; congenital conditions, e.g. cerebral palsy due to damage to the brain during the pre-, peri- or immediate post-natal period and spina bifida, often associated with hydrocephalus, due to neural tube defects. Other common causes include: rheumatoid and osteo-arthritis; amputations; vascular and circulatory disease; respiratory disease, muscular disorders; congenital abnormalities; trauma.

The prevalence of disability increases with age. A UK population survey in 1971 found that approximately half the sample aged over sixty-five had some disability. Conditions with the highest prevalence rates causing disability include arthritis, stroke, Parkinson's disease and cerebral palsy. Those causing the most severe disability, however, have lower prevalence rates, such as multiple sclerosis, motor neuron disease, severe head or spinal injuries. They lead to greater dependence on others, and account for most admissions into residential care establishments, be-cause of lack of adequate community or home care.

The causes of disability change. Since the introduction of vaccines against poliomyelitis, and amniocentesis to test for spina bifida, the incidence of new cases has almost disappeared. But better intensive care facilities and special care baby units may mean that in future more critically injured people will survive accidents with more severe disabilities, and that more low birthweight babies will live with the possibility of disability than do at present.

There are six main areas in the rehabilitation of physically disabled people where psychological factors may be involved in treatment.

1. Physical difficulties with movement are always present. Drugs, physiotherapy, orthoses, aides and equipment all help. Psychologists sometimes add their knowledge of enhancing methods of learning to improve motor control. BIOFEEDBACK is an example of this.

2. Sensory problems are often present, which can include visual disturbance, altered tactile sensation and pain. All could involve interventions from psychologists. For example strategies for coping with chronic pain (Fordyce 1976).

3. Cognitive difficulties may be a direct result of brain impairment, affecting such abilities as language, attention, perception, reasoning, planning, learning and memory. These may impose limits on coping with other problems. Treatment approaches are encouraging (Wilson and Moffatt 1984). People disabled from childhood may have lower intellectual attainments than expected because of limited opportunities, unstimulating environments, social isolation, and, until recently, restricted school curricula. Early attendance at playschool, structured advice for parents of disabled children and integration into mainstream schooling should eventually remove this source of disadvantage.

4. Emotional difficulties may accompany a physical impairment. Brain stem damage can cause emotional lability, with easily provoked tears or laughter. Multiple sclerosis is sometimes said to cause inappropriate affect and patients have been

described, often incorrectly, as "euphoric" whereas they are frequently depressed. People with sudden onset of physical impairment may pass through stages of emotional response similar to those who have undergone a bereavement or other major loss. Some may have ANXIETY symptoms while others may show LEARNED HELPLESSNESS or DEPRESSION. Counseling, cognitive or behavioral psychotherapy can all help (Wilson and Staples 1985).

5. Behavioral problems: tantrums, screaming and physical violence are sometimes a feature of severe head injury, and psychological treatments based on operant conditioning are very effective (Eames and Wood 1985).

6. Personality disturbances may develop as a result of neurological impairment such as bilateral frontal lobe damage or environmental factors such as over-protection or rejection by family and friends. Early intervention may help prevent them.

The many branches of medicine are probably most effective at the level of impairment, by helping to restore the lost or reduced anatomical or physiological properties by surgery or drugs.

The skills of remedial therapists are paramount at the level of residual disability. They include physiotherapy, occupational and speech therapy, prosthetics, orthotics, mechanical and electronic engineering. They work to increase function by re-education, teaching alternative strategies, and the use and provision of aids, appliances and equipment. For disabled people to make use of these services, however, they must have the ability and desire to learn. It is here that psychological factors such as motivation, mood, cognitive abilities, expectations and interests, play a vital role in modifying disability.

At the level of handicap it is the behavior of society in general and politicians in particular which finally determines how much social and environmental disadvantage disabled people experience. They themselves are aware of this and many of the more articulate are involved in pressure groups aimed at legislative change. Others are concerned with the provision of information and support to individuals, through telephone advice lines, self-help groups and Centers of Independent Living (Zola and Crewe, 1983).   DS

Bibliography

Eames, P. and Wood, R. 1985: Rehabilitation after severe brain injury: a follow-up of a behavior modification approach. *Journal of neurological and neurosurgical psychiatry* 48, 613–19.

Fordyce, W.E. 1976: *Behavioral methods in chronic pain and illness*. St. Louis: C.V. Mosby.

Wilson, B. and Moffat, N. 1984: *The clinical management of memory problems*. London: Croom Helm.

Wilson, B. and Staples, D. 1985: Working with people with physical handicap. In *Clinical psychology*. eds. J. Hall and J. Marzillier. Oxford: Oxford University Press.

Zola, I. and Crewe, N. 1983: *Independent living for physically disabled people*. New York: Jossey Bass.

pineal gland A small brain structure (weight approximately 150 mg) lying along the quadrigeminate groove between the superior colliculi (see BRAIN AND CENTRAL NERVOUS SYSTEM: ILLUSTRATIONS, fig. 6). The gland was first described in the third century BC by Alexandrian anatomists who believed it was a sphincter which regulated the flow of thought. According to Descartes (1596–1650) the gland was the site of the "rational mind". In fish and amphibia the pineal cells have an eye-like, light-sensitive function. The function of the pineal gland in higher vertebrates, including man, has not been established unequivocally, though it clearly has an endocrine role, probably related to gonadal function. The nerve supply to the pineal gland consists of postganglionic sympathetic fibers. Part of the input to the pineal gland via these fibers originates from the hypothalamic suprachiasmatic nucleus (figs. 15 and 20) which is believed to be a biological "clock". The pineal gland contains, and probably secretes, a number of biologically active compounds. These are mainly small peptides and biogenic amines, among which the serotonin derivative melatonin has been most extensively studied. The activity of pineal enzymes, e.g.

those involved in melatonin synthesis, is dependent on the light-dark cycle. DHGV

Bibliography

Kappers, J.A. and Pénet, P. 1979: *The pineal gland of vertebrates including man. Progress in brain research.* vol. 52. Amsterdam: Elsevier.

pituitary A gland at the base of the brain which is connected to the ventral surface of the HYPOTHALAMUS (see BRAIN AND CENTRAL NERVOUS SYSTEM: ILLUSTRATIONS, figs. 15 and 20). The pituitary has two lobes which are critical in neuroendocrine-behaviour relationships (see BRAIN AND CENTRAL NERVOUS SYSTEM: CHEMISTRY OF). The posterior lobe (or neurohypophysis) is derived embryologically from neural tissue, while the anterior lobe (or adenohypophysis) is derived from the same tissue as the roof of the mouth. The neuropeptide hormones, vasopressin and oxytocin, are synthesized in the hypothalamus but are stored and released upon hypothalamic stimulation from the posterior PITUITARY into the blood stream. The anterior pituitary releases several hormones into the blood stream, including ACTH, thyrotropin, somatotropin, gonadotropins and prolactin. The release of anterior pituitary hormones is controlled by releasing factors secreted by the hypothalamus and carried in the hypophysial portal system to the anterior pituitary. GPH

Bibliography

O'Riordan, J.L.H., Malan, P.G. and Gould, R.P. 1982: *Essentials of endocrinology.* Oxford: Blackwell Scientific Publications.

plasticity: physiological concept
Plasticity refers to the capacity of neurons in the central nervous system to grow beyond their normal developmental period, or to regenerate or reorganize after injury or environmental change. Although the term is sometimes used to refer to any reorganization of neural connections observed after an experimental manipulation, its use is most appropriate when referring to changes that have functional significance for the organism. At the level of the neuron, or nerve cell, the structural changes that subserve plasticity involve the growth of axons and dendrites, which are fibers that extend from the cell body of the NEURON, and are involved in the transmission of neural impulses, as well as the formation of new synapses, which are the interconnections between neurons. Such structural changes are most prominent during early development, but may be possible throughout adulthood in fish and amphibians. In mammals, a significant capacity for plasticity appears to be limited to a period early in post-natal development, which has been called the "sensitive" or "critical" period (see CRITICAL PERIOD). In addition to referring to the structural changes that can be observed in axons, DENDRITES and SYNAPSES the term plasticity is used to refer to functional changes that are not accompanied by observable alterations in structure. The functional changes to which the term is applied may occur at the neuronal level, where the function of pre-existing synapses may change, or at the behavioral level, where the recovery of some behaviour after neurological damage occurs without evidence of neural growth.

Plasticity has been studied with several procedures, each of which emphasizes a different aspect of change in the central nervous system. Where the emphasis is on observing structural changes in neurons, tissue samples can be obtained, and a staining agent applied so that neurons can be identified microscopically. With this technique the axons, dendrites and synapses of normal tissue samples can be compared with those identified in tissue obtained from organisms that were subjected to some type of experimental manipulation, such as a radical environmental change or a surgical lesion. At this level of analysis, plasticity may be observed in any or all of several ways. Particular neurons form synapses at identifiable points, called target areas, with other specific neurons. Plasticity can occur through the formation of new synapses at an old target area (sprouting), or through the formation of new synapses in a different target area of the same neuron (spreading). A third type of plastic change can be observed when synapses are formed between neurons that do not typically share target areas. This third type of change is called extension.

Although the microscopic observation of stained tissue samples provides direct evidence of structural neuronal changes, it does not yield evidence of functional neuronal changes. The demonstration of functional change requires that the activity of neurons be measured in a behaving organism. One way in which this can be achieved is by recording the electrical activity of neurons. This approach, known as electrophysiology, encompasses a variety of techniques ranging from recording the activity of a single neuron using a micro-electrode implanted in the cell itself, to recording the gross activity of whole regions of the brain using electrodes placed on the scalp. Electrophysiological recordings of single neurons have been used extensively to study plasticity, especially in the visual system.

In the visual cortex of many mammals there are neurons that only respond to stimulation of one eye, as well as those that respond to stimulation of either eye. The former are called monocular cells, the latter are called binocular cells. Although most neurons in the visual cortex are binocular, binocular cells tend to have a bias in their responding. That is, in normally raised animals, binocular cells on one side of the brain are more effectively activated by stimulation of the eye on the opposite side. So, for example, stimulation of the right eye will produce a greater response in the binocular cells of the left visual cortex than will stimulation of the left eye. This bias is known as ocular dominance, and it reflects an organizational principle in the central nervous system that is subject to both plasticity and a sensitive period.

The phenomenon of ocular dominance can be observed by making electrophysiological recordings of the activity of neurons in the visual cortex of normally raised experimental animals, such as cats. Plasticity can be induced, however, by radically altering the animal's environment during early development. Kittens normally open their eyes after the first eight to ten days of life. If the lid of one eye is stitched closed at some point during the first few months of life, a physiological reorganization can be observed in the visual cortex. After a period of monocular deprivation during early development, almost all of the binocular cells are lost and the remaining monocular cells respond only to stimulation of the experienced eye. If the animal is allowed to use only the eye that had previously been sutured, it is functionally blind. There is a specific period of time during which the developing kitten is susceptible to the effects of monocular deprivation. This sensitive period begins at about the third week of life and extends to about the fourth month. The visual cortex appears to be extremely plastic during this time, when as few as three days of monocular deprivation during the fourth week of life is sufficient to produce changes in the normal pattern of ocular dominance.

In humans there is some indication that the brain remains plastic for language during a critical period in development. In most adults language functions are lateralized to the left cerebral hemisphere. For the right-handed population, the incidence of left hemisphere language is well above 90 per cent. Most left-handed individuals also have left hemisphere language, but as a group, there is a higher incidence of language being represented in either the right hemisphere, or both hemispheres (see LATERALIZATION). One of the consequences of language lateralization is that for right-handed people, damage to the left hemisphere due to stroke, tumor or trauma will frequently produce a language dysfunction. However, comparable damage to the right hemisphere in right handed adults rarely produces problems with language. The prognosis for recovery of language function after left hemisphere damage depends on the extent of the damage and the type of language dysfunction present. Although the physiological basis for recovery of function in adults is not well understood, it is generally acknowledged that the observed improvement is not due to the plastic changes seen during the early development of the central nervous system.

In very young children, on the other hand, there tends to be a much greater recovery of function following lateralized brain injury than is observed in adults. Young children who have suffered extensive damage to, or even surgical removal of the left hemisphere lose the language function they have developed just as adults do after left hemisphere injury. If the left hemisphere of a young child is damaged prior to the acquisition of language, however, language may develop in the intact right hemisphere. In the developing human, then, there appears to be some plasticity for language function in so far as the hemisphere not normally involved in language may acquire this function in response to severe damage to the language hemisphere. Such plasticity in language development is found only in childhood, and although there is no general agreement as to the length of the critical period, it appears that plasticity in language function sharply declines after the initial acquisition of language.

The term plasticity, then, generally refers to functional changes in the developing organism that are induced by external influences, and are referable to the organization of the central nervous system. Plasticity is observable at synaptic connections between axons and dendrites, in the electrical activity of single neurons, and in the behavioral recovery of function after damage to the central nervous system. (See also NEURAL CONTROL OF HIGHER MENTAL PROCESSES; RECOVERY OF FUNCTION AFTER BRAIN DAMAGE; SENSORY DEPRIVATION AND ENRICHMENT; SPEECH DISORDERS.)   JJS

Bibliography

Blakemore, C. and Cooper, G. 1970: Development of the brain depends on the visual environment. *Nature* 228, 477–8.

Gazzaniga, M.S., Steen, D. and Volpe, B.T. 1979: *Functional neuroscience*. New York and London: Harper and Row.

Hubel, D.H., Wiesel, T.N. and Le Vay, S. 1977: Plasticity of ocular dominance columns in monkey striate cortex. *Philosophical transactions, Royal Society of Biology* 278, 377–409.

Jacobson, M. 1978: *Developmental neurobiology*. New York and London: Plenum Press.

LeVay, S., Wiesel, T.N. and Hubel, D.H. 1980: The development of ocular dominance columns in normal and visually deprived monkeys. *Journal of comparative neurology* 191, 1–51.

Lund, R.D. 1978: *Development and plasticity of the brain: an introduction*. Oxford: Oxford University Press.

Marshall, J.F. 1984: Brain function. *Annual review of psychology* 35, 277–308.

Woods, B.T. and Carey, S. 1979: Language deficits after apparent clinical recovery from childhood aphasia. *Annals of neurology* 6, 405–9.

Woods, B.T. and Teuber, H.L. 1978: Changing patterns of childhood aphasia. *Annals of neurology* 3, 273–80.

primal therapy A clinical system, formulated by A. Janov (*The primal scream*, 1973), which forces patients to relive painful emotional experiences in order to free them from NEUROSIS. The term "clinical" is appropriate in that Janov is reductionistic, biologically rather than psychologically orientated: 'We don't recall with emotion – the Freudian abreaction. We relive. Recall and "remember" are mind phenomena; relive is a total neurophysiologic one ...' (quoted in Rosen, 1978, p.156; cf. Janov, 1978). His system leaves no room for the therapeutic efficacy of understanding and reformulating the circumstances and current self commitments which engender suffering (see PSYCHOTHERAPY and PSYCHOANALYSIS). It is a subterranean therapy, emotions working according to processes which lie below meaning-infused mental operations; it is anti-cognitive: 'The beginning of feeling is the end of philosophy'. Working with a psychodynamic or hydraulic model, Janov attributes neurosis to early childhood experiences. The child's basic needs, in particular to be loved, are not gratified. The primal trauma (anger, pain) results, and the child responds defensively. The defense system, providing 'a set of behaviors which automatically function to block primal feelings' (Janov, 1973, p.60), is manifested in neurotic activities: bed wetting and the like, or, having been stored, in smoking, over-eating and so on during adult life.

Blocking the pain produces neurosis;

feeling the pain undoes it. Therapy is required to shatter defenses, allowing the patient to get in touch with his pain and then purge what he could not cope with as a child. Therapy begins with a twenty-four hour period of isolation during which the patient is not permitted to nurture his defenses (no tension-diverting activities). There follows a three-week period during which the patient receives one open-ended therapy session a day from a qualified therapist who aims to "bust" (not have "head trips" with) his subject. Spread-eagled on a couch, the patient is encouraged to call out for his parents, and, if all goes well, he erupts with primal screams: "I hate you; Daddy, for Christ's sake, *be* nice". Group sessions follow over a six-month period (or, as with Janovian-inspired communities such as Atlantis in Ireland, become the basis of a life-style (James, 1980)). Having gone through the hell of reliving his pains, the post-primal person has satisfied or completed his childhood needs; he no longer has to ask for the love that he needed but did not receive. He has vented his pain and anger. He no longer has any need for energy consuming defenses because the energy is now used to improve physiological functioning, etc. (see Janov, 1978). Without neurotic defenses, he is more "real", "feels" everything, and can build on the basically good nature which existed before adverse childhood experiences.

Would that life (and therapy) were so simple and true (Janov does not accept that any other approach is valid). Criticisms are legion, the most important being that there is no evidence that endogenous processes *alone* govern the paths of emotions and neurosis. However, it should be born in mind that patients do undergo primal therapy, the results being "remarkable" (Kovel 1978, p.195), and that Freud himself never entirely relinquished the idea that emotional display can be consummative in the therapeutic setting. We know so little about how the emotions work. By emphasizing endogenous processes, by treating traumas in psychodynamic fashion, Janov at the very least has set up an interesting naturalistic experiment.   PLFH

Bibliography

*James, Jenny 1980: *They call us the screamers!* Firle: Caliban Books.

*Janov, Arthur 1973: *The primal scream.* London: Sphere Books.

——— 1978: *The anatomy of mental illness.* London: Sphere Books.

Kovel, Joel 1978: *A complete guide to therapy.* Harmondsworth: Penguin.

Rosen, R. 1978: *Psychobabble.* London: Wildwood House.

projective tests Psychological tests devised to measure global aspects of personality and personality dynamics. They include a range of instruments such as the Rorschach, Thematic Apperception Test (TAT), Sentence Completion, and Draw-A-Person Test, which provide generally vague, ambiguous stimuli and require the subject to respond with his or her own constructions. The individual's response, since it cannot be attributed to the stimulus itself, is believed to reflect the individual's basic personality makeup. Projective tests have been popular instruments in clinical settings as a means of gaining understanding about the patient's psychodynamics. Recently, however, projective tests have waned in popularity partly as a result of their generally low reliability, questionable validity and the increased emphasis upon behavior treatment in clinical settings.   JNB

pseudo dementia This term is used to designate a mental condition in which there are symptoms and signs which erroneously suggest dementia, that is, progressive and irreversible loss of intellectual function (see ORGANIC MENTAL STATES). The sufferer presents with loss of memory, of attention span and general knowledge. His apparent dementia may be caused by drug intoxication or other sources of transient confusion; or by depression, which in the elderly may be initially difficult to distinguish from dementia; or by a state of hysterical dissociation; or more rarely by malingering.   DLJ

Bibliography

Lishman, W.A. 1978: *Organic psychiatry: the psychological consequences of cerebral disorder.* Oxford: Blackwell Scientific Publications; St Louis, Missouri: C.V. Mosby.

psychiatry The branch of medical science concerned with the study, diagnosis, treatment and prevention of mental disorders. Psychiatry deals with disorders which present mainly with disturbances of emotion, thought, perception and behavior, whereas the subject of neurology is disease of identifiable parts of the nervous system. There is much overlap between these two disciplines since both are concerned with aspects of brain function, and in some countries they are practiced as one (see NEUROPSYCHIATRY).

Psychiatry has been slow to develop within the framework of medicine, detaching itself with difficulty from mythology and religion, and more recently from philosophy and politics. Until the nineteenth century there were two popular theories as to the nature of mental disorder. One was that the sufferer was possessed by demons, and could be cured by prayer, confession, exorcism or execution. The second view, propounded by Hippocrates (c.470–c.400 BC) held that madness resulted from an imbalance of the elements (earth, water, air and fire) and of the humors (blood, phlegm and bile). The humors were thought to determine the four temperaments: sanguine, choleric, phlegmatic and melancholic. Treatment was directed at redressing the imbalance through baths, diets and emetics, as recommended by Galen (AD 129–199).

The nineteenth century witnessed the introduction of scientific principles. KRAEPELIN studied the evolution of his patients' illnesses and their family histories, and established the basis of our present system of classification. JASPERS described and categorized mental phenomena as a basis for the discipline of psychopathology. Since then the various disciplines have developed to illuminate mental mechanisms and disorders. Neuroanatomy and physiology have identified brain pathways subserving alertness (RETICULAR ACTIVATING SYSTEM), emotion (LIMBIC SYSTEM), drive and motivation, as well as centers for the control of many endocrine functions and of the AUTONOMIC NERVOUS SYSTEM. Biochemistry and pharmacology are discovering various TRANSMITTER SUBSTANCES in the brain responsible for passing a nerve impulse from one cell to another; some disorders (particularly manic-depression and schizophrenia) are thought to be associated with abnormalities of these transmitters, and treatment can be directed at correcting these.

Psychology has contributed many concepts and techniques important to the understanding of mental disorder. One area of knowledge concerns child development, the growth of affectional bonds, and intelligence. Another area, that of learning theory and conditioning, is relevant to neurotic problems and to BEHAVIOR THERAPY. A further field of study has made it possible to measure certain aspects of intellectual and emotional functioning. Anthropology (the study of man, especially in relation to cultural influences), sociology (the study of humans in groups) and ethology (the study of animals in their natural environment) all continue to contribute to the foundations of psychiatry.

Psychiatric NOSOLOGY (the science of the definition of disease entities) encompasses many different approaches (Clare 1985). Some conditions, for example brain infections, may readily be viewed as disorders with a specifiable etiology and pathology. Others may be defined in terms of clusters of symptoms and signs, as with depression or schizophrenia. But with many disorders there is a need to specify several other aspects of the case, and multi-axial classification may be advocated; one such system in child psychiatry involves three axes: (1) the clinical psychiatric syndrome; (2) intellectual level; and (3) associated or etiological physical conditions. A radically different approach is to abandon the concept of diagnostic categories, and to describe the individual in terms of his position on a number of dimensions, for example Eysenck's psychoticism, neuroticism and introversion/extraversion dimensions for which reliable methods of measurement are available. The terms psychosis and neurosis feature in most classification systems. PSYCHOSIS denotes severe disruption of psychological function, often with DELUSION, HALLUCINATION and loss of insight, whereas a NEUROSIS can be understood as an exaggeration of a natural reaction, often comprising ANXIETY. No single classification of mental disorders commands the allegiance of all psychiatrists, so the following should be viewed as a sample.

Organic psychoses (see ORGANIC MENTAL STATES): there is manifest brain pathology of a toxic, metabolic, infective, traumatic or neoplastic nature, and the symptoms usually include disorientation and disturbed consciousness. The alternative term "symptomatic psychoses" indicates that the psychological disturbance must be recognized as evidence of physical disease which should be the target of treatment. A typical example would be brain tumor.

Functional psychoses: No certain pathology and no associated disorientation are to be found, but a typical cluster of symptoms for each of two psychoses comprising this group. SCHIZOPHRENIA (initially called by Kraepelin "dementia praecox") is characterized by specific disturbances of perception and thinking together with variable impairment of emotional responsiveness and drive. A good response is to be expected in many cases with medication and rehabilitative measures, but relapse is common and schizophrenics still constitute a high proportion of those needing long-term psychiatric hospitalization. AFFECTIVE DISORDERS comprise extreme mood swings into DEPRESSION or mania, and recurrent episodes may be solely of one extreme – unipolar, or of both extremes – bipolar. Treatment usually relies heavily on medication or ELECTROCONVULSIVE THERAPY (ECT), and recurrences may often be prevented by long-continued medication; sometimes it is possible to identify and eradicate precipitant stresses.

Neuroses can usually be understood as exaggerations of natural reactions, anxiety being one major component. Examples of the neuroses are pure anxiety states, PHOBIAS where the symptoms are evoked by particular situations or objects, obsessive-compulsive disorders and hysterical states. PSYCHOSOMATIC DISORDERS may be included here. Treatment can be usefully directed at resolving associated stresses, at unlearning neurotic patterns of responding and learning appropriate behavior (see BEHAVIOR THERAPY). Medication has some part to play. PERSONALITY DISORDERS and behavior disorders comprise a mixture of conditions in which there is an ingrained maladaptive pattern of behavior. Subcategories are based on the identification of a particularly prominent and troublesome character trait or type of activity, for example, schizoid (withdrawn), obsessive or psychopathic personality disorders, or ALCOHOLISM and DRUG DEPENDENCE. Treatment, where appropriate, may include some form of PSYCHOTHERAPY. MENTAL HANDICAP (retardation, subnormality) is a condition of arrested or incomplete development of mind, characterized especially by subnormality of intelligence. It may occur without other pathology as part of the natural distribution of intelligence, or in association with genetically determined anomalies or brain damage. Special schooling, occupational and residential arrangements may be needed.

From this basic classification it is evident that psychiatry is concerned with a wide range of disorders: at the one extreme those identifiable in terms of physical pathology and amenable to conventional medical treatments, at the other those where variants of natural attributes and behavior patterns are viewed in relation to social norms and where management relies on counseling and social or penal measures. The middle ground is occupied by disorders – schizophrenia and manic-depressive psychosis – where the functional disturbances may be so gross that the failure so far to find an organic cause (other than tentatively in terms of biochemistry) is surprising. The diversity and ambiguity inherent in psychiatry have promoted many changes in the discipline. Firstly, there has been a proliferation of subspecialities, facilitating both more specialized research and more specific provision of service: CHILD AND ADOLESCENT PSY-CHIATRY, FORENSIC PSYCHIATRY, PSYCHOGERI-ATRICS, MENTAL HANDICAP. SOCIAL PSYCHIATRY is among the latest offspring, concerning itself with the many environmental factors that influence the course of an illness, and in the treatment sphere with rehabilitative processes. Secondly, psychiatry has allied itself with several other disciplines not only in the broadening of its scientific basis – which we have already seen – but in the enrichment of its therapeutic skills: PSY-CHOANALYSIS, various schools of counseling, social work, CLINICAL PSYCHOLOGY, these have made such major contributions that Eysenck (1975) has put forward the controversial proposal that psychological (as distinct from physical) treatments should become the province of a discipline distinct from medicine.

Finally it is evident that psychiatry is an area for debate and controversy. Szasz, who challenged the concept of mental illness, is seen as one of the leaders of the "anti-psychiatry" movement. Several of the controversial issues have been reviewed by Clare (1980). Such vigorous controversy indicates that psychiatry has now reached a healthy adolescence.   DLJ

Bibliography

*Alexander, F.G., and Selesnick, S.T. 1967: *The history of psychiatry*. London: Allen and Unwin; New York: Harper and Row.

Clare, A.W. 1980: *Psychiatry in dissent*. 2nd edn. London: Tavistock.

––––– 1985: The disease concept. In *Essentials of postgraduate psychiatry*. 2nd edn, eds. P. Hill, R. Murray and A. Thorley. London: Academic Press; New York: Grune and Stratton.

Eysenck, H.J. 1975: *The future of psychiatry*. London and New York: Methuen.

psychiatry: physical treatments

There is a long tradition in psychiatry of the use of physical methods in the management of psychological symptoms. Treatments have often varied from the naive to the bizarre, and many widely applied treatments of the past, such as insulin coma therapy, have no present day relevance. Three main forms of physical treatment are in current use and clinical practice. These are psychosurgery, electroconvulsive therapy and chemotherapy.

PSYCHOSURGERY aims at the removal or modification of certain symptoms or disordered behavior by the selective destruction of discrete areas of the brain which are presumed to be involved in their pathogenesis or their expression. The term does not refer to the surgical treatment of patients with psychiatric symptoms who are also suffering from recognizable lesions in the brain such as tumors, cysts, scars, epileptic foci and vascular anomalies. The first operations, which were pioneered by Egar Moniz, were frontal lobotomies in patients with severe phobias, severe anxiety and severe obsessionality. The standard leucotomy was devised by Freeman and Watts in the 1950s and was widely applied, but these early operations involved relatively large lesions and led to damaging effects on the patients' subsequent adjustment. Indeed, despite improved techniques and a restriction of the size of lesions to the minimum necessary, fewer patients are now offered psychosurgery as less invasive alternative treatments have become available. The indications are therefore limited and are restricted to a relatively small group of patients suffering from intractable anxiety or obsessional symptoms who have not responded to any other treatments. In addition, a strict code of practice ensures that valid consent to psychosurgery is given and, in the absence of consent, that the reasons for surgery are agreed by independent specialists.

ELECTROCONVULSIVE THERAPY (ECT) involves the induction of a generalized convulsion by the controlled passage of an electrical current through the brain. The use of electrical stimulation in the treatment of cerebral conditions dates back to Galen who treated patients with headaches by applying the electrically charged torpedo fish to the body. John Wesley spoke in 1756 of the "unspeakable good" done to patients by the delivery of electrical shocks, but the current use of ECT stemmed from the relatively recent work of Cerletti and Bini in the 1930s. The passage of an electrical current through the brain has marked and widespread effects in the body. These include a massive seizure discharge all over the brain, an activation of the peripheral AUTONOMIC NERVOUS SYSTEM, an increase in the output of HORMONES from endocrine glands and marked muscle contractions. Thus, although there is no shortage of biochemical or physiological concomitants to ECT, there have been difficulties in identifying those changes induced by ECT that are crucial to its therapeutic effects. The mode of action of ECT has, therefore, yet to be clarified, but most recent research suggests that its therapeutic action could be mediated by an increase in the sensitivity of receptors in the central nervous system induced by the convulsions.

Although ECT was initially used in a wide range of psychiatric disorders, recent research has shown that its efficacy is most readily confirmed in patients suffering from severe forms of retarded DEPRESSION. It is however also used in mania and in the treatment of depressive symptoms in SCHI-ZOPHRENIA. Most patients receive between six and twelve treatments and side effects are minimal. While ECT is acknowledged to be an effective acute treatment of severe depressive illness, there is however no evidence to suggest that it exerts any significant influence on the subsequent natural course of a depressive episode. It is therefore frequently used in conjunction with chemotherapy.

Chemotherapy, the rationale for treatment of psychological symptoms with drugs is that, if biological processes are involved in the pathogenesis of mental disorders, drugs acting on or influencing such processes should have an effect on the course or nature of mental illness. PSYCHO-PHARMACOLOGY is the branch of clinical pharmacology that is concerned with the classification and the investigation of the pharmacokinetics, pharmacodynamic effects and the mode of therapeutic action of drugs used in the treatment of psychiatric disorders. The clinical use of these drugs is monitored in the UK by the Committee on Safety of Medicines and there is a wide range of preparations available. The groups of drugs in most common use are the anxiolytic drugs,

antidepressant drugs and the neuroleptic (antipsychotic) drugs.

Anxiolytic drugs are represented chiefly by the benzodiazepines which are widely prescribed for the relief of symptoms of ANXIETY, whether these are primary or secondary. They are reported to exert a calming and sedative effect and can also induce sleep. They induce changes in physiological measures of AROUSAL which accompany their clinical effects and, while their efficacy in relieving anxiety symptoms is recognized, their relevance to chronic anxiety states has been questioned, parti-cularly as it is now known that both psychological and physical dependence can occur with this group of drugs.

Antidepressant drugs are the treatment of choice for depressive illnesses in which there is evidence of an underlying biologi-cal disturbance. Such evidence is usually based on the presence of certain clinical signs as there are no clear biochemical markers of depressive illness. A distinction is therefore made in clinical practice between changes in mood occurring in association with a presumed dysfunction in cerebral mechanisms mediating mood and changes in mood that have no clear association with any underlying distur-bance and which usually reflect life crises.

Antidepressant drugs are presumed to act by increasing the amount of brain monoamines at postsynaptic receptor sites. The rationale for their use is based on the monoamine theory of depression which holds that depressed mood is associated with a deficiency of functionally active monoamines at critical receptor sites in the brain, and that antidepressant drugs compensate for such a deficiency. The most widely used have been the tricyclic antidepressants and the monoamine oxidase inhibitors (MAOI), though clinical trials have tended to favor tricyclic antide-pressants over MAOIs. A new generation of non-tricyclic antidepressants is now available and these are reputed to be as effective as tricyclic antidepressants.

Neuroleptic drugs are the mainstay of the treatment of SCHIZOPHRENIA and of psychotic symptoms occurring in other forms of psychiatric illness. The parent drug in this group, chlorpromazine, was synthesized in 1950 and was first given to patients in 1952. Initial results were significant and convincing and this gave rise to a wave of therapeutic enthusiasm that has had few parallels in the history of medicine. The more overtly non-specific physical treatments of the past could be safely abandoned and clinical psychiatry could claim a place among other specialities in clinical medicine. Hitherto unrevealed potential for rehabilitation in previously inaccessible patients was dramatically unveiled, and for many of these a return to the community was finally possible. The efficacy of these drugs in acute schizophrenia has been confirmed in a large number of studies, but their role in chronic schizophrenia has been questioned. Despite difficulties raised by such studies and some continuing controversy, neuroleptic drugs are still firmly established in the clinical management of both acute and chronic schizophrenia. All neuroleptic drugs block dopamine receptors in the central nervous system and DOPAMINE blockade is believed to be crucial to their therapeutic action. This has led to the dopamine hypothesis of schizophrenia, which suggests that schizophrenia may be due to a hyperdopaminergic state in the mesolimbic cortex.

Physical treatments in psychiatry have tended to follow, albeit erratically at times, developments in research on the pathophysiology of mental disorders. The non-specific treatments used in the early part of this century reflected a paucity of knowledge about the etiology of mental illness which is still apparent today, despite significant advances in neuroanatomy, neurophysiology and neurochemistry. The physical treatments described above could therefore prove to be equally non-specific in the future.   MWO

Bibliography

Sargant, W. and Slater, Elliot 1972: *Introduction to physical methods of treatment in psychiatry*. 5th edn. London: Churchill Livingstone.

psychoanalysis A subject linked inextricably with the name of its originator, Sigmund FREUD. Freud (1916) pointed out that the word as he used it referred to three subjects: a general psychology, a treatment (a form of PSYCHOTHERAPY), and a research methodology. It is difficult to consider any one of these aspects without at the same time considering the other two. The problem of definition is still more complex because over the passage of time psychoanalysis has also come to refer to a highly organized movement which, apart from being involved in training, treatment and research into psychoanalysis, is a quasi-political organization in the sense that it attempts to influence the training of psychiatrists, clinical psychologists and social workers. In addition, and despite a specific denial of this from Freud, psychoanalysis has become part of general culture. ('As a specialist science, a branch of psychology ... it is quite unfit to construct a *Weltanschauung* of its own.' Freud 1933: 158). It has become an influence within sociology (Parsons 1965); anthropology; literary criticism (Faber 1970) and philosophy (Wollheim 1974) and, especially in certain circles, it has become an intrinsic part of intellectual attitudes and verbal currency. Because psychoanalysis has been in existence for nearly 100 years, because of the many highly speculative and imaginative aspects of its writings and, above all, because of its widespread and imprecise applications, definitions of the essence of the subject are extremely difficult. The following five features have been organized as "the basic assumptions" (Sandler, Dare and Holder 1972) and summarize many disparate attempts to encapsulate its nature.

The first assumption is that despite its origins in the consulting rooms of a psychotherapist in private practice in Vienna at the turn of the nineteenth century, psychoanalysis is a general psychology and not solely a psychopathology: a continuity between the mental functioning of "normality" and "abnormality" is assumed, just as there is central belief in a causal continuity between mental states in infancy, childhood and adulthood. Within these continuities the function of motivational instinctual drives and conflict of motivation affecting all aspects of mental life are extremely important and are mentioned later.

Secondly, and this embodies a particular view of the philosophical issue of the body/mind relationship, psychoanalysis supposes the existence of a "mental apparatus", a construct implying a mental system in interaction, that is, making an input to and having an input from the physiological systems such as the cardio-vascular and the nervous systems. The mental apparatus is discussed in terms of structures (that is to say with processes whose rate of change is slow) and with non-structural elements which are experiential. This latter is a very crucial notion, for the basic topic of psychoanalysis is that of subjective experience rather than the observable actions, behavior, or verbal communications themselves which are the source of information about subjective experience.

Thirdly, the concept of psychological adaptation is embodied in all versions of psychoanalytic psychology. Adaptation is always assumed to be an attempt to reach a "steady" state (by analogy with the physiological notion of homeostatic equilibrium) in the face of pressures from external, environmental sources; from internal, physiological sources and from equally important and powerful sources within the mental apparatus itself. Here again it can be seen that conflict is regarded as inevitable as an organizer of psychoanalytic psychology. DEFENSE MECHANISMS, postulated as omnipresent in the control and modification of conflicting motivational tendencies, are constant elements in the psychoanalytic understanding of short-term and long-term adaptational processes. The adaptational change of mental functioning over the course of psychological development, leading to the persisting imprint of many such adaptations at different stages of life, is an important part of the psychoanalytic view of the mental world.

Fourthly, psychoanalysis is based upon an assumption of what is somewhat confusingly called determinism. Because of philosophical controversies current at the time of his education it was necessary for Freud to take a strong stand as to the possibility of finding causes for all mental activity without resort to elements either of divine inspiration or governance or of chance. Psychoanalysts still hold to this view, although it seems much less necessary to argue the case at length. The concept of psychic determinism has become combined with the principle of overdetermination, whereby most mental events are believed to become outwardly expressed because of their origins in multiple, converging psychological processes.

Fifthly, and of extreme importance, psychoanalysis is built on the assumption that mental life can be thought of as progressing both in ways that can be brought into consciousness and at levels of functioning which, as a rule, are quite inaccessible to introspective awareness. The unconscious aspects of thought which are for the largest part inaccessible to the conscious mind, are described as being dynamically unconscious. They are thought to become consciously registered only under specific circumstances such as dreams, in some psychotic states, or are implied by the symbolic meanings of symptoms, parapraxes and slips of the tongue and, above all, can be constructed by the process of the clinical method of psychoanalysis.

The five assumptions underlie the different models of mental functioning which were developed by Freud and have been extended and modified by the generations of psychoanalysts since. There has been an increasing move away from an emphasis upon sexual drives as the major motivational system. First there has been the inclusion and integration of an aggressive drive paralleling the sexual drive ("the libido"). Until the 1950s there was little challenge from within psychoanalysis of Freud's suggestions of sexual and aggressive drives as specific sources of particular mental energies. Over recent years, however, this has no longer been thought to be the case. Experiences in the early stages of life are consolidated to interact with innate tendencies for the infant to be orientated toward the mother and attendant caretakers. The mental apparatus is now thought to be structured by the pressure to remain close to and to enact specific relationship needs. The psychoanalysts who have developed these ideas are referred to as the "object relations" school (e.g. KLEIN 1965, Winnicott 1972, Balint 1952, Bowlby 1969, 1973, 1980).

The change away from a model emphasizing the impingement of specific drives toward an accentuation of the object-attaching quality of the thrust of mental life, can be seen as the outcome of 100 years of psychotherapeutic practice, which remains the major field of activity of psychoanalysts.

Initially Freud saw himself as reconstructing features of the patient's unconscious mental life by the constructions he was able to put upon the patient's encouraged flow of thoughts ("free associations"). Symptoms, casual thoughts and dreams were the principal stimuli for freely expressed thoughts. Interpretation of the psychoanalyst's understanding of the unconscious meaning of the stream of thought was held to be therapeutic by a process of enlightenment. The balance of conflicting forces within the mind was thought to be changed. Over time, however, Freud came to realize that the main interest of the psychoanalytic provision of confidentiality and reliability in frequent (usually daily) sessions, lay in revelations about the nature of the patient's thoughts and beliefs, attitudes and longings, hatred and loves concerning the analyst. These complex feelings ("transferences") demonstrated the many experiences structured by the infantile and juvenile mind in relation to crucial people in the patient's earlier life. The provision of a new, ambiguous but reliable relationship with the analyst, combined with a careful discussion with the patient of the meaning of the unconscious mental orientations toward the psychoanalyst, has become the major activity of psychoanalytic psychotherapy; it is believed to be the source of the therapeutic improvement in the patient's abilities to make satisfactory relationships outside the therapy and to develop realistic life goals.

The analysis of the therapeutic relationship can be seen to be likely to direct the theoretical thinking of the psychoanalyst toward relationship models ("object relations theory") of the mind. It can also be seen to be related to the application of psychoanalytic ideas to therapy in stranger groups ("group analysis" or family therapies. (See OBJECT RELATIONS, GROUP THERAPY, FAMILY THERAPY.)

The peculiar nature of the psychoanalytic treatment setting consists in the unusual feature of the communications. The patient is encouraged to speak simply and as completely as possible the thoughts that come into his mind. The psychoanalyst gives no commitment to speak or respond in any way, other than to facilitate the flow and understanding of the supposedly underlying meaning of the thoughts. Questions from the patient are unlikely to be regularly answered and requests for reassurance about the patient's present condition or its future course will not, usually, elicit a response. Yet the psychoanalyst expresses a concerned and detailed interest in all aspects of the patient's life and devotes up to 200 hours a year to helping the patient. This devotion, combined with the unpredictability and peculiarities of the timing of the psychoanalyst's responses and the rule of free association, give a very special quality to the nature of the material expressed by the patient. The uniqueness of the communications, within the setting, contribute the research interest of psychoanalysis. Using the psychoanalytic method gives particular and special insights into the nature of mental life in differing psychological states.   CD

Bibliography

Balint, M. 1952: *Primary love and psycho-analytic technique.* London: Tavistock.

Bowlby, J. 1969, 1973 and 1980: *Attachment and loss.* 3 vols. London: Hogarth Press; New York: Basic Books.

Faber, M.D. (ed.) 1970: *The design within: psychoanalytic approaches to Shakespeare.* New York: Science House.

Freud, S. 1915–16: Introductory lectures on psychoanalysis. Reprinted in *Standard edition*, vols. 15 and 16.

──── 1933: New introductory lectures on psycho-analysis. Reprinted in *Standard edition of the complete psychological works of Sigmund Freud*, vol. 22. London: Hogarth; New York: Norton.

Klein, M. 1965: *Envy and gratitude and other works 1946–1963*. London: Hogarth Press; Boston, Mass.: Seymour Lawrence.

Parsons, T. 1965: *Social structure and personality*. Glencoe, Ill.: Free Press.

Sandler, J., Dare, C. and Holder, A. 1972: Frames of reference in psychoanalytic psychology, III. A note on the basic assumptions. *British journal of medical psychology* 45, 143–7.

Winnicot, D.W. 1972: *The maturational processes and the facilitating environment*. London: Hogarth Press; New York: International Universities Press.

Wollheim, R. (ed.) 1974: *Philosophers on Freud*. New York: Jason Aronson.

psychodrama A range of therapeutic techniques in which the individual acts out various roles designed to engender catharsis-like experiences and insights into self and/or others. The term is generally attributed to J.L. Moreno, a Rumanian born psychiatrist, and founder of the Psychodramatic Institute in Beacon, New York. In psychodrama the individual typically performs before a therapist-trainer and a support group, the latter usually enjoined to furnish insightful reactions to the performance. A variety of techniques are employed within psychodrama, including the soliloquy (in which the individual verbalizes his or her psychological reactions to various imagined or remembered events), the self-presentation technique (in which the individual plays the part of various significant others), the self-realization technique (in which the individual enacts his or her life plan), role reversal (in which the individual takes the part of another person with whom he or she is interacting) and the mirror technique (in which a member of the audience attempts to copy the behavior of the individual so that he or she may see self from another's standpoint).   KJG

Bibliography

Moreno, J.L. and Ennis, J.M. 1950: *Hypnodrama and psychodrama*. Boston: Beacon House.

Greenberg, I.A., ed., 1974: *Psychodrama: theory and therapy*. New York: Behavioral Publications.

psychogeriatrics The term is probably best used to refer to the branch of psychiatry concerned with all types of mental disorder in elderly people, that is, those aged sixty-five and over. In some contexts it may refer only to confused elderly people, and in other contexts to those in whom physical and mental disease occur concurrently. Its claim to be considered as a discipline distinct from general adult psychiatry rests firstly on its greater concern with organic disorders, particularly dementias, and secondly on the need to liaise closely with a specialized range of community facilities.

The demand for psychogeriatric services is increasing rapidly. In western Europe some 13 to 16 percent of the population are aged sixty-five or over; approximately 10 percent of these show some degree of dementia and a further 13 percent have other psychiatric disorders.   DLJ

Bibliography

Albert, M.L. ed. 1984: *Clinical neurology of aging*. New York and Oxford: Oxford University Press.

psychopathic personality A PERSONALITY DISORDER characterized by antisocial, irresponsible, aggressive and impulsive behavior. However the term has an alternative meaning and Schneider (1950) and some other German writers have used it to cover the whole range of personality disorders and NEUROSES. Because of the pejorative associations of the word "psychopathic" and of the very considerable confusion as to its precise definition, the alternatives of antisocial or SOCIOPATHIC PERSONALITY are often preferred. Psychopathic personality is associated with parental deprivation (see DEPRIVATION: HUMAN PARENTAL) and a history of childhood disturbance. Aggressive traits are most obvious in early adult life, but although these improve, other features do not. Lack of motivation to change and lack of insight both make treatment difficult, but limited success can be obtained by longterm support and by residential GROUP THERAPY in a therapeutic community. Psychopathic personality is a common finding among recidivist offenders. The diagnosis has an important legal status in many jurisdictions as a reason for compulsory psychiatric hospital admission for both offenders and non-offenders.   DLJ

Bibliography
*Kaplan, H.I., Freedman and Sadock, B.J. 1980: *Comprehensive textbook of psychiatry*. 3rd edn. Baltimore: Williams and Wilkins.
Schneider, K. 1950: *Psychopathic personality*. 9th edn. Vienna: F. Deuticke.

psychopathology The area of scientific study concerned with the manifestations of psychological disturbance and the mechanisms underlying these. The term can also be used to designate a body of knowledge and theories related to the specified topic, for example, the psychopathology of aggression. There are two main branches of study: descriptive psychopathology deals with the definition and classification of morbid symptoms and signs (also called phenomenology), JASPERS (1962) being one of its leading exponents; etiological psychopathology explores the ways in which morbid manifestations are generated by various influences, such as genetic, physiological and psychological. Among the latter, dynamic psychopathology is of interest to PSYCHOANALYSIS in postulating links between early childhood experiences and later illness patterns. Taylor (1966) provides a critical account.

The terms psychopath and psychopathy are misleading since they no longer refer to disorders within the whole field of psychopathology but are restricted to those involving persistently aggressive and antisocial behavior. In current usage the term SOCIOPATHIC PERSONALITY may be preferred so as to avoid this confusion.

Psychopathology has developed as a science since the end of the nineteenth century (Kraft-Ebbing first used the word in 1875). Hippocrates (c.470–c.400 BC) had of course recognized the brain as the seat of the emotions and of mental illness, but later centuries had lost sight of this in the pursuit of fanciful notions of possession by demons, an imbalance in the elements and humors, and, in women, the supposed migration of the womb within the body as the basis of HYSTERIA. The growth of neurology in the last century revived interest in the central nervous system and with it the hope that neuropathologists would discover macroscopic and histological changes in the brain of those with mental illness, thereby explaining the symptoms. As this hope was fulfilled in only a minority of illnessess, there arose a need for the separate study of mental pathology.

Descriptive psychopathology, in defining and classifying the manifestations of mental disturbance, provides the raw material for on the one hand the making of diagnoses based on clusters of symptoms and signs, and on the other hand the understanding of causation. It is concerned with patterns of behavior and communication, both verbal and non-verbal, in relation to form and content, and with all types of subjective experience. The latter can be grouped into cognitive (percepts, images, thoughts, memories), affective (emotions, moods), and conative (impulses, desires, motives); a further dimension is added by introspection and self-observation.

For a description and discussion of individual symptoms the reader is referred to a more detailed text such as Jaspers (1962) and Taylor (1966). Among the most important symptoms of cognitive disorder are: illusions, HALLUCINATIONS, DELUSIONS, THOUGHT DISORDERS, obsessions, MEMORY DISORDERS and dementia. In the field of affective disturbance we have: emotional lability, ANXIETY, PHOBIAS, manic and depressive mood, and emotional blunting. In the conative field: states of overactivity and stupor, compulsive disorders, sexual perversions and amotivational states. All types of function may be affected by CONSCIOUSNESS DISORDERS. It is interesting to note that all these symptoms may be experienced by normal subjects, but mildly (as with phobias), transiently (as with amnesia), in a drowsy state (as with hallucinations), or in a hypnotic trance (as with psychogenic anesthesia).

Recent research into descriptive psychopathology has aimed at achieving greater reliability in the recognition of symptoms, and at identifying and rating morbid states by means of questionnaires (Mann and Murray 1979).

The second main area of work in psychopathology is concerned with the etiology of mental disorders. It is helpful to think in terms of two groups of causes: precipitant causes are those events, experiences and physiological mechanisms which lead immediately to the emergence of morbid symptoms; predisposing causes are those which enhance an individual's vulnerability without producing symptoms. Of course, these two groups of causes are not necessarily different in nature; the same cause, for example lack of oxygen supply to the brain, may have either a predisposing or a precipitant role. Furthermore, different causes are commonly seen to act in combination, having an additive effect. Such is the complexity of predisposing factors in any individual that it is often difficult to predict the effect of a specific precipitant. A severe blow on the head may predictably cause unconsciousness, but the death of a pet dog may lead to anything from a mild transient distress to the most severe and protracted psychotic DEPRESSION. Nevertheless, some success has been achieved in allotting relative weights to various stressful experiences in such a way as to compile for an individual at a particular time a life events score which gives a rough guide to the likelihood of mental symptoms developing (Paykel et al. 1976). Experimental work tends to be restricted by practical and ethical considerations, and the limitations of using animals instead of human subjects.

Precipitant causes need to be understood in terms of both physiological and psychological mechanisms. The central nervous system may be seen from one viewpoint as a network of NEURONS, many with specialist functions, supported by a complex apparatus to maintain nutrition and homeostasis; if the integrity and physical harmony of that system are disturbed, symptoms may result. This can occur, for example, through changes in cerebral circulation, oxygenation, chemical balance, hormone regulation, temperature and electrical potential; or through alterations in the pharmacology of the brain, particularly its diverse NEUROTRANSMITTERS which transfer messages from one cell to another. Alcohol and drugs, or their withdrawal, readily unbalance the system. Two subsystems of crucial importance are the RETICULAR ACTIVATING SYSTEM, which regulates the level of consciousness, and the AUTONOMIC NERVOUS SYSTEM, which controls involuntary function such as heart rate and sweating and which can generate widespread and varied symptoms.

From another viewpoint the central nervous system emerges as a means of receiving and filtering information from the body and the environment, assessing it in relation to past experiences and current aims, and responding to it affectively and conatively. Difficulties may arise if there is too little incoming information (sensory deprivation) or too much; or when the information is incomprehensible or excessively alarming; when it reawakens disturbing or distorted memories; when it faces the individual with challenges he sees himself as unable to meet (see LEARNED HELPLESSNESS).

The nature of the precipitant cause will not usually by itself determine the nature of the morbid manifestation. However, it may be true that the more immediate and dramatic causes, especially physiological ones, tend to lead to a specific form of disturbance. For example, a high fever provokes a confusional state; nevertheless the content of an individual's talk when confused is determined by his pre-existing thoughts and memories. Most psychological precipitants result in disorders whose form and content are both largely dependent on the individual's predisposition and mental apparatus.

FREUD and his associates emphasized the importance of internal psychological precipitants. These are seen as arising from primitive impulses (usually erotic and aggressive) from the unconscious threatening to break into consciousness; they are resisted by the ego with the aid of various defense mechanisms such as denial or sublimation (see Taylor 1966 p.290). But the defense itself may be so extreme as to lead to symptom formation; for example, denial may bring hysterical dissociation. Psychoanalysts have also described related predisposing causes in the shape of traumatic childhood experiences and conflicts; when incompletely assimilated and resolved, these may be re-awakened later, and, along with them, pathogenic ways of coping with the associated anxiety. This theme has been extensively developed (see Brown 1964).

There are many other formulations of psychological predisposing causes. Genetic factors as well as early experiences undoubtedly play a major role in personality development, and Eysenck (1967) has claimed to measure two stable attributes, neuroticism and introversion-extraversion, which show correlations with subsequent symptom patterns. Learning theory accounts for the evolution of maladaptive patterns of behavior in terms of classical or respondent conditioning; this has important implications for the understanding of phobias, obsessions and some forms of depression. Social theories ascribe a major role to the social environment in conditions such as sociopathy and reactive depression.

Physiological predisposing causes may sometimes be more easily recognized, as in the case of brain damage, neurological disease or aging processes. However, many more subtle mechanisms undoubtedly await discovery in a way that will revolutionize our view of the etiology of the functional psychoses (manic-depressive illness and SCHIZOPHRENIA).   DLJ

Bibliography

Adams, H. and Sutker, P. 1984: *Comprehensive handbook of psychopathology*. New York: Plenum.

Brown, J.A.C. 1964: *Freud and the post-Freudians*. Harmondsworth: Penguin.

Eysenck, H.J. 1967: *Biological basis of personality*. Springfield: C. Thomas.

*Jaspers, Karl 1962: *General psychopathology*. Trans. J. Hoenig and M.W. Hamilton. Manchester: Manchester University Press; Chicago: University of Chicago Press.

Mann, A. and Murray, R. 1985: Measurement in psychiatry. In *Essentials of postgraduate psychiatry*. 2nd edn, eds. P. Hill, R. Murray and A. Thorley. London: Academic Press; New York: Grune and Stratton.

Paykel, E.S., McGuiness, B. and Gomez, J. 1976: An Anglo-American comparison of the scaling of life events. *British journal of medical psychology* 49, 237–47.

*Taylor, F. Kräupl 1966: *Psychopathology. Its causes and symptoms*. London: Butterworth.

psychopharmacology A discipline concerned with chemical substances (psychotropic drugs) that influence behavior, emotions, perceptions and thought processes by direct action on the central nervous system. Drugs with these actions may be divided (with some overlap) into three main categories:
(1) those mainly used for social, non-medical or culture-specific purposes; (2) drugs employed for the treatment of mental illness; and (3) the psychotomimetics, now used mainly in research.
(1) Centrally acting drugs have been used for social and non-medical purposes at least since the dawn of history. In many cultures alcohol has been and remains an outstanding example, although worldwide it is probable that more caffeine (from tea and coffee) is consumed. The psychological effects of smoking or chewing tobacco are mainly due to the central action of the nicotine present in tobacco. Other examples abound: cannabis in Muslim cultures; cocaine (from chewing the leaves of the coca plant) among Andean Indians; and hallucinogens, also of plant origin, in many tropical forest cultures. Abuse of drugs in this category leads to psychological and eventual physical dependence (or addiction) and severe, and sometimes fatal, reactions on withdrawal. Addiction to narcotics (e.g. opium, heroin) is one extreme example, but the abuse of many other drugs, taken for non-medical reasons, such as barbiturates and amphetamines, leads to similar results.

(2) The past thirty years have seen a phenomenal increase in the number and variety of drugs used for the treatment of mental illness. Until around 1950 only non-specific sedatives and hypnotics, such as chloral hydrate, and the barbiturates were available. The revolution began with the introduction of chlorpromazine for the treatment of schizophrenia and continued a few years later with the discovery of the antidepressants. The outstanding feature of these new drugs which distinguished them from their predecessors was their ability to alleviate the symptoms of mental illness without inducing disabling sedation, stupor or sleep. The main classes are summarized in the table.

The neuroleptics, of which more than twenty are available, are used for the treatment of schizophrenia and also in the short term to quieten acutely disturbed patients whatever the underlying psychopathology. They are mainly represented by three chemical groupings: the phenothiazines (e.g. chlorpromazine), the thioxanthenes (e.g. thioridazine) and the butyrophenones (e.g. haloperidol). In acute SCHIZOPHRENIA the neuroleptics alleviate the DELUSIONS, HALLUCINATIONS and THOUGHT DISORDER characteristic of the condition to the extent that many patients are able to lead normal lives in the community. Some schizophrenics only require treatment with these drugs during the acute phase, but for others long-term treatment is needed to prevent relapse. The neuroleptics are, however, less effective against the apathy and withdrawal characteristics of some cases of chronic schizophrenia. Their main drawback is a tendency to induce extrapyramidal symptoms or disturbances of voluntary movements which may become particularly distressing during long-term treatment.

For the relief of anxiety and mild insomnia a new class of drugs – the benzodiazepines – has almost entirely replaced the barbiturates. A major advantage of these drugs is that they are less toxic and therefore safer in overdose than the barbiturates. The best known example is diazepam (or Valium) which is probably at present the most widely prescribed psychotropic drug. Chronic use of benzodiazepines may lead to dependence and on withdrawal to symptoms of agitation, tension and insomnia; convulsions may occur after chronic use of high doses.

There are two main groups of antidepressants: the tricyclics (structurally related to the phenothiazines) and the monoamineoxidase inhibitors (MAOIs). There are now nearly twenty tricyclics available, of which imipramine was the first. In appropriate patients (not all respond) they alleviate severe depression and decrease fatigue, but often at the expense of unwanted side-effects (see table). It is of interest to note that the tricyclics have no effect on mood in normal subjects. The MAOIs have similar clinical actions but their administration requires strict control of diet and the intake of other drugs. This is because many foods and drugs contain amines with potent pharmacological actions on the cardiovascular system. In normal circumstances these amines are inactivated by the enzyme monoamine oxidase (MAO, mainly in the liver) before reaching the systemic circulation.

Lithium salts were introduced in the late 1950s for the treatment of acute attacks of mania. Lithium carbonate was found to be remarkably effective in quietening overactive euphoric patients. Later work demonstrated conclusively that given prophylactically lithium salts also stabilize mood in patients suffering cyclic swings of mania and depression and they are now widely used for this purpose. The main problem with their administration is their narrow therapeutic/toxic ratio which makes it essential to monitor plasma lithium concentrations during treatment. Toxic effects from too high a dose are potentially hazardous and may be fatal.

Stimulant drugs, represented by the amphetamines, are rarely used in clinical practice. They have no useful antidepressant action. Their proven ability to delay the onset of fatigue in normal subjects is well known, but after this effect has worn off most subjects experience lassitude, depressed mood and tension. The long-term effects of taking amphetamines

Some drugs used in clinical psychopharmacology

Class	Typical drugs	Main clinical effects	Unwanted side-effects
Major tranquilizers or neuroleptics	Chlor-promazine Thioridazine Haloperidol	Sedation without impairment of consciousness; ameliorate psychotic symptoms including thought disorder.	Most serious are disturbances in the control of voluntary movements (dystonia, akathisia and tardive dyskinesia); also hypotension.
Anxiolytics and hypnotics	Diazepam Chlor-diazepoxide Nitrazepam	Alleviate severe anxiety and induce mild sedation (anxiolytics) and sleep (hypnotics).	Include drowsiness, dependence and occasionally severe withdrawal reactions after long-term administration.
Anti-depressants	(1) *Tricyclics* Imipramine Amitriptyline Mianserin (2) *Monoamine-Oxidase Inhibitors* Phenelzine Tranyl cypromine	Alleviate severe depression; decrease fatigue. In appropriate patients similar to the tricyclics but with less sedation.	Many, and may include constipation, blurred vision and sweating, and with some drugs sedation. As with tricyclics. Also administration requires strict dietary control to avoid interactions resulting in severe cardiovascular problems.
Mood-stabilizing agents	Lithium salts	Specific use to quieten overactive, euphoric patients suffering attacks of mania; also prevents depression in manic-depressive psychosis.	Many, depending on dose and including gastrointestinal symptoms, weight gain and tremor. Severe toxic reactions result from too high a dose.
Stimulants	Dexam-phetamine Methyl-phenidate	Main clinical use to increase wakeful periods in narcolepsy. No useful anti-depressant action. In normal subjects may improve psycho-motor performance and counteract fatigue.	Many, and include insomnia, anxiety and anorexia. Chronic use frequently leads to dependence and severe paranoid psychosis.

habitually are serious and may result in psychopathic behavior and even paranoid psychosis resembling acute schizophrenia. (3) Although certain of the psychotomimetics are used in primitive cultures for ritual purposes and are sometimes abused by addicts in western society, they are mainly of interest as research tools. Administered to normal subjects at relatively low dosage they induce profound disturbances in perception, thought and mood; these drugs are often said to elicit a "model psychosis",

but the resemblance to clinical psychosis is only partial.

The main chemical groups of the psychotomimetics are: lysergic acid derivatives (e.g. lysergide or LSD); certain phenylethylamines (e.g. mescaline); methylated indolalkylamines (e.g. dimethyltryptamine); and miscellaneous compounds such as the anticholinergic drug N-methyl-3-piperidyl benzilate and phencyclidine (known as "angel dust").

The syndromes elicited by the first three

groups are similar, but differ in time course. The effects of the first two last for seven to twelve hours, while those of the third group have a short duration (one to three hours). All three stimulate sympathetic centers and induce marked somatic reactions – nausea, sweating, tremor are common. As these subside the central effects increase. These may include intense visual hallucinations, anxiety succeeded by euphoria, paranoia and cognitive disturbances. True loss of insight is rare, but withdrawal and inability to communicate or recall sensations are common. However, individuals differ markedly in their reactions and the variety and intensity of symptoms seem to be partly determined by the personality of the subject.

Piperidyl benzilate and certain other anti-cholinergics induce a syndrome characterized by disorientation in time and space, incoherence and hallucinations, usually with loss of insight. The effects of phencyclidine are complex, but include disturbances in position and touch senses and in cognitive functions. However, hallucinations are rare and somatic effects less marked than with the other drugs.

Psychotropic drugs have proved extremely powerful tools in investigating the chemistry and physiology of normal behavior and in providing clues as to etiology of mental illnesses. For example, the most effective neuroleptics used in the treatment of schizophrenia block neurotransmission at dopaminergic synapses, suggesting that this TRANSMITTER SYSTEM may be overactive in the disorder. The tricyclics, among other actions, inhibit the re-uptake of NORADRENALINE and SEROTONIN in the synaptic cleft, leading to the suggestion of a deficiency of these transmitters in depression. The receptor for the benzodiazepine drugs in the brain is closely associated with the function of the γ-aminobutyric acid neurotransmitter system. In rats high doses of amphetamine give rise to a syndrome of stereotypy which some consider an animal model for schizophrenia. These and many other observations using psychotropic drugs are providing powerful insights into the molecular basis of brain function. (See also NEUROCHEMISTRY AND BEHAVIOR, PSYCHIATRY: PHYSICAL TREATMENTS.)   RR

Bibliography

Cooper, J.R., Bloom, F.E. and Roth, R.H. 1982: *The biochemical basis of neuropharmacology*. 4th edn. Oxford and New York: Oxford University Press.

Lader, M.H. 1980: *Introduction to psychopharmacology*. Kalamazoo: Upjohn.

Lipton, M.A., DiMascio, A. and Killam, K.F. 1978: *Psychopharmacology: a generation of progress*. New York: Raven Press.

Shepherd, M., Lader, M.H., and Rodnight, R. 1968. *Clinical psychopharmacology*. London: English Universities Press.

psychosexual disorders Seriously impaired sexual performance of various kinds.

Disorders

The more common sexual disorders of women are: impaired libido – interest in sex is reduced or absent; orgasmic dysfunction – inability to obtain orgasm, or great difficulty in doing so; vaginismus – sexual intercourse is difficult or impossible because of spasm of the muscles surrounding the entrance to the vagina; dyspareunia – discomfort or pain is experienced during sexual intercourse. The sexual disorders of men are: impaired libido; erectile impotence – difficulty in obtaining or sustaining an erection; premature ejaculation – ejaculation occurs very soon after vaginal penetration, or even beforehand; ejaculatory failure – ejaculation is either impossible, or never occurs with a partner, or is very delayed.

Sexual disorders can also be classified as primary (the problem has always been present) or secondary (normal sexual functioning preceded the onset of the problem). They can be caused by a wide range of psychological and physical factors. Until the advent of sex therapy the causes of sexual disorders were usually understood in terms of Freudian theory of early sexual development and how this might be disturbed (see FREUD). The causes are now usually postulated in terms of simple psychological mechanisms (Hawton 1985). The most common cause of sexual disorders is ANXIETY, which may result from many factors including fear of failure, sexual inhibition and lack of confidence about personal appearance. Another contributing factor is ignorance, including lack of sexual information, and belief in incorrect facts or sexual myths. Sexual disorders are often accompanied by other marital or relationship disorders; sometimes they are the cause of these problems, but more commonly they are the result of such difficulties. Poor communication between partners is also likely to contribute to sexual disorders. DEPRESSION usually causes impaired libido and may cause other sexual problems.

Many physical illnesses can cause sexual disorders. These include, for example, ENDOCRINE DISORDERS, especially affecting the production of sex hormones, and also diabetes, neurological diseases such as multiple sclerosis, and heart and kidney disease. Sexual disorders may also occur in some patients following surgery, including mastectomy, prostatectomy and amputation. Sometimes the disorder is the result of a direct effect of the illness or operation on anatomical mechanisms responsible for sexual response; in other cases it is the result of the psychological responses to the illness or procedure.

A number of medicines can cause sexual disorders, including some used to treat hypertension, major tranquilizers and antidepressants. Sexual disorders are common in individuals who suffer from ALCOHOLISM or DRUG DEPENDENCE.

The treatment of couples with sexual disorders was revolutionized in 1970 when Masters and Johnson introduced their approach to sex therapy. Treatment consists of a careful assessment of each partner, after which the couple are given instructions in a step-by-step program through which they gradually rebuild their sexual relationship beginning with non-genital caressing exercises. Advice is given on how to improve verbal and non-verbal communication. Treatment is provided by either two co-therapists, one male and one female, or by one therapist. The couple are

seen daily and at each session report back on progress. Any difficulties which they may have encountered are discussed and means of overcoming them found. Education is provided about sexual anatomy and response. The Masters and Johnson approach has been successfully modified for use in the National Health Service in the United Kingdom (Hawton 1985).

Patients without partners can also be helped. Barbach (1975) has introduced a masturbation training program for women who have not been able to have an orgasm; sometimes such treatment is provided in groups of five to eight women by two female therapists. Zilbergeld (1979) has suggested ways of helping with the sexual disorders of men who do not have partners. This treatment may also be provided in a group.

The principles of sex therapy can be used in the treatment of some disabled patients and those with chronic physical illness. Where medicine is the cause of sexual disorder, management consists of finding a suitable alternative treatment whenever possible. Sexual disorders resulting from abnormalities of sex hormones can be treated by hormone replacement. For sexual disorders which are the result of marital disharmony, some form of marital therapy rather than sex therapy is usually indicated.

The results of sex therapy reported by Masters and Johnson (1970) were outstanding. Other workers report more modest results, with two-thirds of couples usually having a good outcome (Hawton 1982). The best results are obtained in the treatment of orgasmic dysfunction, vaginismus and premature ejaculation. Severe marital disharmony and psychiatric disorder in one or other partner often indicate a poor prognosis. Although Masters and Johnson (1970) found that hardly any of the couples they had treated successfully had relapsed five years later, little other information is available concerning the long-term prognosis following sex therapy, or of the prognosis of people with sexual disorders who do not receive treatment.

Deviations

The term sexual deviation is used to

describe any sexual activity that is preferred to, or displaces, heterosexual intercourse, or one that involves very unusual methods of sexual arousal, especially when the activity violates the norms of society. Whether a form of sexual behavior is regarded as deviant depends to a great degree on social values. These can change with time.

Homosexuality describes both sexual behavior with, and sexual interest in, members of a person's own sex. The sexual interest of some people exclusively involves their own sex; others may show a range of sexual interest in both their own sex and the other sex, and may be referred to as bisexual. The precise incidence of homosexuality in the general population is not known. Kinsey and colleagues (1948) estimated that among men aged thirty, 7 per cent were largely or entirely homosexual in their orientation. It has also been estimated that between 2 and 4 per cent of females are homosexual. In the United Kingdom, under the Sexual Offences Act of 1967, the legal age of consent for male homosexuality is twenty-one. Except in the armed forces there are no laws specifically concerning female homosexuality.

A transsexual is a person who has a disturbance of gender indentity and has a powerful urge to change sex. Transsexuals may be of either sex although male transsexuals are more common. They usually seek surgery and hormone treatments to bring about sex change.

Fetishism describes sexual behavior in which an object, usually a particular form of clothing, is the main source of sexual arousal. It is probably confined to men. Similarly transvestism refers to cross-dressing in which a man gets pleasure and usually sexual satisfaction from wearing female clothing.

Exhibitionism describes behavior in which gratification is sought through displaying the genitals to members of the opposite sex, usually strangers in public places. Indecent exposure is the legal offense associated with this behavior. This is the most common sexual offense in the United Kingdom and is frequently committed by young males.

There is no definite information, but a large number of theories, about the causes of sexual deviations. It has been suggested that disturbed relationships with parents may contribute to the development of homosexuality but evidence is lacking. Similarly, the disturbance of gender identity found in transsexualism has been related to disturbed upbringing in which behavior more appropriate to the opposite sex is encouraged. Genetic causes have also been postulated. It has been suggested that genetic factors may make an individual susceptible to becoming homosexual if he or she is later exposed to appropriate environmental influences. Abnormalities in levels of sex hormones before or shortly after birth have also been suggested; this has some support from experiments in animals. However, no reliable differences are found between homosexual and heterosexual adults in terms of either their hormonal or physical characteristics. It has been postulated that transvestism and fetishism are the result of conditioning in which sexual arousal at an early age occurs by chance in relation to a particular object or female clothing.

Exhibitionists often suffer from sexual dysfunction and inferiority, and the deviant behavior may be a means of compensating for these difficulties.

Patients often seek treatment to rid themselves of their deviant interest when this is either not appropriate (e.g. well-established homosexual interest in middle-aged men with no heterosexual interest) or they are not well-motivated (e.g. after having been convicted of a sexual offense). Very careful assessment of the patient is therefore imperative. Sometimes deviant sexual interest appears to be related to sexual inadequacy – when treatment as for a sexual disorder may be indicated.

AVERSION THERAPY, in which electric shocks or drug-induced nausea are paired with deviant sexual thoughts or activities, used to be popular. It is now rarely used, because of ethical problems and lack of efficacy. Other self-control techniques may be used (see BEHAVIOR THERAPY). These have been well described by Bancroft (1974). Sometimes patients need help to improve their skills in forming a relationship with a member of the opposite sex (see SOCIAL SKILLS TRAINING). Drugs which suppress libido are occasionally used, but can have dangerous side-effects and can pose ethical problems. Some patients do not wish to give up their deviant sexual interest but require help in adjusting to it. There are now wide ranges of self-help organizations suitable for such patients. Transsexual patients usually seek sex reassignment, including hormonal treatment, social skills training and surgery.

Treatment aimed at modification of homosexual interest is not very successful, especially if the interest has been long established and there is no current or previous heterosexual interest. Treatment aimed at helping patients develop control over exhibitionism, fetishistic or transvestite behavior is more successful, especially with well-motivated patients. However, patients who commit more than one sexual offense (e.g. exhibitionists) usually have a poor prognosis.   KEH

Bibliography

*Bancroft, J. 1974: *Deviant sexual behaviour: modification and assessment*. Oxford: Oxford University Press.

Barbach, L. 1975: *For yourself: the fulfillment of female sexuality*. New York: Doubleday.

Hawton, K. 1982: The behavioural treatment of sexual dysfunction. *British journal of psychiatry* 140, 94–101.

——— 1985: Sex therapy: a practical guide. Oxford: Oxford University Press.

*Kaplan, H. 1974: *The new sex therapy*. London: Baillière Tindall.

Kinsey, A.C., Pomeroy, W.B. and Martin, C.E. 1948: *Sexual behavior in the human male*. Philadephia: Saunders.

*Masters, W.H. and Johnson, V.E. 1970: *Human sexual inadequacy*. London: Churchill; Boston: Little, Brown.

Zilbergeld, B. 1979: *Men and sex*. London: Souvenir Press.

psychosis This term is commonly used to denote a serious disorder of mental functioning, as in organic, affective or schizophrenic psychosis. Beyond this there is no general agreement on its usage. In some contexts it denotes a disturbance that has the features of a clear-cut illness (for example, a psychosis resulting from thyroid under-activity) as opposed to a condition that could be seen to evolve from natural reactions and personality characteristics, which would be termed a NEUROSIS. In other contexts it specifies a mental state encompassing DELUSIONS and HALLUCINATIONS, or the loss of insight. Psychoanalysts view the mental content of psychoses as deriving from the unconscious Id which erupts unchecked into consciousness. JASPERS draws a distinction between mental phenomena which can be understood empathically, and others (encountered in the psychoses) which are accessible only to causal explanations.   DLJ

psychosomatic disorders Illnesses whose development is thought to be importantly determined by psychological factors. Among the diseases speculatively grouped under this heading are: various skin conditions, essential hypertension, coronary artery disease, asthma, peptic ulcers and ulcerative colitis. Studies attempting to define the mechanism of the psychological contribution have explored the possibility of a common personality type, a specific emotional conflict, a particular set of childhood experiences, or a certain life stress. Alternative terms are psychophysiological disorders and organ neuroses, the latter being used especially by psychoanalysts to refer to situations where a persistent emotional disturbance leads to change in the physiology of an organ.   DLJ

Bibliography

Alexander, F. 1952: *Psychosomatic medicine, its principles and applications*. London: Allen and Unwin.

psychosurgery A method of treating severe psychological disorders with brain surgery. Psychosurgery became an accepted treatment in the 1930s after experimental studies showed that selective brain lesions have a calming effect on animals displaying abnormal emotional behavior in stressful or conflict situations. The most common psychosurgical procedure is the frontal lobotomy which involves severing connections between the frontal cortex and the thalamus. The temporal lobe and its related structures have been another important target area, particularly in the control of aggressive behavior. Despite early reports of success it soon became apparent that many patients were not benefiting from psychosurgery and that some may indeed have deteriorated as a result of the operation. Psychosurgery patients often displayed decreased initiative, apathy, impaired concentration, general indifference, and personality changes that precluded the resumption of normal life. There have been attempts to reduce these side-effects by developing more sophisticated surgical techniques whereby localized damage is produced stereotaxically in specific brain regions (e.g. the hypothalamus, amygdala), thought to be directly involved in emotional behavior. Results, however, are mixed and psychosurgery, for clinical and ethical reasons, remains a highly controversial treatment.

(See PSYCHIATRY: PHYSICAL TREATMENTS.)

GWi

psychosynthesis Created by the Italian psychiatrist Roberto Assagioli. Soon after having completed psychoanalytic training and having been considered by FREUD and JUNG as a representative of PSYCHOANALYSIS in Italy in 1910, Assagioli broke away from Freudian orthodoxy and gradually created his own approach. In 1926 he founded the Istituto di Psicosintesi in Rome. A few years later, the hostility of the fascist regime forced this institute to close. Persecution, fascist at first then Nazi, prevented Assagioli from continuing his work. When the war was over, he started a new cycle of writing and teaching. He also began to encourage the creation of new psychosynthesis centers throughout the world. His two main books *Psychosynthesis* and *The act of will* were published respectively in 1965 and 1973.

Assagioli noticed that a great deal of psychological pain, imbalance and meaninglessness are felt when the diverse inner elements in the psyche exist unconnected side by side, or clash with one another. But he also observed that when they merge in successively greater wholes, the individual experiences a release of energy, a sense of well-being, and a deeper meaning in his life. Seeing that this process tends to occur naturally in all human beings, but that it often gets blocked, Assagioli devised various ways of evoking and facilitating it, and gave this system the name of psychosynthesis.

Assagioli's typology has been expressed in his well known "egg diagram" which represents our total psyche. The three horizontal divisions of the oval stand for our past, present and future. All three are active in us, although in different ways. The "lower unconscious" (1) mainly represents our personal psychological past in the form of repressed complexes and long-forgotten memories.

If we wish to encourage our growth we need to investigate *our* lower unconscious. Otherwise it may be the source of trouble, storing repressed energy, controlling our actions, and robbing us of our freedom.

The "middle unconscious" (2) is where all skills and states of mind reside which can be brought at will into our "field of consciousness" (4).

Our evolutionary future comprises the states of being, of knowing, and of feeling which we call the "superconscious" (3). In the words of Assagioli, the superconscious is the region from which 'we receive our higher intuitions and inspirations – artistic, philosophical or scientific, ethical "imperatives" and urges to humanitarian and heroic action. It is the source of higher feelings, such as altruistic love; of genius and of the states of contemplation, illumination and ecstasy'.

The distinction between the "lower" and the "higher" unconscious, or superconscious, is developmental, not moralistic. The lower unconscious merely represents the most primitive part of ourselves. Conversely, the superconscious constitutes all that we can still reach in the course of our

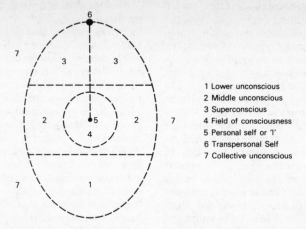

1 Lower unconscious
2 Middle unconscious
3 Superconscious
4 Field of consciousness
5 Personal self or 'I'
6 Transpersonal Self
7 Collective unconscious

evolution. It is not, however, a mere abstract possibility, but a living reality, with an existence and powers of its own.

Our psyche is bathed in the sea of what Carl Jung called the "collective unconscious" (7). In Jung's words, the collective unconscious is 'the precondition of each individual psyche, just as the sea is the carrier of the individual wave'. In the diagram all the lines are dotted to signify that no rigid compartments impede interplay among all levels.

The Self experiences all these levels. In the earlier stages of human development, awareness of the Self is nonexistent. For most of us, it exists later in a more or less veiled and confused way. But it can be experienced in its pure state as the personal self, or "I" (5).

The personal self is a reflection or outpost of the Transpersonal Self (6) – enough to give us a sense of centeredness and identity. It lives at the level of individuality, where it can learn to regulate and direct the various elements of the personality. Awareness of the personal self is a precondition for psychological health.

Identification with the Transpersonal Self is a rare occurrence – for some individuals, the culmination of years of discipline; for others, a spontaneous extraordinary experience. It was described in ancient times with the Sanskrit words *sat-chit-ananda:* being – consciousness – bliss. The Transpersonal Self, while retaining a sense of individuality, lives at the level of universality, in a realm where personal plans and concerns are overshadowed by the wider vision of the whole. The realization of the Transpersonal Self is the mark of spiritual fulfillment.

Personal and Transpersonal Self are in fact the same reality experienced at different levels.

The psychosynthetic approach is primarily pragmatic. It uses a number of techniques which could be grouped into the following categories:

Analytical techniques. These help to assess the blocks and the potentials of the personality, enable the exploration of the underworld of the unconscious, and reach the roots of psychological complexes. Imagery, free drawing, critical analysis, writing and subpersonality work are used for these purposes.

Mastery techniques. Full awareness and understanding of harmful images and complexes may help to disintegrate them, but does not necessarily produce permanent positive change. The cognitive work needs to be complemented by the active and gradual training of all psychological functions, (sensation, desire, impulse, feeling, imagination, thinking, intuition, will). Special emphasis here is given to the discovery of the "I" and to the cultivation of the will as a skillful agent.

Transformation techniques. The step beyond understanding and mastery consists in enabling the seeds of change to come to full bloom. This phase, often the most spectacular, may bring about reversals in values, and other profound developments. Of particular relevance in this phase is visualization, with its power to trigger significant psychological and behavioral changes. The end goal is the reconstruction of the personality around a new center.

Meditative techniques. Specific tools are designed for exploring the superconscious. Various forms of MEDITATION help the individual to awaken the intuition, stimulate imagination, creativity, release higher feelings, and facilitate a wider integration.

Grounding techniques. Although superconscious experiences may be beautiful and satisfying it is better for the individual if he can express the meaning of these and if they play a role in shaping his attitudes and behavior. Higher states of consciousness when improperly handled, can cause a wide variety of problems. Psychosynthesis attempts to harmonize the personal with the superconscious realm and to enable free and effective expression at all levels.

Relational techniques. Healthy interpersonal relationships are the natural counterpart of individual growth.

From a historical perspective, because of its emphasis on the creative potentialities inherent in every human being, psychosynthesis can be regarded as a humanistic and transpersonal psychology, along with the work of pioneers such as A.H. Maslow, R. May, V. Frankl, and C. Rogers. However the attempt to relate eastern insight to western research, the variety of practical methods and the richness of possible applications make of Assagioli's work an unusual contribution to contemporary psychology.   DW

Bibliography

Assagioli, Roberto, 1965: *Psychosynthesis: a manual of principles and techniques*. Harmondsworth: Penguin Books.

——— 1973: *The act of will*. London: Turnstone Press; New York: Viking Press.

psychotherapy The treatment of emotional and personality difficulties by psychological means. Most definitions of psychotherapy highlight the role of the therapist-patient relationship. For example Hans Strupp, a distinguished American psychotherapy researcher, has described psychotherapy as "an interpersonal process designed to bring about modifications of feelings, cognitions, attitudes and behavior which have proved troublesome to the person seeking help from a trained professional" (Strupp 1978). The therapist–patient relationship is different from other forms of relationship in important and basic ways: the person who makes himself or herself available as a therapist is in effect a socially sanctioned healer, a professional who commits himself to help others in need of his expertise.

The person who seeks out the therapist does so usually because of an overwhelming need. It may be to reduce distress, or to learn how to cope more effectively with life's demands or to discover how to live more creatively and fulfillingly. In many patients the need is somewhat blurred and may amount to a general sense of dissatisfaction and malaise. But however covert the problems, the essential point is that the patient decides that he or she is in need of help and chooses someone who has been socially sanctioned as able to provide that help.

Psychotherapy is a generic term under whose rubric are to be found literally dozens of different forms of treatment. In an attempt to classify treatments that are customarily regarded as examples of psychotherapy the plural form of the term is more appropriate. One classification revolves around theory. We have FREUD's PSYCHOANALYSIS, analytic therapy and its many variants, devised by such theorists as JUNG, Adler and KLEIN; the client-centered therapy of ROGERS; EXISTENTIAL ANALYSIS; GESTALT THERAPY; TRANSACTIONAL ANALYSIS; BEHAVIOR THERAPY; COGNITIVE THERAPY; and many more beside (Patterson 1980).

An alternative approach to classification is according to the target of treatment (Bloch 1979). The examples here include FAMILY THERAPY and marital therapy, in which attention is given to the relationship between members of a family on the premise that the problem lies in relationships, and sex therapy, where the focus is obviously some difficulty in a sexual relationship (see PSYCHOSEXUAL DISORDERS).

A third way to classify the therapies is in terms of the aims of treatment (Bloch 1979). Categorizing the psychotherapies thus shows up their diverse nature, as no standard classification is available. The following represents a commonly cited approach. First, *crisis intervention* – as the name indicates the therapist intervenes in the midst of a crisis which has overwhelmed the patient, and the therapist's aim is that of helping the patient to overcome the crisis. Second, *supportive psychotherapy* – the term depicts the goal of therapy, which is the provision of support to a patient who cannot manage without it, either in the short- or long-term. There is an obvious overlap between crisis intervention and supportive psychotherapy inasmuch as support is fundamental to both, but supportive therapy is the term commonly applied to treatment of those patients with a need for prolonged support, often life-long: for example, patients with chronic SCHIZOPHRENIA or severe PERSONALITY DISORDERS. Third, *symptom-oriented psychotherapy* – no substantial change in personality is attempted and there is no need for the patient to achieve understanding about the nature and origins of his problems. The therapist sets out specifically to help the patient gain relief from distressing or disabling symptoms. Examples of this form of psychotherapy are the various psychological procedures to reduce anxiety; a wide range of techniques is practiced, from Eastern approaches like transcendental MEDITATION and yoga to muscular relaxation.

A fourth approach is *insight-oriented psychotherapy* – the category of psychological treatment usually referred to when the generic term of psychotherapy is mentioned. Insight-oriented therapy is the opposite of the previous category because its chief goal is that the patient will acquire insight into what has been formerly unintelligible and bewildering. The Freudian notion (Freud 1917) that therapy should seek to make conscious what was previously unconscious is at the core of this category of therapy: three chief elements are involved. The first is the recognition and understanding of the unconsciously determined form of relationship that evolves between patient and therapist during the course of treatment, the so-called transference. According to the concept of transference, the patient transfers on to the therapist feelings and attitudes which have their roots in an earlier crucial relationship, usually with a parent or sibling. Teasing out the transference patterns enables the patient to achieve important insights about the nature and origins of his problems. The second element is the patient's identification of the unconsciously determined strategies he has used customarily to ward off unpleasant or threatening feelings, thoughts and fantasies. These mechanisms of defense include REPRESSION – a process of active forgetting of material, which is kept under control in the unconscious, denial – a self deception, whereby the harsh truth of a situation is avoided, and projection – placing intolerable feelings outside of oneself and attributing them to others. The third strand of insight involves the exploration and understanding of the relationship between current personal qualities and patterns of behavior, and key events of the past, usually from childhood.

The issue of insight raises the question of whether it is automatically followed by behavioral or personality change. One body of opinion holds that once a patient acquires self-knowledge behavioral change is inevitable on the grounds that normal psychological growth is no longer blocked by his neurosis and can develop freely.

The function of insight is best examined in the context of the basic factors which appear to underlie all forms of psychotherapy. It is highly likely that these explain the common finding that practitioners of different theoretical schools of therapy by and large achieve similar results (Smith, Glass and Miller 1980). J.D. Frank (1971) the doyen of psychotherapy research, has highlighted the relevance of specific features of psychotherapy which are shared by most clinical approaches. He regards the following six factors as common to all forms of treatment, and necessary, although not sufficient in themselves, for treatment to operate:

1. An intense, emotionally charged confiding relationship with a helping person. The description of the type of relationship is revealing. Unlike an ordinary social interaction it has an intense quality with patient and therapist meeting on serious business. The relationship could not be otherwise but emotionally charged since the patient is invariably distressed or disabled and often desperate for help. The confiding nature of the relationship is intrinsic to psychotherapy. For therapy to work the patient must disclose his problems, feelings and fantasies – disclosures which are typically painful, threatening or embarrassing – and he must feel secure that everything he does reveal is completely confidential.

2. A rationale which contains an explanation of the patient's problems and of the methods of treatment for their solution. A person who seeks help through psychotherapy is usually baffled by his experience. The therapist's provision of a rationale – even giving a symptom a name is helpful – contributes to a reduction in the patient's bewildered state. Paradoxically, the content of the rationale does not seem crucial. More important is the confidence held by the therapist that his theoretical propositions and the related practical methods he applies in treatment are beneficial. Equally important is the patient's acceptance of the rationale as making sense and offering some order to his state of disarray.

3. The provision of new information about the nature and origin of the patient's problems and of ways of dealing with them. This factor is closely allied to that of insight, mentioned earlier. It is not so much the learning by the patient of a precisely accurate explanation of his problems, but an account which is coherent, logical and illuminating. In some schools of psychotherapy the learning process is one of self-discovery, with the therapist acting as a facilitator. In other approaches the therapist assumes a more strictly pedagogic role, teaches the patient about the nature and causes of his difficulties and/or instructs him on how to set about solving them.

4. Hope in the patient that he can expect help from the therapist. A person consults a therapist in the belief that he will benefit (Wilkins 1973). His choice of a professional helper is not accidental: he usually has some idea about the professional status of the therapist and surmises that he has undertaken a program of training and must, therefore, know something about the job of helping people like himself. The other side of the effect of hope is the therapist's personal qualities. The therapist who displays a sense of optimism will usually transmit that optimism to his patient. The mere fact that the therapist takes on the patient for treatment indicates that he has some confidence that improvement is possible.

5. An opportunity for experiences of success during the course of therapy and a consequent enhancement of the sense of mastery. Often a patient enters therapy with the idea that his achievements are negligible and his chances of enjoying success slender. Therapy allows him to reverse this image: as he overcomes his difficulties, begins to appreciate the nature of his problems, and enjoys new favorable experiences during therapy, he develops a growing feeling of self-confidence and a sense that he is capable (Bandura 1977).

6. The facilitation of emotional arousal. Psychotherapy devoid of emotion is most unlikely to prove profitable. A patient's detached, rational view of himself is rarely followed by a substantial change. In ways which are difficult to define, the patient must repeatedly enter into a state of emotional arousal. Through such a process he begins to discover the feelings that are central to his experience and to appreciate what relevance they have to his problems.

SB

Bibliography

Bandura, A. 1977: Self-efficacy: towards a unifying theory of behavioral change. *Psychological review* 84, 191–215.

Bloch, S. ed. 1979: *An introduction to the psychotherapies*. Oxford: Oxford University Press.

*—— 1982: *What is psychotherapy?* Oxford: Oxford University Press.

Frank, J.D. 1971: Therapeutic factors in psychotherapy. *American journal of psychotherapy* 25, 350–61.

Freud, S. 1917 (1963): *Introductory lectures on psychoanalysis*, vols. 15 and 16. In *Standard edition of the complete psychological works of Sigmund Freud*. London: Hogarth Press; New York: Norton.

Parloff, M.B., London, P. and Wolfe, B. 1986: Individual psychotherapy and behavior change. *Annual review of psychology* 37, 321–49.

Patterson, C.H. 1980: *Theories of counseling and psychotherapy*. New York: Harper and Row.

Smith, M.L., Glass, C.V. and Miller, T.I. 1980: *The benefits of psychotherapy*. Baltimore: Johns Hopkins University Press.

Strupp, H.H. 1978: Psychotherapy research and practice: an overview. In: *Handbook of psychotherapy and behavior change*, eds. S. Garfield and A. Bergin. New York: Wiley.

Wilkins, W. 1973: Expectancy of therapeutic gain: an empirical and conceptual critique. *Journal of consulting and clinical psychology* 40, 69–77.

psychotomimetic drugs *See* psychopharmacology.

psychotropic drugs *See* psychopharmacology.

puberty The process of sexual maturation and other physical changes marking the transition from childhood to adult maturity. It is accompanied by the development of secondary sexual characteristics and culminates in the capacity for reproduction. Various psychological changes, e.g. cognitive development, also take place.

Puberty is initiated and controlled by changes in hypothalamic and anterior pituitary function. Changes in the reproductive system occur over two to three years and are related to the adolescent growth spurt. Puberty occurs approximately eighteen to twenty-four months later in boys than in girls and the growth spurt takes place at an earlier point in the pubertal sequence in girls than in boys. The sequence of outward signs in boys is, accelerated growth of the testes and scrotum with the appearance of pubic hair; penile growth, coinciding with the onset of the growth spurt; the first seminal discharge; deepening of the voice. In girls the process begins with the appearance of breast buds and of pubic hair. Menstruation begins near the completion of the sequence, after the peak velocity of the growth spurt (see MENARCHE). Tanner (1962) has described stages in breast growth in girls and genital development in boys.

There is wide individual variation in the age of onset and rate of progress, with different psychological correlates. Late maturation in boys, for example, may be followed by difficulties in personal adjustment.   WLIP-J

Bibliography

Johnson, M. and Everitt, B. 1980: *Essential reproduction*. Oxford: Blackwell Scientific Publications, pp. 143–68.

Reiter, E.O. and Grumbach, M.M. 1982: Neuroendocrine control mechanisms and the onset of puberty. *Annual review of physiology* 42, 595–614.

Tanner, James M. 1962: *Growth at adolescence*. Oxford: Blackwell Scientific; Springfield, Ill.: Thomas.

R

radical therapy In 1967 an extraordinary book appeared – *The politics of experience*, by R.D. LAING. During the next ten years, all the issues raised in that book were acted on in various ways by different groups. In England, *People not psychiatry* was formed as a network of people willing to help each other, the Philadelphia Association was formed by Laing and others, and the Arbours Association followed, with Joe Berke and Morton Schatzman among others. The theoretical issues in psychology were taken up by magazines such as *Red rat* and *Humpty dumpty*, which were angry, campaigning and radical. As a result of these efforts, the medical model has now been widely abandoned even by the orthodox: the very conservative British Psychological Society, for example, came out in the late 1970s as saying that neurosis was not a medical but a psychological problem; and in America the highly respectable five-volume *Handbook of social psychology* said the same thing. Also as a result of these efforts, there is much more general awareness of problems such as racism, sexism, classism and ageism; for example, the US Department of Health, Education and Welfare issued an official kit entitled *Shattering sex-role stereotypes*, which went to all agencies concerned with alcohol, drug abuse and mental health. The same tendency was also reflected in legal changes and changes in quota regulations, etc. In the US, for example, the use of intelligence and personality tests was severely curtailed by legislation and court decisions following the contention that they were used to discriminate against blacks and others. Leon Kamin's book *The science and politics of IQ* was important in this area.

Perhaps the biggest positive change was the enormous increase in various kinds of peer counseling, starting with Re-evaluation Counseling and resulting in 1982 in four different networks of co-counseling in Britain alone. Harvey Jackins's *The human side of human beings* is where the idea began but there are more recent books by Rose Evison and Richard Horobin, and by John Southgate and Rosemary Randall, which make the technique much more accessible and understandable through the copious use of cartoons and diagrams. Self-help groups also increased, and there is now an Association of Self Help and Community Groups in Britain. One of the most influential groups was *Red therapy* in the late 1970s, and out of this came the Ernst and Goodison book *In our own hands*, basically addressed to the women's liberation movement but also useful to mixed groups or men's groups. The main point it makes is that consciousness-raising is not enough, because 'unconscious feelings formed by our childhood conditioning would continue to sabotage our conscious choices for liberation'. So what is needed is "unconsciousness raising", and in their book they describe how this is to be done.

Radical therapy sees the individual as part of a wider social scene, and believes that social problems need social solutions. The difficult task of relating the personal to the social so as to do justice to both was tackled by Nick Heather (*Radical perspectives in psychology*) and by John Rowan (*Ordinary ecstasy*) on the theoretical level, and by the organizations mentioned above in a practical way – to which we may now add the Institute of Psychotherapy and Social Studies in London, which is running courses based on this view of therapy. There are also some classic anthologies in this field which are still worth reading, such as *Radical psychology* (Phil Brown), *The radical therapist* (R.T. Collective), *Going crazy* (H.M. Ruitenbeek) and *Readings in radical psychiatry* (Claude Steiner). JCR

Bibliography

Brown, Phil 1973: *Radical psychology*. London: Tavistock Publications.

*Ernst, S. and Goodison, L. 1981: *In our own hands: a book of self-help therapy*. London: Women's Press.

Evison, R. and Horobin, R. 1979: *How to change yourself and your world*. Sheffield: Co-counselling Phoenix.

*Heather, N. 1976: *Radical perspectives in psychology*. London: Methuen.

Jackins, H. 1965: *The human side of human beings: the theory of re-evaluation counseling*. Seattle: Rational Island Press.

Kamin, L. 1974: *The science and politics of IQ*. New York: John Wiley.

*Laing, R.D. 1967: *The politics of experience* and *The bird of paradise*. Harmondsworth: Penguin.

R.T. Collective 1974: *The radical therapist*. Harmondsworth: Penguin.

Rowan, J. 1976: *Ordinary ecstasy: humanistic psychology in action*. London: Routledge and Kegan Paul.

Ruitenbeek, H.M. 1972: *Going crazy*. New York: Bantam Books.

Southgate, J. and Randall, R. 1978: *The barefoot psychoanalyst*. London: AKHPC.

Steiner, C. et al. 1975: *Readings in radical psychiatry*. New York: Grove Press.

reafference A theory that sets out to explain how animals distinguish between stimuli that result from their own behavior and those emanating from the environment. For example when we move our eyes in a voluntary manner the image moves on the retina, but we have no perception of movement, but when the image on the retina moves as a result of movement of an object in the environment, we do see movement. Reafference theory explains this difference by assuming that during voluntary movement the brain forms an image (known as the efference copy) of the expected consequences of the movement. If the actual (reafferent) consequences correspond to the expected consequences, no movement is perceived. Stimuli emanating from the environment (exafferent stimuli) do not correspond to any efference copy and so their perception is not canceled.

The reafference principle was developed by von Holst and Mittelstaedt (1950) and has been applied to many aspects of animal behavior, including perception, orientation and motivation. DJM

Bibliography

von Holst, Erich and Mittelstaedt, Horst 1950: Das Reafferenzprinzip: Wechselwirkungen zwischen Zentralnervensystem und Peripherie. *Naturgewissenschaft* 37, 464–76.

recovery of function after brain damage The return to normal levels of performance by the brain-damaged subject following any initially disruptive effects. There are several hypotheses which emphasize events and mechanisms occurring over time which may be relevant to the recovery from brain damage. Functional substitution refers to the condition whereby one neural subsystem can take over the role of another in the event of damage to the latter. This is particularly relevant to recovery from brain damage sustained in infancy where assignments of function to structure are considered to exhibit a degree of plasticity. This view has grown from observations on the restoration of speech in patients suffering early damage to the left hemisphere speech areas (see CRITICAL PERIODS AND THE NERVOUS SYSTEM). Diaschisis, functional shock suggests that some aspects of recovery can be attributed to the re-emergence of function of depressed neural areas outside the primary site of damage. Re-organizational compensation, whereby neural subsystems interact in a new way to solve an old problem, may also account for the recovery. Similarly with behavioral compensation the use of novel behavioral strategies compensates for lost skills and abilities. (See also PLASTICITY: PHYSIOLOGICAL CONCEPT.) RCS/BER

reflex An automatic reaction to external stimulation. In a simple reflex the central nervous system receives a message from a sense organ and converts this directly into instructions for muscular contraction or glandular secretion. For example, an increase in illumination on the retina results in a reflex contraction of the iris so that the pupil of the eye becomes smaller, cutting down the amount of light falling on the retina.

Reflexes are particularly important in the co-ordination of limb muscles. Changes in the length of muscles, measured by muscle spindles, or in muscular tension, measured by tendon organs, are automatically signaled to the spinal cord where there are connexions with the nerves responsible for controlling muscular tension. The postural reflexes enable muscles to adjust to the mechanical forces that result from shifts in the centre of gravity during locomotion. Such reflexes often work in reciprocation, so that incompatible sets of muscles can operate in succession, thus achieving smooth co-ordination of limb movements.

PAVLOV discovered that, although many reflexes are inborn, some can be modified or established by conditioning. The automatic depression of the brake pedal by a car driver in an emergency is an example of such a conditioned reflex.   DJM

Bibliography

Homma, S. 1976: *Understanding the stretch reflex. Progress in brain research*, vol. 44. Amsterdam: Elsevier.

regression In common use, the appearance of behavior appropriate to an earlier life stage, triggered by stress. Examples include the adolescent who "regresses" to whining or tantrums when parental demands are imposed; the young child who "regresses" to bedwetting or thumbsucking with the birth of a younger sibling. The term derives from Freud's ontogenetic model of development, in which the individual passes through a series of developmental stages. Ideally, progress requires a balance of gratification and frustration; either excessive frustration or excessive gratification leads to fixation. In reality, normal development inevitably entails a less than perfect balance, and earlier stages leave residues in the form of minor fixations. Regression represents a return to an earlier stage, commonly a stage at which gratification was experienced. ND

regression, in statistics is used in two distinct ways. In regression analysis values of a dependent variable are predicted from a linear function: $y = bx + a$, where y is the value of the dependent variable, b is a constant by which values of the independent variable x are multiplied, and a is a constant which is added in every case. We are therefore able to predict how much increase or decrease in the value of the independent variable x will produce a stated increase or decrease in the value of the dependent variable y. In multiple regression the values of the dependent variable y are predicted from the values of several independent variables $x_1 \ldots x_j$ rather than one.

The other use of the word "regression" is in the phrase "regression to the mean". This was a phenomenon noted by Galton, who found that the children of two tall parents tend to be shorter than their parents, although still taller than average. This seemed to imply that the population was continuously getting closer to the mean. But this was clearly not happening. The solution to this conundrum lies in the fact that in a normally distributed population the majority of members have heights (or weights, or abilities) which are close to the mean. The probability of any individual deviating far from the mean is therefore very small. Hence it is very unlikely that a child of two extremely tall parents would also be extremely tall. RL

Bibliography

Winer, B.J. 1962: *Statistical principles in experimental design*. New York: Holt, Rinehart and Winston.

rehabilitation In psychiatric practice is concerned with the prevention of social disablement following mental illness, especially SCHIZOPHRENIA. Social disablement results from:
1. Continuing psychological dysfunctions

(e.g. THOUGHT DISORDER, DELUSIONS and HALLUCINATIONS).

2. Social disadvantages; for example, unemployment.

3. Personal reactions to the two previous factors (Wing and Morris 1981).

The impoverished environment and custodial attitudes of psychiatric hospitals in the past increased the patients' disabilities, leading to the apathetic and dependent state of institutionalism (Barton 1959; Wing and Brown 1970). The provision of useful occupation (e.g. in sheltered workshops) has often been the first step in reform, and it remains important.

Rehabilitation starts with the assessment of an individual's assets as well as handicaps, allowing realistic goals to be formulated and necessary actions decided. Methods used include BEHAVIOR THERAPY, especially a form of operant conditioning, the "token economy", in which staff reward deserved behavior with tokens exchangeable for cigarettes, meals, etc. SOCIAL THERAPY, with its emphasis on activity, freedom and responsibility, relies upon social pressures and rewards, and attempts to develop self-esteem and self-motivation. Any psychiatric rehabilitation service must provide a wide range of programs and facilities, available for as long as the patient requires, in order to meet the varied and persisting needs of the disabled (Gloag 1985). GPP

Bibliography

Barton, R. 1959: *Institutional neurosis.* Bristol: John Wright and Sons.

*Clark. D.H. 1981: *Social therapy in psychiatry.* 2nd edn. Edinburgh: Churchill Livingstone.

Gloag, D. 1985: Needs and opportunities in rehabilitation. *British medical journal* 290, 981–84, 1059–62, 1201–03.

Wing, J.K. and Brown, G.W. 1970: *Institutionalism and schizophrenia.* Cambridge: Cambridge University Press.

Wing, J.K. and Morris, B. 1981: *Handbook of psychiatric rehabilitation practice.* Oxford: Oxford University Press.

repression The principal DEFENSE MECHANISM in psychoanalytic theory (see FREUD). The process by which a wish, idea etc. is kept out of consciousness because it is unacceptable either to the ego (because maladaptive) or the superego (because offensive to moral precepts). "Primary" repression is what prevents the idea of an instinctual impulse from ever emerging into consciousness, so that much of the unconscious mind consists of id-impulses; while "secondary" repression rejects from consciousness also ideas associated with, or symbolic of, such an impulse (Freud 1915). Repression differs from inhibition in that in the former the energy of the impulse is opposed by a counter-force, whereas in the latter the energy of the impulse itself is withdrawn. If repression is excessive, impulses find indirect expression in neurotic symptoms rather than in constructive sublimations, and normally repressed material is expressed in disguised form in dreams (see DREAMING) or in the mild disruption of everyday psychological functioning (see PARAPRAXIS). NMC

Bibliography

Freud, S. 1915 (1957): *Repression.* In *The standard edition of the complete psychological works of Sigmund Freud,* vol. 14. pp. 143–58. London: Hogarth Press; New York: Norton.

reticular activating system Arousal of the brain is a primary function of the reticular activating system (RAS) (see BRAIN AND CENTRAL NERVOUS SYSTEM: ILLUSTRATIONS, figs. 6 and 9). The reticular formation is composed of a diffuse collection of neurons which extend from medial regions of the medulla through the pons and mid-brain to the THALAMUS. Injury of this brain structure produces persistent sleep, while electrical stimulation of the reticular formation will arouse a sleeping animal. Not only does activation of the RAS lead to awakening, but it also produces increased levels of arousal and attention once awake. All ascending sensory pathways send branches to the RAS. Although this sensory information is very nonspecific, it serves to stimulate the RAS which, in turn, sends messages which activate the cortex so that the incoming sensory messages can be interpreted. Additionally, there are descending neural pathways from the cortex that serve to excite the RAS which will, in turn, more fully activate the cortex.   RAJ

rhythms Periodically repeated features of behavior which may recur over time scales of any duration. Rhythms can arise as a result of clock-driven behavior, as a result of responses to rhythmically occurring external stimuli, or as relaxation oscillations which arise as a result of the physiological or mechanical organization of the animal.

Clock-driven rhythms result from the endogenous time-keeping ability of animals, and may give rise to circannual, circalunar or circadian periodicity in behavior. The timing of annual migration and hibernation is organized in this way, as are the daily routines of many animals.

Responses to exogenous rhythmicity occur in adjustment to the seasons, the weather and daily fluctuations in the availablity of food. Relaxation oscillations occur whenever there is a build-up and release of behavioral potential, as in hunger and in many aspects of locomotion. (See also CIRCADIAN RHYTHMS.)   DJM

Rogers, Carl Ransom The proponent of "client-centered therapy" (nondirective counseling) and the 'father of humanistic psychology'. Rogers was born in Illinois in 1902. His family were farmers with, according to Rogers himself (1959) 'almost fundamentalist' religious beliefs. He went to agricultural college at the University of Wisconsin (1919), but decided to become a minister. Rogers graduated from the Union Theological Seminary in New York in 1924. After that he attended the Columbia University Teachers College, where he studied clinical psychology (PhD 1931). He was an intern at the psychoanalytically oriented Institute for Child Guidance in New York, and from 1928 to 1940 he was a psychologist in the child study department of the Society for Prevention of Cruelty to Children in Rochester, and its replacement the Rochester Guidance Center. During

this period Rogers recognized the patient's (or, as he would say 'the client's') capacity to gain insight into his or her own problems and to find a solution. He argued that listening to the client is better than guiding. In 1939 he published *The clinical treatment of the problem child* and in 1942 he published *Counseling and psychotherapy* which contained the transcript of the tapes of an eight session therapy.

In 1940 Rogers became a professor at Ohio State University. In 1945 he joined the University of Chicago as professor of psychology and head of the counseling center. He now argued that the self-concept is central in the organization of the personality (1947), and that the recognition and clarification of feelings are basic to therapy. During this period he worked out his ideas about the best approach for therapists to take. His views (1957, 1966) were that beneficial change would occur if the therapist was able to provide "congruence" (genuineness), unconditional positive regard, and empathic understanding. The genuine therapist can be him- or herself without putting on an act. Rogers believed that the client is 'likely to sense' that put-on concern is false. The "positive regard" for the client is a (genuine) display of care by the therapist, which is not conditional on the client behaving in any particular way. The therapist must also display empathy and show that he understands the client's feelings and takes them seriously. There is evidence that these characteristics do distinguish inexperienced therapists from good therapists, regardless of theoretical orientation (Frank 1971).

In 1957 Rogers became professor of psychology and psychiatry at the University of Wisconsin. He went on to the Western Behavioral Sciences Institute in La Jolla, California in 1964. He and several colleagues set up the Center for the Study of Persons in 1968. In doing this he dissociated himself from academic psychology, declaring himself 'rather "turned-off" by the ... methods of studying (people) as "objects" for research' (1972).

Rogers is considered important not only as a theorist (and practitioner) of psychotherapy, but also for his ideas about the self. His conceptions of personality and therapy revolve around these ideas. He believes in the 'fundamental predominance of the subjective', and that 'man lives essentially in his own personal and subjective world' (1959). In Rogers' view the individual has an organized set of perceptions of his or her own self and its relationship to others. The self-concept is not fragmented, but a gestalt with a coherent and integrated pattern. It is also conscious. Rogers' experience with the sudden reversals of clients' self-concepts during therapy persuaded him that 'the alteration of one minor aspect could completely alter the whole pattern' (1959).

In addition to the self-concept the individual has an IDEAL SELF, i.e. what he or she would like or thinks one ought to be. Rogers takes the discrepancy between the self-concept and the ideal self as a measure of maladjustment, but the evidence does not entirely support this suggestion. Katz and Zigler (1967), for example, found that older and more intelligent children had greater discrepancies, and argued that this was because they had higher ideals and were more realistic about themselves. On the other hand some of the findings on TYPE-A PERSONALITY, Burger's (1984) work on need for control and Higgins et al.'s (1985) work on self-discrepancy imply that a belief that one is not living up to one's ideals may be a risk factor in mental and physical illness. Rogerians consider that support for the discrepancy model of maladjustment is provided by evidence that discrepancy is reduced by non-directive counseling (Butler and Haigh 1954). This, however, only shows (at best) that after this kind of therapy recovery is associated with such a reduction.

The only motive recognized in Rogers' theory is the "basic actualizing tendency", i.e. 'the inherent tendency of the organism to develop all its capacities in ways which serve to maintain or enhance the organism' (1959). This tendency 'expresses itself . . . in the actualization of . . . the self'. In Rogers' 1959 description of the development of his ideas about the self he says

that from what his clients said, 'it seemed clear that in some odd sense (a client's) goal was to become his 'real self'. Self-actualization, however, has never become a conceptually clear or empirically useful idea.

According to Rogers, there is frequently a discrepancy between the concept of oneself and the reality. He calls this "incongruence". People are vulnerable to anxiety when their self-concepts do not tally with reality. If experience does not support one's view of oneself, one is likely to employ various DEFENSE MECHANISMS such as distortion or denial. In therapy, on the other hand, clients appear to revise their self-concepts. Rogers believes that 'psychological adjustment exists when the concept of the self is such that all the . . . experiences of the organism are . . . assimilated . . . into a consistent relationship with the concept of self' (1951). The maintenance of consistency has, of course, been proposed as a major motive by many psychologists and has led to a great deal of empirical research.

Apart from the "basic actualizing tendency", Rogers also thinks everyone has a secondary or learnt "need for positive regard" (i.e. to be valued for him- or herself). This has already been mentioned as a necessary element in client-centered therapy. Rogers also has the more general belief that acceptance of oneself and high self-esteem are the result of being brought up in a family which shows such positive regard (1951). Coopersmith (1967) provided evidence that children have high self-esteem when their parents have an attitude of acceptance, which is neither too cloying nor too detached, and which does not preclude control or punishment.

Rogers' ideas developed in the practice of therapy, and the things he says (as well as the things he does) show that he has remained suspicious of many of the presumptions of academic psychology. This has possibly produced a tension between his systematic theorizing self and his pastoral self. He effects a reconciliation by claiming that 'research is not . . . an activity in which one engages to gain professional kudos. It is the persistent, disciplined effort to make sense and order out of the phenomena of subjective experience.' Rogers has clearly been of major importance in advancing understanding of psychotherapy. His theories about the self are more difficult to evaluate. Although they often seem to have appealed most to the enthusiastically woolly-minded, they have had sufficient strength and empirical support to provide a valuable counter to some of the more reductive and bizarre assumptions about human psychology which have been popular in Rogers' lifetime.   RL

Bibliography

Burger, J.M. 1984: Desire for control, locus of control, and proneness to depression. *Journal of personality* 52, 71–89.

Butler, J.M. and Haigh, G.V. 1954: Changes in the relation between self-concepts and ideal concepts consequent upon client centered counseling. In *Psychotherapy and personality change* eds. C.R. Rogers and R.F. Dymond. Chicago: University of Chicago Press.

Coopersmith, S. 1967: *The antecedents of self-esteem*. San Francisco: Freeman.

Frank, J.D. 1971: Therapeutic factors in psychotherapy. *American journal of psychotherapy* 25, 350–61.

Higgins, E.T., Klein, R. and Strauman, T. 1985: Self-concept discrepancy theory: a psychological model for distinguishing among different aspects of depression and anxiety. *Social cognition* 3, 51–76.

Katz, P. and Zigler, E. 1967: Self-image disparity: a developmental approach. *Journal of personality and social psychology* 5, 186–95.

Rogers, C.R. 1939: *The clinical treatment of the problem child*. Boston: Houghton Mifflin.

—— 1942: *Counseling and psychotherapy*. Boston: Houghton Mifflin.

—— 1947: Some observations on the organization of personality. *American psychologist* 2, 358–68.

—— 1951: *Client-centered therapy*. Boston: Houghton Mifflin.

—— 1957: The necessary and sufficient conditions of therapeutic personality change. *Journal of consulting psychology* 2, 95–103.

—— 1959: A theory of therapy, personality, and interpersonal relationships, as developed in the client-centered framework. In *Psychology: a study of a science*, vol. 3, ed. S. Koch. New York and London: McGraw-Hill.

—— 1966: Client-centered therapy. In *American handbook of psychiatry*, ed. S. Arieti. New York: Basic Books.

—— 1972: My personal growth. In *Twelve therapists*, ed. A. Burton. San Francisco: Jossey-Bass.

RNA, DNA The two major nucleic acids in virtually all living organisms. DNA (deoxyribonucleic acid) is found primarily in the nucleus of all cells and contains the genetic blueprint for the entire organism. It is present as a double-stranded helix whose backbone comprises an alternating arrangement of sugar and phosphate molecules. The stairs of the helix are formed by pairing four bases: cytosine, guanine, thymine and adenine. Base pairings are always complementary, with adenine binding to thymine and cytosine to

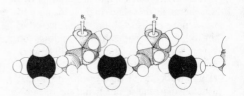

guanine. A linear arrangement of these four bases forms the genetic code, which is read as a series of triplets, each coding for one amino acid. During transcription the two strands of DNA separate, breaking the base pairings, and a single stranded molecule of RNA (ribonucleic acid) is transcribed in complementary fashion from the DNA template. In RNA, uracil replaces thymine. The messenger RNA thus formed migrates to the cytoplasm and associates with ribosomes to initiate protein synthesis, a process called translation. A separate species, transfer RNA, brings molecules of amino acids over to the ribosomes in an order specified by the sequence of bases in the messenger. These amino acids are joined sequentially by peptide bonding to form a polypeptide. When translation is complete, the polypep- tide breaks away from the ribosome and assumes the configuration of a protein.

GPH

S

sado-masochism Abnormal sexual practices (paraphilias) involving the infliction of suffering or pain. The term derives from the Marquis de Sade (1740–1814) in whose novel *Justine* sexual gratification was associated with pain, and L. von S. Masoch (1836–1895), an Austrian novelist who first described pain as a sexual stimulant. Sadism and masochism are found in both homo- and heterosexual relationships, and both sexes. Since these practices are complementary, clinical literature reports many couples, one of whom is a sadist and the other a masochist in a stable relationship; though masochism is apparently more common (Davison and Neale 1982).

Both psychoanalytic and conditioning theories have been proposed to explain the origins of the condition. The psychoanalytic theory connects sadism to castration fear (and so is inapplicable to women), while the conditioning theory depends on the rather implausible thesis that the arousal involved in inflicting and experiencing pain is similar to sexual excitement. Neither theory is well supported empirically. RHa

Bibliography

Davison, G.C. and Neale, J.M. 1982: *Abnormal psychology*. 3rd edn. New York: Wiley.

schizophrenia A mental illness (or group of illnesses), in which there is a fundamental disturbance of the personality characterized by disturbances of thinking, motivation and mood together with delusions and hallucinations, but in which cognition is normal. The peak incidence is in early adult life and approximately one percent of adults suffer from it at some time in their lives. Amidst the wide range of symptoms and variability in their course, there are three basic groupings (1) acute syndrome, often precipitated by stress, with little chronic impairment (2) chronic schizophrenia with no acute episodes, and (3) acute episodes together with long-term abnormalities.

Schizophrenia may affect all aspects of the personality. The acute syndromes are characterized by positive psychological symptoms, such as DELUSIONS, HALLUCINATIONS and THOUGHT DISORDER as well as disturbance in mood and behavior. More chronic schizophrenia is dominated by negative symptoms which include social withdrawal, apathy, lack of volition and decreased emotional expression ("blunting of affect"). The symptoms are greatly worsened by lack of environmental stimulation, as in INSTITUTIONALIZATION. Four main clinical patterns have been described, although most recent evidence suggests that the subtypes cannot be clearly distinguished genetically or clinically:

1. *Hebephrenia* The prominent symptoms are changes of affect, shallowness of mood and thought disorder. Delusions and hallucinations are not obvious. It is said to begin in late adolescence or early adult life.

2. *Catatonia* Psychomotor symptoms of over or underactivity. Abnormal postures may be maintained for long periods or there may be stupor, excitement or abnormal movements. Said to have been common in the large asylums it is now rare.

3. *Paranoid* Most often seen with later onset, paranoid delusions are the most prominent symptom and personality is relatively well preserved. There is no clear distinction from "paraphrenia" of middle age or "late paraphrenia" of the elderly (see PARANOID STATES).

4. *Simple* Progressive decline in personality and social achievement without obvious psychiatric symptoms. The most doubtful category and one which it is difficult to diagnose.

The problem of definition

The greatest problem in describing schizophrenia is the difficulty in diagnosis, although most psychiatrists agree about patients with typical symptoms. The condition was first clearly identified by the German psychiatrist Emil KRAEPELIN (1919) who distinguished two major groups of psychiatric illness, dementia praecox and manic-depressive psychosis. In describing the former (later called schizophrenia), he emphasized the effects on personality, emotion and volition. Kraepelin based his account on descriptions of symptoms and observations of long-term outcome and his conclusions have remained the basis for all more recent concepts. Eugen BLEULER enlarged clinical understanding and also attempted to identify underlying basic symptoms. He introduced the term schizophrenia to emphasize "splitting" of psychic functions, and identified *fundamental* symptoms: disturbance of associations, thought disorder, changes in emotional reactions, autism. Inevitably the dependence of diagnosis upon psychopathological mechanisms rather than overt symptoms meant much less precision than in Kraepelin's approach. More recent attempts to define the concepts of schizophrenia have derived from these two different approaches. Schneider (1959) emphasized the importance of precise diagnosis and suggested the value of a number of symptoms of special diagnostic importance, "first rank symptoms". His criteria have been widely used in Europe and continue to have a major influence on later systems. This relatively narrow and precise definition is in contrast to the broader and vaguer definitions derived from Bleuler's account of psychological mechanisms which have been especially popular in the United States. In recent years increasing awareness of the problems caused by wide international variations in diagnostic criteria (WHO 1978) have led to considerable efforts to develop clear operational criteria. A number of overlapping definitions are available, the best known being that of the current American classification, DSM III (American Psychiatric Association 1980). All these definitions require the presence of certain key symptoms and some also emphasize chronicity of course in terms of abnormal pre-illness personality or of prolonged duration of symptoms.

Related Syndromes Modern narrow definitions emphasize difficulties in classifying typical illnesses. After careful examination some can be classified as AFFECTIVE DISORDER or PERSONALITY DISORDER while others can be placed in tentative categories such as PARANOID STATE. It is still uncertain whether there is an intermediate or subsyndrome of acute, good prognosis psychosis, precipitated by stress and characterized by persistent mood disturbance and perplexity. Among the overlapping terms are good prognosis schizophrenia, schizophreniform state, cycloid psychosis, bouffée delirante and schizoaffective state. The last of these terms has been particularly widely used, both in this sense and also for conditions which satisfy diagnostic criteria for both schizophrenia and affective disorder.

Etiology Much the strongest evidence of predisposing factors comes from genetic studies. These show the occurrence of the condition in arount 10 percent of first degree relatives. Study of identical and non-identical twins and of children of a schizophrenic pair adopted at birth strongly suggest an inherited predisposition, although the mechanism and inheritance are uncertain (Shields 1978). However, it is clear that inheritance is not a complete explanation and this has encouraged much research on environmental factors, including social class, social deprivation and migration. Since FREUD's discussion (Freud 1958) of the autobiography of a paranoid judge, Schreber, there have been numerous psychodynamic theories but the most popular current interest is in the role of patterns of communications within the family (Wynne 1981). The central difficulty in evaluating hypotheses is that it is not possible to determine whether abnormal communication follows the onset of schizophrenia in a family member or precedes it. The limitations of retrospective evidence have led to "high risk research", that is prospective study of populations thought to have a greatly increased risk of schizophrenia. In addition to these *predisposing* factors there is evidence that physical factors and social stresses may precipitate the initial onset and relapse of illness. Study of mediating mechanisms is concentrated in two broad areas: first, psychological abnormalities in arousal, attention and thinking and secondly upon biochemical processes. Research in the latter area has been partly encouraged by advances in PSYCHOPHARMACOLOGY. However, even though there is much evidence of the mode of action of antipsychotic drugs it cannot be concluded that similar mechanisms are the biochemical basis of schizophrenia. Most current interest centers on abnormalities in the neurotransmitter DOPAMINE.

Prognosis The incorporation of evidence of chronicity in some diagnostic concepts makes it difficult to review and compare follow-up evidence. It would appear that about a fifth of patients suffering a first illness have a complete remission of symptoms and about a fifth have a poor prognosis with chronic or relapsing illness (M. Bleuler 1974). Others have further episodes of acute illness or social difficulties but manage with medical care and social support to live largely independent lives. Predictors of a good outcome are: sudden onset, good pre-morbid personality, good previous adjustment, and precipitation of the illness by an obvious stress. Prognosis is substantially affected by social influences. Understimulation encourages the signs of "institutionalization" whereas overstimulation (such as may be caused by stressful LIFE EVENTS or stresses within families) may precipitate florid acute symptoms. There are some indications that the prognosis for social recovery is better in under-developed countries and this may be due to the better social support.

Treatment Treatment of the acute florid symptoms largely depends upon psychotropic medication, particularly the phenothiazine group, although sympathetic care is also essential. This is usually best provided in hospital. Patients with chronic handicaps or who have had recurrent illnesses require long-term treatment.

This has two aims, the prevention of further acute episodes and rehabilitation to minimize chronic handicaps (Wing 1978). The former depends upon the reduction of social and family stresses and usually also upon long-term medication. Rehabilitation is primarily social although many patients also require maintenance medication for control of symptoms. The nature and complexity of their treatment plan will depend upon continuing clinical assessment. Those with the poorest outlook and the greatest handicaps may require considerable medical and social care over many years. A small minority will require sheltered employment and accommodation. The reform of the mental hospitals has rarely been accompanied by the development of adequate community services. This means that it is often difficult to provide the best long-term care for severely handicapped chronic patients.   RAM

Bibliography

American Psychiatric Association 1980: *Diagnostic and statistical manual III*.

Bleuler, E. 1950: *Dementia praecox: the group of schizophrenias*. New York: International Universities Press.

Bleuler, M. 1974: The long term course of the schizophrenic psychoses. *Psychological medicine* 4, 244–54.

Freud, S. 1958: Psychoanalytic notes on an autobiographical account of a case of paranoia. *Standard edition of the complete psychological works of Sigmund Freud*, vol. 12. London: Hogarth; New York: Norton.

*Kaplan, H.I., Freedman and Sadock, B.J. 1980: *Comprehensive textbook of psychiatry*. 3rd edn. Baltimore: Williams and Wilkins.

Kraepelin, E. 1919: *Dementia praecox and paraphrenia*. Edinburgh: Livingstone.

Neuferlech, K. and Davson, M. 1984: Information processing and attentional functioning in the developmental course of schizophrenic disorders. *Schizophrenia bulletin* 10, 160–203.

Schneider, K. 1959: *Clinical psychopathology*. New York: Grune and Stratten.

Serban, G. ed. 1978: *Cognitive deficits in the development of mental illness*. New York: Brunner/ Mazel.

Shields, J. 1978: Genetics. In J.K. Wing ed. op. cit.

*Wing, J.K. ed. 1978: *Schizophrenia: a new synthesis*. London: Academic Press.

World Health Organisation 1978: *Mental disorders: glossary and guide to their classification in accordance with the ninth revision of the international classification of diseases*. Geneva: WHO.

Wynne, L.C. 1981: Current concepts about schizophrenics and family relationships. *Journal of nervous and mental diseases* 169, 82–9.

senses: chemical and the nervous system

The neural structures which participate in the detection of chemicals in the air or mouth and lead to the sensations and perceptions of taste and smell.

Sensory transduction in the gustatory system occurs in the tastebuds of the tongue and palate. Tastebuds are associated with specialized papillae on the tongue (fungiform papillae on the front of the tongue, foliate papillae on the sides, and circumvallate papillae on the back of the tongue). Although individual taste afferent fibers are not selectively responsive to the four qualities of taste (sweet, salty, sour and bitter), sensitivity to sweet is greatest at the tip of the tongue; sensitivity to bitter, at the back; and to sour and salty, along the sides. Nonetheless, the encoding of gustatory information appears to involve the pattern of firing of the population of taste afferents since each fiber responds to some degree to a wide variety of stimuli. Tastebuds are innervated by the facial, glossopharyngeal and vagus nerves whose cell bodies lie in the geniculate, superior petrosal and nodose ganglia respectively. Taste afferents terminate in the solitary nucleus of the medulla. The gustatory relay nuclei lie in the ventromedial portion of the ventral posterior THALAMUS (see BRAIN AND CENTRAL NERVOUS SYSTEM: ILLUSTRATIONS, fig. 19). Two gustatory cortical regions have been identified. One occupies a portion of parietal cortex next to the somatosensory cortex representing the oral cavity (figs. 2, 3 and 4). The other lies in the anterior opercular-insular cortex overlying the claustrum adjacent to the oral representation in the second somatosensory cortical field.

Olfactory receptors, located in the olfactory mucosa of the posterior nasal cavity, detect the presence of odorants. The receptors themselves bear axons which terminate in the glomeruli of the olfactory bulb (fig. 16). Like taste fibers, olfactory fibers are responsive to a variety of stimuli, and the spatial and temporal characteristics of the responses of the whole population of olfactory afferents may encode the perceived features of odor stimuli. The olfactory bulb projects to the anterior olfactory nucleus, the olfactory tubercule, the prepyriform cortex, the amygdaloid complex and the transitional entorhinal cortex. These structures variously project to the HYPOTHALAMUS (figs. 15 and 20) and the same regions of ventromedial, ventroposterior thalamus (figs. 15 and 19) that receive gustatory inputs. The projection from thalamus is to the same region of the parietal lobe of CEREBRAL CORTEX that receives gustatory projections. The olfactory system thus has two regions of primary cortex, one in paleocortex (prepyriform cortex), which evolved early in the vertebrate line, and later connections through the thalamus to a second region in neocortex (parietal cortex). Like the auditory system, the olfactory system has a significant system of descending fibers. Centrifugal fibers from higher centers innervate the glomeruli of the olfactory bulb where they modulate the sensory input at the level of the second order of olfactory neurons. scc

Bibliography

Beidler, L.M., ed. 1971: *Handbook of sensory physiology*, vol. 5, *Chemical senses*. Part 2. *Taste*. Berlin and New York: Springer-Verlag.

—— 1971: *Handbook of sensory physiology*, vol. 4, *Chemical senses*. Part 1. *Olfaction*. Berlin and New York: Springer-Verlag.

—— 1980: The chemical senses: gustation and olfaction. In *Medical Physiology*. 14th edn, ed. V.B. Mountcastle. St. Louis and London: C.V. Mosby.

Shepard, G.M. 1979: *The synaptic organization of the brain*. 2nd edn. Oxford and New York: Oxford University Press.

Shepard, G.M., Getchell, T.V. and Kauer, J.S. 1975: Analysis of structure and function in the olfactory pathway. In *The nervous system*, vol. 1. *The basic neurosciences*, ed. R.O. Brady. New York: Haven Press.

senses: electromagnetic The ability to detect electric or magnetic fields. Many fish are capable of electroreception. For example, dogfish and sharks have electroreceptive sense organs, called *ampullae Lorenzini*, which are distributed over the body surface and usually concentrated in the region of the head. Some dogfish even when buried under sand, can detect prey by the local distortion of the geophysical electric field. Some fish, especially the gymnotid eels, generate their own weak electric fields and are sensitive to distortions of their own field caused by objects in the environment. They usually live in conditions of poor visibility. The fish are sensitive to the electric discharges of other members of the species, and may communicate with each other through this medium. Fish such as the electric ray and the electric eel produce strong electric discharges capable of stunning prey and some predators. However, they do not seem to be capable of electroreception.

Many different animals are sensitive to magnetic fields. Orientation to magnetic north has been found in bacteria, flatworms and snails. Magnetic sensitivity is also used in navigation in pigeons and in bees. Pigeons and other birds effectively have a magnetic compass which they deploy when the sun is obscured by clouds, or when navigating at night. There is some evidence for a similar ability in man (Baker 1981).

DJM

Bibliography

Baker, Reginald R. 1981: *Human navigation and the sixth sense*. London: Hodder and Stoughton; New York: Simon and Schuster (1982).

senses: mechanical The detection of mechanical disturbances in the environment and within the animal's body. Mechanoreceptors are involved in many senses, including hearing, balance, pressure detection and touch.

Information from mechanoreceptors in the limb joints and muscles is particularly important in coordination and locomotion. Postural reflexes are triggered by receptors in the limbs and in the maculae, the organs of balance in the vertebrate ear. Invertebrates often have analogous mechanisms. Thus the statocysts of the octopus are analogous to the maculae of vertebrates and enable the animal to maintain its orientation with respect to gravity.

The array of mechanical senses with which an animal is equipped is partly determined by its way of life. Pigeons have a small vesicle in the ear which gives them a high sensitivity to barometric pressure. This organ is especially well developed in diving birds and is also found in sharks. Other fish detect hydrostatic pressure by means of mechanoreceptors attached to the swim bladder, an organ which does not occur in sharks. DJM

sensory deprivation and enrichment Rearing in either enriched or deprived multi-sensory environments may produce significant effects upon the adult nervous system, including biochemical, anatomical and behavioral changes (see also CRITICAL PERIODS AND THE NERVOUS SYSTEM). For example cells in the cortex show greater dendritic branching, more dendritic spines, and larger synaptic regions in animals reared in complex environments relative to littermates reared in impoverished environments. There is also a consistent increase in the overall cortical thickness of rats reared in enriched environments, which is accompanied by a greater cortical weight. The increased weight is at least partially due to greater protein and RNA content in brain tissue, and there is a greater ratio of RNA to DNA, suggesting increased metabolic activity.

At the behavioral level, selective rearing in an enriched environment produces more efficient maze learning, but the results on tasks such as visual discrimination learning are less consistent. In general, the evidence supports the conclusion that differential rearing produces behaviorally different animals, but it may be misleading to use terms like "intelligence" to refer to such differences. Selective rearing is known to produce long-lasting effects upon emotionality and exploration: multi-sensory deprivation decreases exploratory tendencies and increases diffused, undirected fear reactions, whereas enrichment conditions produce more purposeful patterns of exploratory and avoidance behavior. It is these changes which may account for the deprived animal's inferior performance on learning tasks.   BER/RCS

sensory neglect A set of abnormalities exhibited by patients with cerebral lesions usually characterized by the failure to respond to sensory stimuli presented to the side contralateral to the lesion, even though there is no peripheral sensory or motor defect. The neglect syndrome accompanies lesions, most often caused by cerebral infarction or rapidly-growing malignant tumors, to the inferior parietal lobule, dorsolateral frontal lobe, cingulate gyrus, neostriatum, or thalamus.

Clinically patients often fail to turn towards stimuli contralateral to the lesion (hemiakinesia). They may fail to use extremities on the contralateral side. Some patients refer contralateral sensory stimuli to the ipsilateral side (allesthesia), for example reporting that they were touched on the same side as the lesion when the tactile stimulus is applied to the side opposite the lesion. When asked to draw, patients may produce only half of an object and may quarter rather than bisect a line (hemispatial neglect). Patients may fail to dress the abnormal side, may deny that affected extremities belong to their bodies (anosognosia) or may read only part of a word ("grandmother" may be read as "mother") (paralexia). Finally, patients showing sensory neglect are often also hypokinetic, showing little interest in their environment, and appearing unconcerned about their illness and apathetic about events in general. Patients with initial hemisensory neglect who ignore contralateral stimuli or refer them to the unaffected side often improve later and are able to lateralize stimuli successfully to the affected side. These patients still often fail to report stimulation of the affected side when both sides are simultaneously stimulated (sensory extinction).

The mechanisms of sensory neglect have proved difficult to determine. The combinations of symptoms shown by patients are variable and depend greatly on what is measured clinically and how. Numerous theories have been advanced to explain the symptoms and sets of symptoms of sensory neglect. Of these the hypothesis that neglect results from defects in the attention-arousal mechanisms is consistent with much of the extant data (Heilman and Valenstein 1972).   SCC

Bibliography
*Heilman, K.M. 1979: Neglect and related disorders. In *Clinical neuropsychology*. eds. K.M. Heilman and E. Valenstein. Oxford and New York: Oxford University Press.

Heilman, K.M. and Valenstein, E. 1972: Frontal lobe neglect in man. *Neurology* 22, 660–64.

sensory systems, neural bases of The mechanisms by which the nervous system responds to physical energy in the environment to produce sensory experience. A number of different sensory systems can be distinguished on the basis of the kinds of environmental stimulation to which they respond. These systems fall into three broad categories. The first, called exteroceptive, is concerned with stimuli arising outside the body and provides information about events in the external world. There are five exteroceptive sensory systems: the olfactory system is concerned with the sense of smell, the gustatory system with taste, the visual system with sight, the auditory system with hearing, and the somatic system with feeling stimuli that contact the body surface. The second broad category of sensory systems, called proprioceptive, is stimulated by the action of the body itself and provides information about the activity and position of the body and limbs. Within this category the vestibular system is concerned with the static position of the head (relative to gravity) and with linear or rotational movement of the head. The kinesthetic system is concerned with sensations originating from the muscles, tendons, and joints and provides information about the position of the limbs and body. The third category of sensory systems is called interoceptive, and is stimulated by the internal organs and viscera. This system is concerned with sensations of pain, pressure, and temperature of the internal organs.

The first step in neural processing for each of these sensory systems is conversion of environmental stimuli into the electrochemical activity of NEURONS. This conversion, called sensory transduction, is accomplished by specialized sensory receptors. In many sensory systems, the environmental stimulus directly contacts the receptors. For example the soluble molecules that produce tastes come into direct contact with the gustatory receptors on the tongue and other regions of the mouth and throat. However, some sensory systems have accessory structures that focus, amplify, or otherwise modify the environmental stimulus before it impinges upon the receptor. For example external and middle ear structures collect sound waves (vibrations) in the air, amplify the pressure of the vibrations, and convert them into moving waves in a fluid in the inner ear. These moving waves cause a membrane in the inner ear to vibrate in the fluid. The auditory receptors contact this membrane, and are stimulated by its vibration. Thus, sensory receptors may be stimulated only indirectly by complex accessory structures.

In general the receptors are specialized cells that are uniquely sensitive to particular kinds of environmental stimuli. For example olfactory receptors are cells with membranes that are particularly sensitive to airborn gaseous molecules. Visual receptor cells contain pigments that absorb light of particular wavelengths. Auditory receptors have specialized hairs (or cilia) that are sensitive to the vibrations of the inner ear membrane that they contact. In each case stimulation of the receptor cell produces a small voltage change (a few thousandths of a volt) across the receptor cell membrane. This results in release of a chemical transmitter substance from the receptor cell, which makes contact (see SYNAPSE AND SYNAPTIC TRANSMISSION) with one or more neurons. The neurons in turn generate electrochemical impulses (see ACTION POTENTIAL) that are propagated along their axons into the sensory pathways of the brain.

In some sensory systems (somatic, kinesthetic, and interoceptive), the sensory receptors are specialized nerve endings of neurons rather than separate receptor cells. In these cases, environmental stimulation produces a small voltage change directly in the nerve ending, and this results in action potential generation.

Thus, in every sensory system, environmental stimulation leads directly or indirectly to action potentials in neurons. It is this activity of the neurons, transmitted along axons into the sensory pathways of the brain, that forms the neural basis of sensory experience. Which sensory modality we experience (taste, sound, touch, etc.) depends upon which of these pathways is activated.

Within each sensory system specific properties of sensory stimulation (type of stimulus, its location, intensity, etc.) as well as complex perceptual phenomena are coded by the action potentials generated in neurons. Because all action potentials of all neurons have basically the same form specific sensory information can be coded in only two ways: by which neurons are active, and by the frequency or pattern of action potentials generated by the neurons. Both these methods of stimulus coding appear to be utilized by all sensory systems.

In many sensory systems the location of a stimulus in the environment is coded according to which neurons are active. This happens because the spatial layout of the receptor surface is projected into the brain in a topographic manner by the sensory neurons. Thus, throughout the somatic sensory pathways there is a topographic representation of the body surface, and stimulation of a particular location on the body activates the neurons that receive inputs from that location. Likewise the visual receptor cells lie in a sheet at the back of the eye (the retina), and this receptor sheet is represented topographically in the visual pathways of the brain. Consequently stimulation of a particular retinal location by a light source activates only particular neurons in the visual system.

Stimulus quality may also be coded according to which neurons are active. For example, light touch, pressure, or temperature changes on the skin lead to activation of different neurons in the somatic sensory system. This is due largely to the presence of specific sensory receptors in the skin, each of which activates different sensory neurons. Specific tastes, odors, sound frequencies (pitch), and other sensory qualities may also be coded in a similar fashion.

In general the frequency of action potentials generated by sensory neurons is related to stimulus intensity. More intense stimuli (brighter lights, louder sounds, etc.) cause larger voltage changes in the receptors and this leads to more action potentials (higher discharge frequency) in the sensory neurons. However, discharge frequency can also code stimulus quality, and in some cases both discharge frequency and the discharging neurons can be involved in stimulus coding. Color information is coded this way in the visual system. Certain colors produce activity in certain neurons but not in others. In addition, different colors may activate the same neurons with different patterns of activity. Thus for some neurons blue light increases discharge frequency and yellow light decreases it. For other neurons red light increases activity while green light decreases it. In a similar manner some vestibular system neurons increase their activity when the head turns in one direction and decrease their activity for movement in the opposite direction.

Relatively little is known about the neural bases of more complex sensory experience and perception. Some neurons have been found to discharge only to certain perceptual or abstract aspects of sensory stimuli. For example some neurons in the visual system discharge only when contours of certain orientations move in certain directions with specific velocities through the visual field. It is possible that other neurons (yet to be found) respond selectively to more complex aspects of the environment, such as specific visual objects or spoken

words. However, the most widely held view is that such complex sensory stimuli are coded by the discharges of many thousands (perhaps millions) of neurons, each of which responds to specific components of the overall stimulus. For example when we look at an object different neurons discharge in different patterns to the various contours, colors, and light intensities that occur in different locations in the object. It is this ensemble of neuronal activity that is thought to form the neural basis of complex sensory experience. See also AUDITORY NERVOUS SYSTEM; SENSES, CHEMICAL, AND THE NERVOUS SYSTEM; PAIN AND THE NERVOUS SYSTEM; SOMATOSENSORY NERVOUS SYSTEM; VISUAL NERVOUS SYSTEM.   PDS

Bibliography

Geldard, Frank A. 1972: *The human senses*. 2nd edn. New York and London: John Wiley and Sons.

Thompson, Richard F. 1967: *Foundations of physiological psychology*. New York: Harper and Row.

Uttal, William R. 1973: *The psychobiology of sensory coding*. New York and London: Harper and Row.

separation   A term derived from psychoanalytic theory to describe the anxiety held to be generated by the absence of a person believed necessary for survival (prototypically the mother) and to denote a major developmental process – separation-individuation (Mahler, Pine and Bergman 1975). Mahler and her co-workers described sub-phases of differentiation, practicing and rapprochement to account for development from a symbiotic phase in the middle of the first year when the infant and mother are still primarily a unit, to the autonomy or separation of the three-year-old from its mother. More widely known are the three phases – protest, despair and detachment – described by Bowlby as the young child's response to separation from its primary caregiver and his hypothesis relating maternal loss or deprivation and psychiatric illness. Research in the past thirty years has supported and clarified this proposed relationship but also shown the need to distinguish between bonding failure and bond disruption, between qualitative differences in care and their effects on intellectual, social and emotional factors, between long- and short-term effects and the influence of individual differences on outcomes (Rutter 1981).

(See also DEPRIVATION: HUMAN PARENTAL.)

BBL

Bibliography

Bowlby, J. 1973: *Separation: anger and anxiety*, vol. 2. *Attachment and loss*. London: Hogarth Press; New York: Basic Books; Harmondsworth: Penguin Books (1978).
Mahler, M.S., Pine, F. and Bergman, A. 1975: *The psychological birth of the human infant*. London: Hutchinson; New York: Basic Books.
Rutter, M. 1981: *Maternal deprivation reassessed*. 2nd edn. Harmondsworth: Penguin.

serial vs. parallel processing The sense organs receive information in parallel: many receptors are stimulated simultaneously in normal life. Central information processing however appears often to deal with only one message at a time. For example, we can visually fixate either a picture on our left or on our right. Conscious decision making and thought can deal with only one message at a time even if the receptors do not point to a source, such as trying to attend to two conversations at once. Central processing is therefore serial. The main exception is in the case of highly practiced skills. When behavior becomes automatic it can often be performed in parallel with other behavior.

NM

Bibliography

Hinton, G.E. and Anderson, J.A. 1981: *Parallel models of associative memory*. New Jersey: Erlbaum.
Stone, J. 1983: *Parallel processing in the visual system*. New York: New York and Co.

serotonin (5-hydroxytryptamine) A monoamine neurotransmitter in both the peripheral and central nervous systems. It is synthesized from the amino acid, tryptophan, which comes from the diet.

Centrally, serotonergic cell bodies are located in the pineal gland, and in discrete nuclei of the BRAIN STEM, especially in the nuclei of the raphé system. Descending serotonergic neurons form synapses in the SPINAL CORD. Ascending serotonergic fibers include projections from the raphé nuclei to a number of other neural structures, including the RETICULAR ACTIVATING SYSTEM (some serotonergic cell bodies are also found here), HYPOTHALAMUS, HIPPOCAMPUS, CEREBRAL CORTEX, CEREBELLUM, and a portion of the BASAL GANGLIA. The majority of serotonergic synapses seem to be inhibitory. Serotonergic pathways appear to be involved in a number of physiological functions, including thermoregulation, sleep and the perception of pain, as well as mediating the action of certain hallucinogens.

GPH

Bibliography

Fuller, R.W. 1980: Pharmacology of central serotonin neurons. *Annual review of pharmacology* 20, 111–27.
Green, A.R. and Grahame-Smith, D.S. 1975; 5 HT in CNS function. In *Handbook of psychopharmacology*, vol. 3, eds. L.L. Iversen, S.D. Iversen and S.H. Snyder. New York: Plenum Press.

sexual behavior and the nervous system The nervous system plays a complex role in controlling sexual behavior through the interaction of neuronal and hormonal activity. The HYPOTHALAMUS initiates and regulates sexual behavior by controlling the pituitary gland's production of gonadotrophic hormones which stimulate the sex organs (gonads). The amount of sex hormones produced by the gonads at the sequential stages of sexual behavior is monitored by the hypothalamus via feedback through the blood. Although these hormones play an important role in the activation of such behavior, the nervous system controls its form and direction.

The hypothalamus does not act alone within the nervous system in controlling sexual behavior. The LIMBIC SYSTEM, and particularly the AMYGDALA, is important for the discrimination of environmental and social factors which dictate the appearance of sex behavior and its appropriate expression. The amygdala achieves this control by inhibiting the hypothalamic influence on the pituitary gland. In cases where the amygdala has been removed in man and animals, inappropriate sexual behavior is elicited.   RCS/BER

Bibliography

Hutchinson, J.B. 1978: *Biological determinants of sexual behavior*. New York: John Wiley and Son.
Johnson, M. and Everitt, B. 1980: *Essential reproduction*. Oxford: Blackwell Scientific Publications, ch. 8.
Sachar, E.J. ed. 1979: *Sex hormones and behavior*. *Ciba Foundation Symposium Proceedings* 62. London.

sexual differentiation and the nervous system Adult sexual behavior may be influenced by circulating levels of hormones, but its expression is controlled by the neural circuitry of the brain and spinal cord (see SEXUAL BEHAVIOR AND THE NERVOUS SYSTEM). This neural organization is determined early in development, when the presence of sex hormones may act to organize brain circuitry differentially in males and females. For example, exposure to androgens, male sex hormones, around the time of birth is known to influence sexual behaviour in adult rodents long after the circulating effectiveness of the hormones has ceased. Anatomical differences between the sexes in the pre-optic area of the HYPOTHALAMUS can be abolished by giving androgen to newborn females or by castrating newborn males. Likewise, the presence of ESTROGENS, female sex hormones, may influence both brain development and consequent adult sexual behavior.

While such studies help to elucidate the role of HORMONES in neural development, they continue to elicit controversy regarding their relevance to the psychological study of sex differences in humans.

                                    ER/RCS

Sherrington, Sir Charles (1857–1952) Sherrington's father died while he was an infant and he was brought up in the

household of his stepfather, Dr Caleb Rose. Rose was a remarkable man with a wide circle of friends, both artistic and scientific. His house at Ipswich was a center of the kind of diverse interests that Sherrington believed had inspired his own many-sided career. After Ipswich School Sherrington did his preliminary medical training at St Thomas's Hospital in London and then went on to Caius College, Cambridge to study physiology. From 1884 to 1887 he studied in various places in Continental Europe, working with Goltz, Virchow and finally in Berlin with Koch. He returned to England in 1887 to become Lecturer in Physiology at St Thomas's. In 1891 he married Ethel Wright and in the same year was appointed superintendent of Brown's Institute, a hospital for animals. He was elected to the Holt chair of physiology in Liverpool in 1895, leaving that post for the Waynflete professorship in Oxford in 1913. He remained in Oxford for the rest of his academic career.

Sherrington was a man of great energy and wide interests. He wrote and published poetry, philosophy and history as well as scientific texts and manuals. Among his hobbies was parachute jumping! The excellence of his scientific work was immediately and universally acknowledged and his career shows no sign of any painful struggle for recognition. His work in physiology of the nervous system has often been compared to that of Newton in physics, and like Newton he was President of the Royal Society. He became a member of the Order of Merit in 1924 and, somewhat belatedly, was awarded the Nobel Prize for medicine and physiology in 1932.

His scientific work was based on the broad principle that function must be subserved by structure. Putting this principle to work led him to begin his epoch-making work on the reflex response of the spinal cord with a detailed anatomical study of the structure of the nervous system. This was also the basis of his work on the integrated (co-ordinated) action of the nervous system. His central concept was "reciprocal innervation" meaning that 'inhibitory and excitatory spinal reflexes occur together'. It has been said that modern neurophysiology owes not only its basic theories but also its nomenclature to Sherrington. Another of his important innovations was the recognition and naming of the SYNAPSE, the peculiar kind of connection without continuity by which nerve cells are linked together. This idea, combined with the neuron theory of Ramon y Cajal, that nervous impulses follow definite pathways, set the line for all future neurological research. Sherrington showed how complex behavior could be understood by the use of the same set of concepts. This led him to the idea of "integrative action" which he took to be the key to the working of the nervous systems of all animals. In 1906 he published his classic work *The integrative action of the nervous system* in which his researches were summed up in a comprehensive account of neurophysiology.

The war of 1914–18 interrupted his scientific work, but he threw himself into studies of industrial fatigue. It is said that his first step in this line of investigation was to join a munitions factory anonymously to find out for himself what production line work was like.

His work in Oxford that followed the war was largely a massive and meticulous development of the basic theories of integrative action. To this he added the important concept of "motor unit". This is a single spinal neuron that controls hundreds of muscle fibers. It was for the work on motor units that he received (with Lord Adrian) the Nobel Prize.

As a philosopher Sherrington was much concerned with the "mind-brain" problem. He took a firmly dualistic line, but imposed on it his own concept of integrative function. This led him to a three level theory, each with its own mode of integration: mind, mind with brain and brain.

He died at Eastbourne in 1952.   RHa

Bibliography

Liddell, E.G.T. 1960: *The discovery of the reflexes.* Oxford: Oxford University Press.

Sherrington, Sir Charles S. 1906: *The integrative action of the nervous system.* New Haven: Yale University Press.

Sherrington, Sir C.S. with Creed, R.S. 1932: *Reflex activity of the spinal cord.* Oxford: Oxford University Press.

Sherrington, Sir C.S. 1941: *Man on his nature.* Cambridge: Cambridge University Press.

Skinner, Burrhus Frederic (born 1904)

Experimental psychologist responsible for the development of operant techniques. Skinner was born in Pennsylvania and from 1922 to 1926 attended Hamilton College, N.Y., where he majored in English. He then entered Harvard College to study psychology, and remained there for five years after taking his doctorate. He joined the faculty at the university of Minnesota in 1936, and moved to the university of Indiana in 1945. In 1948 he returned to Harvard where he remained for the rest of his career.

Skinner showed that animal and human behavior could be modified by reinforcement and that animals could in this way be trained to carry out particular tasks to obtain reward, or avoid punishment. His belief that any reinforcer could be used to modify any aspect of behavior was subsequently shown to be incorrect. Nevertheless, his operant conditioning techniques came to be widely used in training and studying animals, and in the modification of human behavior in teaching and clinical situations.

Skinner developed a thorough-going philosophy of behaviorism which he promulgated in his many books. The most important of these were *The behavior of organisms, Verbal behaviour* and *About behaviorism*. He also published three autobiographical works: *Cumulative record, Particulars of my life* and *The shaping of a behaviorist.*   DJM

Bibliography

Skinner, B.F. 1938: *The behavior of organisms.* New York and London: Appleton-Century.

—— 1957: *Verbal behavior.* New York: Appleton-Century-Crofts; London: Methuen 1959.

—— 1959: *Cumulative record.* New York: Appleton-Century-Crofts; London: Methuen 1961.

——— 1974: *About behaviorism*. New York: Knopf; London: Cape.

——— 1976: *Particulars of my life*. New York: Knopf; London: Cape.

——— 1979: *The shaping of a behaviorist*. New York: Knopf: Oxford: Holdan Books.

sleep and arousal: physiological bases

States characterized by changes in consciousness leading in the former, to a decreased responsiveness to the external environment, and in the latter to an efficient interaction with it. Although these two extremes of activity can easily be distinguished by visual observation, a more reliable definition has to describe sleep and wakefulness as a biological rhythm only accurately identified by electrophysiological recording techniques (see, for example, ELECTROENCEPHALOGRAM). Using such techniques, it is well accepted that birds, mammals and primates, including man, present at least two basic patterns of sleep. The first, called slow wave sleep (SWS) or non-REM sleep, is characterized electroencephalographically (EEG) by the appearance of 14 – 18 Hz cortical spindles, which as sleep deepens are replaced by 2–4 Hz slow waves. At the same time high voltage (500–800v) sharp waves are recorded from the hippocampus (see BRAIN AND CENTRAL NERVOUS SYSTEM: ILLUSTRATIONS, fig. 17), while the electromyogram (EMG) or muscle tone decreases slightly. Usually after 30 to 40 min the rapid-eye-movement (REM) sleep phase appears, characterized by the appearance of low voltage fast activity in the cortical EEG, a regular hippocampal theta rhythm (5–6 Hz), an isoelectric EMG (total loss of muscle tone) and bursts of rapid eye movements. Approximately half a minute before the onset of the REM sleep phase (and continuous throughout it), high-voltage EEG spikes appear in the pontine reticular formation (fig. 6), the lateral geniculate nucleus (LGN) and the occipital cortex (fig. 23). These spikes are called PGO and have a fairly constant daily rate of about 14,000 in the cat.

Human EEG sleep stages are more differentiated and consist of four non-REM sleep stages: Stage I, loss of alpha; Stage II, spindles and isolated short waves called K complexes, on a low voltage background activity; Stage III, high amplitude delta activity (slow waves 1–3 Hz); Stage IV, with over 50 percent of delta activity, and one REM stage characterized by low-voltage theta activity, with no spindles or K complexes, and accompanied of course by eye movements and loss of muscle tone (figs. 33 and 34). It is in this stage that DREAMING occurs. During this stage there is also generally speaking an increase in mean value and variability of the heart rate, respiratory rate and blood pressure (see NEUROMETRICS).

The events occurring during REM sleep have been classed as phasic and tonic. The phasic events are represented by activities such as eye movement bursts, middle ear muscle activity (MEMA), cardiovascular irregularities, respiratory changes, muscular twitches, changes in pupil diameter, fluctuations in penile erection, and PGO spikes. The tonic events are represented by low-voltage fast EEG activity, EMG

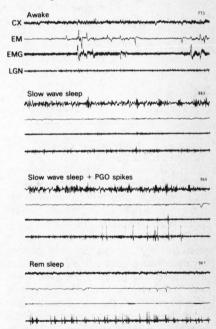

Electrophysiological signs of sleep and wakefulness in the cat. Cortex (CX) Movements (EM) electromyogram (EMG) geniculate nucleus (LGN)

Electrophysiological and Behavioral Correlates of Sleep and Wakefulness in the Cat

| | Arousal | | Sleep | |
	attentive	relaxed	slow wave sleep	REM sleep
Cortical activity	low-voltage fast waves	spindles mixed with mostly low-voltage fast waves	spindles and high voltage slow waves	low voltage fast waves
Hippocampal activity	regular rhythmic theta waves	rhythmic theta waves	irregular high-voltage slow waves	very regular rhythmic theta waves
EMG	high amplitude	medium amplitude	low amplitude	isoelectric with twitches
Eye movements	biphasic continuous	practically none	none	biphasic bursts
PGO	none	none	present only before transition to REM	present (14,000 per day)
Behavior	exploratory attentive	sitting up or lying, head up, eyes open	lying on the side, eyes closed, respiration and heart beat slow	lying curled up, twitching of extremities, neck muscles and vibrissae, irregular respiration
Time spent 24 hr/day	35% alternating between the two		50%	15%

suppression, temperature elevation and increased blood flow.

Since the discovery of REM sleep in the 1950s physiologists have attempted to locate the brain structures responsible for the two phases of sleep through experiments whereby specific areas of the brain are lesioned and subsequent effects on sleep analyzed. Although it is now thought highly doubtful that specific centers exist, there is relative agreement that the sleep-wake rhythm is a brain stem regulated phenomenon with the added involvement of the basal forebrain in regulating SWS. It should be pointed out, however, that in animals which have very definite sleep and waking rhythms, i.e., rodents, the supra-chiasmatic nucleus (SCN) seems to play an

important role (see fig. 20). For example rodents sleep mostly during the day and are active at night. If the SCN is lesioned this rhythm is disrupted, but interestingly the total amount of sleep and waking remains unchanged. It therefore seems that sleep is controlled by several interrelated mechanisms originating from widespread areas of the brain. One group of structures around the HYPOTHALAMUS would seem to regulate its basic rhythms, while other structures mainly located along the BRAIN STEM would be responsible for triggering its onset and/or maintaining its duration.

Coincident with the search for brain regulating structures in sleep there has been a great deal of interest in identifying the chemical substances utilized by these structures in producing sleep. Here again it is more than likely that several substances participate, although theories favoring one over another have been put forward. The most commonly known is the monoamine theory which suggests that slow wave sleep is initiated by the release of SEROTONIN (5–HT) from neurons of the dorsal raphé nuclei in the brain stem, while REM sleep is triggered by the release of 5-HT from neurons of the caudal raphé nuclei. Once initiated, the "executive" mechanisms of REM sleep are governed by catecholamines: the catecholamine (NE) containing neurons of the caudal third of the locus ceruleus are responsible for the muscle atonia associated with REM sleep, and those of the medial third of the locus ceruleus function as a pacemaker for PGO activity. On the other hand wakefulness and cortical arousal are dependent on NE-containing neurons of the anterior locus ceruleus, dopamine-containing neurons of the midbrain reticular formation and cholinergic neurons in the cortex. In other theories the monoamines do not play such a central role, and the main triggering mechanisms of sleep revolve around peptides. Although some such peptides have been isolated, and have been referred to as sleep factors there is as yet no conclusive evidence that they are in fact sleep inducing substances. Other hypotheses revolve around the idea that protein synthesis or a particular group of proteins are most likely to be involved in the production of REM sleep through a kind of "gating" mechanism which modulates the excitability levels of the various neuronal groups involved in producing the electrophysiological signs of REM sleep episodes. Whatever the eventual answer to the neurochemistry of sleep will be, it is more than likely that all these systems and probably more are involved through a rather complicated interaction.

Besides the attempts to understand the mechanisms by which the brain produces the sleep-wake cycle, one of the most nagging questions is the function of sleep. Several theories have been advanced, most of which have some points in common, and which may be reduced to the following five:

(1) the restorative theory which holds that sleep is a period of restoration of physiological and/or psychological states, with SWS restoring the body and REM sleep restoring the brain; (2) the protective theory which suggests that sleep gives the organism a period whereby it can protect itself from excessive wear and tear; (3) the energy conservation theory which holds that sleep serves the function of conserving energy by limiting metabolic requirements; (4) the ethological theory which holds that sleep and wakefulness are control systems which enhance survival and thus protect the species; and (5) the instinctive theory which holds that sleep is an instinct and therefore to be seen as innate behavior rather than as a need. Probably none of these theories alone can explain the function of sleep, but a combination of all might answer the question why we sleep.

Finally, it is important to note that although sleep abnormalities have dramatic influences on waking performances and moods, it is only recently that a reasonable understanding of sleep pathologies has been reached. Sleep disorders can essentially be divided into primary and secondary.

Primary sleep disorders are those in which the abnormalities related to sleep are the cardinal signs or symptoms from which the patient suffers. In these cases a malfunction of the basic neurophysiological and/or neurochemical mechanisms involved in regulating the sleep-wake cycle is presupposed. There are four principal primary sleep disorders. One is narcolepsy, in which the patient goes directly from waking to REM sleep. It is characterized by four symptoms (the so called narcolepsy tetrad): (a) short, but almost irresistible, daytime sleep attacks; (b) cataplexy (ranging from transient weakness to total paralysis of all voluntary muscles); (c) sleep paralysis, a disorder characterized by a sudden inability to execute voluntary movements either at the onset of sleep or upon awakening during the night or in the morning; and (d) hypnagogic hallucinations, so called because they occur as the patient is falling asleep. Another primary sleep disorder is apnea: in this disease the patients literally stop breathing whenever they fall asleep. Three types of apneas are typically observed: central apneas, defined by an absence of any respiratory effort; upper airway apneas which involve a collapse of the upper airway; mixed apneas in which there is a combination of both. There are three clinical subtypes of the sleep apnea syndrome: (a) hypersomnia-hypoventilation syndrome, in which upper airway apneas predominate and which occurs mostly but not necessarily in overweight (Pickwickian) patients (here patients complain of excessive daytime sleepiness on account of the frequent awakenings at night due to the apneas); (b) insomnia-sleep apnea syndrome, in which central sleep apneas predominate and although patients awaken often during the night they do not sleep during the day; (c) sleep apnea in children, which is thought to cause the sudden infant death syndrome (SIDS), although SIDS is itself a much more complicated syndrome. In the remaining two primary sleep disorders, primary insomnia and hypersomnia, the patients do not present significant medical, psychiatric and/or behavioral pathologies, and the disorder is therefore probably associated with a basic dysfunction of the physiology and chemistry of sleep.

The secondary sleep disorders are those in which the basic pathology is medical, i.e., neurological or psychiatric, and sleep disturbances are one of many symptoms. As such we have epilepsies, thyroid dysfunctions, drug and alcohol abuse, depression, schizophrenia and so on.

Finally, there are a series of activities which are normal in waking but erupt in sleep and create various problems. These are the parasomnias, among which are: somnambulism, enuresis (bedwetting), nightmares and night terrors, bruxism (teeth grinding), to name only a few.

The fields of pharmacology of sleep, dreams and development are being very actively pursued in various laboratories and it is only through the interactions of all these fields of sleep research that a solid understanding of the sleep-wakefulness cycle will be forthcoming.   RD-C

Bibliography

Dement, William C. 1972: *Some must watch while some must sleep*. Stanford, Calif.: Stanford Alumnic Assoc.; reptd 1978; New York and London: Norton.

Drucker-Colin, René R., Shkurovich, M. and Sterman, M.B. eds. 1979: *The functions of sleep*. New York and London: Academic Press.

Jouvet, M. 1972: The role of monoamines and acetycholine in the regulation of the sleep-waking cycle. *Ergebnisse der Physiologie* 64, 166–307.

McConnell, P.S., Boer, G.J., Romijn, N.J., van der Poll, N.E. and Corner, M.A. 1980: *Adaptive capabilities of the nervous system*. Amsterdam, Elsevier. Section III, pp.253–356.

Moruzzi, G. 1972: The sleep-waking cycle. *Ergebnisse der Physiologie* 66, 1–165.

Orem, John and Barnes, Charles D. eds. 1980: *Physiology in sleep*. New York and London: Academic Press.

Roffwarg, H.P., Chairman. 1979: Association of Sleep Disorders Centers. *Diagnostic classification of sleep and arousal disorders*. First Edition, prepared by the Sleep Disorders Classification Committee, *Sleep* 2: 1–137.

social psychiatry A series of topics linked by the epidemiological method. The topics include all aspects of the social causes, concomitants and consequences of psychiatric disorder, together with social techniques for dealing with them. The discovery of the social causes of disorder may lead to the rational development of social methods of prevention, while social influences on the course and outcome of disorder may suggest techniques of social treatment and rehabilitation. These issues may involve the psychiatrist in the planning and evaluation of social and medical services or in the assessment of the psychiatric implications of public policy on such matters as employment, education, and housing.

The main tool of the social psychiatrist is the epidemiological method. This is essentially the study of human populations based on rates of illnesses. Two main types of rate are used, incidence and prevalence. Incidence is the number of cases of the disease in question newly appearing in a unit population at risk (often 100,000) during a given period, usually one year. Prevalence is the number of cases present in a unit population at a given time (point prevalence) or during a given period (period prevalence). Prevalence is a function of incidence and the duration of the disorder from onset to recovery or from onset to death.

The establishment of each of these rates requires the definition of a numerator (the number of cases) and a denominator (the reference population). For the rates to be comparable in different studies, the definition of both numerator and denominator must be standard. Case definition implies that mental abnormalities are often most usefully regarded as diseases. The social psychiatrist is orientated toward the use of "disease" theories (see MEDICAL MODELS) in psychiatry (Wing 1978) and toward defining given diseases with more and more precision. The implication of defining SCHIZOPHRENIA say, as a characteristic psychopathological syndrome is that by doing so we hope to find out consistent and useful correlates, for example, of cause, course, outcome and response to intervention. However, not all the phenomena studied by social psychiatrists come so easily into the category of disease. SUICIDE is a clear exception, ALCOHOLISM a more contentious one.

Social psychiatrists rely on no single underlying theory, but borrow at will from the disciplines of biology, psychology and sociology. The relation to sociology is particularly interesting as there is overlap of both topic and method. Because sociologists are concerned with, among other things, beliefs and values and their role in social structure and function, they are likely to be interested in the various social phenomena reflected in the relationship of society to mental illness and its sufferers. Durkheim, for instance, regarded suicide as crucial to his ideas about the integration of society. Important contributions to the ideas used in social psychiatry also come from sociological studies of the family, of small groups and of social networks. Other ideas have come from studies of deviance, stratification, collective behavior and institutions. Both sociologists and social psychiatrists study populations and sociologists may also study illness rates in those populations, although they will in addition be interested in the social processes involved in the recognition of illness.

In the search for associations between variables, epidemiology relies on two main strategies for studying populations. The first is the *case-control study*. Where illness is the dependent variable this has to be retrospective as illness must already be present for the case group to be identified. The *cohort study* on the other hand may be prospective or retrospective. In the prospective version, the population is divided into a group defined by the antecedent variable and a group defined by its absence. These groups are followed up and the subsequent development of illness is monitored. For both of these types of study, the selection of the control group is of paramount importance. Another type of cohort study is retrospective: whole populations are examined and the association between illness and the various antecedent variables examined. In such a study variables can be controlled for in analysis. Sophisticated statistical procedures are now used for doing this.

A major issue of interpretation in these cross-sectional epidemiological surveys is that of *causal direction*. In some cases this can be decided on logical grounds, but in others conclusions must remain tentative (see Susser 1973). One example of this problem is the association of psychiatric disorder with low social class. Does this arise because the strains involved in working-class life can precipitate psychiatric illness or because the psychiatrically ill move down the social scale? The burden of evidence favors the latter interpretation in schizophrenia, the former in minor depressions.

Epidemiological work in psychiatry has been facilitated by certain technological innovations. One of these is the use of *case registers* in which all persons using certain services in a given area are recorded. The advantages of such registers include the avoidance of selection biases and duplicate counting, reference to a defined population and the possibility of longitudinal study (Wing and Hailey 1972). The problem with the study of referred populations is that it is not possible to separate factors which influence referral from those which influence the onset of a disorder. For this reason there has always been an interest in social psychiatric *surveys of the general population.* The major problem with these has been cost, which in the past led to the use of questionnaires to detect psychiatric disorders. These were really incapable of doing more than suggesting the likelihood that some kind of psychiatric disorder was present. Standardized instruments for case detection have been recently introduced. These can be linked to computer programs and incorporate procedures corresponding to those involved in psychiatric diagnosis. These include the Present State Examination in Britain and the Schedule for Affective Disorders and Schizophrenia (SADS) in the United States. Further innovations include reliable measures of other social variables, such as LIFE EVENTS and the quality of interaction between relatives (EXPRESSED EMOTION).

Because of the nature and limitations of the epidemiological method, theories of social causation have tended to rely on simple linear models and to take little account of the fact that people not only are influenced by their social circumstances but have some responsibility for them.

Social causes can be regarded as *predisposing* or *precipitating.* The first group contains a variety of influences, early or late, which affect the way people respond to later circumstances. These may operate for instance by their effect on HORMONES and AUTONOMIC NERVOUS SYSTEM activity, on the practical options open to the person, or on the way he sees the world. Ideas about precipitating factors rely heavily on the concept of psychosocial STRESS, but there have been theories such as those of Wynne and Singer in which a cognitive factor has played a part. The advances which have been made in social explanations of psychiatric disorders have arisen because of refinements in the definition and measurement of stress. Examples include life events and the way the stressful behavior of

the relatives of some schizophrenics is tapped by the rating of "expressed emotion". Recently workers in social psychiatry have become interested in the concept of the *social network* and the related idea of *social support.* These have possible implications for the modifications of stress. Henderson and his colleagues have introduced two extensive interviews designed to discover a variety of aspects of a subject's social relations and the support he obtains from them.

A distinction has been made between *strategic* and tactical research. The former has major implications for treatment and care. Tactical research is more concerned with the action taken on the basis of such implications. Evaluation of services is an area of tactical research in social psychiatry.

Psychiatric services are made available with the object of diminishing or containing psychiatric morbidity. They are concerned, therefore, with the social consequences of psychiatric disease and they operate by affecting the treatment of the disease, by preventing chronic disabilities and by preventing the accumulation of secondary handicaps which arise because of the response of the patient and those around him to the fact of his illness. Full evaluation of a psychiatric service firstly requires an assessment of *need, demand* and *utilization.* The patterns of contact must be established, together with the needs of those who do contact the services being studied. An indication of the effectiveness of the current treatment and management implies explicit definitions of the treatments involved, and ways of assessing them. The requirements of those who have disorders but do not use the services must be known. Research may sometimes suggest possible new types of service, and these services should ideally be assessed when they become available. The controlled trial of social treatments involves difficulties greater than those involved in, say, a drug trial, but these difficulties should not in practice be insuperable. The principles of evaluation in social psychiatric services are laid down by Wing (1972).　　PBe

Bibliography

*Bebbington, P.E. 1978: The epidemiology of depressive disorder. *Culture, medicine and psychiatry* 2, 297–341.

*Brown, George W. and Harris, Tirril 1978: *The social origins of depression.* London: Tavistock; New York: Free Press.

*Lloyd, G. and Bebbington, P. 1985: Social and transcultural psychiatry. In *Essentials of postgraduate psychiatry.* 2nd. edn, eds. P. Hill. R Murray and A. Thorley. London: Academic Press.

Susser, M. 1973: *Causal thinking in the health sciences.* London: Oxford University Press.

Wing, J.K. 1972: Principles of evaluation. In *Evaluating a community psychiatric service. The Camberwell Register 1967–71,* eds. J.K. Wing and A.M. Hailey. London: Oxford University Press.

—— 1978: *Reasoning about madness.* London: Oxford University Press.

—— 1980: Innovations in social psychiatry. *Psychological medicine* 10, 219–30.

—— and Hailey, A.M. eds. 1972: *Evaluating a community psychiatric service.* London: Oxford University Press.

Wing, J.K. et al. 1978: The concept of a "case" in psychiatric population surveys. *Psychological medicine* 8, 203–17.

social skills training

A practical procedure by means of which new forms of social behavior can be learned, or existing behavior modified. The aim of SST is to help clients to organize or improve their social skills, namely behavioral sequences which conform to social norms and which enable people to achieve desired social goals more efficiently and acceptably. SST has been developed and scientifically tested by many university, hospital and business based research teams, and has acquired variable support (modest to good) for its effectiveness. The training consists of instruction (description of applicable skills); modeling or demonstration by competent others; imitation and rehearsal by the client; teaching and feedback from others or from video-recordings; re-inforcement for achieving set standards; homework practice in which the client applies the new skill in a real-life situation. SST is used for training psychiatric patients, as well as managers and other industrial and business personnel, teachers, social workers, doctors and other professionals. It is also used for improving intercultural communication.   PET

Bibliography

Trower, P., Bryant, B.M. and Argyle, M. 1978: *Social skills and mental health.* London: Methuen.

social therapy

This is a form of psychiatric treatment in which the patient's social setting is specifically designed and operated so as to be in itself a major therapeutic factor.

The late eighteenth century, the "Age of Reason", saw a gradual awareness of the cruel manner in which the mentally ill were often treated: in prisons, in private "madhouses", and in institutions such as Bethlem in London and the Bicêtre and the Salpêtrière in Paris. Pinel, as physician-in-chief of the Bicêtre, in 1793 released the patients from chains and forbade many of the traditional treatments such as bleeding, purging and drugs. (Pinel 1801, 1809). In England the Quaker Tuke in 1796 opened "The Retreat" at York which was run on humanitarian lines (Tuke 1813). The "non-restraint" movement flourished under the leadership of men such as Conolly (1856) at the many institutions built in England after the passing of the Asylums Act 1845. These reforms, however, were not merely humanitarian: Pinel, Tuke and Conolly all subscribed to the theory of treatment called "moral management". (In the mid nineteenth century the word moral was still a synonym for psychological.) Moral treatment consisted of providing a peaceful and pleasant environment together with purposeful activities. The normality of the patients was emphasized rather than their sickness.

In the second half of the nineteenth century, however, many asylums grew unmanageably large and the staff in them grew increasingly pessimistic as to the curability of the mentally ill. These institutions tended to develop restrictive and repressive regimes encouraging the development of institutionalism (see REHABILITATION). When active treatment was provided it was usually according to the MEDICAL MODEL in which the patient is a passive recipient, and little emphasis is placed upon the treatment environment.

Before the second world war psychodynamic theories (see PSYCHOANALYSIS) had had little influence upon the treatment of the institutionalized mentally ill, but during the war a number of analysts became responsible for hospital wards catering for psychoneurotic ex-soldiers. Experiments were conducted into forms of patient self-government and the use of the newly developing forms of GROUP THERAPY. Following his experiences at Northfield Hospital, Birmingham, Main coined the term "therapeutic community" which he described as

an attempt to use a hospital not as an organisation run by doctors in the interests of their own greater technical efficiency, but as a community with the immediate aim of full participation of all its members in its daily life and the eventual aim of resocialisation of the neurotic individual for life in ordinary society (Main 1946).

Maxwell Jones continued work in social therapy after the war at the Industrial Neurosis Unit at Belmont Hospital (later renamed Henderson Hospital) where most of the characteristic features of the therapeutic community were developed. The most important perhaps is the emphasis upon the therapeutic potential of all activities and interactions, summarized by Jones's phrase the "living-learning situation". Every therapeutic community has a community meeting, usually daily, in which the day's events can be analyzed. These meetings, which are attended by all residents and all staff working in the unit, vary in detail, but all concentrate upon "here and now" problems and tasks. In most communities the rest of the day is divided between formal psychotherapeutic activities, often group therapy, and the carrying out of daily living tasks such as cleaning and cooking.

A team of sociologists led by Rapoport studied the Henderson Hospital (1960) and concluded that the therapeutic regimen could be summarized by four themes: democratization, communalism, permissiveness and reality confrontation. The therapeutic community approach, like "moral management", tends to emphasize its clients' normality rather than their illnesses, but in addition every community member is also seen as having therapeutic potential. The therapeutic community would appear to be the treatment of choice for certain PERSONALITY DISORDERS (Whiteley 1972).

The post war years also saw the start of the "open door movement" within mental hospitals, followed in the 1950s by the introduction of effective major tranquilizers such as chlorpromazine. Clark (1981) described the application of social therapy in a large psychiatric hospital in terms of "activity, freedom and responsibility". The provision of sheltered workshops and industrial therapy units has become very widespread, but it would appear that the opportunity to experience freedom and responsibility are equally important. Wing and Brown (1970) in a comparative study of three mental hospitals clearly demonstrated the effectiveness of social therapy in institutionalism and SCHIZOPHRENIA. Social therapeutic programs have also been used in a variety of other settings, for example prisons and hostels (see Jansen 1980).

Social therapy is an empirical treatment developed in response to clinical problems and is, therefore, not directly based upon any one particular theory. Historically it has tended to be associated with liberal and radical values, with a rejection of the medical model of man. Attempts have, however, been made to describe social therapy using psychodynamic concepts. Cumming and Cumming (1962) in a theoretical analysis suggested that the therapeutic community, 'encourages ego growth through successful crisis resolution'. Therapeutic communities have also been studied by sociologists (e.g. Rapoport 1960), social psychologists and anthropologists.

In general, it seems to be agreed that social therapy, by providing a model social group ("communal" and "democratic") permits the learning by experience ("permissiveness") of more appropriate forms of behavior. The most important treatment factor is probably a communication system (usually including the community meeting) which ensures prompt and accurate feedback to the individual and to the group ("reality confrontation"). GPP

Bibliography

*Clark, D.H. 1981: *Social therapy in psychiatry*. 2nd edn. Edinburgh: Churchill Livingstone.

Conolly, J. 1856: *The treatment of the insane without mechanical restraints*. London: Smith, Elder.

Cumming, J. and Cumming, E. 1962: *Ego and milieu*. New York: Atherton Press; London: Prentice Hall International.

*Hinshelwood, R.D. and Manning, N.P. eds. 1979: *Therapeutic communities: reflections and progress*. London and Boston: Routledge and Kegan Paul.

*Jansen, E., ed. 1980: *The therapeutic community outside the hospital*. London: Croom Helm.

Jones, M. 1968: *Social psychiatry in practice*. London: Penguin.

Kennard, D. 1983: *An introduction to therapeutic communities*. London: Routledge and Kegan Paul.

Main, T.F. 1946: The hospital as a therapeutic community. *Bulletin of the Menninger clinic* 10, 66–70.

Pinel, P. 1801 (*1962*): *A treatise on insanity*. 2nd English edn. New York: Hathner Publishing Co.

Rapoport, R.N. 1960: *Community as doctor*. London: Tavistock; Springfield Ill.: Charles C.Thomas.

Tuke, S. 1813: *Description of the retreat*. York: W. Alexander.

Whiteley, S. 1972: Henderson. In *Dealing with deviants*. eds. S. Whiteley, D. Briggs and M. Turner. London: Hogarth Press; Toronto: Clarke, Irwin and Co.

Wing, J.K. and Brown, G.W. 1970: *Institutionalism and schizophrenia*. Cambridge: Cambridge University Press.

sociopathic personality Refers to a typical cluster of character traits in an individual who is repeatedly at variance with society. He is unable to make deep and stable relationships, is lacking in concern for others and incapable of guilt and remorse; he is self-centered, irritable and impatient, being liable to emotional and aggressive outbursts in the face of frustrations and delays in the gratification of his wishes. The term is virtually synonymous with PSYCHOPATHIC PERSONALITY, with the exclusion of the inadequate (that is, neurotic) and the creative psychopathic subgroups.

The sociopath is said to score high on tests of extroversion and low on neuroticism, and to be relatively resistant to attempts to modify his behavior through psychotherapy or behavioral treatments, although slow improvement usually occurs through delayed maturational processes. However, sociopathic personality should probably not be seen as a clear-cut diagnostic entity, but rather as part of the wide and varied spectrum of PERSONALITY DISORDERS. DLJ

Bibliography

Craft, Michael 1966: *Psychopathic disorders and their assessment*. London: Pergamon.

somatosensory nervous system Those neural structures which participate in the conversion of the stimulation of body tissues into the sensations and perceptions of touch, position, temperature, and pain. As a physically large system with several submodalities, the somatosensory system has several identifiable subsystems. Spatially, all parts of the body except the face are innervated by somatic afferents from segments of the spinal cord. The face is innervated by afferents of the trigeminal nerve. Functionally and structurally the spinal segmental system is subdivided into the dorsal column-medial lemniscal system and the anterolateral system. The same dichotomy is present in the trigeminal system.

The dorsal column-medial lemniscal system subserves touch, pressure and position sense. (See BRAIN AND CENTRAL NERVOUS SYSTEM: ILLUSTRATIONS, fig. 28.) Its primary afferents are all myelinated fibers from peripheral mechanoreceptors (e.g. Pacinian corpuscles, Meissner corpuscles, Merkel disks, etc.) where sensory transduction occurs. The cell bodies for these fibers are in the dorsal root ganglia of the SPINAL CORD. Afferent axons ascend ipsilaterally in the dorsal columns of the spinal cord to the dorsal column nuclei. These project contralaterally via the medial lemniscus to the posterior nuclear group and the ventral posterior lateral (VPL) nucleus of the thalamus (fig. 19). VPL projects to two somatosensory cortical regions, the primary cortex (SI) of the post central gyrus of the parietal lobe and the secondary cortex (SII) on the upper bank of the Sylvian fissure (figs. 2 and 3). The posterior nuclear group projects primarily to SII and the somatosensory association cortex just behind SI. All these structures are somatotopically organized with continuous mapping of body site onto neural structure (fig. 4).

The anterolateral system subserves pain, temperature sense and crude touch (fig. 29). Primary afferents whose cell bodies lie in the dorsal root ganglia, synapse on neurons in the dorsal horn of the spinal cord. These cells project contralaterally in the lateral spinal columns to the reticular formation of the brainstem (figs. 6 and 9) and to the same regions of the thalamus innervated by the dorsal column nuclei. Projections from THALAMUS to the CEREBRAL CORTEX (SI, SII, and somatosensory association cortex) follow the patterns of the dorsal column-medial lemniscal system.

Like other neocortex, somatosensory cortex is organized into vertical columns. Each column contains vertical sets of neurons sensitive to the same submodality and innervated from the same small region of peripheral sensory organ (see VISUAL NERVOUS SYSTEM for another example of the columnar organization of neocortex).

Descending connections directly from the cortex and those through subcortical relays influence the afferent input at many levels down to the dorsal horn of the spinal cord. These centrifugal neurons appear to contribute to the shaping of sensory input, perhaps selectively increasing spatial resolution in a particular region. They also play a role in facilitating portions of afferent pathways about to be stimulated by body movement.   SCC

Bibliography

Iggo, A., ed. 1973: *Handbook of sensory physiology*, vol. 2. Somatosensory system. Berlin and New York: Springer-Verlag.

Kandel, E.R. and Schwartz, J.H., eds. 1981: *Principles of neural science*. New York and Oxford: Elsevier/North-Holland.

Mountcastle, V.B. 1980: Neural mechanisms in somesthesia. In *Medical physiology*. 14th edn, vol. 1, ed. V.B. Mountcastle. St. Louis and London: C.V. Mosby.

speech disorders Pathological disturbances in an individual's behavior, the study of which is speech pathology. This is not the only possible definition. At one time the term "speech disorder" referred only to disabilities involving the motor function of the vocal organs, thereby ruling out the more "central" disorders such as aphasia. At the other extreme some therapists have taken the term to apply to all mental and physical disabilities which hinder verbal communication, including SCHIZOPHRENIA, DEAFNESS AND HEARING IMPAIRMENT, cleft palate, and reading and writing disorders such as DYSLEXIA. "Speech disorders" here refers only to those communicational disorders which specifically concern the production and reception of speech. This excludes abnormalities of speech which arise as repercussions from other non-language disturbances: for instance, the distinctively disordered speech of the schizophrenic or of many of the deaf.

Speech disorders can arise from a variety of causes. If a particular disorder can be traced to a lesion or malfunctioning in the brain or nervous system, the disorder will be referred to as "organic". If no such cause can be found, or assumed, the disorder will be deemed "functional". The most common types of organic speech disorders result from cerebro-vascular accidents or "strokes". Speech disorders may also be caused by brain tumors, birth injury, infectious diseases (such as meningitis), headwounds, etc.

Although speech disorders are mentioned in texts dating as far back as the ancient Egyptian era, they did not become the subject of scientific investigation until the nineteenth century. Medical scientists, such as Pierre Broca (1865) and Carl Wernicke (1908) first undertook the study of speech disorders with the aim of locating the area(s) in the brain specifically concerned with speech (see BRAIN AND CENTRAL NERVOUS SYSTEM: ILLUSTRATIONS, figs. 2 and 3). These investigations centered on the CEREBRAL CORTEX or surface gray matter covering the major part of the brain. The areas which these early investigators found to be the seat of language functions were located in the left of the cortex (for right-handed people: see LATERALIZATION) at or near the junction between the temporal, frontal, and parietal lobes. Two such areas were found to be essential to coherent speech. The first, Broca's area, is located at the inferior gyrus of the left frontal lobe. A second speech area, known as Wernicke's area, is found in the superior gyrus of the left temporal lobe. Lesions in Broca's area were said to lead to "motor" or "expressive" speech disorders: that is, disorders affecting the production of speech. Lesions in Wernicke's area were thought to be the cause of "sensory" or "receptive" disorders: i.e. disorders affecting the reception of speech.

Much of this early medical framework is still part of speech pathology today. Both the expressive/receptive dichotomy and the notion of speech centers in the brain continue to exert an influence on contemporary theories of NEUROLINGUISTICS and speech pathology. Recent work, however, has turned more to the specification of the behavioral aspects of speech disorders, framed in the vocabulary of modern linguistics. The linguistic character of a disorder had hitherto been analyzed only in very general, pre-theoretical terms. The dominant notion was that of language modalities: speaking, hearing, reading, and writing. Today these commonsense descriptions have largely been replaced by a variety of competing descriptive frameworks, culled from contemporary linguistic theories. As yet, there is little conclusive evidence about the relative merits of these frameworks; consequently there is no standard classification of speech disorders. However, it is convenient (and

not uncommon) to group them into three basic types: central disorders, output (or production) disorders, and input (or reception) disorders.

Most central disorders are grouped under the general heading of aphasia, which has received more scientific attention than any other speech disorder primarily because it is thought to reveal the nature of the speaker/hearer's knowledge of his language as well as of the ways in which that knowledge is cognitively processed.

Whether, in the contemporary theoretical context, aphasia is to be seen as a disorder of competence or performance is, however, controversial (see Whitaker 1970; Weigl and Bierwisch 1970).

One influential analysis of aphasia was first suggested by Roman Jakobson (1964) on the basis of investigations by the Soviet psychologist LURIA (1970, 1976). This linguistic classification has been modified and extended (see Sabouraud, Gagnepain, and Sabouraud 1963, and Gagnepain 1973, 1982). Gagnepain and the Sabourauds model their analysis on two fundamental linguistic dichotomies. The first concerns the distinction between syntagmatic (combinatory) and paradigmatic (selectional) processes. Aphasics with a lesion in Broca's area are said to have difficulty combining linguistic items in coherent sequence. On the other hand, a Wernicke's aphasic is unable to make an effective selection of appropriate linguistic items. The second dichotomy is drawn between two types of linguistic unit: the phoneme and the word. This is sometimes referred to as "the dual articulation of language" and is a dichotomy between the primary significant units of language (words) and the primary non-significant units (phonemes). While phonology concerns the language-user's ability to select and combine phonemes in order to construct words; semiology, according to this theory, refers to the ability to select and combine words in the construction of utterances.

As a result of the intersection of these two dichotomies, the earlier distinction between "expressive" and "receptive" aphasia has been replaced by a more complex division into four fundamental types of aphasia. The Broca's aphasic with a semiological disorder is unable to combine words effectively into a syntactic structure. His vocalizations are often described as telegraphic or as exhibiting a-grammatism. When there is a-grammatism, an absence of the grammatical markers (prepositions, conjunctions, inflectional endings) needed to combine words into sentences is observed. Should a phonological disorder affect the Broca's aphasic he will be unable to combine phonemes into coherent words. This may result in utterances consisting of many unconnected syllabic fragments spoken with an a-rhythmical and monotonous pitch pattern.

The Wernicke's aphasic with a semiological disorder will produce a fluent stream of words, with no lack of grammatical markers, but a word-finding difficulty (anomia) may be observed. This may in turn lead to frequent circumlocution in order to avoid selection difficulties and/or to the use of vague pronouns and "semantically empty" words such as *thing, whatsitsname*, and *the one*. In addition paraphasia (the production of inappropriate words) or jargon (the production of meaningless words) may occur. The speech of the Wernicke's aphasic with a phonological disorder will be characterized by frequent inappropriate selections from the stock of phonemes. Again, jargon and paraphasia may result, but at the syllabic level. Related to this will be the inability, often attributed to dysarthria (see below), to realize the basic paradigmatic oppositions which distinguish one phoneme from another. Thus the word *bit* may be pronounced as *pit* or *bid* or *bet*.

The most frequently studied output disorders are stuttering (or "stammering") and cluttering. A variety of features characterize stuttering. These include erratic rhythm and tempo patterns, abnormal prolongations of sound segments, and greater than usual amounts of pausing, repetition, self-correction, and incomplete grammatical structures. In addition there may be blocking – a unique characteristic of the stutterer which results from the inability to release the tension built up prior to articulation. There has, as yet, been no accepted organic explanation of stuttering, but much progress has been made in its functional study, including the specification of psychological factors which may cause a child to acquire a stutter.

Cluttering is often confused with stuttering. The clutterer tends to speak too quickly, omitting linguistic units of various levels, telescoping units into one another, and even inverting the sequential order of units. There is also the characteristic "flat" intonation of the clutterer. Because general personality differences have been found between clutterers and stutterers – the former tend to be aggressive and extraverted while the latter are timid and introspective – there are some speech pathologists who take them not as disorders specific to speech, but as resulting from an influence of character traits on speech.

On the borderline between central and output disorders are dysarthria and apraxia (or dyspraxia) of speech. Both involve disability in the articulation of speech and may result either from malfunctioning in central linguistic processes or from more general malfunctions in the neuromuscular command of articulatory performance. Since there are other behaviorial apraxias – for instance, apraxia of tool use (which affects writing ability) and apraxia of dress – all of which involve a difficulty in performing voluntary and purposive movements, it has been argued (Gagnepain 1973, 1982) that apraxia is not a disability specific to language, and so not, strictly speaking, a speech disorder.

Two disorders are primarily concerned with input. Auditory agnosia is diagnosed when the hearer is not able to recognize what should be familiar speech sounds. He is not able to recognize as instances of the same linguistic unit two occurrences of a particular phoneme or syllable. With "pure word deafness", on the other hand, the recognition of sounds is not impaired. But the patient is unable to take a group of sounds as forming a recognizable word. As with many of the types of speech disorders the distinction between agnosia and "pure word deafness" is largely theoretical, in practice it is difficult to distinguish between them. The inexplicitness of both the linguistic and the neurological criteria which define such categories is a problem which continues to plague the study and remedial treatment of speech disorders. (See also NEUROLINGUISTICS.)   TJT

Bibliography

Broca, P. 1865: Sur le siège de la faculté du language articulé. Reprinted in *La Naissance de la neuropsychologie du language*, eds. H. Hécaen and J. Dubois. Paris: Flammarion, 1969.

*Crystal, D. 1980: *Introduction to language pathology*. London: Edward Arnold.

Crystal, D., Fletcher, P., and Garman, M. 1976: *The grammatical analysis of language disability*. London: Edward Arnold.

*Dalton, P. and Hardcastle, W.J. 1977: *Disorders of fluency*. London: Edward Arnold.

Gagnepain, J. 1973: Discours et méthode. *Actes du Colloque International d'Aphasiologie*. Brussels.

——— 1982: *Du vouloir dire: traité d'epistemologie des sciences humaines*. Oxford and New York: Pergamon.

Hécaen, H. and Albert, M.L. 1978: *Human neurophysiology*. New York: John Wiley.

Jakobson, R. 1964: Towards a linguistic typology of aphasia impairments. In *Disorders of language*, eds. A. De Reuck and M. O'Connor. London: Churchill.

*Lesser, R. 1978: *Linguistic investigations of aphasia*. London: Edward Arnold.

Luria, A.R. 1970: *Traumatic aphasia*. The Hague: Mouton.

——— 1976: *Basic problems of neurolinguistics*. The Hague: Mouton.

Sabouraud, O., Gagnepain, J., and Sabouraud, A. 1963: *Vers une approche linguistique des problèmes de l'aphasie*. Rennes. (Also in *Revue de Neuropsychiatrie de l'Ouest*, 1963.)

Weigl, E. and Bierwisch, M. 1970: Neuropsychology and linguistics: topics of common research. *Foundations of language* 6, 1–18.

Wernicke, C. 1908: The symptom-complex of aphasia. In *Disorders of the nervous system*, ed. A. Church. New York: Appleton.

Whitaker, H. 1970: Linguistic competence: evidence from aphasia, *Glossa* 4, 46–53.

Sperry, Roger Wolcott An American neurobiologist who exactly forty years after his first professional appointment shared, in 1981, the Nobel Prize in Medicine and Physiology. In this period (and since) he has produced a massive body of research which has been found as significant to philosophers and psychologists as to his co-workers. This is the less surprising in that among his numerous honors and awards is also to be found an award for science journalism.

Although it is tempting to summarize his research as making radical innovations in two different fields of inquiry – his discovery of the chemoaffinity theory, and his research into the higher functions of the conscious human brain – Sperry himself (1975) sees the two as closely linked. When he started his research (he worked first with Paul Weiss, and postdoctorally with Karl Lashley, but was about to diverge from the major claims of both) the popular view of nervous networks emphasized anticonnectionism, extreme plasticity, and cortical equipotentiality. This view was further supported when in the early 1940s it seemed that complete transection of the corpus callosum produced no definite functional symptoms (Akelaitis 1943). Sperry's research, based particularly on the retinotectal system of amphibians, showed that the alleged functional PLASTICITY was incapable of correcting the animals' opto-kinetic responses when the eyeball was rotated through 180° on the optic axis; moreover, even after section of the optic nerve, regenerating fibers restored the original functional relations (i.e. ignoring the rotated eyeball) between retina and visual centers. So motor and sensory nerves were not functionally interchangeable after surgical transposition; they rather revealed a very precisely programed axonal outgrowth through astonishingly complex pathways to exactingly selective targets. Sperry's explanation for this was his chemoaffinity theory, postulating selective matching of the chemical codes in neurons, axonal pathways – perhaps involving billions of chemically distinct brain cells – and synapses: functional convenience comes second to this chemical code. Current research is, correspondingly, largely devoted to the hunt for the molecular basis of these affinities. Anticonnectionism was further challenged when, in papers dating from the 1950s, Sperry showed that commissurotomy led to numerous cross-communication deficits in animals (cats and monkeys) and, in papers dating from the 1960s, in humans too. The hemispheres emphatically proved not to be equipollent, and research into their respective areas of expertise has since proceeded apace.

Sperry was encouraged by his split-brain studies to pursue the vexed problem of higher mental competences, consciousness in particular. In the 1950s, consciousness was regarded either as a global property of the brain as a whole, or the mesencephalon was considered to be the most crucial site for it. However, the split-brain findings showed that a divided neocortex (but an *intact* brainstem) split many of the higher psychological functions in complex and complementary ways, and this forced a revision of the whole subject of the cerebral basis of consciousness. Moreover, this revision required one to investigate the possibility of relatively selective localization.

Sperry has produced a theory that ascribes to the conscious mind a causal role in regulating brain processes. He sees it as a "holistic emergent" of brain activity, but something over and above the neural events of which it is composed; indeed, he has described himself (1966) as 'in a 0.1 percent mentalist minority'. His theory is nevertheless offered as a compromise and resolution of the materialist and dualist debate over the mind-brain problem, and as a theory with implications for tackling humanistic problems like the determinism/free will debate. Given the nests of difficulties in these areas, it is little criticism to say that many want to know more about the nature of this emergentism, and in what respects the emergent mental is "different from" its constituent neural events – just how is Sperry a "mentalist"? We see emergentism, as Sperry has himself pointed out, in unquestionably "physical" relationships: what if anything is special or extra, specifically "mental", about the sort of emergentism found with consciousness?

Whatever the future of the theory, though, the fact that the mind-brain problem has now advanced a very considerable distance from the oversimple dichotomy between crude identity theories or behaviorism on the one hand, the implausible dualism on the other, or has advanced from an *eliminative* reductionism towards a more generous interpretation of what reduction might involve, is due very largely to Sperry's work.   KVW

Bibliography

Akelaitis, A.J. 1943: Studies on the corpus callosum, vol. 7.: study of language functions (tactile and visual lexia and graphia, unilaterally following section of corpus callosum. *Journal of neuropathology and experimental neurology* 2, 226–62.

Sperry, R.W. 1966: Mind, brain, and humanist values. *Bulletin of the atomic scientists* 22, 2–6.

—— 1975: In search of psyche. In *The neurosciences: paths of discovery*, eds. F.G. Worden, J.P. Swazey and G. Adelman. Cambridge, Mass.: MIT Press.

spinal cord A portion of the central nervous system that begins at the base of the brain and extends caudally as a long tapering tube within the spinal column (see BRAIN AND CENTRAL NERVOUS SYSTEM: ILLUSTRATIONS, fig. 10). The spinal cord of humans is composed of 24 segments which divide into cervical, thoracic, lumbar, and sacral regions. A cross-section of the spinal cord at any level reveals a central canal, containing cerebrospinal fluid, surrounded by a butterfly-shaped core of gray matter, made up mainly of three types of cell bodies: (1) sensory neurons (generally located in the dorsal aspect of the cord), which receive input conveyed by peripheral nerves from receptors; (2) motor neurons (concentrated in the ventral portions), which project motor signals to response or effector mechanisms; (3) interneurons, which connect spinal neurons in proximity to each other. The gray matter is surrounded by a mass of white matter, consisting of myelinated fiber columns that carry ascending and descending information between spinal segments and higher brain regions. An additional function of the spinal cord is the mediation of reflexes (i.e. simple, involuntary responses) under the control of specific stimuli (e.g. knee-jerk reflex). In its most elementary form this is accomplished when a stimulus excites a sensory fiber that synapses directly with the cell body of a motor neuron which, in turn, projects directly to a muscle, activating a response. This is an example of a monosynaptic reflex; other reflexes, also mediated within the spinal cord, have more complicated neural circuitry, involving one or more interneurons.   GWi

split-brain preparation A surgical procedure in which the corpus collosum and other fibers connecting the two cerebral hemispheres are severed (see BRAIN AND CENTRAL NERVOUS SYSTEM: ILLUSTRATIONS, figs. 1 and 6). This operation eliminates interhemispheric transfer of information and, when the optic chiasm (fig. 23) is also cut abolishing interocular transfer, the effect is to create virtually two functionally independent brains. Used initially in experiments with animals, this technique has proved useful in studying how the brain integrates and processes information. Surgical sectioning of the corpus callosum has also been performed on humans to prevent the spread of epileptic seizures in the brain. Observations based on such patients have confirmed the functional asymmetry of the human brain. Thus stimuli can be identified verbally by split-brain patients when projected to the left but not the right hemisphere. Conversely, nonverbal tasks can be performed better when the information is processed in the right hemisphere. These and related findings emphasize the respective dominance of the left and right hemispheres with respect to linguistic and nonverbal operations. (See NEURAL CONTROL OF HIGHER MENTAL PROCESSES; SPERRY.)   GWi

steroids: adrenal and gonadal Two important groups of hormones which are structurally related to cholesterol. In humans, the primary adrenal steroid is cortisol. The synthesis and release of cortisol is promoted by stressful stimulation (see ACTH). Increased cortisol levels stimulate glucose formation from protein, suppress inflammation and inhibit the further release of ACTH (inhibitory feedback control). Aldosterone, another adrenal steroid, is involved with the regulation of the concentration of sodium ions in body fluids. There are three major gonadal steroid hormones, each of which is important in regulating sexual behavior (see also SEXUAL BEHAVIOR AND THE NERVOUS SYSTEM). In addition, testosterone, the primary male gonadal steroid, interacts with other hormones in the development, maturation and maintenance of sperm formation and secondary sexual characteristics. The primary female gonadal steroids, estrogens and progesterone, play an integral role in the monthly menstrual cycle of nonpregnant adult females.   GPH

Bibliography

Johnson, M. and Everitt, B. 1980: *Essential reproduction*. Oxford: Blackwell Scientific Publications.

stress The definition of the term "stress" has been the source of much debate: there are at least three different ways of defining it and thus of approaching its study (Cox 1978). The simplest definitions are those that have been termed the stimulus-based (used by engineers) and the response-based (favored by clinical practitioners and physiologists). The former concept treats and measures "stress" as a noxious or aversive characteristic of the person's environment, in terms of degrees of temperature, for example, as sound pressure level (excessive noise), as hours of restraint (animal studies), or as speed of machine-paced work. Conversely, and largely following from the work of Hans Selye (1976) the response-based approach defines and measures stress in terms of the non-specific elements of the (physiological) response to noxious or aversive stimuli. In practice, there has been a tendency to concentrate on sympathetic-adrenal medullary activity and on pituitary-adrenal cortical activity as representative of the non-specific stress response. For a variety of reasons these approaches have been seen as inadequate by most psychologists, who have advanced more interactive models. These have tended to focus on the person's dynamic relationship with their environment, and to emphasize the critical importance of perceptual-cognitive processes and of individual differences (see Kaplan 1983). Several models of stress now treat it, not as "stimulus" or "response", but as a process. The process is that which describes the way in which people realize and identify their problems, how they react to them and attempt to cope with them, and the "cost" of doing so. Such models usually combine social psychological and psycho-physiological perspectives, and attempt to identify the structural characteristics of problems in terms of the demands made on the person, the support and resources made available for coping (or problem solving), and the constraints on coping. Situations involving high demand and high constraint, but involving poor problem-solving resources or low support are perceived and reported as aversive or problematic, and are often associated with the sort of changes in behavior and in physiological state which have been taken as diagnostic of stress. The term "stress" is thus to be treated as an economic descriptor of a particular problem-oriented process.

Given the confirmed existence of "stressful" problems, and the reactions they evoke, the individual shows increased risk of a number of psychological and physical disorders. Among those chronic physical disorders commonly associated with the existence of stress are coronary heart disease, gastric ulcers and, more recently, disorders of the immune system. Attempts at coping with stress may involve direct action (eg. avoidance or escape behavior, aggression or palliative behavior) or may be more cognitive (cognitive defense).

(See also LIFE EVENTS, WORK STRESS.)   TRC

Bibliography

Cox, Tom 1978: *Stress*. London: Macmillan.

Kaplan, H.B. ed. 1983: *Psychosocial stress*. New York: Academic Press.

Selye, Hans 1976: *Stress in health and disease*. Reading, Mass.: Butterworth.

stupor A condition of mutism and lack of movement and responsiveness in which there is evidence of relative preservation of consciousness. The term has been used in various senses but it is agreed that it must be clearly distinguished from coma, in which consciousness is impaired, and that it has organic and psychiatric causes. Among the former are lesions of the upper mid brain (e.g. tumors, strokes, meningitis and encephalitis), senile and pre-senile dementia, and raised intracranial pressure and severe alcohol or drug intoxication. The most common psychiatric causes are DEPRESSION and SCHIZOPHRENIA, but HYSTERIA and other neuroses are also rare causes. Diagnosis depends upon meticulous physical examination and a detailed psychiatric history from other informants.   RAM

Bibliography

Lishman, W.A. 1978: *Organic psychiatry: the psychological consequences of cerebral disorder*. Oxford: Blackwell Scientific Publications; St Louis, Missouri: C.V. Mosby.

subception The phenomenon of autonomic response to a stimulus which is not consciously recognized. McCleary and Lazarus (1949) introduced the term subception to suggest an apparently autonomic, perhaps subcortical form of perception. Subjects were shown nonsense syllables, half of which had previously been associated with shock, and the other half of which were neutral. With tachistoscopic exposures too short for conscious recognition, subjects still showed an elevated GALVANIC SKIN RESPONSE to the syllables previously paired with shock. This important study led to a series of investigations concerning the possible effects of unconscious phenomena on bodily processes and overt actions. Although there is considerable controversy, it is possible to interpret the findings as consistent with views of defensiveness promulgated by theorists such as FREUD and ROGERS.   SRM

Bibliography

McCleary, Robert A. and Lazarus, Richard S. 1949: Autonomic discrimination without awareness. *Journal of personality* 18, 171–9.

suicide The deliberate act of taking one's life; the term attempted suicide is often more loosely used of acts which carry some risk but are not necessarily aimed at death – parasuicide is an alternative term. Durkheim (1951) described four types of motivation: egoistic, anomic (where the individual is poorly integrated into society), altruistic and fatalistic. In western cultures suicide tends to be slightly more common among men than women, and for both sexes the risks are higher in the elderly, those living alone, in poor health or suffering from psychotic depression (especially with delusions of guilt and worthlessness; see AFFECTIVE DISORDERS). The majority give some prior warning of their suicidal intentions. Alcoholism and drug abuse greatly increase the risk of suicide.

DLJ

Bibliography

Durkheim, Émil 1951: *Suicide*. Glencoe, Ill.: Free Press.
*Stengel, F. 1973: *Suicide and attempted suicide*. Harmondsworth: Penguin; New York: Jason Aronson.

synapse and synaptic transmission
The site and process of the communication of information from one NEURON to another (see BRAIN AND CENTRAL NERVOUS SYSTEM: ILLUSTRATIONS, figs. 30 and 32). The term synapse describes the junction between two neurons or other excitable cells. The conduction of nervous impulses along a neuron is an electrical process, while the transmission of information from one neuron to the next is (with few exceptions) chemical and is termed synaptic transmission (see NEUROTRANSMITTER SYSTEMS). The presynaptic axon terminals of a neuron contain many synaptic vesicles, which in turn contain molecules of neurotransmitters. In general, any one neuron contains only one type of neurotransmitter. When an ACTION POTENTIAL reaches the axon terminal, it effects a quantal release of neurotransmitter into the synaptic cleft, a 200 angstrom gap between the presynaptic and postsynaptic neural elements. The interaction of the neurotransmitter and its receptor on the postsynaptic neural membrane causes certain changes in the permeability of that membrane to specific ions. This permeability change makes it either more or less likely that the post-synaptic neuron will initiate an action potential. Since each neuron may receive input from 1,000 or more synapses, the "decision" to fire is based on the spatial and temporal summation of these various signals. Once released, the action of the neurotransmitter may be terminated by enzymatic degradation or by reuptake into the presynaptic neuron.

GPH

T

T-group (training group) A method for improving individuals' sensitivity to themselves and others. The primary objectives are to increase individuals' awareness of their own feelings, the reactions of other people, and their impact on others, as well as their awareness of how people interrelate and of how groups operate. The T-group seeks to improve the individual's skills in listening to people, in understanding them empathically, in expressing feelings, and in providing feedback to other people.

The T-group is not structured at the outset but evolves its own organization. The evolving structure is continuously examined by members through looking at the social process of the group. The interactions that take place focus on the sharing of feelings about interpersonal behavior. Lectures, skill-building games, process observation experiences, simulations, and other structured experiences are sometimes used to support T-group activities.

The T-group is helped by a trainer whose role is to participate and provide some leadership in helping people get in touch with themselves and to share their thoughts openly with each other. There are two main types of trainer: those who emphasize the personal growth of the individual participant, and those who focus on the processes of group development and operation. T-groups are most commonly found in educational and business settings. Each group consists of approximately ten to fifteen people, including one or two trainers. The group is usually scheduled for one or two meetings each day over a period of one or two weeks. The meetings typically last for around two hours.

ALP/NMT

thalamus A major structure in the diencephalon, located centrally in the brain between the third ventral and posterior limbs of the internal capsule (see BRAIN AND CENTRAL NERVOUS SYSTEM: ILLUSTRATIONS, figs. 15 and 19). A Y-shaped band of myelinated fibers anatomically divides the thalamus into several nuclear groups containing nuclei which fall into three functional categories.
1. Sensory relay nuclei which receive input from ascending sensory pathways and project to specific cortical projection areas. This category includes lateral and medial geniculate bodies which, respectively, are parts of the visual and auditory systems, and the postero-ventral nucleus which represents somasthetic and kinesthetic senses. The postero-ventral nucleus is also the termination point for pain, temperature, and gustatory senses. The lateral ventral nucleus relays motor signals between subcortical areas (e.g., CEREBELLUM, BASAL GANGLIA), and the frontal cortex.
2. Association nuclei which have reciprocal connections with association areas of the cortex and are concerned with memory and integrative functions. They include pulvinar, dorsolateral, and dorsomedial nuclei.
3. Mid-line nuclei which include periventricular and intralaminar nuclei which receive input from the brain stem reticular formation as well as other thalamic and subcortical nuclei. As part of the ascending activating system, these nuclei project diffusely throughout the cortex, serving a cortical arousal function. GWi

Bibliography

Wright, Samson 1982: *Applied physiology*. 13th edn, eds. C.A. Keele, E. Neil and N. Joels. Oxford: Oxford University Press, pp. 313–15.

thermoregulation The maintenance of an optimal temperature. Animals function most effectively at a particular temperature, below which their metabolism progressively slows down. Above the optimal temperature the metabolic rate rises rapidly and energy is utilized wastefully. For most species there is a lethal limit in the region of 47°C.

Animals are able to influence their own body temperature by appropriate behavior and by specialized physiological mechanisms. In both cases some degree of thermoreception is essential. Nerve endings sensitive to the temperature at the surface of the animal have been studied in insects, fish, amphibia, reptiles, birds and mammals. The temperature sense is especially well developed in pit vipers (*Crotalidae*) which have special sense organs sensitive to infra-red radiation. These endow the animal with a directional temperature sense and enable it to attack warm-blooded prey when visibility is poor. Some animals also have thermoreceptors in the internal organs, particularly the brain. In mammals there are distinct heat and cold receptors in the skin, and there are also thermoreceptors in the veins, spinal cord and brain. The thermoreceptors in the veins and spinal cord can initiate shivering even though the temperature of the brain and at the skin remains constant. This sometimes happens when people drink a large quantity of cold water.

The metabolic reactions of the body produce heat continuously and animals can easily become overheated, especially when they are active. Overheating can also occur in especially hot environments or when heat dissipation is impaired. Because the lethal body temperature is not much above the normal body temperature of many animals, cooling mechanisms have to be especially rapid and effective.

There are four principal ways of losing heat from the body.

1. Conduction of heat occurs through the tissues and between the body and external objects, such as the ground. The degree of conduction depends upon the temperature differences between these, and upon the degree of insulation. Insulation is provided by layers of fat within the body and by layers of air trapped in hair or feathers at the body surface. Animals can to some extent control the rate at which the body cools by altering these insulating properties. Long-term regulation can be effected by increasing deposition of fat and hair growth in winter and decreasing these in summer. Short-term changes can be achieved by raising or lowering hair and feathers, and by altering body posture in relation to the prevailing weather. Surface insulation is influenced by wind and wetness. Wet hair increases heat loss by conduction. When a mammal lies or sits on the ground the hair is compressed and holds less air. Heat is then conducted into the ground, particularly when the ground is wet. It is for this reason that cows frequently lie down before rain comes.

2. Convection occurs as a result of the circulation of warm blood from the interior of the body to the cooler surface tissues. The control of blood flow provides an important means of temperature regulation. When the hand of a European is plunged into cold water there is an increase in the flow of blood to the hand, but his is only half the increase an Eskimo could obtain, to keep his hand warm and usable. The Lapps, a people of European origin, respond in the same way as other Europeans even though they inhabit conditions similar to those of Eskimos.

Convection is also important at the surface of the body. Free convection occurs as warm air ascends from a heated surface, and is of some importance in warm-blooded animals. Forced convection occurs when the surface is subject to an airstream so that heat lost from the body is quickly removed. The angle at which wind strikes the body and the direction of hair growth in relation to wind direction can to some extent be controlled by the animal. Much more heat is lost if the wind blows against the direction of hair or feather growth and most resting mammals and birds face into the wind to prevent this.

3. Radiation heat loss is proportional to the area of the radiating surface and is roughly proportional to the temperature difference between the animal and its environment.

An animal's color makes no significant difference to its heat loss by radiation, but it does affect heat gain. Thus black animals gain more heat by absorption of radiation than do white ones which have greater reflection. Animals can affect radiant heat losses by behavioral means. for example, certain fiddler crabs (*Uca*), ground squirrels (*Ammospermophilus leucurus*), and other burrowing animals, make sorties between their cool burrows and the warm external environment. In this way they can easily cool off by radiation if they become overheated. Camels (*Camelus dromedarius*) allow their body temperature to rise during the day time and dissipate the excess heat by radiation during the cold desert night.

4. Evaporation from the body surface occurs in most animals, but its extent depends upon the type of body covering. Insects which have a hard surface covered with wax lose very little water by evaporation, but earthworms (*Lumbricus*) suffer rapid desiccation of the surface of the body in a dry atmosphere. Most animals also lose water in respiration and this form of water loss is particularly important as a means of cooling in reptiles and birds.

Evaporative water loss through the skin is uncontrolled in amphibians, reptiles and birds, but in mammals it is regulated by the sweat glands. These are present in all higher mammals except rodents and lagomorphs (rabbits). In man, the sweat glands on the palms are emotionally controlled, while those on the rest of the body normally respond to thermal control. Sweating is controlled by thermoreceptors in the brain and not by those in the skin. Thus we usually sweat during exercise but not when sitting by a hot fire. Some animals enhance evaporative cooling by moistening the body surface with saliva, or wetting themselves with water as in the case of elephants.

Respiratory evaporation is to some extent controlled in most animals. Crocodiles, snakes and some lizards gape widely when hot. The desert iguana (*Dipsosaurus*) pants like a dog. Because so much water is lost in respiratory evaporation it tends to be used only in emergencies. Birds and mammals pant only when their body temperature approaches the lethal temperature. Flying birds generate a lot of heat and rely primarily upon respiratory evaporation to dissipate it. The camel does not pant at all, but relies on radiant cooling during the night. Camels do not store water to a greater extent than other species, and cannot afford to expend water in keeping cool.

Animals can increase their body temperature in two main ways: by increasing heat production or heat gain and by reducing heat losses. Many invertebrates are cold-blooded in the sense that their body temperature tends to conform to that of their environment. Because the rate of metabolic reactions is determined by the temperature at which they occur, it is difficult for such animals to increase metabolic rate in response to cold. They can raise their body temperature only by moving to a warmer environment. In warm-blooded animals heat production can be raised by muscular activity such as shivering, and by raising metabolic rate under the influence of hormones. Food intake also serves to increase heat production, because heat is released during digestion.

Heat losses can be reduced by increasing insulation at the body surface. Birds fluff their feathers, mammals raise their fur, and people put on extra clothes when cold. These rapid responses can be supplemented in the long term by increasing the amount of fur or subcutaneous fat. Heat losses can also be reduced by behavioral means. The most effective of these is to move to less cold surroundings. Heat loss by radiation can be reduced by curling up and so reducing the apparent area of the body surface. The warming effects of sunlight can be exploited by color change. Many lizards change color in accordance with their thermal requirements. In the early morning when temperatures are low they adopt a dark coloration which aids the absorption of radiant heat. As the temperature rises throughout the day, the lizards become pale, thus reflecting solar radiation to a greater extent. Heat can also be obtained by conduction from hot surfaces. The lizard (*Aporosaura anchietae*), which inhabits the Namib desert, emerges from beneath the sand where it spends the night and presses its body against the sun-warmed surface of the sand so that it can quickly raise its body temperature and become active.

Some animals, called poikilotherms, have a body temperature that is the same as the environmental temperature. This is particularly true for small invertebrates and for fish. Aquatic animals cannot lose water from the body by evaporation and so can never achieve a body temperature that is lower than that of their surroundings. The heat generated by muscular exercise is rapidly removed from the body by conduction and this can be prevented only by efficient insulation as in marine animals such as whales. Heat lost from the body is rapidly removed by convection due to the flow of water over the surface.

Poikilotherms have a difficult time on land, because temperatures fluctuate much more widely on land than in water. The necessity to avoid temperature extremes severely restricts the range of behavior of such animals. These restrictions can to some extent be overcome by behavior which enables the animal to attain a body temperature higher than that of the environment. Sun bathing serves this purpose in many animals and reptiles. For example, the frog (*Rana clamitans*) can maintain a body temperature 17°C above that of the environment by basking in full sun. Such animals are generally called ectotherms (heat source from without) in contrast to endotherms (heat source from within) which applies to mammals, birds and large reptiles which control body temperature on a basis of internally produced heat.

Most ectotherms are able to regulate their body temperature to a limited extent. Amphibia can keep cool by evaporation of water from the body surface. The frog (*Rana pipiens*) can maintain a body temperature of 36.8°C at an environmental temperature of 50°C. Reptiles have a more limited ability to cool themselves and tend to avoid very hot conditions. The Namib desert lizard (*Aporosaura anchietae*) burrows into the sand when the midday temperature climbs above 40°C.

True thermal HOMEOSTASIS is found in birds and mammals, which are able to maintain a constant body temperature despite fluctuations in environmental temperature. Their high metabolic rate provides an internal source of heat and their insulated body surface prevents uncontrolled dissipation of this heat. Birds and mammals maintain a body temperature that is generally higher than that of their surroundings. The brain receives information about the temperature of the body and is able to exercise control over the mechanisms of warming and cooling. When the brain temperature becomes too high the cooling mechanisms are activated, and if it becomes too cool heat losses are reduced and warming mechanisms are activated. This FEEDBACK principle is the same as that found in a thermostatically controlled electric heater.

Fine control of body temperature occurs in man who has an early warning system consisting of numerous thermoreceptors in the skin. On the basis of this type of information people are able to take anticipatory action and so forestall any undue fluctuations in body temperature. Controlled temperature changes do occur in birds and mammals, often on a diurnal basis. The phenomenon is particularly marked in birds which generally reduce their body temperature by several degrees at night, probably as a means of energy conservation. The average human body temperature is 36.7°C in the early morning and 37.5°C in the late afternoon.

The degree of thermoregulation varies considerably among species within the animal kingdom. Although partly due to the requirements of different ways of life, this variation reflects evolutionary advances. Primitive animals tend to conform to the dictates of the environment. The ability to control body temperature in the face of environmental changes is characteristic of higher mammals and birds and enables them to exploit a wide range of habitats. DJM

Bibliography

*Hokanson, J.E. 1969: *The physiological bases of motivation*. New York: J. Wiley and Sons.
*Whitlow, G.C. ed. 1970: *Comparative physiology*

of thermoregulation. vols. 1 and 2. New York: Academic Press.

thought disorder This term is employed in its broadest sense to describe four types of abnormality in thinking: the form of thought (the way in which thoughts are linked together by logical associations), possession of thought (the feeling that one's thoughts are not one's own), content of thought (delusions and other related morbid ideas), and stream of thought in which the speed and abundancy of thoughts is abnormal. The term is also sometimes used in a narrow sense restricted to formal thought disorder. This includes phenomena such as thought blocking (a feeling that thoughts have come to a sudden stop), flight of ideas and a general loosening of associations. The latter may be so severe that the result is totally incoherent speech. Thought disorder has been classified in a variety of ways, none entirely satisfactory. There have also been a range of explanatory theories. Thought disorder is characteristic of SCHIZOPHRENIA, MANIA and ORGANIC MENTAL STATE and precise description of its nature has diagnostic significance. JC

Bibliography
Fish, F. 1967: *Clinical psychopathology*. Bristol: John Wright.
Kaplan, H.I., Freedman, A.M. and Sadock, B.J. 1980: *Comprehensive textbook of psychiatry*. 3rd edn. Baltimore: Williams and Wilkins.

trace storage A term used by Melton (1963) to refer to the retention of experienced events, in contradistinction to trace formation and trace utilization. (A memory trace is usually defined as the neurophysiological record of an attended-to event.) Trace storage is said to intervene between trace formation, or the initial acquisition of information, and trace utilization, or the retrieval of information that has been stored.

The gestalt psychologists of the 1930s believed that the memory trace undergoes systematic changes in the course of storage; but the results of well controlled experiments have failed to support that hypothesis. There is no evidence, moreover, that memory traces decay autonomously in time while they are in storage. NCW

Bibliography
Melton, A.W. 1963: Implications of short-term memory for a general theory of memory. *Journal of verbal learning and verbal behavior* 1, 1–21.

traits A trait is a characteristic of a person or animal which varies from one individual to another. Traits may be physical (e.g. height, eye color) or psychological (e.g. intelligence and aggressiveness). The concept is one of particular relevance to personality psychology because the major effort in recent years has been directed at establishing the main dimensions of temperament on which people differ as a first step towards explaining these individual differences. Traits are conceived as reasonably stable and enduring attributes, distinguishing them from *states*, which are temporary behavioral predispositions. Because a person is anxious in the dentist's chair this does not mean he or she is necessarily anxious in general.

It has been estimated that there are about 4500 trait-descriptive adjectives in the English language, many of which are heavily overlapping (e.g. pompous, vain, arrogant, conceited, presumptuous, egotistical, snobbish, smug and haughty). The first task of the psychologist is therefore, to reduce the list to manageable proportions and identify those that are of central importance. A statistical method for doing this is called *factor analysis*. This is a technique of classification which starts with a matrix of correlations among test items and looks for the simplest patterns that might account for it. Not uncommonly, a hierarchical pattern emerges; a large number of trait clusters are found at what is called the *primary factor level* which, because they are themselves intercorrelated, may be reduced to a smaller number of more independent *higher-order factors*. Some critics of factor analysis claim that the method yields contradictory results on different occasions, but this is usually not true; apparent contradictions arise because researchers favor solutions at different levels of generality. American psychologists, notably R.B. Cattell, have generally concentrated upon the primary factor level (the Sixteen Personality Factor Questionnaire being a well known measuring instrument) while European psychologists, such as H.J. Eysenck, have preferred to work with a more general but reliable higher order level.

Eysenck stresses the importance of three major dimensions which are largely independent of one another: extraversion versus introversion, neuroticism versus stability and psychoticism versus empathy. These are the three scales provided in the Eysenck Personality Questionnaire. If three dimensions seems a very small number within which to describe the many different personalities that we encounter it is worth remembering that all of the 25,000 or so colors we can distinguish may be identified by their positions in relation to just three variables: hue, saturation and brightness. Indeed, research has shown that the multi-trait profiles yielded by many personality tests such as the MMPI can be reduced to three scores with little loss of information.

Eysenck has devoted a great deal of research to the question of the biological basis of these three main dimensions. His theory of extraversion concerns the level of AROUSAL typically prevailing in the CEREBRAL CORTEX, which in turn depends upon the physiological functioning of the brain-stem RETICULAR ACTIVATING SYSTEM. Introverts are believed to have a higher level of chronic arousal than extraverts, who are therefore less in control of their impulses and more sensation-hungry in their behavior. Neuroticism is thought to be related to the degree of lability of the emotional midbrain (which controls the AUTONOMIC NERVOUS SYSTEM and therefore factors such as fearfulness and irritability). Psychoticism is assumed to have some kind of biochemical basis that is as yet unknown but involves the balance of sex HORMONES or the chemistry of SYNAPSES. Jeffrey Gray has proposed a rival theory that ANXIETY and impulsiveness are basic temperamental variables, relating at the neurological level to pain avoidance and reward-seeking mechanisms respectively. Both theories have assembled considerable experimental support but there are many issues still to be settled.

Other personality variables that have been widely researched because of their theoretical and practical significance are authoritarianism, dogmatism, internal versus external control, aggressiveness, achievement motivation and field dependence. Within the clinical field there are other particularly relevant variables, such as depression, obsessionality, anxiety and thought disorder.

Measurement of traits is most commonly undertaken with questionnaires and adjective check-lists, although there are many other techniques that may be used for special purposes, such as behavioral observation and ratings, projective devices and performance in laboratory tasks. All such measures are samples of behavior that have direct or theoretical relevance to the trait in question. Color preferences, for example, may be used as a clue to extraversion since it is known that extraverts tend to choose bright, garish colors while introverts prefer subtle, reserved colors.

In recent years, some psychologists, such as W. Mischel, have questioned the usefulness of the trait concept, claiming that situational factors are much more important determinants of behavior. They illustrate this argument by referring, among others, to a 1928 study by Hartshorne and May which found that dishonesty in school children did not generalize greatly from one situation to another. Thus a child who cheated in exams would not necessarily steal from a shop or lie to his parents. Since only low correlations are found among such behaviors Mischel has argued that behavior is very largely situation-specific.

Trait theorists such as Eysenck reply that the low correlations occur because these different situations place variable degrees of stress on the child's honesty and that a whole battery of such items is needed before stable and valid trait measurement is achieved. They cite the parallel case of intelligence in which a child may pass one

IQ test item and fail another because one is more difficult than the other. This does not mean that intelligence does not exist as a trait, merely that a large number of problems are needed to comprise a satisfactory IQ scale.

The specificity theory gained considerable popularity among American psychologists because it was consonant with the environmentalist *Zeitgeist* of the 1960s and 70s. Today, however, it is recognized that although situational factors need to be considered in a full account of human motivation and behavior, the measurement of temperamental traits is also a necessary exercise for many purposes. Developmental studies have confirmed that emotional tendencies, strongly predictive of similar characteristics in later childhood, can be identified in infants within a few weeks of birth.

Another criticism of the trait approach is the argument that every individual is totally unique and therefore it is not possible to classify people with respect to preselected factors. This is a misunderstanding of the nature of scientific thought, which depends heavily upon classification and generalization. It is true that nobody is perfectly duplicated, not even by their identical twin, but such a statement is utterly unhelpful. Every banana is unique, but it is sometimes useful to classify bananas as large or small, straight or bent, green, ripe or bad. The unique individual may be of interest to the novelist, dramatist or clinician, but it would be difficult even to describe him without resort to higher order (summary) concepts.

Trait measurement is of particular interest in the field of behavior genetics, where concern is with the degree of heritability of factors such as height, intelligence, musical ability, and psychoticism. Modern techniques of genetic analysis based on comparisons of identical and fraternal twins can also reveal the approximate number of different genes that are involved in determining the individual's position on a trait and whether the family or other aspects of the environment are the more influential in modifying it. The old, naive heredity versus environment argument has given way to a comprehensive partitioning of variance of a trait into different kinds of genetic and environmental influence.

Among the complications of genetic analysis are assortative mating, dominance and epistasis. *Assortative mating* refers to the fact that humans tend to marry or pair on the basis of similarity on a great number of traits such as height, intelligence, attractiveness and political conservatism. This causes a certain degree of polarization within the population on the trait in question and an increase in the kinship correlations that has to be put into the equations of the behavioral geneticist.

Dominance refers to the fact that some genes predominate over others (called recessives) in terms of the degree to which they are manifested in body or behavior. The best known example is eye color, in which brown is dominant over blue. In the field of behavior it is found that most of the genes determining high IQ are dominant (some evidence for this being seen in the phenomena of *inbreeding depression* and *hybrid vigor*), but neither end of the extraversion – introversion dimension predominates over the other. It is likely that this reflects the fact that high extraversion and introversion are roughly equally adaptive to the individual in evolutionary terms.

Epistasis refers to the fact that the expression of a gene may be modified by the action of a non-coinciding gene, possibly even one that is located on a different chromosome. Since the effect of this is to lower all kinship correlations except those for identical twins, epistasis is often difficult to distinguish from dominance. It may, however, account for some part of the variance in IQ and other traits that has previously been attributed to the environment.

Trait psychology (and indeed the science of psychometrics) may be said to have originated in the last century when Sir Francis Galton took a variety of anatomical and behavioral measurements on a large sample of visitors to the great Crystal Palace Exhibition in Kensington and sought to intercorrelate them. We have come a long way since then in terms of measurement techniques, experimental procedures and genetic analysis, although there are problems yet to be solved. Criticisms of the trait concept have had little impact on this progress, and with the decline of psychoanalytic approaches to the explanation of behavior, the psychology of personality has come to be regarded by many writers as synonymous with the study of traits.   GDW

Bibliography

Blass, T., ed. 1977: *Personality variables in social behavior*. Hillsdale, N.J.: Lawrence Erlbaum.

Lynn, R. 1981: *Dimensions of personality*. Oxford and New York: Pergamon.

Mischel, W. 1968: *Personality and assessment*. New York and London: Wiley.

transactional analysis (TA) A theory of personality and social behavior, used as a vehicle for psychotherapy and more general social change. It was born out of Eric Berne's early interest in intuition (1949) and his desire to produce a language of behavior which would be universally understood (1972).

Central to TA is the concept and practice colloquially known as "stroking" – the process of stimulating and giving recognition to fellow human beings. Stroking patterns form a common theme in the main sub-sections of TA.

Personality structure is formed by the inter-relationship of Parent, Adult and Child. These labels do not bear their common meaning but denote "egostates", coherent systems of external behavior and internal process. They are formed from the early beginnings of human development. The Parent egostate is based on limit-setting and nurturing as modeled by an individual's own parent figures. The Adult comprises reality testing and probability computing. The Child is an expression of feelings, creativity or adaptations which were originally experienced during actual childhood. TA prescribes methods for achieving a balance of energy among the egostates which is held to be essential for the well-being of the individual, the family or the organization.

Communication is defined as a series of stimuli and responses from the egostates between individuals. TA pays particular attention to the stimuli and responses which occur at a psychological level, usually non-verbally and outside the awareness of the participants. These are "ulterior" transactions and it is believed they decide the real outcome of an exchange. They are the powerful means which we adopt to influence each other.

Games, arguably the most original construct in TA (Berne 1964), are created by a regular use of ulterior transactions leading to a conclusion in which all participants lose. They are played from the psychological roles of Persecutor, Rescuer or Victim and constitute set routines to structure time, provide excitement and avoid intimacy. They can range from low-level teasing to criminal involvement and occupy a large part of everyday activity.

Feelings analysis is focused on the possible repertoire of anger, fear, sadness and joy or those feelings like guilt, hurt, boredom or jealousy which are compounds of two or more of the basic four. They can be experienced as reactions – appropriate contemporary responses; as "rubber-bands" – old feelings reactivated by a trigger in the present; or as "rackets" – favorite permitted or displaced feelings generated as a background accompaniment to living.

Script analysis examines plans decided upon in early childhood under parental influence, which are intended to shape the most important aspects of life. They consist of myths arising out of messages received about self and the world and are perpetuated by games and rackets. They fall into the main categories of "winner", breeding success, "non-winner", which are tolerable but unsatisfying and "loser", which presents problems of varying degree. Scripts may be changed through redecisions which will replace old internal frames of reference with a realistic and more accurate world view.   CT

Bibliography

Berne, E. 1949: The nature of intuition. *Psychiatric quarterly* 23, 203–26. Reprinted in E. Berne, 1977: *Intuition and egostates*. San Francisco: TA Press.

―――― 1964: *Games people play*. New York: Grove Press; London: André Deutsch (1966).

―――― 1972: *What do you say after you say hello?* New York and London: André Deutsch (1974).

Woollams, S. and Brown, M. 1978: *Transactional analysis*. Michigan: Huron Valley Press.

transmitter substances: neurotransmitters Chemical entities which are synthesized and stored in neurons (see NEURON) and released into the synaptic cleft during nerve activity. They interact with specific receptors on postsynaptic membranes, thereby inducing a change in the activity of the postsynaptic cells (see SYNAPSE AND SYNAPTIC TRANSMISSION).

Criteria have been formulated which need to be met before a substance can be considered to be a transmitter (Elliott and Darchas 1980). There is not yet definite proof of a transmitter role for many putative transmitters, both in the periphery and in the central nervous system. A further complication is that it seems likely that substances traditionally classified as transmitters may also be neuromodulators or have a neuromodulator function (see NEUROMODULATORS).

In 1921 the German physiologist Otto Loewi provided the first conclusive evidence for the concept of neurohumoral transmission. He made the classical demonstration that a chemical substance released by one frog heart *in vitro* could inhibit the activity of a second heart. The "Vagusstoff" of Loewi was later shown to be ACETYLCHOLINE, the transmitter of the postganglionic parasympathetic nerves. Similarly, a cardiac excitatory substance was called "Acceleransstoff" by Loewi, who believed it to be EPINEPHRINE. In 1946 Von Euler was finally able to end a long and sometimes heated dispute by proving that, in higher vertebrates including man, NOREPINEPHRINE rather than epinephrine is the transmitter of the postganglionic sympathetic nerves. Other chemical substances which might also be acting as transmitter substances in the periphery include DOPAMINE, SEROTONIN (5-hydroxytryptamine) and adenosine nucleotides. Acetylcholine, norepinephrine, dopamine, adrenaline, serotonin and γ-amino-acid (GABA) are well known and proven transmitter substances in the central nervous system. Evidence for a transmitter role has been presented for a number of amino acids, among which are glycine, glutamate, aspartate, histidine, proline and taurine. At least some of the many peptides which have been shown to occur in distinct neuronal systems in the central nervous system are very likely candidates for a transmitter role (see NEUROMODULATORS). DHGV

Bibliography

Bousfield, D. 1985: *Neurotransmitters in action*. New York: Elsevier.

Elliott, G.R. and Darchas, J.D. 1980: Changing concepts about neuroregulation: neurotransmitters and neuromodulators. In *Hormones and the brain*, eds. D. De Wied and P.A. Van Keep. Lancaster: MTP Press.

type-A personality Friedman and Rosenman (1974) observed a statistically significant relationship between certain behavior patterns and the prevalence of coronary heart disease (CHD). Individuals significantly at risk were referred to as exhibiting 'the coronary-prone behavior pattern, Type A' as distinct from Type B (low risk of CHD). Type A people showed the overt behavioral syndrome or style of living characterized by 'extremes of competetiveness, striving for achievement, restlessness, hyper-alertness, explosiveness of speech, tenseness of facial musculature and feelings of being under pressure of time and under the challenge of responsibility'. Type Bs possess the opposite extremes of the attributes above.

In the early studies, persons were designated as either Type A or Type B on the basis of clinical judgments by doctors and psychologists or through peer ratings. These studies found higher incidence of CHD among Type A than Type B. Many inherent methodological weaknesses were overcome by the classic Western Collaborative Group Study (Rosenman, Friedman and Strauss 1964, 1966). This was a prospective national study of over 3,400 men free of CHD. All these men were rated as Type A or B by psychiatrists after intensive interviews, without knowledge of any biological data about them and without the individuals being seen by a cardiologist. Diagnosis was made by an electrocardiographer and independent medical internist, who were not informed about the subjects' behavioral patterns. Results included the following: after two and a half years of the study, Type A men between the ages of forty and forty-nine and fifty and fifty-nine had 6.5 and 1.9 CHD more than Type B men. (See CORONARY-PRONE BEHAVIOR.) CLC

Bibliography

Friedman, M. and Rosenman, R.H. 1974: *Type A behavior and your heart*. Greenwich, Connecticut: Fawcett Publications, Inc.

Rosenman, R.H., Friedman, M., and Strauss, R. 1964: A predictive study of CHD. *Journal of the American medical association* 189, 15–22.

———— 1966: CHD in the Western Collaborative Group Study. *Journal of the American medical association* 195, 86–92.

U

unconscious drive A psychoanalytic concept used to describe a basic urge that is associated with a state of psychic energy and which leads to a specific form of behavior that discharges the energy. The word drive is used interchangeably with instinct, both being derived from the German word *Trieb*. There is no agreed classification of drives, and terms overlap. Examples are sex, life, death and aggressive drives. The expression of drives is affected by the DEFENSE MECHANISMS. RAM

V

visual nervous system (See BRAIN AND CENTRAL NERVOUS SYSTEM: ILLUSTRATIONS, fig. 23) The neural structures which participate in the conversion of light into the sensations and perceptions of vision. Light rays are focused by the cornea and lens of the eye onto the retinal mosaic of rods and cones (figs. 24 and 25). Absorption of photons of light by these photoreceptors causes sensory transduction, initiating the chain of neural events that result in seeing. The retina, unlike the peripheral neural structures of other sensory systems, is an evagination of the brain and complex processing occurs before information is forwarded along the optic nerve. There is a trend toward ENCEPHALIZATION of visual processing in the retinae of vertebrates with lower animals performing more processing peripherally and higher animals doing more centrally. Central projections of the optic nerve innervate six areas of the brain in vertebrates: the HYPOTHALAMUS (suprachiasmatic nuclei: fig. 20) and accessory optic tract nuclei, the dorsal THALAMUS (dorsal lateral geniculate nucleus), the ventral thalamus (ventral lateral geniculate nucleus) (fig. 19), the pretectal region and the optic tectum (superior colliculus: figs 6 and 7). In most of these structures, the organization of the optic nerve fiber terminals preserves the arrangement of their source in the retina producing a retinotopic map.

These various retinal inputs serve identifiable, separate, visual systems which are interconnected in complex ways to produce visually guided behavior. The connections to the hypothalamus serve to synchronize biological rhythms to the light-dark cycle of the environment, and may not lead directly to visual perception. The connections to the pretectal areas mediate the pupillary response to light and likewise do not lead directly to VISUAL

PERCEPTION. The functions of the accessory optic system and the ventral lateral geniculate nucleus are not yet clear. The two most studied visual subsystems are the retino-geniculate-striate cortex system which serves form vision, and the retinotectal system which moves the eyes.

Optic nerve fibers from corresponding parts of the retinae of both eyes innervate adjacent layers of the dorsal lateral geniculate nucleus (LGN), bringing into registration retinotopic maps from the two eyes. The LGN projects via the optic radiation to the striate cortex (area 17) on the banks of the calcarine fissure in the parietal lobe of CEREBRAL CORTEX (figs 2 and 3). The striate cortex projects to the peristriate cortex (areas 18 and 19) which finally projects to the infratemporal cortex in the temporal lobe. The connections in this subsystem appear to be hierarchical with simpler response properties in cells closer to the retina leading to more and more complex response properties in cells further up the neuronal chain. Striate cortex has highly structured arrangements of cortical columns to abstract stimulus pattern information from retinogeniculate inputs (see Hubel and Wiesel 1977).

Besides visual inputs, the superior colliculus also receives sensory inputs from other modalities and interconnects directly or indirectly with visual cortex, the pulvinar of the thalamus, the CEREBELLUM (fig. 6), vestibular nuclei and the motor nuclei of the extraocular muscles which move the eyes. The retinotectal system is involved with voluntary and involuntary eye movements, with the direction of visual gaze toward the source of a sensory stimulus, with preservation of gaze during body movements, etc. The retinotectal and geniculostriate subsystems are strongly interconnected.

Descending connections from striate

cortex to the LGN are well known in mammals. Neural feedback to the retina itself, however, has only recently become a relatively popular concept with the suggestion that centrifugal fibers in the optic nerve may regulate photoreceptor membrane turnover (see Teirstein et al. 1980; Itaya 1980).   SCC

Bibliography

Cornsweet, T.N. 1970: *Visual perception*. New York and London: Academic Press.

Ebbeson, S.O.E. 1970: On the organization of central visual pathways in vertebrates. *Brain, behavior and evolution* 3, 178–94.

Fein, A. and Szuts, E.Z. 1982: *Photoreceptors. Their role in vision*. Cambridge: Cambridge University Press.

Gregory, R.L. 1966: *Eye and brain, the psychology of seeing*. New York: World University Library, McGraw-Hill.

Hubel, D.H. and Wiesel, T.N. 1977: Ferrier Lecture: functional architecture of macaque monkey visual cortex. *Proceedings of the Royal Society of London, Series B, biological sciences* 198: 1–59.

Itaya, S.K. 1980: Retinal efferents from the pretectal area in the rat. *Brain research* 201, 436–41.

Jung, R., ed. 1973: *Handbook of sensory physiology*. vol. 7/3. *Central visual information. A: integrative functions and comparative data*; and *B: Visual centers in the brain*. Berlin and New York: Springer-Verlag.

Rodieck, R.W. 1973: *The vertebrate retina*. San Francisco: W.H. Freeman.

———— 1979: Visual pathways. *Annual review of neuroscience* 2, 193–225.

Teirstein, P.S., Goldman, A.I. and O'Brien, P.J. 1980: Evidence for both local and central regulation of rat rod outer segment disc shedding. *Investigative ophthalmology and visual science* 19, 1268–73.

Van Essen, D.C. 1979: Visual areas of the mammalian cerebral cortex. *Annual review of neuroscience* 2, 227–63.

visual perception The subjective experience arising from sensory stimulation of the visual system and brain. Its complete and proper study encompasses not only the visual domains of neurophysiology, psychophysics and psychology, but also encroaches upon the related fields of learning, memory and artificial intelligence (pattern recognition).

The process of visual perception starts with the absorption of photons in the four types of retinal photoreceptors, the rods and cones (see COLOR VISION). These sensory transducers receive a two-dimensional real image of external objects, reduced and inverted by the lens. The image is not perfect, but is degraded and blurred in part by the lens itself and in part by the other ocular media interposed in front of the retina. It is an amazing fact of visual perception that, in spite of the optical limitations of the eye, the final image we see is both erect and (normally) in sharp focus.

The photoreceptors convert the image into a code of electro-chemical impulses, which is subsequently analyzed by a multitude of NEURONS into many different dimensions: contrast, orientation, spatial frequency, color, stereoscopic disparity, direction, velocity, and so forth. Such analysis unavoidably alters the input so that an object's representation becomes an abstraction with certain elements enhanced or elaborated and others degraded or lost.

The abstraction begins in the retina where ganglion cells with concentric receptive field organization (see VISUAL NERVOUS SYSTEM) code an object by its spatial changes in contrast: accentuating regions of change (contours or edges) and disregarding regions of uniformity. At higher levels in the cortex, other neurons advance the process of feature extraction. They respond selectively to specific elements such as edges of a particular orientation or moving in a particular direction. Of course the activity of individual neurons *per se* does not code orientation or direction. This is probably done by the relative distribution of activity among neurons with different but overlapping sensitivities. Such groups of neurons, hierarchically arranged within parallel processing networks, compose what are frequently referred to as neural channels. Much psychophysical and electrophysical evidence suggests that distinct channels exist for coding the various stimulus dimensions. However, there is still considerable debate about how separate and independent the channels are and to what degree they are localized in separate cortical areas (see SENSORY SYSTEMS, NEURAL BASES). After all, it must not be forgotten that any given neuron may transmit information about a number of different stimulus dimensions (for example, contrast, orientation and spatial frequency) and may therefore contribute to a number of different analyzing systems.

Regardless of the precise neurophysiological details, one way or another the visual system has the necessary machinery for analyzing the visual image into values along particular stimulus dimensions. This, obviously, is an essential preliminary to recognizing or perceiving objects in the visual world, but it must not be mistaken for the process of perception itself. Perception requires not only detecting the presence or absence of features in the visual image, but also defining their relationship to one another and assigning them to separate objects. To achieve this end, perception cannot merely be a passive extracting process. It must also be an active integrating one, associating and organizing the sensory information (see PERCEPTION: PSYCHOLOGICAL ISSUES).

Consider first the process of dividing the visual image into discrete objects. This is a process which is so fundamental to perception that we generally take it for granted. It involves organizing the extracted elements of the retinal image so that information corresponding to the boundaries between surfaces and objects can be recognized. This is in itself a difficult task because boundaries may be marked by differences in reflectance (or luminance), orientation and texture or by discontinuities in stereoscopic depth and relative movement (see below). Even more difficult, however, is the task of identifying those regions of the retinal image that are not part of any particular object or figure, but compose the background. This organizing of extracted elements into figure and ground seems to be fundamental to vision in that it is present at first sight as far as can be determined from the early behavior of infants and from the behavior of the congenitally blind who are given sight at maturity.

Figure-ground analysis segregates an image into objects and results in their appearing qualitatively very different from the background. It does not provide detailed information about their size, shape, distance or their position in visual space. Further perceptual processes must be involved in making these precise visual judgments. For instance we have considerable perceptual information available to us about the distance of objects or their depth in the visual field; a three-dimensional awareness that cannot be simply obtained from feature analyzing and reconstructing the two-dimensional retinal image. Some information about depth is provided by straightforward binocular cues that vary monotonically with distance: the convergence of the eyes (i.e. the relative positional relation of the two eyes depends upon the distance of the objects being viewed) and the disparity of the two retinal images (i.e. they differ slightly in size, shape and location as the result of the geometry of the light rays). More information, however, is provided by monocular cues derived from further organizing and processing of the extracted elements of the retinal image: (i) *Interposition*, perceiving that nearer objects often partially occlude those further away; (ii) *Kinetic Parallax*, perceiving that moving objects have typical expansive and constrictive patterns associated with them; (iii) *Motion Parallax*, perceiving that head or body movements differentially displace objects at different distances in the visual field; (iv) *Attached Shadows*, perceiving that the attached shadows of objects change with object distance and relative position in the visual field; (v) *Size Perspective*, perceiving that the retinal image gets progressively smaller with increasing distance (this is particularly useful as a cue to the distance of such familiar objects as people and cars, whose true size is roughly known); (vi) *Linear Perspective*, perceiving that the convergence of parallel lines and texture gradients leading away from the observer provide frameworks of relative distance for locating objects; and (vii) *Aerial Perspective*, perceiving that the surface details of distant objects are diminished in contrast and saturation (caused by the veiling of atmospheric haze).

The perceptual processes also extract from the retinal image considerable information about object direction and movement in space. And they do this despite two major problems. First, they must overcome the limitation that visual neurons have spatially discrete receptive fields and can resolve the continuous motion of objects transversing the retina only into a series of discrete excitations. Second, they must overcome the confounding effects of eye movements which shift the image of fixed objects around the retina. Thus, there must be active compensatory mechanisms restoring perceived motion and subtracting out the constantly changing position of the eyes. Information about eye position may come from monitoring the proprioceptive signals originating from the eye muscles and the central (efferent) signals originating from the cortical neurons commanding head, body and eye movements.

Besides permitting us to locate reliably the distance and direction of objects in visual space, perceptual processes allow us to judge accurately their size, shape and color. And they allow us to do this, despite wide changes in the viewing conditions that significantly vary the retinal image. For example, a tall person walking away from you is still perceived as tall even though his or her retinal image is rapidly decreasing in size (i.e. perceived size cannot correspond exactly with visual angle subtended at the retina). Likewise, a round object viewed obliquely is still perceived as circular even though its retinal image is elliptical (i.e. perceived shape cannot correspond exactly with the object's retinal image); and white paper viewed under moonlight is still perceived as white even though it reflects less light than carbon paper viewed under direct sunlight (i.e. perceived lightness/color cannot correspond exactly with the incident retinal illumination). In short, objects are generally judged to be constant in size, shape and lightness/color over an enormous range of viewing conditions that change their phenomenological appear-

ance. The perceptual system must derive this constancy from the various retinal images by taking into account other information obtained directly from the adjacent objects and surfaces and indirectly from the short term memory stores. (This problem of how we recognize objects as being constant is related to the more complex problem of pattern recognition in general, of how we recognize a very diverse set of objects as belonging to a single significant category.)

The few examples that could be discussed above should suffice to demonstrate that perception is not determined merely by passive neural analysis of the retinal input, but also involves active organizing of the sensory information. This fact has several consequences. First, it means that perception is not immediate. Time is required to extract perceptual information either from the retinal image or from the accessible memory stores. Second, it means that perception is not a fixed, immutable process. It is affected not only by a general knowledge of what are likely properties of objects, but also by the specific knowledge of what sorts of objects are likely to be met in particular situations (i.e. the role of expectancy and selection in recognition). Third, it means that perception is fallible. Our perceptual hypotheses about objects may conform to the sensory information, but they are by no means inevitably proven by it. They may be false, nonsensical or nonveridical. Fourth, it means that perception may be modified by experience and learning (see MEMORY AND LEARNING: PHYSIOLOGICAL BASES). Early visual exposure during maturation and specific environmental conditions even in adulthood can affect the development and functioning of perceptual mechanisms.

LTS

Bibliography

Boring, E.D. 1942: *Sensation and perception in the history of experimental psychology*. New York: Appleton-Century Crofts.

Braddick, O.J. and Atkinson, J. 1982: Higher functions in vision. In *The senses*, eds. H.B. Harlow and J.D. Mollon. Cambridge and New York: Cambridge University Press.

*Frisby, J. 1979: *Seeing*. Oxford and New York: Oxford University Press.

Gibson, J.J. 1966: *The senses considered as perceptual systems*. Boston: Houghton Mifflin.

*Gregory, R.L. 1970: *The intelligent eye*. London: Weidenfeld and Nicolson; New York: McGraw-Hill.

Jung, R. 1973: Visual perception and neurophysiology. In *Handbook of sensory physiology*, ed. R. Jung, vol. 7/3, Central processing of visual information. Part A. Heidelberg: Springer-Verlag.

*Held, R., Leibowitz, H.W. and Teuber, H.-L., eds. 1978: *Handbook of sensory physiology*. vol. 8. Perception. Heidelberg: Springer-Verlag.

—— and Richards, W. eds. 1972: *Perception: mechanisms and models*. (Readings from Scientific American.) San Francisco: W.H. Freeman.

Marr, D. 1982: *Vision: a computational investigation into the human representation and processing of visual information*. San Francisco: W.H. Freeman and Company.

W

Weber's law The rule that $\triangle I / I$ is constant, where I is the magnitude of a stimulus and $\triangle I$ is the just noticeable change in that magnitude. Weber proposed the principle in his *De Tactu* (Leipzig 1834): 'In observando discrimine rerum inter se comparatarum non differentiam rerum, sed rationem differentiae ad magnitudinem rerum inter se comparatarum percipimus'. In support of his law, Weber advanced his own observations on weight perception and on the visual perception of the length of lines; and the law has since been found to hold, approximately, for a large variety of sensory dimensions, ranging from the auditory discrimination of frequency to the visual discrimination of velocity. The value $\triangle I$ is often called the *Weber fraction*; in the discrimination of luminance it has a value of less than 1 per cent under optimal conditions.   JDM

Bibliography

Ross, H.E. and Murray, D.J. 1978: *E.H. Weber: the sense of touch*. London, Academic Press.

Shapley, R. and Enroth-Cugell, C. 1984: Visual adaptation and retinal gain controls. *Progress in retinal research* 3, 263–343.

Wernicke's syndrome (or Wernicke's encephalopathy) An acute neurological disorder described by Wernicke in 1881. Its main features are impaired consciousness, disorientation, ataxia (uncoordinated bodily movements) and ophthalmoplegia (paralysis of eye movements). As Wernicke demonstrated, post mortem examination of the brain reveals hemorrhagic lesions in the gray matter around the third and fourth ventricles and the aqueduct. The condition sometimes occurs after many years of alcohol abuse, and is often followed by KORSAKOV'S SYNDROME.   DG

word association test A word association test (WAT) is elegantly simple: provide someone with a stimulus word, and ask for the first word that comes to mind. For example, say "table", and the response may well be "chair". Psychologists examine the nature and probabilities of response words, and sometimes how long it takes for a response. Word associations reveal people's verbal habits, the structure of their verbal memory, thought processes, and occasionally even emotional states and personality. They can be used both to understand individual people and to study the structure of language itself.

Response patterns. The father of WAT was the British scientist Galton, who in the nineteenth century tested one subject, himself. In a less personal WAT in 1901 the German linguist-psychologist team, Thumb and Marbe, used eight subjects and sixty stimulus words. They found the following response trends, which have also been found in many subsequent WATs.

Words of one type evoked a response of the same type: e.g., "brother" led to "sister"; a noun led to another noun.

More common responses occurred more rapidly than less common ones: e.g., to "table", the most frequent response "chair" might occur within 1.3 sec; the next most frequent "furniture", within 1.6 sec; the third "eat", within 2 sec, and so on.

A given stimulus word often elicited an identical response from different subjects.

In the first large-scale WAT, Kent and Rosanoff (1910) tested 1,000 subjects' responses to 100 stimulus words, establishing a set of norms for future WATs. Between 1910 and 1954, there was an increase in primary (the most frequently given) responses. For example, to "table", the primary response "chair" was given by 26.7 percent in 1910; 33.8 percent in 1928; and 84.0 percent in 1954. Idiosyncratic responses (such as "mensa", which was given to "table" by 1 out of 1,008 subjects) became rarer. These trends may be due to the influence of mass media, to advertising, and to the standardization of school instruction. We are in the "group-think" age.

Response patterns of various groups of people differ. Among speakers of three kindred languages – American-English, German, and French, primary responses are similar, but the American group tend to react much more uniformly to a stimulus word than do the German and French groups.

Between men and women, response times tend to be faster for men (1.3 sec for educated, 1.8 for uneducated) than for women (1.7 sec for educated, 2.2 for uneducated) (Jung 1918). Males tend to respond with antonyms and females with synonyms (Goodenough 1940). At every age female subjects may be characterized as stereotyped: compared to males, females give fewer different responses to each stimulus, and are more likely to give one of the four most frequent responses.

Conformity-minded people or people who are exposed to uniform mass media are likely to show more common responses, or less richness. All groups may be moving toward giving more common responses over the years.

Adults vs. children. The character of WAT responses changes with age. The table compares how often four US age groups gave the primary response (for the age group) to nine Kent-Rosanoff words, chosen because they elicited large (65 per cent or more) primary responses in adults.

The table reveals the following trends:
1. Primary responses are more probable for adults than for children.
2. In adults, all adjective stimuli elicited adjective antonyms. According to Deese (1965), contrast is the basic association pattern for adjectives. He notes that dictionaries often define an adjective by giving its opposite.
3. At age 10 some stimuli and responses are from the same word class but are synonyms rather than antonyms ("bitter-sour" and "dark-black").
4. At age 6 the stimulus and response are from different word classes, and are related in sound but not in meaning ("bitter-butter"). Children are responding to superficial, phonetic aspect of words.
5. At kindergarten (age 5), in "bitter-better", the stimulus and the response are

Comparison of Primary Responses by Four Age Groups

Stimulus	Response	Adult	Grade V	Grade I	Kindergarten
bitter	sweet	65.2	24.2 (sour)	6.8 (butter)	5.0 (better)
black	white	75.1	36.2 (dark)	12.1	6.5 (crayon)
dark	light	82.9	40.4	30.4	13.5 (night)
hard	soft	67.4	34.2	19.6	8.0 (rock)
high	low	67.5	46.4	21.8	8.5
long	short	75.8	47.0	20.0	8.0 (grass)
man	woman	76.7	18.8	12.9	9.5
slow	fast	75.2	51.6	35.7	18.0
table	chair	84.0	39.2	36.1	32.0

(Children's responses that differ from those of adults are given in parentheses.) Data of adults from Russell and Jenkins, 1954; of Grade V from Palermo and Jenkins, 1964; of Grade I and Kindergarten from Entwisle 1966).

from the same word class (perhaps fortuitously), but are related in sound rather than in meaning. In "black-crayon", "dark-night", "hard-rock" and "long-grass", the stimulus and the response are from different word classes, but are likely word sequences in running speech.

Adults typically respond to a noun with another noun, to an adjective with another adjective; they give *paradigmatic* responses. Children, by contrast, respond to an adjective (black) with a noun (crayon) that follows the stimulus in a sentence; they give syntagmatic responses.

The shift from syntagmatic to paradigmatic occurs between ages five and nine. Between 1916 and 1961, paradigmatic responses among school children increased for both nouns and adjectives by 10 percent or more. And paradigmatic responding was associated with increased use of contrasts. Both effects may be related to test-taking practice and linguistic sophistication through mass media.

Diagnostic use of WAT.

WATs can reveal a person's emotional state. The noted Swiss psychoanalyst JUNG (1918) pioneered the use of word association in clinical diagnosis. He used emotionally loaded words to probe into patients' repressed images, wishes, or emotions. Both the time it takes for a person to produce a response word and the type of response word are supposed to reflect the emotional state. For example, a thirty-seven year old female teacher, single, came to him with a severe problem of insomnia. She responded with an unusual word "home-sick" to the stimulus "foreign", taking 14.8 sec (compared to normal people's 2 sec in responding to neutral words). In a subsequent interview, she revealed her love affair with a foreigner who left her without saying good-bye.

Generally, people who give a large number of unusual responses are considered to have some form of mental disturbance. Goodenough (1946) reports that single and divorced women, compared to married women, give many unusual responses.

In earlier times, schizophrenics were believed to have unusual and "unlogical" associations, remote associations and clang associations (or rhymes). Modern word association tests show that schizophrenics have intact associative structure, though they tend to have longer response times, fewer common responses, and more repetitions, than do normals (Mefford 1979).

Rapaport and his associates at the Menninger Clinic developed a diagnostic WAT, containing sixty stimulus words, of which twenty are such "traumatic" words as "love, breast, suicide, masturbate, bite", and the rest are such neutral words as "hat, chair, man, city". Here is one illustrative case. A thirty-two year old surgeon, married and childless, with severe anxiety, responded to "breast" with "mammary gland", taking an extraordinarily long time of 4 min 5 sec. The diagnostician's comment on this response was "neurotic intellectualizing" (Rapaport, Gill and Schafer 1946). Out of sixty stimulus words twelve elicited responses requiring specific comments.

Shiomi (1979) in Japan used the words of Rapaport et al. to study personality of normal people. For male adults response times of extraverts to "traumatic" words were shorter than those of introverts. According to Shiomi, introverts defend themselves against responding to traumatic words whereas extraverts do not.

Goodenough (1946) used WATs to test leadership among a large number of women in the US Army. The proportion of active verbs (e.g., "fish", rather than "fishing" to "rod") among the responses given by officer candidates was many times greater than by the enlisted women.

In a WAT a person is free to respond, free to reveal, unconsciously, aspects of his or her inner life.   IT

Bibliography

Deese, J. 1965: *The structure of associations in language and thought.* Baltimore: Johns Hopkins University Press.

Entwisle, D. 1966: *Word associations of young children.* Baltimore: Johns Hopkins University Press.

Goodenough, F.L. 1946: Semantic choice and personality structure. *Science* 104, 451–6.

Jung, C.G. 1918: *Studies in word-association.* London: W. Heinemann.

Kent, H.G. and Rosanoff, A.J. 1910: A study of association in insanity. *American journal of insanity* 67, 37–96.

Mefford, R.B. Jr. 1979: Word association: capacity of chronic schizophrenics to follow formal semantic, syntactic, and instructional rules. *Psychological reports* 45, 431–42.

Palermo, D.S. and Jenkins, J.J. 1964: *Word association norms. Grade school through college.* Minneapolis: University of Minnesota Press.

Rapaport, D., Gill, M. and Schafer, R. 1946: *Diagnostic psychological testing.* Chicago: Yearbook Publications.

Russell, W.A. and Jenkins, J.J. 1954: *The complete Minnesota norms for responses to 100 words from the Kent-Rosanoff word association test.* Minneapolis: Technical Report No. 11, 1954.

Shiomi, K. 1979: Differences in RTs of extroverts and introverts to Rapaport's word association test. *Psychological reports*, 45, 75–80.

work stress Many of the current definitions of stress come from homeostatic, energy-exchange models of physical phenomena espoused by earlier scientists such as Boyle, Cannon, etc. (Hinkle 1973), suggesting that stress results from the interaction of stimuli and an organism. Lazarus (1971) summarizes the definition in human stress terms thus: 'Stress refers to a very broad class of problems differentiated from other problem areas because it deals with *any demands which tax the system*, whether it is a physiological system, a social system, or a psychological system, *and the response of that system.*'

In any form of paid employment there are a large number of potential sources of stress: the characteristics of the job itself, the role of the person in the organization, interpersonal relationships at work, career development pressures, the climate and structure of the organization, and problems associated with the interface between the organization and the outside world.

Factors intrinsic to the job were a first and vital focus of study for early researchers in stress. Stress can be caused by too much or too little work, time pressures and deadlines, having to make too many decisions, fatigue from the physical strains of the work environment (e.g. an assembly line), excessive travel, long hours, having to cope with changes at work, and the expenses (monetary and career) of making mistakes.

Another major source of work stress is associated with a person's role in the organization. A great deal of research in this area has concentrated on role ambiguity and conflict.

A third major source of stress at work has to do with the nature of relationships with superiors, subordinates, and colleagues. A number of writers (e.g. Argyris 1964, Cooper and Marshall 1978) have suggested that good relationships between members of a work group are a central factor in individual and organizational health.

Buck (1972) focused on the attitude of workers and managers to their immediate bosses and their relationships with them, using Fleishman's (1969) leadership questionnaire on consideration and initiating structure. As described in Chapter 10, the consideration factor is associated with behavior indicative of friendship, mutual trust, respect and a certain warmth between boss and subordinate. Buck found that those workers who felt that their bosses were low on consideration reported feeling more job pressure. Workers who were under pressure reported that their bosses did not give them criticism in a helpful way, played favorites with subordinates, "pulled rank", and took advantage of them whenever they got a chance. Buck concludes that the 'lack of considerate behaviour of supervisors appears to have contributed significantly to feelings of job pressure'.

Officially one of the most critical functions of a manager is his supervision of other people's work. It has long been accepted that "inability to delegate" can be a problem, but now a new strain is being put on the manager's interpersonal skills: he must learn to work "participatively". In respect of relationships with colleagues more generally stress can be caused not only by interpersonal rivalry and competition but also by a lack of adequate social support in difficult situations (Lazarus

1966). At highly competitive managerial levels, for example, it is likely that problem sharing will be inhibited for fear of appearing weak, and much American literature identifies the isolated life of the top executive as an added source of strain.

Two major clusters of potential stressors have been identified in the area of career development: lack of job security and fear of redundancy, obsolescence or early retirement; and status incongruity (under- or over-promotion) or frustration at having reached a career ceiling.

For many workers, especially managers and professional staff, career progression is of overriding importance: by promotion they earn not only money, but also enhanced status and the new job challenges for which they strive. Typically, in the early years at work this striving and the ability to come to terms quickly with a rapidly changing environment is fostered and suitably rewarded by the company. At middle age a person's career becomes more problematic, and most employees find their progress slowed if not actually stopped. Job opportunities become fewer, those jobs that are available take longer to master, past (mistaken?) decisions cannot be revoked, old knowledge and methods become obsolete, energies may be flagging or demanded for family activities, and there is the press of fresh young recruits to face in competition.

A fifth potential source of work stress is simply "being in the organization", and the threat to an individual's freedom, autonomy and identity that this poses. Criticisms such as little or no participation in the decision making process, no sense of belonging, lack of effective consultation and communication, restrictions on behavior (e.g. through tight budgets) and office politics are frequent.

The sixth and final source of work stress is more a "catch-all" for all those exchanges between life outside and life inside the organization that might put pressure on an individual: family problems (Pahl and Pahl 1971), life crises (Cooper and Marshall 1978), financial difficulties, conflict of personal beliefs with those of the

company, and the conflict of company with family demands.

The individual worker has two stress-related problems with respect to his family and his work. The first is that of managing time and conflicting commitments. Not only does the busy work life leave few resources to cope with other people's needs, but in order to do a job well, the individual usually needs support from others to cope with the details of home management, to relieve stress when possible, and to maintain contact with the world outside work. The second problem, often a result of the first, is the spill-over of crises or stresses from one system to the other.

(See STRESS.)   CLC

Bibliography

Argyris, C. 1964: *Integrating the individual and the organisation*. New York: Wiley.

Buck, V.E. 1972: *Working under pressure*. London: Staples Press; New York: Crane Rusak.

Cooper, C.L. and Marshall, J. 1978: *Understanding executive stress*. London: Macmillan.

Fleishman, E.A. 1969: *Manual for the leadership opinion questionnaire*. Science Research Associates.

Hinkle, L.W. 1973: The concept of "stress" in the biological and social sciences. *Science, medicine and man* 1, 31–48.

Lazarus, R.S. 1966: *Psychological stress and the coping process*. New York: McGraw-Hill.

Lazarus, R.S. 1971: The concepts of stress and disease. In *Society, stress and disease*, ed. L. Levi. Oxford: Oxford University Press.

Pahl, J.M. and R.E. 1971: *Managers and their wives*. London: Allen Lane.

Wundt, Wilhelm (1832–1920) 'the senior psychologist in the history of psychology', as Boring put it, was among the most prolific scholars of all time. His published books went well beyond the now traditional topics of psychology and included logic, anthropology and (even) a biography of Leibniz. His thorough grounding in the biological sciences was not at the expense of the larger learning, and in all of his most influential writings there is evidence of a broad and discerning intelligence that has barely survived the usual treatments he has received in secondary sources.

Although prepared as a physician, Wundt was from the first deeply interested in the experimental sciences, especially physiology. He interrupted his course of study at Heidelberg so that he could spend time in Johannes Müller's famous Institute at Berlin (1856), receiving his doctorate at Heidelberg in the same year. And it was at Heidelberg, too, that he delivered a series of lectures (1862) later published as *Lectures on human and animal psychology*, in which many of his most mature thoughts and proposals are richly anticipated. It was in these lectures that Wundt noted the conceptual limitations faced by psychology; limitations arising from the irreducible nature of significant social, historical and moral phenomena. The discipline of psychology *qua* psychology could and should aspire to be at once experimental, scientific and "physiological", but such a discipline could not claim for itself proprietorship over the broader range of genuinely *human* affairs. Such affairs proceed from complex motivations, subtle and often remote influences. They are, then, not elements in a *causal* chain, but phenomena arising in the realms of reasons and goals. (The distinction, of course, is one that Kant had made famous and one that Leibniz pressed in his *Monadology*.)

But the "physiological" psychology developed in these *Lectures* is physiological in the (nineteenth century) sense of "scientific", "naturalistic". It is also, therefore, *physiological* in the current sense but not exclusively so. Indeed, Wundt was more inclined in the direction of psychophysics and what is now called information-processing than toward experimental

neurosurgery and the kindred methods that now define physiological psychology. He founded the journal *Philosophische Studien* (1881) to provide a forum for research of this sort. Neither biological nor clinical psychology figured in any central way during the years of Wundt's editorial control, nor does the list of his best known students – Cattell, Külpe, Titchener, Klemm – include an important person in physiological psychology or psychobiology.

It would be fair to say that Wundt's chief part in the specialities that now define physiological psychology was his defense of experimental modes of inquiry, his emphasis upon psychology as a branch of the natural sciences, and his authorship of immensely influential texts in which psychological issues were examined within the context of developments in the neural sciences. Nevertheless, he opposed radical versions of reductionism, defended a species of psychophysical parallelism (in the manner of Leibniz) and insisted that '... psychical can only be adequately explained from psychical, just as motion can only be derived from motion, and never from a mental process ...' (*Lectures*, p. 442). Such arguments preserved the psychological side of the psychophysical relationship at a time when psychology's issues might otherwise and wrongly have been absorbed by physiology.   DNR

Bibliography

Robinson, D.N. 1982: *Toward a science of human nature: essays on the psychologies of Hegel, Mill, Wundt and James*. New York: Columbia University Press.

Wundt, W. 1904: *Lectures on human and animal psychology*. Trans. J.E. Creighton and E.B. Titchener. New York: Macmillan (originally published 1863–1864).

Index

The figures in **bold** index the main article on that subject. Columns (designated a & b) are only differentiated where the subject is restricted to one column on any page.

Sullivan, Harry Stack 163b
sugar *see* glucose
suicide 5a, **277**
  life events **142**
sulcus/-i 47a
superconscious 236b
superego 65a, 103b, 153a
superior colliculus 44a, 89b
superior olivary complex 10b
superior temporal gyrus 11a
superiority, striving for 169b
supportive psychotherapy 238b
suprachiasmatic nucleus (SCN)
  214b, 262a
sweating
  galvanic skin response **105**
  heat regulation 12a
  water balance 121a
SWS *see* slow wave sleep
sympathetic nervous system 12a
  emotion 86a
symptom-oriented psychotherapy
  238b
symptomatic psychosis *see* organic
  mental state
synapse/synaptic transmission 1a,
  2a, 3a, 39a, 63b, 67b, 74b,
  277, 156a, 187a, 192b, 258b,
  260a
  plasticity 215b
synaptic growth theory 158b
synaptic modulator *see* neuromodulator

"tactual window" 21b
Tai Chi 23a
Tai Kwan Do 23a
talk *see* speech
tantra meditation 150a
target, synapse 186b
taste 119b, 253a
Tay-Sachs disease 108a
tectum 44a, 89b
teeth grinding 264a
tegmentum 44a, 89b
telegraphic speech 272a
telencephalon 142b
temporal lobe 8a, 235b
tension, reduction of 149a
test/s personality **167**
testis/-es 116b
testosterone 118b, 275b
T-group (training group) **278**
thalamus 1a, 10b, 13a, 67b, 124a,
  188b, 201b, 235b, 253a, **278**,
  289a
thalidomide 164b
thanatos (death instinct) 103b,
  128a
therapeutic community 78a
therapist *see* analyst
therapy
  action based 111a
  behavior **16–19**
  body-centered **23–4**
  cathartic 129a

gestalt **108–9**
group **111**
  primal **217–18**
  radical **242–3**
  see also psychotherapy
thermoregulation **279–81**
thermostatic mechanism 119b
theta rhythm 82b
thioridazine 229b
thioxanthines 229b
thirst **120–21**
thought disorder 20a, 250b, **282**
Thudicum, J L W 25b
thumb-sucking 48b
thymine 248b
  deficiency 135a
thyroid gland deficiency 4b, 117a
thyrotopin releasing hormone
  (TRH) 185b, 215a
thyroxine 117a
tic 486
tissue aspiration/transection 40b
TM *see* transcendental/meditation
"token economy" 245a
tolerance 75b, 77a
tonotopic organization 10b
topography, neural 173a
touch, sense of *see* somatosensory
  nervous system
toxemia, 164b
trace storage **282**
traits **282–5**
training group *see* T-group
trance *see* hypnosis; meditation
tranquilizers 5b
transactional analysis (TA) 111b,
  238b, **285**
transcendental meditation (TM)
  149a
transcription (genetic code) 158b,
  248b
transducer/transduction, sensory
  see sensory transduction
transfer RNA 248b
transference 102b, 136b, 225a,
  239a
translation (in protein synthesis)
  249b
transpersonal self 236b
transmitter *see* neurotransmitter
transsexuality 233b
transsynaptic modulation 186b
tranylcypromine 5a
trauma
  and aphasia 177a
  brain 7b, 144b, 161a, 198b
  emotional 102b
  primal 217b
  effect on memory 151a
treatment *see* chemical psychology;
  psychiatry; therapy
tremor 13a, 41a, 42b
TRH *see* thyrotropin releasing
  hormone
trichromacy ("three-color-ness")
  53b

tricyclic antidepressant 222b, 230a
trieb 127b, 137b, 288b
trigeminal nerve/systm 269b
trisomy 21, 75a, 106b
"trioka" 144a
trophic hormones 117a
tryptophan 258a
tuberose sclerosis 164a
Turner's syndrome 15a, 106b
twilight states 60a
twin studies in behavior 15b, 106b,
  144a
type-A personality **286–7**

U, inverted curve (on graph) 10a
ulcer/s, gastric 276a
unconditioned reflex *see* reflex
unconscious 65a, 102a, 132a,
  137a, 152a, 207a, 212b
  collective *see* collective
    unconscious
  drive 228b, 223b, **288**
  lower/middle/higher 236a
  in psychoanalysis 224b
  subception 276b
unilateral (brain) *see* lateralization
unipolar depression 4b, 68a, 220a
univariance principle 55a
uracil 249a

vaginismus 232a
vagus nerves 253a
valium 230a
variation, evolutionary *see* genetics
vasoactive *see* VIP
vasopressin 117b, 185b, 215a
ventromedial hypothalamic
  syndrome 120b
vestibular apparatus 70b, 185b
VIP (vasoactive intestinal peptide)
  185b
vipassana 149b
visceral events, hunger, 119a
vision **289–93**
  color *see* color vision
  reafference in **243**
  tachistoscopic 180a
visual after-effects, contingent **60a**
visual cortex **89**, 216a
visual discrimination 294a
visual perception **290–3**
visual illusions 209b
visual impairment *see* blindness
visual nervous system 47a, **289–90**,
  255b
  evolution of 2b
  plasticity of 2b
  and perception 208b
visuo-spatial relationship 2b
  agnosia 173a
  disabilities 172a
vitamins 38a
  deficiency 195b
voluntary/involuntary behavior 58b
vomiting, self-induced 45b
volemic adipsia 121b
VPL nucleus 270a